Maqāṣid al-Sharīʿah

Explorations and Implications

MAQĀṢID AL-SHARĪ‘AH

Explorations and Implications

Edited and with Introduction by
MOHAMED EL-TAHIR EL-MESAWI

IBT
Islamic Book Trust
Kuala Lumpur

Published by
Islamic Book Trust
607 Mutiara Majestic
Jalan Othman
46000 Petaling Jaya
Selangor, Malaysia
www.ibtbooks.com

Islamic Book Trust is affiliated with The Other Press.

Perpustakaan Negara Malaysia Cataloguing-in-Publication Data

Maqasid al-Shari'ah: Exploration and Implications / Edited and with an
Introduction by: Mohamed El-Tahir El-Mesawi
ISBN 978-967-0526-55-3
eISBN 978-967-0526-56-0
1. Maqasid (Islamic law).
2. Islamic law.
I. El-Mesawi, Mohamed El-Tahir.
340.5911

This book is published in collaboration with International Institute for Muslim Unity, IIMU, International Islamic University Malaysia, IIUM.

Printed by
SS Graphic Printers (M) Sdn. Bhd.
Lot 7 & 8, Jalan TIB 3
Taman Industri Bolton
68100 Batu Caves, Selangor

Acknowledgements

My appointment as Deputy Director of the International Institute for Muslim Unity, IIMU at the International Islamic University Malaysia, IIUM for *Maqaṣid* and *Wasaṭiyyah* gave me an invaluable opportunity and great impetus to work on the editing of this book. I should therefore sincerely thank the Rector of IIUM Professor Zaleeha Kamruddin for entrusting me with this responsibility.

The Dirctor of IIMU Professor Waleed Fikry Fares has been very encouraging and considerate and relieved me from many day-to-day administrative tasks, thus enabling me to devote much of my available time to this work. I am very much indebted to him for the understanding and sympathy he has shown to me in this undertaking. I must also record here my high appreciation of the kindness, technical assistance and moral support provided me by the IIMU adimistrative staff: Fazlina Abu Bakar, Raja Rozlinda Abdullah, Sermahal Usad and Norohani Azizi. The Institute' family spirit and social warmth have been a real blessing for me and made my task much easier. Thanks to all of them.

My wife and daughters deserve special expression of gratitude for the love, warmth and understanding they have always overwhelmed me with.

Certainly, without the seriousness and cooperation of the learned scholars in the process of reviewing, revising and editing their respective chapters, I would not have been able to bring it to where it is. They all, individuallay and collectively, deserve my special gratitude for, and high valuation of, their expertise and friendship; and I look forward to more opportunities of collaboration with them and their likes on the path of meaningful intellectualism and sound scholarship.

Above and before all, it is with the grace, blessing and guidance of God Almighty that whatever efforts we make bear fruit and be useful and beneficial. However much we may praise and thank Him, we can never meet an ounce of His countless bounties on us.

Mohamed El-Tahir El-Mesawi

Kuala Lumpur
Rabīʿ al-Awwal/al-Ākhir 1439
December 2017

Contents

Acknowledgements v

Introduction ix

1. The Purposefulness of the Law:
Sayf al-Dīn al-Āmidī on *Maqāṣid al-Sharīʿah* 1
— Bernard G. Weiss

2. Beyond *Uṣūl al-Fiqh*:
Ibn Ashur's *ʿIlm Maqāṣid al-Sharīʿah* 31
— Mohamed El-Tahir El-Mesawi

3. Apprehending and Concretizing *Maqāṣid al-Sharīʿah*
in the Modern World...95
— Sherman A.Jackson

4. *Maqāṣid al-Sharīʿah* and the Challenge of Modernity 121
— Wael B. Hallaq

5. Jurisprudence: The Ultimate Arena For Existential
Clash or Cooperation Within and among Civilizations 155
— Robert Dickson Crane

6. *Maqāṣid al-Sharīʿah* and Rethinking Political Rights in Modern Society 189
— Louay M. Safi

7. *Maqāṣid al-Sharīʿah*, *Maṣlaḥah*, and Corporate Social Responsibility 215
— Asyraf Wajdi Dusuki & Nurdianawati Irwani Abdullah

8. *Maqāṣid* and the Codification of Islamic Penal Rules: The Sudanese Experiment 243
— Ibrahem M. Zein

9. *Maqāṣid* and Related Islamic Legal Concepts on Current Bioethical Issues: Critical Reflections 281
— Anke Iman Bouzenita

10. *Maqāṣid al-Sharīʿah* in the Prohibition of *Ribā* and their Implications for Modern Islamic Finance 311
— Monzer Kahf

11. *Dharāʾiʿ* and *Maqāṣid al-Sharīʿah*: A Study of Aspects of Islamic Insurance 347
— Akhtarzaite Binti Abdulaziz

12. Re-embedding *Maqāṣid al-Sharīʿah* in the Essential Methodology of Islamic Economics 373
— Mehmet Asutay & Isa Yilmaz

Notes on the Contributors 419

Select Bibliography 431

Index 437

Introduction

Until quite recently in the late 20th century, the term *maqāṣid al-sharī'ah* was rarely used in academic circles in the Muslim world, let alone in general public discourses. A doctoral candidate at al-Azhar University in the late 1960s had to change the title of his dissertation and use the term *ahdāf* instead of *maqāṣid*, as the latter did not appeal to some members of the examining committee who were suspicious about the idea behind it, despite its being supervised by one of the foremost scholars in that institution at that time.[1] Books bearing in their titles such term could easily be counted on the fingers of one hand. This was generally the situation in Muslim countries, including the Arab world, until well the late 1980s. Only very few of the textbooks written in Arabic by 20th century authors on Islamic legal theory (*uṣūl al-fiqh*) included a section or chapter on the subject on *maqāṣid al-sharī'ah*, though it was in this discipline that systematic discussion of this topic had developed over the centuries, since at least the time of Abū al-Ma'ālī al-Juwaynī (419-478H), notwithstanding the fact

[1] This was what had happened to my late teacher at Oumdurman Islamic University, Sudan Professor Sheikh Yusuf Hamid al-'Alim (1937-1988), who was supervised by Sheikh 'Abd al-Ghani 'Abd al-Khaliq (1908-1983). See his book *al-Maqāṣid al-'Āmmah li al-Sharī'ah al-Islāmiyyah* (Herndon, Virgina: International Institute of Islamic Thought, 1415/1994), p. 12.

that a number of studies had appeared which dealt with the subject of *maṣlaḥah*, or the doctrine of utility, which actually constitutes the axis of *maqāṣid al-sharīʿah.*[1]

This was literally the situation despite the fact that two of the most important contributions to the study of *maqāṣid al-sharīʿah* had been written by two eminent scholars belonging to some of the erstwhile institutions of traditional Islamic learning and education. These were Muhammad al-Tahir Ibn Ashur of Tunisia (1879-1973) whose name is usually associated with the Zaytuna Grand Mosque University and the Moroccan Mohamed Allal al-Fasi (1910-1974), one of the well-known scholars of al-Quaraouiyine (al-Qarawiyyīn) University; the former had published his work in 1946 while the latter published his in 1963. A third, less known, book by Mohammad Anis Ubadah was published in 1968.[2]

In the English language especially, one cannot think of any book or article on the subject of *maqāṣid* prior to 1973, although this language had registered a number of works on Islamic jurisprudence and legal theory by eminent Orientalists and Arabists. The earliest study I am aware of in this respect was a doctoral dissertation on the work of Abū Isḥāq al-Shāṭibī (d. 790/1388) submitted by the Pakistani Muhammad Khalid Masud to the Faculty of Graduate Studies, McGill University in 1973 and first published in revised form by the Islamic Research Institute, Islamabad in 1977. This work had to wait until 1992 to be followed by Bernard G. Weiss's extensive study on al-Āmidī

---

[1] Reference can be made here, for example, to the works of people like Mustafa Zayd (*al-Maṣlaḥah fī al-Tashrīʿ al-Islāmī wa Najm al-Dīn al-Ṭūfī,* 1954), Muhammad Saʿid Ramadan al-Buti (*Ḍawābiṭ al-Maṣlaḥah fī al-Sharīʿah al-Iālamiyyah,* 1965), Hossain Hamid Hassan (*Naẓariyat al-Maṣlaḥah fī al-Fiqh al-Islāmī,* 1971); the dates given being those of the submission of these works as doctoral or MA dissertations, whilst their publication in book form took place years later.

[2] The titles of their books are, respectively, *Maqāṣid al-Sharīʿah al-Islāmiyyah, Maqāṣid al-Sharīʿah al-Islāmiyyah wa Makārimuhā* and *Maqāṣid al-Sharīʿah.*

(d. 631H) in which he devoted considerable space to the purposes of Islamic Law.

However, a "sudden" development took place towards the early 1990s wherein one can see a total reversal of the tide. This development took both institutional and research forms. Institutionally, courses on *maqāṣid al-sharīʿah* have been introduced at the postgraduate and undergraduate levels in many universities and colleges in the Muslim world from Morocco in North-West Africa to Indonesia in South-East Asia; specialized journals have been launched that are totally dedicated to publishing *maqāṣid* related materials; and even centers and institutes have been established to specifically cater for the promotion of study and publication in the field of *maqāṣid al-sharīʿah.* On the level of research and publication over the last three decades mainly, especially in the Arabic language, scores of journal articles, books, book chapters and doctoral dissertations and Master's theses are produced every year at a remarkably increasing rate; no one year passes without at least a dozen of conferences, seminars and workshops being organized in different places in the Muslim world.

This *maqāṣid* awakening (*ṣaḥwah maqāṣidiyyah*), as the present writer described it ten years ago,[1] has resulted in an increasingly large body of literature covering different aspects in the study of *maqāṣid:* conceptual, methodological, historical and practical. One can thus speak of a surge or boom in the study of *maqāṣid al-sharīʿah* that involves not only students of Islamic jurisprudence and Sharīʿah scholars, but also different categories of researchers and writers from the various disciplines of the humanities and social sciences to the natural and hard sciences, including such disciplines as engineering and ICT. Perhaps one may dub this development as something of a fashion! But before venturing into any such kind of judgment, a general

---

[1] In a book review of Abdel Majid al-Najjar's *Maqāṣid al-Sharīʿah bi-Abʿād Jadīdah* (Beirut, 2006), *at-Tajdid*, vol. 11, No. 22 (1428/2007), pp. 227-236.

survey seems to be in order so as to map out what may be described as the 'field of *maqāṣid* studies' or '*maqāṣid al-sharīʿah* studies', just as one could talk of fields of language studies, Qur'anic studies, Ḥadīth studies, *uṣūl al-fiqh* studies, etc. Taking leave of the academic technicalities of referencing and documentation, we shall pinpoint what we deem major or broad trends in this field of study over the last three to four decades, based on more than fifteen years of personal experience of researching and teaching in *maqāṣid al-sharīʿah.* While doing so, we consider our categorization of such trends as only tentative; hence further analytical and critical study is needed.

The first trend that immediately comes to mind can be described as exploratory and historical in nature. Authors falling under this category are mainly concerned with unearthing the works of previous Islamic scholars, especially legal theorists and jurists, of the 'pre-modern' periods of Islamic intellectual history and explicating their views and doctrines, be that on individual basis or in a comparative context. Likewise, we come across works on Mālik b. Anas, al-Shāfiʿī, al-Juwaynī, al-Ghazālī, ʿIzz al-Dīn b. ʿAbd al-Salām, Ibn Taymiyyah, Ibn Qayyim al-Jawziyyah, al-Shāṭibī, Ibn Ashur, etc., that explore and bring to light their contributions to the study of *maqāṣid al-sharīʿah.* Another trend can be discerned in the growing literature in our field that is of chiefly theoretical/conceptual and methodological interest in the study of *maqāṣid al-sharīʿah.* It aims at elucidating the conceptual foundations on which the doctrine of of *maqāṣid al-sharīʿah* stands and how its different components termed as *ḍarūriyyāt*, *ḥājiyyāt* and *taḥsīniyyāt* are inferred from the textual sources of the Sharīʿah. Discussion is also made of whether the specific taxonomy of the *ḍarūriyyāt* as consisting of safeguarding and promoting what al-Ghazālī described as the five fundamentals (*al-uṣūl al-khamsah*) is conclusive and final or rather other things could be included as part of the fundamental and ultimate objectives of the Sharīʿah.

A third trend that can be clearly seen in the growing *maqāṣid* literature is concerned with investigating the theoretical implications of our knowledge of *maqāṣid al-sharīʿah.* This concern has two main aspects. The first one pertains to the question whether, once inferred and identified from the textual sources, *maqāṣid al-sharīʿah* would bear back on the way those sources themselves are interpreted and understood. In other words, can *maqāṣid al-sharīʿah* have what might be considered as evaluative and corrective role in respect of the methodological approaches that have been used by Muslim scholars of the past and present in the interpretation and explication of the Qur'an and Sunnah as well as in respect of the actual understandings and intellectual constructs that have resulted from that process. Some might even go as far as raising the question as to whether *maqāṣid al-sharīʿah* can be used not only as a tool for reviewing and correcting previous interpretations and understandings, but also for suspending or abrogating meanings that have been expressed by unequivocal textual statements of the Sharīʿah. The second aspect of the same concern relates to the possibilities that *maqāṣid al-sharīʿah* could open up for the way we may express and formulate the principles, values and commands of the Sharīʿah in a such a systematic manner as would reflect their internal structure, dynamics and order of priorities.

Finally, a fourth, but not less important, trend is more practice-oriented, having to do with the procedures and operational modalities of the implementation of the Sharīʿah principles and commands and the realization of its values within the context of the realities and complexities of the contemporary world, especially in the arenas of collective and public life, without neglecting matters pertaining to personal and family life. This applies to explicitly spelled out rules established by the Sharīʿah in its original textual sources as well as the inferences and formulations made through valid processes of *ijtihād* grounded in those sources whether in the past or in the present. Without belittling the efforts made in the various areas of human social life covered by the Sharīʿah, it can be claimed that the field of Islamic banking and finance has got the lion's share of *maqāṣid* studies dealing with practical issues. This phenomenon may be explained by the fact that this field has over the last three decades witnessed a steady growth and wide expansion both institutionally and in terms of the variety and volume of its products and operations.

These are, broadly speaking, what may be seen as general trends expressing major intellectual interests in the study of *maqāṣid al-sharīʿah.* Such concerns, however, are not mutually exclusive, nor sharply divided. Rather, they overlap not only in the trends outlined above, but may also be found to be overlapping at the level of the same author, indeed sometimes in the same work. By mapping out the different trends axing the growing literature on *maqāṣid al-sharīʿah,* it has not been our aim to make any critical evaluation thereof or pass any particular judgment thereon. Our aim has rather been to put in context the book we here present as part of that literature.

However, three major and general observations can be made here. 1. A grand purpose, so to speak, underlies and informs most of the works coming under the rubric of *maqāṣid* studies which is to revitalize jurisprudential *ijtihād* in particular and Islamic thought in general by pushing its frontiers to new horizons and opening for it new vistas in terms of both method and substance; the ultimate aim being to come to grips with the intellectual, cultural and existential challenges facing Muslims in the contemporary world, irrespective of the quality and soundness of such works. 2. No overall systematic study exists that analytically traces the conceptual and methodological developments of the idea of *maqāṣid al-sharīʿah* since its early beginnings until at least the time of al-Shāṭibī whose work is considered a landmark in that development. In other words, a grand critical history of the study of *maqāṣid al-sharīʿah* is seriously lacking. 3. Despite the growing academic interest to teach *maqāṣid al-sharīʿah* in most universities in the Muslim world, no soundly and pedagogically produced standard textbook can be pointed out that reflects the historical and current status of knowledge attained in this field.

The present book has its origins back in the year 2006. Excepting the last chapter, all other chapters are the result of a three-day trilingual conference organized in August of that year by the International Islamic University Malaysia, through the Department of Fiqh and Usul al-Fiqh in collaboration with the Jeddah-based International Islamic Fiqh Academy. It was the first international conference ever convened specifically to deliberate on different aspects and dimensions of the doctrine of *maqāṣid al-sharīʿah* and its relationships to various disciplines. More than 240 participants from Muslim and Western countries attended this unprecedented event in which 93 papers were presented; more than a dozen and half of them were by specifically invited speakers by virtue of their acknowledged scholarship in the field, including the Secretary General of the said academy.[1]

The eleven chapters included in this volume were selected from the English section of those papers, including the ones by the invited scholars. Three main criteria can be said to have generally guided the selection process: 1. intellectual originality and methodological soundness; 2. diversity as well as novelty of the topics addressed; and 3. coherence of style and linguistic accuracy. In fact, these are not the only material that was initially selected; other papers had also been included, but were later dropped for different reasons, chief amongst them is the relatively large size of the volume. Though some of these chapters may have been published as journal articles, their reproduction here has gone its own way of reviewing and evaluating them and having them revised and amended accordingly by their respective authors. In order to fill the gap

---

[1] For more see a report on this conference in *at-Tajdid,* vol. 10, No. 20 (2006/1427), pp. 229-242.

in an important dimension in Muslim intellectuals' reflections on *maqāṣid al-sharīʿah*, namely Islamic economics and finance, as well as to keep abreast with critical concerns in this field, it was deemed appropriate and beneficial to solicit the contribution of expert scholars; hence the twelfth chapter by Asutay and Yilmaz.

While the first and second chapters by Weiss and El-Mesawi respectively may be seen as mainly theoretical and historical in nature, they actually provide illuminating accounts of the study of *maqāṣid al-sharīʿah* at two crucial moments of its development.

Standing almost halfway between al-Juwaynī who initiated the first discussion of *maqāṣid al-sharīʿah* in *uṣūl al-fiqh* and al-Shāṭibī who attempted a total restructuring of this discipline around the theme of *maqāṣid al-sharīʿah*, al-Āmidī's ideas are the focus of Weiss's chapter. The author offers a profound analysis and succinct exposition of al-Āmidī's deliberations on and arguments for causality (*taʿlīl*) and suitability or "suitedness" in the context of his elaboration and validation of analogy (*qiyās*) as being the foremost method of *ijtihād* in Islamic jurisprudence. These two interrelated concepts of causality and suitability constitute the solid basis for the notion of purposefulness in the Sharīʿah commands as previously argued by al-Ghazālī and Fakhr al-Dīn al-Rāzī (d. 606H), and later extensively expounded and passionately defended by al-Āmidī himself, and wherefrom emerged the hierarchical tripartite classification of the Sharīʿah goals.

Having thus demonstrated the epistemological and methodological framework of the theory of *maqāṣid al-sharīʿah* in al-Āmidī's work, Weiss then addresses a crucial aspect of the Sharīʿah legal injunctions; what he calls "the moralistic bent" which is "closely tied to the very idea of the purposefulness of Islamic law." On this account, he argues, the "spirit of Islamic law is in the balance more communalistic and directive, less individualistic and facilitative, than that of Western law. The

Muslim jurists were animated by a social vision that they firmly believed to be of divine provenance;" this social vision is implicit in the five cardinal values of "religion, life, rationality, offspring and property." All these fundamental issues compressed here Weiss has discussed at length throughout the three main sections of his chapter.

In his chapter El-Mesawi undertakes to analyze Ibn Ashur's theorization on *maqāṣid al-sharīʿah* whereby the latter aimed at freeing this subject from the confines of *uṣūl al-fiqh* and reworking it as a new independent discipline by the name of *ʿIlm Maqāṣid al-Sharīʿah.* Taking stock of what classical and post-classical Muslim scholars, from al-Juwaynī to al-Shāṭibī, had contrinbuted to the development and refinement of the conceptual structure of *maqāṣid al-sharīʿah*, Ibn Ashur felt the pressing need of grounding that structure in a still more fundemantal conceptual framework that would help put into strong relief the universality of the goals of the Sharīʿah legal order and the enduring values underlying them. This anchoring took the form of quite original exposition of the two key concepts of *fiṭrah* and *mīthāq* which have both ontological and epistemological implications for dealing with the human condition and affairs. Likewise, the universality of the Sharīʿah commands and the values and norms Islam meant to govern human affairs does not simply derive from revelational declarations, but more importantly from the fact that their essence is part and parcel of the God-given primordial nature of the human being.

According to the author, Ibn Ashur took for granted the categorization and taxonomy of the goals of Sharīʿah that had become the subject of an almost universal consensus among previous Muslim jurisprudents. Yet it was his awareness of, and engagement with, the intellectual and cultural challenges of his time that drove him to think out of the box by not confining himself to a narrow legalistic approach to *maqāṣid al-sharīʿah*. This explains his effort to rework this juristic theory by exploring and demonstrating its sociological and civilizational implications and dimensions and elaborate its ontological significance for human life and existence. It also explains his concern about systematically grounding in the core of *maqāṣid al-sharīʿah* many of the essential notions that became watchcry and motivating forces of the modern age, such as freedom, justice, and equality. Thus, his reformulation of the discourse on *maqāṣid al-sharīʿah* was a well-thought-out response to the philosophical and scoio-cultural challenges posed to Muslim societies by modern (Western) civilization with its dominant secular worldview.

With close affinity of concern to the first two chapters in both method and substance, Jackson's contribution is a reflection on some central epistemological and methodological issues in the study of *maqāṣid al-sharīʿah* and a consideration of how those *maqāṣid* can be apprehended and concretized in modern socio-cultural settings. On the first level, Jackson ponders on the age-long literalist versus non-literalist problematic of understanding the Sharīʿah by linking it to modern epistemic debates on empiricism and other approaches to knowledge. In this respect, he argues that juristic empiricism, a derivative of "the epistemological theory of empiricism, has a common tendency with literalism in a common tendency upholding "the self-sufficiency and finality of individual texts." That is, advocates of juristic empiricism look with suspiscion "at all *a priori* claims to knowledge of the Sharīʿah that go beyond and cannot be explicitly documented in the sources." In contradistinction to juristic empiricism, juristic induction upholds the view that "the aggregate of a number of texts, *lietrally* interpreted, point to a meaning that transcends each text individually but explicitly inheres in the group," notwithstanding the fact that juristic induction makes use of literalism just as juristic empiricism does.

According to Jackson, juristic empiricism and juristic induction, as two interpretative modalities, reflect a "fissure in the Islamic legal tradition that persisted from its early centuries," with juristic empiricism gaining upper hand over "all other approaches to law." In his view, it is against this background that al-Shāṭibī's effort could better be appreciated as he set out "to vindicate and gain more formal recognition for an alternative, or perhaps more properly, supplemental, means of apprehending the law" through his notion of *istiqrā'*. In this alternative approach, "a text's weight was to be based neither on its substance nor its authenticity alone but on its relationship to a universe of meanings and values that were inductively extrapolated from an *aggregate* of texts;" hence "legal matters were to be resolved by reference to inductively established values and principles, even in the absence of explicit texts."

On the second level, Jakcson mainly ponders on the issue of *ḥifẓ al-ʿaql* as one of the five essential goals of the Sharīʿah. He points out an important pradox in this regard, what he describes as "strange and debilitating paradox": while theorists on *maqāṣid al-sharīʿah* from al-Ghazālī downwards base their arguments on induction as the royal path to discovering and identifying those goals, when it comes to the preservation of reason they mainly rely on the prohibition of the consumption of inebriants. This situation runs the danger that the consideration *ḥifẓ al-ʿaql* as a universal (*kulliyyah*) would turn out "to be substantively and practically empty," since the "very idea and value of universality" intimately depends on "juristic empiricism;" hence the emergence of "the problem of the false universal." In order to overcome this paradox, Jackson proposes recourse to the nominalist position taken by Ibn Taymiyyah, who considered that "abstract universals, qua universals, exist only in the mind and that the only meaningful manifestation of a concept, value, or principle is in the concrete." In line with this stand, rather than defining *ʿaql* "as the ability to engage in *a priori* abstraction," Jackson endorses what he considers as "the more general and common-sense description suggested by Ibn Taymiyyah that *ʿaql* is simply the primordial, instinctive ability (*gharīzah*) to 'know' or 'understand'." These reflections lead the author to further investigate the implications of *ʿaql* and its preservation thus apprehended to the current situations where Blackamerican Muslims, Muslims and others in general live under the hegemonic effect of what he calls "normalized domination' by the "white West". To explain what this means, I just cite what the author says about it in a self-explanatory way:

> To the extent that regimes of normalized domination exist, clearly the preservation of "*reason*", or "the ability to know", would have to go beyond the mere proscription of drugs and alcohol. For the ability to know is clearly affected by more than the essentially private acts of self-administered corruption of the mind. Indeed, regimes of normalized domination corrupt reason on a far grander scale and provide in many instances the very incentives for drug and alcohol abuse. In this context, *ḥifẓ al-ʿaql*, if it is to be effective, would have to take on a much more public and political dimension. What this translates into in terms of concrete rules and principles will depend on the realities on the ground in the various contexts in which *ḥifẓ al-ʿaql* is concretized.

While the last three chapters are closely interralted by the fact that they mainly focus on *maqāṣid al-sharīʿah* as such, the next three chapters by Hallaq, Crane and Safi respectively have also their specific thread of connectedness. They all reflect on the special relationship(s) and interaction of the idea of *maqāṣid al-sharīʿah* with modern and postmodern worlds with all their complexities and tensions.

After an instructive exposition of the theory of *maqāṣid al-sharīʿah* as it developed and matured in the works of Muslim legal theorists, Hallaq delves into the problematic of his chapter relating to Muslim legal thinkers' encounters with modernity, in the context of the nation-state and national identities of the post-caliphate system. In this context, Hallaq opines, "[t]he most salient problem facing legal modernizers may be captured in the contrast between the essential qualities defining language, especially one of Qur'anic pedigree, and modernity. However much we believe that the reader constructs the text, it is at least equally true that words have meanings whose range cannot but stop at a particular point in the semantic field."

The major problem that arises in this respect is the following. Due to the realities of linguistic diversity in Muslim lands, Hallaq argues, the semantic field enshrined in the Arabic language "is no longer able to constitute the hermeneutical foundations of the law." Similarly, the utilitarian/secularist approach to legal construction "has proven to lack legitimacy in most parts of the Muslim world." The question then is: can "the five universals of *ḍarūriyyāt*, together with *maṣāliḥ mursalah*, form a new foundation of legal reasoning?"

Based on profound analysis of the place and power of the nation-state that has both dislocated the Sharīʿah and appropriated under its legislative and jural function, Hallaq pinpoints a very fundamental reality concerning the hegemonic transformations that have taken place in the social and moral fabric of Muslim societies. And it is within this context that Muslims have to come to grips with the greatest challenge in their encounter with modernity. That is,

> The overarching estrangement of the *maqāṣid* from their native soil does not alter only their form but also their substantive meaning and material contents. Perhaps most central in this transformation is the loss of the moral *order*, or the moral community, upon which the application of Islamic law depended and which it presupposed. If the *maqāṣid* universals are to have any genuine Islamic meaning and content, they must be situated in a morally-based community, in the sense that the socially-embedded moral code is systematically maintained as the driving engine of the law, not the other way around. The loss of the moral community is the quintessential triumph of modernity. How this community can be revived under the clutches of the modern project is perhaps the most central and urgent question of all.

The crucial issue which Crane brings into focus is that of positivist versus normative law, which he formulates in the fundamental question of whether law is "instrumentally created and sustained by human command," or "is a system of heuristic norms that always wait to be discovered." In the wake of the triumph of philosophical positivism in jurisprudence in the West and its influence on the rest of the world, especially Muslim societies, as Crane shows quoting Cammak on Indonesia, the "driving force for the 'modernization' of Islamic law, perhaps especially in the realm of male/female gender equity, is not justice reflecting the essentials or universal purposes (*maqāṣid*) of Islamic jurisprudence, but the felt need to 'adapt the Islamic legal tradition to political realities inherent in the nation state'." As is well known, this is a universal phenomenon characterizing all Muslim countries with almost no exception.

Commenting on Ibn Ashur's statement that "one of the most important qualities of human beings is their God-given disposition for, and acceptability of, civilization, whose greatest manifestation is the making of laws to regulate their lives," Crane argues that this is "precisely why jurisprudence goes to the heart of cultural identity and forms the ultimate arena for either cooperation or clash among civilizations." In an attempt to relate his reflections on *maqāṣid al-sharīʿah* to the American experience, and clearly drawing on Ibn Ashur's treatment of the concept of human rights a "new in the history of human thought," the author observes that "[w]ithin the religious context of both classical American and classical Islamic thought, which is universal in human history, human rights have always been explored and developed as part of the higher concept of justice." Accordingly, justice "is the most universal value in all civilizations."

For Crane, it is plainly clear that the theory of *maqāṣid al-sharīʿah* has some affinity and perhaps a kind of complementary relationship with what has come to be known in some philosophical and religious circles as *Sophia prennis*, or universal and eternal wisdom. Seen from the prism of this tradition, the "essence of every religion, and especially of Islam, consists of three modes or levels: ultimate reality, thought, and practice." These three levels represent what might be termed as "the religion's classical identity."

Safi starts his submission from the observation that the "question of political rights under Islam is the subject of intense debate in Muslim societies and beyond," a debate at the heart of which "lies the question of how the application of the Sharīʿah affects non-Muslims and women, and how such application relates, in general, to the efforts of democratization." In other words, the central question for him in this respect is: which "parts of the Sharīʿah pertain to morality, "and hence fall within the realm of education and voluntary compliance, and what parts are legal, and can therefore be enforced by society?"

Following a short discussion of epistemological and methodological issues related to understanding the textual sources of the Sharīʿah generally and apprehending the *maqāṣid* in particular, Safi offers a distinction of what he calls layers and spheres of the Sharīʿah wherefrom he advances the following proposition:

> The purpose of the Sharīʿah, therefore, is to provide the standards and criteria that would determine the ends prescribed by revelation. According to Islamic legal theory, justice, as the ultimate value that justifies the existence of law and as the ultimate criterion for the evaluation of social behavior, cannot be realized apart from the understanding of the purpose of human existence. Such understanding cannot be discovered by human reasoning, as natural law theory asserts. It must be acquired by direct exposure to the Divine Will through revelation. Therefore, justice may only be fully realized when Divine Law is recognized and implemented by society.

Safi then engages in a critical evaluation of historical Islamic political thought and experience from the inception of the Muslim political society in Madīnah up to the modern times where he discusses a number of crucial issues, especially those of religion and the state, civil society and the state, and Islam, civil society and the state, together with ensuing sub-issues of personal freedom, social autonomy, plurality, theory of right, rights of non-Muslims, etc. This discussion is meant to pave the way for the suggestion that Muslim scholars are called upon "to engage in new thinking that aims at redefining political principles and authority;" this requires them "to transcend the historical models of political organizations in Muslim society," the reason being that the "political structures and procedures adopted by early Muslim societies are directly linked to their social structures, economic and technological developments, and political experiences." Not neglecting the fact that "historical Islamic models provide a mine of knowledge for contemporary Muslims to utilize," the author insists that "any workable formulation of the modern Islamic model of a state that is true to Islamic values and ethos must emerge out of fresh thinking that takes into account the structure of modern society."

As far as political rights and social justice are concerned, especially with regard to non-Muslims, Safi proposes the principle of reciprocity as the means to attaining them. In his view, being "central to all religious and secular ethics," this principle "lies at the core of the Islamic concept of justice." This entails that "the development of the theory of *maqāṣid* and its implementation in modern society is crucial for thinking afresh and preventing the imposition of historically-bound rules developed by early Muslim scholars, who lived under different social and political conditions."

From generally historical and theoretical issues treated in the first six chapters of the book, we move in the next six chapters to more specific subjects of practical nature. Three of these chapters revolve within the realm of economics and finance, namely those by Kahf, Abdulaziz, and Asutay and Yilmaz; the other three being concerned with issues of social responsibility (Dasuki and Abdullah), bioethics (Bouzenita), and legal codification (Zein).

In the seventh chapter, Dasuki and Abdullah discuss the subject of corporate social responsibility which has been one of the contentious issues in socio-political and economic thought for at least the last seventy years and have gained more momentum with the rise of business ethics thinking. The authors take the theory of *maqāṣid al-sharīʿah* and the doctrine of *maṣlaḥah* as a framework to a holistic and dynamic view on CSR that takes into consideration "reality and ever-changing circumstances." Far from ignoring Western humanistic theories that have offered a wealth of insights on this crucial issue, the authors argue, the Islamic perspective based on *maqāṣid al-sharīʿah* and the doctrine of *maṣlaḥah* enriches the matter through its integralistic spiritual view which bears on the human agent's interaction with fellow human beings and nature in his capacity as God's trustee on earth, thus linking his business behavior and sense of responsibility to the "transcendental aspect of human existence."

According to Dasuki and Abdullah, "the Sharīʿah is predicated on benefiting the individual and the community, and its laws are designed to protect these benefits and facilitate the improvement and perfection of human life in this world. This perfection corresponds to the purposes of the Hereafter." In other words, each of its five grand purposes that are to be realized in this world (viz., preserving faith, life, posterity, intellect, and wealth) "is meant to serve the single religious purpose of the Hereafter." All these five objectives "revolve around compassion and guidance whereby it "seeks to establish justice, eliminate prejudice, and alleviate hardship by promoting cooperation and mutual support within the family and society at large."

Translated in terms of social corporate responsibility, the authors underline, the doctrines of *maqāṣid al-sharīʿah* and *maṣlaḥah* provide the needed "ethical guidance to executives and entrepreneurs who must decide which course to pursue and how much to commit to it." This is mainly articulated via the dynamic pyramid of *maṣlaḥah* as classified into *ḍarūriyyāt*, *ḥājiyyāt* and *taḥsīniyyāt*, and attended to by the principle of preventing harm and supported by a set of maxims, all of which "provide a framework for managers to deal with potential conflicts arising from the diverse expectations and interests of the corporation's stakeholders, especially with respect to CSR." Likewise, "they can make better choices, especially when facing situations that involve trade-offs."

In chapter eight on the codification of Islamic penal commands, Zein takes the Sudanese 1983 experiment as a case for reflection, evaluation and theorization through the prism of *maqāṣid al-sharīʿah*. Looking at this experiment in the context of the post-colonial history of the Sudan, the writer maintains that it actually was "the sum-total of a highly complicated negotiation between the traditional formation of Islamic jurisprudential principles and modernity." To demonstrate this, he provides a detailed exposition of the legal history of the country over a few centuries, especially the nineteenth and twentieth, during which it witnessed an amalgam of legal systems and judicial regimes that differed in origin, philosophy and procedure, according to the type of political authority of the day. This historical account has been necessary to situate what has been dubbed as the "Judicial Revolution" in proper perspective as a reasonably natural development *in tandem* with the Sudan's overall socio-cultural and political development and historical self-awareness.

From that Zein moves on to carefully examine the different legal documents and tools constituting the above-mentioned revolution. To reconstruct the story or narrative of the said experiment, he complements this examination with extensive interviews with different kinds of players in, and witnesses to, the advent and unfolding of the Sudanese experiment to bring the Sharīʿah penal commandments into the heart of modern state legislature and law enforcement as codified laws. Notwithstanding the fact that the experiment met with different reactions, from unreserved support to outright opposition, both internally and externally, the truth remains that it was a manifestation of what some intellectuals described as a search for "cultural authenticity."

The author then turns to a very important dimension that was not absent in the Sharīʿah penal code enacted in September 1983 and then supplemented by a series of laws and explanatory decrees, namely the issue of the philosophy of punishment, which directly brings into play the subject of *maqāṣid al-sharīʿah*. This issue bears not only on the substance and goals of the law and the procedures and mechanisms of its promulgation and implementation, but also on the form, set-up and aftermath of implementation. In this respect, Zein detects a stream of thinking that seems to have matured from the very dynamics and tensions that accompanied the whole process, the crux of which relates to the question of values in terms of their apprehension, systematization and translation in legal systems and forms. In line with this realization, he devotes the last section to discussing the import of *maqāṣid al-sharīʿah* for the systematization of values and their implications for codifying the Sharīʿah corpus of penal precepts and rulings. In this regard, he points out the need to distinguish between values governing the process of codification and values regulating the process of implementation.

As far as the Sudanese experiment of codifying Islamic penal precepts and rules is concerned, the author argues that it had to come to terms in a balanced manner with the existing common-law penal code inherited from the colonial era. This meant not doing away with that system altogether, but rather reorienting and harmonizing its hierarchy of values with that of the Sharīʿah, based on the premise that the codification of Islamic penal teachings should "benefit from the human wisdom regardless of its sources."

From codification of penal law, we are taken to bioethics in chapter nine by Anke Iman Bouzenita. As she avers from the very beginning, the author's purpose is not to develop a *maqāṣid*-based framework for dealing with bioethical issues, but to critically examine the use of *maqāṣid al-sharīʿah* and related concepts by contemporary Muslim scholars in their discussions of such issues. As a prelude to that, she ponders on Muslims' encounter with modern science as it grew in the West with both a secular and secularizing spirit. This encounter has resulted in what she considers as a *paradigm shift* which has been reshaping their "lives, value systems and way of thinking" through "an increasingly secularizing process", thus creating a dichotomous situation in their existence. Due to many different reasons, according to Bouzenita, and despite the fact that while Muslims have adopted the Western model of science as it is, they have failed to excel in scientific research let alone to show any originality, be it in medicine or the other natural sciences. In her view, this situation has its roots in the colonial history of the Muslim world.

From her review and examination of a wide range of material on a variety of bioethical issues especially in medicine (such as organ transplantation, genetic engineering and cloning) where different scholars resorted to *maqāṣid al-sharīʿah* to formulate their juristic views, Bouzenita comes to the following realization:

> [M]most of the scholars outweigh probable benefits over probable harms in their treatment of cloning and genetic engineering in animals and plants. Issues like free and uncontrolled mutations of plants, possible side effects on human health or the equilibrium of creation are hardly discussed as harms that should at least be heeded. Another striking characteristic in their debates is that there is hardly any consideration of the probability factor

which is inherent to experimental sciences. What *might* accrue in terms of benefit is often treated as a real or existent benefit.

Explaining this situation by the hegemonic presence of the secular paradigm in Muslim thinking and lifestyles, the author surmises that her conclusions "are not confined to the biomedical field." Instead, they reflect a total phenomenon consisting of a dichotomy between Islamic values and rules on one side and implemented non-Islamic systems on the other. Accordingly, she argues that countering this dichotomy by resorting to *maqāṣid al-sharīʿah* within a non-Islamic framework does not only fail to "provide a solution to the problem," but it also runs the risk of the "closing of ranks with utilitarianism, thaus propagating particular interests in the garb of Islam."

As alluded to earlier, the last three chapters of this book are concerned with the realm of economics and finance. Kahf takes up the old-new issue of usury (*ribā*) which occupies a central and critical place in Islamic economic thought and no discussion of economic and financial matters can ignore it. His aim is to look into the purposes behind the Sharīʿah banning of usurious dealings among individuals and institutions, especially in personal financing, in order to trace their implications for financial transactions and products in Islamic banking and finance. At the outset, he suggests that in order to comprehend the meaning of *ribā* and reasons for its ban according to the language of the Qur'an, there is need to understand the basic concept of debts. A debt, Kahf explains, "is an inter-personal relation that is a liability on one party and an abstract asset to another." As such and in real life "a debt is not liable to increase or decrease," nor is it "able to produce increments because it has no intrinsic utility other than being an ingredient of wealth." Likewise, "a debt cannot have different values at different times and places unless we create additions in the form of assumptions; that is by creating a debt market and valuating or assessing debts in relation to time." Moreover, the increment thus created in debts is assumptive; it depends on the conditions and externalities in the imaginary market that we create for debts." That is the nature and essence of *ribā* simply and straightforwardly put.

According to Kahf, "understanding the differences between interest-loan-based financing and debt-creating sale financing is extremely essential to comprehend the objectives of the prohibition of *ribā*" by virtue of the fact that "these differences elucidate the crucial point of the distinction between seemingly similar transactions." Put in a nutshell, the fundamental difference between interest financing and Islamic financing is that the former is done in loan contracts. Likewise, it is "based on a postulate that a debt may be assigned or may give entitlement to an increment while in reality a debt cannot produce any increment," and is at the same time very much linked to, or constitutes another facet of, the property rights which "entitle the owner of an asset to all and any increments that may happen in her/his asset and preclude any other person from any claim on increments that may happen in other persons' assets." And this is a distortion of the reality and nature of things.

From this follows the author's enumeration of eight objectives as being intended by the prohibition of *ribā* in the Sharīʿah after which he dedicates considerable attention to outlining the implications of those objectives in terms of determining the nature and characteristics of Islamic financial intermediation. This boils down to one thing: that the distinctive feature of Islamic financial intermediation as opposed to direct commercial credit is that "Islamic financial intermediaries must not act on their own initiatives in creating a financing process; they must only act on an initiative by a customer," meaning that Islamic financial intermediary is not a direct investment industry and is instead "a support institution of businesses" providing financing to customers investments and purchases. This also implies that whenever Islamic banks undertake buying or owning assets on their own initiatives (outside buying goods and services for their own personal needs to practice their business), they actually violate "the basic definition of Islamic financial intermediation and turn into merchant direct commercial credit providers!"

However, Kahf finally warns, the matter is not as simple as it might appear from his exposition on *ribā*, *maqāṣid* and financing. Rather, there is within the limits of *maqāṣid* underlying the prohibition of *ribā* a host of means that make risk management in innovative Islamic financial engineering a challenging arena which does not leave room to resort to dubious and counterproductive interest-mimicking approaches of financing that contradict "the essence and basic objectives of the prohibition of interest as well as other regulations of Islamic financing."

In her turn, Akhtarzaite binti Abdulaziz studies some aspects of Islamic insurance in light of *maqāṣid al-sharīʿah* and as can be assessed based on the theory of means or *dharāʾiʿ*. She first explicates the meaning and categories of *dharāʾiʿ* and demonstrates their close relationship with the doctrine of *maqāṣid* whereby the central concepts of *maṣlaḥah* and *mafsadah* are put into strong relief as being the subject matter around which both *maqāṣid* and *dharāʾiʿ* ultimately revolve. The author then provides a condense summary of the hierarchical order of human interests as delineated through the different categories of *maqāṣid al-sharīʿah* with a clear attempt at bringing to light their compact structure and internal dynamic. This is followed by a special look into the specific purposes of the Sharīʿah in respect of the acquisition and management of wealth and property as can be inferred from multiple instances of texts and ordinances. All this is meant as a platform on which to deal with the issue of insurance in Islam.

Accordingly, Abdulaziz examines what has been developed and established in the Islamic finance industry over the last forty years as *takāful* insurance put in practice in many Muslim countries from the Gulf to South East Asia and elsewhere.

Based on cooperation and mutual assistance, the *takāful* model of insurance, the author indicates, provides through a set of schemes and products effective means to realizing "*maqāṣid al-sharīʿah* in financial transactions and wealth and property management", whereby the Sharīʿah purposes relating to wealth and property (wide circulation, transparency, certainty, justice, acquisition, and investment) are to be achieved.

Last but not least, Asutay and Yilmaz devote chapter twelve to a critical examination of, and reflection on, the place and use of *maqāṣid al-sharīʿah* in Islamic economic thought over the last forty to fifty years. In the authors' opinion, "Islamic economics emerged as a project to develop a new economic theory based on Islamic normative principles and substantive morality" with the aim of overcoming the deficiencies of prevailing materialistic conceptions of the economy and rescuing "the meaning and function of human agency, land, labor and capital within the Islamic social formation based on participatory and sharing economy." However, a drift from this vision took place towards a narrow legalistic approach by which "Islamic economic thinking has been reduced and limited to banking activities and financial transactions mostly divorced or, to just put it in a milder way, weakly connected to the realm of real economy, with an unsophisticated and theoretically shallow conception of Islamic finance." This has resulted in mere "mimicry of conventional finance through the adoption of a hybrid of financial services."

For Asutay and Yilmaz, this drift was quite detrimental to Islamic economics and poses the urgent challenge of bringing it back on the right track by doing two things: 1. Freeing the notion of *maqāṣid* from the selective use and abuse it has undergone which turned it into an umbrella to just adopt and incorporate existing concepts of capitalist socio-economic thinking into Islamic economic thought. 2. Re-embedding the theory of *maqāṣid al-sharīʿah* in the essential methodology of Islamic economic thinking in such a way as to cast it in "the theoretical underpinnings of Islamic economics to function as substantial methodology in deriving developmentalist oriented public policy."

With this main purpose in view, the authors embark on a critical exposition and review of the *maqāṣid* related literature on Islamic economics and finance over the last few decades. A major conclusion emerges from this exercise. Characterized by a clear degree of both slowness and homogeneity in its development, theorizing on Islamic economics has been mainly moving "within the boundaries of the Ghazālian *maqāṣid* framework" without casting *maqāṣid al-sharīʿah* with their five cardinal values or universal necessities at the heart of the methodology and substance of that economy. This situation is worsened by the fact that proponents of Islamic finance "are even narrowing the scope of *maqāṣid* to the preservation of wealth," a matter that is evidenced by empirical studies on IBF. A closely related observation made by the authors is that "Muslim scholars have not systematically paid sufficient attention to methodological issues in theorizing Islamic economics," and consequently "they oscillated between two opposite poles: the 'step-by-step approach' and the 'all-or-nothing approach'.

Hence, according to Asutay and Yilmaz, what is needed is an adoption of *maqāṣid al-sharīʿah* that encompasses both the intentionalist and consequentialist approaches to economics and economic life. But this re-embedding and operationalization of *maqāṣid* in Islamic economics requires a revision of its Ghazālian formulation which, in the authors' view, is deficient on two counts. The first pertains to its 'individual orientedness' or self-centredness, thus "lacking explicit emphasis on societal aspects within each objective;" the second deficiency lies in its 'lack of proactivity' reflected by such words of safeguarding, preservation, prevention and protection; all referring to al-Ghazālī's term *ḥifẓ*, which "evokes a closed system of objectives that is far from being dynamic in nature and hence unable to be adaptive to and molder of changing circumstances."

According to the writers, what is expected to emerge from this revision and re-embedding process is a proactive *maqāṣid* framework with purposefulness as its essential feature that "stands against the liberal notion of instrumentalism, as *maqāṣid al-sharīʿah* itself evokes a purposeful character beyond attaching an instrumental role to each dealing separately. Therefore, every step in fulfilling a particular objective creates interdependent purposes, in a holistic way, complementing one another, without considering any of them as an instrumental part. In articulating purposefulness into Islamic economics, it is essential to accommodate 'substantive morality' at the core of its theorization, for the moral dimension must be embedded by its very nature of being a value-loaded system aiming to fulfil a particular objective." Beyond purposefulness, the instrumentalist approach breeds the notion of 'instrumental morality', which basically deals with things as mere tools and erodes their essence.

As such, the present book opens with investigation and intimation of the history and epistemology of *maqāṣid al-sharīʿah* and ends up with critical evaluation and futuristic consideration thereof; while in-between it expands over its dimensions and explores its implications. One fundamental idea which runs underneath the different theses developed by the contributors thereto and animates their arguments is what may be described as a unity of vision of the human condition. One might suggest that this unity of vision is actually entailed by the very logic of *maqāṣid al-sharīʿah* by virtue of its rootedness in the *Tawḥīdī* paradigm governing all the teachings of Islam. As a reflection of this, the emphasis on the centrality of morality and values as both the soul and thread of human life and existence is quite clear in all the chapters of the book.

As far as the present writer is aware, this is the first single volume that presents *maqāṣid al-sharīʿah* in such a comprehensive and diversified manner critically covering historical, theoretical and practical aspects of it. The authors' sense of intellectual commitment and responsibility and their serious and sound scholarship are certainly what accounts for its quality.

CHAPTER ONE

The Purposefulness of the Law: Sayf al-Dīn al-Āmidī on *Maqāṣid al-Sharīʿah*

Bernard G. Weiss

Introduction

My task in this chapter will be to explore the thinking of one of the great masters of Islamic jurisprudence—Abū al-Ḥasan ʿAlī b. Abī ʿAlī Sayf al-Dīn al-Āmidī (551-631/1156-1233)—on the subject of the purposes of the law and the controversies surrounding it. Al-Āmidī's treatment of this topic is an invaluable source, not only for the study of his own ideas, but also for the study of the dynamics of Muslim juristic thinking about this important topic in his time. The primary passages are to be found in his compendium of legal methodology (*uṣūl al-fiqh*) entitled *al-Iḥkām fi uṣūl al-Aḥkām* (hereafter to be referred to simply as *Iḥkām*).[1] It should be noted in passing that al-Āmidī's fame rests

[1] ʿAlī Abū ʿAlī Sayf al-Dīn al-Āmidī, *al-Iḥkām fī Uṣūl al-Aḥkām* (Cairo: Dār al-Kutub al-Khidīwiyya, 1914), vol. 4, pp. 277-315 & 387-405. This study is based mainly on the pages thus indicated. *Cf.* Bernard G. Weiss, *The Search for God's Law: Islamic Jurisprudence in the Writings of Sayf al-Dīn al-Āmidī* (Salt Lake City: University of Utah Press & Herndon, Virginia: International Institute of Islamic Thought, revised edition, 2010), pp. 550-73 & 595-620. Editor's note: Since the edition of al-Amidi's *Iḥkām* used by the author is no more available or not easily accessible, I have provided equivalent references based on the

not only this *opus magnum* in jurisprudence but also upon an equally important *opus magnum* in theology, his *Abkār al-Afkār.* This attainment of such high standing in both fields puts him among the truly great minds of classical Islam and reflects his conviction that theology and jurisprudence were closely connected.

Born into a Hanbali family in the largely Kurdish town of Āmid, near Diyar Bakr in Western Anatolia, al-Āmidī took up studies in law and subjects ancillary to it in Baghdad while still an adolescent, first under Hanbali teachers, then, after some years, under Shāfiʿī teachers. This change of schools apparently gave him greater liberty to explore philosophy and theology, even though neither was in good standing in the circles of legal studies of the time, even among the Shāfiʿīs. Al-Āmidī became highly skilled in dialectic, and it appears that it was his invincibility in public debate along with his interest in philosophy that stirred up enmity toward him among his more conservative peers, causing him to move from city to city four times during his career.[1]

As both theologian and legal theorist with unmistakable inclination to philosophical inquiry, al-Āmidī had a lot to offer in terms of systematic theorization on the understanding and interpretation of the legal legal texts of the Qur'an or the Sharīʿah commands. This is clearly reflected in his discussions of analogical reasoning and especially of the occasioning factor of the Sharīʿah rule and its underying rationale brought into focus through the criterian of suitabality. From such discussions has emerged the crucial idea of the purposefulness of Islamic Law as expressed by the term *maqāṣid al-sharīʿah.* This topic

most recent and reliable edition thereof revised by Afifi. See, ʿAlī b. Muḥammad al-Āmidī, *al-Iḥkām fi Uṣūl al-Aḥkām,* ed. Abdul Razzaq Afifi (Riyadh: Dār al-Ṣamīʿī, 1st edn, 1424/2003), vol. 2/3, pp. 277-381 & vol. 2/4, pp. 5-144.

[1] For a brief biographical sketch of Āmidī, see my *The Search for God's Law,* pp. 27-29.

constitutes the axis around which this chapter revolves. As will be shown in the following pages, Muslim jurists's deliberations in this respect are informed by an unmistakably moralistic orientation whereby legal thinking and ethical considerations are not severed.

Analogical Reasoning and the Roots of *Maqāṣid al-Sharīʿah*

Classical Islamic jurisprudence may, I think, be described as fundamentally textualist. By that I mean that it considers all law worthy to be called Sharīʿah law as derived ultimately from the two corpora of revelatory texts: the Qur'an and the Sunnah. The great majority of the issues debated within the pages of the *Iḥkām* presuppose this textualist framework. No law that is fundamentally and conceptually independent of the divine law can hold the status of Sharīʿah law.

The purposes of the law, in al-Āmidī's treatment, have their place in the context of discussions of reasoning by analogy (*qiyās*) as a method of legal construction. This subject is in all probability well known to most readers of these pages and need not be gone into in any great length. It was a controversial method of arriving at knowledge of Sharīʿah law, and not all Muslim jurists accepted it. But even among those who did, there was disagreement concerning how it should work and what was required to construct an analogy.

To review briefly what is involved in the juristic use of analogy, we shall take as our example the classic case of *khamr*-drinking. Every argument making use of analogy rests on what al-Āmidī calls the four "pillars" (*arkān*) of analogy: an original case (*khamr*-drinking), an analogous case (*nabidh*-drinking), a judgment (*ḥukm*) concerning the original case (i.e. that *khamr*-drinking is forbidden), a connecting attribute (*waṣf jāmiʿ*), meaning an attribute on account of which the original case (*aṣ*) was judged as it was which is found in the analogous case (*farʿ*) as well. When these "pillars" are all in place, a judgment regarding the analogous case (*nabīdh*-drinking) follows; needless to say, the analogous case—the drinking of *nabīdh*—is judged as forbidden.[1]

The discussions of the various issues surrounding the topic of analogy take us into one of the most dynamic arenas of Muslim jurisprudential thought. I believe we can discern four different parties in the debate. Together they form a continuum ranging from total rejection of analogy to advocacy of a type of analogy in which place is given to rational principles such as the grand purposes of the law. Most famous among those who reject analogy are the Shīʿīs and the Ẓāhirīs. The Shīʿīs replace analogical reasoning with rational argument under the heading of *ʿaql*. The Ẓāhirīs cling solely to the texts but develop an exegetical approach that stretches the meaning of the texts to its utmost limit. Since they have to develop a law with the same wide coverage of topics as that of the analogists, their rejection of analogy can hardly mean a reduction of the law.[2] The historical roots of this approach are no doubt to be found in the *ahl al-ḥadīth* movement of earlier days. This movement bred a devotion to the revealed text so steadfast as to make the use of analogical reasoning seem like a kind of human intrusion into the realm of divine law.

Next in order within the continuum are those who accept the use of analogy in legal argumentation but do not give place within the argumentation to rationalizing principles such as the grand purposes of the law. They say, in effect, we only need to know that *khamr*-drinking is intoxicating in order to know that it is forbidden and that *nabīdh* is forbidden.[3] This may be considered the minimalist approach to constructing analogies. With this simple information, one could, upon finding the same

---

[1] al-Āmidī, *al-Iḥkām*: Khidiwiyya, vol. 4, pp. 273-76; Afifi, vol. 2/3, pp. 237-40.

[2] See Abū Muḥammad ʿAlī b. Aḥmad b. Saʿīd Ibn Ḥazm, *al-Iḥkām fī Uṣūl al-Aḥkām*, ed. Muhammad M. Tamir (Beirut: Dār al-Kutub al-ʿIlmiyyah, 1st edn, 1424/2004).

[3] al-Āmidī, *al-Iḥkām*: Afifi, vol. 2/4, pp. 68-69.

attribute in a different case, make an argument for an analogy. But how does one determine, by this minimalist approach, which of the multiple attributes one is dealing with is the one that signals this? The answer, it seems, is that the scholar who has spent many years poring over scriptural texts and *fiqh* texts gets a sense of what sorts of things come under the heading of *ʿillah*. We should keep in mind, too, that these texts frequently make explicit *ʿillat al-ḥukm*. This is especially the case with the famous category of *al-ʿillah al-manṣūṣ ʿalayhā,* the "textually stated" *ʿillah*. Jurists in this camp do not concern themselves with purposes, do not ask "Why?" but only "How is it?" And the answer to "How is it?" is always "Well, that is how this or that authoritative text has it." Going back to the classical example, it is more important *that* we know (thanks to the sign) that *khamr*-drinking is forbidden than that we know why it is forbidden. Why it is forbidden may be an interesting question, but this interest is extraneous to the basic analogizing enterprise.

The next group—our third group in the continuum—takes us into the realm of rationalized analogy. For them it is not enough to know that intoxicants are forbidden. We must go further; we must know that intoxication is harmful to the mind and that it violates the principle of the inviolability of human rationality. It is not enough just to know which attribute of a thing renders it forbidden. The approach of this group is all about purposiveness. It places a premium on rationality and insists upon providing rationales as means of identifying an attribute as the ground of a judgment. These rationales take us into the realm of the law's wisdom and ultimately elevate us to the level of the grand purposes of the law.

Wisdom and the law of God are, after all, closely associated with each other in all monotheistic religions focused on a divine lawgiver. Wisdom is the kind of knowledge that leads to the good life, and the good life entails, among other things, preservation of human rationality. No attribute of a human action subjected to a normative judgment could be regarded as the ground of that judgment unless prompted by considerations of the law's wisdom. To hold that an attribute may betoken a normative judgment in the passive manner of a sign is, for al-Āmidī, sheer mindlessness; the attribute must actively elicit (*bāʿith*) the judgment by virtue of its connection with the wisdom of the law.

Thus, the power to intoxicate—the decisive attribute of *khamr*-drinking—does not just signal a judgment of forbiddenness; it elicits such a judgment. But it does even more than that. It concretizes the divine wisdom so as to make it fit a particular case one is dealing with. The Arabic word is *ḍābiṭ*. The power to intoxicate elicits and it concretizes. It functions as a kind of conduit through which the law's wisdom passes into the world, becoming more focused and constant and case-specific as it is brought to bear upon the raw data of everyday life. By itself the law's wisdom tends to be vague, inconstant, and varied in degree of applicability to concrete situations. The attribute nails the wisdom down so to speak, holds it in place (*ḍābiṭ*), rendering it constant so that it will become applicable to a particular situation.

Here we have an approach to analogical reasoning that takes us upward to a higher plane of discourse where we are able, in dealing with the question "Why should humans not become intoxicated?", bring in our deliberations an exploration of the grand purposes of the law. And here we find the answer to our particular question: humans should not become intoxicated because intoxication interferes with the sound workings of the human mind (*ʿaql*), a condition vital to the proper conduct of worship and of one's social and family duties. With this answer we are in the presence of an important strand in the law's wisdom (*ḥikmah*), namely, the principle of the inviolability of the human mind. This principle is what enables us to treat intoxication as the reason for the prohibition of *khamr*. Without this principle the power to intoxicate would have no special significance and the treatment of it as the *ʿillah* of the prohibition of *khamr* would have no validity.

I have spoken above of the continuum on which the various positions taken by Muslim jurists in regard to analogy, connecting attributes, rationales and higher purposes of the law, can be placed. It is vitally important, if we are to have a correct understanding of the matters covered in these pages, to keep in mind an enormously fundamental point. All parties to these juristic debates were textualists in the sense adumbrated in the opening page of this essay. Methodologically speaking, the starting point for all juristic thought was the revealed Word. We must therefore understand the continuum as reflecting a gradation of textualist approaches that stretch from one end to the other. The radical textualists in their rejection of analogy were not necessarily more textualist than others. They were simply textualist in a different way than others.

Even those who were radical in an opposite direction from the anti-analogists were none the less seriously textualist. These were the jurists who envisioned the possibility that any purpose of the law could descend into the workings of an analogy and become the *ʿillah*. In so doing they in effect ousted the attribute of the case or act being judged. Their formula was no longer "*khamr*-drinking is forbidden by virtue of its power to intoxicate." It became "*khamr*-drinking is forbidden by virtue of the harm it does to the human mind." All reference to intoxication is excised and a grand purpose of the law takes over its role. It *was* a problem, however, because of the consequences it had for legal interpretation. The legal process prefers what is specific, concrete, tailored to the facts of a case. If intoxication is the catalyst for the prohibition of *khamr*-drinking, a practitioner of the law has a fairly easy time applying the prohibition to a case. If we removed *khamr*-drinking and replace it with a principle so general as "inviolability of the rational faculties," we open up vistas of interpretation so broad and vague as to be out of control and possibility too vulnerable to human intrusions. After all, many human actions can work havoc on the mind without being subsumable under intoxicative actions.

Nowhere on the continuum of Muslim juristic thought do we find an abandonment of the idea of a revealed law. The revealed Word is always central in Islamic jurisprudence. And no matter how much importance may be attached to notions of necessity, need or embellishment as concerns of the law, it is always from God that the law ultimately proceeds. The assurance that the law always intends what is in the best interests of the creature is an assurance that we always must derive, not from any innate powers of reasoning, but from God's Word; and in that Word we are assured that God does nothing in vain, nothing mindless, nothing frivolous, nothing without a purpose. And in our endeavor to learn what His purposes are, we have no better place to begin than amid the dialectic of the great jurists of Islam such as Sayf al-Dīn al-Āmidī. No matter what extremes of this continuum might be, "the textualist-intentionalist bent in classical Islamic jurisprudence is firmly grounded in a rich legacy of reflection and argumentation."[1]

Maqāṣid al-Sharīʿah: Meaning and Taxonomy

Al-Āmidī elaborates on the concept of the purposes of the law in the course of his discussion of the various ways of determining which attribute of a particular human act constitutes the ground (*ʿillah*) of the judgment made concerning that act.[2] Every human act may be presumed to be a complex of attributes. Only one, however, may be counted the ground for a judgment concerning the act. If an authoritative text indicates which attribute of the act as the basis of the judgment, nothing remains to be done.

---

[1] Bernard G. Weiss, *The Spirit of Islamic Law* (Athens, USA & London: The University of Georgia Press, 1998), p. 65.

[2] Al-Āmidī, *al-Iḥkām*: Khidiwiyya, vol. 4, pp. 387-408; Afifi, vol. 2/3, pp. 317-381.

However, when the authoritative texts provide no such indication, then some other method of determining which attribute is the *ʿillah* must be adopted. The one that receives the greatest amount of attention from al-Āmidī employs the criterion of "suitedness," meaning suitedness to be considered the *ʿillah*. What this entails is a correlation between the judgment elicited by the attribute and the realization of a higher purpose of the law.[1]

In fact, *munāsabah* does not just operate as a criterion, but also as a method for ascertaning the *ʿillah* or occasioning factor of a Sharīʿah judgment is *munāsabah*. In this method, the *mujtahid* applies what we may describe as the suitability test to a particular feature of a case in order to establish that it "suits" being the ground for the *ḥukm*. The suitability test requires that the *mujtahid* have an awareness of the objectives of the Legislator, for "suitable" means suitable in the light of some objective. Al-Āmidī takes his discussion of this fifth method as an opportunity to explore at length, not only the concept of suitability itself, but also the closely related concept of the objectives of the Legislator. It is in the implementation of this method that the awareness of the objective behind a rule becomes absolutely crucial.[2]

It is only when the suitability test is central to one's method of ascertaining the occasioning factor behind a rule that an awareness of the Legislator's objectives becomes crucial. When the occasioning factor is indicated in a text in a manner that does not require that suitability be taken into account, the objective, however much it may be presumed to exist, may be ignored. The objective acquires relevance only as a touchstone of suitability. Since it cannot, in the view of the majority of jurisprudents, function as an occasioning factor in its own right, its only function can be to enable the *mujtahid* to determine which of several features of a case is the occasioning factor in

---

[1] Al-Āmidī, *al-Iḥkām*: Afifi, vol. 2/3, pp. 339-40.

[2] See especially al-Āmidī, *al-Iḥkām*: Afifi, vol.2/3, pp. 338-45.

situations where no consensus or Sunnaic or Qur'anic text has sufficed. Only if a feature possesses the quality of suitability can it have the role of giving determinacy to a rationale. Or, to state the point slightly differently, a feature can give determinacy to a rationale only if it is such that the rationale comes to be realized as the result of a rule's becoming operative in conjunction with its presence.

The classic example of the prohibition against drinking *khamr* will again provide the needed clarification. As we have previously noted, the power to intoxicate, which is commonly regarded as the occasioning factor behind the prohibition, serves to give determinacy to the rationale of preventing mental confusion, thus promoting rationality: it is not just any threat to rationality that is being warded off, but the particular threat represented by intoxicants. Clearly, to say that the power to intoxicate gives determinacy to the rationale is tantamount to saying that it is "suitable" in the sense defined here. Thus, the power of *khamr* to intoxicate gives determinacy to the objective of preventing mental confusion by virtue of its being such that this objective comes to be realized as a result of a prohibition's coming into effect whenever it is present.

To borrow from the definition just mentioned: if a prohibition is made to become operative whenever the power to intoxicate is present, a safeguarding of rationality necessarily results, and this safeguarding certainly qualifies, by virtue of its being known to be among the objectives that the law serves, to be regarded as the objective underlying this prohibition. The power to intoxicate thus possesses the quality of suitability.

It will be noticed that the higher purpose (*maqṣūd*) in this example is something we have previously encountered under the heading of the law's wisdom (*ḥikmah*). That is, one and the same principle emerges under both headings. The objective that the Legislator has in mind in ordaining a particular rule of law may consist of the realization of a benefit, the prevention of a harm, or a combination of the two. The benefit or harm thus realized or prevented will pertain exclusively to the human creature, since God is above benefit or harm. The Legislator's purpose may also become the purpose of the human creature in that it is especially pertinent to him and in that he, as a rational being, will embrace it. The realization of benefit or prevention of harm may occur either in this life or in the hereafter. If it occurs in this life, then the establishment of the rule will have the effect either of *giving rise* to the condition in which a benefit is realized or a harm prevented or of *maintaining* that condition or of *enhancing* it. Thus, the Legislator, by according validity to certain property transactions, establishes a rule that gives rise to enjoyment of property; in forbidding murder and requiring retaliatory justice he establishes a rule that maintains security of life; and in making witnesses and a fair dowry a condition of validity of marriage he establishes a rule that enhances marital well-being. As for, the realization of a benefit or prevention of harm in the hereafter, these consist exclusively of attaining a reward in paradise and escaping from the punishments of hell.

This takes us to an important observation. The concept of purposes of the law is an elaboration of the law's wisdom. We may in fact go so far as to say that the purposes of the law are the law's own self-articulations of its wisdom, its revelation of its own contents. Bereft of all knowledge of the purposes of the law, we would be left with a notion of wisdom that would be wisdom in name only. Thanks to the laying out in detail of the purposes of the law in the *Iḥkām* and other works of Islamic jurisprudence, we know what the wisdom of the law consists of.

The purposes of the law constitute for al-Āmidī—as they do for certain other Muslim jurists before and after his time—two basic sets of types, one that may be described as vertical (in the sense of hierarchically arranged) and the other as horizontal. These objectives, first of all, either relate to universal requirements of human well-being or they do not. If they do not, then they relate either to no universal requirements of human well-being *(ḥājāt al-nās)* or to those things that enhance human well-being without being requisite to it. Likewise, we have, at the outset, three major categories of objectives: those that relate to universal necessities, those that relate to human needs that, though genuine, are not universal, and those that relate to the advancement of human well-being beyond the level of actual need.

The vertical categories are three: purposes that are concerned with the absolutely vital, universal and unchanging necessities of human societies, purposes that are concerned with the variable and conditional needs of people, and purposes that are concerned with the niceties of human life, things that do not fall under the heading of necessity or need. The horizontal categories are two: I shall call these core purposes and supplementary purposes.[1] They are found within the first two vertical categories only. Combining the two sets of categories, we end up with seven categories:

1. core necessity-related purposes,
2. supplementary necessity-related purposes,
3. core need-related purposes,
4. supplementary need-related purposes,
5. life-enhancing purposes.

Crucial to this classification of purposes of the law is the distinction between necessity and need—in Arabic, *ḍarūrah* and *ḥājah*. The term *ḍarūrah* (corresponding adjective, *ḍarūrī*) has wide currency in Muslim scholarly literature. It refers to those things that the very survival of a community is dependent on and on account of which something less vital may on occasion

---

[1] al-Āmidī's Arabic reads: "*fa-'imma an yakūna aṣlan aw lā yakūna aṣlan.*" I think "core" captures the sense of *aṣl*, which literally means "root" or (as an extension of this literal meaning) "principle." Instead of calling the other category "non-core," following the lead of al-Āmidī's method of classification (*taqsīm*), I am utilizing terminology that he introduces later in his discussion, viz. *takmilah, tatimmah.* (*al-Iḥkām,* vol. 2/3, p. 343-44; Afif's edition).

have to be foregone. For example, in war time the survival of the Muslim community may require sacrificing a finite number of Muslims held captive behind enemy lines. Whatever is *ḍarūrah* takes precedence over anything that is not. Although many examples of such necessity can be given, al-Āmidī's classification limits those necessities that are the concern of the core necessity-related values to five: religion (*dīn*), the soul (*nafs*), the mind (*ʿaql*), progeny (*nasl*), and property (*māl*). Why these five? Are there not others? Al-Āmidī's answer is that we are led by simple reflection (*naẓar*) upon the real world (*al-wāqiʿ*) to regard these five necessities as absolutely fundamental and prior to all else that we may experience as necessary. Through such reflection we know that, *fī al-ʿādah*, there is no absolutely vital necessity outside these five. I leave this last phrase in its Arabic form since it is not amenable to easy definition and bears lengthy explanation. Suffice it to say *al-ʿādah* is a term of Islamic theology that refers to the observable world as a world subject to the ongoing orderly creative energy of God as manifest in both the natural and the social realm. That is, the divine custom embraces all those regularities that are discernible in the created order. As we reflect upon the human part of the created order, that is to say, upon human life, we discover patterns of need and aspiration that are as much a part of the divine custom as patterns visible in the nonhuman part of the created order. Implied in the use of this phrase by al-Āmidī[1] is a reference to the inductive method of investigation. When we examine the world as constituted by God empirically and inductively we discover at the end of our investigation that these five necessities and these alone are fundamental to everything else. They relate to the purposes of the law as the things the law is first and foremost concerned to preserve over time.

Since the five objectives constituting the first category both relate to vital necessities and are principal, they stand at the top

---

[1] al-Āmidī, *al-Iḥkām*, vol. 1/3, p. 343 (Afif's edition).

of the hierarchy of objectives of the law. As for the ancillary objectives, these relate to things that contribute to the perfect realization of the five principal objectives. To use a metaphor drawn from rabbinic usage, the ancillary objectives build a hedge around the weightier matters of the law.

Al-Āmidī provides the following four examples to help us understand the core necessities:

1. In order to preserve religion, the law prescribes that the unbeliever who leads others astray be put to death and that the one who attracts people to heretical doctrines be punished.

2. In order to preserve the soul, the law prescribes retaliation for homicide and bodily harm.

3. In order to preserve the mind, the law prescribes a special punishment for imbibing an intoxicant.

4. In order to preserve property, the law puts restraints on those who would steal or in any way wrongfully appropriate what is not theirs.

Al-Āmidī does not give an example relating to preservation of progeny, although one can think of many examples from Muslim family and inheritance law that he could cite. One could multiply examples even further. In fact, it is quite possible to use the five core necessities as a framework for an account of the social vision informing the legal thinking of the Muslim jurists.

As an example of a supplementary necessity, al-Āmidī mentions the prohibition of moderate drinking, that is, drinking amounts of *khamr* that do not result in inebriation. How does this contribute to the preservation of the human mind? It seems that in this case the mind is not in jeopardy. Al-Āmidī's response is that the prohibition of moderate drinking prevents an individual from taking a first step in the direction of heavier drinking. It therefore blocks entrance onto the slippery slope that leads to perdition. Moderate drinking does seem to stay clear of the attribute of potential for intoxication, if the attribute pertains only to heavy drinking as opposed to moderate or light drinking. The main point is that a judgment that declares moderate amounts of *khamr* forbidden is a distinct rule in and of itself—that is, distinct from the general prohibition of *khamr*—and therefore can be regarded as a supplement to the general rule, bringing out what is not obvious from that rule.[1]

It should be noted that, whereas the core necessities form a finite set of five, needs and niceties do not seem to be quantifiable. This is as one would expect. It stands to reason that those things that are universally vital to the very existence of community life, past, present and future should be seen as finite in number, while the other categories, by their non-universality and their embeddedness in the variables of local custom and taste, should seem to be an open-ended category. The only thing about them that may be described as universal is that wherever human societies exist there will predictably be some sort of customs and esthetic traditions, however different these may be among societies. On the other hand, it is not as though within the spheres of custom and nicety anything goes. Needs and tastes may not contradict any of the purposes of the law that are concerned with the core necessities and their implementation. In that sense, there are limits to what humans are permitted to do under the headings of need and enjoyments of life. The five core necessities provide the groundwork for all else.

Of the various categories of objectives just reviewed, those objectives that relate to universal necessities and that are principal are *sui generis* inasmuch as they alone are found in all legal orders (*sharā'i'*) based on a divine law. In other words, these objectives not only relate to universal necessities; they *are* themselves universal. No legal order based on a divine law can be imagined to be without them. All other objectives are no universal. These include not only objectives that relate to no

[1] *Ibid.*, p. 344.

universal needs but also objectives that *relate* to universal necessities *but are not principial.* Since these latter objectives are ancillary to the universal five and since the ways in which they may contribute to the perfect realization of the universal five vary from time to time and from place to place, they lack universality.

To put it in somewhat different terms, once we have explored the purposes of the law as they bear on the categories necessity, need and embellishment, we should find ourselves in a better position to understand the inner workings of the law's wisdom, for that wisdom consists precisely of the pursuit of the law's purposes. At the center of the law's wisdom are the universal, unchanging purposes. They are the constants of the law. Surrounding them are the purposes that are continually adapting to new conditions. These are the purposes that take into account cultural and esthetical variables. The law's wisdom is thus uncompromising in regard to universals, adaptable in regard to all else.

Maqāṣid and Morality in Islamic Law

Having surveyed the dynamics and structure of the purposefulness of Islamic law as elucidated by al-Āmidī, it is appropriate to turn to an important aspect that is closely tied to the very idea of the purposefulness of Islamic law. Anyone who takes up the study of *fiqh* literature cannot fail to notice a feature of that literature that I shall call the moralistic bent.[1] Although the law contained in the school manuals, commentaries, and *fatwā* collections accords a large measure of freedom to human beings and takes pains to safeguard their legitimate rights, the primary emphasis of that law lies not so much on the side of rights and freedom as on the side of duties and constraints. The law is in large measure the conscience of every Muslim—a moral code as

[1] This section draws on the author's book *The Spirit of Islamic Law*, especially chapter seven (pp. 145-171).

well as a legal one. It is the path of rectitude an individual must follow in order to achieve happiness in this life and in the life to come. Some clarification is required here. Since the Sharīʿah includes norms beyond those that constitute law in the strict sense, it is incorrect to equate Sharīʿah and law *simpliciter* as is often done. In other words, law is clearly a part of the Sharīʿah in Muslim thinking and must always be understood as such. Its most fundamental terms emanate from a primordial covenantal encounter between Lord and subject, between divine Addressor and human adressee, in which all rights belong to the Lord and duties alone belong to the subject. Any rights, any measure of freedom, which the subject may enjoy, must have been granted to him or her by the Lord.[1]

Within this perspective, personal freedom is, however, by no means without positive value. The Muslim jurists acknowledge that there is a large sphere in which human beings must be able to conduct their own affairs so as to achieve maximal advantage for themselves. Humans are presumed to be endowed with an intelligence that enables them to define and pursue ends beneficial to themselves, and self-initiated efforts to achieve those ends are seen as indispensable to true self-fulfilment. Though humans are in principle servants of God, their existence is not meant to be slavish. God's servants are in many ways self-determining free agents; they are clearly not automatons.

But in all human social life, freedom must have its limits, and Islamic law stands in contrast to the liberalism of the West in the drawing of these limits. The spirit of Islamic law is in the balance more communalistic and directive, less individualistic and facilitative, than that of Western law. The Muslim jurists were animated by a social vision that they firmly believed to be

---

[1] On the notion of covenant see the author's "Covenant and Law in Islam," in Edwin B. Firmage, Bernard G. Weiss & John W. Welch, eds., *Religion and Law: Biblical-Judaic and Islamic Perspectives* (Winoma Lake: Eisenbrauns, 1990), pp. 49-83.

of divine provenance and that they saw the law as always serving. This social vision is implicit in the five cardinal values of the law discussed earlier, namely religion, life, rationality offspring, and property. These values were normally discussed as topics in their own right in the rather limited context of discussion of analogy and were linked to a specific method of analogical reasoning that not all analogists shared, not to mention the opponents of analogy; and these discussions are found in the literature of *uṣūl al-fiqh*, not the literature of *fiqh*. That this is so does not, however, detract from their suitability as indicators of the social vision that animated all the jurists. Those analogists who discussed them systematically, after all, believed them to be firmly rooted in the foundational texts and clearly evident to anyone who reflected deeply upon those texts. Although the specific method of analogy that entailed reference to these values may have been controversial, the values themselves could hardly have been a matter of controversy.

It is significant that while the five values are not universally listed in a particular order, the first and second to be mentioned are usually religion and life. The Arabic term here translated as "*religion,*" namely *dīn*, has a wide range of meanings but generally, at least in the writings of the Muslim jurists and theologians, including al-Āmidī, refers to the total body of beliefs and practices, including ritual practices, to which individuals adhere as a matter of duty toward God and of affiliation with a particular religious community. *Dīn* comprises in particular the five acts of worship that constitute the famous "pillars" of Islam: confession of faith, ritual prayer, alms, fasting during the month of Ramadan, and pilgrimage to sacred places in the vicinity of Makkah. The specific duties entailed in these acts of worship comprise the ritual law, discussion of which fills the opening chapters of every *fiqh* book.

The inclusion of religion among the vital interests of humans reflects the grounding of Muslim juriprudnece in a natural theology that makes the knowledge of God's existence the result of rational reflection. If humans can naturally know that God exists, then they can naturally know that it is their interests to render to God any service that He may require. As seen above, the Lord-subject relationship is built into human consciousness prior to the reception of revelation. The institutionalization of this relationship through the institutions of ritual law is thus a prerequisite of human happiness.

Worship is not a realm in which one expects to find the accent on human freedom or rights. In worship one is extolling and serving one's Lord, and in so doing one is expressing one's subordination to the Lord. Worship flows from the realization that one is indeed a creature and subject to the dominion of the Creator. One does not choose this status any more than one chooses who shall be one's Lord or decides whether to have a Lord. In worship one is carried back to the primordial covenantal moment in which all rights lie on the side of the addressing Lord and all duties lie on the side of the addressed subject. Through worship one is keeping one's self and one's life in proper perspective. "Thee do we worship" *(iyyāka naʿbud),* declares the worshiper at the beginning of each of the five daily ritual prayers.

Worship encompasses not only the realm of overt ritual—the physical acts the worshiper performs—but also the inner realm of intention and belief. Without intention *(niyyah)* no ritual act is valid. Mind and body must both be involved in serving the Lord. Even the confession of faith—the most pervasive ritual in the entire system of worship and the one must crucial to Muslim identity—has both an outer and inner aspect. One confesses with one's mouth "There is no god but God, and Muhammad is the Messenger of God." But this confession is hypocrisy and sham of the highest order if it is not the expression of genuine inner belief. Belief, the assent of the mind to the verities contained within the confession, is as much a part of worship as the actual recitation of the words of the confession. Again, all is duty. One does not choose what to believe. The truth about

God and about his Messenger is not for humans to take or leave. It is man's duty to embrace and declare it. Believers are those who have performed this duty, unbelievers are those who have not. Not only must the two cardinal tenets be embraced; so too must all truths that follow from those tenets. To confess that Muhammad is the Prophet of God is to declare belief in all that the revelation of which he was the bearer contains in the way of teachings about God and his prophets, about history, about the Day of Judgment and the hereafter.

The pervasiveness of the confession of faith within the Islamic religion is due to its being a vital component of three of the four other pillars of Islam. It is part of the call to prayer voiced by the *muezzin* from atop the minaret and part of the ritual prayer itself, and since the ritual prayer is an indispensable part of the pious activities that occur during the fast and the pilgrimage, the confession of faith becomes a virtually omnipresent mark of the religion.

Religion is crucial not only to the life of the individual Muslim but to the common life of Muslims as a community. The classical jurists all shared a view of human community that made religion the primary foundation of such community, which they variously called *ummah*, *millah,* or *diyānah.* The last of these terms is in fact a cognate of *dīn.* Religion-based communities are, for al-Āmidī and classical Muslim authors in general, the primary actors on the stage of history. History is in fact the story of the succession of such communities. The Muslim community is the youngest of these communities and the one destined to remain intact until the Day of Judgment. Preservation of the Islamic religion is thus tantamount to preservation of Muslim community.

The law as elaborated by the jurists assures the preservation of the Islamic religion in various ways. It does not compel humans to embrace the religion in the sense of providing penal sanctions against those who do not. Whether a non-Muslim chooses to be a Muslim or not is an issue that the law leaves entirely in the realm of private deliberation. But the law clearly gives the religion of Muslims a predominant position within the domain of public life. The social order envisioned by the jurists is a mosaic of religion-based communities—Muslim, Jewish, Christian, Zoroastrian, and others—that live peacefully side by side but in the context of a public life designed to give preeminence to the religion of Muslims. In the cities of the medieval Muslim world, the different religious communities lived in their respective residential quarters; but the public area of the city—the area in which the marketplace and official buildings were located and in which people of all faiths assembled to do business—had a definite Islamic character.

An important symbol of this Islamic character was the congregational mosque, where Friday prayer services were conducted. The main congregational mosque of a city was usually located adjacent to the city's marketplace; it towered over Muslim and non-Muslim alike, although it was a place of worship for Muslims alone. The law made the ruler or his delegate responsible for the holding of Friday services and for seeing to it that shops were closed and business suspended during the services. Anything that interfered with or undermined this all-important collective expression of commitment to the religion of Islam could be subjected to punitive action. Although all other daily performances of the ritual prayer were left to the conscience of the individual Muslim, the Friday congregational prayer was a clear public duty for Muslims, and participation in it could, if the need arose, be enforced. Muslim places of business were to be closed during the Friday service, and offenders could be punished.

Churches, synagogues, and other non-Muslim places of worship were restricted to locations outside the central public areas of the city. Usually they were located in the residential quarters where those who frequented them lived. The law placed restrictions on the building of new non-Muslim places of worship, even though these restrictions were not always enforced. In principle, non-Muslim communities remained constant, while only the community of Muslims was free to grow by way of proselytization. New mosques could therefore be built as needed, but non-Muslim places of worship could for the most part be only repaired or replaced.

To the extent that the law allowed non-Muslims to remain faithful to their ancestral faiths we may say that it granted freedom of religion. But it was a freedom that was subject to many qualifications. Non-Muslims enjoyed the protection of the Muslim state only by virtue of a contractual relationship predicated upon payment of a communal tax. They were not allowed to show disrespect for Islam or for things sacred to Muslims, nor were they permitted to drink wine or eat pork in public. They could not marry Muslim women, ride on horseback, bear arms, perform religious services in a loud voice, or attempt to convert Muslims. Muslims, on the other hand, were not free to change their religion. Any Muslim who renounced Islam and persisted in his renunciation despite efforts to convince him of the truth of Islam and wrongness of his renunciation was subject to the death penalty. Determined apostates posed a serious threat to the religion and could not be allowed to live lest they have a pernicious influence on others.

Warfare was justified entirely with reference to religion. The jurists divided the world between two realms, the abode of Islam and the abode of war. The abode of Islam embraced those areas in which the Muslim community held the reins of power and government was Islamic; the abode of war embraced all other areas. That latter was so named because only in these areas could warfare rightfully be undertaken. Warfare within the abode of Islam amounted to civil strife among Muslims and was anathema to the jurists. Security within the abode of Islam, however, required that the Muslim government exercise policing functions and that rebellions launched by unworthy claimants to power be put down. These functions did not technically constitute warfare in the true sense, for which the Arabic designations were *ḥarb* and *jihād*.

Warfare against non-Muslims living outside the abode of Islam was not only permitted but was a communal duty (*farḍ kifāyah*). The ultimate objective of all warfare was to incorporate the entire world into the abode of Islam, and until this objective was achieved (if it would ever be), Muslims were duty bound to engage in warfare whenever there was a reasonable prospect of success. Warfare was not, however, a duty that rested upon every Muslim. Rather, it was, as a communal duty, normally discharged by Muslim armies on behalf of the community as a whole. When the prospects of success were poor and the interests of the Muslim community were likely to be jeopardized rather than served by war, it was acceptable for the Muslim government to establish treaties of peace with non-Muslim powers. Such treaties were always to be regarded as temporary, however, since peace could in principle never be permanent until the abode of Islam encompassed the entire world.

Warfare did not necessarily entail fighting. The jurists were very clear in their demand that the Muslim commanding authority issue a call to the enemy either to embrace Islam (which would be tantamount to submission) or to submit as non-Muslims to Muslim rule. If the latter alternative was chosen, the enemy agreed to live within the interreligious Islamic social mosaic and to pay a special tax to the Muslim state in return for a protected status. Ideally, therefore, warfare would produce its desired result peacefully and without bloodshed. Combat was always to be a last resort.

The law of war and peace and the constitutional theory erected by the Muslim jurists thus derive their justification in large part from a social vision in which the Islamic religion formed the foundation of the ideal social order and preservation of that religion was a paramount value. The purpose of war was to make the world safe for Islam, to create (as in the earliest days of Islam), maintain, and enlarge a domain within which the religion of Muslims was secure against malicious forces that might oppose it. True peace was possible only where the religion was secure, in other words, within the abode of Islam.

Preservation of the religion was also assured, on the domestic front, by certain aspects of family law. The Muslim family is well defined in Islamic jurisprudence. All male members and those female members born within the family are necessarily Muslim. Only females who become members through marriage may be non-Muslim, providing they had never previously been Muslim. Although a Muslim man could marry a non-Muslim woman, marriage to a Muslim woman was preferable. A Muslim woman, on the other hand, could under no circumstances marry a non-Muslim man. The structure of family life was essentially patriarchal. A wife's religious affiliation was not nearly as crucial as the husband's, for a wife's role vis-á-vis children was limited to physical nurturing in the early years of life, whereas the responsibility for religious education and upbringing of children belonged solely to the husband and other males of the family. Typically, boys—and occasionally girls—began learning to recite the Qur'an shortly after reaching the age of seven. Children learned to perform the duties of worship by observing and imitating their Muslim elders. Inheritance law—a subject to which we will return shortly—made provision only for Muslim members of the family.

"Life" is my rendering of the Arabic term *nafs*, which embraces a host of meanings including "self," "psyche," "soul," "animus," "living being." It is not life in an abstract biological sense that is meant by *nafs* but rather the life of the individual person. There can obviously be no worship, no religion, without living worshipers. Unlike Sharīʿah, which has God as its subject, *dīn* (religion) has the human as its subject. In order for din to be preserved, nafs must therefore be preserved.

This second cardinal value of the law lies at the core of much of the family law.[3] Life begins in the midst of the family. A newborn child is an utterly dependent being; if its life is to be preserved, responsible adults must provide food, clothing, and shelter. These three necessities are what the Muslim law of maintenance *(nafaqah)* is meant to guarantee. This law of maintenance presupposes a patriarchal family structure. Only adult male members of the family are expected to be fully independent beings capable of maintaining themselves without assistance from others. But their duty under the law includes maintenance not only of themselves but also of dependent members of the family, that is to say, children as well as adult females. Both children and adult females may be owners of property and recipients of income derived from property. This ability does not, however, diminish their right to maintenance, since they are assumed not to be in a position to earn an ongoing livelihood. For them property is a security against future need. The proper place of children and adult females is in the home. Home is the setting in which children grow up and in which adult females provide for their basic needs. Adult females are thus nurturers and providers of care in an environment of food, clothing, and shelter supplied by adult males. Adult males are themselves also recipients of this care. Normally, adult females are members of the Muslim family by virtue of marriage, although where a daughter does not marry after reaching adulthood she retains her right to maintenance by her father until she does marry. Divorced adult females may also return to the families of their parents with a right to maintenance.

But the life of the individual not only must be sustained by means of food, clothing, and shelter but must also be protected against those who would extinguish it without just cause, in other words, would-be murderers. Here again the setting of the patriarchal family is decisive, for the Muslim law of homicide operates within this setting. Homicide does not belong within the domain of criminal law, strictly speaking; it is not an offense against society as such calling for public prosecution.[4] Rather, it belongs under the rubric of a *lex talionis* in which the family unit

—or, more precisely, the *ʿāqilah*, which comprises certain male agnates—is the primary actor; it is an offense against the family, and the family must decide how to deal with it. The *talio* is a right, not a duty, and the family—more specifically a near male relative of the victim acting on behalf of the family—may or may not exercise it, although in the normal course of events it predictably will. The slogan of the lex talionis as it relates to homicide is "a life for a life," although the victim's family may elect to receive blood money in lieu of the life of the offender. Forgiveness is also an option for the victim's family.

The *talio* gives the family the right to demand the death penalty but does not empower the family to execute it without due process. The proper implementation of the death penalty is the responsibility of the state, as is the review of evidence and the determination of guilt. The courts' role in homicide cases is thus more civil than criminal. They uphold and enforce private decisions of families.

Within the setting of patriarchal family life as envisioned by the Muslim jurists, the talio operates as a highly effective deterrent to homicide and as a means of preserving life. Every individual, including the one inclined to take the life of another, is part of a tightly knit extended family unit. The murderer therefore does not act alone but rather represents his family in an act inimical to another family, for the victim too represents a family. All human life is embedded in the web of kinship. Just as the family cradles life during the crucial years of its formation, so it affords protection of life throughout the longer span of time between birth and natural death. When one kills without cause, one therefore is as much accountable to one's own family, which incurs responsibility for appropriate action, as to the family of the victim. Therein lies the deterrent force of the talio within a society founded on ties of kinship.

Muslim family law bristles with the spirit of moral directiveness, and concern for the preservation of the life of the individual in large measure explains why. Only the extended family can function with optimal effectiveness as the cradle and safe haven of human life. Any restructuring of the family along other lines can be said most assuredly to be contrary to the spirit of Islamic law. Family life requires a hierarchy in which females and children are under the authority of males, although males must exercise that authority responsibly and with kindness. Males are endowed with the mental and physical qualities that suit them for this role. The same qualities that make for success in earning a livelihood in the world outside the family equip males to provide leadership and direction within the family. Within the nuclear unit, it is the husband/father who provides this leadership; within the larger extended family, adult males form a hierarchy in which leadership is exercised by the more senior males. (A woman, it should be noted, remains part of her original biological family inasmuch as her father or brother still functions as protector of her interests.)

The law's commitment to maintaining the integrity of the extended family is especially apparent in the lex talionis, which we have just discussed, as well as in the law of inheritance, a salient feature of which is the restriction of bequests to one-third of an estate. Muslim inheritance law works on the principle of fixed shares, and while first consideration goes to members of the nuclear family, other relatives as well are assured entitlements in amounts and under conditions stipulated by the law and calculated according to a highly complex system. A person facing death cannot dispose of his earthly goods as he pleases; the interests of the family take precedence over his personal wishes.

The law presupposes that membership in a family is a natural condition among humans and that individuals will rarely become totally bereft of family connections. When this unlikely condition does occur as a result of warfare, plague, or other disasters and the individual is without the means to sustain life, as can occur especially in the case of orphans and widows, he or she then comes under the care of the community as a whole by virtue of an entitlement to a share in goods donated for charitable purposes. The law guarantees that a certain level of provision for such unfortunate persons will "always be available by imposing on those with means the duty of *zakāh*, a progressive tax on merchandise or wealth the revenue from which is designated for partly charitable or religious purposes. Otherwise the law leaves the welfare of these persons in the hands of voluntary benefactors on the supposition that benevolence will always be for Muslims a supreme form of piety. The Qur'an itself, in innumerable passages, makes it clear that those who from their wealth provide for the destitute attain greater closeness to God.

To the life of the individual as a fundamental value that the law seeks to preserve, is closely tied progeny *(nasl)*. Humans not only live their own lives in this world; through sexual reproduction they give rise to lives other than their own. Although some individuals may not marry, the classical jurists considered marriage to be the normal ultimate state of human beings, and they saw marriage as inevitably resulting under normal circumstances in offspring. Through progeny human life —and with it the worship of God and communal life of the faithful—continues from generation to generation. To the extent that the law is concerned with the preservation of life across generations, it is bound to be concerned with the preservation of progeny.

But progeny is more than a mere continuation of life across generations considered in the abstract. Progeny is always the progeny of particular persons. Just as one has one's own life to consider, one's *nafs,* so one must give consideration to one's offspring, or *nasl.* In keeping with the patriarchal structure of the family, progeny is reckoned in patrilineal terms. It is the man who has nasal, not the woman. The woman is the necessary partner in procreation, but the offspring is reckoned to be the man's. The justification for this patriarchalism has already been intimated.

Preservation of the patrilineal progeny requires first of all that procreation occur solely within the bounds of legal marriage. A social order in which men and women could have sexual intercourse freely and at will was unthinkable to the classical jurists. In such a situation, men would be unable to identify their offspring, and chaos and corruption of human life would ensue. Nowhere in the *fiqh* literature is the moralistic bent of the jurists more evident than in the sections that deal with marriage and sexual behavior. Marriage is for them largely a means of regulating human procreation in such a way that the identification of offspring and assignment of responsibility for nurture and maintenance will be assured. Since paternity is presumptive, the law must lay down the conditions for a valid presumption. Decisions about paternity cannot be left to the whims of individuals.

Marriage is the all-important ground for a presumption of paternity. According to the commonly accepted rule, a man is presumed to be the father of a child if the child is known to have been born to his wife at least six months after their marriage.

Conclusion

What have we learned about the place given to purposes of the law in the thinking of al-Āmidī and the classical Muslim jurists? The following points come to mind:

1. The purposes of the law are not, for the vast majority of jurists, a source for rules or a basis for judging cases. They are too general for that. They can, however, have a bearing on the formulation and application of law by being incorporated into legal analogies and made to fit into a world of multiple facts through the concretizing impact of the *ʿillah*.

2. What is general is not necessarily devoid of usefulness. In many ways, the preambles of many constitutions of the modern world sound themes very much like the five purposes of Islamic thought. One need only think of the

preamble of the American constitution, which refers to themes such as "We the People," "a more perfect Union," "Justice," "domestic Tranquility," "the common defense," "the general Welfare," "the Blessings of Liberty", all preceded by the phrase "in Order to".[1] In other words, these are the grand purposes of the American legal system. Turning to the Indonesian constitution of 1945, we find somewhat different content due to different circumstances, but the same overriding concern with purposes: "freedom as a right of nations," "protection of the people," "public welfare," "unity," "guided democracy," "social justice," to mention just a few.

3. The purposes of the law are anchored in the sacred texts and are discovered therein through an inductive process of understanding over centuries. They do not therefore disconnect the community from the divine sources of law and morality.

4. The purposes of the law can be useful as a focal point for discussions of the ideal social order as envisaged in Islam. This is a role that has become especially important in recent times, with the advancement of a field of study and reflection often known in Muslim circles as *'Ilm Maqāṣid al-Sharī'ah.*

5. The theorization on the purposefulness of Islamic law in Muslim jurisprudential thought is clearly embedded in a moral vision that is in turn grounded in a worldview in which the primorodial covenant between God and human beings is the cornerstone. This provides the ontological basis of individual human life and communal existence as well as of the fundamental values proping them up.

---

[1] *The Constitution of the United States of America* (Washington: United States Government Printing Office, 2007), p. 1.

CHAPTER TWO

Beyond *Uṣūl al-Fiqh*: Ibn Ashur's *ʿIlm Maqāṣid al-Sharīʿah*

Mohamed El-Tahir El-Mesawi

Introduction

Maqāṣid al-sharīʿah or intents and objectives of Islamic Law can be regarded as the greatest development in Islamic juristic thought next to *uṣūl al-fiqh,* the discipline which deals with issues related to the sources and methodology of Islamic Law, thus generally standing as the equivalent of the philosophy of law as usually understood in secular jurisprudence. Many scholars of Islamic jurisprudence contributed to this crucial development, right from Abū al-Maʿālī al-Juwaynī (419/1028-478/1085) in the classical period of Muslim history up to Muhammad al-Tahir Ibn Ashur (1296/1879-1393/1973) in modern times. Realizing the importance of the idea of *maqāṣid,* the Andalusian jurist Abū Isḥāq al-Shāṭibī (d. 790/1388) attempted to reconstruct the whole of *uṣūl al-fiqh* around the *maqāṣid,* thus making them the unifying theme of the issues and topics usually dealt with almost independently of one another by *uṣūl* works. With him the *maqāṣid* became the axis of *uṣūl al-fiqh.* In modern times, Ibn Ashur sought to reformulate the *maqāṣid* not only as a doctrine in Islamic jurisprudence and central theme in *uṣūl al-fiqh*, but as an independent discipline by the name of *ʿIlm al-Maqāṣid.* Just as a matter of clarification, while *uṣūl al-fiqh* deals with issues of legal theory and methodology revolving around the sources of the Law and the methods of deriving its rules therefrom, *maqāṣid al-sharīʿah* can be seen as mainly pertaining to the philosophy and ends of the law.[1]

In the understanding of the present writer, the idea of *maqāṣid al-sharīʿah* as conceived and developed by Muslim scholars throughout the centuries is about the sociopolitical and moral order of human society. Thus, it does not only reflect the objectives of the legal system of the Sharīʿah, but it is also a manifestation of the Islamic world-view itself and an embodiment of the system of values which Islam has brought for human life individually and collectively. Likewise, it has been an important tool for formulating the fundamental principles and cardinal values pertaining to human good and welfare according to a classification of human needs into a descending order. It has also served as a means to articulate a systematic and comprehensive understanding of the values and goals underlying Islamic teachings. This definitely implies certain outlook on human nature and a specific view of the dynamics of human society.

Among the scholars who dealt with the subject of *maqāṣid al-sharīʿah* Ibn Ashur exhibited clear awareness of the importance of human nature for the study of the objectives of the Sharīʿah. He devoted considerable effort to elaborate on it through a discussion of the Qura'nic concept of *fiṭrah.* It is therefore appropriate that his views on *fiṭrah* and other related concepts, especially *mīthāq* and *wāziʿ*, should be analyzed in our

[1] The reservation implied here is intended in order not to equate the term *law* in its current prevalent sense with of *Sharīʿah* as used in the Qur'an and as undersatood by the majority of Muslims both in the past and present. As rightly pointed out by Weiss, "Since the Sharīʿah includes norms beyond those that constitute law in the strict sense, it is incorrect to equate Sharīʿa and law *simpliciter* as is often done. On the other hand, law is clearly a part of the Sharīʿa, in Muslim thinking, and must always be understood as such." Bernard G. Weiss, *The Spirit of Islamic Law* (Athens & London: The University of Georgia Press, 1998), p. 8.

attempt to study his project of establishing *maqāṣid al-sharīʿah* as an independent discipline enabling Muslims to respond more efficiently and on their own terms to the challenges of modern times. Furthermore, by linking the doctrine of the higher objectives of the Sharīʿah to the subject of human nature through the term *fiṭrah* as done by Ibn Ashur, we are provided an appropriate framework to assess the deep crisis tormenting contemporary societies in terms of the shattering of value systems and the loss of meaning expressed in different forms and various levels of individual and collective life the world over.

Human Nature and the Roots of the Ethico-socio-political Order

1. In the Aftermath of Secular Humanism

The issue of human nature is central to any discussion of human society and the values and ideals propping the human socio-political order with its relations and institutions. This is because much of the differences and conflict between social philosophies and political ideologies and systems as well as the antagonistic attitudes toward religion and religious belief and values, lies at the fundamental level of the predominant views of human nature.[1] Depending on their views of human nature and the place of man in the universe and in the wider context of being and existence, individuals and groups develop their understanding of values and formulate their theories about individual and collective human life, on which basis they devise social institutions and political systems. As a leading political scientist put it, "Since the time of Socrates, political theory has been devoted to an inquiry into

---

[1] For further detail, see Mohamed El-Tahir El-Mesawi, *A Muslim Theory of Human Society: an Investigation into the Sociological Thought of Malik Bennabi* (Kuala Lumpur: Thinker's Library, 1998), pp. 13-23.

human nature and its consequences for social life."[1] Likewise, without a clear and sound understanding of human nature and of what makes human beings distinct from other creatures on earth, and without arriving at a common understanding of what such distinctness entails in terms of values and institutions, there is indeed little hope that the wide ideological gaps and cultural and political chasms dividing humanity and accounting for many of the bloody events in human history could one day be bridged or even narrowed.

The problem of human nature has reached unprecedented measures of gravity reaching far beyond the implications of the reductionist and secular theories of human nature that have prevailed in Western thought since the Renaissance and Enlightenment periods and affected in varying degrees philosophical and social thought in the world. Not only have such theories distorted our understanding of human nature, but they have also been at the origin of a process of systematic denial thereof. This denial has been quite universally expressed by the notion of the 'blank slate' or *tabula rasa.* According to this epistemological position, individual human beings are born without any innate or built-in mental and spiritual content, which means that their entire stock of knowledge is merely the result of impressions gradually acquired from their experiences and sensory perceptions of the outside world.

The alarming gravity resulting from that cultural and historical process amounts to no less than mischievous manipulation of human constitution to reengineer human beings and make them come into existence at will and upon demand. Carried out in the name of science and progress, this manipulation, Fukuyama has rightly warned, threatens not only of undermining the human socio-political order by sapping the philosophical and moral ideas supporting it, but it also threatens

---

[1] Roger D. Masters, *The Nature of Politics* (New Haven and London: Yale University Press, 1989), p. 249.

to bring nearer what he calls our "post-human future". Even those Western thinkers who attempted to formulate theories that would overcome the empiricist-and-positivist biology-based conceptions of human nature fell short of transcending the secularist paradigm that gave rise to such conceptions.[1] One need not be a believer in any religion to be apprehensive of the consequences of the unfettered intervention in the creation in the name of science, with a tendency to playing God. Non-relgionists too who might be sheer atheists do express similar concerns, seeing in that intervention an unfolding of the process of degradation of mankind and emptying it of its essence.[2]

2. Fiṭrah and the Original God-given Human Nature

Ibn Ashur dealt at length with the concept of *fiṭrah* in many of his works, including his commentary on the Qur'an. It would be appropriate first to look at his explanation of the general meaning of this term before examining his interpretation thereof in relation to the teachings of Islam. In his view, the term *fiṭrah* refers to the natural disposition or the system that God has put in every created being. Thus, man's *fiṭrah* is the inward and outward states in which man has been created, that is to say, at the physical and intellectual levels. Accordingly, walking on his feet is an aspect of man's physical *fiṭrah,* while trying to hold things with his feet is against that *fiṭrah*. Similarly, relating effects to their causes

---

[1] *Cf.* David Martin, *A General Theory of Secularization* (London & New York: Harper & Colophon Books, 1979); Steven Pinker: *The Blank Slate: The Modern Denial of Human Nature* (London & New York: Viking Penguin, 2002); Francis Fukuyama, *Our Posthuman Future: Consequences of Biotechnology Revolution* (London: Profile Book Ltd, 2002); Edgar Morin, *L'Humanité de l'humanité : L'Identité Humaine,* vol. 5 of his *La Mé thode* (Paris: Editions du Seuil, 2001); Charles Taylor, *A Secular Age* (Cambridge, USA, and London, UK: The Belknap Press of Harvard University Press, 2007).

[2] See for example, Raymond Tallis, *Aping Mankind: Neuromania, Darwinitis and the Misrepresentation of Humanity* (Durham: Acuman, 2012), also *The Explicit Animal: A Defence of Human Consciousness* (London: Macmillan Press Ltd, 1999); Ted Peters, *Playing God? Genetic Dterminism and Guman Freedom* (New York & London: Routledge, 2003).

and inferring conclusions from their proper premises is an intellectual *fiṭrah*, whereas attempting to infer things not from their right causes is contrary to the intellectual *fiṭrah*; hence, it is considered in the art of argumentation as invalidity of argument. Thus, asserting that things have a reality of their own independently from our perception of them is part of the intellectual *fiṭrah*, contrary to the Sophists who stand against that *fiṭrah* by denying the reality of things.[1] To further elaborate the intellectual aspect of *fiṭrah*, Ibn Ashur leaned quite heavily on a long passage from the great Muslim Peripatetic philosopher Abū ʿAlī Ibn Sīnā (Lat. Avicenna) that he quoted integrally in the works pointed out above.[2]

Ibn Sīnā explained the meaning of *fiṭrah* in his discussion of demonstrative proof in the part of his book *al-Najāt* (Healing) dealing with logic. This he did as follows: Let us imagine that a person has come into existence fully mature and with perfect consciousness and intelligence all at once, without having known any thoughts, or adopted any faith, or mixed with any people, or experienced any politics; yet, he has seen the *sensibilia* (*maḥsūsāt*) from which he derives images (*khayālāt*). If this person then examines something and doubt finds its way to his mind concerning it, this means that the thing he has doubts in is not confirmed by the *fiṭrah;* if he cannot doubt it, then it is what *fiṭrah* necessitates. However, Ibn Sīnā remarked, not all that man's *fiṭrah* confirms is true; only things confirmed by the faculty of it known as intellect (*ʿaql*) are so.[3]

---

[1] Muhammad al-Tahir Ibn Ashur, *Treatise on Maqāṣid al-Sharīʿah* (hereinafter *Treatise*), trans. Mohamed El-Tahir El-Mesawi (London & Washington: The International Institute of Islamic Thought 1427/2006), p. 81; *Uṣūl al-Niẓām al-Ijtimāʿī fī al-Islām,* hereinafter *Uṣūl*, ed. Mohamed El-Tahir El-Mesawi (Amman: Dār al-Nafaes, 1421/2001), p. 36; *Tafsīr al-Taḥrīr wa al-Tanwīr*, hereinafter *Taḥrīr* (Tunis: Maison Souhnoun, 1997), vol. 10/21, p. 90.

[2] Ibn Ashur, *Treatise*, pp. 81-82; *Uṣūl*, p. 37; *Taḥrir*, vol. 1/3, p. 193 & 10/21, pp. 90-91.

[3] Al-Sheikh al-Ra'īs al-Husayn Abū ʿAlī Ibn Sīnā, *Kitāb al-Najāt fī al-Ḥikmah al-*

As Ibn Ashur argued, the Sharīʿah commands are meant to restore human nature in all its aspects and free it from all that has encroached upon it. For example, marriage, cooperation for the common good and survival of the species, protection of life and lineage all flow from the spring of human nature. Building a righteous humane civilization and pursuing useful knowledge are also a manifestation of that same nature which is inclined to express itself through human intellectual creativity and inventions.[1] Thus, because Islam is intimately linked to what is confirmed by human nature and agreeable to it, it has been considered as man's *fiṭrah* as if it were that nature itself.[2]

3. Human Nature and the Primordial Covenant

The Islamic view of human nature as expressed by the term *fiṭrah* is closely linked to another concept that occupies a prominent place in Islamic thought, that is, the notion of *mīthāq* or covenant.[3] As can be realized from the foregoing discussion, we are presented with a holistic and balanced understanding of human nature that emphasizes the spiritual and, for that matter, metaphysical and transcendental dimensions of man without alienating him from the material world or trying to portray him as an angelic being. It is a vision fully aware of both the strengths and weaknesses of human nature. In so doing Ibn Ashur benefited clearly from the contributions of previous Muslim

---

Manṭiqiyyah wa al-Tabīʿiyyah wa al-Ilāhiyyah, ed. Majid Fakhri (Beirut: Dār al-Āfāq al-Jadīdah, 1405/1985), p. 99. Cf. his *al-Ishārāt wa al-Tanbīhāt*, ed. Sulayman Duniya (Cairo: Dār al-Maʿārif, 1983), vol. 1, p. 352.

[1] Ibn Ashur, *Treatise*, p. 85.

[2] Ibn Ashur, *Uṣūl*, p. 40; *Taḥrīr*, vol. 1/3, p. 194.

[3] For an indepth treatment of this concept in the Qur'an, see Bernard G. Weiss, "Covenant and Law in Islam," in Edwin B. Firmage, Bernard G. Weiss & John W. Welch, eds., *Religion and Law: Biblical-Judaic and Islamic Perspectives* (Winona Lake, USA: Eisenbrauns, 1990), pp. 49-83; Wadad (Kadi) al-Qadi, "The Promordial Covenant and Human Hsitory in the Qur'an," *Poceedings of The American Philosophical Society*, Vol. 147, No. 4 (December 2003), pp. 332-338; Joseph E.B. Lumbard, "Covenant and Covenants in the Qur'an," *Journal of Qur'anic Studies*, vol. 17, No. 2 (2015), pp. 1-23.

scholars and thinkers irrespective of their specific disciplinary background or intellectual orientation in the vast sphere of classical Islamic scholarship. But it is also of equal importance to note that, in formulating his ideas on the relation of religion and human nature, he was not unaware of the philosophical discussions that animated European Enlightenment thought in this respect, especially in France.[1] As the following paragraphs will show, the Islamic view of human nature is based on a deeper philosophical and theological ground expressed by the idea of covenant. To state it more specifically, the question here depends on the ontological framework underlying the Islamic conception of human nature.

According to the Qur'an, man's instinctive cognition of God and his natural inclination to submit to His will are rooted in a more fundamental metaphysical reality pertaining to the human beings' ontological bond with their Creator. Thus, we read that God "brought[2] forth from the loins of the Children of Adam their offspring" and "called upon them to witness about themselves: 'Am I not your Lord?' They answered: 'Yea, we do bear witness thereto." (Q. 7: 172). This is, as Ibn Ashur commented, a metaphorical description of a metaphysical situation exemplifying God's creational power in determining the essence and qualities of the creatures in accordance with His will. It is a representation of something whose nature and essence cannot be apprehended by human intelligence, but

---

[1] See his remarks on Voltaire, Diderot and Rousseau in *Uṣūl*, p. 39.

[2] We have here followed Abdullah Yusuf Ali's use of the past tense which is in the original. But it is a characteristic of the Arabic language and of the Qur'anic discourse in particular that the past tense is not used to only indicate events or processes that occurred in the past and have ceased to exist. It is also used to indicate and stress continuous recurrence. Hence, Muhammad Asad has rightly suggested using the present tense to bring out more clearly this aspect whereby the 'question' and 'answer' mentioned in the verse are portrayed as a continuous recurrence in the Divine act of creation. Muhammad Asad, *The Message of the Qur'an* (Gibraltar: Dar al-Andalus, 1984), p. 230, note 139.

which the Qur'an makes more immediate through metaphoric analogy. This metaphoric representation is an indication of the fact that "God has impressed in man since his creation the capacity to comprehend the proofs of [His] oneness and put in his natural intelligence the propensity for pursuing and acquiring that knowledge, provided he is free from the influence of adverse factors that might corrupt his inborn disposition."[1]

This Qur'anic account has suggested to Muslim scholars the fundamental idea of an original covenant (*mīthāq*) between man and God. According to the contemporary Tunisian scholar Mohamed Talbi, this *mīthāq* refers to "a solemn and pre-eternal engagement that had already fixed and determined, in the ontological time of pre-eternity, the relation of man to God."[2] Thanks to this primordial ontological covenant, man finds the stamp of the faith engaging him toward his Lord and Creator deeply sealed in his heart. From this has followed the notion of original religion which successive prophets came to confirm and revive.[3] It is beyond our power as humans to uncover the hidden reality lying behind the symbolism of this primordial covenant. However, this does not mean that it is merely "a matter of gratuitous abstraction, or ineffective myth."[4] On the contrary, it points to man's essential nature and the purpose of his worldly existence both as God's servant (*ʿabd*) and vicegerent (*khalīfah*) on earth.[5] In this respect, al-Attas has argued that the notion of man's covenant with God "is the starting point in the Islamic conception of religion, and is the dominant element in all other Islamic concepts bound up with

---

[1] Ibn Ashur, *Taḥrīr*, vol. 5/9, p. 168 & 7/13, pp. 125-26.

[2] Mohamed Talbi, "Quelle clé pour lire le Coran" in Mohamed Talbi and Maurice Bucaille, *Reflections sur le Coran* (Paris: Seghers, 1989), pp. 108-109.

[3] *Ibid.* p. 109.

[4] *Ibid.* p. 110.

[5] Syed Muhammad Naquib al-Attas, *Islam and Secularism* (Kuala (Lumpur: International Institute of Islamic Thought and Civilization, ISTAC, 1993), pp. 139-140.

it, such as those of freedom, responsibility, justice, knowledge, virtue, brotherhood, etc."[1]

Grounded in the idea of the primordial covenant, the Islamic view of human nature thus lays down the foundation for man's noble position and mission in the world whereby he is the sole amongst all creatures to bear God's trust or *amānah* (Q. 33: 72) as the stewart of earth. As pertinently indicated by Talbi, if we divest man of these dimensions, he will be reduced to a mere "stomach and sex, that is, to a purposeless twofold function of maintenance and reproduction: producing and procreating to consume, and consuming and producing to procreate… Through an endless rotation the circle closes up on emptiness, absurdity and despair, which is the real disease" of our time since Nietzsche announced the death of God.[2] By estabilshing such essential bond between human nature and Islam, the Qur'an actually aims at unifying inborn natural and revealed religion, hence the significance of the description of Islam as *dīn al-fiṭrah* whereby a solid relationship is established between "ethical values and ontological realities."[3] This unification finds its expression in its basic beliefs and universal Law whose precepts and commands conform to the natural needs and longings of the human beings. Likewise, in the Islamic worldview, the inborn natural guidance prepares man to

---

[1] Syed Muhammad Naquib al-Attas, *Prolegomena to the Metaphysics of Islam* (Kuala (Lumpur: International Institute of Islamic Thought and Civilization, ISTAC, 1995), p. 75.

[2] Talbi, *op. cit.*, p. 114.

[3] A. Ezzati, *Islam and Natural Law* (London: Islamic College for Advanced Studies Press, 1st edn, 2002), p. 103. For more elaboration on the notion of the unity between natural and revealed religion in Islam, see Ezzati, *op. cit.,* especially chapter 3; Jacques Jomier, *Dieu et l'Homme dans le Coran: l'aspect religieux de la nature humaine joint á l'obeissance au Prophete de l'islam* (Paris: Les Edition du Cerf, 1996), pp. 31-52 & 139-183; Abu Yaarub al-Marzouki, *Waḥdat al-Fikrayn al-Dīnī wa al-Falsafī* (Damascus: Dār al-Fikr, 1st edn, 2001).

recognize and accept the revealed guidance embodied in the Qur'an and Prophetic traditions.[1]

4. *Wāzi*ʿ *and the Dynamics of Human Socio-historical Existence*

Another important concept closely rlated to the issue of human nature which Ibn Ashur deployed in his project of establishing *ʿIlm Maqāṣid al-Sharīʿah* is that of *wāziʿ*. To introduce this concept, he advanced the following proposition. Unlike worldly reformers, an infallible reformer (*muṣliḥ maʿṣūm* or *ilāhī*), cannot be content with simply preaching and showing people what is right and warning them against what is wrong or merely exhorting them to do good and abstain from evil. Rather, such a reformer is as much concerned about making them act accordingly as about their perseverance and consistency to do so. Therefore, there is need for more than just the inculcation of right faith and sound thinking, in order to ensure the continuity of human action in conformity with the new ideas and values and prevent human personality from reverting to the undesired old ways and practices or deviating to any other kinds of misconduct.

For Ibn Ashur, there is always in the human self a conflict where old habits and evil forces do not just retreat in front of the good tendencies and new ways and habits acquired thanks to the reformative measures taken by Islam to remold and change the human personality and condition. Those old elements would always resist such reforms and strive to push them out or at least minimize their effect on man's action and behavior, aided in that by a natural inclination in human beings to stick to their earlier customary practices and succumb to their whims and desires. This conflict is what the Prophet Muhammad (*pbuh*) meant by *jihād akbar*, that is, greater struggle

---

[1] Cf. Al-Sheikh Muhammad ʿAbdu, *al-Aʿmāl al-Kāmilah*, ed. Muhammad ʿImarah (Cairo: Dār al-Shurūq, 1414/1993), vol. 3, pp. 501-503; Abdulaziz Sachedina, *Islamic Roots of Democratic Pluralism* (Oxford & New York: Oxford University Press, 2001), pp. 91-93.

which everyone has to undertake within one's own self. This struggle in the human self occurs between the conflicting forces and inclinations of good and evil which pull in opposing directions so as to make one type of conduct and action prevail over the other. The role of *wāziʿ* is to enable the person to win the battle by curbing the negative and evil tendencies and promoting the positive and good qualities in human behavior.[1]

Of course, the idea of such restraining force is not new in Islamic thought. In fact, the concept of *wāziʿ* was an important component of classical Islamic political theory used by many scholars to establish the necessity of political authority and rule in human society. The following statement by Ibn Khaldūn aptly summarizes this point, though in a different terminology from the jargon of most of the jurists. "When mankind has achieved social organization, as we have stated, and when civilization in the world has thus become a fact, people need a restraining force (*wāziʿ*) to keep them from committing aggression against one another, for aggressiveness and injustice are in the animal nature of man."[2] But, as we shall see below, Ibn Ashur does not confine the meaning and function of *wāziʿ*

---

[1] Ibn Ashur, *Uṣūl,* pp. 135-136.

[2] ʿAbd ar-Raḥmān ibn Muhammad Ibn Khaldun, *The Muqaddimah: An Introduction to History,* translated from the Arabic by Franz Rosenthal (London: Routledge, & Kegan Paul, 1967), vol. 1, p. 91. There seems to be a general agreement in Muslim intellectual traditions on this aspect of the function of the state in society. *Cf.* for example Abū al-Ḥasan ʿAlī ibn Muhammad ibn Ḥabīb al-Māwardī, *al-Aḥkām al-Sulṭāniyyah wa al-Wilāyāt al-Dīniyyah*, ed. Khalid A. A. al-ʿAlami (Beirut: Dār al-Kitāb al-ʿArabī, 1415/1994), pp. 29-30; Ḍiyāʾ al-Dīn Abū al-Maʿālī ʿAbd al-Malik ibn ʿAbd Allāh al-Juwaynī, *al-Ghayyāthī: Ghayyāth al-Umam fī Iltiyāth al-Ẓulam*, ed. Abdul Azim Mahmud al-Deeb (Jeddah: Dār al-Minhāj, 1432/2011), p. 217; Abū ʿAbd Allāh Muḥammad ibn ʿAlī al-Qalʿī (d. 630 H), *Tahdhīb al-Riyāsah wa Tartīb al-Siyāsah*, ed. Ibrahim Y. Mustapha ʿAjjī, al-Zarqa (Amman: Maktabat al-Manār, 1405/1985), pp. 94-97; Abū Naṣr al-Fārābī, *Fuṣū Muntaẓʿah*, ed. Fauzi Mitri Najjar (Beirut: Dār al-Mashriq, 2nd edn, 1992), p. 65-78; also *Kitāb Ahl al-Madīnah al-Fāḍilah*, ed. Albert Nasri Nader (Beirut: Dār al-Mashriq, 8th edn, 2002), p. 117-136; Abū al-Ḥasan al-ʿĀmirī, *al-Iʿlām bi-Manāqib al-Islām*, ed. Ahmed Abdul Hamid Ghurab (Riyadh: Muʾassassat Dār al-Aṣālah, 1408/1988), pp. 158-159.

to the external aspect that is undertaken by the state seen as an arbiter whose task is to maintain peace and order in society and settle disputes between its members, as clearly expressed by Ibn Khaldūn.

For Ibn Ashur, this is only one aspect of the complex meaning of *wāzi*ʿ. Islam's holistic approach in dealing with human affairs is clearly reflected in his understanding and formulation of the meaning of this concept. In his view, *wāzi*ʿ consists of three kinds: natural (*jibillī*), spirituo-religious (*dīnī*) and governmental (*sulṭānī*).[1] Before discussing the scope and dynamic of each of these types of *wāzi*ʿ, it is appropriate to have a quick look at an interesting point raised by Ibn Ashur in this respect. As his reasoning implies, a question might be asked as to the need for a restraining force once the right faith has been inculcated based on rational evidence and intellectual conviction. In other words, is not the right faith sufficient by itself to make human beings behave properly and continue undertaking the good deeds enjoined upon them and not revert to old practices?

Ibn Ashur's answer to this question is clearly in the negative. As he argued, right beliefs, which are based on indubitable evidence and firm rational conviction, are far from being easily falsified or contradicted. Once established in the intellect and imbibed in the soul, truth rarely yields to falsehood. Moreover, when people have embraced a faith out of conviction in its truthfulness and in such a way that it becomes a determinant factor of their personality and identity, they are

---

[1] Ibn Ashur, *Treatise*, p. 231. It is worth noting here that the great Hanbali scholar Ibn Qayyim al-Jawziyyah dealt extensively in many of his works with the concept of *wāzi*ʿespecially in conjuction with his discussion of the institution of punishments in the Sharīʿah which, as he argued, are needed when people's natural (*wāziʿ ṭabʿī*) and religious restraining force fail to hold them from transgression and aggression. See for example, Abū ʻAbd Allāh Muḥammad ibn Abī Bakr ibn Ayyūb Ibn Qayyim al-Jawziyyah, *Ighāthat al-Lahfān fī Maṣā'id al-Shayṭān*, ed. Muhammad Aziz Shams (Makkah: Dār ʻĀlam al-Fawā'id, 2nd edn, 1436), vol. 2, pp. 871-888.

usually less prone to be shaken by adverse factors opposing it. Thus, Ibn Ashur contends, faith is not in need of continuous sustenance to keep it alive. Deeds, on the contrary, are in need for much more care and protection because they are more vulnerable to such adverse influences for at least two reasons. One reason has already been mentioned above, which consists of the psychological propensity of human beings to revert to their old practices and to follow their whims and desires. The second reason is epistemological. Proofs on the validity and righteousness of acts and deeds are not always of the same degree of certainty and conviction as those pertaining to faith and belief; therefore, they are less compelling to the mind.[1] In addition to these two reasons, a third one can be adduced which concerns the influence of perverse external factors preventing people from keeping their good practices and enticing them to evil acts. Though not expressly stated by Ibn Ashur, this reason can be deduced from his sociological reasoning.

As indicated earlier, *wāziʿ* is classified into three kinds: two internal to the human self and one external. The latter type is what Ibn Ashur calls *wāziʿ sulṭānī.* It refers to the state power and political authority whose role is to implement and enforce law and maintain order in society. He mainly addressed this aspect in his book on the principles and cardinal values of the Islamic social system, *Uṣūl al-Niẓām al-Ijtimāʿī fī al-Islām.* In his view, the other two types of *wāziʿ* precede, both ontologically and historically, the coercive power of the state. Being the religion of human nature or *dīn al-fiṭrah*, Islam does not intend to ignore or suppress the inborn forces and propensities of human beings. To express this point in Cassirer's words, it is not the aim of religion (and Islam in particular) "to suppress or eradicate the deepest instincts of mankind."[2] On the contrary, it

---

[1] *Ibid.* p. 137.

[2] Ernst Cassirer, *An Essay on Man* (New Haven: Yale University Press, 1972 [1944]), p. 95.

recognizes them as legitimate impulses and essential aspects of the constitution of the human species that must be satisfied and valued. These instincts consist of impulses such as nutrition, sex, self-defense, protection of spouse and offspring, etc. Fulfilling them is part of of human beings' overall well-being which Islam aims to realize. However, the Sharīʿah is not very much concerned with providing specific prescriptions to the effect of requiring people to satisfy these drives or warning them against harmful things in this respect. This is because they are naturally motivated to do so due to inbuilt mechanisms. Yet, Islam does not want human beings to live by merely following their instinctive drives like other animal species.[1] The Islamic view of human nature as expressed by the term *fiṭrah* discussed above brings into focus the singularity of the human race. Therefore, while legitimizing man's instincts and encouraging their satisfaction as an essential dimension of his nature, the Sharīʿah also aims at channeling and orienting them according to its moral values and ideals embedded in the Islamic worldview.

The essential link established by the Qur'an between natural and revealed religion through the concepts of *fiṭrah* and *mīthāq*, clearly epitomizes its view of the singularity and uniqueness of mankind among other creatures. Thus, yearning for the beyond and the transcendental is ingrained in the human self. It is here that the second type of *wāziʿ* comes into play. Emanating from sincere and deep faith in God and the message He revealed to the Prophet and nurtured by continuous education, the psycho-religious and spiritual restraining factor (*wāziʿ dīnī nafsānī*) plays a very crucial role in Islam. Its importance lies in the fact that the implementation of most of the Sharīʿah rules and ordinances greatly depends on it.[2]

---

[1] Mohamed El-Tahir El-Mesawi, ed., *Jamhrat Maqālāt wa Rasā'il al-Shaykh al-Imām Muḍammad al-Ṭāhir Ibn ʿĀshūr*, hereafter *Jamharah* (Amman: Dār al-Nafaes, 1st edn, 1536/2015), vol. 1, pp. 324-325.

[2] Ibid. p. 387.

This explains the Qur'an's special interest in building and nurturing it in the human psyche. For this, Islam has adopted a unique approach to educating and refining the human personality that combines a number of things. First, it has strongly and repeatedly emphasized the notion of reward and punishment for the acts the individual consciously undertakes as a matter of worship and submission to God's command or as a matter of disobedience to Him, hence establishing and strengthening the sense of responsibility and accountability. Second, in order to stimulate people to good action by following the Sharīʿah prescriptions and avoiding its proscriptions, Islam nurtures in the human being the feelings of awe and fear as well as of love and hope towards God. Moreover, its approach in this regard rather consists of cultivating the feeling of love and hope and making it overweigh that of mere fear and awe so that obedience to the Sharīʿah becomes an act of willing submission to the Divine Will it exemplifies.[1] The third method used by Islam to strengthen the *wāziʿ dīnī* consists in inculcating in the believer's psyche the feeling of hatred and repulsion toward all evil thinking or desire by reminding him of its origin as a result of devil's whispering. Fourth, Islam consistently links good deeds and obedience to belief and wrongdoings and disobedience to disbelief.[2] Likewise, Ibn Ashur's conception of the meaning of *wāziʿ* is comprehensive. It is not confined to the negative aspect, i.e., that of restraining and deterring from undesired deeds and conduct, as the term might at first sight suggest. Indeed, it is equally, if not more, concerned with the positive and proactive aspects, that is, of stimulating good action and encouraging good behavior.

---

[1] Ibn Ashur, *Uṣūl*, pp. 140-141; *Treatise*, p. 387.
[2] Ibn Ashur, *Uṣūl*, pp. 142-143.

Fiṭrah and the Comprehension of the Sharīʿah

The positive and optimistic interpretation of *fiṭrah* as elaborated by Ibn Ashur and his predecessors has far-reaching implications which it is beyond our purpose to delve into.[1] Some of those implications discussed by Ibn Ashur will, however, be highlighted here, which mainly concern his historical dynamic perception of the Sharīʿah as well as his understanding of its general structure and characteristics and the way its injunctions and precepts should be comprehended and implemented. At the outset we need to re-emphasize one important point that has already been mentioned. The successive Divine messages vouchsafed to select individuals (i.e., prophets) have always aimed, according to the Qur'an, at reminding people of the essential truth engrained in their inborn nature and calling them to live in accordance with its demands. External Divine guidance through revelation has accompanied mankind since very early stages of her history. Its function consisted in reviving, purging, complementing, and bringing to better actualization the inner guidance God has instilled in the human species. In Ibn Ashur's view, this Divine education for mankind has followed a gradual process in respect of the laws and principles of legislation brought by each messenger so that the specific conditions of his respective audience are taken into consideration.[2]

It is part of God's design that mankind should follow a gradual process of intellectual and socio-cultural development in which every stage, which might span many centuries, would differ from the previous one in terms of the density of social organization and needs as well as contacts, conflicts and movement among the different communities and peoples of the world. According to Ibn Ashur, all this led to mutual knowing

---

[1] For a fairly informative treatment of the metaphysical, epistemological, ethical, psychological and legal implications of the concept of *fiṭrah,* see Yasien Mohamed, *Human Nature in Islam* (Kuala Lumpur: A.S. Noordeen, 1419/1998), pp. 84-132.

[2] Ibn Ashur, *Taḥrīr,* vol. 3/3, p. 190.

(*ta'āruf*) and cultural exchange between different communities and consolidated the sense of universal society and global civilization. This has been indicated by the Qur'an as one great aspect of God's purpose in making mankind into "nations and tribes" (Q. 49: 13).[1] Subsequent stages in that historical evolution are thus seen as progress and advancement over earlier ones. In this respect, he provided a panoramic description of the major stages in the history of legislation for human life and social organization where both divine and man-made laws are mentioned side by side as reflecting human intellectual and socio-cultural development. Likewise, the teachings and laws of Abraham, Hamurabi, Brahma, Ancient Egypt, Moses, Zoroaster, Confucius, Solon and Jesus are mentioned as representing the human heritage that had been available when the Qur'an—God's last word to mankind carrying to them the universal Sharī'ah that would regulate their life in all its aspects—was revealed to Prophet Muhammad in Arabia. None of them, Ibn Ashur argues, had the characteristics of universality that would make it transcend the specific socio-cultural and geographical context in which it appeared, including the great Sharī'ah of Moses.[2] The context-bound nature of those religio-legal traditions does not mean, however, the absence of mutual cultural and social borrowing among the communities associated with them, which took both peaceful and conflictual forms.[3]

However, Islam did not appear in any of the areas where those traditions had taken deep roots. Its advent was rather in an area that had preserved a considerable measure of simplicity in respect of social organization and cultural heritage and had remained almost totally isolated from the major civilizational spheres of the ancient world where those traditions had made

---

[1] Ibn Ashur, *Taḥrīr*, vol. 12/26, pp. 259-261.
[2] *Ibid.* vol. 3/3, p. 192; *cf.* vol. 2, pp. 299-300.
[3] *Ibid.* vol. 3/3, pp. 192-193.

lasting and deep impact on man and society. For Ibn Ashur, an unfathomable wisdom underlies this cultural and spiritual aloofness of the immediate geographical and social context of the Qur'anic Revelation. As a religion whose universal character the Qur'an proclaimed from the very beginning,[1] Islam required in its first bearers certain essential qualities that would allow them to carry it out worldwide easily. Ibn Ashur believes that four major qualities were manifested in the Arabs who first received the call of Prophet Muhammad. Besides the simplicity or primitiveness of their social organization and culture and their aloofness from the cotemporary nations of their time, these people were distinguished by fine minds and strong memories.[2] In his view, the significance of these qualities is that those who possessed them were nearer to the original human nature (*fiṭrah*) and not burdened with such legal and cultural tradition that would prevent them from embracing the new message and carrying it to other peoples.[3] Ibn Ashur seems to imply that the social milieu in which Islam dawned had preserved a considereable degree of pristine human nature

Thus, he seems to suggest that there was a general disposition and positive attitude among the Arabs to identify with Islam and respond positively and energetically to its calling thanks to their freedom from deep-rooted and long-established spiritual and intellectual traditions that would burden their souls and imprison their minds. Hence, the message of Islam was not to be confined within the specific socio-cultural context of Arabia both in terms of its scriptural sources (especially the Qur'an) and its historical unfolding. This historical perspective on the advent of Islam and its position in the chain of revealed

---

[1] Al-Attas, *Islam and Secularism*, p. 100.

[2] Ibn Ashur, *Treatise*, p. 153; *cf.* Ibn Khaldun, *The Muqaddimah,* vol. 1, pp. 250-265.

[3] To further support this point, Ibn Ashur indicates that, with only a few exceptions, Arab Christians and the Jews in Madīnah obstinately refused to accept Islam because they believed themselves to be on a right religious tradition. Ibid. p. 136, note 2.

religion enabled Ibn Ashur to identify the following features marking the universality of the Sharīʿah in relation to human nature. In what follows we shall outline the main implications of his positive interpretation of *fiṭrah* for the understanding and implementation of the precepts and injunctions of the Sharīʿah.

Moderation and balance constitute, for Ibn Ashur, one of the major characteristics of Islamic teachings and a fundamental principle of the Islamic social system.[1] In his opinion, the reflections of Muslim sages and scholars on the qualities and conditions of the human mind and soul can be summarized in the following dictum: "moderateness constitutes the backbone of all virtuous qualities."[2] It constitutes the golden mean of all human virtues. Likewise, all extreme inclinations in the form of both negligence (*tafrīṭ*) and excessiveness (*ifrāṭ*) are the result of aberration and corruption in human nature caused by indulgence in vain desires and strayness. Such deviation from the norm of balanced sound nature emanates either from submission to one's own caprices and passions or from falling under the influence of subvert people who would drive others into such aberrations and vices.[3] Moderation and balance, however, should not be equated with half-heartedness, expediency or mediocrity, nor should they be understood to mean compromising other values in order to please this or that.

Since it is part of the main goals of the Sharīʿah to safeguard and restore human nature, its precepts and commandments have been devised in such a way as to shun all types of extremism in human thinking, belief and behavior. Hence, the Qur'an describes the Muslim *ummah* as "a community of the middle way)" (Q. 2: 143), which the Prophet, as reported by al-Bukhārī, interpreted as being just (*ʿadl*).[4] This means keeping

---

[1] Ibn Ashur, *Uṣūl*, p. 45.
[2] Ibn Ashur, *Treatise*, p. 268; *Uṣūl*. pp. 45-46. See also *Jamhrah*, vol. 1, p. 309.
[3] Ibn Ashur, *Uṣūl*, p. 26.
[4] Ibn Ashur, *Treatise*, pp. 87-88; *Uṣūl*, p. 47.

"an equitable balance between extremes" and being "realistic in its appreciation of man's nature and possibilities."[1] According to Ibn Ashur, the middlemost position to which the Qur'an invites mankind stems from its sense of justice on the basis of which everything is put in its right place and given its due without excess or deficiency.[2] Moreover, the grounding of moderateness and middle-way position in the concept of justice in its comprehensive meaning makes it, in Ibn Ashur's opinion, the fountainhead of all virtues and nobility.[3]

To express this point in Asad's pertinent words, we can say that this attribute of the Sharīʿah can be seen to summarize "the Islamic attitude towards the problem of man's existence as such: a denial of the view that there is an inherent conflict between the spirit and the flesh, and a bold affirmation of the natural, God-willed unity in this twofold aspect of human life"—such balanced attitude being a direct consequence of "the concept of God's oneness and, hence, of the unity of purpose underlying all His creation."[4] It is this balanced attitude that accounts, according to Ibn Ashur, for the Muslim *ummah*'s being the "best community brought forth for [the good of][5] mankind" (Q. 3: 110) and "bearing witness to the truth before all mankind" (Q. 2: 143).[6]

Another equally important feature of the Sharīʿah, flowing from Islam's compatibility with human nature, is *samāḥah*. For Ibn Ashur, this characteristic derives from the quality of moderateness and middlemost position discussed above.[7] It consists of seeking ease and comfort and avoiding hardship and

---

[1] Asad, *The Message of the Qur'an*, p. 30 (note 118).
[2] Ibn Ashur, *Uṣūl*, p. 47.
[3] Ibn Ashur, *Treatise*, p. 87; *Uṣūl*, p. 47.
[4] Asad, pp. 268-69.
[5] This explanatory phrase is by Muhammad Asad.
[6] Ibn Ashur, *Taḥrīr*, vol. 2, pp. 19-21.
[7] Ibn Ashur, *Treatise*, p. 87; *Uṣūl*, p. 50.

difficulty in all dealings and undertakings.[1] Likewise, *samāḥah* is "commendable easiness in matters in which people usually tend toward sternness and intransigence (*tashdīd*) in such a way that does not lead to harm or an evil."[2] Textual evidence supporting this aspect of the Sharīʿah is abundant both in the Qur'an and the Prophet's Sunnah.[3] More important even, according to Ibn Ashur's reasoning, are the principle and wisdom underlying the the Qur'anic and Prophetic emphasis on *samāḥah* as one of the foremost characteristics of Islamic teachings. Human nature abhors and eschews hardship and sternness. And since Islam is *dīn fiṭrah*, its teachings both in their fundamentals and details are agreeably accepted and implemented by human beings,[4] thanks to their harmony with the latter's physical constitution and their inherent spiritual and mental disposition.[5]

In other words, this characteristic of *samāḥah* is behind the suitability of the precepts and commands of the Sharīʿah to all human beings and brings comfort to both the individual and society.[6] The impact of this aspect of the Sharīʿah can best be seen in the fast and wide spread and historical continuity of Islam.[7] It has been a norm of history that the rapidity and readiness with which different peoples submit to certain religious laws (*sharāʾiʿ*) and their persistence in so doing are commensurate with the level of ease and facility of those laws and, hence, of the degree of their compatibility with human nature.[8]

The third characteristic of the Sharīʿah treated at some length by Ibn Ashur is the universality (*ʿumūm*) of its teachings

---

[1] Ibn Ashur, *Treatise*, p. 87.
[2] Ibn Ashur, *Treatise*, p. 269; *Uṣūl*, p. 49.
[3] See such evidences as quoted by Ibn Ashur, *Treatise*, pp. 88-89; *Uṣūl*, pp. 49-51.
[4] Ibn Ashur, *Treatise*, pp. 89-90; *Uṣūl*, p. 51.
[5] Ismail al-Hassani, *Naẓariyat al-Maqāṣid ʿinda al-Imām Muḥammad al-Ṭāhir Ibn ʿĀshūr ʿĀshūr* (Washington: The International Institute of Islamic Thought, 1425/1995), p. 271.
[6] Ibn Ashur, *Treatise*, p. 90.
[7] *Ibid.*; *Uṣūl*, p. 51.
[8] Ibn Ashur, *Uṣūl*, pp. 51-52.

and principles. In this respect, he proceeds in what can be described as an inverse reasoning whereby the conclusion provides the proof of the premise. Since it has been God's wisdom and will that Islam be the last religion through which His word is addressed to mankind, this means that it should be based on a universal attribute shared by all human beings and deeply rooted in their souls in such a way that sound reason would readily recognize it. That attribute is nothing but *fiṭrah* or the primordial disposition with which God has created the human species.[1] Thus, the universality of the Sharīʿah derives from the suitability of its injunctions and commands to human nature in all its dimensions. According to Ibn Ashur, the universality of the Sharīʿah entails that its commands (*aḥkām*) be applicable to all nations and individuals equally regardless of circumstances and custom, for it is this universal applicability of laws and values that actually helps bringing about social unity and cohesion.[2]

This argument has important epistemological and methodological consequences for the way Ibn Ashur looked at the two main textual sources of the Sharīʿah (i.e., the Qur'an and the Prophet's traditions) and his formulation of the relationship between them. As a general rule, the Qur'an, in his opinion, is predominantly concerned with setting up universal principles or simply universals, whereas the Sunnah deals mainly with particulars or specific cases. Qur'anic universals, Ibn Ashur explains, are expressed in both "literal/verbal" (*lafẓiyyah*) and thematic (*maʿnawiyyah*) forms. For him, these forms are definitive for what they stand for.[3]

Ibn Ashur's exposition of the second type of universals clearly builds on the same argument[4] based on the idea of

---

[1] Ibn Ashur, *Treatise*, pp. 134-135.
[2] *Ibid.* p. 136.
[3] *Ibid,*. pp. 137-138.
[4] See his discussion of the importance and steps of thematic induction in *Treatise*, pp. 14-17.

thematic induction (*istiqrā' maʿnawī*) as elaborated by al-Shāṭibī. However, his view concerning the validity of what he calls "literal universals" can be said to be a clear departure from the view held by many classical legal theorists. By this expression he seems to refer to what is known in classical *uṣūl* theory as absolute (*muṭlaq*) and general (*ʿāmm*) expressions. For those scholars, such expressions, in general, must not be understood in their apparent meaning for their connotation is speculative rather than definitive. Therefore, they require interpretation through qualification or particularization in order for their true import to be properly determined.[1] According to Ibn Ashur, this view is erroneous and has led Muslim jurists to liberal and sometimes far-fetched and inaccurate application of particularization and other techniques. In his opinion, most of general and absolute statements, especially in the Qur'an, are intended as generic terms meaning what is conveyed by their literal forms.[2] Hence, they are of equal weight to thematic inferences in denoting certainty and expressing universal meanings or concepts.

As for the Prophet's traditions, Ibn Ashur is of the view that they mostly consist of particular cases related to specific situations. Such cases, he argued, cannot be readily considered as a basis for universal legislation, since they are equally open to both generalization and particularization. This probability, he maintains, is at the origin of disagreement among jurists on legal argumentation on the basis of such individual cases. It is in this light, he clearly indicates, that the Prophet's interdiction of the Companions to record anything other than the Qur'an should be understood. In his view, the reason why the Prophet did not allow the writing down of something except the Qur'anic verses

---

[1] For further details, see Muhammad Hashim Kamali, *Principles of Islamic Jurisprudence* (Petaling Jaya, Malaysia: Ilmiah Publishers, 2001), pp. 104-116; Wael B. Hallaq, *A History of Islamic legal Theories* (Cambridge, UK: Cambridge University Press, 1999), 45-46.

[2] Ibn Ashur, *Treatise*, pp. 137-138.

was the fear that "particular cases be taken as universal rules"[1] and "universal and permanent legislation" be "confused with temporary and particular cases."[2] This is because observing the specific mores and customs of different nations in a binding universal legislation is against the rule. However, this does not mean ignoring such manners and customs altogether. On the contrary, they find their proper place and value under the principle of permissibility.[3] Thus, for Ibn Ashur, there should be no doubt that,

> [N]o one has the right to impose the customs and mores of a particular people on them or on other people as 'legislation'. Of course, Islamic legislation takes into account such customs and mores so long as their followers have not altered them. This is because people's adherence to those customs and mores and the latter's continuance as part of their lives endow them with the status of default terms and conditions.[4]

This means that, unlike the Qur'an, a good deal of the Prohetic traditions was embedded in the socio-cultural environment in which the Prophet lived and fulfilled his mission as God's Messenger and leader of the rising Muslim community. Likewise, there is a pressing need for a proper approach to distinguish in those traditions what pertains to the

---

[1] *Ibid.* p. 138.

[2] *Ibid.* p. 140.

[3] *Ibid.* p. 138; *Taḥrīr,* vol. 1/3, pp. 195-96.

[4] Ibn Ashur, *Treatise*, p. 139. It is worthy of mention here that Ibn Ashur's concern with the issue of the general and specific in the Prophetic traditions is so strong that he devoted a complete chapter to tackling it. Building on the work done in this respect by the eminent Mālikī jurist Shihāb al-Dīn al-Qarāfī, he set out to examine and identify the various capacities (*maqāmāt*) in which the Prophet made statements and carried out actions. He enumerated twelve such *maqāmāt* that need to be taken into consideration if any proper understanding of the Sunnah is to be achieved. *Traetise*, pp. 212-230; *cf.* Muhammad Mahdi Shams al-Din, *al-Ijtihād wa al-Tjdīd fī al-Fiqh al-Islāmī* (Beirut: al-Mu'assasah al-Dawliyyah, 1419/1999), pp. 86-87.

specific socio-historical circumstances of Arabia at that time from what is general and transcends those circumstances, thus expressing the universal teachings enshrined in the Qur'an.[1] As he further made it clear, the universality of the Sharīʿah and its suitability to all mankind

> [S]hould in no way be understood to mean that all human beings are required to follow the customs and manners of a particular people or nation, such as the Arabs during the time of Revelation. Nor should it mean that other nations are bound to follow the special rulings and specific cases that conferred certain benefits on those who lived the time of Revelation, whether or not they could be appropriate.[2]

Accordingly, Ibn Ashur suggested that the universality and suitability of the Sharīʿah can be conceived in two different, yet interrelated, ways. First, its fundamental rules, universal principles and commands are applicable to all circumstances without any difficulty or hardship. Second, the situations and conditions of all peoples and nations in all times and climes can also be transformed and reshaped in accordance with Islamic teachings without any difficulty or hardship.[3] In his reasoning, it is this level of universality and flexibility of the Sharīʿah that gives *ijtihād* its function and utmost importance. We may express this point in Muhammad Iqbal's words by saying that it is here that *ijtihād* reveals its real significance as a manifestation of "the principle of movement in the structure of Islam."[4] Thus, the universality and suitability of the Sharīʿah

---

[1] Ibn Ashur, *Treatise*, pp. 140-141.

[2] *Ibid.* pp. 142-143. It should be indicated here that the particular cases of the Sunnah, though not always of general purport, provide us with pertinent practical modalities of the implementation of the general and universal meanings conveyed by the Qur'an. Hence, they cannot be disposed of as some anti-Sunnah groups have been teaching.

[3] *Ibid.* pp. 142-143.

[4] Muhammad Iqbal, *Reconstruction of Religious Thought in Islam,* new edition annotated by M. Saeed Sheikh (Standord, Ca: Standford University Press,

to all mankind throughout the ages means that its commands consist of universal principles and enduring values concerning human good and welbeing, which can be translated into various systems and rulings to regulate human life, diverse in form but unified in purpose.[1]

From this, according to Ibn Ashur, follows the twofold strategy of the Sharīʿah in dealing with the human life and condition, which operates at two complementary and closely related levels: change and transformation on the one hand and confirmation or sanction on the other. Change consists of removing all kinds of corruption and categorically declaring their evilness. It might take the form of more rigorous and severe measures to eradicate slackness and indifference in human behavior out of consideration for the human good. It might also take the form of alleviation and easing as a measure to prevent excessive or extremist attitudes. For Ibn Ashur, the basis of this aspect of the Islamic approach to social and culatural change is clearly laid down in the Qur'an. It only suffices to reflect upon the following two verses: "God is the Protector of those who have faith, taking them out of deep darkness into light" (Q.2: 257), "through which [i.e., clear divine writ] God shows unto all who seek His pleasure the paths leading, by His grace, to salvation and brings them out of the depths of darkness into light and guides them onto a straight way." (Q. 5:16)[2]

The second aspect of the abovementioned strategy consists of confirming and sanctioning all the good norms and virtuous practices mankind has followed over the ages. If we examine the history of mankind, Ibn Ashur believes, we will discover that many of the virtues and positive good values forming the foundation of human culture and civilization are inherited from

---

2012), pp. 116-142.

[1] *Ibn* Ashur, *Treatise*, p. 143.

[2] *Ibid.* pp. 165-166.

the teachings, advices and wisdom of prophets, patriarchs, sages and just rulers in such a way that they have become deeply rooted in human consciousness and experience. These virtues and good values sanctioned and promoted by Islam are, according to Ibn Ashur, expressed in the Qur'anic phrase "enjoins upon them the doing of what is right."[1]

In other words, it is not part of the Islamic legislation for human life to destroy and eradicate all the values, ideas, practices and institutions that have preceded it and start human experience from a *tabula rasa* as if all that is merely vice and wrong. On the contrary, Islam, based on its positive and optimistic conception of human nature discussed earlier, aims at renewing people's spirituality and morality by linking it to the primordial tree of *Tawḥīd* and goodness rooted in human nature. Likewise, all values and practices that do not conflict with its teachings and promote human good are assimilated in its system and oriented in accordance with its basic parameters. This attitude, it should be recalled, stems from a firm belief in the essential unity of human nature no matter how much corrupting influences might affect it.[2] Informed with this understanding of the relationship of the Sharīʿah and human nature, Ibn Ashur set out to reformulate the idea of *maqāṣid al-sharīʿah* in an attempt to develop it into a self-contained discipline, i.e., *ʿIilm Maqāṣid al-Sahrīʿah.*

Categorization of the *Maqāṣid al-Sharīʿah* and the Scheme of Values and Human Interests

A major criticism leveled by Ibn Ashur against *uṣūl al-fiqh* in particular and Islamic jurisprudence in general is that the idea of *maqāṣid* was only marginally treated in it. In his historical

---

[1] *Ibid.* pp. 166-167.

[2] *Cf.* Eltigani Abdelgadir Hamid, *The Qur'an and Politics* (London & Washington: The International Institute of Islamic Thought, 1416/1995), pp. 22-23.

review of the development of the notion of *maqāṣid*, he singled out ʿIzz al-Dīn ibn ʿAbd al-Salām (d. 660H) and Shihāb al-Dīn al-Qarāfī (d. 684H) as the most outstanding scholars, before al-Shāṭibī, who attempted to establish the systematic study of *maqāṣid al-sharīʿah*. But it is al-Shāṭibī, whom he credited as the "genius", who succeeded in so doing. His achievement consisted of what may be considered an epistemological and methodological restructuring of the *uṣūl* by making the subject of *maqāṣid* the central theme informing the study of all its component parts. However, the ingenuity and achievement of the Andalusian scholar could not spare him Ibn Ashur's criticism. In his view, al-Shāṭibī's effort fell short of achieving its full purpose, thus leaving much to be done in terms of establishing *ʿIlm Maqāṣid al-Sharīʿah*.[1]

The subject of *maqāṣid* had preoccupied Ibn Ashur for a long time since his youth days as a fresh graduate.[2] As he set out to develop his views on the matter, he reasserted his position on the inadequacy of *uṣūl al-fiqh* epistemology and methodology to lead to certainty (*qaṭʿ*) in legal reasoning for reasons mentioned

[1] Ibn Ashur, *Treatise*, p. xxiii. This feeling was shared by his contemporary and colleague, the Mālikī *mufti* Sheikh Muhammad al-ʿAziz Djait (1303/1889-1386/1970). According to this scholar, one could hardly find in the vast literature of Islamic jurisprudence one comprehensive work that "systematically brings together the *maqāṣid al-sharīʿah* and articulates the inner wisdom of [Islamic] legislation." Only scattered fragments and inarticulate thoughts could be found immersed in *fiqh* books which "bring no heal to whom would content himself with them." This jurist hoped that some of the contemporary skilled scholars striving for Islamic reform (*iṣlāḥ*) would undertake the task of "collecting the scattered material [on *maqāṣid*] and casting it into a systematic construct that would make it easily accessible." *al-Majallah al-Zaytūniyyah*, vol. 1, No. 2 (1355/1936), p. 124.

[2] As far back as the early years of the first decade of the 20th century, Ibn Ashur attributed the stagnation and decadence of Islamic jurisprudence to marginalization and neglect of the study of *maqāṣid al-sharīʿah* in both *uṣūl al-fiqh* and *fiqh* compendia and classes. Al-ʿAllamah al-Sheikh al-Imām Muhammad al-Tahir Ibn Ashur, *Alaysa al-Subḥ bi-Qarīb? al-Taʿlīm al-ʿArabī al-Islāmī: Dirāsah Tārīkhiyyah wa-ʾĀrāʾ Iṣlāḥiyyah,* ed. Mohamed El-Tahir El-Mesawi (Aleppo: Dar al-Multaqa / Khartoum: Hay'at al-Amal al-Fikriyyah, 1st edn, 1431/2010), p. 352 & 359.

there. But this did not mean for him that the *uṣūl* legacy had to be abandoned altogether as useless. For him, what was needed was rather a critical appreciation of its propositions and methodological rules to free it from historical accretions and epistemologically irrelevant discussions and inquiries that were brought into its fold under specific historical and intellectual circumstances and which do not serve the purpose of discovering the intentions of the Lawgiver and deeper wisdom of the Sharīʿah. Once such sifting has been done, much of the remaining material must be recast into a new discipline that would constitute the independent *ʿIlm Maqāṣid al-Sharīʿah* proposed by Ibn Ashur.[1]

At this juncture, he is quite clear about one important point. The material to be derived from the legacy of Islamic jurisprudence is scarce and therefore not sufficient for edifying the new discipline. This is due to the fact that the doctors of *fiqh* and *uṣūl* focused most of their juristic reasoning and inquiry on devotional matters (*ʿibādāt*) and a limited number of instances of *ḥalāl* and *ḥarām* relating to sales contracts (*buyūʿ*). Ibn Ashur further explains that since he is mainly concerned with the goals of Islamic teachings pertaining to the laws of social conduct and inter-individual dealings (*muʿāmalāt*) as well as the laws concerning the reform (*iṣlāḥ*) and preservation (*ḥifẓ*) of the socio-political order, the work of earlier scholars is of little help for him in this challenging enterprise.[2] By this criticism Ibn Ashur seems to point out an aspect of classical Islamic jurisprudence and legal thought that was to be brought into more focus by an increasing number of Muslim thinkers and scholars after him. That is, an atomistic approach dominated the thinking of classical Muslim jurists in dealing with the injunctions and rules of the Sharīʿah. Thus, they focused on individual matters and lost sight of society as a global or all-

---

[1] Ibn Ashur, *Treatise*, p. xxii.
[2] *Ibid.* pp. xxiv-xxv.

encompassing world with its own logic and dynamic.[1]

In our discussion of the implications of Ibn Ashur's optimistic interpretation of *fiṭrah*, we saw how he conceived the universality of Islamic teachings with regard to human nature. Drawing on the same argument, he advanced the proposition that the Sharīʿah objectives are grounded in man's *fiṭrah*, which is the utmost attribute of the Sharīʿah. So, how does this grounding take place? To answer this question, Ibn Ashur resorted to an epistemological argument whereby he classified the *maqāṣid* into two categories: real ideas or meanings (*maʿānī ḥaqīqiyyah*) and universal conventional ideas (*maʿānī ʿurfiyyah ʿāmmah*). The first category refers to notions or concepts that have a being of their own (*taḥaqquq fī nafsihā*); thus, sound minds would realize their suitability (*mulā'amah*) or incongruity (*munāfarah*) with what is good (*maṣlaḥah*), i.e., they lead either to the realization of a universal benefit or the causing of a general harm. According to Ibn Ashur, our perception of this category takes place independently of any previous knowledge of any law or custom; hence, their universality and commonality among different nations in different civilizations. Of the examples he mentioned in this respect we would only mention one that clearly reveals his theological position. Realizing that justice (*ʿadl*) is good in itself does not, in his view, depend on any

---

[1] This issue has been taken up on somewhat similar lines by an increasing number of scholars and thinkers over the last decades after Ibn Ashur's death. See for example Hassan al-Turabi, *Qaḍāyā al-Tajdīd: Naḥwa Manhaj Uṣūlī* (Khartoum: Institute of Research and Social Studies, 1411/1990); Muhammad Mahdi Shamsuddin, "al-Ijtihād fī al-Islām", *al-Ijtihād*, No. 9, Beirut 1411/1990, and *al-Ijtihād wa al-Tajdīd fī al-Fiqh al-Islāmī* (Beirut: al-Mu'assassah al-Dawliyyah, 1419/1999); Fazlur Rahman, *Islam and Modernity: Transformation of an Intellectual Tradition* (Chicago and London: The University of Chicago Press, 1982); AbdulHamid A. AbuSulayman, *Towards an Islamic Theory of International Relations: New Directions for Methodology and Thought* (Herndon, VA: The International Institute of Islamic Thought, IIIT, 1414/1993), and also., *Crisis in the Muslim Mind* (Washigton: The International Institute of Islamic Thought, 1414/1993).

formal prior knowledge.[1] Our knowledge of them would fall under what some Muslim philosophers call knowledge by presence (*ʿilm ḥuḍūrī*).[2] In other words, such perception may be said to pertain to the category of self-evident primary truths that are immediately accessible to the human mind. Thus, the cognition of such truths is rooted in the human mind itself, and hence they constitute, as seen earlier, part of man's inborn nature or *fiṭrah*.

The second category refers to time-tested notions resulting from historical experience. These perceptions are such that they are agreeable and intimately linked to the psychology of the public because they are at the origin of the realization of good or the repulsion of evil. Believing that benevolence is suitable and necessary for strengthening social relations or that punishing criminals is required to deter them from recidivism and to prevent others from committing crimes or that filthiness should be removed are instances of this kind of perception.[3] The difference between the two categories is the same as that between nature and nurture. That is, knowledge of the real ideas is necessary as they are rooted in human nature, while that of the conventional ideas is acquired, and depends on education and socialization, or simply on history as a manifestation of the wisdom of human experience.

Moreover, in Ibn Ashur's view, the veracity of these two categories of ideas depends on their satisfying four main criteria, namely certainty, evidence, consistency, and regularity. This can be explained in the following manner. Firstly, the existence of these ideas must be definitive or of high probability bordering

---

[1] Ibn Ashur, *Treatise,* p. 71.

[2] In contradistinction to *ʿilm ḥuṣūlī* which is knowledge attained by demonstration, *ʿilm ḥuḍūrī* may be seen as intuitive knowledge which one finds ingrained in oneself requiring no external proof. See in this regard, Mehdi Ha'iri Yazdi, *The Principles of Epistemology in Islamic Philosophy: Knowledge by Presence* (Albany: State University of New York Press, 1992).

[3] *Ibid.* p. 72.

on certainty. Secondly, they must be evident in such a way that nobody will disagree over their meaning. Thirdly, they must be clearly distinct so that they are not confused with other things. The last criterion is that they must be constant, which means they must obtain in all situations regardless of the circumstances of space, time or social organization.[1] Clearly, Ibn Ashur is attempting to reformulate at a higher and more general epistemological level a set of notions which classical legal theorists used to discuss within the narrow context of *ʿillah* and its conditions in analogical reasoning. This can be seen as an implementation of the recasting strategy he suggested.[2]

The concept of *maṣlaḥah* occupies a central place in the doctrine of *maqāṣid* as expounded by Muslim jurisprudents. The meaning of this crucial concept is so comprehensive in Islamic jurisprudence that it encompasses all aspects of human good both at the individual and collective levels. As Bagby has pertinently observed, the theory of *maṣlaḥah* in Islamic jurisprudence is "a type of utilitarianism that is universal (not egocentric), ideal (not hedonistic), and rule-based (not act-based)."[3] But, as observed elsewhere, despite its centrality, it is difficult to speak of an agreed upon inclusive-exclusive definition of *maṣlaḥah*. This might be due to the broadness of its meaning. Of course, it is not our purpose here to attempt such a definition, nor would that be much desired in the context of the present study. It would suffice to only provide a workable definition that would bring to light the general import of this fundamental concept.

---

[1] *Ibid.*

[2] It would be intellectually interesting and historically significant to carry out a comparative inquiry on the issue of the origin, being and role of values in human life involving Ibn Ashur's views and those of Nicolai Hartmann and Max Scheler who are among the most eminent 20th-century scholars who devoted considerable effort to this crucial subject.

[3] Ihsan Abdul-Wajid Bagby, *Utility in Classical Islamic Law: The Concept of Maṣlaḥah* in *Uṣūl al-Fiqh*, unpublished Ph.D. thesis (the University of Michigan, 1986), p. 43.

After reviewing some definitions of *maṣlaḥah* by previous jurists, Ibn Ashur suggested that it should be defined as follows. The term of *maṣlaḥah* is derived either from the root verb *ṣalaḥa* or *ṣaluḥa* (to be good, right, useful, etc.) or from the verbal noun *ṣalāḥ* (goodness, rightness, utility).[1] By virtue of its morphological form *mafʿalah*, which denotes the density of that from which the term is derived, *maṣlaḥah* signifies the prevalence and intensity of goodness, rightness and utility in the context to which it is applied. Accordingly, *maṣlaḥah* can be defined as "an attribute of the act *(fiʿl)* whereby righteousness and goodness takes place, that is to say utility and benefit (*nafʿ*), always or mostly for the public or individuals."[2] This definition, according to Ibn Ashur, underlines the following main features of *maṣlaḥah*: 1. *Maṣlaḥah* can be an absolute benefit taking place under all circumstances or merely a predominant benefit that takes place in most of the cases; 2. It is of two kinds, public and private. While the first kind concerns the whole or most of the society, the second concerns the individuals.[3] As for *mafsadah*, the opposite of *maṣlaḥah*, it can be defined by simply reversing the definition of the latter.[4]

Ibn Ashur then reminds us of a major characteristic of Qur'anic legislation. As seen above, the Qur'an is mostly concerned with laying down the foundations for collective or universal good, whereas it is the task of the Prophet's Sunnah to legislate for the individual or personal good obtaining in specific situations. This does not, of course, suggest the absence of specific legislations from the Qur'an or of universal legislations from the Sunnah. What is even more important, according to Ibn Ashur, is that the distinction between personal and public

---

[1] This indecision is due to the difference among Arab linguists on whether the verb *(fiʿl)* or the verbal noun (*maṣdar*) is the basis of the derivative system in the Arabic language.

[2] Ibn Ashur, *Treatise*, p. 96.

[3] *Ibid.* pp. 96-97.

[4] *Ibid.* p. 96.

good is not always definitive nor is it desirable in the Islamic context. On the contrary, *maṣlaḥah ʿāmmah* does not lose sight of the individuals who make up the society. Similarly, *maṣlaḥah khāṣṣah* results, indirectly, in the collective good of society. In other words, we can speak of continuity or mutual consolidation rather than divorce or rupture or even conflict between the notions of personal and collective good in the Islam. Another point, which is equally important to him, needs to be highlighted here. In some instances, it might appear that *maṣlaḥah* is overweighed by its opposite, *mafsadah*, or does not obtain altogether. Implicitly warning against superficial and hasty decisions, Ibn Ashur insists that only profound reflection and broad consideration of all aspects can enable us to perceive the truth in such situations.[1]

An extreme example can sufficiently clarify this point. Consider the case of a destitute, ignorant, old person torn by disease. Such a person cannot be of any use or help, neither for him/herself nor for others. It would thus seem reasonable and even preferable that the life of such a person should be terminated out of mercy for him/her, that is, in order to put an end to his/her suffering. This kind of reasoning, Ibn Ashur strongly argued, is totally unsound and unacceptable in Islam. Human life is sanctified and has to be always preserved under all conditions. The so-called painless killing or, to just use the technical term, euthanasia, can by no means be a solution and can in no case be justified. This is because the preservation and good of the order of the world (*niẓām al-ʿālam*) depend on the sanctity and preservation of individual souls. If we were to subject it to considerations of this kind, a matter that varies according to people's discretion, situation, perspective, and even interest and vagaries, then a wide breach will be open from which indifference and inconsiderateness in dealing with human life will sweep into people's minds. By emphaszing the necessity

[1] *Ibid.* pp. 97-98.

to preserve and sanctify human life even under such severe conditions as in the above example, the Sharīʿah aims at safeguarding it from being prey to the whims and temperaments of individuals and groups and to protect the order of the world from being sapped at one of its very deep bases.[1]

From this discussion of the meaning and scope of *maṣlaḥah*, the Tunisian scholar proceeds to outline the structure of the *maqāṣid* in terms of the proposed new discipline. Let us recall here what was said about the overall goal of the Sharīʿah, namely that it consists of realizing the well-being of mankind. From this all-purpose principle flows the tripartite vertical hierarchical order of *maqāṣid al-sharīʿah*. The question that must be asked here is: what are these *maqāṣid*? Differently from the concept of *maṣlaḥah*, classical *uṣūl* literature on the subject does not provide a clear definition of what *maqāṣid* are. Even al-Shāṭibī to whom we owe much for its systematic and comprehensive treatment did not attempt to give such a definition.[2] Only in modern times do we find attempts to define *maqāṣid*. In this context, Ibn Ashur can surely be considered the first scholar to have undertaken such a task. He was followed seventeen years later by the Moroccan scholar and politician Allal al-Fasī in his book *Maqāṣid al-Sharīʿah al-Islāmiyyah wa Makārimuhā*.[3] What came afterwards did not actually transcend the general framework set up by these two scholars.

Ibn Ashur's attempt to define *maqāṣid* consists of three steps. The first step deals with the definition of the most general

---

[1] *Ibid.* p. 98.

[2] For further detail see Ahmad al-Raysuni, *Imām al-Shāṭibī's Theory of the Higher Objectives and Intents of Islamic Law,* translated from the Arabic by Nancy Roberts (London-Washington: The International Institute of Islamic Thought, 1427/2006), p. xxi; Yusuf Ahmad Muhammad al-Badawi, *Maqāṣid al-Sharīʿah ʿnda Ibn Taymiyyah* (Amman: Dār al-Nafaes, 1421/2000), pp. 43-47.

[3] While Ibn Ashur's book on *maqāṣid* was completed in 1360/1940 and first published in 1366/1946, the work of al-Fāsī was completed and published in 1382/1963.

goal of the Sharīʿah constituting its all-purpose principle. This is what he means by the *maqṣad ʿāmm* to which he devoted a whole chapter in his *Treatise on Maqāṣid al-Sharīʿah*. It can be considered a genus encompassing a number of less general goals. This all-encompassing objective is "to preserve the social order of the community and insure its healthy progress by promoting the well-being and righteousness (*ṣalāḥ*) of that which prevails in it, namely, the human species;" wherein the well-being and virtue of people "consist of the soundness of their intellect, the righteousness of their deeds as well as the goodness of the things of the word where they live that are put at their disposal."[1] As the following exposition will hopefully show, we are here proceeding from the most general and universal to the most particular and specific. The second step in Ibn Ashur's process of definition is to identify the Sharīʿah objectives that branch out of its all-purpose principle, thus forming a category of less general or more particular goals. This category includes what he calls the general objectives, *maqāṣid ʿāmmah*. Although he uses here the same term employed to express the overall goal of the Sharīʿah, the only variation being the plural instead of the singular form, the difference is made clear by the definition given to this category. As he indicates,

> The general objectives of Islamic legislation consist of deeper meanings (*maʿānī*) and inner aspects of wisdom (*ḥikam*) considered by the Lawgiver (*shāriʿ*) in all or most of the areas and circumstances of legislation (*aḥwāl al-tashrīʿ*). They are not confined to a particular type of the Sharīʿah commands… They also include certain meanings and notions that are present in many, though not all, of the Sharīʿah commands.[2]

It should be noted here that some of the general

---

[1] Ibn Ashur, *Treatise*, p. 91.
[2] Ibn Ashur, *Treatise*, p. 71.

characteristics (*awṣāf ʿāmmah*) of the Sharīʿah, such as *samāḥah*, are also included in this category of *maqāṣid.* This is by virtue of the fact that one of the great ends of Islamic teachings is to remove hardship and bring ease and comfort in human life.[1] Accordingly, these characteristics have a twofold nature: they are both properties and goals of the Sharīʿah depending on how we look at them.

The last step involves determining the meaning of the specific goals of each particular area of Islamic legislation. This class of *maqāṣid khāṣṣah* consists of the methods or modalities "intended by the Lawgiver for realizing the useful purposes of the human beings or preserving their public interests (*maṣāliḥ ʿāmmah*) relating to their private conduct. The aim here is to prevent people's pursuit of their personal interests from leading to the undermining of their established public interests, owing to carelessness, whimsical errors, and vain desires."[2] As indicated by Ibn Ashur, to this category belong all reasons underlying the institution of particular rules regulating people's activities and undertakings, such as establishing the family and household by marriage contract or avoiding continuous harm through divorce, etc.[3]

An important idea in the conceptualization of *maqāṣid* is introduced here. The particular rules and commands (*qawāʿid wa aḥkām*) relating to the different spheres of human activity are not ends in themselves. Rather, they are means to ends. More

---

[1] *Ibid.* This is how the Qur'an has described the role of teachings and of its conveyor's mission contrary to prtevious revelations: "those who shall follow the [last] Apostle, the unlettered Prophet whom they shall find described in the Torah that is with them, and [later on] in the Gospel: [the Prophet] who will enjoin upon them the doing of what is right and forbid them the doing of what is wrong, and make lawful to them the good things of life and forbid them the bad things, and *lift from them their burdens and the shackles that were upon them* [aforetime]." (Q., 7:157). For an elaborate commentary by Ibn Ashur on this verse, see *Taḥrīr*, vol. 5/9, pp.129-139.

[2] Ibn Ashur, *Treatise*, p. 231.

[3] *Ibid.*

specifically, the Sharīʿah does not content itself with merely setting out a number of goals or ends for human beings and then leave it to them to follow whatever course of action or adopt any kind of means for achieving them. There is, in the Sharīʿah system, not only a correlation but inseparability between ends and means, whereby the former cannot justify the latter, except under extreme necessity (*ḍarūrah*) in very specific situations and for the sake of preserving a higher value for which there is not a means that is in itself itslef permissible.[1] Seen from a specific angle, the third part of Ibn Ashur's book on *maqāṣid* (devoted to the particular objectives of the various dealings [*muʿāmalāt*] among people)[2] is a detailed and profound analysis of the issue of ends and means in the Sharīʿah. In it he dealt with three important areas in Islamic legislation, namely the family, wealth and economic transactions, and legal justice and juridical procedures. His treatment of these crucial topics has been prefaced by a remarkably deep and comprehensive analysis of the meaning and types of right both from the sociological and legal points of view.

Likewise, a general picture emerges as to the vertical descending order of the Sharīʿah objectives according to their scope thus proceeding from the most general and abstract to the most specific and tangible. It would be interesting to dwell on the hermeneutical methods and modes of juristic reasoning Ibn Ashur used to develop his views in this and other respects.[3] However, this will take us beyond the specific purpose of this study; i.e. delineating the general framework he developed to deal with the higher objectives of the Sharīʿah and exploring their theoretical and methodological implications for social theorizing. As the previous exposition attempted to show, Ibn

---

[1] *Ibid.* pp. 231-237.

[2] This last part of the book covers a complete one hundred and six pages, from 413 to 518.

[3] For a fair treatment of this aspect, see al-Hassani, *Naẓariyat al-Maqāṣid ʿinda al-Imām Muḥammad al-Ṭāhir Ibn ʿĀshūr*, pp. 325-414.

Ashur's work has offered us a novel presepective on dealing with this crucial subject in Islamic jurisprudence. The philosophical importance of his grounding of *maqāṣid* in a holistic understanding of human nature has now become so clear that it does not need further emphasis. In fact, Ibn Ashur's contribution in this respect can better be appreciated in contrast with a general feature that has characterized most of the theological discussions of *kalām* scholars. In their rational arguments and different formulations of the articles of Islamic faith, Muslim theologians seldom addressed the issue of human nature to establish its relationship with Islam. As Fazlur Rahman rightly observed, theologians "have been too much preoccupied with God and His power."[1] Even the jurists who were concerned with elaborating the Islamic legal system cannot be said to have been more attentive to this issue. Exception can be made, however, of Ibn Taymiyya and his close disciple Ibn al-Qayyim for whom the concept of *fiṭrah* was central in most of their theological and juristic deliberations. Thus, man's nature and function in relation to God's commands have remained outside the purview of the systematic formulations of most theologians and jurists. As Fazlur Rahman further argued, "A science of Islamic morals can be possible only when man is put in the center of interest, for the Word of God has come to man for the sake of man."[2]

The foregoing discussion has brought us to a vantage point wherefrom we can proceed to examine the fundamental aspect of the Sharīʿah objectives, namely their classification according to their importance and impact in human life and existence. Again, we should keep in mind the all-purpose principle of the Sharīʿah consisting of the preservation of the order of the world.

---

[1] Fazlur Rahman, "Functional Interdependence between Law and Theology", in G.E. von Grunebum, ed., *Theology and Law in Islam* (Wiesbaden: Otto Harrassowitz, 1971), p. 97.

[2] Rahman, "Functional Interdependence between Law and Theology", p. 97.

We are further told that the pathway to that goal is by "regulating the conduct of human beings in it by preventing them from inflicting corruption and destruction upon one another."[1] The strategy for attaining this is summarized in the brief phrase of "realizing the good and preventing the evil (*taḥṣīl al-maṣāliḥ wa ijtināb al-mafāsid*)."[2] Seen from the perspective of their impact and importance in human life and socio-historical existence, the *maqāṣid*-cum-*maṣāliḥ* are classified into three categories following a vertical order. They consist of the *ḍarūriyyāt,* the *ḥājiyyāt* and the *taḥsīniyyāt.* As mentioned there, the general scheme of this hierarchical classification was initiated by al-Juwaynī and subsequently adopted by the majority of mainstream legal theorists as a basic framework for understanding the essential connection between the Sharīʿah and human life and existence.

Ibn Ashur is no exception to this almost universal consensus on that basic framework. Therefore, if that is the case, then what is the purpose of returning to a topic that has already been dealt with quite fairly? To answer this question, one might say that original contributions to human thought and knowledge do not always and necessarily consist of the discovery or invention of things hitherto hidden or completely unknown. They may take the form of improving and reconstructing existing knowledge, which can be attained through various ways and at different levels. They can be through the systematization of certain areas of inquiry; they can also be by shedding new lights on already known things and highlighting dimensions of them not previously attended to carefully or sufficiently, etc. Despite his passionate call for *ʿIilm al-Maqāṣid*, Ibn Ashur did not claim making new discoveries. He rather humbly declared that he would follow in the footsteps of his predecessors, especially al-Shāṭibī without, however, merely

---

[1] Ibn Ashur, *Treatise*, p. 116.

[2] *Ibid.*

reproducing their works.[1] It should be mentioned here that this is not an apology for Ibn Ashur. It is only a statement of an ordinary, yet very important, fact about the nature and development of human thought and knowledge. Neglecting this fact often results in false and sometimes damaging verdicts on people, ideas and events.

Be that as it may, what interests us in Ibn Ashur's discussion of the issue at hand is his clear concern about the social dimensions and implications of the *maqāṣid.* To put this aspect of his thought into stronger relief, it would be appropriate to recall here al-Ghazālī's definition of the *ḍarūriyyāt.* The main objective of the Sharīʿah (*maqṣūd al-Sharʿ*) in human beings, al-Ghazālī indicates,

> Consists of [realizing] five things, namely to protect their faith and religion (*dīn*), their life (*nafs*), their intellect (*ʿaql*), their offspring (*nasl*) and their property (*māl*). Anything involving the protection of these fundamentals (*uṣūl*) is a benefit (*maṣlaḥah*), and anything involving the omission thereof is harm (*mafsadah*) whose removal is a benefit.[2]

No human society or legal system meant for the good of mankind, be it based on divine revelation or otherwise, al-Ghazālī strongly argues, can exist without these five universal things, which he considers as the ultimate and foundational principles (*uṣūl*) of all good.[3] Muslim legal theorists considered the limitation of the category of the *ḍarūriyyāt* to these five as a matter of necessary knowledge. According to al-Āmidī, this limitation is based on "the nature of existence (*wuqūʿ*) and on our knowledge of the nonexistence of any necessary objectives beyond them in the usual course of things (*ʿādah*)."[4] For Ibn

---

[1] *Ibid.* p. 174.

[2] Abū Ḥāmid al-Ghazālī, *al-Mustaṣfā min ʿIlm al-Uṣūl,* ed. Muhammad Sulayman al-Ashqar (Beirut: Mu'assassat al-Risālah, 1st edn, 1417/1997), vol. 1, p. 417.

[3] *Ibid.*

[4] ʿAlī b. Muḥammad al-Āmidī, *al-Iḥkām fi Uṣūl al-Aḥkām* (Riyadh: Dār al-Ṣamīʿī, 1st

Ashur, the *ḍarūriyyāt* are those *maṣāliḥ* the realization of which "is essential for the community both collectively and individually" in such a way that its social order "will not function properly if there is any defect in these *maṣāliḥ*."[1] In his view, any defect in this category of *maṣāliḥ* results in the decline and disintegration of the community. However, the disintegration of the *ummah*'s social order does not imply her immediate destruction and extinction from the world, for this is a fate that even "the most idolatrous and barbaric peoples are spared."[2] This means that the community would degenerate into an anarchic and primitive status nearing savagery such that in the long run Muslim society faces the danger of eventual extinction either by internal strife and self-destruction or by subjugation by external forces.[3] Certainly, Ibn Ashur's quest here is not merely for the juristic aspects and legal implications of the idea of *maqāṣid*. He is rather trying here to capture its civilizational dimensions and cultural and political significance as a foundational framework for the socio-historical existence of the Muslim *ummah* and mankind at large.[4]

This intellectual concern can also be seen in his discussion of the five universal necessities or *ḍarūriyyāt*. Speaking of the protection of faith and religion (*ḥifẓ al-dīn*), he indicates that it means safeguarding each individual from anything that might cause confusion to his/her faith or bring corruption in his/her conduct and deeds which are based on that faith. As for the *ummah* as a whole, *ḥifẓ al-dīn* means preventing all that might undermine the fundamentals of religion pertaining to both faith and conduct. It includes, among other things, preserving the independence and sovereignty of the *ummah* and ensuring continuity between her generations through basic

---

edn, 1424/2003), Vol. 2/3, p. 343; *cf.* Weiss, *The Search of God's Law*, pp. 613-15.

[1] Ibn Ashur, *Treatise*, p. 118.

[2] *Ibid.*

[3] *Ibid.*

[4] Al-Rysuni, *Naẓariyat al-Maqāṣid*, pp. 295-99.

Islamic education so as to consolidate Muslim cultural unity and social integration.[1]

In a similar vein, he examines the other four with clear emphasis on their sociological and cultural dimensions both at the material and non-material levels. For example, when talking about the protection of human life (*ḥifẓ al-nafs*) he brings in the idea of mutual dependence or reciprocal relationship between the individual and society. Thus, for him, *ḥifẓ al-nafs* consists of protecting human lives individually and collectively, which means that care must be equally taken of the individual and cmmunity.[2] True, a the individual cannot survive and flourish outside society, but this does not mean that a person is totally dissolved into the social whole considered by Ibn Ashur, as seen above, as a reality *sui generis* with its own properties, thus exerting constraint on individuals and shaping their persoanlity and conduct. As he put it, each one of the individual members making up human society is endowed with qualities and dispositions on which the existence and preservation of the social order ultimately depend.[3]

In this respect, Ibn Ashur takes classical jurists to task. To demonstrate the concern of the Sharīʿah for the protection of human life, they adduced the case of the law of just retribution (*qiṣāṣ*) as the main example. According to him, "just retribution is the weakest means for protecting human souls, because it consists of only a partial remedy of the loss. Thus, the most important way to protect human life is to prevent harm and ruin before they happen, such as combating and eradicating epidemics."[4] A jurist may answer this argument by referring to the deterring effect of the law of retribution that consists of preventing people from committing homicide. But Ibn Ashur

---

[1] Ibn Ashur, *Treatise*, p. 120.
[2] *Ibid.*
[3] *Ibid.*
[4] *Ibid.* p. 120.

seems to be concerned about more than just an appreciation of what can be seen as reactive measures or strategy of the Sharīʿah in dealing with human affairs. His concern seems to be more about the positive aspect and proactive strategy of the Sharīʿah not only to protect but also to promote human life and endow it with better quality. Likewise, eradicating the socio-cultural and political roots of crime against human life would fit well in his line of reasoning.

It is not the purpose of the present discussion to go into the details of Ibn Ashur's elaboration on each of the five necessary universals (*kulliyyāt ḍarūriyyah*). However, some aspects in his analysis must not escape our attention here due to their methodological and epistemological significance. In line with this, he raised an important question as to whether there is a necessary correlation in the Sharīʿah between the institution of *ḥudūd* punishments and what is considered indispensable (*ḍarūrī*) in the scheme of its objectives (*maqāṣid*). In other words, are *ḥudūd* penalties meant exclusively for the protection of the *ḍarūrī* category? Or are these penalties the only criteria of what is a universal necessity?

For many classical jurists, the answer is in the affirmative. The institution of a *ḥadd* punishment, they would argue, is a clear indication and decisive criterion as to the indispensability of that to which it pertains.[1] In contrast, Ibn Ashur views that we need not subscribe to such a type of correlation for considering some types of *maṣlaḥah* as indispensable. In other words, *ḥudūd* in the Sharīʿah are not necessarily and always linked to what is indispensable. They may also be instituted for the protection of *maṣāliḥ* belonging to the second category,

---

[1] See for example ʿAbd al-Raḥmān b. Jār Allāh al-Banānī, *Ḥāshiyat al-Banānī ʿalā Jamʿ al-Jawāmiʿ* (a commentary on Tāj al-Dīn al-Subkī's *Jamʿ al-Jawāmiʿ*), (Cairo: Maṭbaʿat wa Maktabat Muṣṭafā Bābī al-Ḥalabī, 1356/1937, vol. 2, p. 280; Najm al-Dīn al-Ṭūfī, *Sharḥ Mukhtaṣar al-Rawḍah*, ed. Abdullah al-Torki (Beirut: Mu'assassat al-Risālah, 1410/1990), vol. 3, p. 209.

namely the *ḥājiyyāt.*[1] This mode of reasoning is in tune with Ibn Ashur's epistemological and methodological position concerning the issue of establishing universals in which thematic induction occupies, as mentioned earlier, a central place.

This argument is developed in conjunction with his discussion of the protection of progeny or offspring (*ḥifẓ al-nasl*). Mentioning the jurists' use of another term, i.e., *ḥifẓ al-ansāb*, to express the same thing, Ibn Ashur lamented over their confusion in determining its precise meaning. To overcome that confusion, he advanced the following clarifications. If it is meant by *ḥifẓ al-nasl* to safeguard human procreation and reproduction from cessation, then there is no doubt that it belongs to the *ḍarūrī* category. The reason is obvious: it is through procreation that the individuals of the species are replaced. If it decreases or ceases, this will result in the danger of the diminution or extinction of the species. But if *ḥifẓ al-nasl* is understood to mean establishing a person's ancestral line or lineal identity for which purpose the Sharīʿah has provided specific regulations for marriage, prohibited adultery and set up a penalty for it, then there is no clear reason to consider it among the *ḍarūriyyāt.* As he further indicated, "there is no imperative reason for the community to know that X is the offspring of Y. Rather, what is necessary is the existence of the individuals of the species and the proper management of their affairs" through their integration into the social order.[2]

However, Islam looks beyond the mere biological survival and physical continuation of the species. Its concern about lineal association and identity of offspring through the regulation of marriage and the institution of the family as a basic social unit contemplates a very important purpose in human life. It aims at cultivating and fostering the natural or inborn inclination (*mayl jibillī*) in the parents to take care of their children until they reach

---

[1] Ibn Ashur, *Treatise*, p. 123.
[2] *Ibid.* p. 122.

maturity and self-reliance. If lineal association and identity are dubious or unclear, that parental natural inclination will be weakened, a phenomenon that is naturally paralleled by the feeling of ingratitude and the absence of filial devotion on the part of the children. In Ibn Ashur's view, there is no doubt that such a situation involves a great harm.[1] But such harm, he avers, is no sufficient reason to raising *ḥifẓ al-ansāb* to the level of the *ḍarūrī* category, for the survival and continuation of the human species does not indispensably depend on it.

What seems to be suggested here is to disentangle the different aspects of the issue, a task that earlier jurists fell short of fulfilling. In his view, the reason behind their confusion lies in the epistemological and methodological mistake of assuming a necessary correlation between the institution of *ḥudūd* penalties and the protection and promotion of indispensable benefits, in the present discussion between the *ḥadd* punishment for adultery and *ḥifẓ al-nasl.* Accordingly, he clearly distinguishes between *ḥifẓ al-nasl* and *ḥifẓal-ansāb* as two terms expressing two different things that belong differently. While the first pertains to the *ḍarūrī* category, the second belongs to the category of *ḥājiyyāt* that comes next to it in importance and is strongly linked to it.[2] This argument also applies to the question of the punishment which the Sharīʿah has prescribed for slander (*qadhf*). Based on a consideration of the severity of the *ḥadd* penalty on *qadhf*, some jurists have included the protection of honor (*ḥifẓ al-ʿirḍ*) in the *ḍarūrī* category.[3] Ibn Ashur argues against this view as follows. For society and even for the individual, honor (*ʿirḍ*) is undoubtedly less important than lineal association and identity

---

[1] *Ibid.* p. 122.

[2] *Ibid.*

[3] This is, for example, the view of the Shāfiʿī jurist Tāj al-Dīn al-Subkī (d. 771 H) and his commentator al-Jalāl Shams al-Dīn al-Maḥallī (d. 864 h). See *Ḥāshiyat al-ʿAllāmah al-Banānī ʿalā Sharḥ al-Jalāl al-Maḥallī ʿalā Matn Jamʿ al-Jawāmiʿ*, ed. Muhammad Abd al-Qadir Shahin (Beirut: Dār al-Kutub al-ʿIlmiyyah, 1418/1998), vol. 2, pp. 432-33.

and it cannot, therefore, be part of what is necessary or indispensable for human social existence. However, the Sharīʿah has raised its protection to the status of *ḥājiyyāt* and enacted a severe penalty for slander (eighty lashes) in order to prevent people from offending one another with the slightest form of offense even verbally.[1] Thus grounded in spiritual and ethical considerations, the concern of the Sharīʿah to cultivate and enhance these essential emotional and spiritual bonds aims at realizing its objectives in the best humane manner possible.

Coming next to the *ḍarūriyyāt,* the *ḥājī* category consists, according to Ibn Ashur, of what is highly or extremely needed by society for "the achievement of its interests and the proper functioning of its affairs."[2] Failing to realize this category of benefits or ignoring them altogether does not actually cause the social order to collapse all at once, "but it will not function well", and this will lead to instability and hardship in people's lives, which ultimately will end in the disintegration of society. Accordingly, the Sharīʿah has considered such things like legal marriage, sales and trade, protection of lineal identity and honour, etc., as part of this important category.[3] Since the well-being of human society depends on the realization of these *maṣāliḥ*, "the importance given by the Sharīʿah to the *ḥājī* almost equals its concern about the *ḍarūrī*".[4] We need here to recall our discussion of the implications of Ibn Ashur's theorizing on *fiṭrah* for comprehending the characteristics and objectives of the Sharīʿah. As seen before, one major feature of the Sharīʿah, which is at the same time one of its universal goals, is to remove hardship (*mashaqqah*) and promote ease and comfort (*yusr*) in human life, which has a strong bearing on its universality and compatibility with human nature. Likewise, the *ḥājiyyāt* are a

---

[1] Ibn Ashur, *Treatise*, pp. 120-124.
[2] *Ibid.* p. 123.
[3] *Ibid.* pp. 123-124.
[4] *Ibid.* p. 124.

necessary complement to the *ḍarūriyyāt* without which hardship cannot be removed and ease cannot be attained.[1]

Finally, the third category of *maṣāliḥ* in the Islamic scheme of human good is that of the *taḥsīniyyāt.* For Ibn Ashur, this category consists of things that bring perfection and beauty to the social order and lifestyle of the *ummah.* The *taḥsīniyyāt* are such that they would enable people to live a comfortable quality life and become a social model attracting others to belong to the *ummah* or to at least seek friendship with her.[2] Enhancing good manners and blocking the means to evil belong to this category.[3] As it appears from his analysis, the significance of the *taḥsīniyyāt* is that they aim at freeing human life from the rules of necessity just as the *ḥājiyyāt* contemplate raising human society above the level of the primordial laws of nature and instinctive impulses. Not only that, this category aims at embellishing and beautifying human life and existence.

The reason for expounding these categories of *maṣāliḥ* is not, for Ibn Ashur, merely to show that the Sharīʿah has taken care of them, nor is it to demonstrate how specific cases can be dealt with through *qiyās* by relating them to established precedents. To him, this is only a partial aspect of the understanding of the Sharīʿah that belongs to the task of the jurist and falls short of the purpose of *ʿIlm al-Maqāṣid.*[4] What is of utmost importance for him is to arrive at a knowledge and formulation of the general principles and universal genres (*ṣuwar kulliyyah*) of the *maṣāliḥ* intended by the Sharīʿah. Once this is attained, he ascertains, we can face new situations with much confidence that the solutions we develop are grounded in the value system of Islam and conform to its commands and teachings. As he argued,

---

[1] *Ibid.*

[2] *Ibid.*

[3] *Ibid.* pp. 124-125.

[4] *Ibid.* 125.

> Thus, whenever we are faced with new cases and emergent issues which did not exist during the time of Revelation and which have no equivalent in the precedents whose rules have been established in the Sharīʿah sources, we will know how to classify and judge them according to the relevant rules (*aḥkām*). We will then be confident that we have formulated valid Sharīʿah judgments.[1]

Besides the vertical categorization of *maṣlaḥah* according to its structural place and weight in human existence, there are other criteria according to which the Sharīʿah objectives are also examined and categorized. Allusion has already been made to such considerations. We shall therefore not expand much on them. A brief survey thereof will be sufficient for the purpose of outlining the general framework of Ibn Ashur's thinking on *maṣlaḥah*. Thus, *maṣlaḥah* is further categorized according to two criteria. The first concerns its scope seen in terms of its universal and private character, whereas the second pertains to the degree and strength of evidence establishing its veracity.

According to the first criterion, *maṣlaḥah* is classified into two types: universal (*kulliyyah* or *ʿāmmah*) and particular (*juzʾiyyah* or *khāṣah*). The first type concerns the whole society. Universal *maṣaḥah* is "that which equally concerns the whole community, very large numbers of its individuals or one whole country."[2] In his opinion, the universal type of *maṣlaḥah* pertaining to the whole *ummah* is rare. It includes things like the protection of Muslim unity and sovereignty, safeguarding the Islamic faith from being undermined, preserving the Qur'an from distortion and propagating its message, protecting the main sanctuaries of Islam from falling under non-Muslim dominance, etc. Some components of the *ḍaruriyyāt* and *ḥājiyyāt* belong, according to Ibn Ashur, to this type of universal *maṣlaḥah*.[3]

---

[1] *Ibid.* pp. 125-126.
[2] *Ibid.* p. 130.
[3] *Ibid.*

Universal *maṣaḥah* can be equated with what is known in the jargon of modern social and political thought as general or public interest. It includes whatever in the categories of *ḍarūriyyāt* and *ḥājiyyāt* concerns the whole Muslim *ummah* or large portions of it such as a region, a country or a people, or a number of countries or peoples. In Ibn Ashur's view, there are in these two categories permanent types of *maṣlaḥah ʿāmmah* that are not subject to any alteration throughout the ages, such as the protection of the two sanctuaries of Makkah and Madīnah which have an essential spiritual and historical value and function for every Muslim at any time. There are also changing types of *maṣlaḥah ʿāmmah* that vary according to the needs and socio-historical development of the Muslim *ummah* both as one universal community and as countries and peoples. As examples of the changing forms of *maṣlaḥah ʿāmmah*, he mentions establishing judicial institutions and court systems to settle disputes among the people, entering into agreements with non-Muslim governments to ensure the safety of Muslims and protect Muslim interests in their dominion, etc.[1]

Maṣlaḥah juzʾiyyah or *khāṣṣah* includes all that concerns "the interest of individuals or small numbers of individuals. In other words, it pertains to the private rights and properties. According to Ibn Ashur, the protection and promotion of this type of *maṣlaḥah* "has been covered by the rules and commands regulating the different types of transactions."[2]

A closely tied up with this classification of *maṣlaḥah* into *kulliyyah* and *juzʾiyyah* is another more fundamental one that can actually be considered as the basis for all other classifications. Although this kind of classification was pointed out earlier, it is not inappropriate to repeat it here for two main reasons. Firstly, it sheds further light on Ibn Ashur's view on the relationship between the prescriptive teachings of the

---

[1] *Ibid.* pp. 130-131.
[2] *Ibid.* p. 131.

Sharīʿah and those human acts emanating from instinctive impulses. Secondly, it helps making the main argument of the present discussion clearer. This classification includes two types of *maṣlaḥah*. On the one hand, there are those interests that are readily realizable by human beings because they conform to their immediate instictoid impulses. Such interests have to do with man's instinctive needs and inclinations and people would naturally seek to satisfy them by themselves without external stimuli or motivation. They include such things as sexual desire, food, shelter, etc. On the other hand, there are those interests in which the lot of particular individuals is less evident than in the first category. In Ibn Ashur's view, only when such things are missed would people realize their importance for their own well-being. Paving roads, establishing security systems, etc., are examples of such *maṣāliḥ* that constitute what is called public interest.

As seen above, and this is again emphasized in the present context, it is not the purpose of the Sharīʿah to order human beings to pursue the first type of *maṣlaḥah* whose benefits are obvious and readily perceivable. Being satisfied with their natural impulses that would drive them to do so, the Sharīʿah is rather more concerned to remove the obstacles to achieving those benefits. In contrast, the second type of *maṣlaḥah* whose benefits are less obvious have been positively handled by the Sharīʿah in order to ensure that they are not abandoned or violated. Its strategy for that has taken two forms. The first one consists of making such things personal obligations on each and every individual (*farḍ ʿayn*) or collective duties (*farḍ kifāyah*) on the community, whereas the second consists of enacting specific penalties for neglecting or infringing upon them.[1]

However, the noninterference of the Sharīʿah in the first type of *maṣlaḥah* is not unconditional, meaning that it leaves human beings totally to their instinctive drives or natural

---

[1] *Ibid.* p. 110.

impulses. People might be influenced by perversive or corruptive teachings or bad habits in such a way that their original disposition (*jibillah*) is adversely affected and their behavior becomes abnormal. Killing girl children for fear of dishonor or poverty because of them, torturing oneself by not taking food because of some irrational thought or as a kind of asceticism for the sake of spiritual pursuit, abstaining from marriage and sexual intercourse in order not to be the cause of the suffering of the child who will be born out of that are, Ibn Ashur tells us, some instances reported by history which testify to such a corruption of human nature. People might also become so self-centred and egoistic that they would only care about their own interests and use whatever means to attain them no matter how much harm they would cause to others. As such attitudes run counter to Islam's purpose to restore and safeguard man's original nature (*fiṭrah*) and promote human good for the individual and society on the material as well as spiritual levels, the Sharīʿah has devised proper measures to combat deviations from its ideal of the natural human norm. These measures vary from mere exhortation to law enforcement up to punishment, depending on the situation.[1]

The third criterion on the basis of which *maṣlaḥah* is further considered is evidence. Accordingly, it is classified in a descending order into three kinds, definitive (*qaṭʿiyyah*), probable or conjectural (*ẓanniyyah*) and illusionary (*wahmiyyah*). A definitive *maṣlaḥah* is usually established on explicit textual or rational evidence whose meaning does not require any interpretation. To this belongs what Ibn Ashur called *kulliyyāt naṣṣiyyah*, meaning those expressions in the Qur'an and Prophet's traditions whose meaning is definitive. Similarly, when the mind in its inquiry reaches a stage where it is compelled to accept something as certain, this also constitutes a valid and definitive basis for the consideration of *maṣlaḥah*. The five universal necessities belong

[1] *Ibid.* pp. 110-111; *Jamharah*, vol. 1, pp. 465-468; *Taḥrīr*, vol. 13/27, pp. 420-437.

to this category. A conjectural *maṣlaḥah* is one that has been established only as likelihood, whether through textual or rational evidence. "Illusionary *maṣlaḥah* is what appears to create benefit, but when subjected to investigation, it is revealed to be harmful."[1]

From the foregoing exposition of the classification of *maṣlaḥah* according to the criterion of evidence an important feature of Ibn Ashur's thinking comes to the fore. It relates to his optimistic view of the power of human reason to know what is good and beneficial (*maṣlaḥah*) and distinguish it from what is evil and harmful (*mafsadah*), thus making him at variance with the view maintained by many earlier *uṣūl* scholars, especially the Ashʿarites. This brings him once again closer to the position of the Muʿtazilah and Ibn Taymiyyah. Whatever the case, it is not our purpose to trace Ibn Ashur's sources or to investigate his indebtedness to a particular school or scholar. Our concern has been mainly to bring into focus those features of his thought whereby he has pushed the understanding of the idea of the protection and promotion of this type of *maqāṣid al-sharīʿah* beyond the boundaries of the traditional legalistic approach that has dominated most of Muslim scholars' works on the subject well until the present.

Before recapitulating some of the major points that have emerged in the preceding discussion, a few words are in order here to clarify an important point pertaining to our discussion of the various considerations according to which *maṣlaḥah* is classified. Throughout that discussion in which the different criteria for the taxonomy of *maṣlaḥah* were briefly analyzed, mention was only made of this concept without its opposite, i.e., *mafsadah*. This might give the impression that the latter does not come under the purview of those criteria. Of course, this is not the case. The three types of classification on the basis of weight and impact, scope and evidence apply equally to the concept of

---

[1] *Ibid.* pp. 131-132.

mafsadah. Let us now recapitulate some of the important points in the previous discussion. This, it is hoped, will enable us to highlight some directions for further study not only of Ibn Ashur's work and legacy, but of Islamic jurisprudence in general and the subject of *maqāṣid* in particular. Two main point are of special interest for us here

Firstly, in addition to his tacit and explicit criticisms of *uṣūl al-fiqh* both at the methodological and epistemological levels, Ibn Ashur's attempt at reformulating the theory of *maqāṣid* not only allowed him to free it from the narrow legalistic approach that has dominated it, but it also placed this important subject at the centre of the philosophical and methodological concerns of theorizing on human social existence. By grounding the notion of *maqāṣid* in a positive and optimistic view of human nature as expressed by the concept of *fiṭrah*, he has pushed the frontiers of Islamic legal and social thinking to higher and challenging intellectual horizons. No one before, nor even after, him has tried to systematically tie up the study of *maqāṣid* or the Sharīʿah commands in general to the issue of human nature in such a systematic fashion as he did. His insistence that the study of *maqāṣid* should be done within a wider understanding of the social system and its dynamics as envisioned by Islam is quite original.

The second point concerns his methodological insights with regard to the ground on which to identify the component elements of the *ḍarūriyyāt*. His argument with classical jurists on the non-necessary correlation between the institution of *ḥudūd* penalties and what belongs to this category has far-reaching implications for the understanding of the Sharīʿah commands. We shall not expand on this here. Only a few brief remarks will be made, while more will be said in the next section of this chapter. Not only did that argument allow Ibn Ashur to question and even reject some classical positions, but it is most probably what has enabled him to introduce into the scheme of *maqāṣid* some crucial concepts in a totally different way from the way most of classical and modern Muslim jurists usually treat them. Foremost among those concepts are freedom (*ḥurriyyah*), justice (*ʿadl*) and tolerance (*tasāmuḥ*).[1] He thus can be said to have broadened the scope of thinking about the objectives of the Sharīʿah far beyond what earlier and even contemporary writers could attain, including al-Shāṭibī himself. This aspect of Ibn Ashur's thought is of special interest for us here due to its implications for the systematization of values.[2]

From the Doctrine of *Maqāṣid* to *ʿIlm al-Maqāṣid*

To what extent has Ibn Ashur succeeded in developing the study of *maqāṣid al-sharīʿah* into what he called *ʿIlm al-Maqāṣid*? Let it be noted at the outset that in order to stand as an independent and self-contained discipline, any field of study has to satisfy some basic requirements. To put it briefly in the words of Ibn Khaldun, an independent science (*ʿilm*) must have "its own peculiar object (*mawḍūʿ*)" and "its own peculiar problems (*masāʾil*)."[3] Of course, these two essential requirements can be subjected to a more detailed analysis as can be found in epistemological and methodological studies. However, it would suffice here to quote a

---

[1] For a detailed and systematic analysis of Ibn Ashur's political thought consisting of these and other concepts, see Mohamed El-Tahir El-Mesawi, "Towards an Integrated Islamic Political theory: A Systematic Analysis of Ibn Ashur's Political Thought", in Zeenath Kausar, ed., *Islamic Political Thought in Modern and Contemporary Times (*Kuala Lumpur: Research Centre, International Islamic University Malaysia, 2005), pp. 69-112.

[2] Despite the importance of this aspect in the study of *maqāṣid,* only very few efforts have been devoted to it. See for example, Fahmi Muhammad Alwan, *al-Qiyam al-Ḍarūriyyah wa Maqāṣid al-Tashrīʿ al-Islāmī* (Cairo: al-Hay'ah al-Miṣriyyah al-ʿĀmmah li al-Kitāb, 1989); Taha Abderrahmne, *Tajdīd al-Manhaj fī Taqwīm al-Turāth* (Casablanca/Beirut: al-Markaz al-Thaqāfī al-ʿArabī, 3rd edn, 2007 [1994]), pp. 93-129, and also, "Mashrūʿ Tajdīd ʿIlmī li-Mabḥath Maqāṣid al-Sharīʿah," *al-Muslim al-Muʿāṣir,* Vol. 26, No. 103 (1422-2002), pp. 41-64; Noura Bouhannach, *Maqāṣid al-Sharīʿah ʿinda al-Shāṭibī wa Taʾṣīl al-Akhlāq fī al-Fikr al-ʿArabī al-Islāmī* (Algiers & Beirut: Manshūrāt Ḍifāf, 1st edn, 1433/2012).

[3] Ibn Khaldun, *The Muqaddimah*, trans. Frenz Rosenthal (London: Routledge and Kegan Paul, 1967), vol. 1, p. 77.

definition of science—in the sense of specific discipline or field of study—that can, together with the previous quotation, help us formulate a tentative answer to the above question. According to a prominent French philosopher, science is

> The body of knowledge and research having a sufficient degree of unity and generality and allowing its pursuers to reach consistent conclusions that are the result neither of arbitrary conventions nor of the personal tastes and interests of the individuals sharing them, but of objective relations that me gradually discovered and can be confirmed by precise methods of verification.[1]

Without being unaware of the natural-science bias in Lalande's definition, we can however infer from his and Ibn Khaldun's statements four major criteria. An independent scientific discipline must have a specific subject matter, a set of clear general propositions, a body of rules and methods guiding the steps of research in it and allowing its pursuers to arrive at objective conclusions that can be tested and verified, and thus must enjoy a sufficient level of unity and internal cohesion.

From a general review of the material arrangement, methodological structure and way of reasoning of Ibn Ashur's book on *maqāṣid* it can be said that these requirements have been adequately observed. In the first part of the book consisting of almost seventy pages, the author argues two main things. The first point is that the Sharīʿah has purposes and objectives underlying its commands and teachings. This is established through a discussion of the issue of *taʿlīl* and a refutation of the literalist approach to the textual sources of the Sharīʿah.[2] Hence, the case is made for a distinct object of *ʿIlm al-Maqāṣid* as an independent discipline. The second point is dealt with through an analysis of the various methodological

[1] André Lalande, *Vocabulaire technique et critique de la philosophie* (Paris: Presses Universitaires de France, 1988 [1947]), vol. 2, p. 954.

[2] Ibn Ashur, *Treatise*, pp. 26-67.

rules and steps that should be followed to discover those purposes and objectives.[1]

In the second part covering almost half of the book, the subject matter of the proposed new discipline is taken up again. The author undertakes a more detailed analysis of its components and elaboration of their classification according to a descending hierarchical order branching out of the all-purpose principle of the Sharīʿah to which he devotes a whole chapter.[2] Throughout this part Ibn Ashur's main concern is to show how the *maqāṣid* constitute a specific area worthy of independent inquiry that transcends the limited interest and atomistic methods of the traditional jurist and is informed by an underlying logic knitting its components together.[3] A major feature of his reasoning in this respect is to establish the universality of the *maqāṣid* d by virtue of the compatibility of Islamic teachings with human nature as expounded on the basis of the Qur'anic concept of *fiṭrah.* As mentioned above, al-Shaṭibī succeeded to reformulate the idea of *maqāṣid* as the central and unifying theme of Islamic legal theory. He thus paved the ground, both epistemologically and methodologically, for Ibn Ashur to free that study from the narrow legalistic approach and language of both legists and legal theorists. Although his declared objective was to narrow down juristic differences and transcend doctrinal fanaticism between the *fuqahā'* by providing a frame of reference consisting of the definitive universals (*kulliyyāt qaṭʿiyyah*) of the Sharīʿah,[4] our inter-textual analysis of his works has, however, clearly shown that his contribution went far beyond that limited purpose and addressed fundamental issues relating to the study of human social existence. By grounding the study of *maqāṣid al-sharīʿah* in

---

[1] *Ibid.* pp. 13-25.
[2] *Ibid.* pp. 91-95.
[3] *Ibid.* pp. 91-186.
[4] *Ibid.* p. xvi.

a comprehensive understanding of human nature and condition and addressing fundamental questions on the origin and universality of values, Ibn Ashur has paved the way for a kind of social theorizing capable of transcending the reductionist epistemological and methodological tendencies and materialistic philosophies prevailing in much of the literature on man and society.

In the third part of the aforementioned book, Ibn Ashur undertakes what can be considered an applied study of the main ideas and concepts developed in the preceding parts. A number of areas in human social life and dealings are discussed to show how the idea of *maqāṣid* is manifested in them through the different modes of Islamic legislation. They include domains like the specification and determination of rights, family and kinship, economic activity and wealth, justice and juridical procedures, punishment and the penal code, etc. All this is prefaced with an insightful analysis of the relationship between means and ends showing both the dynamic and pragmatic nature of that relationship and its imbeddeness in moral considerations.[1]

Reflecting on our expostion of Ibn Ashur's reformuation of the idea of *maqāṣid al-sharīʿah* such as would suit his purpose of edifying a new discipline, the following can be said. Muslim legal theorists' insistence on the centrality and universality of the five necessities is of special significance for the proper understanding of, and approach to solving, human problems. It tells a lot about what makes the ultimate truth of human socio-historical existence and determines its functioning and dynamics. Identifying the ultimate purpose of the Sharīʿah as being the protection and promotion of those universals means that they constitute the necessary and *sine qua none* condition for a specific mode of life that ensures human well-being. To borrow a famous term in Jung's analytical psychology, the five indispensable universals constitute the *archetypes* of human

---

[1] Ibn Ashur, *Treatise,* pp. 229-340.

society[1] without which its existence and continuity would be inconceivable. They represent the level beneath which human socio-historical existence becomes practically impossible. As can be understood from the line of argument followed by legal theorists in this respect, these fundamental universal values are not the result of mere intellectual speculation or theological stipulation, nor are they sheer theoretical abstractions or constructs. They are rather deeply rooted in the ontological and empirical reality of human nature and likewise constitute real and practical conditions necessary for human life. From this, they derive their importance as the highest or ultimate criteria for both human good and conduct on the individual as well as collective levels.[2]

However, in the discourse of legal theorists, these fundamental values do not operate in vacuum or in isolation from the wider scheme of the Sharīʿah. On the contrary, they constitute a core which is consolidated and complemented by a whole gamut of values aiming at promoting human well-being in its comprehensive sense as discussed above. In other words, they are so comprehensive and universal that any value we could think about can be subsumed under them no matter how important it might be. This crucial aspect of the *ḍarūriyyāt* seems to have escaped the attention of those who have advocated the reconsideration of limiting them to the five universals. It may also account for Ibn Ashur's wavering view as to the place of some very important values, such as freedom,

---

[1] For a detailed discussion of the origin and function of Jung's notion of artchetypes as constitutive of his theory of the unconscious and human's instinctual structure, see Sonu Shamdasani, *Jung and the Making of Modern Psychology: The Dream of a Science* (Cambridge-New York: Cambridge University Press, 2003), especially chapter 3: pp. 163-270; also Michael Vannoy Adams, "The Archetypal School," in Polly Young-Eisendratth & Terence Dawson (eds.), *The Camdridge Companion to Jung* (Camdridge-New York: Cambridge University Press, 2008), pp. 107-124.

[2] Alwan, *al-Qiyam al-Ḍarūriyyah wa Maqāṣid al-Tashrīʿ* , p. 95.

justice, equality and tolerance, which he included under what he called *maqāṣid ʿāmmah*;[1] a hesitation reflected in the fact that he did not subsume these values under any of the three categories of *ḍarūriyyāt*, *ḥājiyyāt* and *taḥsīniyyāt*, despite his strong emphasis on them as general objectives and essential characteristics of the Sharīʿah reflecting its universality and the compatibility of its teachings with human nature. The previous observations do not mean, however, that classical Muslim scholars said the last word and that no room is left for further inquiry. What those remarks aim at is that hasty judgements and the lack of profound and learned appreciation of received wisdom are detrimental to the development of solidly grounded scholarship and viable thought.

Whatever the case might be concerning the finality or open-ended nature of the *ḍarūriyyāt*, the main interest of the present study has been to explore the possibility of taking the idea of *maqāṣid* as a basic framework for understanding human socio-historical existence. As we have seen in our journey with Ibn Ashur, his articulation of this important theme in Islamic legal theory on the basis of a positive and optimistic interpretation of *fiṭrah* presents us with an opportunity to overcome the inadequacies of both the positivistic and formal approaches to the study of man and society through an integrated methodology in which the empirical and the theoretical are cast together. The *maqāṣid* thus restated provide an appropriate framework for a science of ethics and values rooted in an integrated and holistic understanding of human nature and reality, for without a clear and comprehensive conception of what makes the reality and nature of human beings any theorizing on ethics and values will be meaningless.

In fact, as mentioned at the beginning of this study, the disagreement on the understanding of what human nature

---

[1] See an analysis of these concepts in El-Mesawi, "Towards an Integrated Islamic Political theory", *op. cit.*

means is the fundamental cause of much of the differences and conflicts between social philosophies and political ideologies as well as the antagonistic intellectual attitudes toward religion and religious belief and thought in the modern and post-modern worlds. Individuals and groups develop their understanding of values and formulate their theories about human individual and collective life as well as social and political institutions according to their conception of that nature and the place of human beings within the wider ontological context of existence. There is little hope, if any at all, in bridging the wide ideological divides and overcoming the cultural and political conflicts among peoples and nations if no common understanding of what makes human beings distinct from other creatures and of what such distinctness entails in terms of the values and institutions is not achieved beyond the materialist paradigm of secular humanism. It is with this essential question of human nature in mind that the the present author attempted to provide a detailed exposition of Ibn Ashur's optimistic understanding of the concept of *fiṭrah* as the cornerstone in his reformulation of the theory of *maqāṣid al-sharīʿah.*

By Way of Conclusion

It is our belief that Islam's claim to universality cannot be properly appreciated and the relevance of its teachings to the human condition cannot be soundly established unless its fundamental proposition that it is *dīn al-fiṭrah* is clearly understood. As seen throughout this study, Ibn Ashur's work on *maqāṣid* offers a well-argued case in this respect. It presents us with an unprecedented and inspiring attempt at social theorization solidly grounded in the Islamic world-view and value system. Without this grounding, one would venture to say, any effort to face the pressing intellectual and philosophical challenges of the secular materialist thought and vision of the world perpetuated by Western modern and postmodern trends will remain inadequate. Humanity at present is in dire need to restore not only the meaning of human nature but also that of reality, for reality is indeed at risk as a contemporary philosopher has pertinently argued.[1] Otherwise, and due to the unscrupulous manipulations of man and nature carried out in the name of science and progress, we should only expect, as recently argued by Francis Fukuyama, the near approaching of the post-human future of mankind. As he rightly put it, "any meaningful definition of rights must be based on substantive judgments about human nature."[2]

The idea of *maqāṣid* as reformulated by Ibn Ashur and as further work on it is deemed to yield, provides an appropriate framework to address crucial issues pertaining to human socio-historical existence and to salvage man and society from the increasing dehumanization that has been at work for quite a long time.[3] Under the systematic onslaught of the modern secular mind and nihilistic philosophical tendencies, humanity at the present stage of her development is alarmingly losing sense of the fundamental values capable of preserving the humanness of man and sanctity of life. As Dubos warned more than three decades ago, the desecration of life and nature is at the center of man's problems in the modern world and is at the origin of the process of dehumanization just mentioned.

---

[1] See Roger Trigg, *Reality at Risk* (Sussex & New Jersey: The Harvester Press & Barnes and Noble Books, 1980).

[2] Francis Fukuyama, *Our Posthuman Future: Consequences of the Biotechnology Revolution* (London: Profile Books Ltd, 2002), p. 13.

[3] *Cf.* Pitirim Sorkin, *The Crisis of the Age* (Oxford, UK: Oneworld Publications Ltd, 1992 [1941]); René Dubos, *So Human an Animal* (New York: Charles Scribner's Sons, 1968); Wilhelm Röpke, *The Social Crisis of our Time*, translated from the German by Annette and Peter Schiffer Jacobsohn (Chicago: The University of Chicago Press, 1959); Seyyed Hossein Nasr, *Man and Nature: The Spiritual Crisis in Modern Man* (Chicago: ABC International Group, Inc, 1997).Raymond Tallis, *Aping Mankind: Neuromania, Darwinitis and the Misinterpretation of Humanity* (Durham, UK: Acumen, 2011).

CHAPTER THREE

Apprehending and Concretizing *Maqāṣid al-Sharīʿah* in the Modern World

Sherman A. Jackson

Introduction

It was in the nineteenth century that the "scientific" study of Islam approached maturity in the West. This was also the period during which the hegemonic rise of the hard sciences and "higher criticism" in religious studies opened a new chapter in the age-old conflict between "reason" and revelation. Among the most important by-products of this development was the rise of religious Fundamentalism, in which Christian—more specifically Protestant—scholars and theologians moved to erect a dike of literalism around the Bible to stave off doctrinal erosion and compromise. [1] To their opponents, secular and Christian

[1] The term "Fundamentalism" is taken from a twelve-volume series entitled, *The Fundamentals*, published by a group of conservative Protestant scholars and theologians between 1909 and 1919, financed by two brothers, Wyman and Milton Stewart, in response to liberal re-interpretations of Christianity. There were five main fundamentals: (1) the inspiration and infallibility of Christian Scripture; (2) the deity of Jesus (including his virgin birth); (3) the substitutionary atonement of Jesus' death; (4) the literal resurrection of Jesus; and (5) the literal second coming of Jesus. For a good introduction to fundamentalism, see Ed. Dobson *et al.*, *The Fundamentalist Phenomenon: The Resurgence of Conservative Christianity* (Grand Rapids, MI: Baker Book House, 2nd edn, 1986), pp. 48-49.

"progressives" alike,[1] literalism came to represent the antithesis of both modernity and reason. This attitude would soon permeate the academy where it informed the study of religion in general and Islam more particularly. As the Western academy settled into its new "post-religious" identity, almost every criticism that could be directed at religion in general was assumed *a fortiori* to apply to Islam. Literalism, in this context, as the Believer's last-ditch effort to find refuge from the deluge of modern secularism, came to be identified with any and every serious commitment to Islam.[2]

Literalism, certainly as institutionalized in Western Fundamentalism, assumes that meaning is restricted to the strictly lexical sense of words and that allegorical, figurative, or metaphorical interpretations are most often attempts to escape or distort the true meaning of scripture. Similarly, the idea that science, history, church authority, *ijmāʿ* (unanimous consensus), or social reality might suggest or compel non-literal renderings is regarded with suspicion if not contempt. On this understanding, any move by modern Muslims towards more felicitous interpretations of Islam is commonly assumed to *require* a move away from literalism. Literalism, in other words, is assumed to be the root-cause of Islam's maladjustment to modernity. It is in this context that the approach to scriptural interpretation that proceeds from what classical jurists identified as the *maqāṣid al-sharīʿah*, (broader aims and objectives of the law) has acquired almost panacean expectations among modern Muslims. This is

---

[1] A pristine example of this is reflected in the important and controversial sermon, "Shall the Fundamentalists Win?" delivered in 1922 by the then most prominent leader of emergent Christian liberalism, Harry Emerson Fosdick. *See* Harry Emerson Fosdick, *"Shall the Fundamentalists Win?": Defending Liberal Protestantism in the 1920s*, http://historymatters.gmu.edu/d/5070 (last visited May 15, 2007).

[2] Indeed, aspects of this bias were even retrojected back into medieval times, where it informed our perception of the substance, value, and significance of the Traditionalist movement. For more on this point, see Sherman A. Jackson, *Islam and the Blackamerican: Looking toward the Third Resurrection* (Oxford/New York: Oxford University Press, 2005).

based on the belief that interpretations that are violent, intolerant or misogynistic, or culturally, economically or politically stultifying or ineffective are almost invariably grounded in a literalism that cannot stand in the face of appeals to the broader aims and objectives of the law. These expectations, however, are routinely thwarted by two interrelated oversights. The first is the failure to differentiate between literalism, on the one hand, and what I term "juristic empiricism," on the other. The second is the inability to move beyond the pre-modern jurists' abstractions of the *maqāṣid al-sharīʿah* to practical concretions that are responsive to the realities of the modern world.

This chapter attempts to undo this confusion between literalism and juristic empiricism, allowing for the introduction of the notion of "juristic induction" as the theoretical basis of *maqāṣid al-sharīʿah.* The chapter then moves to a more functionally pragmatic concretion of one of the *maqāṣid*, namely, *ḥifẓ al-ʿaql* (preservation of reason). This shall entail a number of interrelated questions: What is the meaning of *ʿaql* and how expansive or restrictive a construct is it? Is *ʿaql* a mere paper tiger, invoked primarily to insulate existing doctrine, or is it a more generative principle capable of moving the law beyond the status quo? Are received notions of *ʿaql* adequate? If not, what adjustments might render *ḥifẓ al-ʿaql* a more useful tool for interpreting Islamic law in the modern world?

Literalism, Juristic Empiricism, and Juristic Induction

My use of the term "juristic empiricism" is derived from the epistemological theory of empiricism, according to which only sense-observation and experiment can decide our acceptance or rejection of a proposition. In the same way that philosophical and scientific empiricists deny all knowledge beyond the senses and restrict it to *a posteriori* observation, juristic empiricists look askance at all *a priori* claims to knowledge of the Sharīʿah that go *beyond* and cannot be explicitly documented in the sources. To be sure, there is a thin line between literalism and juristic empiricism, inasmuch as both seek to promote the primacy of texts and to banish extra-textual biases, hunches, speculation, and presupposition. Literalism, however, can also be placed in the service of another approach to legal interpretation, namely "juristic induction." Here the aggregate of a number of texts, *literally* interpreted, point to a meaning that transcends each text individually but implicitly inheres in the group, the whole equalling more than the sum of its parts. Literalism and juristic empiricism meet in their common tendency to uphold the self-sufficiency and finality of individual texts. With juristic induction, however, literalism actually generates meaning *beyond* the individual texts. These different applications of literalism may be likened to the difference between direct and alternating electrical currents. While both constitute electric power, where electrons flow from negative to positive, alternating current has characteristics (for example, distance and ease in adjusting voltage) that make it more advantageous for many more commercial and domestic applications.

To demonstrate the difference between these two applications of literalism, take a series of commands, for example, to open the window, fetch a fan, turn off the lights, and pour a glass of water. One can separate these commands, interpret them literally, and stop at that. Or one can combine them and interpret them literally, in which case they might generate a cumulative meaning to the effect that, "It's hot!" On this understanding, it would be proper to do anything that could effectively counter the heat (for example, buy an air-conditioner) and to do nothing that might increase the heat (for example, turn on the oven). In neither case, however, does the status of these ancillary actions depend on any explicit command or prohibition. Nor does it depend on any figurative interpretation of any of the commands themselves. Rather, the propriety and impropriety of these ancillary actions reclines upon a *literal* interpretation of the original commands in the aggregate. In other words, the illocutionary force that is produced by aggregation, *not* the semantic possibilities opened up by figurative interpretation, that allows (or perhaps even compels) us to go beyond these commands.

The point here is that literalism is not the antithesis of juristic induction, even if the latter is capable of producing *results* that transcend the former. Juristic induction, however, *is* the antithesis of juristic empiricism. For, according to the latter, everything one did to counter or increase the heat in the above example would require an explicit text that commanded or prohibited these actions, respectively.

These two interpretive modalities, juristic empiricism and juristic induction, along with their respective relationships to literalism, reflect a major fissure in the Islamic legal tradition that has persisted from its early centuries. It reached crisis proportions in the time of al-Shāfiʿī (d. 204/819-20), one of the eponyms of the four Sunni schools of law, who wrote the first known work on legal theory, *al-Risālah* (The Epistle) in large part as a direct response to this fissure. Contrary to the traditional view, however, still maintained in some circles,[1] classical legal theory (*uṣūl al-fiqh*) was not a mere extension of al-Shāfiʿī's thesis. In fact, it was a reaction *against* al-Shāfiʿī's rather crass nativism.[2] Closely examined, al-Shāfiʿī's writings reveal a deep concern over the presence of what he deemed to be "interpretive viruses," which he feared were going undetected because they were sublated into the realm of "plain speech" by peoples whose language was now that of the Arabians but

---

[1] Notable exceptions include Sherman A. Jackson, "Fiction and Formalism: Towards a Functional Analysis of *Uṣūl al-Fiqh*," in Bernard G. Weiss ed., *Studies in Islamic Legal Theory* (Leiden/Boston/Köln: Brill), 2002, pp. 177 & 186-92; Wael B. Hallaq, "Was al-Shāfiʿī the Master Architect of Islamic Jurisprudence?," *International Journal of Middle East Studies*, vol. 25, No. 4 (1993), p. 587.

[2] For more on this point, see Jackson, *Fiction and Formalism*, *supra* note 4, at 186-92.

whose interpretive presuppositions were emphatically not.[1] In al-Shāfiʿī's view, many of those who now swelled the ranks of the Muslims—Arabicized non-Arabs—could be justifiably told what the philologist and narrator of one of the seven readings (*qirā'āt*) of the Qur'ān, ʿAmr b. al-ʿAlā' (d. 154/770), told the proto-Muʿtazilite, ʿAmr b. ʿUbayd (d. 144/761): "You are a non-Arab (*aʿjamī*), not in your language but in your understanding..."[2]

Given his recognition of the role of interpretive presuppositions in legal interpretation, al-Shāfiʿī understood that the meaning of a statement, for example, "The thief, male and female, cut off their hands," was as contingent upon prior notions about the "character" of God as it was upon the words themselves. In this light, he wanted to ensure that the primordial presuppositions of the Arabs, or more properly the Arabians, continued to reign supreme. Otherwise, a command to amputate the hands of thieves might be interpreted away by those whose inherited notions of God pre-empted the possibility that He might actually sanction literal amputation.

The reaction to al-Shāfiʿī, however, was ultimately to reject his thesis in favor of an interpretive theory that was grounded in linguistic formalism, according to which meaning was restricted, *mutatis mutandis*, to the observable features of language (morphology, syntax, grammar). This was the beginning of what Prof. Bernard Weiss referred to as "exotericism" in Islamic law, according to which all biases, hunches, and presuppositions were to be extracted from the realm of subjective consciousness, packaged in the guise of objective language, and presented as the plain dictates of revelatory speech.[3] The

---

[1] *See, e.g.*, Muḥammad b. Idrīs al-Shāfiʿī, *al-Umm* (Cairo: al-Dār al-Miṣiyyah li al-Ta'līf wa al-Tarjamah, n.d.), vol. 4. p. 134 & 141.

[2] *See* Aḥmad bin Yaḥayā bin al-Murtaḍā, *Tabaqāṭ al-Muʿtazilah,* edited by S. Diwald-Wilzer (Wiesbaden/Beirut: Franz Steiner, 1380/1961), p. 83 (author's translation).

[3] Bernard B. Weiss, "Exotericism and Objectivity in Islamic Jurisprudence", in Nicholas Heer & Farhat Jacob Ziadeh, eds., *Islamic Law and Jurisprudence*

implication here was that *all* presuppositions—Arabian and non-Arabian alike—were equally suspect and equally threatening to the integrity of scripture.[1] As such, legal arguments were to be judged solely on the basis of their linguistic fidelity to sources and heuristic methods located in the public domain, where they could be assumed to be equidistant *from* and equally accessible *to* everyone. This trend, which came to dominate *uṣūl al-fiqh*, had the ultimate (and in my view plainly intended) effect of levelling the playing field between those who began versus those who ended their genealogy as Arabs.

In this context, the main thrust of classical *uṣūl al-fiqh* came to constitute a consciously-maintained form of the above-cited juristic empiricism. Indeed, Islam developed not simply into a nomocratic civilization, but into what might be termed, to borrow W.W. Bartley's nomenclature, a "justificationist" one.[2] In this culture, all assertions of legal doctrine, legal rights, and legal obligations had to be justified or authenticated on the basis of *objective* legal proofs.

Yet, Islam's subscription to juristic empiricism has been routinely mistaken (both in Western scholarship and under its hegemonic influence by Muslims of various stripes) for a commitment to literalism. Nowhere, perhaps, is this more clearly manifested than in the ubiquitous tendency to identify the movement known as Ẓāhirism as an expression of

---

(Seattle: University of Washington Press, 1990), pp. 53-71.

[1] One wonders, in this regard, if the palpably less-developed state of such sciences as *asbāb al-nuzūl* (Occasions of Revelation) or even *Sīrah* (Prophetic Biography) may also be a reflection of the attempt to downplay everything that would result in a possible interpretive advantage for those who hailed from Arabia. Even if no authentic body of material existed on, for example, the Occasions of Revelation, if the science itself had been as valued as much as, for example Ḥadīth, certainly there would have been a more cogent attempt to *invent* material, just as is claimed to have occurred with Ḥadīth.

[2] *See* William Warren Bartley III, *The Retreat to Commitment* (La Salle/London: Open Court Publishing Company, 2d ed. 1984), pp. 73, 88, 91-92, 97-98, 102.

"Literalism."[1] Carefully examined, Ẓāhirism reveals itself to have been neither an aberration nor unduly committed to literalism. It was merely a more entrenched (and perhaps consistent) commitment to the already established and increasingly hegemonic principle of juristic empiricism. The Ẓāhirites, as is well known, went furthest in rejecting *a priori* presumptions in legal reasoning, including those underlying the method known as *qiyās* (analogy)![2] They were equally diligent in rejecting all mediating factors that were external to scripture, such as the unanimous consensus of the jurists (though not that handed down from the Prophet himself, which they clearly saw as a constituent of scripture, part of the Prophetic Sunnah) or the opinions of individual Companions.[3] Meanwhile, the only complete work on Ẓāhirite legal theory that has come down to us, *al-Iḥkām* by the Spaniard Ibn Ḥazm (d. 456/1064), clearly establishes Ẓāhirism as ultimately no more literalistic than any other legal school.[4]

> If they say, 'How do we know what diverts a statement from its apparent meaning?' It is said to them, and by God the Exalted is success, 'We know this by information we gain from the apparent meaning of another text, or by an

---

[1] *See, e.g.*, Nicholson J. Coulson, *A History of Islamic Law* (Edinburgh: Edinburgh University Press, 1964), p. 71; N. Calder, "Law", in John L. Esposito, *The Oxford Encyclopedia of the Modern Islamic World* (Oxford/New York: Oxford University Press, 1995), vol. 2, p. 450; Khaled Abou El Fadl, *Speaking in God's Name: Islamic Law, Authority and Women* (London: Oneworld Publications, 2001), p. 309; Wael B. Hallaq, *A History of Islamic Legal Theories: An Introduction to Sunnī uṣūl al-fiqh* (Cambridge/New York: Cambridge University Press 1999), p. 207.

[2] *See, e.g.*, Abū Muḥammad ʿAlī Ibn Ḥazm, *al-Iḥkām fī Uṣūl al-Aḥkām*, ed. Ahmad Muhammad Shākir (Beirut: Dār al-Āfāq al-Jadīdah, 1403/1983), vol. 8, pp. 2-123 [hereinafter *Iḥkām*].

[3] *See, e.g.*, Ibn Ḥazm, *Iḥkām*, *supra* note 12, at vol. 2, pp. 12-21.

[4] Devin Stewart has extracted parts of a Ẓāhirite work by the son of the founder of Ẓāhirism from the writings of the Ismāʿīlī jurist, al-Qāḍī Nuʿmān (d. 363/974). However, these parts do not appear to include treatment of such topics as literal versus figurative meaning. *See* Devin Stewart, "*Muhammad b. Dāʾûd al-Ẓāhirī's Manual of Jurisprudence: Al-Wuṣūl ilā maʿrifat al-uṣūl,*" in Weiss, ed., *Studies in Islamic Legal Theory*.

> absolutely certain unanimous consensus handed down on the authority of the Prophet, God's blessings and salutations be upon him ...[1]

In the same work, Ibn Ḥazm expands this when dealing specifically with the topic of literal verses' metaphorical meaning (*ḥaqīqah wa majāz*). Here he denounces those who deny the use of metaphorical language in the Qur'an and insists that:

> Whenever we have certainty, based on a univocal text (*naṣṣ*), a unanimous consensus (*ijmāʿ*) or natural reason (*ṭabīʿah*), that a word has been diverted from the meaning it was coined to have in the language to another meaning, we must interpret it thus (*wajaba al-wuqūf ʿindah*).[2]

This is quite standard among the schools of law. All begin with a *prima facie* deference to literal meaning, only agreeing to set it aside on the basis of other textual or non-textual justifications. In this regard, Ẓāhirism was right in step with the mainstream. Where Ẓāhirism departed from the mainstream was in its rejection of analogy and unanimous consensus. But this was related not to literalism but to its more emphatic and uncompromising commitment to juristic empiricism. In other words, the whole point of rejecting these synthetic accoutrements was to promote and preserve the primacy of scripture by insulating it from any and all potential competitors, explicit or implied, subversive or well-meaning.[3]

---

[1] Ibn Ḥazm, *Iḥkām*, *supra* note 12, at p. 41 (translated by author).

[2] *Id.* at 28. For example, he notes that the verse, The Qur'an, *Sūra al-Isrā'* 17:24, "*wa' khfiḍ lahumā janāḥ al-dhulli min al-raḥmah*," can only be taken to mean that we must incline in humble mercy to our parents, not that humility literally has a wing. *See* Ibn Ḥazm, *Iḥkām*, vol. 3, *supra* note 12, p. 29.

[3] As far back as 1883, even without the benefit of Ibn Ḥazm's *al-Iḥkām*, the celebrated Hungarian Islamicist Ignaz Goldziher was able to discern that Ẓāhirism was not at all about literalism but constituted an attempt to combat *ra'y*, that is, "what the individual insight of a legist or judge, in real or apparent dependance [*sic*] on those indisputable sources, recognizes as truth emanating from their spirit." *See* Ignaz Goldziher, *The Ẓāhirīs: Their Doctrine and their History*, trans. Wolfgang Behn

Meanwhile, mainstream classical legal theory's acceptance of *qiyās* and *ijmāʿ* was essentially an attempt in the same direction. This was aimed at curbing the speculative, *a priori* forays of the jurists, binding them to deductions from scripture. In other words, even the reaction to Ẓāhirism reflected a shared, *prima facie* commitment to the principle that knowledge of the law was (ideally) limited to the locutionary dictates of *texts* and could go little beyond this.[1]

All this leads to a conclusion of far-reaching implications for modern Muslim legal discourse: contrary to popular belief, Islamic law neither produced nor recognized a literalist canon of the Western Fundamentalist genre. Muslim jurists only produced an empiricist canon. The confusion, however, between these two modalities is a major impediment to the production and acceptance of modern interpretations that purportedly recline upon *maqāṣid al-sharīʿah.* This is because literalism is essentially a false problem in whose resolution the real challenge, juristic empiricism, remains in full effect. On this oversight, interpretations that transcend literalism via reliance upon *maqāṣid al-sharīʿah* leave in place the requirement of justification by reference to specific, individual texts. Thus, to return to the hypothetical example, any claim about the propriety of purchasing an air-conditioner or the impropriety of turning on an oven would be met with the unfulfillable demand to produce explicit (individual) texts to substantiate these claims.

Juristic Induction and the *Maqāṣid al-Sharīʿah*

Historically, juristic empiricism has dominated and marginalized

---

and with introduction by Camilla Adang (Leiden/Boston: Brill, 2008), p. 3.

[1] This is not to deny that such interpretive instruments as *dalīl al-khiṭāb* (disjunctive inference), *faḥwā al-khiṭāb* (*a fortiori* inference), and even *al-ʿāmm yurādu bihi al-khuṣūṣ* (general expressions used for restricted referents) invest in the illocutionary force of words. But these are quite limited by the range of what the *conventional use* of Arabic language allows, as a means of controlling how much can be invested in a purely figurative interpretation.

all other approaches to law. From surprisingly early on, however, there was a growing recognition of some of its drawbacks and limitations. Early Ḥanafī attempts to vindicate *istiḥsān* (equity) are a clear manifestation of this;[1] so are the efforts of such later Ḥanbalīs as Ibn Taymiyyah (d. 728/1328) and Ibn Qayyim al-Jawziyyah (d. 751/1350), as reflected, for example, in their gallantly anti-empiricist work, *al-Ṭuruq al-Ḥukmiyyah fī al-Siyāsah al-Sharʿiyyah*;[2] so are the ubiquitous Mālikī and other (for example, Najm al-Dīn al-Ṭūfī (d. 716/1316)) attempts to vindicate the principle of *maṣlaḥah* (public utility).[3] Even Shāfiʿīs, for example al-Ghazālī, would devote words to the anti-positivist, extra-empirical instrument of *maṣaḥah*, and later Shāfiʿīs would go so far as to engage in outright induction. Al-ʿIzz b. ʿAbd al-Salām (d. 660/1261), for example, explicitly proclaims such acts as cursing the Prophet or smearing feces on the Kaʿbah to be "the greatest of major sins, even though the religious law [read individual texts] does not explicitly identify any of this as a major sin."[4]

Still, where such efforts were not marginal, they remained invariably apologetic.[5] It was against this backdrop that the now

[1] However, as Kamali observed, none of these attempts are convincing, for clearly *istiḥsān* is not a form of analogy but a reaction to it. Juristic empiricism could only accommodate methods that were sufficiently bound to the *a-posteriori* dictates of scripture and thus sought, through a tortuous logic to cast *istiḥsān* as such a move. Mohammad Hashim Kamali, *Principles of Islamic Jurisprudence* (Cambridge: The Islamic Texts Society, 3rd edn, 2003), p. 344.

[2] Ibn Qayyim al-Jawziyyah, *al-Ṭuruq al-Ḥukmiyyah fī al-Siyāsah al- Sharʿiyyah* (Cairo: al-Mu'assasah al-ʿArabiyyah li al-Ṭibāʿah wa al-Nashr, 1381/1961); Taqī al-Dīn Abū al-ʿAbbās Aḥmad Ibn Taymiyyah, *al-Siyāsah al-Sharʿiyyah fī Iṣlāḥ al-Rāʿī wa al-Raʿiyyah* (Beirut: Dār al-Afāq al-Jadīdah, 1403/1983).

[3] Najm al-Dīn al-Ṭūfī, *Risālah fī Riʿāyat al-Maṣaḥah*, ed. Ahmad Abdulhamid al-Sayih (Cairo: al-Dār al-Miṣriyyah al-Lubnāniyyah, 1413/1993), pp. 25-48.

[4] ʿIzz al-Dīn ʿAbd al-ʿAzīz ibn ʿAbd al-Salām, *al-Qawāʿid al-Kubrā* known as *Qawāʿid al-Aḥkām fī Iṣlāḥ al-Anām*, ed. Nazih Hammad & Othman Damiriyya (Damasucs: Dār al-Qalam, 1st edn, 1421/2000), vol. 1, p. 29.

[5] This is confirmed by the modern jurist Ibn Ashur. *See* Muhammad al-Tahir Ibn Ashur, *Maqāṣid al-Sharīʿah al-Islāmiyyah,* ed. Mohamed El-Tahir El-Mesawi, (Amman: Dār Alnafaes, 2nd edn, 1421/2001), p. 167 (hereinafter *Maqāṣid*).

much celebrated Ibrāhīm ibn Mūsā al-Shāṭibī (d. 790/1388) would launch his campaign to vindicate and gain more formal recognition for an alternative, or perhaps more properly, supplemental, means of apprehending the law. Al-Shāṭibī's "juristic induction," literally *istiqrā'*, as he called it, sought to break the near monopoly of the reigning juristic empiricism and go beyond its uncompromising deductive syllogism, which read something like the following: All X's (*and only* X's) are binding; Y is an X; Y (and only what can be validly considered Y) is therefore binding (where X represents the Qur'ān and Sunnah and Y represents individual texts of these). For al-Shāṭibī, a text's weight was to be based neither on its substance nor its authenticity alone but on its relationship to a universe of meanings and values that were inductively extrapolated from an *aggregate* of texts. On this understanding, legal matters were to be resolved by reference to inductively established values and principles, even in the absence of explicit texts.[1]

We should note, however, that it was not al-Shāṭibī's aim to execute an act of "epistemicide," whereby juristic empiricism would be denied all validity. On the contrary, he readily recognized that juristic empiricism was integral to the very process of juristic induction itself, for it was through a straightforward reading of an undetermined quantity of actual texts that the broader aims and objectives of the Sharīʿah were to be inductively established.[2] In other words, al-Shāṭibī's primary commitment remained to a text-driven, as opposed to a purely speculative, approach. His aim was simply to vindicate juristic induction or *istiqrā'* as a valid *legal* epistemology, such that juristic empiricism, as a particular *way* of reading texts,

---

[1] Abū Isḥāq Ibrāhīm ibn Mūsā al-Shāṭibī, *al-Muwāfaqāt fī Uṣūl al-Sharīʿah,* ed. Abd Allah Draz et al (Beirut: Dār al-Kutub al-ʿIlmiyyah, 1st edn, 1424/2004), vol. 1/1, pp. 18-28 & vol. 1/2, pp. 37-42 (hereinafter *al-Muwāfaqāt*).

[2] This is almost certainly the point behind al-Shāṭibī's banning anyone who had not mastered traditional *fiqh* and legal theory from reading his work. *See* 1 *al-Muwāfaqāt*, vol. 1/1, p. 61.

would not be the only basis for arriving at or judging legal conclusions. Through this process of juristic induction or *istiqrā'*, pre-modern jurists (al-Shāṭibī being simply among the most emphatic) extracted and vindicated the so-called *maqāṣid al-sharīʿah.* Al-Ghazālī, for example, makes a point of clarifying that the *maqāṣid* are known "not on the basis of any single proof-text (*dalīl*) nor on the basis of any specific principle but on the cumulative strength of proofs too many to enumerate."[1] In a similar vein, al-Shāṭibī declares that,

> The entire community agrees, nay all religious communities agree, that the religious law was instituted for the protection of the five absolute necessities: religion, life, progeny, property and reason. This community (i.e., the Muslim community) has unassailable (*ḍarūrī*) knowledge of this. But this has not been established on the basis of any specific proof-text nor confirmed by any specific principle that we could isolate and invoke. Rather, its appropriateness to the religious law is simply known on the basis of an aggregate of proofs too numerous to count.[2]

Preservation of Reason (*Ḥifẓ al-ʿAql*): One of the *Maqāṣid al-Sharīʿah*

On the above approach, typical vindications of the preservation of reason (*ḥifẓ al-ʿaql*) as one of the *maqāṣid* point to the depth and breadth of scriptural prohibitions on consuming intoxicants. Al-Qarāfī (d. 684/1285), for example, derives the value of *ḥifẓ al-ʿaql* from the fact that, "God the Exalted has never (in any

---

[1] Abū Ḥāmid Muḥammad ibn Muḥammad al-Ghazālī, *al-Mustaṣfā min ʿIlm al-Uṣūl,* ed. Muhammad Sulayman al-Ashqar (Beirut: Mu'assassat al-Risālah, 1st edn, 1417/1997), vol. 1, pp. 420 & 430. Indeed, al-Ghazālī's whole point in this section is to vindicate inductive reasoning from the grip of judgments and criteria of validation that are grounded in juristic empiricism.

[2] al-Shāṭibī, *al-Muwāfaqāt,* vol. 1/1, p. 26.

dispensation) sanctioned ... the abuse of one's faculties by allowing drunkenness."[1] In a typical display of circumspection, he adds that even religious communities that allow the consumption of alcohol, do not countenance inebriation.[2] Meanwhile, the famed Fakhr al-Dīn al-Rāzī insists "reason ... is protected via the prohibition of intoxicants, and God the Exalted has alluded to this via such statements as, '*Satan simply desires to sow dissention and hatred among you through intoxicants...*'"[3] Earlier, al-Ghazālī had neatly summed up the matter by suggesting that, "the imposition of prescribed punishments upon those who consume intoxicants is a means of protecting the faculty of reason, upon which all legal responsibility (*taklīf*) hinges."[4]

Directly or indirectly, all of these writers implicate induction in the process of establishing *ḥifẓ al-ʿaql* as a *maqṣid*. When we turn, however, to the actual application of this principle, we are confronted with a strange and debilitating paradox. *Ḥifẓ al-ʿaql* is supposed to be a *maqṣid*, a "broader interest" inductively extracted from the aggregate of prohibitions on consuming intoxicants. This mode of extrapolation presumably takes *ḥifẓ al-ʿaql* beyond the more conservatively-deduced *ʿillah* (*ration essendi*) or *ḥikmah* (underlying rationale) involved in the process of analogy (*qiyās*).[5] Indeed, the whole point of inductively validating *ḥifẓ al-ʿaql* would seem to be to authenticate conclusions that

---

[1] Shihāb al-Dīn Aḥmad ibn Idrīs al-Qarāfī, *Sharḥ Tanqīḥ al-Fuṣūl fī Ikhtiṣār al-Maḥṣūl fī al-Uṣūl*, ed. Ahmad Farid al-Mazidi (Dār al-Kutub al-ʿIlmiyyah, 1428/2007), p. 377.

[2] *Id.*

[3] Fakhr al-Dīn Nuḥammad b. ʿUmar b. al-Ḥusain al-Rāzi, *al-Maḥṣūl fī ʿIlm al-Uṣūl*, ed. Taha Jabir al-Alwani (Cairo: Dār al-Salām, 1st edn, 1432/2011), vol. 3, p. 1248; Shihāb al-Dīn Aḥmad ibn Idrīs al-Qarāfī, *Nafā'is al-Uṣūl fi Sharḥ al-Maḥṣūl,* ed. Mohammad Ahmad Ata (Beirut: Dār al-Kutub al-'Ilmîyah, 1421/2000), vol. 4, p. 166.

[4] al-Ghazālī, *al-Mustaṣfā*, vol. 1, p. 418.

[5] The *ʿillah* of the prohibition on consuming intoxicants would be that the latter intoxicate. The *ḥikmah* would speak to the underlying wisdom behind this, that is, why intoxication itself is bad.

could *not* be supported on the basis of *qiyās*. Yet, for all the hopes and expectations modern Muslims place in the *maqāṣid* this is precisely what we tend *not* to find in the actual application of the principle, *ḥifẓ al-ʿaql*.

In what is perhaps the most widely cited (if not most authoritative) work on the subject by a modern jurist, *Maqāṣid al-Sharīʿah al-Islāmiyyah* (*The Broader Aims and Objectives of Islamic Law*), the late Muhammad al-Tahir Ibn Ashur (d. 1393/1973), spelled out the practical implications of *ḥifẓ al-ʿaql* as a *maqṣid* in the following terms:

> The meaning of preservation of reason (*ḥifẓ al-ʿaql*) is to prevent damage from befalling the minds of people. For, damage befalling the minds of people leads to great corruption, in the form of their losing control over their actions. Damage befalling the minds of individuals leads to micro-cosmic corruption, while damage befalling the minds of groups and nations is greater still. Thus, it is as necessary to prevent individuals from becoming intoxicated as it is necessary to prevent intoxication from spreading among nations. Likewise, it is necessary to prevent the spread of such corrupting agents as hashish, opium, morphine, cocaine, heroin and similar substances whose use has become wide-spread in the 20th century.[1]

It is difficult to discern the point of this exercise, for none of these prohibitions require anything approaching the kind of juristic induction that Ibn Ashur (like al-Shāṭibī and others before him) claimed to be the very basis of the *maqāṣid*. Indeed, if this is the sole or universally-recognized application of *ḥifẓ al-ʿaql*, it is unclear that juristic induction offers any real advantage over mainstream (to be distinguished from Ẓāhirite) juristic empiricism.

We should note, however, in fairness to Ibn Ashur that this particular application is not exclusive to him. On the contrary, it

---

[1] Ibn Ashur, *Maqāṣid*, p. 417.

represents the only application of *ḥifẓ al-ʿaql* that I have ever encountered—*wa ʿadam al-ʿilm laysa ʿilman bi al-ʿadam.* Among its most obvious redeeming features is perhaps its universality (which Ibn Ashur and others cite as one of the criteria for a valid juristic induction).[1] In other words, what sustains this application is the fact that it—and perhaps *only* it—is recognized as the application that is relevant and suitable to all peoples in all times and all places. As such, it satisfies, in its own way, the surreptitious yet enduring criterion of objectivity (read juristic empiricism) that extends, as we have seen, all the way back to the reaction to Imām al-Shāfiʿī.

At any rate, what we end up with is a universal, a *kullīyah, ḥifẓ al-ʿaql,* which, if applied as such across time and space, turns out to be substantively and practically empty. This very idea and value of universality is intimately indebted, however, to juristic empiricism. Its function is to negate the impact of time, space, and perspective—the implication being that in the absence of these, our conclusions can be solely and justifiably attributed to texts. However, what we gain in the way of theoretical neatness and empirical justification, we lose in the way of concrete, practical utility. Moreover, the entire arch of meaning generated by our inductive reading of the sources is sacrificed to an undetected addiction to juristic empiricism.

This problem of universalism (keeping in mind its indebtedness to juristic empiricism) is far more pervasive and problematic than may initially meet the eye. Typically, rather than negate perspective, claims to universalism tend only to disguise it. Elsewhere, I have referred to this conflation as the problem of the false universal, according to which only those who share one's specific concretions of "justice," "reason," "beauty," etc., are justified in laying any claims to these.[2] The

---

[1] *See, e.g., Maqāṣid,* pp. 252-253.

[2] See, e.g., Sherman Jackson, "Islam(s) East and West: Pluralism between No-Frills and Designer Fundamentalism," *in Mary L. Dudziak ed.,* September 11 in

false universal conceals itself in the habit of speaking as if the shape that one's values assume in concrete social, political, or interpersonal contexts is not grounded in cultural, historical, or even ideological perspectives but is reflective of a natural order that is obvious to all, save the stupid, the primitive, or morally depraved.

Several modern critiques, from Afrocentrism to feminism to postmodernism, have succeeded in exposing the false universalism in the hegemonic claims of the modern West.[1] Less apparent is how Muslim articulations of such constructs as *maqāṣid al-sharīʿah* are also prone to this tendency. This is precisely what is reflected, however, in the tendency toward a uniform application of *ḥifẓ al-ʿaql*, despite the racial, ethnic, cultural, and historical differences separating modern Muslims from one another and their past. Such unanimity reflects a belief in the irrelevance of history or perspective and suggests the propriety of subsuming the massive diversity of the modern Muslim community under a single application of the principle, "preservation of reason."

As an alternative, I propose a position already marked out by the Ḥanbalite jurist Ibn Taymiyyah, according to whom abstract universals, *qua* universals, exist only in the mind and that the only meaningful manifestation or application of a concept, value, or principle is in the concrete.[2] On this understanding, taking Ibn Ashur's "preventing damage from befalling the mind"[3] as our abstract universal whose status and validity is grounded in induction (which means that its purpose

---

History: A Watershed Moment? *(Durham, NC: Duke University Press, 2003), p. 113.*

[1] See, *e.g.*, Molefi Kete Asante, *Afrocentricity: The Theory of Social Change* (Philadelphia: Temple University Press, 1988); Linda Alcoff & Elizabeth (eds.), *Feminist Epistemologies* (New York: Routledge, 1993).

[2] On this point, see Wael B. Hallaq, *Ibn Taymiyya Against the Greek Logicians* (Oxford, USA: Oxford University Press, 1993), pp. xxii-xxiii.

[3] Ibn Ashur, *Maqāṣid*, p. 184.

must reach beyond the prohibitions and exhortations of specific texts), this principle's actual concrete application must assume different modalities, qualities, and characteristics for different times, places, and peoples.

Al-ʿAql: Beyond False Universals

Part of the difficulty in settling on a functionally meaningful application of *ḥifẓ al-ʿaql* is connected to traditional definitions of *ʿaql* itself. Typically, *ʿaql* is equated with the faculty for *a priori* conceptualization and synthesis. Ibn ʿĀshir's (d. 1040/1630) standard mnemonic text on the basics of Islamic law and jurisprudence, *al-Murshid al-Muʿīn ʿalā al-Ḍarūrī min ʿUlūm al-Dīn*, provides a classic example:

> A rational judgment (*ḥukm ʿaqlī*) is one whose validity is confirmed by neither custom nor convention.[1]

In his commentary on this text, Mayyārah (Muhammad b. Ahmad al-Fāsī, d. 1047/1637) explains that any judgment or assignment of a relationship (for example, the world is temporal) not based on experience or revelation is a rational judgment.[2] In other words, the essence of reason is the ability to go beyond the senses and construct and sustain logically consistent, abstract judgments.

To be sure, Muslim tradition—most specifically the rationalist theologians, who exerted a disproportionate influence on Islamic legal theory—developed the habit of conflating the *ability to use* reason with *particular uses of* reason, such that only those whose views confirmed a particular regime of reason, for example Muʿtazilism or Māturīdism or Ashʿarism, were recognized as having any justifiable claim to *ʿaql*. On this

---

[1] ʿAbd al-Wāḥid ibn ʿĀshir, *al-Murshid al-Muʿīn ʿalā al-Ḍarūrī min ʿUlūm al-Dīn* (Beirut: Dār al-Fikr, 1416/1996), p. 3.

[2] Abū ʿAbd Allāh Muḥammad ibn al-Ṭālib, *Ḥāshiyat al-ʿAllāmah Abī ʿAbd Allāh Muḥammad ibn al-Ṭālib ʿalā Sharḥ al-ʿAllāmah Muḥammad ibn Aḥmad al-Fāsī* (Cairo: Mustafā Bābī al-Ḥalabī, n. d.), vol. 1, pp. 17-18.

conflation, it appears that the damage to be prevented from befalling the mind, for example, by banning all species of intoxicants, is a damage that would impede not one's ability to employ reason on the common sense understanding but to engage in systematic theology or law.

It is questionable, however, whether this particular notion of *ʿaql* can be reconciled with the content of the texts from which *ḥifẓ al-ʿaql* as a *maqṣid* is presumably extracted. The Sunnaic material on intoxicants is quite explicit in targeting not the ability to engage in abstract reasoning, but the propensity towards violence and bellicosity. The Qur'anic material confirms this (Qur'an, 5 [*al-Mā'idah*]: 90-91), and further implicates, *inter alia*, ego, social anxiety, and cultural convention in the corruption, suppression, or misuse of *ʿaql*. "Have you seen the one who takes his undisciplined passions as his god? Are you to be his caretaker? Or do you think that most of them hear or use their reason (*yaʿqilūn*)?" (Qur'an, 49 [*al-Hujurat*]: 4) "God has not sanctioned any dedications to the idols, *baḥīrah*, *sā'ibah*, *waṣīlah*, or *ḥām*. But those who disbelieve invent lies against God, and most of them do not use their reason." (Qur'an, 5 [*al-Mā'idah*]: 103) "And when it is said to them, 'Follow what God has revealed,' they say, 'Nay, we follow what we found our forefathers following.' What? Even if their forefathers understood (*yaʿqilūn*) nothing and were not guided?" (Qur'an, 2 [*al-Baqarah*]: 170)

It may be, however, that the ancients, in their own time and place, given Islam's general triumph over paganism and the pervasiveness of decentralized, "weak" states that were incapable of engineering "national characters" or "indigenous cultures," simply isolated self-induced intoxicants as the most meaningful target of the Qur'anic and Sunnaic prohibitions. In the end, though, however they may have reached their conclusions, it is we, the custodial generation, not they, the transmitting generation, who have the ability to turn their specific concretions into universally valid and binding prescriptions.

Concretizing *Ḥifẓ al-ʿAql* in the Modern World

In attempting to arrive at a more meaningful modern application of *ḥifẓ al-ʿaql*, I introduce alternative constructions of both *ʿaql* and *ḥifẓ*. These modifications are informed by my own historical context in the same way that the constructs invoked by the pre-modern jurists were informed by theirs. In this context, my approach can be seen to be procedurally consistent with that of the ancients. Beginning with *ʿaql*, rather than define it as the ability to engage in *a priori* abstraction, I endorse the more general and common-sense description suggested by Ibn Taymiyyah that *ʿaql* is simply the primordial, instinctive ability (*gharīzah*) to "know" or "understand."[1] As for *ḥifẓ*, rather than restrict it to potential internal, self-induced corrupters such as drugs or alcohol, I consider the possibility that external, that is, socio-political and cultural factors may be equally or perhaps even more corruptive. In my effort to concretize these adjustments, I take the socio-political experience of Blackamericans as my point of departure. Such referencing should be understood, however, as merely the beginning, rather than the ultimate, objective of my approach.

Students of religious studies are familiar with Rudolph Otto's concept of *mysterium tremendum*, which referred to that inscrutable awe and trembling that accompanies the experience of encountering the divine.[2] According to Otto, *mysterium tremendum* lay at the heart of all theistic religion, from primitive times down to the present.[3] In an insightful addendum to Otto, however, the American scholar Charles Long wrote of a spurious or false *mysterium tremendum* that befell America's

---

[1] *See* Abu al-Abbas Ahmad Ibn Taymiyyah, *Muwāfaqat Ṣaḥīḥ al-Manqūl li Ṣarīḥ al-Maʿqūl* (Beirut: Dār al-Kutub al-'Ilmiyyah, 1405/1985), vol. 1, p. 83

[2] *See* Charles H. Long's chapter 10, "The Oppressive Element in Religion and the Religions of the Oppressed," in his *Significations: Signs, Symbol and Images in the Interpretation of Religion* (Aurora, CO: The Davies Group Publishers, 1995).

[3] *See id.*

enslaved Africans and their descendents during the course of their introduction into the New World.[1] This was a *mysterium tremendum* in which the awesome, fear-inspiring, inescapable other was not God but the white man and the critical categories of modernity he created: civilization, (biological) race, culture, primitiveness, I.Q., and so on.[2]

In a real sense, blacks in America, like all other orphans of modernity ("Third-Worlders," "primitives," or even "Middle Easterners") were "created" by the forces of white supremacy and the theoretical disciplines of the (French) Enlightenment. This "second creation" had the cumulative effect of placing between blacks and primordial knowledge a normative regime of sense that was sponsored and controlled by the dominant group. At the same time, the invisibility of whiteness (only non-whites were raced) placed whites in the position of being "just people," who could speak not only in the name of their specific group, but also for humanity as a whole. This had the effect of conferring upon their fears, assumptions, proclivities, prejudices, and specific genius, the status of "normal." In effect, this reflected a transcendent natural order, whose validity was obvious to all, save the stupid, the primitive, or the morally depraved.

The tacit (or in some instances, not so tacit) requirement that blacks recognize and conform to this normative regime of sense and "normal" behavior translated into a socio-cultural order I refer to elsewhere as "normalized domination." Normalized domination occurs when humans are reduced to such a state of self-doubt and/or self-contempt that they internalize the vague but inextricable feeling that they can only redeem themselves by living up to the norms and expectations of those who seek to exploit them.

---

[1] *See id.*
[2] *See id.*

When this happens, their ability to engage in reasoned critiques of the prevailing order is drastically reduced, because the feelings of triumph that occur as they approach redemption tend to obliterate any recognition of the provenance or falseness of the criterion upon which their redemption is based. In this context, ontological and even meta-cognitive truths that contradict the reigning paradigm are confronted agnostically, and one is given over to formalized ideologies, popular morality, or simply "the ways of the forefathers."[1]

Elsewhere, I identified normalized domination with the Qur'anic concept of "*fitnah*."[2] At bottom, *fitnah* turns on the simultaneous recognition and exploitation of the human condition and the contingent nature of much of human knowledge. Humans cannot really *know* how smart, dumb, handsome, or unattractive they are without other subjectivities to confirm this. This has obvious and far-reaching implications for any ability to "know." For in the context of any regime of normalized domination, even the most obvious truths can evade acknowledgment or be undermined. This seems to be the clear implication of any number of Qur'anic verses.[3]

In sum, regimes of normalized domination achieve in psychological effect what politically predatory regimes achieve in

---

[1] For a more in-depth treatment of these issues, see Sherman A. Jackson, *Islam and the Blackamerican: Looking Toward the Third Resurrection* (Oxford/New York: Oxford University Press, 2005) pp. 172-183.

[2] *See, e.g.*, Sherman A. Jackson, "Islam and Affirmative Action," *Journal of Law and Religion*, vol. 14, No. 2 (2000), p. 405.

[3] "If you ask them, 'Who created you?' they will exclaim, 'God!' How, then, are they given to lies?" (Qur'an, *al-Zukhruf* 43:87); "Say [O Muhammad]: Who provides you with sustenance from the heavens and the earth? Is it He who dispenses hearing and sight? And who draws life out of the dead and death out of the living? And who orders the affairs (of the universe)? They will say, 'God.' Will they not, then, be God-conscious?" (Qur'an, *Yūnus* 10:30-31); "If you ask them, 'Who sent down rain from the sky through which the earth is brought to life after death?.' They will say, 'God.' Say, 'Praise be to God.' But most of them do not reason (*yaʿqilūn*)." (Qur'an, *al-ʿAnkabūt* 29:63).

behavioral effect, namely acquiescence that seeks to mollify itself by equating itself with the simple acceptance of truth. This is painfully captured in the crowning scene of George Orwell's classic, *1984*, where the state wants to be assured that the protagonist, Winston, sees reality only as it wants him to see it. To this end, Winston is placed in a "pain chair," and the state-official holds up four fingers and asks, "How many fingers am I holding up, Winston?" Winston answers, "Four," but the official insists that there are five and continues to tweak the dial on the pain-chair until Winston exclaims that he is trying to abandon his senses and see five fingers![1]

To the extent that regimes of normalized domination exist, clearly the preservation of "*reason,*" or "the ability to know," would have to go beyond the mere proscription of drugs and alcohol. For the ability to know is clearly affected by more than the essentially private acts of self-administered corruption of the mind. Indeed, regimes of normalized domination corrupt reason on a far grander scale and provide in many instances the very incentives for drug and alcohol abuse. In this context, *ḥifẓ al-ʿaql*, if it is to be effective, would have to take on a much more public and political dimension. It would have to deal not simply with individuals but with political, social, cultural, educational, and economic institutions. This conception and application of *ḥifẓ al-ʿaql* is in no way limited to the plight of Blackamericans or the socio-political reality of the United States. White supremacy is now a global phenomenon—however reluctant Muslims in the Muslim world may be to say so out loud (which is perhaps a confirmation of the depth and degree of normalized domination). Moreover, white supremacy is now a force that can call to its service a technological capability unprecedented in human history, providing it with the ability to produce, sustain, and disseminate ideas and images of itself and of others as never before. Through these instrumentalities, Muslims—and, indeed,

---

[1] George Orwell, *Nineteen Eighty Four* (London: Secker & Warburg,1949), p. 253.

non-Muslims—are today routinely afflicted with the mental disease that W.E.B. Du Bois famously referred to as "double-consciousness."[1] Commercially, socio-culturally, and politically crafted images of what it means to be "modern," "civilized," or "liberated," place them in the position of having to struggle, on the one hand, *to be* Muslims and, on the other hand, *against being* Muslims, that is, if they are to be redeemed as modern, reasonable, or civilized. In such a context, the enterprise of acquiring or apprehending bona fide "knowledge" about Islam —again, for Muslims and non-Muslims alike—becomes extremely difficult, if not moot.

The Western tendency to invoke false universals may be the most feared and widely felt, but it is by no means the only instantiation of this reality. The Muslim world (read Middle East) is equally prone to the tendency to promote false universals whenever the subject is Islam or Islamic law. Routinely, the realities and priorities of the Muslim world are passed off as the proper object of legal contemplation for Muslims everywhere. And it is the conclusions reached in contemplation of *these* realities that are deemed to constitute the norm, other realities being dealt with not directly but analogously on the basis of these. As a result, it is often through only the most tortuous logic and years of back and forth that legal precepts commonly invoked in the Muslim world[2] find any meaningful, concrete application in the West.[3] *Ḥifẓ al-ʿaql* is

---

[1] W.E.B. Du Bois, *The Souls of Black Folks: Essays and Sketches* (Chicago: A. C. McClurh & Co., 2nd edn, 1968).

[2] For example, "absolute necessity renders the unlawful lawful (*al-ḍarūrāt tubīḥu al-maḥẓūrāt*)."

[3] For example, the now defunct Sharīʿah Scholars' Association of North America (SSANA) held a conference in Detroit in 1999, where several Muslim jurists from the Muslim world were invited to discuss the pressing legal (*fiqhī*) questions confronting Muslims in America. Among these was the question of home mortgages, the problem being that Western banks typically deal in interest, which many equate with the Qur'ānically banned institution of *ribā*. The suggestion that owning a home in America was an "absolute necessity (*ḍarūah*)"

no exception in this regard.

Conclusion

On an inductive reading of the sources, it would appear justified to equate *ʿaql* with "the ability to know" and to direct the value and imperative of its "preservation," or *ḥifẓ*, towards things (whether internal or external) that most fundamentally and systematically threaten the human ability to know. What this translates into in terms of concrete rules and principles will depend on the realities on the ground in the various contexts in which *ḥifẓ al-ʿaql* is concretized. On this understanding, *maqāṣid al-sharīʿah*—or at least one of them—might be converted from a largely inert, mental abstraction into a concrete instrument for transforming the modern world, particularly those aspects that appear so impervious to the instrumentalities provided by and insisted upon by the reigning juristic empiricism.

---

was strongly resisted if not rejected outright, because the presence of alternatives, such as renting, negated any absolute necessity. "Absolute necessity," in other words, in contemplating Western reality, was equated with matters of life and death. Meanwhile, in a standard textbook on Mālikī law, still used at al-Azhar today, *al-Kawākib al-Durriyyah fī Fiqh al-Mālikiyyah*, 2, 160ff (Cairo: al-Maktabah al-Azhariyyah li al-Turāth, 2001), the requirement that sellers and buyers know the exact quantity of each counter exchange, as part of the ban on *ribā*, is relaxed in cases of "absolute necessity." None of the examples given have to do with "life and death." Rather, all relate to the realities of an agrarian society where counting certain counter-exchanges, (for example, the ears of corn in a corn-field), would simply be impractical. Now, based on such rulings, Muslims in the West could freely estimate in sales of corn-fields, though this may technically entail *ribā*. But they could not freely determine home-ownership through mortgages to be an absolute necessity, homemortgages incidentally being the exception rather than the rule in the Middle East.

CHAPTER FOUR

Maqāṣid al-Sharīʿah and the Challenge of Modernity

Wael B. Hallaq

Introduction

A central feature of public Muslim discourse over the past two or three decades has been the call to restore the Sharīʿah in one form or another. Some reformers have proposed a new theoretical underpinning for this restoration, arguing for the adoption of foundational concepts that bear little, if any, resemblance to their pre-modern counterparts.[1] The majority of writers and movements, however, and almost all political platforms appear to espouse a revival of the historical Sharīʿah or a modernized version thereof. What is notable about this espousal is that, despite its variants, it seems to hold a perception of pre-modern Sharīʿah that makes serious claims to objectivity. Put differently, a particular practice anchored in a particular law and theory is posited to have actually existed, and

---

[1] A radical example is Muhammad Shahrur whose views, as intellectually impressive as they are, have not been received well. For a summary of his proposed reform, see Wael B. Hallaq, *A History of Islamic Legal Theories* (Cambridge: Cambridge University Press, 1997), pp. 245-54. See also Dale Eickelman, "Islamic Liberalism Strikes Back," *Middle East Studies Association Bulletin*, 27 (1993), pp. 163-68.

all that is needed now is simply to revive this practice subject only to certain modifications that accommodate the exigencies of the modern world. In a sense, I see this conference as an attempt at partaking in this very discourse.

It is, I believe, accurate to argue that any serious project aiming at refashioning a conception of the Sharīʿah must claim history and pre-modern legal culture as its frame of reference. But which history? This is an eminently urgent and fundamental question. And to this extent of seeking reference, several of the modernizing *Sharʿī*-minded reforms seem to be, in principle, on the right track. The Western model has provided, for the past two centuries, the parameter for jural experiment, one that now appears to have failed as an exclusive alternative to Muslim indigenous traditions. Yet, because the need for legal modernization remains little contested, an aporia has resulted. The reconciliation between the exigencies of modernity and the placing of a premium on legal "heritage" thus not only give rise to this aporia but also exacerbate it epistemically. For what is involved is not merely the challenge of bringing the one to coexist with the other—if not coexist in a necessary state of symbiosis,—but also of informing this symbiosis with a particular construction, or a particular narrative, of legal history. That the latter constitutes a colonialist product makes the challenge all the more formidable.

A central question that ineluctably emerges in this aporia is: What narrative must be adopted as the representation of the historical Sharīʿah, the Sharīʿah that prevailed until the early portion of the nineteenth century? If the colonial narrative is *ipso facto* programmatic and teleological, and if it served and still serves the purposes of all but those of the subaltern majority, then what other narrative must be adopted in the project of creating the new symbiosis? And if the jural voices of the subaltern are to come in for serious consideration, then how are we to represent them, if we can at all?[1] And if we cannot, then into what espistemic predicament, if not a perennial aporia, does this throw both the privileged scholar and the reformer /intellectual? This chapter does not provide answers to these questions but rather addresses the problematics that these and related questions raise in dealing with the challenge of introducing into the modern Muslim condition one form of Islamic law or another.

The Theory

Yet, although these questions are not answerable at this stage of scholarly and intellectual-reformist development, a beginning must be made somewhere, preferably at a site that can claim centrality in the dialogic intersection between legal history and tradition, on the one hand, and the theoretical and substantive imperatives of modernity, on the other. Accordingly, there is perhaps no better site to accomplish these analytical tasks than what has inductively emerged in post-classical jurisprudence as *maqāṣid al-sharīʿah*, rendered into English best as the "universal aims of the law." The claim of this site as a supreme and, indeed, foundational analytical unit is due in good part to the fact that these aims sum up the range of desiderata produced by the law, its theory and practices over several centuries, but desiderata that have been inferred through a spaciotemporal and empirical means. Induction in the law, having its own rules of logic,[2] was seen to yield conclusions that would become, under certain conditions, the basis of further deductive arguments. It is in this sphere that the theory of *maqāṣid* provided, no less than the

---

[1] Gayatri Chakravorty Spivak, "Can the Subaltern Speak?" in Patrick Williams and Laura Chrisman, eds., *Colonial Discourse and Post-Colonial Theory: A Reader* (New York: Columbia University Press, 1994), pp. 66-111.

[2] Namely, that for purposes of the law, incomplete induction acts as a categorical and perfect induction, yielding conclusions that are demonstrative. For a detailed discussion of this matter in al-Shāṭibī's thought, see Hallaq, *History*, p. 169 ff.

mukhtaṣarāt,[1] the closest simulacrum of codification (though the many crucial differences must bar claims to further analogies). But more importantly, it is in this sphere — which squarely belonged to the *maqāṣid* — that the meaning, intent, purposes and Weltanschauungen of the law were articulated. In the context of the dialogic intersection of the post-classical and modern legal imperatives, to what extent do these *maqāṣid* retain value in terms of modern relevance?

An instructive point of entry into the theory of *maqāṣid* is the paradigmatic domain of *taʿlīl*, the theoretic that aims to identify and verify the *ratio legis* lying behind a particular ruling. *Ratio*s come in various shapes and forms, depending on the semantic-hermeneutic connection between the "novel" case at hand and the language of revelation, be it Qur'anic or Sunnaic. The connection itself, Arabicate in form and content, is therefore determined by the quality of the text's relevance, that semantic-conceptual bridge which presumably permits the jurist to cross the divide between social order and what is nothing less than God's textual episteme. The bridge may lie at any point on a spectrum that ranges from relatively clear textual evidence to a textual hint or cue. But God, insofar as the two primary sources are concerned, can also be silent. What if such connections, however faint, are not to be found? What if no textual evidence can attest, affirmatively or negatively, to a case for which a legal norm is sought?

The absence of a text that bears upon a new case does not leave the jurist stranded. In addressing this issue, al-Ghazālī begins with the prototypical case involving the consumption of inebriants.[2] In the Qur'an, wine is forbidden because it

[1] Cf. Mohammad Fadel, "The Social Logic of *Taqlīd* and the Rise of the *Mukhtaṣar*," *Islamic Law and Society*, vol. 3, No. 2 (1996), pp. 193-233.

[2] Abū Ḥāmid al-Ghazālī gives a detailed discussion of *munāsabah* and *maqāṣid* in his *Shifāʾ al-Ghalīl fī Bayān al-Shabah wal-Mukhīl wa-Masālik al-Taʿlīl*, ed. AbdelHakim al-Saʿdi (Baghdad: Maṭbaʿat al-Irshād, 1390/1971), pp. 142-266.

possesses the property of intoxication, deemed prohibited as it prevents the mind from exercising normal cognition, thereby leading its victim into misconduct, including the neglect of religious duties and an increasing tendency to violence. If we were to assume, for the sake of argument, that the Qur'an did not stipulate the reason for the prohibition, we would still, al-Ghazālī argues, come to the conclusion that the consumption of alcohol is prohibited, and this we know because of the harmful consequences of inebriants. This, al-Ghazālī insists, amounts to reasoning on the basis of suitability (*munāsabah*), since we, independently of revelation, know that there is certain harm in allowing the consumption of wine and a particular benefit that accrues from its prohibition.

Since suitability is rationally conceived and emanates neither from the direct nor oblique meaning of the revealed texts, its applicability to the law cannot be universal. In other words, since the law cannot always be analyzed and comprehended in rational ways, reason and its products are not always in agreement with the legal premises and their conclusions. Suitability, therefore, may at times be relevant (*mulā'im*) to the law, and irrelevant (*gharīb*) at others. No *ratio legis* may be deemed suitable without being relevant. Any irrelevant *ratio* becomes, *ipso facto*, unsuitable, and this precludes it from any further juristic consideration. The obligation to pray, for instance, is waived under circumstances of hardship. The *ratio* of hardship is deemed relevant to the spirit and positive commands of the law, since a great number of obligatory acts cease to be obligatory under extreme circumstances, such as illness and travel. But in the case of barring guardianship over divorced women who are of minor age, suitability is irrelevant, and therefore inadmissible. A divorcee who has reached the age of majority may remarry without a guardian, since she is thought to have acquired a sufficient degree of experience of worldly affairs during her last marriage.

This reasoning, however, though equally applicable to the

divorcee who is a minor, is considered inappropriate in the context of the Sharīʿah since it runs counter to the aims of the law in protecting the interests and welfare of minors. Thus, the validity of suitability rests on whether or not God took it into consideration as a legal norm, and whether or not it can be shown that the norm became operative when the feature of suitability in question was also present in the case attested by the revealed sources. Both the operative legal norm and the feature of suitability must coexist in order to satisfy the requirement of the *ratio.*[1]

Be that as it may, the ultimate goal of suitability is thus the protection of public interest (*maṣlaḥah*) in accordance with the fundamental principles of the law.[2] But in determining the *ratio legis* by the method of suitability, the jurist does not deal directly with the texts, since the *ratio* is not, strictly speaking, textual. Rather, he infers it through his rational faculty, though it must be in agreement with what may be called the spirit of the law. The law is known to prohibit that which is harmful and to protect and promote that which is beneficial to Muslims in this world and in the hereafter. For after all, if God is a merciful and rational being—the assumption being that he is preeminently so —then the combination of these attributes must rationally yield the conclusion that He aims to promote the interests of his *ʿibād.* Although we have no demonstrative proof that He should do so as a rational necessity, we are nonetheless left with the predominant likelihood that He does act to promote these

---

[1] See Sayf al-Dīn al-Āmidī's discussion in Bernard Weiss, *The Search for God's Law: Islamic Jurisprudence in the Writings of Sayf al-Dīn al-Āmidī* (Salt Lake City: University of Utah Press & Herndon, Va: International Institute of Islamic Thought, 2010), p. 596-609.

[2] In fact, the Zaydite al-Shawkānī, expressing a Sunnite *uṣūlī* view, states that the term "*munāsabah*" (suitability) is interchangeable with '*maṣlaḥah*,' '*istidlāl*,' and the 'protection of the law's aims' (*riʿāyat al-maqāṣid*). See Muḥammad b. ʿAlī al-Shawkānī, *Irshād al-Fuḥūl ilā Taḥqīq al-Ḥaqq min ʿIlm al-Uṣūl* (Surabaya: Sharikat Maktabat Aḥmad b. Saʿīd b. Nabhān, n.d.), p. 214.

objectives. In fact, the majority of, if not all, jurists held that God acts according to the best interests of his subjects. As al-Shāṭibī put it: "The Sharīʿah was instituted for [the promotion of] the good of believers."[1]

It thus follows that, in the jurist's reasoning, what is deemed detrimental to this good, the objective of the law, must be avoided, and whatever promotes harm must be prohibited. The constant and consistent promotion of benefit and exclusion of harm are the aims of the law, and it is to these aims that the rational argument of suitability must conform. The protection of life (*nafs*), property (*māl*), religion (*dīn*), mind (*ʿaql*) and offspring (*nasl*) represents a central aim of the law. Accordingly, the penalty of the murderer is death, a penalty instituted with the aim of deterring homicide and preserving life. "Had it not been for this penalty, people would rise up, threatening with collapse the order of public interest."[2]

The protection of property is achieved in "civil" matters through imposing compensatory damages upon the wrongdoer or unlawful appropriator (*ghāṣib*), while in criminal matters the thief is punished with amputation or a stiff discretionary penalty. All of these measures are intended to protect property, the prop of sustenance. Offspring are protected by prohibiting fornication and adultery (*zinā*), and by imposing another stiff penalty upon those who commit them. Fornication and adultery furthermore constitute not merely the diametrical moral and logical opposites of marriage, but they stand *vis-á-vis* this institution as mutually exclusive. Nor is this exclusivity limited to the logical and the moral, for the law, with its deliberate designs, consciously battles *zinā* through the promotion of marriage. Religion is protected and promoted through a. the

---

[1] Abū Isḥāq al-Shāṭibī, *al-Muwāfaqāt fī Uṣūl al-Aḥkām*, ed. Muḥyi al-Dīn ʿAbd al-Ḥamīd, 4 vols. (Cairo: Maṭbaʿat ʿAlī Muḥammad Ṣubayḥ, 1970), Vol. 2, p. 3: "*al-Sharīʿah wuḍʿat li-maṣāliḥ al-ʿibād.*"

[2] Shawkānī, *Irshād al-Fuḥūl*, p. 216.

application of the death penalty to those Muslims who apostate (*murtadd*), and b. warring against nonbelievers (*jihād*). Finally, the preservation of the mind, quintessential for any act of obedience, is brought about through the prohibition on the consumption of inebriants.

Al-Shawkānī reports that some later jurists (*al-muta'akhkhirūn*) added a sixth category, namely, honor. For people in general are customarily known to sacrifice their lives and property for the sake of preserving and protecting their honor, a fact that *a fortiori* bestows on the latter a position superior to that of the former. A false accusation of unchastity (*qadhf*)[1] has thus come to be punishable by the law precisely in order to promote and preserve honor.

Being many, the aims of the law are multi-faceted, and some are more fundamental than others. Al-Ghazālī offers a hierarchical classification consisting of three levels, the first of which includes those aims that he calls essential (*ḍarūriyyāt*), i.e., those which we have just enumerated, complemented by a class of subsidiary aims that seek to sustain and enhance the essential aims. For instance, the consumption of a small quantity of wine is prohibited because it invites the consumption of a larger quantity. Similarly, the acts of looking at or touching females are prohibited in an effort to sustain and bolster the sanction against adultery and fornication, to give added support to the principal prohibitions on sexual misconduct. Any *ratio legis* determined by suitability and falling within these areas of the law

[1] I.e., accusing someone of *zinā*. For an accusation to hold, the evidence to be satisfied must consist of four male witnesses who testify as eye witnesses to the act of sexual intercourse. Should the four witnesses offer contradictory testimonies or should one of the four be disqualified as a witness (due to being a slave or to some criminal past) or withdraw his testimony (leaving only three witnesses), all four would be liable to the *ḥadd* punishment, which consists of eighty lashes. See Abū Zakariyyā Yaḥyā b. Sharaf al-Dīn al-Nawawī, *Rawḍat al-Ṭālibīn*, ed. Adil Abd al-Mawjud and Ali Awad, 8 vols. (Beirut: Dār al-Kutub al-ʿIlmiyyah, n.d.), vol. 7, p. 322.

must be treated according to the principles governing this level of *maqāṣid.*

The second level, consisting of necessary aims (*ḥājiyyāt*), is distinguished from the first in that its neglect causes a secondary harm, indirectly detrimental to the categories and imperatives of the first level. Examples of necessary aims are the interests served by contracts of rent, for without them the owners of real property would not be entitled to protect the commercial value or usufruct of their assets, leaving them to be exploited by others without compensation.[1] This secondary but necessary aim—of regulating rent—has come to serve and enhance the interests of the higher and essential aim of protecting property. The same can be said of the necessity to appoint a guardian who is charged with the responsibility of giving a female of minor age in marriage. Here, no life is threatened and no property endangered; nevertheless, protecting certain interests, including those of minors, are necessary for ensuring justice in, and the orderly functioning of, society.

Finally, the third and least important level is what al-Ghazālī calls "improvements" (*taḥsīn*, *tawsīʿah*), which enhance the implementation of the higher aims of the law in secondary ways. The slave, for instance, is denied the capacity to act as a witness because his menial social status and servitude impede his independent testimony (the assumption being that evidentiary rectitude is normatively guaranteed by the threat of losing social capital or social standing). While this denial neither serves nor harms the indispensable and necessary aims (first and second levels), it does serve to enhance the aims of the Sharīʿah on the whole by confirming its principles.

Now, the aims of the law play a significant role in determining the so-called *al-maṣāliḥ al-mursalah*, a type of reasoning applied to cases upon which no text can be brought to bear. This was also known as *istidlāl bil-mursal*, and more

---

[1] Al-Shawkānī, *Irshād al-Fuḥūl*, p. 216.

generally, *istidlāl.*[1] Al-Shawkānī, one of the last of the classical jurists who had the benefit of a cumulative knowledge of the *uṣūlī* tradition, could sum up the various stances of the jurists on *maṣlaḥah mursalah.* For many, he observed, *maṣlaḥah* generally meant the preservation of the objectives of the law by means of averting harm, the aim of the law being social order. Yet, as al-Ghazālī held, instead of being grounded in a text of revelation, its rationale is founded in rational suitability. While on the one hand this type of reasoning has been rejected by many jurists, al-Qarāfī asserted that a thorough investigation into the matter reveals that all legal schools heavily resorted to the test of suitability, the cornerstone of *maṣlaḥah.*[2] When the derivation of legal rules is predicated upon the test of suitability-cum-relevancy, a good number of jurists, including the Ḥanafites, admit it as a valid form of reasoning. The Shāfiʿite legist Ibn Barhān added that this position is the choice of the jurists (*al-ḥaqq al-mukhtār*).

The position seemingly adopted by the majority insists on *maṣlaḥah* being "necessary, certain and universal." By necessary it is meant that it must be subsumable under the five *ḍarūriyyāt* enumerated above, namely, the preservation and promotion of life, property, religion, mind and offspring, and by universal, that it should encompass all Muslims. Al-Ghazālī illustrates the meaning of universality by the example of a military conflict between Muslims and non-Muslims, wherein the unbelievers' army is assumed to have captured a group of Muslims and to be using them as a shield. If the shield is not attacked, the army of the enemy will succeed in its design to destroy the Muslim community. In order to repulse the enemy, it is necessary to attack the shield, an act that is sure to result in killing many, if

[1] Abū al-Muẓaffar Manṣūr b. Muḥammad al-Samʿānī, *Qawāṭiʿ al-Adillah fil-Uṣūl*, 2 vols. (Beirut: Dār al-Kutub al-ʿIlmiyyah, 1997), vol. 2, p. 259; al-Shawkānī, *Irshād al-Fuḥūl*, p. 242.

[2] al-Shawkānī, *Irshād al-Fuḥūl*, p. 242: *qāla al-Qarāfī hiya ʿinda al-taḥqīq fī jamīʿ al-madhāhib li'annahum yaqūmūn wa-yaqʿudūn bil-munāsabah.*

not all, the Muslims forming the shield. Although the individuals are not guilty of any offense, and therefore do not deserve any penalty, much less capital punishment, *maṣlaḥah* dictates that the killing of fellow Muslims is "rationally relevant" (*mulā'im*) in light of the accruing benefits, namely, the protection of the wider Muslim community. For if such a sacrifice is not made, the enemy will defeat the Muslim army, destroy the community, and annihilate the shield at any rate.

Entailed by al-Ghazālī's example (famously known as *mas'alat al-turs*) is the certainty that the Sharīʿah aims at minimizing killing when killing cannot be averted at all. The killing of the persons forming the shield thus emerges as a rational certainty that is at once suitable, a certainty that must be so compelling as to override the legal consideration that no innocent soul should be punished in any manner, much less killed. [1] However, the claim to certainty and its "suitable" conclusions will not stand should there be any chance that the army of the enemy may not, in any case, win the battle. On the other hand, the claim to universality is rendered problematic should the situation in question not pose a threat to the entire community. If a ship were to be on the verge of sinking, it is deemed categorically prohibited to jettison some passengers in order to save the ship even though it might appear that such an act will save the day.[2] Needless to say, the extremely hypothetical nature of *mas'alat al-turs* did not escape Al-Ghazālī's colleagues who retorted, *inter alia*, that the average case in the law does not involve the entire community. Al-Ghazālī's point, however, appears to be the balance in favor of certainty that bears on what might be called general public interest, that which affects the community at large.

---

[1] Abū Ḥāmid al-Ghazālī, *al-Mustaṣfā min ʿIlm al-Uṣūl*, 2 vols. (Cairo: al-Maṭbaʿah al-Amīriyyah, 1324/1906), vol. 1, p. 284; al-Shawkānī, *Irshād al-Fuḥūl*, p. 242.

[2] al-Shawkānī, *Irshād al-Fuḥūl*, pp. 242-43.

Modern Encounters

There is little doubt that one of the major problems facing Muslim legal thinkers today is coping, under modern conditions, with the weight of what I have elsewhere called the Arabicate hermeneutic,[1] that juristic tradition which assumes a particular linguistic link between the law and the revealed sources. The link is also specifically Arabicate in the sense that, irrespective of the identity of the national and ethnic group that aims to apply the Sharīʿah to itself, the sources of the law and the means of their interpretation remain bound by the rules of the Arabic language. Even when the ethnic and national character of the group is seen to predetermine the law, as happened in the case of certain Indonesian legal thinkers (mainly with regard to the rules of inheritance),[2] the reasoning which aimed to bring the Qur'an to bear on this specific character could not avoid addressing the hermeneutics and linguistic structures of the revealed text. Thus, even in this radical nationalist exercise, the point of departure was a struggle with the Arabicate hermeneutic.

The linguistic hegemony of Arabicate *fiqh* appears to be daunting. It would not be an exaggeration to state that almost all modern legal thinkers attempting to make sense of Islamic law in the face of modernity—be they Malaysian, Indonesian, Arab or otherwise—have grappled with this hegemony. Rashid Rida, one of the first modern legal "reformers," resorted to a notion of *maṣlaḥah* that culminated in a near-total abandonment of the revealed texts in favor of a utilitarian construction of positive law.[3] Arguably, his juristic rationalization either led to or, at least, encouraged the westernization of both the substance and

---

[1] Wael B. Hallaq, *Sharīʿa: Theory, Practice, Transformations* (Cambridge: Cambridge University Press, 2009), pp. 500-42.

[2] See Mark Cammack, "Islamic Inheritance Law in Indonesia: The Influence of Hazairin's Theory of Bilateral Inheritance," *The Australian Journal of Asian Law*, vol. 4, No. 1 (2002), pp. 295-315.

[3] Hallaq, *History*, pp. 214-20.

form of law in many Arab countries, a phenomenon seen today as intrusive and alien. The Pakistani intellectual Fazlur Rahman proffered his double-movement theory in a clear effort to thwart the Arabicate linguistic hegemony, reducing the constitutive Islamic legal element to an understanding of the situational "intent" of the Lawgiver. His project is one about contexts and general intentionalities, but certainly not about the meaning and significance of individual words and prepositions.[1] Judging by the manner in which he was received in his native country, and by what the course of "Islamicization" in Pakistan has been, his project can hardly be described as successful. Likewise, the Syrian engineer-turned-jurist Muhammad Shahrur managed to develop a theory of law that entirely escapes the Arabicate hermeneutics, although it does erect an interpretive apparatus of its own.[2] Of all these proposed programs, Shahrur's has—now with the benefit of hindsight—been the least well-received.

The most salient problem facing legal modernizers may be captured in the contrast between the essential qualities defining language, especially one of Qur'anic pedigree, and modernity. However much we believe that the reader constructs the text, it is at least equally true that words have meanings whose range cannot but stop at a particular point in the semantic field. For any (legal) reasoning to gain legitimacy, it must, as a first and minimal condition, be believable to its intended audience. Believability is also a necessary, though clearly insufficient, condition for acquiring legitimacy; and legitimacy, or lack of it, is after all constitutive of what may accurately be called a Muslim legal predicament. Especially with the centuries-old weight of linguistic tradition, Qur'anic-Sunnaic language has been endowed with meanings whose semantic range is perforce

---

[1] Hallaq, *History*, pp. 241-45; Tamara Sonn, "Fazlur Rahman's Islamic Methodology," *The Muslim World*, Vol. 81, No. 3-4 (1991), pp. 212-30.
[2] Hallaq, *History*, pp. 245-53.

narrower than that which emerged during the twentieth century. The modern condition has pushed back the limits of this range, but only to a limited extent. Despite its malleability, the semantic field remains limited: a word's connotation, as a rule, cannot be turned into its opposite.

It is precisely in the "liquidity" and "progress"[1] of modernity that the contrast becomes clear. A run-away train,[2] so to speak, modernity has brought about ever-changing conditions with which the semantic fields of the Qur'an and the Sunnah cannot hope to catch up. The changes brought about by nation-states in the field of positive law can hardly be said to emanate from any legitimate hermeneutic, especially as their basis and method are constituted by no more than the will-to-power of the state itself. And the proposed projects of the so-called intellectual Islamic and Islamist reforms have all been caught up, without a successful conclusion, in the opposition between the relatively limited semantic field and the constantly changing conditions of modernity, be they social, moral, economic, technological or otherwise.

If the semantic field is no longer able to constitute the hermeneutical foundations of the law, then what alternative is there? The utilitarian/secularist approach to legal construction, we have already intimated, has proven to lack legitimacy in most parts of the Muslim world. Can, then, the five universals of *ḍarūriyyāt*, together with *maṣāliḥ mursalah*, form a new foundation of legal reasoning? After all, these universals—having been inductively constituted on the basis of both the revealed texts and the law that has presumably emanated therefrom over the centuries—represent the total sum of values upon which the Sharīʿah as well as Islam as religion and culture

---

[1] See, among others, Zygmunt Bauman, *Liquid Modernity* (Oxford: Polity Press, 2000); Jean-François Lyotard, *The Post-Modern Condition* (Minneapolis: University of Minnesota Press, 1985); Anthony Giddens, *The Consequences of Modernity* (Stanford: Stanford University Press, 1990).

[2] In all likelihood, the expression is not mine.

have placed a premium.

If we subsume Shawkānī's category of "honor" under that of "offspring" (as they are interconnected in many ways), it will become obvious that out of the five *maqāṣid* universals, no less than four (religion, life, property and offspring) present significant challenges in coping with modernity's condition.

First, little need be said about religion which stands in paradigmatic antithesis with a largely secular modern world. Once a criterion by which communities defined themselves and were defined by others, it has become, under the secularism of the nation-state, a marginalized definitional element. It is no longer required of the by-gone denizen to believe in religion, this requirement having been replaced by a national ideology whose main objective is the near-total pacification of an otherwise materially productive citizen. The upshot of all this is that the category of the "national citizen" has displaced religious loyalty as the hallmark of political identity, with the distinct implication that the protection and promotion of religion as defined by the *maqāṣid* universals is no longer compatible with the status of religion under the *modern* nation-state. Under the latter, it is true, religion has become a private matter, a natural right of which no individual should be deprived. But this right cannot, at least in theory and in law, be turned into a political privilege.

Accordingly, with this transmutation into the political ideology of national citizenry, the *ahl al-dhimmah* laws of *fiqh* are rendered problematic, at least as set by the standards of the so-called universal human rights and as these standards continue to be harnessed as a means of pressure and interference by the colonialist and quasi-colonialist western states. The fact that the laws of the Muslim countries of today have largely been determined by the direct and indirect control of these states complicates all possible options, which in their oppositions and syntheses may not prove viable. In other words, the practice of an exclusively classical *ahl al-dhimmah* doctrine has been thoroughly quashed by the socio-economic and legal transformations in most parts of the Muslim world, especially as manifested in the collapse of local community structures (exemplified by villages and city quarters) and the pre-modern legal sociology and laws that governed them. On the other hand, the transplantation of a purely western-type law, which would—in theory—fully accommodate the demands made by the universal conception of human rights, has proven to be antithetical to indigenous interests and ways of life. It is an option for which Muslims in general seem to have lost taste. And the synthesis between (and admixture of) these two extremes has not proven to be a happy mean, assuming that the post-colonial condition is a synthesis at all.

Second, and related to the first, is the "preservation of life," where the challenge is posed by the deterrent of capital punishment. This latter is increasingly facing opposition from several international quarters, despite the egregious indifference of the United States (with about three dozen states that continue to mete out this punishment). However, the difficulty arising in this context is representative of multiple problems running the full gamut of the law, namely, the role of the state in the criminal sphere. Whereas Islamic law and the Qur'an defined homicide as a private wrong to be settled by mediation and arbitration, and regulated by general guidelines that allowed for retaliation, compensation or forgiveness (the middle category being the most commonly practiced), the nation-state appropriated this sphere both in Europe and the colonized Muslim world. In fact, this appropriation (together with commercial law) was consistently one of the first acts of colonialist legal change. Retaliation became at that point the prerogative of the state, which not only claimed entitlement to the lives of its subjects but also introduced its own evidentiary procedures, declared to be more "effective" than their "lax" equivalent propounded by Islamic law.[1] This is not to say that deterrence, the central point of *maqāṣid*, cannot be achieved through the agency of the modern nation-state, but it is to assert the point that, inasmuch as dealing with homicide is a fundamental function of the law, dealing with punishment and its social ill-effects are just as important. Islamic law dealt with it within communal bounds, and in terms set by the community's internal interests, needs and desires. The modern nation-state has progressively ignored the interests of these communities whose structures and ways of life it has never stopped transforming.

The third challenge is the range of implications arising from the universal principle of "protecting offspring," the prohibition on fornication and adultery and their dialectical relationship with the laws of marriage in particular and those related to public morality in general. With the emergence of a modern type of public sphere and the role of women in it, these restrictions—which essentially govern females—have been largely forced out of the nation-state's law. Many of the new codes of family law in Muslim countries have come to encompass labor laws that permit women to engage in a range of conduct in the public space and have excluded from their purview all quasi-ritual rules about touching and looking at the female body.[2] Very few codes nowadays continue to prohibit women from exercising their right to work, so that with this newly acquired right, a husband's control over his wife's freedom of movement has, in some

---

[1] See, for example, Radhika Singha, *Despotism of Law: Crime and Justice in Early Colonial India* (Delhi: Oxford University Press, 1998), vol. 2, pp. 49-75.

[2] But I argue, along with Chatterjee, that these acts do not amount to women's liberation, for the state and its nationalism "conferred upon women the honor of a new social responsibility and by associating the task of female emancipation with the historical goal of sovereign nationhood, bound them to a narrow, and yet entirely legitimate, subordination." See Partha Chatterjee, "Colonialism, Nationalism, and Colonized Women: The Contest in India," *American Ethnologist*, vol. 16, No. 4 (1989), pp. 622-33, at 29, but also see pp. 63-32.

spheres, diminished considerably. These changes, effected as much by legislation as by the fundamental transformations in the mode of economic production, have altered religious morality in structural ways, and have significantly reduced both its scope and qualitative effects. That morality once regulated sexuality and that the latter has invariably had a direct bearing on the category of "offspring," are matters that hardly need comment. What needs to be addressed is rather the compatibility of modern morality—or more accurately, counter-morality—with the paramount status Muslims had assigned to sexuality and "offspring."

The same problematic that has arisen earlier with other *maqāṣid* universals must be addressed here too. How do the massive waves of legal westernization in the Muslim world square with the socially-embedded cultural ideals and desiderata that Muslims have developed over the centuries? How does any change in positive law, most particularly those occurring in line with the broad program of western feminism, reduce the centrality and effect of this universal, rendering it devoid of any substantive significance? Can western feminism, with its colonialist stance,[1] as well as so-called Islamic feminism, be accommodated—howsoever partially—while keeping the constitutive elements of this socio-moral category intact? This no doubt constitutes an immediate challenge, and one with which great many Muslim countries will have to deal sooner than later.

A significant obstacle impeding a forthright examination of

---

[1] Chandra T. Mohanty, "Under Western Eyes: Feminist Scholarship and Colonial Discourse," in P. Williams and l. Chrisman, eds., *Colonial Discourse and Post-colonial Theory: A Reader* (New York: Columbia University Press, 1994), pp. 462-82; M. Dube, "Postcolonial, Feminist Spaces, and Religion," in L. E. Donaldson and K. Pui-lan, eds., *Postcolonialism, Feminism, and Religious Discourse* (New York: Routledge, 2002), pp. 100-17; Uma Narayan, "The Project of Feminist Epistemology: Perspectives from a Nonwestern Feminist," in S. Harding, ed., *The Feminist Standpoint: A Theory Reader* (London: Routledge, 2004), pp. 213-24.

this challenge is the close connection between morality and the nature of the material system that evolved in tandem with modernity in a complex dialectical way; for it is undeniable that modernity arose out of capitalism as much as capitalism arose out of modernity. One can safely argue, I think, that the modern project in any society cannot succeed or sustain itself for long without the adoption of an essentially capitalist economy.[1] The recent collapse of the Soviet Union, the doomed struggle of Castro's Cuba, and the subsequent economic transformations in China and Vietnam are abundant testimonies to this. And if we accept this premise, we are faced with a double-pronged challenge: How will Muslims cope with the direct and massive indirect effects of capitalism on their culture-specific moralities, and, more importantly (which is our fourth point), how do they aim to deal with the *maqāṣid* universal relative to property defined as encompassing more than the reductionist notion of the sacrosanct entitlement to own wealth and protect it? How can "Islamic capitalism"—which grew in the shadow of the Sharīʿah and was for centuries highly conducive to the evolution of a distinct yet grandiose material, intellectual and spiritual culture—be prevented from slipping into the socially and morally troublesome forms of unrestrained modern capitalism?

Except for the category of "mind," therefore, all *maqāṣid* universals are plagued by considerable dilemmas, all of which in turn stem from trenchant features of modernity. I have suggested that modern, western-style capitalism has ineluctably reshaped the social landscape which pre-modern Islamic law had presupposed as its operative setting. Yet, the effects of capitalism can hardly exceed those brought about by the importation of the concept and practice of the nation-state into the Muslim world. And it is precisely here that a further complication to the significance of *maqāṣid* and their place in

---

[1] In this context, see I. Wallerstein, *The Modern World-System,* vols. 1 & 2 (New York: Academic Press, 1974, 1980); vol. 3 (San Diego: Academic Press, 1989).

remapping the legal landscape arises. It would hardly be an exaggeration, I believe, to suggest that there is virtually no problem or issue in the modern legal history of Islam that does not hark back to the discord between the thoroughly indigenous Islamic/customary law and the European-grown import that was the nation-state.[1]

An "Ecological" Misfit?

A conceptual analysis of the disharmony between Islamic law and the nation-state (mainly after the middle of the nineteenth-century) is foundational, in that all chronological accounts of the permutations in modern Islamic legal systems presuppose and rest upon the analytical difference between the pre-existing *system* (largely, but by no means exclusively, defined by the Sharīʿah) and the *system* that came to replace it (i.e., the nation-state).[2] The first and starkest feature that renders them incompatible is that both essentially belong to the same genus in that they are, in their own way, machines of governance. Both are designed to organize society and to resolve disputes that threaten to disrupt their respective orders—however different from each other these orders are.

Second, and more specifically, both are legally productive mechanisms or, to put it simply, Lawgivers. But couldn't they, as organs bearing the same specialization, co-exist? The short answer must be in the negative. Judged by historical experience (a venue that perforce renders complex any definition), Islamic

---

[1] There is a great merit to the argument that one of the chief problems that encounter the recently fashionable projects of "nation-building" is the fact that the nation-state that is being exported to Muslim countries has required over five centuries of history to develop in Europe, when nowadays it is expected to be adopted and fully incorporated in non-Western countries within a decade, if not less.

[2] For a general background essay, see Wael B. Hallaq, "Juristic Authority vs. State Power: The Legal Crises of Modern Islam," *Journal of Law and Religion*, Vol. 19, No. 2 (2003-2004), pp. 243-58.

law could and did accommodate a measure of legal intervention by the political sovereign, but never did this measure exceed the peripheral and the marginal, especially in terms of determining the substance of the law. (This relative jural independence is not to be confused with the proposition that the formation of Islamic law was to some degree affected by the institutions of political governance, a proposition which renders the Sharīʿah's marked independence even more remarkable.) While it is a given that Islamic law under the Ottomans—the most state -like dynasty of Islam[1]—was administered by means of state apparatus, the *corpus juris* applied was overwhelmingly of *Sharʿī* pedigree. Thus, while Islamic law is tolerant of administrative competition, it is only thinly tolerant of substantive juristic intervention. The nation-state, on the other hand—also judged by the very fact of its historical evolution[2]—had developed even less tolerance to legislative, administrative and bureaucratic competition. Its staunchly centralized nature *ab initio* precluded any palpable tolerance of other governing systems.[3]

Third, in theory as well as in practice, both systems claim ultimate sovereignty, and it is precisely this opposition that gives rise to serious questions as to *who* determines the *maqāṣid*'s content, form or otherwise. For, at least in juristic political

---

[1] It is imminently arguable that the Ottoman Empire during the fifteenth century and all of the sixteenth had developed as efficient bureaucracy and administration as Atlantic Europe had done during the same period. For an insightful analysis, see Rifaʿat Abou-El-Haj, *Formation of the Modern State: The Ottoman Empire, Sixteenth to Eighteenth Centuries* (Albany: State University of New York Press, 1991).

[2] For an excellent account of the rise of the nation-state, see Martin van Creveld, *The Rise and Decline of the State* (Cambridge/New York: Cambridge University Press, 1999).

[3] It is of course readily admitted, as Sally Merry argues ("Legal Pluralism," *Law and Society Review*, 22, 5 [1988], 869-901), that there exist "competing, contesting, and sometimes contradictory orders outside state law," but the overwhelming scholarly attention to the centrality of state law, and the relatively faint struggle to bring in the discipline of legal pluralism to counterbalance it, are, in themselves, abundant testimony to the pervasive nature and dominant weight of the state and its law.

theory, government (*siyāsah*) is subservient to the Sharīʿah.[1] The *raison d'etre* of *siyāsah* (whose invocation must *always* presuppose and announce the presence of the civil population) is to serve the interests of the law, not the other way round. That legal sovereignty remained, in both theory and practice, within the realm of the Sharīʿah is a fact that hardly squares with the modern nation-state's totalistic appropriation of this paramount form of sovereignty. A nation-state without jural sovereignty is no state at all.

Fourth, Islamic law and the nation-state operated in two opposing directions, the latter compelling and pushing towards an exclusive and ultimate center, and the former demonstrably centrifugal. As typical of Islamic structures (evident in social organization, urban and rural economic organization, mosque architecture, and pre-modern dynastic bureaucracies),[2] the law operated horizontally, so to speak. Aside from judicial appointments which were nominally, if not symbolically, hierarchical, the administration of justice was largely, if not exclusively, limited to the self-structured legal profession. If there was a hierarchy, it was within the profession itself, and was in nature epistemic rather than political or social. Yet, the hierarchy within Islamic law was largely[3] universal and self-sufficient, unlike the hierarchy existing in the judicial system of the nation-state, a hierarchy that ultimately reports to the higher corporate orders of the nation-state. The referential authorities

---

[1] See ʿAlī b. Muḥammad al-Māwardī, *al-Aḥkām al-Sulṭāniyyah* (Cairo: Dār al-Fikr, 1983), p. 3.

[2] With the partial exception of the Ottomans (see n. 29, above). More generally, see Louise Marlow, *Hierarchy and Egalitarianism in Islamic Thought* (Cambridge: Cambridge University Press, 1997).

[3] This is to allow for the occasional but informal complaints that were made to the ruler or provincial governor, a practice falling under the rubric of *maẓālim*. See J. Nielsen, *Secular Justice in an Islamic State* (Leiden: Nedelands Historisch-Archaeologisch Instituut, 1985); F. Zarinebaf-Shahr, "Ottoman Women and the Tradition of Seeking Justice in the Eighteenth Century," in *Women in the Ottoman Empire*, ed., M. Zelfi (Leiden: Brill, 1997), pp. 253-96.

of the *qāḍī* were learned *muftīs* and author-jurists. Hard cases were decided with the juristic assistance of the *muftī*, and appeals did not usually travel upwards in a hierarchy but were heard by the succeeding judge.[1] And even when some complaints were made to the highest offices of the "state" (as happened in the Ottoman Empire), they were made directly and given—with explicit intention—the personal attention of the ruler. Yet more often than not the ruler would send them back to the Sharīʿah judge. This was a personal form of justice, not corporate. By contrast, the nation-state's jural system is perforce hierarchical from within, and answers to a state hierarchy that is external to it, but one that both sustains and envelops it.

Fifth, and stemming from the preceding consideration, is the central fact that Islamic law is a grass-root system that takes form and operates within the social universe; it travels upward with diminishing velocity to affect, in varying degrees and forms, the *modus operandi* of the pre-modern "state" (by definition a minimal political, bureaucratic, administrative organization). The jurists emanate from the very society and societal culture that they serve, and the law as ideology and doctrine requires that they be, and continue to be, so. It is one of the most striking features of Islamic law, as a substantive and jural system, that it is generated at the very social level on which it was applied. In sharp contradistinction, the law of the nation-state (however democratically representative of the "people's concerns") is superimposed from a center in a downward direction, first originated by the mighty powers of the state apparatus and thereafter deployed—in a highly structured but deliberately descending movement—to the individuals of the social order, those individuals who are harnessed as national

---

[1] See David Powers, "On Judicial Review in Islamic Law," *Law and Society Review*, Vol. 26, No. 2 (1992), pp. 315-41. The successor review system was made tenable by virtue of the fact that judges served for short periods of time, an average of six months to two years.

citizens (fathers and mothers in the nation's families; economically productive agents; tax-payers; soldiers, etc.). A society subject to Islamic law is one that is largely self-governing, whereas a society subject to the nation-state is one that is ruled from above. If men (and now women) run the modern bureaucracy and make law on behalf of the corporate entity that is the nation-state, then the latter, as Max Weber and Sayyid Qutb aptly observed, is little more than "the rule of man over man."[1]

Sixth, and finally, while Islamic law and the nation-state shared the general goal of organizing society and adjudicating disputes, they did so to significantly different effects. Intrinsic to its behavior, the nation-state is systemically and systematically geared towards the homogenization of both the social order and the national citizen; and to accomplish these goals, it engages in systemic surveillance, discipline and punishment.[2] Its educational and cultural institutions are designed to manufacture the "good citizen" who is respectful of the law, submissive to notions of order and discipline, industrious and productive. Discipline-cum-punishment is integral to, and a unique feature of, the modern nation-state. The resultant "good citizen" is one who can *efficiently* serve the state, the father—and much less frequently the mother—of all. Obedience to the law, which presupposes submission and—more importantly—discipline, is then the prop upon which the state rests. Without the law and its tools of surveillance and punishment, no state apparatus can exist. Ergo, the centrality of the element of violence, and of the

---

[1] For Weber, see Peter Lassman, "The Rule of Man Over Man: Politics, Power and Legitimation," in Stephen Turner, ed., *The Cambridge Companion to Weber* (Cambridge: Cambridge University Press, 2000), pp. 83-98; For Sayyid Qutb, *Milestones* (Cedar Rapids: The Mother Mosque Foundation, 2003), pp. 94-95, and passim.

[2] Michel Foucault, *Discipline and Punish: The Birth of the Prison*, trans. Alan Sheridan (New York: Vintage Books, 1995); idem., *The Foucault Reader*, ed., Paul Rabinow (New York: Pantheon Books, 1984), pp. 169-256.

threat to use it, in the definition of the nation-state. The state, insofar as I am aware, is the only entity in human history that has arrogated to itself the exclusive right to exercise violence or to threaten its use. That the citizen has accepted—or has been conditioned into accepting—this right of the state is perhaps the most salient success of its project. Islamic law, by contrast, has not concerned itself with creating the national citizen, and to this extent, it shares none of the features of the nation-state in this regard.

Aside from its higher transcendental aims, Islamic law had little interest in the social order beyond resolving disputes in the least possible disruptive manner to this order. Obedience to God, the nominal and theoretical function of Islamic law, was manifested in communal existence. He who breached communal harmony was deemed to have violated God's law. That the general goal of Islamic law has always and everywhere been to restore individuals—to the best extent possible—to their social positions remains one of the most valid generalizations about this legal system. Put differently, unlike the punitive-oriented state which created the citizen only to subdue him/her along with society at large, Islamic law mediated conflicts and arbitrated disputes in a constant effort to mend the ruptures of the social fabric. Its prescribed harsh punishments, whenever applied (and mostly they were not), were conceived of as exemplary, intended to deter the forces of corruption which nearly always translated into disrupting social harmony.

But it seems also true that, because Islamic law never constituted part of a machinery of coercive justice, its prescribed penalties represented the furthest limit to human conduct. This did not mean that punishment was applied wherever an infraction took place (which explains why every large Middle Eastern city boasted, among other subversive features, a healthy population of prostitutes) but the limit was designed as a possible invocation against excesses whenever there was enough social force to call for the strict application of penalties. (This feature of Islamic law perhaps explains why the British, among other colonialists, thought of Islamic criminal law as unduly lenient, lacking in punishments, inefficient, and conducive neither to the propagation of discipline nor to the imposition of "law and order." This also explains why Islamic penal law was one of the first corpuses of law to be replaced by western criminal codes.)

While both Islamic law and the nation-state were constituted as governing organs that by necessity were Lawgivers, they fundamentally differed in the articulation of their *modus operandi* and ultimate objectives (a fact that should constantly be borne in mind when speaking of the modern functions of the *maqāṣid*). As universal lawgivers, the two systems are mutually exclusive. And since their aims and *Weltanschauungen* were so different, such coexistence was precluded *a priori*. It is this teleological difference that pitted the state against Islamic law. In this competition, the latter had no chance of withstanding the assault, much less of winning the jural war, against an entity that is powerfully capitalistic, intrusively bureaucratic-administrative and intensely militaristic. The victory of the nation-state was not only one of displacing Islamic law, but also one which *entailed* the "reordering" of Muslim social structures. The Muslim believer *had* to be converted into the "good national citizen." The rest is legal history.

On a more specific analytical level, the nation-state confronted Islamic law as a purely legislative entity, our second point above. The nation-state's jural *modus vivendi* was codification, a method that entails a conscious harnessing of a particular tool of governance. The *maqāṣid*, however articulated or interpreted, must now fit into this new reality. Codification is a deliberate choice in the exercise of legal and political power, a choice that at once accomplishes a multitude of tasks. The most essential feature of the code is the *production* of order, clarity, concision and authority.[1] Modern codes and acts, the legal experts agree, have come to replace "all previous inconsistent customs, mores, and law,"[2] those very relations that produced Islamic law and its *maqāṣid* philosophy. This replacement is also totalistic, since codes must also fulfill the requirement of completeness and exclusivity. They must comprehensively cover the area they claim to regulate, an act that perforce precludes both the substantive application and—equally significant—the authority of any competing law. Where exceptions are made permitting the co-existence of other forms of (pre-existing) law, it is only by virtue of permission granted by such codes. In other words, modern codes always claim exclusive and superior authority, over and above all previous law.

Nor is this all; codes must be systematic and clear, arranged rationally and logically, and rendered easily accessible to lawyers and judges;[3] and it is into this legal landscape that the *maqāṣid*, once again, must be fitted. By their very nature, codes are not only declaratory and enunciating of their own authority, but also universal in their statement of rules; hence their conciseness. They pay no direct attention to the individual, whether it is the particular case or the human individual. As an enhancement of this feature, they are always abstract, "to the point," and deliberately preclusive of the concrete. It was, for instance, held to be a virtue that the "French and German Civil Codes could be held within the boards of a volume while the common law required a full library."[4] But the premium attribute of the code is

---

[1] Ferdinand F. Stone, "A Primer on Codification," *Tulane Law Review*, Vol. 29 (1954-55), pp. 303-10, at 303-04, acknowledges that codification is a tool of the state, including its reformers, as well as a means to create a "new economic and social order," but all this harks back at a single function of codification, namely, "to state the law clearly and concisely."

[2] S. A. Bayitch, "Codification in Modern Times," in A. N. Yiannopoulos, ed., *Civil Law in the Modern World* (Kingsport: Louisiana State University Press, 1965), pp. 161-91, at 164.

[3] This, according to Stone being the *raison d'etre* of the code ("Primer," pp. 303-04).

[4] Stone, "Primer," p. 306.

its capacity to create uniformity, an attribute subsidiary to the universal modern condition as an uncompromisingly homogenizing one. This also explains why it was to the civil codes of Western Europe—and not to the English Common Law—that the Afro-Asian reformers turned. Thus, codes must create uniformity not only within themselves, but also in their application. The sway of the code's authority therefore overextends its own definition and encroaches upon the administration and implementation of justice.[1]

Islamic law, on the other hand, runs counter to the great majority of the code's attributes. First, Islamic law did not lay any claim to exclusive authority. In fact, it *depended* on the cooperation of customary and royal law (*siyāsah sharʿiyyah*), the former being the systemic prop upon which morality meshed into law as a "rational" system. Nowhere did Islamic law operate exclusively, and everywhere customary law was entwined with it in the realm of practice. Nor, in this connection, was Islamic law declaratory, in that it never pronounced itself as the bearer of exclusive authority, as having come to replace others in the field. By its hermeneutic and highly individualistic nature, Islamic law was not systematic according to the European perception of the world, although an expert in it might have viewed the matter entirely otherwise.

Similarly, from a modern perspective, Islamic law has been described as obscure and complex, unlike the "clear and accessible" code. While the code is clearly more accessible than treatises of *fiqh*, the argument of clarity is no more than a relative one. An expert in *fiqh* may find it as clear as the modern lawyer finds the code. Admittedly, however, Islamic law cannot be said to have internal uniformity, since plurality of opinion—the so-called *ijtihādic* pluralism—is its defining feature par excellence. It is on the diversity of its own character that, interestingly, it thrived (and insisted), and it is *in* it that it found

---

[1] See Bayitch, "Codification," pp. 162-67.

the flexibility to accommodate, through variant legal norms, different situations that would otherwise come under the same codified rule. The plurality of opinion answered not only the multiplicity of particular and special situations but the exigencies of legal change.[1] Its plurality ran counter to the spirit of uniformity, since homogenization—in its modern meaning and effect—was largely absent from its agenda. And since its interest lay in the individual as a singular worshipper of God, there was no need for an abstract and universalizing language. Most importantly, however, it is the declaratory nature of the code as well as its uniformity of substance and legal effect that betrayed a will-to-power that emanated from the higher offices of the nation-state; by contrast, in Islamic law such a will-to-power could not exist on any level beyond the purely abstract and theoretical (if not the metaphysical and theological).

That codes must be systematic, clear and accessible is also a function of the difference in roles played by the *faqīh*, on the one hand, and the modern lawyer-judge, on the other. The modern lawyer-judge is the representative and agent of the nation-state, an extension of its agency, and one who studies and applies the code as technocrat. But he/she does not produce the law of the code, a fact leading to far-reaching effects. The nation-state apparatus of control and surveillance produced the obedient lawyer and judge—obedient, that is, to the commanding powers of the state. Being a technocrat and a specialist in what has been termed "the province of law," the lawyer-judge is confined to the technical study of law, which is the nation-state's tool to accomplish control and order for the sake of efficient management of an economically productive citizenry. The *faqīh*, on the other hand, served a different imperative, for long and for most of the time transcending the limitations of technocracy. Among the *faqīhs*, the *qāḍī*s tended to

[1] Wael B. Hallaq, *Authority, Continuity, and Change in Islamic Law* (Cambridge: Cambridge University Press, 2001), pp. 121-235.

serve as technocrats, but never all of them. For *qāḍī*s wore other hats, so to speak, such as those of the *muftī* and the author-jurist.[1] Thus a significant number, if not a majority, of the *faqīhs* were intellectuals who routinely engaged in specialized studies of other disciplines, from history, theology and literature, to philosophy, logic, medicine and astronomy. Their desideratum was the discovery and articulation of the law, and they marshaled their interdisciplinary knowledge toward the accomplishment of that goal. They produced the law, and they accumulated the highest form of authority, namely, the epistemic. They, the *mujtahid*s and the leading *muftīs*, were thus the public intellectuals who spoke truth to power. This can never be claimed to be an attribute of the modern lawyer-judge.[2]

In Lieu of a Conclusion

With this conceptual background in mind, the *maqāṣid,* if they are to be revived, must be refitted in a world of nation-states, a world that is dramatically different from its pre-modern counterpart and one that shows no signs of disappearing any time soon.[3] The refitting is by no means a mechanical arrangement, but rather one that redefines the very form and content of the *maqāṣid.* The readjustment, furthermore, is one that involves no less than a transplantation into a new legal ecology. Assuming that the

---

[1] Hallaq, *Authority*, pp. 166-74.

[2] The judge's judicial independence in the modern state, and thus his competence —as a judge—to speak truth to power, are limited by the very law that the state installs to regulate the judge's office and function. In other words, the judge's empowerment (or delegated authority) to speak the truth cannot exceed that empowerment itself (or the bounds of that authority). In contrast, in Islamic legal and political cultures, there was no such empowerment since the state in its modern meaning never existed, and the Sharīʿah was itself largely independent of all legal and juristic constraints. Therefore, in the Islamic context, speaking truth to power was not predetermined by power's power to delimit the scope of truth.

[3] Even if the theory of the decline of the state is to be taken seriously, any decline will not occur soon enough to minimize the urgency of this "refitting." On this theory, see Martin van Creveld, *The Rise and Decline of the State.*

maqāṣid's link with Arabicate *ijtihād*ic hermeneutics is successfully severed—the whole point of their rejuvenation as a viable way out of the hermeneutical impasse—they must be accommodated within a body politic wherein legal power is above and beyond them. They must, in other words, depend on an alternative hermeneutic that ensues not from an individualistic, socially-embedded, Arabicate-driven *ijtihād*, but from state-designated councils or committees that operate under the shadow of state interests. Having been formed out of the soil of *ijtihād*ic pluralism, they must now cope with the processes and effects of being recast into code-like forms, the essential *modus operandi* of the nation-state.

In terms of content, on the other hand, the sources (*uṣūl*) of the *maqāṣid* will, under the state, cease to be a hermeneutic that is dialectically based on text and society (which are located in opposition to political power), but rather a hermeneutic that incorporates the will of the state and a vision of enacting the good citizen. The text—however defined here—and the hermeneutic are largely shaped by the state on behalf of the citizen as a social being. The social order *qua* social order does not, in and by itself, generate any law, nor does it remotely have the agency which produced the *muftī*, the author-jurist and the *faqīh*. If law is a reflection of its sources, of its hermeneutic, of the kind of legal profession producing it, then how can the *maqasid* continue to preserve a certain Islamic character (however it may be defined) under dramatically different conditions where the sources, the hermeneutic and the legal profession share little, if anything, with their pre-modern counterpart? How, no less importantly, can the *maqāṣid* law (if we were to add to this mix the inevitable effects of capitalism) under the nation-state order accommodate and give voice to the subaltern?

Furthermore, when once they were seen as the moral underpinning of the social order and as an exemplary guideline of conduct which generated willing submission—but by no means a systematic implementation of "law and order",—they would now, under the nation-state, acquire a disciplinarian fixity with which they had not been associated. Hand mutilation or capital punishment (protecting property and life, respectively) would not be a flexible hermeneutical exercise sporadically used to maintain social harmony (in a specific, localized social group) whenever the jurists and judges felt a limit had been breached, but the all-or-none punishment that must reflect the much-cherished blind-justice. How could the cherished values that characterized—indeed distinguished—Islamic societies and made them what they are be, *mutatis mutandis,* maintained in the face of such hegemonic transformations?

How would the *maqāṣid* maintain that minimalist essence that makes a society Muslim/Islamic, and distinct from others, in the face of modernity's powerfully homogenizing effects?

The overarching estrangement of the *maqāṣid* from their native soil does not alter only their form but also their substantive meaning and material contents. Perhaps most central in this transformation is the loss of the moral *order*, or the moral community, upon which the application of Islamic law depended and which it presupposed. If the *maqāṣid* universals are to have any genuine Islamic meaning and content, they must be situated in a morally-based community, in the sense that the socially-embedded moral code is systematically maintained as the driving engine of the law, not the other way around. The loss of the moral community is the quintessential triumph of modernity. How this community can be revived under the clutches of the modern project is perhaps the most central and urgent question of all.

These challenges are formidable enough in the presence of the irretrievable modern nation-state—whatever form it may take in the future. To install the *maqāṣid* in a legal system in which the state is subservient to the Sharīʿah—as many Muslims call for today—is to argue for a more radical solution, and thus to face an even more formidable challenge. This option would require the construction of a new legal system, a new legal education, a new conception of the law, a new economy, and a new moral community.[1] All this, in other words, would require transcending modernity, the ultimate challenge facing humankind today.

---

[1] See Wael B. Hallaq, "Can the Shariʿa be Restored?" in Yvonne Y. Haddad and Barbara F. Stowasser, eds., *Islamic Law and the Challenges of Modernity* (Walnut Creek: Altamira Press, 2004), pp. 21-53.

CHAPTER FIVE

Jurisprudence: The Ultimate Arena For Existential Clash or Cooperation Within and among Civilizations

Robert Dickson Crane

Introduction

In 1982, as a "Cherokee Indian" and former Ombudsman in the U.S. government's Bureau of Indian Affairs responsible for resolving irresolvable problems, I was invited to represent the indigenous nations and religions of "American Indians" at a gathering above the little village of Baca on the Western Slope of Colorado's Rocky Mountains. Maurice Strong, a Canadian philanthropist and former Under Secretary General of the United Nations, had invited two Buddhist monks from Dharmsala, India, representing the Dalai Lama, to start a monastery as part of a village of monasteries representing all the world religions. I was asked to entertain these monks for five minutes when they arrived. Not knowing how to entertain Buddhist monks, I asked them if they could summarize the essence of Buddhism in five minutes.

They laughed and replied, "We don't need five minutes to explain anything so simple. First, we have Hinayana Buddhism, which teaches that one should avoid attachments to the material world. Second, we have Mahayana Buddhism as a path toward higher awareness of transendent reality, which you may call 'God'. Finally, we have Tantrayana Buddhism, at which level one's highest desire is to bring compassionate justice to every person, every community, and everything in the world."

My immediate response was, "In less than one minute you have just summarized the essence of Islam and of every other world religion, including the indigenous, since the origin of human beings many millions of years ago."

As a lifelong student of comparative jurisprudence, I then and there founded my first think-tank, the Center for Civilizational Renewal, which in 1987 published my book, *Shaping the Future: Challenge and Response,* and led to such publications as my four-volume textbook, *Islam and Muslims: Essence and Practice,* together with my co-author, Muhammad Ali Chaudry, and twenty years later in 2006 to this essay selected as a chapter in Mohamed El-Tahir El-Mesawi's edited book.

Positivist versus Normative Law

From the traditionalist perspective of the world religions, the underlying issue in the world today is whether the ultimate reality is man's autistic pursuit of unlimited power through the modern state with its monopoly of coercion as a substitute for God, or whether a higher reality of universal truth is accessible to persons and communities as guidance for a normative system of compassionate justice.

The conflict between these two paradigms of jurisprudence boils down to the question whether law is "positivist" or "normative." Is it instrumentally created and sustained by human command, or is it a system of heuristic norms that always wait to be discovered?

Orientalists have always used Western positivist law as the base case and thereby set the stage to denigrate Islamic law as non-existent or at least inferior because it is utopian and is not enforced. Traditionalist Muslims, on the other hand, especially the more mystical Shī'a, consider that Islamic law is primarily educational and is designed to motivate both persons and communities to fulfill their spiritual and moral potentials. From this perspective of Islamic law as the base case for comparative jurisprudence, it appears that Western law is grossly inferior. One may legitimately argue that in recent centuries the pragmatic result of the "Western" and the "Eastern" legal systems in the actualization of justice may favor Western law, at least for domestic consumption. Civilizational clash, however, stems more from philosophical points of origin as part of identity politics than from "practical" results.

Perhaps the three most seminal books to appear during the past year or two[1] on the role of jurisprudence in the renewal of civilization as a means to marginalize violent extremists in every religion have been published by Harvard Law School, by the International Institute of Islamic Thought, and by the Institute of Ismaili Studies in London.

The thirteen scholarly chapters in the book from the Harvard Series in Islamic Law, *The Islamic School of Law: Evolution, Devolution, and Progress*, explore the origin, dynamics, and function of the *madhhab* or "school of law", and particularly of its institutionalization as a means to provide legitimacy and effectiveness in government. Of its three editors, namely, Frank Vogel, who is head of Harvard's Legal Studies Program, Peri Bearman, who is his alter ego, and Rudolph Peters, only the latter has contributed a chapter to this symposium.

Professor Peters' chapter on the Ḥanafi school of law adopted by the Ottoman Empire confirms the dynamic and fluid nature of the Islamic Sharīʿah as developed by the four Sunni *madhahib* and the four Shīʿa related ones, especially in their formative period before they became institutionalized as a

---

[1] The author refers to years preceding 2006 when he prepared this chapter for the First International Conference on Maqasid al-Shariah organized by the International Islamic University in collaboration with the Jeddah-based International Fiqh Academy.—(Ed.)

matter of survival in competition with the many now extinct schools of law and as a means to defend their search for truth and justice against the dictates of political oppression. In his introduction, Peters asks how "such a fluid doctrine full of contradictions could be enforced by the courts. Or, in other words, how Islamic legal doctrine with its many conflicting views and rulings could be transformed into positive law?"[1]

This question is central to Western jurisprudence, political science, economics, and sociology. According to *Black's Law Dictionary*, which has been authoritative at Harvard Law School ever since I earned a J.D. there in comparative legal systems half a century ago, positive law is "law actually and specifically enacted or adopted by proper authority for the government of an organized jural society. A 'law,' in the sense in which that term is employed in jurisprudence, is enforced by a sovereign political authority. It is thus distinguished from all rules which, like the principles of morality and the so-called laws of honor and of fashion, are enforced by an indeterminate authority which is either, on the one hand, superhuman or, on the other hand, politically subordinate. In order to emphasize that 'laws', in the strict sense of the term, are thus authoritatively imposed, they are described as *positive laws*."[2]

This definition of law reflects the uniquely Euro-American concept in jurisprudence known as philosophical positivism, typified by the Austinian school of positivist law that has reigned at Harvard since the time of the American Civil War. Legal positivism asserts that all genuine law is man-made. It rejects the existence of natural law, which reigned at Harvard

---

[1]Rudolph Peters, "Chapter Ten: What does it Mean to be an Official *Madhhab*? Hanafism and the Ottoman Empire," in Peri Bearman, Rudolph Peters & Frank E. Vogel (eds.), *The Islamic School of Law: Evolution, Devolution, and Progress* (Cambridge, Massachusetts: Islamic Legal Program, Harvard Law School, 2005), p. 147.

[2] Henry Campbell Black, *A Law Dictionary* (St. Paul, Minn.: West Publishing Co., 2nd edn, 1910), p. 915 (italics in the original).

prior to the Civil War, whether it is derived from divine revelation or from human nature and the *de facto* laws of the physical universe, known in Islamic thought as the *sunnat Allāh*.

The demands of state sovereignty in the modern age and their force as a rationale for "reforming" Islam are presented by Professor Mark Cammack of Southwestern Law School in Los Angeles in his chapter on "Forging an Indonesian *Madhhab*" to reconcile Islam and nationalism. The rise of the *madhhab* movement in the first three Hijrah centuries, he says, resulted from the use of *ijtihād* to develop a consensus or *ijmāʿ* on the limits of disagreement both on the relative priorities of reason and revelation and on the role of customary law in developing the Sharīʿah. He quotes Joseph Schacht's writings of the 1950s contending that much of the substantive content of the law was originally not "Islamic" and suggests that the modern dissolution of the traditional *madhhab* gives rise to the opportunity to develop new *madhhab*s better designed to address social conditions different from the ones of a thousand years ago in the Middle East.[1]

His case in point is the half-century old movement in Indonesia to reshape the laws of inheritance by reinterpreting the Qur'an and Ḥadīth so they will no longer be bound by the patriarchal customs of the Arabs and instead will reflect the matriarchal customs of parts of Indonesia or at least abandon the "two for one" principle and institute "bilateral inheritance law." In support of this argument that the patrilineal model does not reflect the only possible interpretation of the Qur'an, the founder of the Indonesian-*madhhab* movement, Hazairin, who was a reformer rather than a legal theorist, "pointed to the differences between Sunni inheritance rules and Shīʿite

---

[1] Mark E. Cammak, "Chapter Twelve: Islam and Nationalism in Indonesia: Forging an Indonesian Madhhab," in Peri Bearman *et al.*, *The Islamic School of Law*, pp. 175 & 188-189. Editor's Note: see especially Joseph Schacht, *The Origins of Islamic Jurisprudence* (Oxford: The Clarendon Press, 1979).

doctrines, which developed in a different social milieu and grant greater rights to female blood lines." The modern dissolution of the *madhhab* as an instrument of "historically contingent" identity and authority may open the way to revive *ijtihād*, which originally gave rise to the *madhhab* movement in Islamic jurisprudence, and thereby adapt Islamic law to the demands of the nation-state.[1]

The driving force for such "modernization" of Islamic law, perhaps especially in the realm of male/female gender equity, is not justice reflecting the essentials or universal purposes (*maqāṣid*) of Islamic jurisprudence, but the felt need to "adapt the Islamic legal tradition to political realities inherent in the nation state."[2] The issue is not merely whether the law should mirror society's morals, rather than serving as a moral guide to society, but whether the law can serve its positivist role to consolidate political power in the imagined community of the corporate state.

For centuries, the Dutch colonialists accentuated and fostered the differences among the many indigenous cultures in the Indonesian archipelago based on their various forms of customary law or *ʿādāt*, which were rooted in an indigenous, mystically-oriented and syncretic form of Islam known as *abangan*. The object was to counter the threat of Sharīʿah-oriented or *santri* Islam as a potential unifying force against foreign rule. After independence the political incentives were reversed as indigenous nation-building based on a national form of the Sharīʿah, Islam came to serve the interests of centralized power.[3]

Cammack concludes his chapter with the statement that, "the imperative for the creation of national Islamic law is also to some extent universal, since the ideal of national law is inherent

---

[1] *Ibid.*, pp. 178-180.
[2] *Ibid.*, p. 181.
[3] *Ibid.*, pp. 177-178.

in the concept of the nation state, and the nation state has become the ubiquitous model for political organization."[1]

The bulk of this valuable book on the dynamic history of the interpretative communities known as *madhhābib* is by modern scholars who explore the origins and unique natures of the better-known *madhhabs*, as well as the interrelationships among them and with political rulers. Not one of these scholars referred to the term "positive law" except as a synonym for substantive law, *furūʿ al-fiqh*, as distinct from procedure and from legal theory, *uṣūl al-fiqh*. Two of the most valuable chapters are by Camilla Adang of Tel Aviv University dispelling the myths about the role of the currently controversial Andalusian Ibn Ḥazm in the spread of the extinct Ẓāhirī *madhhab*,[2] and by Daphna Ephrat, director of the Islamic section at the Open University of Israel, on the variously competing and reinforcing roles of *madhhabs* and *madrasas* in eleventh-century Baghdad.[3]

At the opposite end of the spectrum from positivist law to sacred law in Harvard Law School's latest production is the chapter by Robert Gleave of the University of Bristol, England, on the Shīʿite conception of the *madhhab* and its role in bringing men and women closer to God.[4]

In Shīʿī Islam, the concept of *madhhab* goes beyond the *furūʿ al-fiqh* and even the *uṣūl al-fiqh* to the broader theological realm of combining reason with revelation. According to Professor Gleave, the principal conflict within the dominant Shiʿa *madhhab*, known as the *madhhab* of the *Ithnā-ʿasharī Imāmiyyah* or the Jaʿfarī *madhhab*, named after the sixth Shiʿite imam, was between the

---

[1] *Ibid.*, p. 190.

[2] Camilla Adang, "Chapter Eight: The Beginnings of the Ẓāhirī Madhhab in al-Andalus," in Peri Bearman *et al.*, *The Islamic School of Law*, pp. 117-125.

[3] Daphna Ephrat, "Chapter Six: Madhhab and Madrasa in Eleventh-Century Baghdad," in Peri Bearman *et al.*, *The Islamic School of Law*, pp. 78-93.

[4] Robert Gleave, "Chapter Nine: Intra-Madhhab *Ikhtilāf* and the Late Classical Imami Shiite Conception of the Madhhab," in Peri Bearman *et al.*, *The Islamic School of Law*, pp. 128-146.

Akhbaris and the traditionists or *Uṣūlīs* who emphasize knowledge of all past scholarship. This use of the term "traditionist" is the opposite of that in Sunnī Islam, as is also the term "*uṣūlī*" or "funda-mentalist." The *Akhbaris* focused exclusively on re-examining the texts of revelation. Their name comes from the verb *khabara*, to know by experience, and the noun *khabar*, message or *ḥadīth*, for which the plural is *akhbār*.

The soundness of the Ithnā-ʿasharī Imāmiyyah *madhhab* is judged by its appeal to authority. This is understood very specifically not in the political sense, because one of the two major differences between Shīʿī and Sunnī jurisprudence are the Shīʿa's emphasis on gender equity and the Shīʿa's condemnation of any moves to combine religious with political authority, Ayatullah Khomeini's doctrine of *wilāyat al-faqīh* being a bizarre modern anomaly.

Authority in the Imāmiyyah and related *madhhabs* includes the ḥadīth or sayings not only of the Prophet Muhammad but of the inspired successors to the spiritual successor of the Prophet Muhammad, namely, ʿAlī b. Abī Ṭālib. It includes also two tiers of scholarly interpretation. The first tier is known as the *ihktilāf* generation of scholars who laid out the range of acceptable diversity of opinion. The second tier consists of the later jurists who summarize and restate the earlier scholarship with explanatory notes. I have compared this with the Jewish concept of the *Talmud* and *Midrash* as successive levels of understanding the *Torah*.

The key to this process is how to "reveal the opinion of the Imam," whether living as in earlier times or later "in occultation." The task is to reach a constructed consensus (*ijmāʿ murakkab*) on possible answers to a legal problem, beyond which no further answers are permitted. The opinion of the Imam by definition supports this range of answers. If further scholarship and *ijtihād* produce a consensus on one of these answers, this then reveals the opinion of the Imam. The Shīʿa concept of authority therefore reflects a body of scholarly opinion that develops over time in response to changing conditions. Since this required continual *ijtihād* or intellectual effort, the Sunnī reliance on analogy *(qiyās)* was unnecessary. Instead, reliance was required on the formulation of basic normative principles from which every *ḥukm* or regulatory rule must derive its meaning.

According to both Sunnī and Shīʿī historiography, Imām ʿAlī always excelled in tracing all decisions to higher principle, as was demanded by the Prophet Muhammad himself in instructing his followers. The deadening practice of *taqlīd*, following detailed rules without informative principles, can produce injustice. Following principle in the search for compassionate justice is the key to combining reason and revelation in always up-do-date understanding and response to changing conditions of life so that both individual persons and the communities derived from them will have optimum conditions to remain close to God and thereby fulfill the purpose of their existence.

The final chapter in the Harvard publication on the Islamic school of law addresses the declining relevance of the traditional *madhhab* and the threat of chaos from individual faux *ijtihād* developed on the internet in the form of what the author Ihsan Yilmaz from Turkey describes as "inter-*madhhab* surfing" in the practice of *talfiq*, which is the syncretic search among madhhabs for whatever supports one's selfish interests.

His solution to this problem is to "raise the level of Islamic consciousness by indicating the connection between reason and revelation [in order to] raise individuals who would meet the criteria of a mujtahid." This can be done only through "faith-based movement leaders with effective organizations to implement their ideas." Ihsan Yilmaz's chapter focuses on the movement of Fethullah Gulen as a model. Other possible models would be the Islamist movements of the past half century modeled after the former Sufi, Hassan al-Banna, who today is still the mentor of enlightened Islamist movements throughout the Sunni world.[1]

Maqāṣid al-Sharīʿah

None of these faith-based movements has succeeded in developing a jurisprudence that is adequate to the demand for Islamic leadership in pursuing human responsibilities and rights as the major requirement for peaceful engagement among civilizations in the third millennium.

The missing dimension has been supplied by perhaps the greatest Islamic legal scholar of the twentieth century, Muhammad al-Tahir Ibn Ashur, who taught at al-Zaitouna Grand Mosque. As a young man he was a follower of the reformer Muhammad ʿAbdu, and rose to become the Grand Mufti of Tunisia. His major work, first published in Arabic in 1946, was translated and annotated for a modern reader with incredibly thorough footnotes by Mohamed El-Tahir El-Mesawi under the title, *Treatise on Maqāṣid al Sharīʿah* and published by the International Institute of Islamic Thought in 2006. This book marked the first serious attention given by Muslims in the Sunnī world to normative Islam in six hundred years.

In this seminal work of scholarship Shaikh Ibn Ashur critiques and updates the work of the master in the *maqāṣid al-sharīʿah*, al-Shāṭibī, who dominated scholarship in the last half of the 8th century hijra until his death in 790, almost exactly a century before Columbus "discovered" America. As a Mālikī jurist, Abū Isḥāq Ibrāhīm b. Mūsā al-Shāṭibī built on the intellectual efforts of his Hanbali predecessor, Ibn Qayyim al-Jawziyyah, who died half a century earlier, because both of these two *madhhabs*, more than the Ḥanafīs and Shāfiʿīs, emphasized the inner purpose of acts rather than merely their form. The corresponding dichotomy between the intent and

[1] Ihsan Yilmaz, "Chapter 13: Inter-Madhhab Surfing, Neo-Ijtihad, and Faith-Based Movement Leaders," Peri Bearman *et al.*, *The Islamic School of Law*, pp. 191-206.

the letter of the law, which exists in all religions but to my knowledge has never been studied from an interfaith perspective, had recently split the Roman Catholic Church both internally and from the Eastern Orthodox Church and thereby consolidated the permanent hostility between the Neo-Roman and Byzantine empires.

Ibn Ashur's preface to his master work begins with the statement, "Nobody would contest that the provisions and ordinances of any divine law (*sharīʿah*) instituted for humankind aim at certain objectives intended by God, the Lawgiver. It is proven beyond doubt that God does not act in vain, as plainly shown in His fashioning of creation. Thus, we are informed in the Qur'an: 'For [thus it is:] We have not created the heavens and the earth and all that is between them in mere idle play. None of this have We created without [an inner] truth: but most of them do not understand it' (Qur'an: 44:38-39) … Moreover, one of the most important qualities of human beings is their God-given disposition for, and acceptability of, civilization, whose greatest manifestation is the making of laws to regulate their lives."[1]

This is precisely why jurisprudence goes to the heart of cultural identity and forms the ultimate arena for either cooperation or clash among civilizations.

Once one accepts the premise that purpose is paramount, one must decide which of the many possible purposes of civilization is number one. The eighteenth-century Whig movement in England, which spawned the American Revolution based on the deeply spiritual Scottish Enlightenment, established order, justice, and freedom as the trinity of ultimate purpose in any civilization. America's founders in the Preamble to the Constitution reordered this to

---

[1] Muhammad al-Tahir Ibn Ashur, *Treatise on Maqāṣid al-Sharīʿah*, translated by Mohamed El-Tahir El-Mesawi (Herndon/London: The International Institute of Islamic Thought, 1427H/2006CE), p. 3.

read justice, order, and liberty, none of which is possible without the others.[1]

Ibn Ashur followed up the above quotation from the Qur'an with the statement, "God sent messengers and revealed laws (*sharāi'i'*) only for the purpose of establishing human order,"[2] by which Ibn Ashur was referring to the Qur'anic concept of *furqān* or "balance" whereby persons can distinguish and weigh right and wrong and live together in equity by avoiding what he calls "the extremes of excessiveness (*ifrāṭ*) and negligence (*tafrīṭ*)."[3]

For "order" he uses the word *niẓām*, which refers to the order of a string of pearls and to constitutional law (*niẓām asāsī*). He uses this term as a synonym for human nature or a person's natural disposition (*khilqah*) to maintain the inward (*bāṭin*) and the outward (*ẓāhir*), the soul and body, in balance.[4] This is known as *fiṭrah nafsiyyah* and *fiṭrat Allāh*, as reflected in the Qur'an 95:4, "We have created man in the best of moulds (*aḥsan taqwīm*)," free to follow the wisdom of divine revelation "for the orderly functioning of the world," but free also, as indicated in 94:4, to "sink to the lowest of the low (*asfala sāfilīn*)."[5]

He refers to *niẓām al-ḥaqq* as the divine order in the Sharīʿah, which, in turn, is a synonym also for *ṣalāḥ* and *maṣlaḥah* in the sense of righteousness and setting things to rights in contrast to corruption.[6] Ibn Ashur even suggests that one higher purpose or *maqṣūd* of the Sharīʿah is the preservation of the *fiṭrah*, since "it is the inner person that actually motivates one to righteous deeds," and "human beings have a natural disposition for

---

[1] *The Constitution of the United States of America as Amended* (Washington: United States Government Printing Office, 2007), p. 1.

[2] Ibn Ashur, *Treatise*, p. 3.

[3] Ibid., p. 87.

[4] Ibid., p. 81.

[5] Ibid., p. 83.

[6] Ibid., pp. 92-96.

perfection."[1]

This contrasts starkly with the positivist concept of order, which refers exclusively to stability through material dominance, superficial security, and short-term expediency without any reference to morality and the Divine Will. This is what Ibn Ashur means by the term *jāhiliyyah* or "law of pagan ignorance" referred to in the Qur'an 5:50.[2]

The entire purpose of classical Islamic jurisprudence, according to Ibn Ashur's *maqāṣid* paradigm, is to raise awareness and respect for *Tawḥīd*, which is the coherent order in diversity that points to the Oneness of its Creator, and to strengthen one's *taqwā* or love of God.

Two of the notable positions of Ibn Ashur were his warning against the doctrine of abrogation, whereby one part of the Qur'an can abrogate another rather then merely augment it, and the doctrine of necessity, whereby the inner or higher purposes of the Sharīʿah were to be invoked only when the external regulations of the Sharīʿah made no sense in the given circumstances. According to the doctrine of necessity, for example, the right to life, *ḥaqq al-hayāh*, is to be applied to eliminate the prohibition against eating pork if one is starving in the desert in the presence of pigs. In Ibn Ashur's system of thought it was incorrect to say that out of necessity the Sharīʿah did not apply, when one could more easily say that the duty to respect life as a universal principle of the Sharīʿah took precedence over the duty to respect health, both of which still applied but with different priorities. Ibn Ashur warns that following the Ẓāhirī reliance on examining individual words without contextually normative content, which led to the doctrine of necessity, "might eventually deny the relevance and applicability of Islamic Sharīʿah at every time and in every

[1] Ibid., pp. 85, 94-95.
[2] Ibid., p. 194.

place."[1] Although Ibn Ashur did recognize a very limited use of abrogation as an interpretative technique[2] he warned that the doctrines of abrogation and necessity could eliminate the coherence not only of the Qur'an but of the entire system of Islamic philosophy of jurisprudence (*maqāṣid al-sharīʿah*) and law (*fiqh*).

The standard set of the *sharʿī* higher purposes, known as *maqāṣid*, and as universals or *kulliyyāt*, and as essentials or *ḍarūriyyāt*, was formulated by Abū Ḥāmid al-Ghazālī in his book *al-Mustasfā* in the early classical period during the fifth Hijra century as *ḥaqq al-dīn* (protection of religion), *ḥaqq al-nafs* (or *nufūs*, protection of the person), *ḥaqq al-nasl* (or *ansāb*, protection of lineage or the family), *ḥaqq al-māl* (or *amwāl*, protection of property), and *ḥaqq al-ʿilm* (or *ʿaql*, *ʿuqūl*, protection of the right to knowledge and critical reason).[3] Others were advanced over the years, such as preserving honor (*ḥifẓ al-ʿirḍ*), which was emphasized during the late classical period of Islam by perhaps the leading Ḥanbalī theoretician of the *maqāṣid*, Najm al-Dīn ibn ʿAbd al-Qawīyy al-Ṭūfī, who preceded the last great Islamic scholar, al-Shāṭibī, by half a century,[4] but these "add-ons" were not taught in places like al-Azhar.

All of the *maqāṣid* were induced by human reason from the two major sources of revelation, the Qur'an and *aḥādīth*, and therefore were thought to be subject to further *ijtihād* or human reason in expanding their number, redefining them, or reordering priorities. Unfortunately, in the Sunnī world, the doctrine of *taqlīd* or mindless following of earlier scholars gained dominance shortly after al-Shāṭibī's death. This "closing of the door of *ijtihād*" killed the entire concept of *maqāṣid al-sharīʿah* and shut down the creativity and dynamism of Islamic

---

[1] Ibid., p. 63.
[2] Ibid. p. 290.
[3] Abū Ḥāmid al-Ghazālī, *al-Mustasfā min ʿIlm al-Uṣūl,* ed. Muhammad Sulayman al-Ashqar (Beirut: Mu'assassat al-Risālah, 1997), vol. 1, p. 417.
[4] Ibn Ashur, *Treatise*, p. 118.

civilization for six hundred years. Ibn Ashur sought to revive it by renewing the *maqāṣid* as a paradigm of thought and as the core of the *sharʿī* systems analysis that six centuries earlier had produced the first code of human rights. This sophisticated paradigm of human responsibilities and corresponding human rights has never been matched since then or even rivaled by any other legal system.

For six hundred years, until the advent of Ibn Ashur, any attempt in the Sunnī world to expand or in any way alter the standard formulation of the *maqāṣid* by what Ibn Ashur called *istiqrā'* (translated as inductive examination or thematic inference),[1] as distinct from *istinbāṭ* or "juristic deduction," was considered to be the grossest *bidʿah* or condemnable innovation and to disqualify the guilty scholar from any teaching position. In fact, this prohibition obtained almost universally in the Sunnī world until quite recently in the 20th century, which is why the very concept of universal principles of jurisprudence has been almost universally unknown. Perhaps the major contribution of the International Institute of Islamic Thought has been to select, translate, and publish the classics in the field of jurisprudence or normative Islamic law and volumes of commentary, including the 441-page book, *Imām al-Shāṭibī's Theory of the Higher Objectives and Intents of Islamic Law* by Ahmad al-Raysuni, with a foreword by the principal pioneer in this field, Dr. Taha Jabir al-Alwani, who is one of the IIIT's early founders and has long been a leading member of the World Fiqh Council in Makkah.

Perhaps the most daring of Ibn Ashur's teachings was his redefinition of the primary *maqṣūd*, *ḥaqq al-dīn*, from its narrowly conceived meaning of "protect the true religion" to "respect and protect freedom of religion," thereby recognizing the principle stated again and again throughout the Qur'an that all paths to God are legitimate providing only that one is aware of God

[1] *Ibid.*, p. 5 & 57.

(*taqwā*), recognizes the justice of God both in this world and the next (*qadr)*, and performs good works (*ṣāliḥāt*). Freedom of religion is important in two other *maqāṣid*, namely, the duty to respect human dignity (*ḥaqq al-karāmah*), including gender equity, and to respect freedom of thought, speech, and association (*ḥaqq al-ʿilm*).

The introduction of freedom as a new *maqṣid* might be considered, however, as a spin-off from *ḥaqq al-ḥurriyyah*, which is the duty to respect political self-determination of both persons and nations. The generic concept of freedom does not appear as a term in the Qur'an, but it is inherent as a result of reasoning from its specific components. Ibn Ashur uses as an example of such "inductive inference… the examination of the repeated commands to free slaves, which means that realizing and implementing freedom is one of the higher objectives of the Sharīʿah."[1] He concludes his chapter on the "Methods of Establishing *Maqāṣid al-Sharīʿah*" with the statement by al-Shāṭibī, "In instituting the commands (*aḥkām*), the Lawgiver [God] has primary and secondary objectives. Some of these are explicitly stated (*manṣūṣ*), some merely alluded to, while others are to be inferred from the texts. We therefore conclude from this that whatever is not clearly stated but can be arrived at from induction, is intended by the Lawgiver."[2]

Ibn Ashur was acutely aware that human rights have not been part of the traditional Muslim's lexicon, but also aware of the fact that the concept of human rights is new in the history of human thought. This concept is a product of the secular thought that originated in the European Renaissance, which was a unique movement to liberate humankind from religion. Most people still view human rights in a religious context. What we today call human rights were always conceived to be the result of virtues. Rights were considered to be the result of carrying

---

[1] Ibid., p. 17.
[2] Ibid., p. 20.

out responsibilities, not as ultimate ends in themselves. The concept of rights, other than the rights of God, was even considered to be a false god. The objective was not to pursue freedom from moral values, as in positivist law, but to practice the values that produce freedom and have been taught in all the world religions.

Classical American thought perfectly illustrates the Islamic position. Thomas Jefferson warned that no people can remain free unless they are properly educated, that education consists primarily in learning virtue, and that no people can remain virtuous unless their entire personal and social lives are infused with awareness and love of God. It is noteworthy that the U.N. Declaration of Human Rights carefully does not refer to God or morality because the Soviet delegate, Maxim Litvinov, refused to sign it unless all references to religion were eliminated.

Within the religious context of both classical American and classical Islamic thought, which is universal in human history, human rights have always been explored and developed as part of the higher concept of justice. Justice is the most universal value in all civilizations, which is why there is so much negative reaction to the failure of American policy-makers to include freedom and democracy within the concept of justice as a higher paradigm of thought.

The core teaching of the Qur'an, though Ibn Ashur did not cite it in his magnum opus, is contained in *surah al-Anʿām* 6:115: *wa tammat kalimatu Rabbika ṣidqan wa ʿadlan,* "The Word of your Lord is perfected and completed in truth and justice."

The purpose of all religion is to empower the truth, which exists independently of human beings but requires religion in order to be translated into principles of compassionate justice. Justice therefore is not produced by majority vote but is transcendent. The classical study of justice is heuristic in the sense that it seeks knowledge about the sources, nature, and praxis of justice, with the challenges lying more in the present as a means to build on the best of the past in search of a better future.

In highly simplified explanation of what required several hundred pages in Ibn Ashur's book on the subject, the architectonics of justice in the Islamic Sharīʿah consist of a hierarchy of levels proceeding from the general to the specific. The highest are the *maqāṣid ḍarūriyyah*, also known as ultimate purposes or *maqāṣid ʿāliyah*. The intermediary or secondary, which spell out and serve as means to implement the *maqāṣid ḍarūriyyah*, are the *ḥājjiyyāt*, also known as *maqāṣid qarībah*. The tertiary level, known as *taḥsīniyyāt*, might be compared to the specific courses of action in program planning.

Differences in interpretation depend in part on whether one is referring to the *maqāṣid* narrowly as law or more broadly as functional guidelines for public policy. The strictest definitions are called *maṣlaḥah muʿtabarah*, the broader as *istiṣlāḥ*, and the broadest as *istiḥsān*.

The *maqāṣid* that seem to be recognized today by general *ijmāʿ* or consensus are seven in number, consisting of *ḥaqq al-dīn* and three related pairs. These form the chapter headings of a book that I have been asked to write, because they are important in both classical American and classical Islamic thought.

The highest priority of the seven irreducibly highest principles is *ḥaqq al-dīn*. This can lead one from the bare level of tolerance expressed in the phrase "I won't kill you yet," to the level of diversity embodied in the phrase, "I can't stand you, but you are here, and I can't do much about it," all the way to the level of pluralism, in which one welcomes those of other religions with the insight, "We have so much to learn from each other because we each have so much to offer."

The first of the three pairs consists of *ḥaqq al-nafs* and *ḥaqq al-nasl*. The first of these, *ḥaqq al-nafs* or *ḥifẓ al-nafs*, requires respect for the human person. At its secondary level it requires respect for life itself (*ḥaqq al-ḥayāh*), including the tertiary principles of the just war doctrine, "because the well-being of society and preservation of the order of the world depend on the sanctity and protection of human souls under all conditions."[1] The second one, *ḥaqq al-nasl,* was reinterpreted by Ibn Ashur to mean not merely respect for one's progeny but respect for the nuclear human family and every level of community all the way to the human species. This introduces the principle of subsidiarity, which recognizes that legitimacy expands upwards from community or nation to state, and not the reverse as in positivist international law and in American occupation policy in Afghanistan and Iraq.

The second set consists of responsibilities that deal with institutionalizing economic and political justice. These are, respectively, *ḥaqq al-māl* and *ḥaqq al-ḥurriyhah.* Both emphasize subsidiarity and self-determination. Ibn Ashur has revolutionary things to say about these two, perhaps even more than on the other five.

The third pair of *maqāṣid* consists of *ḥaqq al-karāmah* and *ḥaqq al-ʿilm.* These are the duties, respectively, to respect human dignity, including especially gender equity based on distinguishing nurture from nature, and the duty to respect knowledge, including the secondary level of *ḥājiyyāt* requiring implementation through freedom of thought, publication, and assembly.

The major place where Ibn Ashur hints that reinterpretation equivalent to abrogation might be in order is Qur'an 4:34 in view of the Prophet Muhammad's strong aversion to the interpretation that calls for chastising one's wife by beating her *(ḍaraba).*[2] The translator helps him out by referring to the publication by the president of the International Institute of Islamic Thought, AbdulHamid AbuSulayman, *Marital Discord: Recapturing the Full Islamic Spirit of Human Dignity*, in which AbuSulayman points out that the term *ḍaraba* has a

---

[1] Ibid., p. 98.
[2] Ibid., p. 145.

dozen different meanings in the Qur'an and that the basic meaning is not 'to beat' but 'to separate'.[1] In his chapter on the family, Ibn Ashur emphasizes that in Islam marriage is not a mere contract with the wife as an object, as it was in the period of *jāhiliyah*, but a sacred bond with a religious purpose.[2] The duty of the husband to support his wife [in every way], according to Ibn Ashur, is part of *infāq*, which is the natural inclination of every person to give rather than merely take in life.[3]

In the field of Islamic economics, which for many decades was and still is dominated by the Marxist paradigm of thought among most Muslim intellectuals, both liberals and conservatives, Ibn Ashur thundered that Marxism is un-Islamic in theory and would be catastrophic in practice.

His most radical proposal in this field in his magnum opus published in 1946 was that wealth in capital intensive economies is created by capital rather than by labor. He thereby stood Karl Marx on his head, who had asserted, contrary to all evidence, that labor is the only factor in wealth creation and that capital is merely a "congealed form" of it. The so-called labor theory of value justified the expropriation of all private ownership of capital by the state on behalf of the workers, who otherwise would be doomed forever to the status of wage-slaves.

Marx recognized the evils of the wealth gap and correctly predicted that in an age of globalization it would continue indefinitely without major changes in human institutions. The principal evil of Marxism was its refusal to recognize the universal human right of every individual to earn from ownership of capital in a capital-intensive age when almost all wealth is produced by machines and only peripherally by their

---

[1] AbdulHamid A. AbuSulayman, *Marital Discord: Recapturing the Full Islamic Spirit of Human Dignity Through the Higher Objectives of Islamic Law* (Herndon/London: The International Institute of Islamic Thought, 2nd edn, 1423AH/2003CE), pp. 19-23.
[2] Ibn Ashur, *Treatise*, p. 152.
[3] Ibid. p. 260.

operators. It therefore failed to recognize that the institutions of society can and should be perfected to make possible the broadening of capital ownership and even its universality as a fundamental human right.

Ibn Ashur devoted an entire chapter of his book to his introduction of a new *maqṣad* which he termed "equality," based on the teaching that "Islam is fundamentally the religion of nature (*dīn al fiṭrah*)."[1] This *maqṣad* calls for equality in the two major categories of *maṣāliḥ* intended by the Sharīʿah; "[i]t thus becomes clear that human beings in the Sharīʿah are equal with regard to what is indispensable (*ḍarūrī*) and necessary (*ḥājī*)."[2]

He related the *maqṣād* of equality to the *maqṣūd* of freedom in a statement very pertinent to the current institution of wage slavery among those who do not have personal, individual ownership of the means of production (including entire nations in hopeless debt from interest-burdened financing) and are dependent on those who own capital for their survival. He wrote, "Having one's hands tied describes a person who, owing to powerlessness, poverty, lack of protection, or pressing need, is driven into a situation similar to that of a slave, in which he or she is subject to the will of someone else in all his or her dealings. One is thus deprived of all sense of self-respect and condemned to accept humiliation."[3]

He included in the *maqāṣid* of equality and freedom the principle of equality of opportunity and associated it with access to and preservation of private wealth. He insisted accordingly that justice calls for free markets and transparency in all transactions. He considered that respect for private property in the means of production and its preservation and safe-guarding (*ḥifẓ*) form the core principle of *ḥaqq al-māl* and a key to both personal and community prosperity. In this regard he quoted

---

[1] Ibid., p. 146.
[2] Ibid., p. 147.
[3] Ibid., p. 155.

the Qur'anic verse 9:41: "and strive hard in God's cause with your possessions and your lives."[1] He posited as a basic principle of subsidiarity that "the preservation of private wealth leads eventually to the preservation of the community's wealth, because the preservation of the whole is achieved by preserving its constituent parts."[2] This principle applies to self-determination in both economics and politics.

Ibn Ashur was almost a century ahead of his time by inventing not merely binary economics but trinary or three-factor economics, which is critical to such tools of expanded capital ownership as community investment corporations. As he wrote, earning (*takassub*) "depends on three primary factors (*uṣūl*): 1) land (*arḍ*), 2) labor (*ʿamal*), and 3) financial capital (*ra's al-māl*)," while owning (*tamalluk*) "is the basis of wealth formation by humans."[3]

He was not equipped to devise specific institutional means to create money and credit based on future rather than on past savings, which is the key to modern binary and trinary economics. His framework, however, leads inevitably to the concept that it is a universal human right for every person to participate in owning productive wealth. This leads to the concept of social justice, according to which it is a universal responsibility of individuals working together in moral community through government to perfect existing institutions in order to make this possible. This is a community obligation or *farḍ kifāyah.*[4]

Ibn Ashur devotes several chapters in his magnum opus to financial transactions in which he reaches clear conclusions on addressing the superficial results of underlying institutional inequities. Thus, he notes that "Islam abolished enslavement in

---

[1] Ibid., p. 172.

[2] Ibid., p. 121

[3] *Ibid.*, p. 282-282

[4] *Ibid.*, pp. 221-225.

payment of debt, a practice that was part of the Roman law,"[1] in which human beings had become 'things'. His conclusions, however, make it clear that fundamental reform in the creation of money and credit designed to broaden rather than constantly narrow the ownership of productive wealth in a globally capital-intensive world is an essential objective of compassionate justice. He was perhaps too far ahead of his time in recognizing that the appellation "the dismal science" applies especially to Islamic economics, with its obsession about the single word *ribā.* He offered hope, however, by stating: "if some or all of the scholars of a given period fail to discover some or all of these objectives, this does not necessarily mean that the scholars who come after them will also fail."[2]

A current example of this hopeful opportunity concerns the ownership of the oil in the Fertile Crescent (nowadays known as Iraq). Ibn Ashur cites the Qur'anic verse 2:29, "He it is Who has created for you all that is on earth," in support of his statement that, "this Qur'anic text stipulates explicitly that all the bounties of the world are the right of humankind."[3] Whatever is owned by state power (*sulṭān*) that could be owned privately therefore should be owned individually as part of a process of expanding capital ownership and narrowing the wealth gap within and among countries. In Iraq this would mean that the oil resources there should be privatized through individual, inalienable voting shares of stock to every person resident there, so that every Sunnī, Shīʿī, and Kurd would have an equal vested interest in maintaining a federal government committed to protecting the profitability of their major source of income against foreign exploitation.

Ibn Ashur discusses the ultimate crime of *ḥirābah*, which is the attack by highway robbers on an entire people; he defines it

---

[1] *Ibid.*, p. 157.
[2] *Ibid.*, p. 66.
[3] *Ibid.*, p. 238.

as "the waging of war."[1] He quotes the sayings of the Prophet Muhammad, "No Muslim's property should be allowed to be taken from him without his own accord," and "Whoever is killed while protecting his property is a martyr."[2]

Ibn Ashur states that he had three objectives in writing his masterpiece, which are: 1. To present the *maqāṣid* paradigm as a frame of reference for both Muslim and non-Muslim students of Islam; 2. To combat extremism and counter hate-filled fanaticism by developing enlightened *ijmāʿ* or consensus among Muslim jurisprudents based on the underlying universal wisdom (*ḥikmah*) of the Sharīʿah (to be distinguished from *ʿilm al-ḥikmah* or the science of philosophical epistemology), including the *ādāb* or polite virtues of leniency and ease (*samāḥah* and *takhfīf*); and 3. To institute a process of global reform (*iṣlāḥ ʿāmm*) for which reason he has emphasized the highest transcendent good of the human community known as *maṣāliḥ*,[3] in contradistinction with the secular utilitarian, individualistic, and "democratic" concept of "the greatest good for the greatest number."

Ibn Ashur has left the subjects of faith (*ʿaqīdah*), spirituality, and personal morality to another of his books, *Uṣūl al Niẓẓm al-Ijtimāʿī fī al-Islīm*, which awaits competent translation and elegant publication. This volume expands on some of the *maqāṣid*, with detailed discussion on the freedom of religion (*ḥurriyat al-iʿtiqād*) and on freedom of expression (*ḥurriyat al-aqwāl*) as part of the freedom for knowledge (*ḥaqq al-ʿilm*).

Sophia Perennis

The most profound of the recent books addressing the past, present, and future of existential clash or cooperation within and among civilizations is the monumental, 558-page, *Festshrift*, entitled *Reason and Inspiration in Islam: Theology, Philosophy, and*

---

[1] *Ibid.*, p. 73.
[2] *Ibid.*, p. 296.
[3] *Ibid.*, pp. 3-4, 56-57, 59, 95, & 366.

Mysticism in Muslim Thought, Essays in Honour of Hermann Landolt, edited by Todd Lawson and published by the Institute of Ismā'īlī Studies in London, 2005. This magnum opus on a major world religion was well worth the more than fifty hours required to read, annotate, and index the work of many scholars, both Ismailis and others, who have devoted their lives to exploring a thousand years of scholarship on the interdependent roles of reason and inspiration in seeking out the Will of God. This task is essentially jurisprudential, because the paradigm of all Islamic thought, and indeed of all religion, is the search for a higher reality of universal truth accessible to persons and communities as guidance for a normative system of compassionate justice.

This collection of studies, each one a model of careful scholarship on the historical development of what is known as Shī'ism and especially of its Ismā'īlī branch, is particularly interesting for the typical American who believes only what he or she has directly experienced and is attracted by the traditionalist Islamic emphasis on immediate awareness and love of God and on its natural manifestation in the search for universal justice. This independence of spirit is why the typical American *ḥanīf* or Muslim by primordial *fiṭrah*, like those in Makkah fourteen hundred years ago, is skeptical of all institutionalized religion but eager to learn about the deeper insights that are obscured in all religions by identity politics. Of course, this is also the reason why ethnic and ideological Muslims from abroad distrust American converts and why such distrust, especially among African Americans, often is reciprocated.

Mysticism is at the core of all religion, including often lapses into superstition and polytheism, which is precisely why a major purpose of divine revelation is to bind it by right reason. The tension between these two capabilities of the human being, the esoteric and the exoteric, is what gave rise in the Muslim world to Sufism.

All the schools or *ṭarīqahs* of Sufism, with the single

exception of the Shādhili *ṭarīqah* from North Africa which provided all the terminology used by Saint John of the Cross, arose in Asia beyond the purvey of Western empires. This may explain why the Arabs almost universally declare that the Lord Buddha was a *kāfir* or heathen, whereas most Muslims from Persia to the Pacific consider him to be not only a Muslim but a prophet.[1]

The magisterial work, *Reason and Inspiration in Islam,* explicates Shīʿism as a path to compassionate justice in the form of what scholars might, but never have, called *ʿilm al-ʿadl*, the combined esoteric/exoteric science of jurisprudence. In point of fact, though not by intention, this tour de force presents a chronological history of Sufism in four stages: Classical Islam, Early Medieval, Later Medieval, and Pre-Modern and Modern.

Following European custom, whereby the individual professor rather than the educational institution carries maximum prestige, this undertaking was prepared by the former students of Hermann Landolt in his honor as a foremost advocate of what nowadays is often termed the *Sophia Perennis* or science of the permanent things. Landolt started his career in his hometown, Basel, Switzerland, where he wrote his dissertation in its then dominant environment of post-war existentialism epitomized by Karl Jaspers and Karl Barth. These were identified as the two leading beasts of the Anti-Christ (*bête noire*) by my professor at the time, the famous Roman Catholic theologian Romano Guardini at the University of Munich, where I was the first American student at a German university after World War II. Landolt left this dead-end corner of intellectual life to earn another diplome under Henry Corbin at the Sorbonne. In 1964 he moved to McGill's Institute of

[1] This is why the Saudi perversion of the Abdullah Yusuf Ali's rendering of the meanings of Qur'an, which has been donated in millions of copies around the world, eliminated the esoteric from Ali's original translation, including his footnote to *Sūrah al-Tīn* indicating that the term *tīn* may refers to the Bo Tree under which the Buddha received enlightenment.

Islamic Studies in Montreal, Canada, founded ten years earlier by Wilfred Cantwell Smith, where Landolt spent the next thirty-five years as a "Persianist" exploring Islamic mysticism, including the controversial subject of *waḥdat al wujūd*, about which I have published an extensive critique in *www.theamericanmuslim.org*, and the legacy of the leading mystical jurisprudents. These ranged from Imām Ja'far al-Ṣādiq, who founded the first of the major schools of Islamic law, and the early Ismā'īlī philosopher Abū al-Ḥasan al-Hujwīrī (Datta Ganjbaksh), the author of *Kashf al-Maḥjūb*, which was the first history of *taṣawwuf* and introduced me to Islam during a two-week *khalwah* on top of a mountain in New Hampsure; to Suhrawardī, who led the cause of *ijtihād* during the Dark Ages; to William Chittick, Toshihiko Izutsu, Seyyed Hossein Nasr, and many others, who carried the flame of *sophia perennis* in the face of the cold winds that threaten to bring on the intellectual winter of a global *nakbah* today.

The studies in this book reflect amazing detective work by many young scholars uncovering the interconnections among the seminal spiritual and intellectual leaders of Islam's Southwestern and Central Asian heartland over the past more than one thousand years, as well as the historical backdrop of their respective eras.

Since this is a compilation for scholars by scholars, the reader would be well advised first to read Seyyed Hossein Nasr's chapter, "The Spectrum of Islam" in his book, *The Heart of Islam*, as background in order to distinguish the more orthodox intellectual and spiritual leaders among the Shī'a from the less orthodox and to identify the movements that originated from the latter but developed into sects within Islam and even into new religions outside its widest boundaries. For example, the *Akhbaris*, mentioned in the Harvard Law School publication on schools of law, flourished in the middle Safavid period (early 1600s) but spawned the Shaykhi movement of the early Qajar period (1700s), which gave rise in the early 1800s to the new

Bahai religion. This modernist response to Western cultural imperialism essentially reversed the mindset of its origins by developing the anti-intellectual piety of the *Akhbaris* into a form of 21st-century post-modernism.[1]

The more mundane backdrop, which is available in textbook accounts of events and their relation to political, military, economic, and sociological trends, is considered by the young scholars only as a framework in which the true prime movers of civilization worked in seeking the higher realities (*ḥaqā'iq*) of the permanent things that have always transcended the ephemeral. Like the great river of Heraclitus, discussed by Ismaʿīl Rājī al-Fārūqī in his book, *Meta-Religion: A Framework for Islamic Moral Theology,* which I was able to rescue from oblivion after his death and publish in 2000,[2] one never steps in the same river again, but the water never ends. New intellectual and political flotsam is always flowing out to the sea, but the life-giving water is always recycling at both its origin and end by God's will.

The knowledge encompassed within the gathering of thirty-eight life-long scholars on Islam in this symposium on reason and inspiration should not be summarized but rather experienced. Here it may be sufficient merely to suggest that a common thread running throughout the symposium is the insight that theology and philosophy are not ends but preliminary paths to mysticism, which in all the world religions is based on awareness that intuition is the highest human faculty, because it has immediate access to the highest reality, unlike sense experience and reason, which are merely mediate. As Golam Dastagir, a Muslim professor of philosophy at Jahangirnagar in Dakka, defines it, "Knowledge by intuition

---

[1] Seyyed Hossein Nasr, *The Heart of Islam: Enduring Values for Humanity* (New York: HarlperCollins Publishers, 2002), pp. 55-112.

[2] Shaeed Ismaʿil Raji al Faruqi, *Meta-Religion: A Framework for Islamic Moral Theology* (Washington, Virginia: Institute for Strategic Studies, 2000).

is immediate in the sense that the subject is merged in the object."[1] This is what mystics in most religious traditions usually express in their path to the Supreme Reality or God. Along the journey to that destination, "the mystic's first and foremost activity is love, which is higher even than acts of complete surrender and supreme perception," a status arrived at through a process of contemplation, rememberance of God, and spiritual purification of the heart, according to Muslim Ṣūfīs.[2] Often, this is connected in the language of mystics with the notion of self-annihilation, or *fanā'*, which means "union of the sould with the divine nature of God."[3] According to Dastagir this "view is shared by the Christian mystic, Meister Eckhart, who says, 'I receive God into myself, and through love I enter into Him… We are transformed into God, so that we may know Him as He is'."[4]

"Truth can be understood," Golam Dastagir writes, "not just in the remembrance of God through prayer but in the realization of God in the pure heart, in which there is no difference between the knower, the known, and the knowledge. Communion of the individual soul with the Divine is the ultimate goal of human life." However, he points out, it should not be forgotten tha the "methods of reaching this goal vary according to peoples' customs, cultures, and beliefs," but what matters most is to "purify our souls from the pollution of blind bondage to world nefarious activities." Dastagir then concludes that the cause of most conflict in the world today is the failure of religious people to recognize this, which is why they are vulnerable to emotions of despair, fear, and hatred.[5]

We fear the specter of growing chasm between civilizations

---

[1] Golam Dastagir, "The Global Mystical Union", *The World and I: Innovative Approaches to Peace* (Winter 2006), p. 45.

[2] *Ibid.*, pp. 46-47.

[3] *Ibid.*, pp. 48.

[4] *Ibid.*

[5] *Ibid.*, p. 50.

in an age of advanced technologies, but Dastagir warns, "the human mind-set is at the center of all contentions and conflicts among divergent faiths and nations... Our first and foremost endeavor should be to bridge the chasm between God and humanity."[1]

This is the task of *ʿilm al-ʿadl*, the science of compassionate justice, which is based on the cycle of apophatic spirituality (the *via negativa* associated with *islām*), cataphatic spirituality (the *via positiva* or "yes" stage of the spiritual path associated with *īmān*), and the highest level of *iḥsān*, which completes the dynamics of *tawḥīd*. This might also be termed *ʿilm al-ʿadl al mutaʿālī* or transcendent law, similar to *al-ḥikmah al-mutaʿāliyah* of the seventeenth-century Shīʿī polymath, Ṣadr al-Dīn al-Shīrāzī, well-known as Mulla Sadra, who, like al-Ghazālī, created a major synthesis of philosophy, doctrinal Sufism or gnosis (*ʿirfān*), and theology (*kalām*) in a new school that Seyyed Hossein Nasr has translated as "transcendent theosophy."[2]

The best modern translation of *ʿilm al-ʿadl*, however, is simply "meta-law." Meta-law is the substance of what America's founders called "traditionalism." In the 379-page Summer/Fall 1987 issue of *Modern Age*, which has long been the most sophisticated journal of functionally Islamic thought in America, Henry Regnery defined traditionalism in terms of its opposite, which for more than a century, has been known as "modernism." Modernism, he says, is "the loss or rejection of the divine paradigm" and is "the desacralization of life."

This concept of traditionalism was further developed in my book, *Shaping the Future; Challenge and Response*, especially the chapter entitled "Moral Law for Cyber-Civilization: A Tawhid Cybernetic Framework for Applying Islamic Thought." The golden rule of meta-law, as first advanced in 1957 by the

---

[1] *Ibid.*, p. 50.
[2] Seyyed Hossein Nasr, *Ṣadr al-Dīn Shīrāzī and his Transcendent Philosophy* (Teheran: Imperial Iranian Academy of Philosophy, 1978), pp.85-97.

unknown mystic, Andrew Haley, is not "do unto others as you would have done unto yourself," but "Do unto others as they would have done unto them." This is a higher level of law designed for relations among sentient beings wherever they live in the universe, because it is based on loving recognition that all beings are divinely created for the same purpose and that one's capacity for self-knowledge is God's greatest gift to every sentient being. Meta-law is the basis of compassionate justice and is the ultimate arena for cooperation both within and among civilizations.

This insight was first brought home to me in 1982 when I was asked to entertain two Buddhist monks who had just arrived at the invitation of the Aspen Institute to found a Buddhist monastery as part of an interfaith community of monasteries in Baca, Colorado, which story I stated at the beginning and recount here. Not knowing how one entertains Buddhist monks deputed by the Dalai Lama for such a mission, especially those with a very tight schedule, I asked them to explain Buddhism in five minutes. They laughed and replied that one minute is more than enough. First, one must understand Hinayana Buddhism, which teaches that one must separate oneself from the material world and the search for illusory power. Next comes Mahayana Buddhism, which teaches that one can then unite with nirvana, which is nothing in the sense of no-thing, i.e., what is beyond the material. Finally comes Tantrayana Buddhism, at which level one will have an over-powering desire to bring compassionate justice to the world.

Although I was a hidden Muslim at the time, invited as an expert on native American religions, I could not help but exclaim, "*al-ḥamdu li Allāh*, you have just explained everything there is to know about the common essence of Islam and every other world religion, including the indigenous, in thirty seconds." In retrospect, I would add that these two Buddhist monks had just identified the jurisprudence of compassionate justice as the ultimate arena for either cooperation or clash among civilizations.

> Justice, Justice, thou shalt pursue (Deuteronomy 16:20).
>
> If you want peace, work for justice (Pope Paul VI).[1]
>
> And the word of your Lord is fulfilled in truth and in justice. (Q., 6:115).

Conclusion

The essence of every religion, and especially of Islam, consists of three modes or levels: ultimate reality, thought, and practice. Together they represent what one might term the religion's classical identity. The first is the level of ontology, which addresses the question "what is ultimate reality?" and the relation between the transcendent and the immanent. The second is the level of epistemology, which addresses how one knows anything and is especially important in classical Islam. The third is the level of axiology, which is the process of developing a paradigm of compassionate justice and applying it through a hierarchy of highest principles or purposes, intermediate goals and objectives, and finally courses of action.

In classical Islam, through a process of reviving the *naẓm* or coherence of divine revelation from the original source and through a process of renewal for contextual application, an architectonics based on several highest principles of respect can be derived. In one formulation of eight such principles, the first four are guiding principles, and the second four are principles of application, all of them dependent on each other.

The four guiding principles are:

1. *ḥaqq al-dīn,* respect for freedom of religion;

2. *ḥaqq al-nafs,* respect for the sacredness of the human person,

---

[1] This statement by was made by the the Pope on January 1, 1972, in his Message for the "Celebration of the Day of Peace".

including respect for life;

3. *ḥaqq al-nasl,* respect for human community at every level from the nuclear family to the nation and on to civilizations and all humanity, as well as to sentient beings elsewhere in the universe; and

4. *ḥaqq al-mahd,* respect for the physical environment.

The four principles of application are:

1. *ḥaqq al-māl,* respect for economic justice, based on expanded or even universal individual capital ownership in a world where as much as 90% of wealth is produced by capital not by human labor;

2. *ḥaqq al-ḥurriyyah,* respect for political self-determination, based on economic justice;

3. *ḥaqq al-karāmah,* respect for human dignity and honor, especially gender equity; and

4. *ḥaqq al-ʿilm,* respect for freedom of thought, publication, and assembly.

This essence and practice of Islam and of every one of the world religions is the key to distinguishing a democracy based on human fiat from a republic based on natural law as the basis for building a future of harmony throughout the world and beyond.

CHAPTER SIX

Maqāṣid al-Sharīʿah and Rethinking Political Rights in Modern Society

Louay M. Safi

Introduction

The question of political rights under Islam is the subject of intense debate in Muslim societies and beyond. Groups calling for reasserting Islam in public life have long insisted that the key to embracing Islamic values in the political sphere is to declare Sharīʿah as the official law of the land. At the heart of the debate lies the question of how the application of the Sharīʿah affects non-Muslims and women, and how such application relates, in general, to the efforts of democratization and ensuring the accountability of public officials and law makers to the public.

The tension over the application of the Sharīʿah in modern society has been highlighted recently in the adultery case against Amina Lawal by a Nigerian Sharīʿah court, the application of *ḥudūd* punishments in Kelantan, Malaysia, and most recently the prosecution of the Afghan convert to Christianity, Abdulrahman, under Afghan Sharīʿah law.

The understanding and application of the Sharīʿah, increasingly demanded by the Muslim masses, is an issue that requires special attention from contemporary Muslim scholars. Concerns over the uncritical implementation of the Sharīʿah is not limited to quarters opposed to Islam but is shared, for completely different reasons, by many Muslim scholars and jurists throughout the world. Concerns over any uncritical implementation of the Sharīʿah include the lack of clear delineation between the moral and the legal in Islamic law.

What parts of the Sharīʿah are moral, and hence fall within the realm of education and voluntary compliance, and what parts are legal, and can therefore be enforced by society? The question of delineating the legal and moral also relate to the issue of state intrusion into individual privacy, and to what extent the state can police individual morality. Also, of concern is the question of due process, rules of evidence, and individual privacy. To what extent can the court rely on circumstantial evidence to convict a person of a crime he or she has not voluntarily confessed? And more importantly, how does implementation of Sharīʿah relate to multi-religious societies, in which people of different religions live side by side and are subject to the same legal jurisdictions.

The Rise and Decline of Juristic Reasoning: *Qiyās, Istiḥsān, Istiṣlāḥ,* and *Maqāṣid*

It is not uncommon today for Muslim jurists to invoke a specific revealed text, or a direct analogy (*qiyās*) to provide answers to moral and legal issues presented to them. Yet the consideration of analogy as a primary tool of juristic reasoning represents a serious setback for the development of Islamic jurisprudence, even when focusing on the history and evolution of *fiqh*.

The use of analogy as the only tool for expanding the rules of Sharīʿah, as was done by Muḥammad ibn Idrīs al-Shāfiʿī, can be considered as an initial stage in the development of juristic reasoning. The majority of Muslim jurists employ more complex and developed means to address the issues of their times, particularly during the zenith of Islamic culture and civilization. Juristic reasoning evolved to include such approaches as *istiḥsān* (juristic preference) and *istiṣlāḥ* (unrestricted common good).

Eventually, Muslim scholars realized that the various rules (*aḥkām*) purport to achieve general principles (*qawāʿid*) and purposes (*maqāṣid*). The work of scholars such as al-Juwaynī and al-Ghazālī that led to the recognition of the five purposes of the Sharīʿah (i.e., the protection of religion, intellect, life, property, and dignity) was developed into a more sophisticated system of general and universal rules by scholars such as al-ʿIzz ibn ʿAbd al-Salām and Abū Isḥāq al-Shāṭibī.

The process of maturation of Islamic jurisprudence took several centuries. With the death of the Prophet and the emergence of new circumstances and issues never before addressed by the Qur'an or the Sunnah, the question arose as to how the Sharīʿah would subsequently be practiced. The answer lay in the exercise of juristic speculation (*ijtihād*), a practice that had already been approved by the Prophet. However, a juristic opinion (*ra'y*) arrived at by the exercise of *ijtihād* could lead only to tentative conclusions or conjectures (*ẓann*). Such judgments were thus considered by jurists as subject to abrogation and refutation. But when juristic opinions arrived at through ijtihād were subjects of general agreement by the jurists (*fuqahā'*), they were considered incontrovertible, and hence binding for the entire community. The juristic speculation of individual jurists (*ijtihād*) and their consensus (*ijmāʿ*) became, after the death of the Prophet, additional sources of the Sharīʿah, and new methods to define Divine Law.

By limiting juristic speculation (*ijtihād*) to analogical reasoning (*qiyās*), al-Shāfiʿī hoped that he could render the former more systematic and, consequently, ensure the unity of law, while opposing the efforts of those who would be tempted to usurp the law for their own personal ends. Analogy (*qiyās*), nonetheless, continued to be considered by a significant number of jurists as only one of several methods through which the principle of *ijtihād* could be practiced. The followers of the Ḥanafī and Mālikī schools of law, for instance, employed the principles of juristic preference (*istiḥsān*) and public good (*istiṣlāḥ*) respectively, regarding them as appropriate methods to derive the rules of the Sharīʿah. Apparently, the former method was employed by the Ḥanafī jurists to counteract the attempts of the Shāfiʿī jurists to limit the concept of juristic speculation to the method of reasoning by analogy. *Istiḥsān* (juristic preference) was an attempt to return to the freedom of juristic opinion (*ra'y*) that permitted jurists to make legal rulings without relying solely on analogy. For the more systematic jurists, however, rulings rendered through the application of *istiḥsān* were nothing more than arbitrary rulings or, as al-Shāfiʿī put it, "*innamā al-istiḥsān taladhudh*" (*istiḥsān* is ruling by caprice).[1]

Istiṣlāḥ (consideration of public good) was another approach employed by Mālikī, and to a lesser extent by Ḥanafī, jurists to escape the rigid form into which the Sharīʿah was gradually cast by more conservative jurists (primarily the Shāfiʿī and Ḥanbalī). The jurists who advocated the use of the *istiṣlāḥ* method argued that the principles of the Sharīʿah aimed at promoting the general interests of the community; therefore, "public good" should guide legal decisions wherever revelation was silent with regard to the question under consideration.[2]

---

[1] Muḥammad ibn Idrīs al-Shāfiʿī, *al-Risālah,* ed. Ahmed Shakir (Cairo: Dār al-Turāth, 2nd edn, 1399/1979), p.507. For further delail see: Noel J. Coulson, *A history of Islamic law* (Edinburgh: Edinburgh University Press, 1964), p.40; Malcolm Kerr, *Islamic Reform: The Political and Legal Theories of Muhammad Abduh and Rashid Rida* (Berkeley, California: University of California Press, 1966), p. 90.

[2] This view has been strongly expressed by a number of eminent scholars from the different juristic schools. See for example, Ḍiyā' al-Dīn Abū al-Maʿālī ʿAbd al-Malik b. ʿAbd Allāh b. Yūsuf al-Juwaynī, *al-Ghayyāthī: Ghiyyāth al-Umam fī Iltiyath al-Ẓulam,* ed. Abdul-Azim al-Deeb (Jeddah: Dār al-Minhāj, 3rd edn, 1432/2011); ʿIzz al-Dīn ʿAbd al-ʿAzīz b. ʿAbd al-Salām, *al-Qawāʿid al-Kubrā: Qawāʿid al-Aḥkām fī Iṣlāḥ al-Anām*, ed. Mazih Kamal Hammad & Othman Jum'ah Damiriyyah (Damascus: Dār al-Qalam, 1sr edn, 1421/2000); Najm al-Dīn al-Ṭūfī, *Risālah fī Riʿāyat al-Maṣaḥah,* ed. Ahmad Abdulhamid al-Sayih (Cairo: al-Dār al-Miṣriyyah al-Lubnāniyyah, 1413/1993), pp. 25-48; Abū ʿAbd Allāh Muḥammad b. Abī Bakr Ibn Qayyim al-Jawziyyah, *al-Ṭuruq al-Ḥukmiyyah fī al-Siyāsah al-Sharʿiyyah,* ed. Nayif bin Ahmad al-Hamad (Makkah al-Mukarramah: Dar Alam al-Fawa'id, 1st edn, 1428H); Abū Isḥāq Ibrāhīm ibn

The introduction of the tools of *istiḥsān* and *istiṣlāḥ* allowed the jurist to deal with issues that arose under more sophisticated and far removed social settings than those experienced by the early Muslim society, while preserving the basic Islamic values and attitudes. The reverting to *qiyās* in contemporary times signifies, therefore, a return to more preliminary juristic reasoning when jurists are confronted with complex issue that do not lend themselves to analogous reasoning. This requires us to reexamine the meaning of the Sharī'ah and explore how the rich body of juristic reasoning can be re-appropriated and developed for modern times.

Layers and Spheres of the Sharī'ah

The term *sharī'ah* is often used by Muslims to denote the divine guidance revealed to the Prophet Mohammad (*pbuh*). Contemporary Muslim jurists have reduced the meaning of the Sharī'ah to the various rules historically derived by Muslim scholars to expound the Qur'anic and Prophetic teachings. The bulk of these rules were elaborated on by the 5th century of the Islamic calendar (12th century CE).

The Sharī'ah was revealed to provide a set of criteria so that right (*ḥaqq*) may be distinguished from wrong (*bāṭil*). By adhering to the rules of law, the Muslims would develop a just society, superior in its moral and material quality to societies which fail to observe the revealed will of God. As such, the Sharī'ah constitutes a comprehensive moral and legal system, and aspires to regulate human behavior to produce conformity with Divine Law. Adhering to the rules and principles of the Sharī'ah not only causes the individual to draw closer to God but also facilitates the development of a just and prosperous society.

The purpose of the Sharī'ah, therefore, is to provide the

Mūsā al-Shāṭibī, *al-Muwāfaqāt fī Uṣūl al-Sharī'ah,* ed. Abd Allah Draz *et al.* (Beirut: Dār al-Kutub al-'Ilmiyyah, 1st edn, 1424/2004), vol. 1/2, pp. 7-312. R standards and criteria that would determine the ends prescribed by revelation. According to Islamic legal theory, justice, as the ultimate value that justifies the existence of law and as the ultimate criterion for the evaluation of social behavior, cannot be realized apart from the understanding of the purpose of human existence. Such understanding cannot be discovered by human reasoning, as natural law theory asserts. It must be acquired by direct exposure to the Divine Will through revelation. Therefore, justice may only be fully realized when Divine Law is recognized and implemented by society.

The question arises here as to what extent the Sharīʿah can be regarded as the manifestation of the Divine Will? To answer this question, we need first to distinguish the levels of meaning that separate the ideal from the existential in Islamic legal thought. In connection with this, the term sharīʿah may refer to any of the following four meanings.

First, law may be perceived as the eternal set of principles which reflect the Divine Will as it is related to the human situation; that is, those principles that relate to the purpose of human existence and the universal rules that must be observed by human beings to achieve that purpose.

Second, law could be regarded as the revelatory verbalization of the eternal principles in the form of a revealed word or message that discloses the Divine Will to mankind. The Qur'an, the manifestation of the Divine Will, consists of two categories of rules: universal rules (*aḥkām kulliyah*) embodied in general Qur'anic statements, and particular rules (*aḥkām farʿiyyah*) revealed in connection with specific instances, which hence may be considered as concrete applications of the universal rules.

Third, law may be viewed as the understanding of revelation as reflected in the oral and written statements of the jurists. The Qur'an was revealed over a 23-year period in piecemeal fashion in response to the various questions and problems facing the evolving Muslim community. In order to define the Divine Will in new situations never before addressed by revelation, Muslim jurists had to develop a legal theory that spelled out the Sharīʿah and establish the methods of deriving and applying its rules. The jurists had to define the overall objectives of the Sharīʿah, and, using inductive reasoning, rediscover the fundamental principles underlying the formulation of the rules of the Sharīʿah. Classical jurists had also to develop the appropriate method that could be used to define the fundamental principles of Sharīʿah and expand their application to new situations.

Finally, law could be seen as the positive rules derived from the theoretical principles of Sharīʿah and used to regulate social and individual behavior. These rules are collected in major encyclopedic works, as well as in numerous handbooks used by the several schools of law. It is this very specific and concrete meaning of law which usually comes to mind in connection with the term *Sharīʿah*.

Evidently, analogical juristic reasoning fails to distinguish the general and abstract ideals of the Sharīʿah from the specific and concrete body of doctrine. That is, it confuses the ideals embodied in the Qur'an and the practice of the early Muslim community with the rules later developed by the jurists. In fact, this confusion did not occur at the early stages of the development of the Sharīʿah but only at a later stage, after the four schools of law began to take shape during the 3rd and 4th centuries of the Islamic calendar, and finally with the formulation of the classical theory of law.

Earlier jurists, including the founders of the major schools of law, recognized the difference between the ideal and doctrinal elements of law, for they did not hesitate to reject previous legal theories and doctrines, replacing them with others. It was this distinction that ensured the dynamism of Sharīʿah and its growth during the early centuries of Islam. By constructing new legal theories and modifying old ones, the connection between the ideal and existential was maintained and the Sharīʿah was thus flexible enough to respond to the concerns of a developing society. However, when the prevailing doctrine of the 5th century was idealized, the Sharīʿah lost its flexibility, and the relationship between law and society was gradually severed. Henceforth, the efforts of the jurists were directed towards resisting any developments that would render social practices incompatible with the existing legal code, instead of modifying legal doctrines so that new social developments could be guided by Islamic ideals.

The four levels of meaning that separate the ideal from the existential elements of law enable us to see the fatal epistemological error that the proponents of the classical legal theory commit when they insist on the infallibility of the principle of *ijmāʿ*. The classical legal theory mistakenly asserts that the ideals which the law aspires to realize have been captured, once and for all, in the legal doctrines formulated by early jurists, and that classical legal doctrines, substantiated by *ijmāʿ*, have attained absolute universality. Implicit in this assertion is the assumption that legal decisions give up their subjectivity and specificity as they move away from the domain of the individual to that of the community. As they finally become the subject of juristic consensus, legal decisions acquire complete objectivity and universality.

Such a perception is manifestly faulty, for it could be true only if we ignore the historical evolution of the human experience. As long as the future state of the society, whether in the material conditions or social organization, is concealed and uncertain, law must keep the way open for new possibilities and changes. It should be emphasized here that the relationship between the third and fourth meanings of the Sharīʿah (i.e., law as interpretation and as positive rules) is dialectical and must be kept that way if law is to be able to function more effectively. For in order for the ideal to have positive effect, its universality and objectivity must be embodied in a specific and concrete doctrine. Only when the universal ideal is reduced to particular and local rules and institutions can it begin to transform the human world. However, the embodiment of the ideal in a concrete rule or institution should always be regarded as tentative, and the possibility for future re-evaluation or modification should likewise be kept open.[1]

The positive rules of the Sharīʿah as well as the legal doctrines that have been formulated by Muslim jurists are therefore tentative, because they have been formulated by fallible human beings situated in specific historical moments. The consensus (*ijmāʿ*) cannot confer universality or absoluteness on rules or decisions agreed upon by any particular generation. All that *ijmāʿ* can do is to make the rules more objective for a specific community situated in a specific time and space. The claim that the positive rules of the Sharīʿah (or more accurately the rules of *fiqh*) and Divine Will are identical is erroneous and ill-founded, for it ignores the historical significance of the legal doctrine and the human agency that has been responsible for its development.

To see how the *maqāṣid* approach to the Sharīʿah can liberate us from a literal and uncritical understanding of how the Sharīʿah relates to a multi-religious society, let us reexamine the prophetic tradition in bringing the Sharīʿah to bear on the Madīnah society he founded at the dawn of Islam.

The Formative Principles of the Madīnah State

The notion of the Islamic state advanced today by populist writers is a mixture of the nationalist structure of the modern state with the communal structure of the historical Sharīʿah. The concept of the state that emerges as a result is in complete contradiction with the nature and purpose of the polity founded by the Prophet or developed historically by successive Muslim generations. A quick review of the guiding principles of the first

---

[1] See Iredell Jenkins, *Social Order and the Limits of Law: A Theoretical Essay* (Princeton, NJ: Princeton University Press, 1980), pp. 333-335.

Islamic polity reveals the disparity between the modern state and the early Islamic polity. The principles and structures of the early Islamic polity are epitomized in the Pact or Covenant of Madīnah (*Ṣaḥīfat al-Madīnah*) that formed the constitutional foundation of the political community established by the Prophet.[1]

The Covenant of Madīnah established a number of important political principles that, formed the political constitution of the first Islamic state and defined the political rights and duties of the members of the newly established political community, Muslims and non-Muslims alike, and drew up the political structure of the nascent society. The most important principles included in this pact are:

First, that the *ummah* is a political society, open to all individuals committed to its principles and values, and ready to shoulder its burdens and responsibilities. It is not a reclusive one, whose membership rights and securities are restricted to a select few. The right to membership in the *ummah* is specified by: (1) accepting the principles of the Madīnah Covenant and manifested in the commitment to adhere to the principles of mutuality and justice; (2) declaring allegiance to the political order defined by the pact, through practical contributions and struggles to actualize its objectives and goals. Thus, allegiance and concern for public good are the principles determining the membership of the *ummah* as defined by the first article of the document: "This is a Compact offered by Muhammad the Prophet, (governing the relations) among the believers and the Muslims of Quraysh and Yathrib (Madīnah), and those who

---

[1] This important document has been preserved in its totality and details and transmitted in early classical sources. For a detailed discussion of its provenance, authenticity and transmission channels, full text, variants, and the parties involved in it, see Muhammad Hamidullah, *Majmūʿat al-Wathāʾiq al-Siyāsiyyah li'l-ʿAhd al-Nabawī wa'l-Khilāfah al-Rāshidah* (Beirut: Dār al-Nafāes, 6th edn, 1407/1987); pp. 57-62; Michael Lecker, *The "Consitution of Medina": Muhammad's First Legal Document* (Princeton, NJ: The Darwin Press, Inc., 2004), pp. 5-203. (ed.)

followed, joined, and labored with them."[1]

Second, a general framework that defined individual norms and the scope of political action within the new society but preserved the basic social and political structures prevalent then in tribal Arabia is delineated in the compact. The Compact of Madīnah preserved tribal structure, while negating tribal spirit and subordinating tribal allegiance to a morally-based legal order. As the compact declared that the nascent political community is "an *ummah* to the exclusion of all people," it approved a tribal division that had already been purged of tribal spirit epitomized by the slogan "my brethren right or wrong," subjecting it to the higher principles of truth and justice. The Compact therefore declared that the emigrants of the Quraysh, Banū al-Ḥārith, Banū al-Aws and other tribes residing in Madīnah, according "to their present customs, shall pay the blood wit they paid previously and that every group shall redeem its prisoners."[2]

Islam's avoidance of the elimination of tribal divisions can be explained by a number of factors that can be summarized in the following three points. (1) The tribal division was not a mere political division but also a social division providing its people with a symbiotic system. Therefore, the abolition of the political and social assistance provided by the tribe before developing an alternative would have been a great loss for the people in this society. (2) Apart from its being a social division, the tribe represented an economic division in harmony with the pastoral economy prevalent in the Arabian Peninsula before and after Islam. The tribal division is the ideal division of the pastoral production as it provides freedom of movement and migration in search of pasture. Any change in this pattern requires taking

---

[1] Abū Muḥammad ʿAbd al-Malik Ibn Hishām, *Al-Sīrah al-Nabawiyyah,* 4 vols., ed. Mustapha al-Saqqa, Ibrahim al-Abiyari & Abdul Hafid Shalabi (Beirut: Dār al-Jīl., 1411/1990), vol. 3, p. 34.
[2] *Ibid.*

an initiative first to change the means and methods of production. (3) Perhaps the most important factor that justified the tribal division within the framework of the *ummah* after the final message had purged the tribal existence of its aggressive and arrogant content, is the maintenance of the society and its protection from the danger of central dictatorship that might come into existence in the absence of a secondary social and political structure, and concentration of political power in the hand of a central authority.

Hence, Islam adopted a political system based on the concept of the one *ummah* as an alternative to the divisional tribal system and upheld the tribal division having cleared it from its aggressive elements. It left the question of changing the political structure to gradual development of economic and production structures. Although the Islamic revelation avoided any arbitrary directives aimed at immediate abolition of the tribal division, it criticized openly tribal and nomadic life.[1]

Third, the Islamic political system adopted the principle of religious autonomy based on the freedom of belief for all members of society. It conceded to the Jews the right to act according to the principles and rulings to which they adhered based on their belief: "'The Jews of Banū ʿAwf are one community with the believers. The Jews have their religion and the Muslims theirs." The pact emphasized the fundamentality of cooperation between Muslims and non-Muslims in establishing justice and defending of Madīnah against foreign aggression. "'The Jews must bear their expenses and the Muslims their expenses. Each must help the other against anyone who attacks the people of this Compact. They must seek mutual advice and consultation." It prohibited the Muslims from doing injustice to the Jews or retaliating for their Muslim brothers against the followers of the Jewish religion without adhering to the principles of truth and justice. "'To the Jew who follows us

[1] See for example Qur'an, 9: 97-99 and 49: 14.

belongs help and equality. He shall not be wronged nor shall his enemies be aided."[1]

Fourth, the Compact stipulated that the social and political activities in the new system must be subject to a set of universal values and standards that treat all people equally. Sovereignty in society would not rest with the rulers, or any particular group, but with the law founded on the basis of justice, goodness, and maintaining the dignity of all. The Compact also emphasized repeatedly and frequently the fundamentality of justice, goodness, and righteousness, and condemned injustice and tyranny. "They would redeem their prisoners with kindness and justice common among the believers," the Compact stated: "The God-conscious believers shall be against the rebellious, and against those who seek to spread injustice, sin, enmity, or corruption among the believers, the hand of every person shall be against him even if he be a son of one of them," it proclaimed.[2]

Fifth, the Compact introduced a number of political rights to be enjoyed by the individuals of the Madīnan state, Muslims and non-Muslims alike, such as (1) the obligation to help the oppressed, (2) outlawing guilt by association which was commonly practiced by pre-Islamic Arab tribes: "A person is not liable for his ally's misdeeds;" (3) freedom of belief: "The Jews have their religion and the Muslims have theirs;" and (4) freedom of movement from and to Madīnah: "Whoever will go out is safe, and whoever will stay in Madīnah is safe except those who wronged (others), or committed sin."[3]

---

[1] *Ibid.*
[2] *Ibid.*
[3] *Ibid.*, p. 35.

Religion and the State in Historical Muslim Society

Adhering to the guidance of revelation, the *ummah* has respected the principle of religious plurality and cultural diversity during the better part of its long history. Successive governments since the Rāshidūn period have preserved the freedom of faith and allowed non-Muslim minorities not only to practice their religious rituals and proclaim their beliefs but also to implement their religious laws according to an autonomous administrative system. Likewise, the *ummah* as a whole has respected the doctrinal plurality with both its conceptual and legal dimensions. It has resisted every attempt to drag the political power into taking sides with sectarian groups, or to prefer one ideological group to another. It has also insisted on downsizing the role of the state and restricting its functions to a limited sphere.

Anyone who undertakes to study the political history of Islam soon realizes that all political practices which violated the principle of religious freedom and plurality were an exception to the rule. For instance, the efforts of the Abbasid caliph al-Ma'mūn to impose doctrinal uniformity in accordance with the Muʿtazilite interpretations, and to use his political authority to support one of the parties involved in doctrinal disputes, were condemned by the *ʿulamā'* and the majority of the *ummah*. His efforts to achieve doctrinal homogeneity through suppression and force eventually clashed with the will of the *ummah*, which refused to solve doctrinal and theoretical problems by the sword. This compelled al-Wāthiq Billāh, the third caliph after al-Ma'mūn, to give up the role assumed by his predecessors and abandon their oppressive measures.[1]

Obviously, Muslims have historically recognized that the

---

[1] The Abbasid caliph al-Ma'mūn attempted to force the Muʿtazilite doctrine of the "creation of the Qur'an" on all Muslim scholars and clashed with Ahmad bin Hanbal and his movement over the issue. For a detailed discussion of the event, see Abū al-Faraj ʿAbd al-Raḥmān b. ʿAlī b. Muḥammad Ibn al-Jawzī, *Manāqib al-Imām Aḥmad Ibn Ḥanbal* (Cairo: Dār Hajar, 2nd edn, 1409 AH), pp. 420-30.

main objective of establishing a political system is to create the general conditions that allow the people to realize their duties as moral agents (*khulafāʾ*) and not to impose the teachings of Islam by force. We, therefore, ascribe the emergence of organizations working to compel the *ummah* to follow a narrow interpretation, and calling for the use of political power to make people obedient to Islamic norms, to the habit of confusing the role and objectives of the *ummah* with the role and objectives of the state. While the *ummah* aims to build the Islamic identity, to provide an atmosphere conducive to spiritual and mental development of the individual, and to grant him or her the opportunity to realize his or her role and aims of life within the general framework of the law, the state makes efforts to coordinate the *ummah*'s activities with the aim to utilize the natural and human resources to overcome the political and economic problems facing society.

Differentiating between the general and particular in the Sharīʿah and distinguishing between the responsibilities of the *ummah* and the state is a necessity if we want to avoid the transformation of political power into a device for advancing particular interests, and to ensure that state agencies and institutions do not arrest intellectual and social progress, or obstruct the spiritual, conceptual, and organizational developments of society.

Differentiating Civil Society and the State

Historically, legislative functions in Muslim society were not restricted to state institutions. Rather, there was a wide range of legislations related to juristic efforts at both the moral and legal levels. Since the major part of legislation relating to transactional and contractual relations among individuals is attached to the juristic legislative bodies, the judicial tasks may be connected directly with the *ummah*, not with the state. The differentiation between civil society and the state can only be maintained by dividing the process of legislation into distinct areas that reflect both the geographical and normative differentiation of political society.

The importance of the differential structure of the law is not limited to its ability to counteract the tendency of centralization of power, which characterizes the Western model of the state. Rather, it is also related to guarantees extended to religious minorities.

The Islamic model maintains the legislative and administrative independence of the followers of different religions, as the sphere of communal legislation does not fall under the governmental authority of the state. On the other hand, the majoritarian model of the democratic state deprives religious minorities of their legal independence; it insists on subjugating all citizens to a single legal system, which often reflects the doctrinal and behavioral values of the ruling majority.

The early Muslim community was cognizant of the need to differentiate law to ensure moral autonomy, while working diligently to ensure equal protection of the law as far as fundamental human rights were concerned. Thus, early jurists recognized that non-Muslims who have entered into a peace covenant with Muslims are entitled to full religious freedom, and equal protection of the law as far as their rights to personal safety and property are concerned. Muḥammad ibn al-Ḥasan al-Shaybānī states in unequivocal terms that when non-Muslims enter into a peace covenant with Muslims, "Muslims should not appropriate any of their [the non-Muslims'] houses and land, nor should they intrude into any of their dwellings. Because they have become party to a covenant of peace, and because on the day of the [peace of] Khaybar, the Prophet's spokesman announced that none of the property of the covenanter is permitted to them [the Muslims]. Also, because they [the non-Muslims] have accepted the peace covenant so as they may enjoy their properties and rights on par with Muslims."[1] Similarly, early Muslim jurists recognized the right of non-Muslims to self-determination and granted them full moral and legal autonomy in the villages and towns under their control. Therefore, al-Shaybānī, the author of the most authoritative work on non-Muslim rights, insists that the Christians who have entered into a peace covenant (*dhimmah*)—and hence became *dhimmī* (covenanters)—have all the freedom to trade in wine and pork in their towns, even though such practice is considered immoral and illegal among Muslims.[2] However, the *dhimmīs* were prohibited from doing the same in towns and villages controlled by Muslims.

Likewise, early Muslim jurists recognized the right of a *dhimmī* to hold public office, including the office of a judge and minister. However, because judges had to refer to laws sanctioned by the religious traditions of the various religious communities, non-Muslim judges could not administer law in Muslim communities, nor were Muslim judges permitted to enforce the rules of Sharīʿah laws on the *dhimmīs*. There was no disagreement among the various schools of jurisprudence on the right of non-Muslims to be ruled according to their laws; they only differed on whether the positions held by non-Muslim magistrates were judicial in nature, and hence the magistrates could be called judges, or whether they were purely political, and therefore the magistrates were indeed political leaders.[3] Al-Māwardī, hence, distinguished between two types of ministerial positions: plenipotentiary minister (*wazīr tafwīḍ*) and executive minister (*wazīr tanfīdh*). The two positions differ in that the former acts independently from the caliph, while the latter has to act on the instructions of the caliph, and within the limitations set by

---

[1] Muḥammad ibn Aḥmad ibn Sahl al-Sarakhsī, *Sharḥ Kitāb al-Siyar al-Kabīr*, 4 vols. (Pakistan: Nusrullah Mansour, 1405/1984), vol. 4, p. 1530.

[2] *Ibid.*

[3] Abū al-Ḥasan al-Māwardī, *Kitāb al-Aḥkām al-Sulṭāniyyah wa'l-Wilāyāt al-Dīniyyah* (Beirut: Dār al-Fikr, 1401/1982), p. 59.

him.[1] Therefore, early jurists permitted the *dhimmīs* to hold the office of the executive but not the plenipotentiary minister.[2]

However, while the Sharī'ah law recognized the civil and political rights and liberties of non-Muslim *dhimmī*, Sharī'ah rules underwent drastic revision, beginning from the 8th century of the Islamic calendar. This was a time of great political turmoil throughout the Muslim world. It was during this time that the Mongols invaded Central and West Asia, inflicting tremendous losses on various dynasties and kingdoms, and destroying the seat of the caliphate in Baghdad. This coincided with the Crusaders' control of Palestine and the coast of Syria. In the West, Muslim power in Spain was being gradually eroded. It was under such conditions of mistrust and suspicion that a set of provisions attributed to an agreement between the caliph Omar and the Syrian Christians were publicized in a treatise written by Ibn al-Qayyim.[3] The origin of these provisions is dubious, but their intent is clear: to humiliate Christian *dhimmīs* and to set them apart in dress code and appearance. Their impact, however, was limited, as the Ottomans, who replaced the Abbasids as the central power in the Muslim world, continued the early practice of granting legal and administrative autonomy to non-Muslim subjects.

Islam, Civil Society and the State

The modern state emerged to foster individual freedom and to protect the individual against arbitrary rule, and to ensure that the members of the political society assume full control over public institutions. To do so, the modern state found it necessary to free public institutions from the control of all exclusive groups, including organized religions. However, despite the clear desire of

[1] Ibid., pp. 20-23.
[2] Ibid., p. 24.
[3] Ibn Qayyim al-Jawziyyah, *Sharḥ al-Shurūṭ al-'Umariyyah* (Beirut: Dār al-'Ilm li'l-Malāyīn, 1381/1961).

the pioneers of the modern state to replace religious morality with civic virtue as the moral foundation of the state, secularism gradually developed anti-religious tendencies, leading to the continuous erosion of the moral consensus. The continuous erosion of morality and the rampant corruption in modern politics threaten to turn the state into an instrument in the hands of corrupt officials and their egoistic cronies.

This has prompted calls for the return of religion and religiously-organized groups into the political arena. Nowhere are these calls louder and clearer than in Muslim societies where Islamic values have historically exerted great influence on the body politic. Unfortunately, the reunion envisaged by the advocates of the Islamic state is often presented in crude and simplistic terms, as it fails to appreciate the great care that was taken by early Muslims to ensure that the state incorporates, both in its objectives and structure, the freedom and interest of all intra- and inter-religious divisions.

This calls upon Muslim scholars to engage in new thinking that aims at redefining political principles and authority. In doing so, Muslim scholars should be fully aware of the need to transcend the historical models of political organizations in Muslim society. Political structures and procedures adopted by early Muslim societies are directly linked to their social structures, economic and technological developments, and political experiences. While historical Islamic models provide a mine of knowledge for contemporary Muslims to utilize, any workable formulation of the modern Islamic model of a state that is true to Islamic values and ethos must emerge out of fresh thinking that takes into account the structure of modern society.

Islamic political thought, I believe, can make a profound contribution towards reclaiming the moral core of social life, and preserving religious traditions, without sacrificing the principle of freedom and equality promoted by the modern state.

The hallmark of the Islamic political experience is the

limitations historical Muslim society was able to place on the actions of rulers, and the presence of vigorous and robust civil society. Many of the functions the secular state assumes today were entrusted to civic institutions, including education, health and legislation. The state was mainly entrusted with matters of security and defence, and was the last resort in matters relating to dispensation of justice. This understanding of state power would potentially free religious communities from intervention of the state and state officials, who tend to enforce their religiously-based values and notions on the members of society, including those who do not share some of those values and beliefs.

The notions of individual freedom and equality are intrinsic to Islamic political thought, and those principles require that individuals have the basic civil liberties offered by the modern state. However, by freeing civil society from the heavy hand of the state, and by extending individual liberties to the community and recognizing the moral autonomy of social groups, social and religious groups under the Islamic conception of law (the Sharīʿah) would have the capacity to legislate their internal morality and affairs in their communities. While the new sphere of freedom acquired under this arrangement allows for differentiation among citizens, equality would have to be maintained as the criteria of justice in the new area of public law, and in access to public institutions—i.e., in matters that relate to the sphere of shared interests and inter-communal relations.

Apostasy Law

The issue of apostasy under Islamic law (the Sharīʿah), brought recently to public attention in the widely-publicized case of the conversion to christianity of an Afghan citizen, raises troubling questions regarding freedom of religion and interfaith relations. The prosecution by the Afghan State of an Afghan man who converted to Christianity in 1990 while working for a Christian non-governmental organization raises in the mind of many the question of the compatibility of Islam with plural democracy and freedom of religion and faith. Although the state court dropped the case under intense outside pressure, the compatibility issue has not been resolved as the judge invoked insanity as the basis for dismissing the case.[1]

The case was presented as an example of conflict between Islam and democratic governance but in many respects the case is rooted in, and influenced by, the forced secularization of Muslim society, and the absence of free debate under authoritarian regimes that currently dominate much of the Muslim world.[2] The issue of apostasy, like many other issues stemming from the application of the Sharīʿah in modern society, is rooted more in the sociopolitical conditions of contemporary Muslim societies than in Islamic values and principles. More particularly, it is rooted in the incomplete transition from traditional to modern socio-political organizations. It is rooted in the decision of many post-colonial Muslim countries to abandon traditional legal codes informed by the *Sharīʿah* in favour of European legal codes developed to suit modern European societies. The new laws were enforced by state elites without any public debate and with little attention for the need to root legal codes in public morality.

Islam is the foundation of moral commitments for the overwhelming majority of Muslims and is increasingly becoming the source of legitimacy for state power and law. Yet the post-colonial state in Muslim societies has done little to encourage debate in the area of Islamic law. The increased interest in adopting legal codes based on Islamic values leaves the majority of Muslims with outdated legal codes that were intended for societies with markedly different social and political organizations and cultures.

---

[1] *Christian Science Monitor*, March 27, 2006.
[2] *New York Times*, March 24, 2006.

Traditionalist scholars have long embraced classical positions on apostasy that consider the rejection of Islam as a capital crime, punishable by death. This uncritical embrace is at the heart of the drama in the case of the Afghan convert to Christianity, and which will more likely be repeated until the debate about Sharīʿah reform and its relevance to state and civil law is examined and elaborated by authentic Muslim voices.

Theory of Right

The Sharīʿah is essentially a moral code with few legal pronouncements, and the question of which precepts are purely moral and which have legal implications is determined through the theory of right. The widely accepted theory of right among jurists divides rights into three types: (1) Rights of God (*Ḥuqūq Allāh*): These consist of all obligations that one has to discharge simply because they are divine commands, even when the human interests or utilities in undertaking them are not apparent, such as prayers, fasting, *ḥajj*, etc.; (2) Rights shared by God and his servants (*Ḥuqūq Allāh wa-l-ʿIbād*): These include acts that are obligatory because they are demanded by God, but they are also intended to protect the public, such as *ḥudūd* law, *jihād, zakāh*, etc., and (3) Rights of God's servants (*Ḥuqūq al-ʿIbād*): These are rights intended to protect individual interests, such as fulfilling promises, paying back debts, and honouring contracts. Still, people are accountable for their fulfilment to God.[1]

As can be seen, the theory of right devised by late classical jurists—around the 8th century of the Islamic calendar—emphasizes that people are ultimately answerable to God in all their dealings. However, by using the term 'rights of God' to underscore the moral duty of the individual, and his/her

[1] ʿIzz al-Dīn Ibn ʿAbd al-Salām, *Qawāʿid al-Aḥkām* (Beirut: Dār al-Kutub al-ʿIlmiyyah, 1999), vol. 1, pp. 113-121; Abū Isḥāq Ibrāhīm ibn Mūsā al-Shāṭibī, *al-Muwāfaqāt*, ed. Abu Ubayda Mahshur Āl Salman (al-Khobar, SA: Dār Ibn ʿAffān, 1417/1997), vol. 2, pp. 539-542.

accountability before God, classical jurists obscured the fact that rights are invoked to support legal claims and to enforce the interests of the right-holder. Because the Qur'an makes it abundantly clear that obeying the divine revelation does not advance the interests of God but only those of the human being, the phrase 'rights of God' signifies only the moral obligations of the believers towards God, and by no means should they be taken as a justification of legal claims.[1] It follows that the 'rights of God' which are exclusively personal should be considered as moral obligations for which people are only answerable to God in the life to come. As such, accepting or rejecting a specific interpretation or a particular religious doctrine, and observing or neglecting fundamental religious practices, including prayer or *ḥajj*, should have no legal implications whatsoever. A legal theory in congruence with the Qur'anic framework should distinguish between moral and legal obligations and should confine the latter to public law that promotes public interests (constitutional, criminal, etc.) and private law that advances private interests (trade, family, personal, etc.).

Unless the above legal reform is undertaken, there is no way to ensure that *takfīr* (charging one with disbelief) and *zandaqah* (charging one with heresy) claims would not become a political weapon in the hands of political groups to be used as a means to eliminate rivals and opponents. Indeed, there is ample evidence to show that *zandaqah* and *takfīr* have been used by the political authorities during the Umayyad and Abbasid dynasties to persecute political dissidents.[2]

---

[1] Legal issues that require enforcement by the state deal mainly with criminal law and tort law or any conflict that involves encroachment of individual and public law. However, most of the Sharīʿah injuncitons pertain to moral and religious obligations and entail accountability before God on the day of judgement.

[2] The persecution of critical voices of the conduct of the ruling elite, such as Ghaylān al-Dimashqī and Ibn al-Muqaffaʿ, and many others was justified by demonizing those critics as *kāfir* or *zindīq*.

Reciprocity and Social Peace

The principle of reciprocity, central to all religious and secular ethics, lies at the core of the Islamic concept of justice. The Qur'an is pervaded with injunctions that encourage Muslims to reciprocate good for good and evil for evil.[1] The principle is, similarly, epitomized in the Golden Rule of the Christian faith, and has been given a secular expression in Kant's categorical imperative: "Act only on that maxim through which you can at the same time will that it become a universal law."[2]

In modern society where people of different faiths live side by side and cooperate under a system of law that recognizes their equal dignity, due attention must be given to the principle of reciprocity as the essence of justice in a multi-religious society. Any attempt by a religious community to place sanctions and apply coercion on its members who choose to convert to another religious group will place a moral obligation on the latter to defend the newcomers who choose to join their faith. Muslims would feel morally obligated to defend the right of a Jew and Christian to freely embrace Islam and, therefore, would not accept any coercive measure intended to restrict the right of Jews and Christians to convert to Islam. A Christian or a Jew who converts to Islam is no longer a Christian or a Jew but a Muslim and must be respected as such. By the same token,

---

[1] Thus, we read: "And fight in God's cause against those who wage war against you, but do not commit aggression—for, verily, God does not love aggressors," "Fight during the sacred months if you are attacked: for a violation of sanctity is [subject to the law of] just retribution. Thus, if anyone commits aggression against you, attack him just as he has attacked you—but remain conscious of God, and know that God is with those who are conscious of Him." (Q., 2: 190 & 194); "As for such [of the unbelievers] as do not fight against you on account of [your] faith, and neither drive you forth from your homelands, God does not forbid you to show them kindness and to behave towards them with full equity:9 for, verily, God loves those who act equitably" (Q., 60: 8).

[2] Immanual Kant, *Groundwork of the Metaphysics of Morals* (London: Routledge, 1993), p. 84.

a Muslim who converts to Christianity is no more a Muslim but a Christian and must be respected as such.

Indeed, there are already signs that the calls by radical voices within Muslim societies to revive apostasy laws have provoked calls by others to restrict conversion to Islam of members of their communities. In December 2004, members of the Coptic community in Egypt cried foul when a Coptic woman converted to Islam. Coptic leaders accused Muslims of forcing the woman to accept Islam and thousands of Christian Copts demonstrated "in various parts of the nation against what they say is the government's failure to protect them against anti-Christian crimes."[1]

Although medieval Christian Europe practiced coercion to force reverse conversions to Christianity, modern societies recognize the freedom of religion of all citizens. Muslim scholars have the obligation to reconsider modern realities and reject any attempt to revive historical claims rooted in classical jurisprudence that are clearly at odds with Qur'anic principles and the Islamic spirit, and with modern society and international conventions and practices. It would be a tragedy, for both social peace in Muslim societies and world peace in an increasingly diverse global society, if religious communities embrace practices that limit freedom of religion and adopt measures that rely on coercion to maintain the integrity of religious communities.

Conclusion

The realization that the particular rules of the Sharī'ah are subsumed under universal rules forced Muslim scholars to reevaluate any particular pronouncements that conflict with

---

[1] Aaron Klein, "Christians protest kidnapping, forced conversion wife of Coptic priest allegedly taken by Muslim extremists in Egypt," *WorldNetDaily.com*, Dec. 6, 2004. Retrieved at *http:www.worldnetdaily.com/news/article.asp?ARTICLE_ID=4180,5* (accessed May 15, 2006).

established Sharīʿah principles that emphasize equal dignity, justice, compassion, and excellence (*iḥsān*). This allowed eminent scholars, such as ʿIzz al-Dīn b. ʿAbd al-Salām and al-Shāṭibī in the seventh and eight centuries of Islam, to reorganize the body of the Sharīʿah around rationally comprehensible pinciples known as *maqāṣid al-sharīʿah*. As we argued in this chapter, the development of the theory of *maqāṣid* and its implementation in modern society is crucial for thinking afresh and perventing the imposition of historically-bound rules developed by early Muslim scholars, who lived under different social and policital conditions.

Indeed, the *maqāṣid* approach is essential for grounding ethics and law in a rationally defensible framework compatible with the principles of equal dignity, justice, freedom, and compassion clearly established by all divine revelations, and enshrined in Qur'anic revelation and Prophetic message. We focused in the arguments advanced above on illustrating that the *maqāṣid* approach to the Sharīʿah provides a solid foundation for an Islamic tradition of human rights. This approach could undoubtedly be utilized to develop a robust system of ethics and law rooted in the transcendental values of the followers of Islam and other revealed traditions.

CHAPTER SEVEN

Maqāṣid al-Sharīʿah, *Maṣlaḥah*, and Corporate Social Responsibility

Asyraf Wajdi Dusuki & Nurdianawati Irwani Abdullah

Introduction

Over the last few decades, the notion of corporate social responsibility (CSR) has blossomed as a framework for the role of business in society and for setting standards of behavior to which a corporation must subscribe in order to impact society in a positive and productive manner. The emergence of social enterprises, business ethics, environmental practices, a human rights approach to recruitment and employment conditions, and investment in the community are examples of such impacts.

Many believe that CSR is the tribute that capitalism everywhere pays to virtue.[1] According to this view, corporations are no longer defined as entities with a mandate to pursue profit and power relentlessly, regardless of the potential harmful consequences. Instead, they are expected to use their extensive resources to soften their self-interest image by presenting

---

[1] See, for example, Jamie Snider, Ronald Paul Hill & Diane Martin, "Corporate Social Responsibility in the 21st Century: A View from the World's Most Successful Firms," *Journal of Business Ethics*, vol. 48, No. 2 (2003), pp. 175-87.

themselves as humane, benevolent, and socially responsible. Due to globalization, corporations undoubtedly govern society, perhaps even more than governments do. Governments are increasingly looking at these giant and resource-rich entities to address socioeconomic problems. For example, multinational corporations are perceived as the key to development through providing jobs, paying taxes, transferring technology, and making charitable contributions to education and health care. The issue of CSR has only grown in importance in light of recent business scandals involving such large corporations as Barings, Enron, Arthur Anderson, WorldCom, and others.

Despite the tremendous efforts to promote CSR among corporations and society at large, this concept is not without criticism. For instance, how can CSR be operationalized effectively and efficiently on the ground, especially in situations that involve trade-offs? The potential conflict arising from the diverse interests and expectations among various constituents in society further hinders CSR initiatives.

This chapter, therefore, delineates the concept of CSR in light of an Islamic perspective. In particular, the following discussion on *maqāṣid al-sharīʿah* (the Sharīʿah objectives) and the principles of *maṣlaḥah* (the public good) serve as foundations for such a perspective. The implications of these principles are discussed in detail to shed light on how Islam perceives CSR in a holistic and dynamic way, taking into consideration social reality and ever-changing circumstances. These principles also provide a better framework that managers can use when faced with potential conflicts arising from diverse expectations and interests of a corporation's stakeholders.

Since this chapter is among the few attempts to discuss CSR from an Islamic perspective, it produces a conceptual justification that might have some practical relevance for business.[1] Indeed, the ensuing discussion fills an important gap

[1] Earlier authors, among them A. B. Obe, J. A. Mohamed, and Zinkin and G. A.

in CSR literature. The following section briefly discusses CSR's evolution in the West. Section 3 describes *maqāṣid al-sharīʿah* together with the principle of *maṣlaḥah*. The *maqasid* bearing on CSR is further elaborated in section 4, and a description of *maṣlaḥah* as a framework for conflict resolution while implementing CSR is offered in the fifth section. The conclusion is presented in the final section.

The Evolution of Corporate Social Responsibility

CSR is defined as denoting corporate activities beyond making profits, such as protecting the environment, caring for employees, being ethical in trading, and getting involved in the local community. Some of its main issues are promoting human rights, community development, human resource management, socially responsible investing, and social reporting. Robert Davies simplifies this: CSR means a set of standards of behavior to which a corporation subscribes in order to have a positive and productive impact on society. Put simply, it is the framework for the role of business in society.[1]

Williams, agree that the idea of CSR is deeply inscribed in the Sharīʿah and thus not alien to Islam. See, for example, Amir Bhatia Obe, "Corporate Social Responsibility in the Context of Islam," in *Workbook on Corporate Social Responsibility*, (2004), pp. 57-68, available at *www.fco.gov.uk/Files/kfile/CSR- WORKBOOKcc0824,0.pdf*, and Javed Akhtar Mohamed, "An Islamic Per- spective of Corporate Social Responsibility" (paper presented at the Islamic Studies Postgraduate Conference, University of Melbourne, 21-22 Nov. 2005) and also his Jawed Akhtar Mohammed, *Corporate Social Responsibility in Islam* (a doctoral dissertation submitted to the Auckland Uinversity of Technology, 2007), for a comprehensive treatment of CSR from an Islamic perspective. Zinkin and Williams also posit that CSR seems to conform closely to Islamic principles and can build bridges between civilizations, especially in our increasingly difficult and turbulent world. For details, refer to their "Islam and CSR: A Study of the Compatibility between the Tenets of Islam and the UN Global Compact" (Feb. 2006), available at *http://ssrn.com/abstract=905201.*

[1] Robert Davies, "The Business Community: Social Responsibility and Corporate Values," in John H. Dunning, ed., *Making Globalization Good: The Moral Challenge of Global Capitalism* (Oxford: Oxford University Press, 2003), pp. 301-319.

In its Western conceptualization, CSR comes in many forms. As a result, its operation is open to a great deal of interpretation and argument. Until now, CSR has been evolving constantly and incorporating different approaches, depending on circumstances and needs. Available literature attempts to delineate the corporation's role *vis-á-vis* CSR. On the one hand, the classical view proounces CSR as an altogether pernicious idea because the corporation's role is limited to providing goods and services in a way that maximizes their owners' wealth. Milton Friedman, a leading American economist, argues that having managers extend their social responsibilities beyond serving their stockholders' interests is fundamentally a misconception of a free economy's character and nature. He asserts categorically that solving social problems belongs to government and social agencies, not businessess.[1] Certainly, his argument reflects the prevailing worldview of neoclassical economics, which has long been entrenched in the notion of the self-interested economic man.

On the other hand, the escalating socioeconomic problems brought about by globalization have raised new questions as well as expectations about corporate governance and social responsibility. As a result of the continued discontent with the restrictive and misleading worldview that is deeply rooted in self-interest, as well as the secularist and hedonistic individualism underlying the Western economic worldview, CSR emerges as a doctrine to broaden the spectrum of corporate responsibility to include both a social and an environmental dimension.

The spectrum takes into account the multi-fiduciary nature of the stakeholder concept in that the corporation recognizes other responsibilities beyond profit maximization. In this

[1] Milton Friedman, *Capitalism and Freedom* (Chicago & London: The University of Chicago Press, 40th Anniversary Edition, 2002), see especially chapters VIII & XII.

context, management sees itself as responsible for satisfying and meeting the demands connected with the corporation's social responsibility to various groups that have direct or indirect connections to it, namely, consumers, employees, share-holders, suppliers, the community or society in general, and the environment.[1]

According to this view, extending their social responsibility to include all possible effects on society is due to the fact that corporations, especially large ones, have great economic and social power. Therefore, in return for granting them legal status as separate entities, society is entitled to expect from them a significant net positive contribution to the general good.

Corporations are starting to realize the negative repercussions of paying inadequate attention to the needs and interests of multiple stakeholders and society at large. Society's perception of corporations is crucial, so much so that it may affect the corporation's survival if it breaches the "social contract," a covenant made between it and the society in which it operates.[2] For example, if a corporation focuses only on efficiency and externalities to the detriment of society, it will ultimately face social sanctions that will, at the very least, increase its costs or perhaps put it out of business. This obligates corporations to engage positively and constructively with such social structures as the family, the local community, the educational system, and religious institutions to help enhance the people's lives and meet their needs.

In other words, the corporate social contract theory used to justify the CSR construct holds that business and society are equal partners, each enjoying a set of rights and reciprocal responsibilities. There is both a direct and an indirect mutual

---

[1] R. Edward Freeman, *Strategic Management: A Stakeholder Approach* (London: Pitman, 1984).

[2] George P. Lantos, "The Boundaries of Strategic Corporate Social Responsibility," *Journal of Consumer Marketing* 18, No. 7 (2001), pp. 597-99.

need between both entities. While the former requires continuous support from the latter in terms of resources and sales, the latter might expect the former to operate in a socially responsible manner, for corporations control a large amount of economic and productive resources (e.g., technology, finances, and labor) that may affect the society in which they operate.

In an attempt to further legitimize the corporation's role in society, an instrumental theory has developed CSR as a strategic tool designed to achieve economic objectives. Its proponents assert that the corporation may choose to support some social programs for reasons of acquiring a good image, public relations, a competitive advantage, or other strategic reasons without jeopardizing the interests of their primary stakeholders: the share-holders. They further argue that maintaining a good corporate reputation through CSR initiatives may add to the "reputational capital" by which corporations may become profitable in the long run, since market forces provide financial incentives for such perceived socially responsible behavior.[1]

Attempts to conceptualize and justify CSR have been criticized for lacking a solid foundation, particularly as regards the diverse moral and ethical standards adopted in construing a corporation's duties to CSR and its various stakeholders. For example, according to a theory of CSR being based on a social contract, the "contract" between business and society has to be renegotiated as society's preferences change.[2] This confirms CSR's relative and transitional nature in the business sense. Since a corporation's legitimacy rests upon the public's perception alone, corporations inevitably need to alter their behavior according to how society expects them to behave.

According to Davies, some corporations argue that they

---

[1] *Ibid.*, pp. 602-04.

[2] See, for example, Thomas Donaldson and Thomas W. Dunfee, "Toward a Unified Conception of Business Ethics: Integrative Social Contracts Theory," *Academy of Management Review*, vol. 19, No. 2 (1994), pp. 252-84.

should respect local values, even if this means having a greater tolerance for low standards and corruption.[1] As a result, science and philosophical arguments, which are perceptible by our senses and rational faculty, cannot really describe, analyze, or even predict human behavior accurately, since human beings do not always behave in a standard normative manner. Thus, people lack concrete and solid normative judgments that may resolve various potential conflicts.

This creates a dilemma for corporations, since social responsibility has no absolute guiding principle of ethical or moral conduct. Frustrated by this situation, James Humber bluntly argues that "we should abandon the quest to develop a special moral theory for use in business and we should not attempt to impose the use of any moral theory upon business, but rather should allow corporations to determine their moral responsibilities in any way they see fit."[2] Such a statement is rather delusory and tends to exacerbate this confusion and moral dilemma. For example, if a corporation is operating in a low standard or corrupt society in which bribery is part of the social norm, does this mean that it should condone bribery? In other words, corporations committed to CSR need more specific moral rules or principles to explain why they should act in one way instead of another.

Notwithstanding the many attempts to provide theoretical and ethical groundings for CSR, such endeavors have also been widely criticized *vis-á-vis* their justification, conceptual clarity, and possible inconsistency. They also fail to give adequate ethical guidance to business executives who must decide which course to pursue and their level of commitment. This problem is especially acute in view of the fact that all choices involve trade-offs. For example, a program to increase minority

---

[1] Davies, "Business," p. 167.

[2] James M. Humber, "Beyond Stockholders and Stakeholders: A Plea for Corporate Moral Autonomy," *Journal of Business Ethics*, vol. 36, No. 3 (2002), p. 215.

employment might reduce efficiency, thereby preventing the corporation from fulfilling its obligations to shareholders and perhaps its other employees while raising prices for consumers. Or, such a program might be adopted at the expense of reducing the amount of pollution generated, which conflicts with another demand: corporate social responsibility.

In contrast to Western humanistic theories, an Islamic view of CSR takes a rather holistic approach by offering an integralistic spiritual view based on the teachings of the Qur'an and Sunnah (the Prophet's sayings and practices). Such an approach provides a better alternative philosophical framework for a person's interaction with nature and his/her fellow human beings.[1] In fact, given that the moral and ethical principles derived from Revelation are more enduring, eternal and absolute; they may serve as better guidelines for corporations exercising their business and social responsibilities simultaneously.

According to al-Shāṭibī, determining what is beneficial and harmful cannot be left to human reason alone (as most western theorists advocate, as in the social contract theory and the normative stakeholder theory). Human reason plays a crucial role within the guiding framework of Revelation.[2] Islam recognizes the role of reason and experience in theorizing economic behavior and business activities only in a manner that embraces the transcendental aspect of human existence, for human beings' inherent limitations "posit a strong reason that requires divine guidance, especially to ascertain what is right and what is wrong."[3] Hence, according to Khaliq Ahmad, our

---

[1] Khaliq Ahmad, "Islamic Ethics in a Changing Environment for Managers," in Khaliq Ahmad & AbulHasan M. Sadeq, eds., *Ethics in Business and Management Islamic and Mainstream Approaches* (London: Asean Academic Press, 2002).

[2] Abū Isḥāq Ibrāhīm ibn Mūsā al-Shāṭibī, *al-Muwāfaqāt fī Uṣū al-Sharīʿah*, ed. Abdullah Draz (Beirut: Dār al-Kutub al-ʿIlmiyyah, 1425/2004), vol.1/2, pp. 33-34.

[3] Imran Ahsan Khan Nyazee, *Islamic Jurisprudence: Uṣūl al-Fiqh* (Islamabad:

rational faculties can—and should only—be used to complement, support, and strengthen ethics and morality as defined by the Sharīʿah. The following section briefly explains the Sharīʿah objectives and the principle of *maṣlaḥah* that provide a framework for managing the natural conflict arising from the stakeholders' diverse expectations and interests.

Maqāṣid al-Sharīʿah

Islam incorporates permanent features and mechanisms for adapting to change. While its fundamentals, among them *ʿaqīdah* (faith), *ʿibādah* (worship), and *akhlāq* (morality and ethics), never change, their manifestations in such secondary areas as economics, business, and other worldly activities require flexibility and development according to time and space.[1] This is embodied in the Sharīʿah, which is central to Islam's worldview.

The Sharīʿah, defined as a system of ethics and values covering all aspects of life (e.g., personal, social, political, economic, and intellectual) with its unchanging bearings as well as its major means of adjusting to change,[2] cannot be separated or isolated from Islam's basic beliefs, values, and objectives. In other words, it reflects the holistic view of Islam, which is a complete and integrated code encompassing all aspects of life, be they individual or social, both in this world and the Hereafter. For instance, economic or political aspects cannot be isolated from moral and spiritual aspects, and vice versa. Therefore, a contemporary understanding of one concept, say *maṣlaḥah* (the public good) according to the Sharīʿah may lead to a theoretical understanding of economics, science and

---

Islamic Research Institute Press, 2000). Nyazee's argument is supported by a number of Qur'anic verses such as 23:71.

[1] Muhammad Hashim Kamali, "Sources, Nature and Objectives of Sharīʿah," *The Islamic Quarterly* (1989), pp. 215-35.

[2] Ziauddin Sardar, *Islam, Postmodernism and Other Futures: A Ziauddin Sardar Reader* (London: Pluto Press, 2003).

technology, the environment, and politics. Similarly, not understanding a key concept may thwart developments in all of these fields. To understand the Sharīʿah, one needs to comprehend its objectives, which allow flexibility, dynamism, and creativity in social policy.[1] According to al-Ghazālī:

> The objective of the Sharīʿah is to promote the well-being of all mankind, which lies in safeguarding their faith (*dīn*), their human self (*nafs*), their intellect (*ʿaql*), their posterity (*nasl*) and their wealth (*māl*). Whatever ensures the safeguard of these five serves public interest and is desirable.[2]

Al-Shāṭibī approves of al-Ghazālī's list and sequence, thereby indicating that they are the most preferable in terms of their harmony with the Sharīʿah's essence.[3] Generally, the Sharīʿah is predicated on benefiting the individual and the community, and its laws are designed to protect these benefits and facilitate the improvement and perfection of human life in this world. This perfection corresponds to the purposes of the Hereafter. In other words, each of its five worldly purposes (viz., preserving faith, life, posterity, intellect, and wealth) is meant to serve the single religious purpose of the Hereafter.

The Sharīʿah uppermost objectives revolve around the concepts of compassion and guidance, as expressed by many verses of the Qur'an.[4] It seeks to establish justice, eliminate prejudice, and alleviate hardship by promoting cooperation and mutual support within the family and society at large. Both of

---

[1] Wael B. Hallaq, *A History of Islamic Legal Theories: An Introduction to Sunni Usul al-Fiqh* (Cambridge: Cambridge University Press, 2004).

[2] Cited by Muhammd Umer Chapra, *The Future of Economics: An Islamic Perspective* (Leicester: The Islamic Foundation, 2000), p. 118. See Abū Ḥāmid Muḥammad bin Muḥammad bin Muḥmmad al-Ghazālī, *al-Mustaṣfā min ʿIlm al-Uṣūl*, ed. Muhammad Sulayman al-Ashqar (Beirut: Mu'assassat al-Risālah, 1st edn, 1417/1997), vol. 1, p. 417.

[3] Nyazee, *Islamic Jurispudence*, p. 121.

[4] See for example Qur'an 21:107 and 10:57.

these concepts are manifested by realizing the public interest that Islamic scholars have generally considered to be the Sharīʿah's all-pervasive value and objective that is, for all intents and purposes, synonymous with compassion. *Maṣlaḥah* sometimes connotes the same meaning as *maqāṣid*, and scholars have used these two terms almost interchangeably.[1] To shed more light on our discussion, especially with regard to the Sharīʿah's goal of preserving the public good, the following section elaborates on the *maṣlaḥah*, an important tool that upholds the Sharīʿah.

Maṣlaḥah (The Public Good)

Maṣlaḥah is a juristic precept established in Islamic legal theory to promote the public good and prevent social evil or corruption. Its plural *maṣāliḥ*, means "welfare, interest, or benefit." Literally, *maṣlaḥah* is defined as seeking benefit and repelling harm. *Maṣlaḥah* and *manfaʿah* (benefit or utility) are treated as synonyms. However, *manfaʿah* is not a technical meaning of *maṣlaḥah*, which Muslim jurists define as seeking benefit and repelling harm, as directed by God in the Sharīʿah.[2]

Among the major Sunnī schools of Islamic jurisprudence, Imam Malik is the leading proponent in upholding *maṣlaḥah* as one of the Sharīʿah sources.[3] He uses the term *al-maṣāliḥ al-*

---

[1] Many classical Muslim jurists advocated the principle of the public good (*maṣlaḥah*) and the Sharīʿah's objectives (*Maqāṣid al-Sharīʿah*) in Islamic legal thought (*fiqh*): e.g., Abū al-Maʿāli al-Juwaynī (d. 1085), Abū Ḥāmid al-Ghazālī (d. 1111), Fakhr al-Dīn al-Rāzī (d. 1209), Sayf al-Dīn al-Āmidī (d. 1233), ʿIzz al-Dīn al-Sulamī (d. 1261), Shihāb al-Dīn al-Qarāfī (d. 1285), Abū al-ʿAbbās Aḥmad Ibn Taymiyyah (d. 1327), Abū Isḥāq al-Shāṭibī (d. 1388), Ibn Qayyim al-Jawziyah (d. 1350), and Najm al-Dīn al-Ṭūfi (1316). See, Deina AbdelKader, "Modernity, the Principles of Public Welfare (*Maṣlaḥah*), and the End Goals of the Sharīʿah (*Maqāṣid*) in Muslim Legal Thought," *Islam and Christian-Muslim Relations,* vol. 14, No. 2 (2003), pp. 164-74.

[2] Cited in Nyazee, *Islamic Jurispudence*, p. 161.

[3] All jurists from the main Sunnī schools of Islamic jurisprudence agree that the Sharīʿah's main sources are the Qur'an, the Sunnah, *ijmāʿ* (the consensus

mursalah to connote interests that are not covered by other sources.[1] Most other jurists, however, reject this as a source, with the exception of al-Ṭūfī (Ḥanbalī) and al-Ghazālī (Shāfiʿī). However, al-Ghazālī uses *istislāḥ* (seeking the better rule for the public good) but does not claim it as the Sharīʿah's fifth source. He also restricts its application to situations deemed to be necessary to serve the public good.[2] He defines *maṣlaḥah* as follows:

> *Maṣlaḥah* is originally an expression denoting the acquisition of benefit or the repulsion of injury or harm, but that is not what we mean by it here, for the acquisition of benefit and aversion of harm by nature constitutes human beings' goals, and their wellbeing consists in attaining such goals. What we mean by *maṣlaḥah*, however, is the preservation of what is inended (*maqṣūd*) by the Divine Law (*sharʿ*). And what is intended by the Law in relation to human beings consists of five things: to safeguard their faith (*dīn*), life (*nafs*), intellect (*ʿaql*), progeny (*nasl*), and property (*māl*)."[3]

---

of Islamic jurists), and *qiyās* (analogical deductions). For a detailed discussion of each source, see to Abdul Karim Zaidan, *al-Madkhal li-Dirāsat al-Sharīʿah al-Islāmiyyah* (Baghdad: Maktabah al-Quds, 1985), pp. 190-215.

[1] The formulation of a rule on the basis of *al-maṣāliḥ al-mursalah* must take into account the public good and conform to the Sharīʿah's objectives. According to the Maliki School, this tool must fulfill three main conditions. First, it must deal only with transactions (*muʿāmalāt*) in which reasoning through one's rational faculty is deemed necessary. This is unlike actions related to religious observance, such as an act of worship (*ʿibadāh*), which is strictly subjected to the Sharīʿah's main sources. Second, the interests should be in harmony with the Sharīʿah's spirit. Third, the interests should be of the essential type, as opposed to the embellishment type. Here, "essential" implies preserving the Sharīʿah's five main objectives. For details, see Sobhi R. Mahmassani, *The Philosophy of Jusrispudence in Islam* (Kuala Lumpur: The Open Press, 2000), pp. 87-89.

[2] *Ibid.*, p. 88.

[3] Abū Ḥāmid Muḥammad b. Muḥammad al-Ghazālī, *al-Mustasfā min ʿIlm al-Uṣūl,* ed. Mohamed Sulyman al-Ashqar (Beirut: Mu'assassat al-Risālah, 1st edn, 1417/1997), vol. 1, pp. 416-417.

Here, al-Ghazālī reinforces the importance of preserving the Sharīʿah objectives as the fundamental meaning of *maṣlaḥah*. Al-Shāṭibī, closely following al-Ghazālī's taxonomy, defines *maṣlaḥah* in his *al-Muwāfaqāt* as a principle that concerns the subsistence of human life, the completion of one's livelihood, and the acquisition of what his/her emotional and intellectual qualities require of him/her in an absolute sense.[1] In fact, he singles *maṣlaḥah* out as being the only overriding Sharīʿah objective broad enough to comprise all measures deemed beneficial to people, including administering justice and worship. He further classifies *maṣlaḥah* into three categories: *ḍarūriyyāt* (the essentials), *ḥājiyyāt* (the complementary), and *taḥsīniyyāt* (the embellishments).[2] These categories are briefly discussed below.

Ḍarūriyyāt: The essentials are the self-interests upon which people essentially depend, such as faith, life, intellect, posterity, and wealth. According to Mohammad H. Kamali, these elements are by definition absolutely necessary for the proper functioning of a person's religious and mundane affairs, to the extent that their destruction and collapse would precipitate chaos and the collapse of society's normal order. Thus, protecting them reflects the effective way of preserving the Sharīʿah, as outlined in its objectives.[3]

Ḥājiyyāt: The complementary interests supplement the essentials and refer to those interests that, if neglected, would lead to hardship but not to the total disruption of life's normal

[1] Hallaq, *History*, p. 168.

[2] Ibid., pp. 168-69.

[3] According to Hallaq, the essentials are maintained by two means: on the one hand, they are enhanced and strengthened, while on the other, all potential harm that may arise to affect them is averted. For example, protecting life and intellect are examples of important elements of the essentials that can be enhanced by providing proper food, shelter, clothing, education, and so on. On the other hand, any potential harm that might threaten these essentials may be averted by means of a penal law or punishment that prohibits alcohol or dumping toxic waste that may cause harm to one's intellect and life, respectively. Hallaq, *History*, p. 168.

order. In other words, they are needed to alleviate hardship so that life may be free from distress and predicament. An example is seen in the sphere of economic transactions, where the Sharīʿahvalidates such contracts as forward sale (*salam*) and lease and hire (*ijarah*), because people need them, notwithstanding a certain anomaly attendant in both.

Taḥsīniyyāt: The embellishments refer to those interests that, if realized, would lead to refinement and perfection in the customs and conduct of people at all levels of achievement. For example, the Sharīʿah encourages charity (beyond the level of *zakāh*) to those who are in need and, in customary matters and relations among people, urges gentleness, pleasant speech and manner, and fair dealing.

Many scholars, among them Muhammad H. Kamali, M. Umer Chapra, Imran Nyazee, Michael Mumisa, Ziauddin Sardar, and Wael Hallaq, assert that the above classification is related to and deeply rooted in the Sharīʿah objectives to ensure that society's interests are preserved in the best fashion both in this world and in the Hereafter. According to their views, such a classification implies how a *maṣlaḥah*-based methodology could be used to derive new rulings from the Sharīʿah, meet society's changing needs, and solve contemporary problems related to socioeconomic endeavours.[1] Thus, these principles can help establish guidelines for moral judgment and balancing the individual's self-interest with social interests.

Maqāṣid Implications for Corporate Social Responsibility

In light of the above discussion on *maqāṣid*, CSR assumes a

---

[1] As a case in point, the validity of an Islamic leasing instrument (*ijārah*) that may be initially of secondary (*ḥājiyyāt*) importance to an individual is elevated to an essential (*ḍarūriyyah*) *maṣlaḥah*, as it is deemed essential for the society at large. Refer to Mohammad Hashim Kamali, *Principles of Islamic Jurisprudence* (Petaling Jaya, Malaysia: Pelanduk Publications, 1989), pp. 352-56.

broader and more holistic significance to Muslim workers, managers, corporations, customers, and society as a whole. Islam's concept of CSR encompasses a broader meaning, embracing God-consciousness (*taqwā*) by which corporations (as groups of individuals) assume their roles and responsibilities as servants and vicegerents of God in all situations. By doing so, they make themselves ultimately responsible to God, the Owner of their very selves and the resources that they utilize and manage. This responsibility is, in fact, a function of the intrinsic quality of each Muslim's life as a trust from God.[1]

For a committed and devout Muslim, concern for others and the surrounding environment are deeply inscribed in the five pillars of Islam. In fact, each Muslim is considered a social being that cannot isolate him/herself or ignore his/her role and responsibility towards society and other human beings in any way, even if for ritual worship. According to Abū Hurayrah:

> One of the Prophet's Companions passed a ravine where a freshwater spring ran. He liked the ravine and said: "How I would like to isolate myself from other people to worship God! I will not do so before asking permission from God's Messenger (may be upon him)." The man told the Prophet of his wish, and the Prophet replied: "Do not do it. Your striving in God's path is better than praying in your house for sixty years."[2]

Therefore, CSR is a moral and religious initiative based on the belief that a corporation should be "good" despite the financial consequences. This is not to suggest that Islam

---

[1] Syed Muhammad Naquib Al-Attas, "The Worldview of Islam: An Outline," in Sharifah Shifa Al-Attas, ed., *Islam and The Challenge of Modernity* (Kuala Lumpur: International Institute of Islamic Thought and Civilization, ISTAC, 1996).

[2] Abū ʿAbd Allāh al-Ḥākim al-Naysābūrī, *al-Mustadrak ʿalā al-Ṣaḥīḥayn* (Cairo: Dār al-Ḥaramayn, 1st edn, 1417/1997), "Kitāb al-Jihād', No. 2437 &.2438, Vol. 2, p. 86; Abū Bakr Aḥmad b. al-Ḥusayn b. ʿAlī al-Bayhaqī, *al-Sunan al-Kubrā,* ed. Mohamed Abdulqadir ʿAta (Beirut: Dār al-Kutub al-ʿIlmiyyah, 3rd edn, 1424/2003), "Kitāb al-Syar", No. 18503 & 18504, vol. 9, p. 270.

opposes making a profit. Rather, it is seen as a necessary condition, though not the sole purpose, of a corporation's existence. Invoking the Sharīʿah and employing a *taqwā*-based business paradigm imply that the entrepreneur is no longer driven by profit maximization alone, but by the pursuit of ultimate happiness in this life and in the Hereafter. In other words, his/her corporation has acknowledged its social and moral responsibility for the well-being of others (e.g., consumers, employees, share-holders, and local communities).

Furthermore, Islamic guidance, enshrined by its principle of justice, brings about a balance between individuals' rights and their duties and responsibilities toward others, and between self-interest and altruism. Islam recognizes self-interest as a natural motivating force in all human life; however, it has to be linked to the overall concepts of goodness and justice.[1] In fact, Islam lays down a moral framework for effort by spelling out values and non-values, as well as what is and is not desirable from a moral, spiritual, and social perspective.[2] The concept of reward is also broadened by incorporating within it reward in this world and in the Hereafter. This provides a strong and self-propelling motivation for good and just behavior, without denying one's natural instinct for personal gain.[3]

Hence, moderation and concern for the needs of others, along with one's own, become an integral part of the Islamic perspective of CSR. Therefore, social responsibility is not solely a duty of the government, as Friedman, Humber, and others would have us believe; rather, it is a duty of all members of the community, including corporations, particularly the better-off ones. Thus, individuals and corporations are encouraged to sacrifice, give up, and spend portions of their wealth on the

---

[1] Syed Nawab Haider Naqvi, *Perspectives of Morality and Well-Being: A Contribution to Islamic Economics* (Leicester: The Islamic Foundation, 2003), pp. 99-110.

[2] Saiyad Fareed Ahmad, "Does Morality Require God?" *Intellectual Discourse,* vol. 11, No. 1 (2003), pp. 51-76.

[3] *Ibid.*, pp. 65-66.

poor and the needy while expecting their reward only from God. This sense of duty, responsibility, and spirit of sacrifice, which Islam nurtures, actually helps remove self-centeredness and covetousness and promotes compassion, caring, cooperation, and harmony among people.

Applying the Concept of *Maṣlaḥah* to CSR

We now turn our discussion to applying the concept of *maṣlaḥah* to CSR. These principles, by implication, reflect how Islam stresses the importance of considering public interests rather than merely individual interests. It provides a framework for making decisions and a mechanism for adapting to change, especially for corporations willing to commit to CSR. Perhaps these principles can further contribute to delineating the role of corporations in terms of their CSR. It also offers guidelines for moral judgment on the part of managers and other stakeholders, particularly in solving conflicts that may arise when pursuing CSR. To shed light on our discussion here, this study depicts these principles in a pyramid form (figure 1).

Figure 1: The Pyramid of Maṣlaḥah

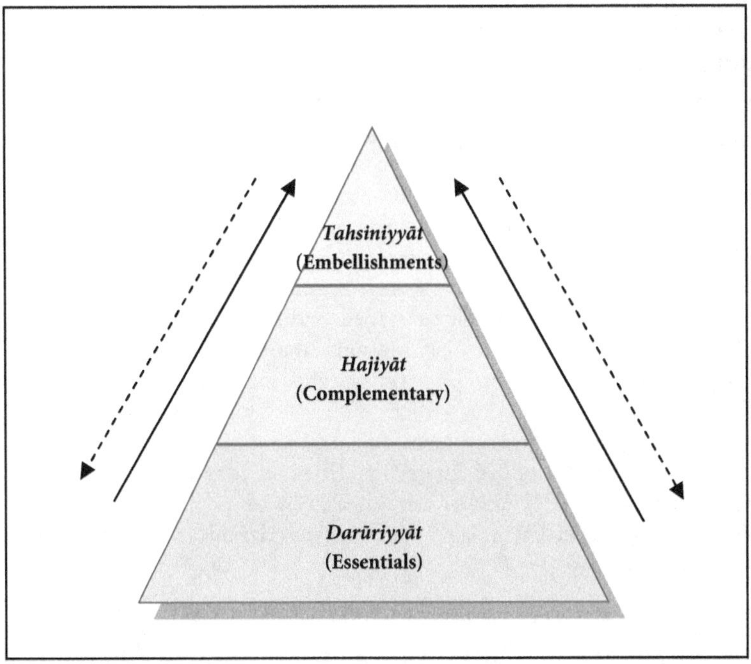

This pyramid, which functions as a framework and a general guideline to an ethical filter mechanism, provides managers with three levels of judgment to resolve the ethical conflicts that inadvertently emerge while applying CSR programs and initiatives. The levels also reflect the different degrees of importance in terms of responsibility fulfillment. The bottom level, the essentials, constitutes the most fundamental responsibility to be fulfilled, as compared to the complementary and the embellishments categories.

Therefore, as the pyramid moves upward, the degree of decision making will be less fundamental, albeit more virtuous, so as to attain society's perfection and well-being.[1] It assumes that individuals will strive for the next level as soon as the previous one has been fulfilled. This presumption is grounded in Islam's principle of motivation, which encourages Muslims to strive continuously and consistently for excellence in order to gain God's pleasure and receive better rewards from Him.[2]

In essence and according to Islamic ethics, a corporation's performance is evaluated according to the fulfillment of its objectives of continuous improvement and sharpening of the edge. The sense of continuous improvement disappears if one cannot make today better than yesterday. Hence managers, shareholders, and workers must not be content with fulfilling the essentials alone; instead, they must always strive to improve

---

[1] According to Islamic scholars, the existence of the complementary and the embellishments depends upon the primary purposes underlying the essentials, in other words, protecting and preserving one's faith, life, intellect, posterity, and wealth. The two categories are structurally subservient and substantively complementary to the essentials, to the extent that violating the latter produces far-reaching consequences. On the other hand, any damage affecting the com- plementary or the embelishments will result in only a minor disturbance to the essentials. Hence, it is essential to preserve the three categories in their order of importance. See the detailed discussion in Michael Mumisa, *Islamic Law: Theory and Interpretation* (Beltsville, MD: Amana publications, 2002). Also refer to Kamali, *Principles*, and Hallaq, *History*.

[2] Mohd Kamal Hasan, "Worldview Orientation and Ethics: A Muslim Perspective," in Ahmad & Sadeq, *op. cit.*

the corporation's fulfillment of its social responsibility, since their personality and character have been shaped by their heightened sense of ultimate accountability to God, from which no one can escape.[1] As mentioned above, this is actually is a manifestation of the God-consciousness (*taqwā*).

The pyramid's three levels are not mutually exclusive; rather, they are inter-related and mutually dependent. The arrows pointing upward and downward reveal the flexibility and mechanism of change in the decision-making process, in the sense that any element comprising one level of *maṣlaḥah* may be elevated upward or pushed downward, depending on the different circumstances concerning the public at large. However, it should be noted that such flexibility is confined within the Sharīʿah framework, and not vice versa.[2]

This reflects the pyramid's dynamism in assisting the decision-making process within each different context, time, and space. For instance, if circumstances change and corporations are encouraged to respond and, as a result, reconsider their roles within society, this will necessitate a realignment of their business institutions (e.g., mission, vision, policy deployment, decision making, reporting, and corporate affairs) to the new *maṣlaḥah*, so long as it does not contradict the principles of the Sharīʿah.

Such contemporary Islamic jurists as Hussain Hamid Hassan, Mohamed S. R. al-Buti and Mustafa Zaid all affirm this dynamism in Islamic jurisprudence (*fiqh*). However, it has to be carefully used when confronting contemporary challenges. The touchstone by which the validity of *maṣlaḥah* is judged consists of the Qur'an and the Sunnah. In his *Ḍawābiṭ al-Maṣlaḥah fī al-*

---

[1] Thus, we read in the Qur'an (9:105): "And say [unto them, O Prophet]: Act! And God will behold your deeds, and [so will] His Apostle, and the believers: and [in the end] you will be brought before Him who knows all that is beyond the reach of a created being's perception as well as all that can be witnessed by a creature's senses or mind."

[2] See further discussion of this aspect in: Mumisa, *Islamic Law.*

Sharī'ah al-Islāmiyyah (1965), al-Buti cautions that the *maṣlaḥah* must not be used at random. He maintains that the effective way to preserve the Sharī'ah in its ideal form is to determine the *maṣlaḥah* via the needs recognized by the Sharī'ah. Otherwise, they will be exposed to extraneous factors opposed to the spirit of the Qur'an and the Sunnah.[1]

To further elucidate our argument, particularly on how the *maṣlaḥah* pyramid can be applied to CSR, we shall analyze the different levels of the decision-making process based on each principle. On the first level (the essentials), managers are expected to strive to preserve and protect their stakeholders' essential needs (viz., religion, life, intellect, posterity, and property) and the public good in general. For example, under the CSR precept, they must protect their employees' welfare or basic needs by providing adequate prayer rooms and protecting the employees' safety and health in the workplace, thereby reflecting their responsibility to safeguard, respectively, the faith and values of life. Moreover, they must confine their operations to those that safeguard the above-mentioned essential values.

Accordingly, corporations have a moral and social duty to avoid any activities that may cause disruption and chaos in people's lives, even though pursuing them may engender higher profits, as clearly taught by the Qur'an (28: 77) which says in its account about Qārūn: "Seek instead, by means of what God has granted thee, [the good of] the life to come, withought forgetting, withal, thine own [rightful] share in this world; and do good [unto] others as God has done unto thee; and seek not to spread corruption on earth: for, verily, God does not love the spreaders of corruption." Such examples include business activities that can endanger people's lives and disrupt their intellects as a result of environmental degradation and manufacturing illicit drugs for public consumption.

As soon as this level's responsibilities have been fulfilled,

---

[1] *Ibid.*, pp. 60-71.

the corporations may strive for the second level: the complementary. Here, it is deemed beneficial to remove difficulties that may not pose a threat to the normal order's survival. For example, managers may want to extend their social responsibility commitment by extending the employees' essential needs, such as fair pay and a safe workplace, to include continuous training and enhanced human quality programs. The latter is not really essential, for neglecting it does not threaten the employees' continued existence. However, assuming such a responsibility fulfills the complementary interest of advancing the workers' intellectual well-being (knowledge and skills).

In some cases, such an effort can be considered one of the essentials. For example, Islamic banks need to provide adequate Sharīʿah training to their employees concerning the offered Islamic financial instruments in order to protect the interests pertaining to the faith. Other examples of such responsibilities include not trading in, manufacturing, or selling tobacco, alcoholic, and pornographic products in order to prevent their negative effects on people's and the society's health and behavior.

At the highest level, the embellishments, corporations are expected to discharge their social responsibilities by engaging in activities or programs that may lead to improving and attaining the perfections and niceties of public life. Giving charity or donating to the poor and the needy, as well as offering scholarships to poor students and providing sufficient, correct, and clear information or advertisement regarding all products, are some of the examples of CSR commitment with respect to realizing this level's goal for society.

On the whole, the *maṣlaḥah* pyramid implies the need for corporations to engage in and manage their businesses and CSR activities according to priorities that have evolved from a deep understanding of the Sharīʿah objectives such that preserving the *maṣlaḥah* is done in a way that is in accord with the different levels of importance and the severity of consequences. For instance, one must not focus on attaining the embellishments while jeopardizing the essentials, nor should one be obsessed with attaining benefits to the extent of harming others. Our discussion of the principle of preventing harm, which is pertinent to our discussion of the *maṣlaḥah's* implications to CSR, is further elaborated in the following section. As pointed out earlier, the concept of *maṣlaḥah* entails understanding the Islamic principle of preventing harm, which states that a corporation cannot harm or cause grief to others while engaging in its economic and business activities. In general terms, two major Sharīʿah axioms clearly reflect this concept: removing hardship (*rafʿ al-ḥaraj*) and preventing harm (*dafʿ al-ḍarar*). This concept occupies a central position in the framework of protecting the social interest, as enshrined in the *maṣlaḥah*, particularly in averting social harm.[1] As such, discussing CSR from an Islamic viewpoint is futile if such an important framework is undermined.

This principle is based on the Prophet's famous ḥadīth narrated by ʿĀ'ishah, Abū Saʿīd al-Khudrī, and Abū Hurayrah that "No harm is to be shall inflicted, nor shall any harm be reciprocated."[2] According to al-Suyūṭī, this ḥadīth enunciates a very important that covers many areas of Islamic jurisprudence. Among the arguments derived from it is the following: If someone has damaged another person's property, the affected person cannot retaliate by damaging that person's property, for

---

[1] For further details in this respect, see Muhammed Abu Zahra, *Uṣūl al-Fiqh* (Cairo: Dār al-Fikr al-ʿArabī, 1958), pp. 364-379; Muhammad Kamaluddin Imam, *al-Maṣlaḥah fī al-Musṭalaḥ al-Maqāṣidī Ru'yah Waẓīfiyyah* (London: al-Furqan Foundation, 2011); Sami al-Daghistani, "Semiotics of Islamic Law, *Maṣaḥa*, and Islamic Economic Thought," *International Journal for the Semiotics of Law*, vol. 29, No. 2 (2016), pp. 389-404.
[2] Mālik b. Anas, *Muwaṭṭa' al-Imām Mālik*, ed. Muhammad Mustfa Alazami (Abu Dhabi: Mu'assassat Zayed bin Sultan Al Nahyan, 1st edn, 1425/2004), "Kitab al-Aqdiyah", No. 2759, vol. 2, p. 1078; ʿAli b. ʿUmar al-Dāraquṭnī, *Sunan al-Dāraquṭnii* ed. Adel A. AbdulMawjud & Ali M. Muawwad (Beirut: Dār al-Maʿrifah, 1st edn, 1422/2001), "Kitāb al-Buyu", No. 3046, vol. 2, p. 684 & "Kitāb fī al-Aqḍiyah wa al-Aḥkām", Nos. 4459-4462, vol. 3, pp. 469-470.

such an action is deemed to aggravate the damage without any providing any benefit in return. Hence it is harmful. The alternative is paying an amount of compensation that has the same value as the damaged property so as to avoid further harm to the owner's property.[1]

Islamic scholars broadly classify harm as that which occurs due to a person's deliberate action to afflict other parties/entities (e.g., the environment) and an action done with a solemn intention and that is permitted by the Sharīʿah. But in this latter case, such an action may harm other parties. While the former is strictly prohibited (*ḥarām*), the latter has to be examined in varying degrees and in various contexts to determine if it is permissible or not.[2]

Preventing harm, along with promoting benefit, has been the subject of wide discussion in the field of Islamic jurisprudence. A number of Islamic legal maxims have been derived from this. For the purpose of this study, we simplify the discussion by summarizing the Islamic maxims derived from the principle of preventing harm. Table 1 summarizes some of the most important of these maxims that are relevant and significant to our discussion. Examples of their application to various CSR-related issues are provided in the corresponding column to further illuminate our understanding of them.

Table 1: The Framework of Harm Prevention in Islam

Islamic Maxim	Description	Examples of Application
Harm is repelled as far as possible	Any potential harm to society has to be prevented as far as possible. This resembles the proverb that "prevention is better than	Dumping toxic waste as a form of externalizing a corporation's cost to society must be averted, such that it must not

[1] Jalāl al-Dīn ʿAbd al-Raḥmān al-Suyūṭī, *al-Ashbāh wa al-Naẓā'ir fī Furūʿ al-Shāfiʿiyyah* (Beirut: Dār al-Kutub al-ʿIlmiyyah, 1st edn, 1403/1984), pp. 83-84.
[2] Mustafa al-Bugha and Muhyiddin Misto, *A Discussion on An-Nawawi's Fourty Hadiths* (Kuala Lumpur: Prospecta Printers Sdn. Bhd., 1998), pp. 346-66.

Islamic Maxim	Description	Examples of Application
	cure." In other words,	even be considered an option
Harm is ended.	Any harm must be stopped or abolished. It is obligatory to remove the harm and try to rectify the damage.	If a corporation disposes its toxic waste in a residential area, it must be stopped. If publiv health problems ensue, the corporation must admit responsibility and pay compensation.
Harm cannot be ended by its like	In the attempt to remove harm, another type of harm, either to the same degree or worse, must not be invoked.	In avoiding risky investments that may harm the shareholders' fund, managers must not invest in prohibited (based on the Shariah viewpoint) activities, even if it will earn higher profits by doing so.
Severe harm is avoided by a lighter harm	If harm is unavoidable, one must choose the lighter harm. A similar maxim states that the lesser of the two harms must be chosen.	If a bank has to lay off some employees or close branches to remain in business, it may do so, because the harm of a collapsed bank is more severe than the suffering of some workers.
To repel a public, a private harm is preferred.	One has to absorb a private harm in order to prevent social harm In other words, a corporation's operation should be biased in favour of society if two harmful acts are in conflict.	Avoiding companies that produce illegal drugs and engage in activities detrimental to public interest in necessary, even if doing so undermines individual profits.
Repelling harm is preferable to attaining benefit	If there is a conflict between harm and benefit, it is obligatory to repeal or lift the harm first even if by so doing it will remove	A bank should not finance activities that might be perceived as productive in terms of profits or as supposedly

Islamic Maxim	Description	Examples of Application
	the benefits. This is because harm can easily spread and cause severe damage, and hence priority ought to be given to the aversion of harm over attaining benefits.	satisfying some demand (e.g., pornography, gambling, prostitution, alcohol), but still contain elements that may severely harm society or the people's morals and health.
Harm must not be sustained	Anything that may cause harm must be abolished, regardless of whether it is old or new. In other words, any preceding harm must not be allowed to continue, although the circumstances that originally caused it might have changed.	An Islamic corporation that acquires another corporation must terminate any of itsprohibited activities or contracts (e.g., investments in alcohol or gambling).

The Islamic legal maxims used in this study were elaborated in the *Majallat al-Aḥkām al-ʿAdliyyah* or the *Mejelle* (the Civil Code of the Ottoman Empire).[1] The *Mejelle* comprises of 851 articles arranged in an introduction and sixteen books. The introduction consists of 100 articles dealing with Islamic legal maxims. However, this study only selects those maxims that are relevant to the discussion of preventing harm within the CSR framework.

The *Mejelle* reinforces the idea that each person is a social

[1] The *Majallah* was promulgated in 1876. This civil code compilation is based on Sharīʿah principles mainly as elaborated within the Hanfi School. Although comprehensive in delineating certain Islamic jurisprudential principles, it does not contain all civil law provisions (e.g., one branch of law pertaining to family law was left out). The purpose of compiling this code was to prepare a book on juridicial transactions that would be correct, easy to understand, free from contradictions, embody the selected opinion of the jurists, and easy for everyone to read. Among the subjects covered are sale (*bayʿ*), hire (*ijārah*), guarantee (*kafālah*), transfer of debt (*ḥawālah*), pledges (*rahn*), trust and trusteeship (*amānah*), and gifts (*hibah*). Cited in, *The Mejelle: Being an English Translation of Majallat al-Aḥkām al-ʿAdliyyah and a Complete Code of Islamic Civil Law* (Kuala Lumpur: Islamic Book Trust, 2001).

being and that social life and responsibility are integral, especially in commercial dealings or transactions. In fact, its first article clearly states: "In view of the fact that man is social in nature, he cannot live in solitude like other animals and is in need of mutual cooperation with his fellow men in order to promote a high civilization."[1] Acknowledging that the individual is, by nature, selfish, the *Mejelle* further reaffirms the major goal of the Sharīʿah to maintain order and justice, especially in balancing the individual's rights with those of society (viz., harmonizing self-interest with social interest). Therefore, in light of this principle, corporations must consider social responsibilities and avoid business practices that harm the well-being of society at large.

Conclusion

Many corporations still wonder how the ideal concept of CSR can be operationalized on the ground. While the primary reason for this is due to the corporation's distorted worldview of self-interest and restrictive role, both of which have long been entrenched in the Western business community as well as around the world, the lack of a concrete and solid framework to manage the conflicting interests arising from its diverse stakeholders further thwarts the endeavor to promote good CSR practices. Therefore, this paper fills an important gap in both CSR and Islamic studies, since it offers an instructive understanding of CSR from an Islamic point of view.

The doctrine of *maqāṣid al-sharīʿah* and *maṣlaḥah* provides adequate ethical guidance to executives and entrepreneurs who must decide which course to pursue and how much to commit to it. In particular, the *maṣlaḥah* pyramid along with the principle of preventing harm provide a framework for managers to deal with potential conflicts arising from the diverse expectations

---

[1] *Ibid.*, pp. 1-2.

and interests of the corporation's stakeholders, especially with respect to CSR. By understanding the principles of preventing harm and promoting benefit as embedded in this framework, for instance, they can make better choices, especially when facing situations that involve trade-offs. For example, a manager who wants to maximize profits may be allowed to do so as long as his/her business activities do not have any negative repercussion on society or the surrounding environment.

The implications of these principles concerning how Islamic corporations, such as banks, should function are clear. Abiding by the rules of the Sharīʿah and observing the principle of *maṣlaḥah* require that such banks should not be solely oriented toward profit; rather, they must seek to promote the social welfare and protect the needs of society as a whole. In addition, they should have a clear financing policy and guidelines to guide them while they are considering a commercial dealing proposal. Likewise, Islamic banks cannot, for instance finance a company dealing in gambling, pornography, alcohol, and other prohibited transactions; a company involved in activities deemed harmful to society (e.g., environmental degradation); or a company dealing with oppressive regimes or those who abuse human rights. Moreover, Islamic banks cannot make excessive profits at their customers' expense or undermine and neglect their social responsibility and commitments to their stakeholders.

To conclude, the concept of CSR is not alien to Islam, for it is deeply inscribed in the Sharīʿah. Therefore, any corporation that claims to follow Sharīʿah-based principles should naturally practice CSR, as it reflects Islam's true spirit. Indeed, Islamic corporations should endeavor to be the epicenter in the business galaxy of promoting good CSR practices. In this respect, assimilating CSR and other Islamic ideals to fulfill stakeholder expectations deserves the utmost consideration, as the desire to do so represents a fundamental difference between Islamic and conventional corporations. Given all of the above factors, this study suggests the importance of CSR training programs that incorporate a Sharīʿah dimension to educate people, especially Muslim executives and entrepreneurs, about CSR best practices. These programs could promote better understanding among the public of why CSR is important, how it could benefit the community as a whole, and eliminate misconceptions that may arise during its implementation. An in-depth understanding of the Sharīʿah, its objectives, and principles may also benefit managers, particularly on how to practice CSR more effectively and efficiently without undermining corporation's viability and long- term sustainability.

CHAPTER EIGHT

Maqāṣid and the Codification of Islamic Penal Rules: The Sudanese Experiment*

Ibrahim M. Zein

Introduction: Historical Background

The Sudanese experiment of codification of the Sharīʿah rules in general and the penal system in particular is, perhaps, the most important one in Sunnī Islam. It has far-reaching implications for the administration of justice in Islam. Admittedly, its distinctive hue is largely due to its *maqāṣidic* approach. This chapter attempts to understand the *maqāṣid* principles that were behind the process of codification. It should be observed that the process of codification of the Islamic penal system is a complex one. It is also true that a number of mechanisms and learned choices have to be taken into account by the legislators in order to codify the corpus of Islamic jurisprudence. It is indeed the sum-total of a highly complicated negotiation between the traditional formation of Islamic jurisprudential principles and modernity. It necessitates a deep look into the post-colonial apparatus of the administration

* In writing this chapter has drawn partly on his unpublished doctoral dissertation submitted at Temple University, USA in 1989 under the title "Religion, Legality and the State: 1983 Sudanese Penal Code".

of justice and the requirements of the Sharīʿah. Thus, the *maqāṣidic* approach plays a significant role in codifying a form of the Sharīʿah that would not start at the zero point.

However, we must first tell the story of modem judiciary in the Sudan: how it came into existence; the different definitions of cultural identity; and how these developed within this particular cultural formation. This will allow us to take the lead in creating a holistic and accurate picture that will avoid the shortcomings of both Sudanese political activists and "orientalist" scholars. The first group represents the historical fallacies of "Orientalism". In this account, I will attempt to restore a missing dimension by seeing history as a living process; then I shall turn to the politics of legal history to demonstrate that this is nothing but an extension of cultural history of Islamic law.

By way of background, it is important to recognize that the history of the law, in the geographical area which became politically known as the Sudan, is far less developed than other fields of administrative history. This is due, to begin with, to the fact that the sources of historiography, in the domain of administrative history, are largely confined to political and educational institutions.[1] On the other hand, the administration of justice by separate official elite, throughout the history of the Sudan, has always been an urban phenomenon, for customary law has always been the effectively practiced law in the countryside.[2]

---

[1] See R.L. Hill, "Historical writing on the Sudan since 1920", in *Historians of the Middle East*, ed. Bernard Lewis and P.M. Holt (London: Oxford University Press,1962), p. 360 and 366; see also G. N. Sanderson. "The Modem Sudan, 1820-1956: The Present Position of Historical studies, *The Journal of African History (1963)*, p. 449; and see also Yousif Fadl Hasan, Some *Aspects of Writing of History in Modern Sudan* (Khartoum: Khartoum University Press), pp. 29-34.

[2] See Zaki Mustafa, *The Common Law in the Sudan* (London: Oxford University Press, 1971), pp. 33-60; Carolyn Fluehr-Lobban, *Islamic Law and Society in the Sudan* (London: Frank Cass and Company Limited, 1987), pp. 22-51. However, the

It should be noted that little has been done to fill the gaps in our understanding of the dispensation of justice by the Sudanese in the countryside. This is because modem Sudanese historians have generally shown a bias against oral evidence. More importantly, the "fetishism of written document[1]" is still the driving force behind modem Sudanese historians, while the evidence evading, customary law is necessarily largely oral in nature.

Given this context, the history of the law in the Sudan has suffered from both neglect and trivialization. However, Nimeiri's "Judicial Revolution" might lead to a reconsideration of this important field. Furthermore, the growing interest in oral tradition among Sudanese folklorists and some historians may end up in collecting more data about customs, ethics, and customary law,[2] thus providing us with information that can reveal the real depth behind the administrative history. Most importantly, an interdisciplinary approach to the study of the phenomenon of the law in the Sudan is required for a better understanding of the subject matter. This would necessitate the joint efforts of historians, social anthropologist, archeologists, linguists and Islamicists.

Our attempt to see the administrative continuity through-

---

customary law receives less attention than the common law, or *Sharīʿah*. See also: J.A. Reid and J.F. P. Madaren, "Arab Court Procedure and Customary Law", in *SNR*, XIX, 1, (1936), pp. 159-161.; M.I. Elnur, "The Role of the Native Courts in the Administration of Justice in the Sudan", SNR. XLI (1969), pp. 78-87; Obeid H. Ali, "The Conversion of Customary Law to Written Law" *SLJR* (1970); Natale Akolawin, "The Compensation in Criminal Proceedings in the Sudan", *SLJR* (1965); To "The Family and the Law of Torts in African Customary Law", *SLJR* (1965); P. P. Howell, *A Manual of Nuer Law Being of Account of Customary Law: Its Evolution and Development in the Courts Established by the Sudan Government* (London: Published for the International African Institute by the Oxford University Press, 1954). This is not to mention the anthropological studies on Southern tribes.

1 Abdullahi Ali Ibrahim, "Sudanese Historiography and Oral Tradition," *History in Africa,* vol. 12 (1985), p. 126

2 *Ibid.*, pp. 125-126.

out the regimes of Sinnar and Darfur, *Turkiyyah*,[1] the Anglo-Egyptian Sudan and the post-independence Sudan is based on the assumption that both Islam and modernization were shared factors throughout that time. Obviously, Islam was over-stressed during certain eras, while modernization or westernization was emphasized during other eras. Yet, the line of development in the structure of the judiciary was somehow kept intact.

It should be noted that Egyptian historiography emphasized some elements of the history of the Egyptian administration in the Sudan during both the *Turkiyyah* period and the Anglo-Egyptian Sudan, while British historiography did the same thing in its account of the same periods. Yet, there are distinguished exceptions whose objectivity outweighs their national political interests.[2] However, this only underlines the fundamental fact that both schools of historiography contribute more to their complete distortion, for quite a long time, of the history of the Sudan. This is in addition to their complete distortion, for quite a long time, of the history of the Mahdist state in the Sudan.[3] Hill summarized two of the essential political agendas behind the thesis of the Egyptian historiography on the Sudan as that "the Mahdist rising was due almost wholly to foreign interference in the internal administration of the Sudan."[4] In contrast, Hill stated that the British general attitude in the literature on the Sudan has been that "Egyptian rule in the Sudan was inefficient, corrupt and cruel", and "General Gordon was the exemplar of the British conception of justice and humanity."[5]

However, the British attitude toward the Egyptian

---

[1] The term *Turkiyyah* refers to era when the Sudan come under the ottoman rule.

[2] For example, P.M. Holt from the British School, and Abdel Majid ʿAbdin and Mustafa Muhammed Musʿad from the Egyptian school.

[3] Hill, "Historical writing..." pp. 362-363; Sanderson, "The Modem ...," p. 438.

[4] Hill, *op. cit.,* p. 36.

[5] Ibid., p. 365.

administration in the Sudan during the *Turkiyyah* period was reflected in two significant studies which may be the only works that actually sketch the history of the judiciary in the Sudan,[1] although one of them was done by a Sudanese legal scholar and the other by an American anthropologist. Both of them reflect the prevailing British attitude towards Egyptian rule in the Sudan during that period. Zaki Mustafa stated that during the *Turkiyyah* era, "excessive cruelty was practiced in the execution of sentences. Accused persons were quite often sentenced to 300 or 500 lashes of the *kurbaj*. Death sentences were executed publicly and quite often by crucifying the accused or mounting him on a *khāzūq*."[2] Then the learned legal scholar concluded that "there was generally nothing like the rule of the law."[3] It should be noted that Mustafa did not forget to point out the humane mission of General Gordon. Carolyn Fluehr-Lobban, throughout her book, showed great deal of sensitivity and a critical attitude towards the body of "orientalist" literature. Yet, she stated that "Turkish rule in the Sudan was notorious for its brutality and its gross commercialism."[4]

It should be noted that these two scholars, because of their failure to do sufficient research, were trapped by British propaganda, so that they ended up echoing it in their accounts. This does not mean that the Egyptian rule during the *Turkiyyah* period was so good, but rather that one should be cautious about passing such sweeping judgments. This is because the ʿAbdin Archives in Cairo regarding the issue of the administration of justice during the *Turkiyyah* period in the Sudan were not yet used seriously by legal historians.[5] Thus, any any such sweeping judgment about justice during this period in the Sudan still reveals the impact of the British literature.

[1] Mustafa, *The Common Law in the Sudan*, and Carolyn Fluehr-Lobban, *op. cit.*
[2] Mustafa, *The Common Law in the Sudan,* p. 36.
[3] Ibid., p. 37
[4] Fluehr-Lobban, *op. cit.,* p. 30.
[5] See Hill, *op. cit.,* p. 360.

Moreover, the same thing is true of any sweeping judgment about the administration of justice during the Mahdiyyah.[1] This is because the Egyptian literature, for political reasons, contributed to the distortion of the history of the Mahdist state in the Sudan.[2] However, this does not mean that the British were free from being biased against the way in which justice was dispensed during the Mahdiyyah era. Clearly, the Mahdiyyah archives concerning the administration of justice, in the Sudan and in Britain, were not yet subjected to serious research.[3] However, both the condominium and the post-independence eras received more considerable attention.[4]

The Mahdiyyah Era (1884-1889)

According to the Mahdi's propaganda, the governors of the Sudan, "the Turks", were "infidel". Thus, the Mahdi launched his *jihād* on the basis of that claim. Indeed, the type of law which was

---

[1] A.B. Theobald, *The Mahdiya* (London: Longman, 7th edn, 19656): pp. 180-181.

[2] See Hill, *op. cit.,* p. 363.

[3] Muhammed Abu al-Qasim Haj Hamad, *al-Sūdān: al-Ma'zaq al-Tārīkhī wa Āfāq al-Mustaqbal* (Beirut: 1980); also, Abu Salim, *al-Ḥarakah al-Fikriyyah fi al-Mahdiyyah* (Beirut: Dār al-Jīl, 1970), pp. 4-9.

[4] See Krishna Vasdev, "Ghosts, evil, witches and the law of homicide in the Sudan," *Sudan Law and Reports* (1961), pp. 238-144; *The Law of Evidence in the Sudan* (London: Butterworths, 1981); also, his "Provocation as a defense in Sudan Criminal Law," *The Sudan Law Journal and Reports* (1968), pp. 167-229. Vasdev also re-produced the last article in his book *Homicide in the Sudan* (London: Butterworth, 1987). See also A. Ahmed al-Naʿim. *al-Qānūn al-Jinā'ī al-Sūdānī: al-Naẓariyyah al-ʿAmmah li al-Mas'ūliyyah al-Jinā'iyyah* (Omdurman: Maṭbaʿat al-Ḥuriyyah, 1986); J.J. Gow, "Law and the Sudan," *The Sudan Notes and Records* (1953), pp. 299-309. A.W.M. Disney, "English Law in the Sudan, 1899-1958," *The Sudan Notes and Records* (1959), pp. 121-123; Wiliam L. Twining, "Some Aspects of Reception," *The Sudan Notes and Records* (1957), pp. 229-252; Cliff Thompson, "The Formative Era of the Law of the Sudan," *The Sudan Law Journal and Reports* (1965), pp. 474-513; and Galal A. Lutfi, "The Future of the English Law in the Sudan," *The Sudan Law Journal and Reports* (1967), pp. 219-249. However, the significant change between the issues of the 1950s and the late 1960s was that instead of talking about the reception of the English law, it became on "the revision of the Sudanese law to comply with the tradition or the Sharīʿah.

applied during the *Turkiyyah* times in the Sudan was the focus of the Mahdi's criticism. It is misleading to characterize the Mahdi's revolution as a return back to the basic sources of Islam (Qurān and Sunnah). Evidently, this is what the Mahdi and his Khalifah 'Abullahi claimed. Yet, a critical analysis of the religious literature of both of them will reveal that their literature was less about "purifying" Islam than providing a synthesis between the process of Islamization in the western Sudan and in the riverine Sudan.[1]

It should be remarked that the essential claim of Mahdism is about *'adl* (justice). Thus, it was not surprising that the judiciary was the focus of the Mahdi's mission, with emphasis on the penal aspect of the Sharī'ah. In addition, it was regarded that the requirements prior to the Mahdi's advent should be considered as the embodiment of *ẓulm* (injustice). This led the Mahdi to rebuke the "Turks' ways" of dispensation of justice. Then, the Mahdi created a system of justice based on the measures which were taken by some Muslim jurists and this led him to cancel the schools of *fiqh*, which allowed him to practice *ijtihād*. To justify this, the Mahdi claimed that he enjoyed *al-ḥaḍrah al-nabawiyyah* (direct contact with the Prophet) in order to give his religious claims a character of divinely inspired works. Soon after the Mahdi's untimely death, the Khalifah 'Abdullahi used that method to organize the Mahdist state.[2]

The Mahdist state was divided into two distinct periods. The first period ended with the death of the Mahdi. Then the second period, led by the Khalifah 'Abdullahi, lasted until the crushing of the Mahdist state by Lord Kitchener. During the first period, the sources of the law were the Qur'an, the Sunnah, and the circulars of the Mahdi, while during the second period,

---

[1] P.M. Holt, *The Mahdist State in the Sudan* (London: Oxford University Press, 2nd edn, 1970), p. 261; Abu Salim, *al-Ḥarakah al-Fikriyyah*, pp. 30-31, talked about *al-wirāthah al-muṣṭafawiyyah* which was used by Khalifah 'Abdullahi al-Ta'āyshī.

[2] Abu Salim, *al-Ḥarakah al-Fikriyyah*, pp. 43-44 & p. 63; also, his *Manshūrāt al-Mahdiyyah* (Beirut: Dār al-Jīl, 1969).

the proclamations of the Khalifah ʿAbdullahi were added to the sources of law. However, the understanding of both the Mahdi and the Khalifah ʿAbdullahi of the Sharīʿah was not dissociated from the traditional Mālikī rulings. Yet the Mahdi insisted on the importance of absolute *ijtihād*.[1]

The judiciary of the Mahdist state evolved eventually with the revolution itself. Obviously, Mahdism itself gave the Mahdi the status of the supreme authority, yet the Mahdi, created during the revolution the office of *Qāḍī al-Islām* (the judge of Islam); Ahmed Jubara was the first to assume this office. Then Ahmed Ali was *Qāḍī al-Islām* for twelve years out of the fourteen years of the Mahdist state. Soon after the conquest of Khartoum, the judiciary was reorganized; there were districts, provinces, and *Qāḍīs* attached to the units of the *Anṣār* army.[2] However, during the Khalifah ʿAbdullahi's period, the judiciary structure was much more complex than the first period. Gradually, the office of *qāḍī al-Islām* was marginalized, and then replaced by the office of *Qāḍī al-Quḍāt* (Chief Justice) with six *nuwwāb* (deputies). The Khalifah ʿAbdullahi added the institution of *dār al-maẓālim* (the House of the rectification of injustices) to the judiciary to preside over cases that involved governors, and commanders.[3] Although the Khalifah ʿAbdullahi was harsh on his political opponents and used the judiciary to crush them, the significant change in the administration of justice, as Fluehr-Lobban observed, was that justice was no longer monopoly of the elite and the merchant class. On the contrary, justice became available for the average Sudanese in the Mahdi's court system.[4]

---

[1] Holt, *The Mahdist State*, pp. 123-132 & pp. 261-264.
[2] Mustafa, *The Common Law in the Sudan*, p. 40
[3] Fluehr-Lobban, *op. cit.*, p. 32
[4] Mustafa, *The Common Law in the Sudan,* p. 44. See also "The Khartoum School of Law Order 1935," *Laws of the Sudan*; Supplement to vol. 3, Section 6(1) and (2).

The Condominium: The Anglo-Egyptian Sudan (1899-1956)

It should be remembered that the British colonial era was established on the remains of the Mahdist state. As has been noted above, the Mahdi focused on the Islamic penal law as the content of justice. It should not be surprising that the first laws to be drafted by the Legal Secretary under special supervision from Lord Kitchener, the Governor General, were the penal code and the code of criminal procedure. Both the Islamic Law and the Egyptian code were entirely excluded. This was due to the fact that the new codes were based on a different understanding of justice. Obviously, it viewed the Mahdiyyah's system of justice as representing the penal aspect of a medieval understanding of criminology, in addition to technical reasons that made this codification of the penal code and the code of the criminal procedure a replica of the English law, rather than a codification of the Sharīʿah understanding of penology.[1]

Though Lord Cromer was the master-architect of the judiciary system in the Sudan, the technical work was entrusted to Edgar Bonham-Carter, an English lawyer, who was aided by William Brunyate, to draft the penal code and the code of the criminal procedure.[2] In spite of the hastiness in the judiciary, this step connected principally the development of the Sudanese law with the rich tradition of the English common law system. Despite the crucial differences between the Sharīʿah and the

---

[1] Mustafa, *The Common Law in the Sudan*, p. 44. See also Gabriel Warburg, *The Sudan Under Wingate* (London: Frank Cass, 1971), pp. 124-136

[2] See Lutfi, "The Furore of the English Law" SLJR, p. 220. Lutfi stated that "the leaders of revolution (1964) preferred to affirm and recognize the continuation of the existing laws but provided in the national chapter The Formation of a Law Revision Committee for the purpose of proposing new laws consistent without tradition". Also, after the National Reconciliation in 1977, a committee was presided by Hasan al-Turabi, Attorney General, was set up to revise the Sudanese laws to comply with the Sharīʿah.

common law system, the modem Sudan could not do away with the experience of the common law system. This precisely explains why the demand for the implementation of the Sharīʿah, during the post-independence era, emphasized the idea that the change was meant to make the Sudanese laws comply with the principles of the Sharīʿah, rather than to do away with the technical achievements of the common law system.[1]

It was the British who established the English common law during the first years of the colonial rule; however, both Egyptian and Sudanese personnel were recruited to run the enforcement mechanisms of justice throughout the following years.[2] Legal education was highly controlled by the British administration, but some Sudanese were able to find their way to Egypt for legal education. Thus, throughout the colonial era, the legal profession in the Sudan was divided between the common law system in the Sudan and the continental Napoleonic law system in Egypt. However, the law of the lawyers, during the condominium period, was the common law. In contrast, the law of the people was the Islamic law, following the Ḥanafī School of fiqh. In addition, customary law was recognized and applied in the countryside. The personal law of the Muslims in the Sudan was judged mostly by Egyptians, while the law of the lawyers was for a long time left to British judges.

The Post-Independence Era: 1956-1983

One can say that it was unfortunate that the modernization of the law in the Sudan was tied to colonialism, since this politicized the law in an artificial manner. More importantly, however, the process of modernization, especially of the penal law, was not sensitive enough to the demands of the traditions of the Sudanese people. In addition, the Sudanese administrators of justice who

---

[1] Mustafa, *The Common Law in the Sudan*, p. 59.

[2] See Lutfi, "The future…", *op. cit.* Thompson, "The Formative Era...," *op. cit.*, and Twining, *op. cit.*

were trained during the colonial era turned into highly westernized elite. This was because legal education was divided between the law of the lawyer (common law) and the law of the people (the Sharīʿah). Thus, a trained law student could only be enrolled in one program. The medium of instruction for the law of the lawyers was English, whereas Arabic was the language for teaching the Sharīʿah. In addition to this, soon after independence, Cairo University established a branch in Khartoum. The law students in this branch were trained in the continental law system, despite the fact that Arabic was the medium of instruction. However, this trilogy of law systems (common, continental, and the Sharīʿah) remained largely intact throughout the post-independence era,[1] and yet, the common law tradition was kept intact.

The period between 1956 and 1964 was the most apparently stable period. This stability, however, was not due to the firm foundation of the judiciary. Immediately prior to this period, all the High Court members from 1950 to 1955 were British except one Sudanese, who became the first Chief Justice between 1955 and 1964, and who was a good example of the highly westernized elite.[2] In contrast, Shaykh Hasan Muddathir, the last Grand Qāḍi in the Sudan submitted to the first Sudanese parliament an appeal for an Islamic constitution. His appeal was based on the premise that "the Sudan is an Islamic country; its social organization is built on Arab customs and Islamic ways."[3] In fact, neither the learned Chief Justice nor the

---

[1] J. O. Voll, *Historical Dictionary of the Sudan* (London: The Scarecrow Press, 1978), p. 29. Also see Vasdev, *Law of Homicide*, *op. cit.*; and "Blood Money and Law of Homicide in the Sudan" in ed. Robert A. Cook, SLJR (1962): pp. 479-480. Although Mansur Khalid in his book *al-Fajr al-Kādhib* (pp. 23-24) played down the element of westernization in Abu Rannat's decisions, yet a critical reading of the examples he presented disproved his claims.

[2] C.F. Thompson, "The Failure of Continental Codes in The Democratic Republic of the Sudan: An Analysis", in *Verfassung und Recht in Ubersee* (1975), pp. 407-421.

[3] Fluehr-Lobban, *op. cit.* P. 47. In addition to Thompson, "The Failure...," the

Grand Qāḍi Shaykh Mudathir was capable of understanding the dynamics of the post-colonial state.

Soon after the October Revolution of 1964, a committee of experts was set up to revise the Sudanese laws to comply with the principles of the Sharīʿah. Furthermore, a parliamentary committee was set up to draft an Islamic constitution. This process was abruptly stopped by the "Revolution of May 1969", led by Nimeiri. However, the fastest developments in the judiciary system and the law took place during Nimeiri's era. First, the law was Arabized. The Egyptian civil law (continental system) had been adopted for a while. Then Zaki Mustafa was appointed to restore the common law. Another reorganization took place in 1980, which led to the restructuring of the judiciary and unified the law of the lawyers (common law or civil) and the law of the people (the Sharīʿah) sections in the Ministry of Justice in one system under the Chief Justice (from the civil section) with four deputies (three from the civil section and one from the Sharīʿah). However, the most important decision was Nimeiri's judiciary revolution of 1983.

Judicial Reform Law and the Development of the Judiciary (1983)

The declaration of the 'Judiciary Revolution' began with the issuance of the Judiciary Act, 1983.[1] From then on, the volume of new legislation amounted to nothing less than a revolution in the substantive laws, the laws of procedure, and others. And yet,

---

discussions about revision of the laws were summarized in: Zaki Abdel Rahman (Attorney General), "Introduction" to *Laws of the Sudan,* vol.1 (1901-1925), 5th edn, 1975), pp. iii-v; Zaki Mustafa (the President's Advisor for Law Revision and Reform), "Preface" *Laws of the Sudan*, Vol. 1(1901-1925), 5th edn, 1975), pp. vii-ix; Zaki Mustafa, "Sudan" in A.N. Allot, ed., *Judicial and Legal Systems in Africa* (London: Butterworths, 1970), pp. 274-288. See also Muhammed Ibrahim Zaid, "Simāt Tanẓīm al-ʿAdalah al-Jināʾiyyah fī al-Sabʿīnāt", *JLJR* (1970), pp. 177-223, concerning change in penal law.

[1] *Al-Ṣaḥāfah.* August 12, 1983.

continuity with the previous legislation was quite evident in the new laws. Obviously, the legal system was transformed to comply with the Sharīʿah, but the method by which this was carried out did not ignore the existing structures. I will confine my analysis here, however, to the penal system. Thus, the following laws are the subject-matter of this analysis:

1. The Penal Code, 1983;
2. The Law of Evidence, 1983;
3. The Criminal Procedure Act, 1983
4. The Basic Rules, 1983;
5. The Judiciary Act, 1983;
6. The Judiciary Act, 1984;
7. The Judiciary circulars issued by the Chief Justice between August, 1983 and September, 1984;
8. The Judiciary circulars issued by Abdel Rahman, the Chief Justice, between October, 1984 and April, 1985;
9. The Explanatory texts issued by the Presidency;
10. The Emergency Rules and Regulations, 1984.[1]

In what follows I will focus on the structures and the actors who codified and implemented these laws; I will divide the process of the inception of the law and development of the judiciary into three periods. The rationale behind this division is that during each period, either the legal actors were changed, or a new set of laws were introduced to restructure the judiciary. Thus, each period had both its specific legal characteristics and its own legal actors. Also, the meaning and structures of justice changed from one period to another.

---

[1] In translating the names of these codes and acts, I have used some of the translations given by Garvey n. Gordon in "The Islamic Legal Revolution: The Case of the Sudan," *The International Lawyer,* vol. 19, No. 3 (1985), pp. 795-796.

Although the distinction between the different phases of Nimeiri's Islamic experiment was blurred in some instances, yet they should be treated separately for a better understanding of the whole experiment. Those distinct features, therefore, were emphasized solely for the purpose of analysis. Throughout the course of Nimeiri's Islamic experiment, we can clearly identify these distinct periods. The first period started with the declaration of the 'Judiciary Revolution', and the issuance of the Judiciary Act, 1983 and ended in April 1984; the second period started with the declaration of the state of emergency in April 1984, and ended in September 1984; and the third period started with the lifting of the state of emergency and the issuance of the Judiciary Act, 1984 and ended with the downfall of Nimeiri's regime.

Each period had different court systems, legal actors and legal procedures. It should be noted that only the substantive law was kept intact throughout the experiment. During the second period, the Criminal Procedure Act (1983) had been replaced by the emergency rule (1984), which was based on the presidential decree no. 285, 1984. The emergency rule of 1984, was supplemented by an explanatory note issued in 1984, and then implemented through the issuance of a number of emergency orders. Moreover, the important legal actors during this period became heads of emergency courts; however, those legal actors were not necessarily from the Judiciary. In contrast to this, during the third period, even the Judiciary Act of 1983 was replaced by the Judiciary Act, 1984. This was done to incorporate the experience of the second period. Moreover, the legal actors of the courts of instantaneous justice during the second period assumed the higher official ranks of the judiciary. For instance, Fuad al-Amin Abdel Rahman was both the Cheif Judge of the panel of the court of instantaneous justice number (9) as well as the Head of the Court of Appeal of the instantaneous justice in Khartoum. However, he was a "shining star" during the second period and he became the Chief Justice instead of Dafaʿ Allah Al-Haj Yusuf.

It should be remarked that the interaction between Islamization and westernization was the major factor behind the history of the judiciary in the modern Sudan. In addition to that the modernization of the judiciary was understood as a process completely different from westernization. Thus, the voices, during the 1960s and 1970s, that called for change were opting for the compliance of the law with the Sudanese tradition, or the Sharīʿah. Clearly, no one dared to call for the demolition of common law system in the Sudan; but rather much of the efforts were directed to call for a revision of that experience. Therefore, the emphasis was on how that experience can comply with the Islamic ideals and most importantly, perhaps, how to achieve *maqāsid al-sharīʿah*, (Objectives of the Sharīʿah) requirements in administration of justice.

Legal Discourse between Historical Formation of the Sharīʿah and *Maqāṣidic* Approach: Religion in the Law[1]

Interestingly, one chapter of the Penal Code, 1983 is titled "Crimes Related to Religions". However, in that chapter, a distinction was clearly made between revealed religions and 'noble heavenly beliefs'. All the Sections of this chapter (242, 243, 244 and 245) are explicit in their concern for, and protection of, revealed religions. On the contrast, only in Section (242a.) are noble heavenly beliefs linked to revealed religions. That provision stipulates the prohibition of using either of them to obtain political goals, or to fuel hatred among different religious groups.

It should be remembered that the structure of the Penal Code, 1974, was in the Penal Code, 1983. Yet, the distinction between revealed religions and noble heavenly beliefs in the

---

[1] Perhaps, the most comprehensive study on Numayri's Islamic experiment in the Sudan is the book by Aharon Layish and Gabriel R. Warbury, *The Reinstatement of Islamic Law in Sudan under Namayri* (Leiden: Brill, 2002).

Penal Code of 1974, was only a description of two different sets of beliefs, whereas in the Penal Code, 1983, the distinction was crucial. Evidently, the phrase 'noble heavenly beliefs' was meant to describe traditional African religions. However, in my interview with Ustaz Awad al-Jeed, member of the committee that drafted the laws, he believed that the distinction in the Penal Code, 1983 was based upon the Islamic understanding of the status of noble heavenly beliefs, (traditional African religions).[1] Most importantly, both Abu Grun, a leading member of the committee that drafted the laws and al-Jeed were very open in admitting that the law shouldn't extend its protection to the noble heavenly beliefs.[2] Al-Jeed even went further, and told me that "it is a sin to protect these beliefs."[3] Both al-Jeed and Abu Grun were aware that the traditional understanding of Islam does not extend the denotation of *ahl al-kitāb* (People of the Book) to 'noble heavenly beliefs'. They are also aware that all the traditional African religions in the Sudan have no sacred books, since they are oral religions.

In my interview with al-Sadiq al-Mahdi, he was very clear on this point: that the traditional understanding of *aḥkām ahl al-dhimmah* (the Rules of the Protected People) should be replaced by the legislation in the document of al-Madīnah. He further argued that this document is much more suitable to our situation in the modern Sudan.[4] This was because the document was based upon a clear understanding of the idea of citizenship in the al-Madīnah regardless of any religious affiliation. Hence, al-Mahdi understood that the document stipulated that all citizens of al- Madīnah are one *ummah*. Thus, the document laid down the foundation for the basic relationship between

---

[1] Author's interview with al-Jeed. (These interviews were conducted between May and August of 1986 in Sudan in addition to these interviews I had a series of extensive interviews with Prof. Abdullah Ahmed An-Naim in UCLA in Jun 1987).

[2] Personal interview with al-Jeed, personal interview with Abu Grun.

[3] Personal interview with al-Jeed.

[4] Personal interview with al-Mahdi.

different religions in the first Islamic state. This was solely based on a citizenship contract. Furthermore, the term, *dīn* (religion) has a much wider application in the Qur'an than *ahl al-kitāb* (the People of the Book). Indeed, pre-Islamic Arabian 'paganism' was regarded by the Qur'an as one form of *dīn*. Therefore, the employment of the Madīnah document principles, according to al-Mahdi, would solve the issue of the non-Muslims in the modern Islamic state.[1]

However, Section (242a.) made a distinction between religion and politics, and thus outlawed the use of religion for political purposes. This provision was both controversial and paradoxical. On the one side, it made a distinction between religion and politics, while the Penal Code was a codification of the Sharī'ah which by its nature does not accept such a distinction. This is because the Sharī'ah is both a religion and a polity. On the other hand, the Penal Code itself was the focus of the 'Judiciary Revolution' which marked the beginning of the regime's Islamic era.

Given this, it is clear that the practice of the regime would make religion inseparable from politics. Hence, this provision was in flat contradiction with the regime's political behavior. It seemed that the provision was not providing any particular interpretation of Islam by the proponents of the regime (or the use of any other religion) against the regime. It should be noted that this provision was consistent with the secular structure of the Penal Code, 1974. Then, when it was incorporated into the Penal Code, 1983, it raised serious problems about the possibility of incorporating any religious understanding of criminology within a positivist secular framework. At a formal level, the provision was in open opposition to Nimeiri's program of Islamization. The only way to avoid that contradiction was to employ a double standard of interpretation of the provision.

[1] *Ibid.*

There are, however, serious concerns to be taken into account as to the real content of this provision. In the first place, both the Muslim Brothers and al-Mahdi's associates considered that this provision was directed against them.[1] When I asked al-Jeed and Abu Grun about the possibility of using this provision against Muslim activists, they completely denied any such possibility.[2] However, al-Jeed went on to say that this provision is quite inapplicable, because it is very difficult to prove that anyone is using religion for political purposes. Moreover, the history of this provision since colonial rule in the Sudan has proven clearly that it is inapplicable.[3] For both al-Jeed and Abu Grun, the provision was there to maintain the structure of the Code, rather than to have any bearing or real content that could be used against any Islamic opposition to the regime. Likewise, it was much less a genuine piece of legislation than a provision that was inherited from the Penal Code, 1974. Nevertheless, the unrestricted form of the provision was very disturbing to both Muslim and non-Muslim activists. More importantly, Shaykh Abu Grun's negation of the possibility of any Islamic opposition to the Islamic leader revealed much about his actual interpretation of this provision. Soon after the imprisonment of the Muslim Brothers, Abu Grun in response to Nur al-Deen Madani considered all political opposition to the Muslim leader, even one who is *fājir* (non-righteous), to be *baghy* and *fitnah* (treason and dissension).[4]

However, it is difficult to accept the interpretations of this provision by both Abu Grun and al-Jeed, as it is equally difficult to buy the Muslim activists' understanding of this provision. This is because the provision could be ignored without affecting either the general structure or the index of the law. Only non-

---

[1] Author's interviews with al-Mahdi, Ibrahim Ahmed Omer and Abdel-Majid.

[2] Interviews with al-Jeed and Abu Grun.

[3] Interview with al-Jeed

[4] *Al-Ṣaḥāfah*, March 29, 1985, p. 7.

Muslims were expected to respond directly against Islamic law. Quite obviously, such a provision was meant as a legal weapon to crush any political opposition to the law. However, it was clearly understood that Nimeiri's 'Judiciary Revolution' would take the wind from the sails of the Muslim activists who opposed the regime for Islamic reasons.[1] Interestingly, Abdellah Jarbuʿ remarked that the provision could be understood as part of the hastiness and inconsistency of the legislators.[2] In addition, al-Mahdi had a low opinion of the legislators of Nimeiri's Islamic program. He believed that they were chosen, much less for their legal competence than for blind loyalty to Nimeiri. More importantly, al-Mahdi added that he considered Nimeiri's Islamic era of terror in the name of religion. In fact, al-Mahdi wrote a *maqāmah* (a generic of Arabic prose) titled *al-tarwīʿ bi al-tashrīʿ* (terror with legislation).[3] Accordingly, for al-Mahdi, Section 242a could be understood in the light of both the incompetence of the legislators and their bad intentions.

In contrast, al-Turabi gave Nimeiri credit for his Islamic measures. Yet he observed that Nimeiri's Islamic legislation was meant to govern the governed only, and not to be extended to the governor.[4] Nonetheless, he believed there were shortcomings in the codification of the laws. Al-Turabi also thought that the idea of a double standard for the governor/governed was the key to understanding Nimeiri's Islamic experiment.

Keeping in mind all these factors, I believe that both bad intentions towards Muslim and non-Muslim activists as well as the inconsistency of the law were behind this provision.

Although the Penal Code, 1983 was supposed to be a codification of the Sharīʿah, only six chapters out of 29 were

---

[1] Mansour Khalid, *Nimeiri and The Revolution of Dis-May* (London: Routledge, 1985), p. 257.

[2] Personal interview with Taha Ibrahim Abdallah (Jarbu').

[3] Personal interview with al-Mahdi.

[4] Personal interview with al- Turabi.

related to the Islamic stipulations. Moreover, as Abdellah Jarbuʿ observed, these six chapters were not more than an attempt to incorporate the Islamic *ḥudūd* (punishment laws) within a framework that originally considered murder, theft, and so on as criminal activities.[1] Thus, the reformulation of these chapters was done in such a way as to preserve both the pluralistic orientation of the law, and the special emphasis on the Sharīʿah. As al-Naʿim told the author, the previous theory of criminal responsibility was preserved intact in the new Penal Code.[2]

However, when I asked Abu Grun, why they left out stoning from Section 318(1) as the punishment for adultery, while it is included in Section 64 in the Penal Code, 1983, and, why apostasy was not in the Penal Code, 1983, his answer was that they were much more concerned with the negative impressions that would be created by these two things, rather than with perfecting the Penal Code from an Islamic point of view.[3] He further pointed out that, as legislators, they were aware of the shortcomings of the law from an Islamic point of view. Yet they kept at the end of each law a general principle that clearly stipulated the non-validity of any provision of the law that contradicts the Sharīʿah. Thus, the strategy of the legislation was to avoid sensitive and controversial issues, while keeping intact the general principle of the sovereignty of the Sharīʿah. Therefore, Abu Grun believed that any apparent contradiction between Islamic principles and any legislation should be understood in the light of the above-mentioned strategy.[4]

However, al-Jeed justified leaving out stoning by the fact that it would not be possible to implement this punishment for practical reasons. In addition, Abdel-Malik al-Jaʿalī, then

---

[1] Personal interview with Abdallah (Jurduʿ).

[2] Author's iinterview with Abdellahi Ahmed An-Naʿim.

[3] Interview with Abu Grun.

[4] Ibid

Minister of Religious Affairs, issued a *fatwā* (legal opinion) to the effect that, due to the circumstances under which Islamic laws were restored, hanging could juridically replace the stoning punishment. Nonetheless, al-Jeed added that Section 64 is an original provision in the Penal Code, whereas Section 318(1) is not. Thus, under normal circumstances Section 64 would rule over Section 318(1).[1]

Evidently, the proclamation of the law of Basic Rules, 1983, was in line with Abu Grun's strategy of legislation. Although it was the only law that was adopted without any change from the legislation passed by al-Turabi's committee, this law, unlike the other legislation, was originally designed to serve the same purpose. However, the law was divided into two sections: 1) how to explain any piece of legislation; 2) what is required from a judge when there is no legislation. Quite obviously, the Basic Rules, 1983 was a general articulation of the principles of *usūl al-fiqh* (Principles of Islamic Jurisprudence).

Moreover, the law was written with an eclectic attitude toward Islamic schools of law. However, they made a distinction between the stipulations of the Sharīʿah and the activity of the *fuqahā'* (Muslim jurists). The law, here, considered the sense of justice, as approved by sound human reason, as a source of guidance that could be used in the absence of Islamic legislation in civil cases. Primarily, then, the law considered the principles of the Sharīʿah, and, next to it the fiqh as the major sources for understanding the legislation. Finally, the law accepted both sound human legislation and the Sudanese precedents as sources of guidance, if, and only if, they did not contradict the principles of the Sharīʿah.

The basic assumption behind this law was that Islam does not contradict the human disposition. Thus, whatever emerges from a sound human disposition ought to comply with Islamic norms and stipulations. Both Abu Grun and al-Jeed asserted

---

[1] Interview with al-Jeed.

that they believe that Islamic legislation came about to purify and enhance the quality of goodness in human beings. Thus, out of this conviction, they believe that Islamic legislation in the Sudan was meant to restore this quality.[1]

Obviously, religious language as well as religious categories of the *fuqahā'* were carefully avoided in the law. This did not, however, drastically affect the content of the law. As al-Jeed mentioned, the objective of the Islamic legislation was not meant to disregard the existence of non-Muslims, neither to estrange the enforcement mechanisms; it was rather meant to add the Islamic sanctions to the Penal Code closely following the spirit of the Penal Code, 1974.[2] One can surmise that the Penal Code, 1983 is an "Islamicized" replica of the Penal Code, 1974. However, it could also be seen as an attempt to 'secularize' the Sharīʿah within the post-colonial state. And yet the architects of the 'Judiciary Revolution' were careful enough to state clearly the sovereignty of the Sharīʿah over and above any provision of these laws. It could also be said that they were much more worried about the criticism of the two extremes, than about the perfect formulation of the law. As a result, for the 'secularists', the emphasis would be on the new code as it is an attempt to "secularize" the Sharīʿah. Whereas for the "fundamentalist", no matter in what framework the Sharīʿah was codified, it was specified that the fundamental law in the legislation was the rule of the Sharīʿah.

The Philosophy of Punishment

Most of the intellectual effort to work out a theory of punishment has been rather devoted to the justification of the implementation of the Sharīʿah. Evidently, this has to do with the obvious tension between Islamization and the post-colonial framework. Thus, instead of working out a philosophy of

---

[1] Interview with al-Jeed, Personal interview with Abu Grun.

[2] Interview with al-Jeed.

punishment from an Islamic viewpoint, the major effort was devoted to justifying the issues of authenticity, liberation, and the Islamization of human knowledge. These were seen as necessary conditions for any practical program of implementing the Sharīʿah.

Thus, a considerable amount of attention was paid to both the justification of punishment and the practical implementation of the Sharīʿah. In this connection, it should be remarked that Mudathir Abdel-Rahim was the first to advocate the importance of 'cultural authenticity' in the Sudanese context.[1] During the 1970s, Abdel-Rahim's argument was understood by the Muslim Brotherhood as a genuine contribution to the process of Islamization. Later, the same argument was used by the government to justify the implementation of the Sharīʿah. Though the religious dimension in Abdel-Rahim's argument was not clear, 'cultural authenticity' could easily be put into an Islamic framework. In my interview with him, Abdel-Rahim confided that he was aware of that dimension in his argument. More importantly, it became generally used in justifying Nimeiri's program of Islamization. And yet, Abdel-Rahim considered it a narrow escape in Nimeiri's case, because, for him, the playing off of the *shūrā* (consultation), against *al-ʿadālah al-ijtimāʿiyyah* (social justice) handicapped Nimeiri's Islamic program. Abdel-Rahim stated that he had expressed these concerns to Nimeiri, after the declaration of the 'Judiciary Revolution', in a meeting with him. Yet Nimeiri responded by equating such concerns with al-Mahdi's criticism of the experiment. Though Abdel-Rahim was black-listed, his intellectual impact was still evident throughout the pages of the Journal of *Jamāʿat al-Fikr al-Islāmī.*[2] Although this intellectual

---

[1] See *Majallat al-Fikr al-Islāmī,* (2) (September 1984), pp. 6-12. See also Mudathir Abdel-Rahim, *Bayn al-Aṣālah wa al-Tabʿiyyah* (Khartoum University Press, 1978).

[2] Interview with Omer. See also *al-Dalīl al-Fikrī li al-Ikhwān al-Muslmīn*

organ was established before the declaration of the 'Judiciary Revolution', by and large its activity reflected the intellectual content of Nimeiri's Islamic era.

On the other hand, Ibrahim Ahmed Omer, a leading member in the Muslim Brotherhood in Sudan who was considered the 'philosopher' of the organization, after Jafar Shaykh Idris, articulated an Islamic epistemology along with his 'philosophy of development'. He developed his epistemology for a 'philosophy of development' within the doctrine of the Islamization of human knowledge. Though Idris ceased to have any active role and considerable influence in the organization due to his reservations concerning the political line of al-Turabi and his associates and to his subsequently self-imposed exile in Saudi Arabia, Omer has never been far from Idris' way of thinking. Both of them regarded Abdel-Rahim's analysis of Sudanese politics highly; they especially admired his thesis of 'cultural authenticity'. In the interview with Omer, he made a distinction between two separate but related issues with regard to 'cultural liberation'. [1] For him, the first issue, the implementation of the Islamic laws, was a crucial step through which they (as Sudanese Muslims) would be able to establish their system in accord with their cultural heritage and beliefs. The second issue was the extent to which they understood Islam, and the extent to which the 'experiment' would succeed in the realization of Islamic goals. For Omer, the distinction between the two issues was crucial, because no matter who led the process of 'cultural liberation' it was inherently a good process. Thus, the shortcomings of the 'experiment' should not be used to belittle the importance of the process of 'cultural liberation' on the legal level. In short, the dictatorship of Nimeiri's regime should not be an excuse for doing away with

---

(unpublished essay) probably written by J'afar Shaykh Idris.

[1] Interview with Omer; Ibrahim Ahmed Omer *Falsafat al-Tanmiyyah: Rwiya Islamiyyah* (unpublished essay, 1986)

the Islamic measures he had introduced. Although Omer believes that there is an Islamic method that governed the process of codification, the context of this process should also have been emphasized.

However, Omer's justification of the theory of punishment in Islam must be understood within the context of his general theory of knowledge in Islam. It is quite evident that no summary of Omer's theory of knowledge in Islam will do justice to it. However, I will try here to recapitulate its main points. Omer regards the *waḥy* (revelation) as *the maṣdar* (the principal source of knowledge). Both the Qur'an and the Sunnah are regarded as the higher *maṣādir*. Then, he accepts the linguistic methods of *usūliyyūn* as valid methods in that domain. Yet there is another important principle that unifies knowledge in the different domains (natural, social and psychological). Thus, the unity of knowledge is constantly stressed here. This unity is established through the most basic concept of Islam which is *al-ḥaqq*. Omer defines *al-ḥaqq* as the characteristic of things described by God. For instance, X a person, a code, or a society will achieve the maximum utility, if X satisfies the requirements of *al-ḥaqq*. Although *al-ḥaqq* is the most central concept in Omer's theory of knowledge, he stresses both utility and beauty. Thus, the theory of punishment in Islam is understood within this theory of knowledge that seeks to unify knowledge and establish the basic philosophic assumptions of Islam. In his philosophy Omer labors to overcome the inherent shortcomings of both deduction and induction and, above all, to work out an axiological stand that fosters unity without adopting ethical sensibility of consequence. Finally, he was fully aware of the human dimension in his understanding of the principal sources of Islam.[1]

After reviewing the legal literature and considering the practice of the Emergency Courts and the Courts of

[1] Interview with Omer.

Instantaneous Justice throughout Nimeiri's Islamic experiment, it can be said that the term *rādiʿah* (deterrent) was employed as the justification for punishment. It should be noted that *rādiʿah* was not the ultimate justification for punishment; but rather reflected the usual understanding of how the law actually functioned in the Sudanese context. This is because the ultimate justification for the infliction of punishment in Islam is that it is *al-ḥaqq* (the persistent). However, the term *al-ḥaqq* is much more difficult and complex. This is the justification at the axiological level. Thus, for administering justice in day-to-day activities, deterrence is clearly emphasized in the legal rationale of the judges. Most importantly, for quite a long time, it was the constant main theme for the news items issued by both the Emergency Courts and the Courts of Instantaneous Justice. In editing the daily reports of these Courts, the Attorney's Office and then the Minister of State for Criminal Affairs in the Attorney General Chamber were clearly emphasizing deterrence as the general philosophy of punishment.

Clearly, deterrence as a justification for punishment was a much less developed concept in these daily reports, than simply a legal jargon. Indeed, there was a tendency to popularize the notion of deterrence in these reports. This was partially due to the fact that these reports were not addressed to members of the legal profession, but rather to the general public. However, this aspect of Nimeiri's legal-Islamic experiment was responsible for popular support for Nimeiri's administration and allowed him to legitimize his rule. Likewise, the overwhelming popular presence of this factor should not be overlooked if we are to reach a proper understanding of this aspect of Nimeiri's Islamic experiment and how it appealed to the general psychology of the people.

When I interviewed Abu Grun about the justification of punishment in the Penal Code (1983), his answer was that punishment is principally justified by the basic belief of the Islamic *ʿaqīdah*. Therefore, he went to say, for us as Muslims, all good objectives including practical ones can be achieved by the correct implementation of Islamic punishment code. Abu Grun believes that punishment, in Islam, is quite justifiable, because it is *al-ḥaqq*. As such, one of its goals is is to maintain the social order. Thus, for Abu, Grun the former justification is the sole justification of punishment for a Muslim. In contrast, the latter can be a justification even for non-Muslims. It should be noted that for him this dual nature of the justification is due to the fundamental fact that the law is meant for both Muslims and non-Muslims.[1]

Interestingly enough, Abu Grun considered that the whole philosophy of the 'Judiciary Revolution' was a genuine search for *aṣālat al-murtakẓ al-qānūnī* (the authenticity of legal authority).[2] He went on to elaborate that Islam provided that for the Sudanese people. Further, these authentic legal sources liberate the human being, as such, from any authority other than God. More importantly, he added that servitude to God is not a constraint hindering the realization of maximum human freedom. For him, this is because servitude to God is ultimate freedom. As a result, for the Muslim, the need to be a law-abiding citizen will not emerge from fear of the law, but rather from a genuine submission to the legislation that is considered to be a part of the belief in God. However, Abu Grun regarded Islam as the only true revelation that can be legally implemented, whereas both Christianity and Judaism lacked, for him, these two qualities of both validity and possibility of implementation. Accordingly, he believed that Islam is the only alternative and 'third force' that could replace both capitalism and communism.[3]

Abu Grun represents the popular Sufi understanding of this issue. It is much less important for them to prove the validity of

---

[1] Interview with Abu Grun.
[2] *Ibid.*
[3] *Ibid.*

their claims about the other alternatives; rather their emphasis falls on Islamic belief. Furthermore, both history and empirical data lack the capability of offering counter-examples to both their beliefs and the sacred details of Islamic history. In short, their *Ṣūfī* dogmatism about every minor detail that could be labeled Islamic is immune to any scientific refutation. And yet Abu Grun was quite capable of admitting that he is "one-sided" in his understanding of Nimeiri's Islamic experiment.[1]

Soon after the declaration of the 'Judiciary Revolution', the Presidency issued an "Explanatory Text" for the Penal Code, 1983.[2] The Explanatory Text was divided into two sections. Section one was confined to criminal responsibility and the theory of punishment, whereas section two was committed to the clarification of the important crimes in the Penal Code, 1983. However, the justification for punishment was dealt with in such a way as to enable the judge to realize the goals of Islamic law when implementing its rules. This is because the judge, according to the 'Judiciary Revolution', was given a wide range of authority both in interpreting the law and in choosing between alternatives ppenalties. Ultimately, deterrence was stressed as a general strategy for punishment. Yet education and reform were thought of as a favorable alternative in some cases, especially in the case of discretionary punishments. Moreover, corporal punishment was stressed, and the judges were directed to avoid imprisonment as far as possible.

In short, the Explanatory Text criticized the prison system as both ineffective deterrent and innovation having not precedent in the Prophetic tradition. It should be remembered that the opening statement in the Explanatory Text emphasized *al-ittibāʿ* (the following of the tradition) and denounced *al-ibtidāʿ* (innovation). However, the Explanatory Text is such more

---

[1] *Ibid.*

[2] *al-Saḥāfa*, October 15, 1984, p. 5; the second part of the Explanatory Note was published in *al-Saḥāfa*, October 18, 1984, p. 5.

faithful to the traditional Islamic literature of penology, *al-ahkām al-salṭāniyyah*, than the Penal Code, 1983. Perhaps, it was meant to restore this missing part in the Penal Code.

Contrary to this emphasis on public deterrence, the actual implementation of punishment was moderate and humane. Although amputation of hands and legs took place in Kober prison, the punishment was administered using a medical knife and was carried out under the supervision of one of the most famous medical doctors in Khartoum. Furthermore, the amputee would be taken directly to the nearby hospital.[1] Thus, the punishment was much less a painful amputation than a surgical amputation of the hand or the leg. However, the presence of medical staff in this type of punishment raised the theoretical question of restoring the hand or the leg; right after the amputation act took place. Likewise, the Islamic requirements would be formally satisfied, while the criminal would not lose his hand or leg forever.[2] This raised a theoretical question whether the goal behind amputation is to get rid of a limb or to inflict suffering. It further posed the question as to whether Islamic punishments were meant to emphasize the reform of the offender or to preserve public order.

These and other issues were raised because of the advances in medical science that have made such restoration possible. It was thus asked whether the Islamic stipulations regarding the amputation of limbs were meant solely to inflict pain, or whether they were designed to affect the complete loss of the limb. This was because it had been reported that a doctor tried to restore the hand of an amputee. Moreover, it was asked whether it was permissible to restore the limb after amputation or not. For this reason, other Muslim legislators were asked to

---

[1] *Al-Saḥāfah*, December 10, 1984, p. 1; the amputation was described in detail.

[2] *Al-Muslimūn: Jarīdat al-Muslimīn al-Dawliyah*, January 21, 1987 p. 5. This issue reviewed a Ph.D. in al-Azhar University that dealt with the problem. More importantly, in the issue of May 2, 1985, p. 1; a report from the Sudan provided the researcher with the law case.

develop a comprehensive philosophy of punishment, in order to resolve this clear tension between the classical understanding of criminology and the modern legal understanding. It is evident that the modern codification of the penal aspect of the Sharīʿah should be organized according to a clear modern understanding of the philosophy of punishment.

As a matter of fact, there were conflicting stands regarding the issue of the philosophy of punishment during the three periods of Nineiri's Islamic experiment. Nimeiri's own stand was outlined in his famous speech on the fifteenth anniversary of the May Revolution. He never altered it throughout the experiment. He threatened the would-be offenders that they would be publicly flogged.[1] He also knew that there was a prevailing belief among the Sudanese that public flogging shouldn't deter courageous people; on the contrary, it is a virtue not to be deterred by such punishment. However, he argued that offenders should be ashamed and consider the public punishment to be the most humiliating of experiences. This is because it is much less a matter of courage in bearing the pain of flogging, than it is an issue of subjecting oneself to degradation. However, for the average Sudanese, it is less a matter of right and wrong than a matter of showing courage and boldness in the face of the pain of punishment itself.[2]

This may be due, basically, to the fact that the law of the lawyers is an urban phenomenon, and for quite a long time it was adjudicated by foreigners. Thus, being courageous, while facing the infliction of pain by the authorities, was considered a highly respected norm by the Sudanese. Nimeiri argued that it was beside the point whether the offender is courageous or not in bearing the pain; rather, the punishment should be looked at as a mark of dishonor. Hence, a decent citizen should save his

---

[1] *Al-Ṣaḥāfah,* May 25, 1984, p. 6.

[2] Tore Nordenstam, *Sudanese Ethics* (Uppsala: The Scandinavian Institute of African Studies, 1968), p. 82.

record from such a thing regardless of the fear of the physical pain. Furthermore, Nimeiri threatened the would-be offenders by saying that the report of the criminal courts would be a permanent item in the news. Thus, public defamation would be another aspect of the punishment.[1] In short, Nimeiri was stressing deterrence as the general principle of punishment. Yet, deterrence was used by Nimeiri much less in the technical sense of the term than in an emotive sense.

Maqāṣid al-Sharīʿah and Systematization of Values

The prime concern of *maqāṣid al-sharīʿah* in the process of codification or implementation of the law is about the specific objectives of the penal system. Though the general objectives of the Sharīʿah will provide the framework where both *maqāṣid al-shāriʿ* (objectives of the Lawgiver) and *maqāṣid al-mukallaf* (objectives of the human being) will be the main principles from which the specific penal laws will be derived, the systematization of penal values will be the main concern of the specific objectives of the Sharīʿah in punishment. In this regard, one can make a distinction between the specific objectives of the Sharīʿah which can be derived from the whole corpus of penal rulings and the specific objectives which have been directing the implementation of these laws. Based on this distinction one will be able to identify the set of values that govern the process of codification and that which govern the process of implementation. The former set of values will reveal the concerns of the legislators, while the latter will reflect the intents of enforcement mechanisms. Therefore, the systematization of values will focus on the two sets of values and how they relate to the objectives of the Sharīʿah and, more to the point, how they relate to the specific objectives of the penal system.

To begin with, I will confine my discussion to the set of

---

1 *Al-Saḥāfa,* May 25, 1984, p. 6.

values that govern the process of codification. One can say that the learned legislators assumed that the act of codifying the Sharīʿah should be taken for granted. To prepare for "The Judiciary Revolution", Nimeiri had set up a committee to draft a number of legislations in order to make the existing laws comply with the Sharīʿah ideals. Thus, *taqnīn al-sharīʿah* (codification of the Sharīʿah) was a non-issue; it was rather taken as the necessary step for the Islamization of the legal system. As a result, the legislators were much less interested in doing away with the existing system of codification or the framework that resulted from it; their main concern was how to maintain a delicate balance between the Sharīʿah values pertaining to crime and punishment and the existing framework of the penal code. It should be pointed out that the existing framework reflected all the values of a secular legal system. Yet the learned legislators were supposed to be careful enough to develop and maintain a delicately balanced Islamized legal system. Admittedly, the values of the post-colonial legal system were in open contradiction with the Islamic ones. It should be remembered that the apparent contradiction was largely due to the hierarchy of values of each system. It is equally important to remark that a value is a value whether it is in the Islamic legal system or a secular one. The only difference will be its position in the hierarchy of values.

In this reespect, a fundamental difference is the systematization of these values in a hierarchical set. The legislators of the 1983 "Judiciary Revolution" decided to keep all the parts of the legal system that would not be in open contradiction with the Sharīʿah. When it was necessary to keep some parts of the existing legislation for technical reasons though they happened to be in contradiction with the Sharīʿah, they were kept. However, as a general principle, the legislators argued that any piece of legislation that contradicts the Sharīʿah values should be considered null and void. It was suggested that all the benefits of the common law system and its experience in the Sudan should be preserved and that the process of Islamization of the legal system was not meant to throw away the baby with the bath-water. A driving idea was that this process was to benefit from the human wisdom regardless of its sources. The existing experience of the common law system in Sudan was meant to be perfected by the addition of the Islamic values. Therefore, these values were seen by the legislators as part and parcel of recognized universal values.

The Islamic way of systematizing these values was regarded as casting them in a new hierarchical order. The values of the existing penal system were recognized and the legislators had to recast them in the new system that maintained a delicate balance between the values of modernization and the Islamic values of criminology. This was taken as a general strategy in the process of codification. Despite the fact that those legislators were careful enough or perhaps were having limited choices in the process of codifying the values of the Sharīʿah in formal laws, they were aware of the importance of benefiting from the existing framework and declaring the Sharīʿah values as supreme values. At this point, one would like to know whether the aims of those experts were in line with the general objectives of the Sharīʿah or not. Obviously, one would not like to give a simple and straightforward answer for such a complicated question, but one could say that the legislators developed a legal system in keeping with both the required values of modernization and the ideals of Islam. By so doing they believed to restore Islamic identity and not to be completely alienated from the process of modernization. It is worthy pointing out that the idea of utilizing human wisdom was the driving force behind their work. This should be in line with the main objectives of the Sharīʿah, but could it equally be relevant to the specific objectives of the codification of the Islamic penal values?

One would not err to say that there is nothing against such a position for codifying the penal values of Islam in the form of a codified law. What is of utmost importance is the conspicuous declaration of shari'ah as the supreme source of values and its hierarchical system should be completely adopted without any reservations. This is exactly what the members of the committee did in the process of codification which resulted in a set of laws, directives and explanatory notes. The main criticism which was leveled against their work was that it was immature in terms of its technical apparatus. Such immaturity was rather expected since the committee was not given either enough time or the freedom to consult other experts who could render invaluable suggestion for such an historical work. Arguably, the ethics of intent that governed the work of the legislators was in line with the objectives of the Sharīʿah in the specific area of criminology. However, the end result of their work suffered a great deal of inconsistencies and a gross violation of the appropriate method of codifying the Sharīʿah values into a form of law. There might be political reasons behind all this, but it certainly deprived this historical experience of the regular process that could have contributed significantly to the success of the codification of the values of the Sharīʿah in a penal code. Consequently, it would be out of context to raise the question whether the process of codification is in line with the specific objectives of the Sharīʿah or not.

Let us now turn our attention to the second part of this discussion. It should be remarked that the values that governed the process of implementation were significantly different from the values that governed the process of codification. This is because the process of implementation was much less about the existing legal framework than about the enforcement mechanisms and the dynamics of the politicization of the law. In addition, the legal actors and the structures of the judiciary were not the same throughout the experiment. As it was suggested earlier, there were three phases through which the process of implementation took place. In each phase there were different legal actors and a new judiciary structure. All this contributed a great deal to the differences in the values that governed the process of implementation.

Certainly, during the first phase of the implementation the main justification of punishment was to deter the would-be offenders. It seemed that both the legal actors and the judicial structure were, essentially, for advocating the deterrence value of the penal system. Deterrence in this regard had nothing to do with the actual implementation of the punishment in order to deter the would-be-offenders. Rather, the deterrence value of the law was the major aspect of the justification regardless of the realization of this value in specific case or not. The mindset of the legal actor and the setup of the judiciary were supposed to carry out this value through the process of the law with it symbolic value as presenting the ideals of Islam. The *ḥudūd* were meant as a reminder for the human being not to cross the boundaries of decenc, and most importantly not to be under the wrath of his Creator.

In contrast, both the second and the third phases of the experiment were dominated by high visibility of the deterrence factor not as justification of punishment, but as a realization of one aspect of this value of delerance. The implementation of the two systems of punishment was meant to deter the would-be-offenders rather than a justification of punishment. This, among other things, can be seen as deterrence directed mainly against would-be-offenders. While in the first phase punishment was not meant to be implemented but rather to be seen as a symbolic representation of the ideals of Islam in penology, in both the second and third phases that the implementation of the punishment was meant to promote the deterrence function of the law. Therefore, it should be kept in mind that deterrence by law is completely different from deterrence by the implementation of the law in order to deter the would-be-offenders. Because of this the second and third phases of the experiment witnessed a politicization of the law and, more specifically, the law was utilized to crush any political dissent. Clearly, the answer to the question whether the objectives of the legal actors, the judiciary structure and the enforcement mechanisms in the second and third phases of the experiment were in line with specific objectives of the Sharīʿah in the area of penology, would be a simple one. The politicization of the law and the urge to inflict pain on others while making a clear distinction between the governed and the governor would defeat the purpose of the penal system in Islam. It would be counterproductive and could be seen as antithetical to the value of justice. This is because the sole justification of punishment in Islam is that it maintains a high quality of justice. Therefore, in a system that showed the slightest deviation from this cardinal value would be remarked null and void.

Finally, one could argue that though this experiment maintained a careful concern about the systematization of the Sharīʿah values in the process of codification, it suffered from a major setback in keeping with the specific objectives of the Sharīʿah during the second and third phases of the process of implementation.

Conclusion

It was stated that the Sudanese Penal Code is a poor replica of the English Law. It was equally noted that the Sudanese Penal Code, 1983 is a poor codification of the Sharīʿah. Perhaps, the shared characteristic between these two legal documents is that hastiness was the rule of the game. Both the British lawyer and the legislators of the 1983 code were rushed to finish up the job. Let it be remembered that the legislators of the 1983 'Judiciary Revolution' were careful enough not to do away with the English law infrastructure; they rather focused on purifying that infrastructure from the provisions that go against the spirit of the Sharīʿah. Thus, for them, the legislative strategy is to maintain the English law framework and to codify the Sharīʿah in such a way that does not nullify the English law experience.

However, the un-codified part of the Sharīʿah can be applied in cases of lacunae in the statutory legislation. Most importantly, perhaps, it was stated in the Basic Rules, 1983 that the court should apply in cases of lacunae the un-codified Sharīʿah, and the Penal Code, 1983 declared that any provision of this law opposing the Sharīʿah is null and void. This legislative strategy of codifying the Sharīʿah that resulted in the 'Judiciary Revolution' provides us with an in-depth understanding of the interplay between the specific *maqāṣidic* approach and the post-colonial state.

CHAPTER NINE

Maqāṣid and Related Islamic Legal Concepts on Current Bioethical Issues: Critical Reflections

Anke Iman Bouzenita

Introduction

This chapter is an analysis of, and reflection upon, Muslim scholars' use of *maqāṣid al-sharīʿah* and related Islamic juristic concepts in their evaluation of contemporary bioethical issues. It does not intend to provide a *maqāṣidic* framework for the derivation of legal rules in the field of bioethics, but rather to highlight some of the problems related to the reference to *maqāṣid* on a meta-level. It tries to figure out a paradigm involving the relationship between Islam and science and expounds the major paradigm shift which has taken place in the Muslim world. The chapter then analyzes the implications of the paradigm shift on the reference to *maqāṣid*. A number of selected contemporary bioethical issues will be discussed to highlight the background of the contemporary reference framework.

A Paradigm and its Development: Islam and Science

Islam is a comprehensive, all-encompassing and universal way of life. Qur'anic verses like "Today, I completed your *dīn* for you" (Q., 5: 3), and "We did not leave out anything in the book" (Q., 6:

38) are clear to the effect that Islam as a way of life covers all aspects of human existence and addresses whatever matters imaginable, from personal hygiene to state affairs. The Islamic legal system known as the Sharīʿah translates this into the different aspects of life, thus transcending the secular meaning of law.

Medical and bioethical issues are part and parcel of the realities of human life. The role of Islamic jurisprudence or *fiqh*, as it is generally known, is to provide legal rulings on any practical aspect of human life based on the Islamic sources. So far, we might state that the role of Islamic law in bio-medical questions is the same as in any other field of human activity, i.e. to incorporate an action or a situation into the framework of the Sharīʿah by evaluating it, on the basis of its sources, as *ḥarām*, *makrūh, mubāḥ, mandūb* or *farḍ*. Accordingly, Islamic jurisprudence has from the earliest times developed and formulated a number of legal rules to those questions related to bio-medicine such as abortion or treatment with prohibited substances or materials *(al-tadāwī bi-l-muḥarramāt)*.

In those past centuries during which the Islamic way of life was established in a holistic manner, Islamic culture and civilization brought about unique contributions in all domains of life, especially in what has come to be known as the natural sciences, including medicine. In total contrast to the Christian medieval experience, Islamic civilization never opposed the development of science. While science and medicine soon florished under the embrella of Islamic culture with sanction from its scriptural sources, the Christian Church was imposing severe obstacles to scientific research and development. Science in the West only developed after the Church's influence on culture and society was drastically reduced, whereas scientific progress in the Muslim world slowed down in the wake of an overall decline linked to a negligence of and deviation from the very foundations of Islamic society and culture.

I am reluctant to speak of a particularly *Islamic* science or a particularly *Islamic* medicine, as some scholars do.[1] However, we may understand *Islamic science* or *Islamic medicine* as a scientific model developed within the framework of an Islamic socio-cultural system and informed by the spiritual and moral values of that system. Obviously, any (medical) research developed in accordance with these outlines cannot be considered un-Islamic. In other words, it is the framework of reference which sets the values and objectives of a society. In an Islamic society, this framework of reference is constituted by what the Qur'ān and Sunnah have determined in terms of rules, values and objectives.[2]

As stated earlier, "Islamic medicine" is a model developed within the framework of an Islamic society. It is not necessarily a medical treatment derived from Islamic texts or sources. Muslim scientists have freely referred to and made use of the scientific heritage bequeathed by preceding cultures and civilizations. The Greek contributions to medicine, once translated into Arabic, laid an important practical and theoretical foundation to build upon. Non-Muslims working within the wider framework of the Islamic civilization contributed to that aspect of Islamic culture. The Muslim scholars who excelled in the natural sciences had generally been polymaths whose

---

[1] See for example, Syed Hossein Nasr, *Science and Civilization in Islam* (Chicago IL: ABC International Group, 2001); Muzaffar Iqbal, *The Making of Islamic Science* (Petaling Jaya, Malaysia: Islamic Book Trust, 2009), also *Science and Islam* (Westport/Connecticut/London: Greenwood Press, 2007); George Saliba, Islamic Science and the Making of the European Renaissance (Camridge, Massachusetts/London: The MIT Press, 2007); Ziaduddin Sardar, *How Do You Know? Reading Ziauddin Sardar on Islam, Science and Cultural Relations*, edited by Ehsan Masood (London/Ann Arbor: Pluto Press, 2006), esp. pp. 91-213.

[2] The term 'Islamic medicine' is sometimes used to designate Prophetic medicine (*al-ṭibb al-nabawī*), meaning the medical advice or statements recorded in the traditions of the Prophet (*s.a.w.*). It might also be used to designate medical treatment with the Qur'an or related methods of alternative medicine used in an Islamic context. This chapter adopts a working definition of *Islamic medicine* as stated above.

education was solidly based on Islamic teachings and values.

It is often referred to the adaptability of Islamic culture, i.e. its ability and aptitude to absorb and adapt knowledge from other cultures ("islamize" it, according to some) and make it its own. Some remarks have to be made here to understand an inherent mechanism Islamic society has enacted in the past because it is still relevant for the relationship of Islam and science today.

We have to differentiate between two forms of science; a universal form which is not bound by a particular point of view in life; and a specific form which is directly linked to a specific point of view. What is universal in technology and science is generally permissible (*mubāḥ*) as it does not have any particular impact on our belief system. God says: "Are you not aware that God has made subservient to you all18 that is in the heavens and all that is on earth, and has lavished upon you His blessings, both outward and inward?" (Q., 31: 20). In other words, it is basically value-free. Its interpretation and usage, however, may be ideologically bound by a particular framework.

Whatever is directly linked to an idea emanating from *other* than the Islamic belief system and values needs to be evaluated in the light of the Islamic parameters. Technical and medical innovations directly emanating from a specific non-Islamic point of view on life, such as human evolution from apes, or attempts to bring about eternal life in humans, are clearly to be rejected from an Islamic point of view.

The Contemporary Context

Humankind has suffered a tremendous loss when the development of a holistic Islamic culture broke down and was then abandoned. Re-enacting Islamic culture today is imperative as it has been severed from the roots of its vitality and real the sources of its dynamism. From being established as an encompassing way of life in the past, Islamic life has been reduced to the area of personal worship and some rules related to personal status. It is generally referred to in limited ethical terms. The political framework needed to implement Islamic systems was abolished.

The scientific (and medical) models prevailing in our age arose from a socio-cultural milieu which stands in diametric opposition to spirit of Islamic culture and worldview. Generated in the so-called developed countries, they have emerged from a distinctly materialist and capitalist worldview. Characteristic of this point of view is, first and foremost, the separation of life from (any) religion. Worldly matters are to be decided by worldly authorities with no reference to revelation. Religion is to be confined to the individual's private sphere and must not influence the public discourse on legal, economic or political matters. Hence, the foundation of human action, its raison d'être, is neither reward nor punishment in the Hereafter. Such action is rather valued and defined on the basis of its material profitability and ensuing interests, thus giving way to sheer utilitarianism.

An ethics (founded on a semi-religious or humanistic basis) has been introduced to bridge the gap between reality and conscience, but ethical boundaries are very hard to delimitate and even harder to realize in a materialistically orientated system. What is profitable is allowed or will be legalised once public opinion has been calmed down and sufficiently re-directed. Negative medical, ethical, and environmental side effects will always be subordinated to the rules of profit. Although most capitalist countries have established advisory ethical committees to set some kind of common sense boundaries, reality proves that there is always a way to serve the goals of interest groups, thus giving them precedence over anything else.

The implications of these ideological foundations are obvious. Research needs to be funded. Next to government funding, it is the big multinational companies which channel research into the direction which is most profitable to them.

Unprofitable innovations or those that harm the globalized market's interests are suppressed. Copyright laws, enacted to protect "intellectual property", have become eternalizers of those companies' profits. To mention only one example of the manifold manifestations of this phenomenon, AIDS medication, i.e. medication slowing down the acceleration of this illness, is available, but so cost-intensive that treatment is and remains unaffordable for those who need it most: millions of AIDS-patients on the African continent.[1]

Ever since the advent of colonialism, the Islamic world has seen the implementation of systems strange to Islam in most spheres of life, in legal and political systems, economy and education. The impact on science and medicine may be summarized as follows: There is virtually no original research stemming from the framework of an Islamic culture which takes Islamic values into account and expresses an Islamic point of view. As scientific education in the Islamic world still follows the syllabus of the former colonial powers and is even being taught in their languages (English or French), the result will in most cases be scientists and medical doctors incorporating an approach foreign to Islamic culture; in the best of cases we will see Muslim scientists trying to individually overcome this bias. The scientific field, in other words, is nothing but another expression of continous imitation and ongoing colonization of the intellect. As in other related fields, we do not find any original research or originality in research emanating from within an Islamic context. The number of successful and prominent Muslim scientists and medical doctors does not necessarily reflect an original Islamic approach in their work. Muslims are taking on concepts developed by others as a reference framework, either by way of using or rejecting them. Experts of Islamic sciences, including *fiqh*, are, and this is

[1] From an Islamic perspective, there is no such copyright. Results of scientific research rather have to be made accessible to mankind in the sense of *taskhīr*.

another result of secularization, generally characterized by a lack of specialized scientific knowledge, their branch of specialization being seen as a remnant of the past with hardly any contemporary relevance.

This alienation from the Islamic worldview and way of life is an encompassing phenomenon. Societies in the Islamic world are governed by non-Islamic legal, economic and political systems. These systems are informed by non-Islamic values and objectives. In other words, a *paradigm shift* has taken place that has been for so many decades reshaping Muslim peoples' lives, value systems and way of thinking in an increasingly secularizing manner. Understanding this dichotomy between revealed knowledge and Islamic law on one hand, and the state of societies in the Islamic world on the other, is *sine qua none* to evaluate the reference to *maqāṣid* and related legal concepts in the debate on biomedical issues.

The reader might ask: why should we care about all these developments and prolegomena to discuss the usage of *maqāṣid* in bioethical questions? Is it not true that the reference to *maqāṣid* constitutes one of the tools of *ijtihād*, and that the objectives of the Sharīʿah are to be found in the Islamic texts, namely the preservation and protection of the five essential values, *dīn*, life, intellect, lineage, and property?

The history of Islamic jurisprudence has registered the names of many eminent scholars who developed the theory that the Islamic legal rules have been legislated for human beings' good and wellbeing (*maṣāliḥ*) in this world and in the Hereafter.[1]

---

[1] See for example, Abū Ḥāmid al-Ghazālī, *al-Mustasfā min ʿIlm al-Uṣūl,* ed. Muhammad Sulayman al-Ashqar (Beirut: Mu'assassat al-Risālah, 1st edn, 1417/1997), vol. 1, pp. 416-421; Sayf al-Dīn al-Āmidī, *al-Iḥkām fī Uṣūl al-Aḥkām,* edited by Abdul Razzaq Afifi (Beirut: al-Maktab al-Islami, 2nd edn, 1402H), vol. 3, pp. 271-275; ʿIzz al-Dīn ʿAbd al-ʿAzīz b. ʿAbd al-Salām, *al-Qawāʿd al-Kubrā: Qawāʿid al-Aḥkām fī Iṣlāḥ al-Anām,* edited by Nazih Kamal Hammad & Othman Jumʿah Damiriyyah (Damascus: Dār al-Qalam, 1st edn, 1421/2000), esp. vol. 5-14; Abū Isḥāq Ibrāhīm b. Mūsā al-Shāṭibī, *al-Muwāfaqāt*

We might annotate here that the theory of benefits underlying every single legal rule has not been accepted by all scholars. Within this context, it is not unusual to hear inaccurate references to Ibn Qayyim al-Jawziyyah as having said that "wherever *maṣlaḥah* obtains, there is the law (*sharʿ*) of God," thus implying an overriding authority of the notion of interest over the scriptural texts.[1] There has been much discussion on the rationalization (*taʿlīl*) of legal rules and whether it can be comprehensive (*ʿāmm*) or specific (*khāṣṣ*). To construe of a possible *ḥikmah* or wisdom of God in certain legal rules as its *ʿillah* or cause of legislating on the basis of which other legal rules can be construed is common to this approach, but it is not undisputed.[2]

It ought to be mentioned here that considered benefits or *maṣāliḥ* have to be established as *sharʿī* benefits, i.e. they are authentic in that the texts testify to them and through this testimony they run in accordance with the higher purposes and limits set by the Lawgiver, God Almighty. Al-Ghazālī clearly pointed out the difference between benefits as intended by the Lawgiver—which need to be observed—and benefits as merely defined by humans according to what they feel is suitable (*mulāʾim*) to them or simply according to their whims.[3]

The role of the reference framework to define a *maṣlaḥah* or *mafsadah* is highly important in the contemporary usage of *maqāṣid.* When deciding a case based on *ijtihād maqāṣidī*, a *faqīh* or Muslim jurist has to evaluate the *sharʿī maqāṣid*, the benefits and

---

fī Uṣūl al-Sharīʿah, edited by Abdullah Draz (Beirut: Dār al-Kutub al-ʿIlmiyyah, 1st edn, 1422/2001), vol. 1/1, p. 26 & vol. 1/2, pp. 7-41.

[1] Ibn al-Qayyim's original statement, itself an elaboration on Ibn Aqil's, reads differently from what is often attributed to him. See, Abū ʿAbd Allāh Muḥammad b. Abī Bakr b. Ayyūb Ibn Qayyim al-Jawziyyah, *al-Turuq al-Ḥukmiyyah fī al-Siyāsah al-Sharʿiyyah*, ed. Naef bin Ahmed al-Hamad (Makkah al-Mukarramah: Dār ʿĀlam al-Fawāʾid, 1st edn, 1428H), pp. 29-32.

[2] See Ahmad al-Raysuni, *Naẓariyat al-maqāṣid ʿinda l-Imām al-Shāṭibī*, (Herndon: The International Institute of Islamic Thought, 1992), pp.5ff

[3] Al-Ghazālī, *al-Mustaṣfā*, vol. 1, pp. 414-416.

harms and their priorities in every particular case. The same applies for the reference to *maṣāliḥ mursalah* or, on a different level, even the definition of necessity (*ḍarūrah*). The scholar depends on an evaluation scheme to define or evaluate the usage of these legal tools. The principles of jurisprudence or *uṣūl al-fiqh* have provided guidelines for this to a certain extent, like the reference to legal maxims.[1] Still, this evaluation scheme is linked to its general reference framework. Bearing in mind the paradigm shift discussed above, this may prove problematic: The current reference framework in the Islamic world is characterized by the lack of realizing the very first of the five objectives, *al-dīn*, which is actually the cornerstone of the *Islamic way of life*.

We might add here that some scholars elaborate on the relation between Islam and science in terms of what we may describe as the *maṣlaḥah-mafsadah* paradigm: Nearly all contributions underline the positive attitude of Islam towards science, but differentiate, though, between the positive and negative aspects of science. The 10th Conference of the Islamic Fiqh Academy in Jeddah stated that Islam does in no way obstruct science, but that science is subject to clear limits set by Islamic law.[2]

Wahba al-Zuhayli states that science is good as long as it serves humanity and leads to the development and well-being of human beings, whereas it is bad where it leads to their harm. He mentions the discovery of the atom and its scientific usage as an example.[3] The Shiʿite scholar Muhammad Mahdi Shams al-Din emphasizes the same distinction between useful and harmful knowledge: Islam supports science where it aims at the

---

[1] Al-Raysuni, *Naẓariyat al-Maqāṣid ʿinda l-Imām al-Shāṭibī*, p. 267.

[2] Islamic Development Bank (IDB) & Islamic Fiqh Academy (IFA), *Resolutions and Recommendations of the Council of the Islamic Fiqh Academy 1985-2000* (Jeddah: Islamic Resaerch Institute, 1st edn, 1421H/2000), p. 204.

[3] Muhammad Husayn Fadlallah, *et al., al-Istinsākh: Jadal al-ʿIlm wa al-Dīn wa al-Akhlāq* (Beirut: Dār al-Fikr al-Muʿāṣir, 1997), p. 122.

realization of a specified aim, but not as an end in itself.[1]

Mahmoud ʿAkkam underlines the necessary limits for research: Knowledge, he believes, is not the highest value; rather the highest values are to be the benefit and welfare of mankind, the realization of its objectives, and the protection of its humanity. The Creator knows best where the welfare of mankind lies; therefore, things are bound by their aims and purposes. Islamic law does not principally forbid science except in cases its aims and results are directed against mankind.[2] "Yes to knowledge serving humankind", he emphasizes, "but a thousand-fold *NO* to a human being who becomes a factor of scientific results."[3]

Misbah, who underlines Islam's openness towards science, clearly states that not every kind of knowledge is useful knowledge.[4] Shams al-Din adds that not every form of science is lawful in Islam. Further, only few people may (for economic reasons) participate in these developments, whereas the entire mankind has to pay the price for transgressing the limits. He rejects the idea of science for its own sake as propagated in the West.[5]

Based on the preceding discussion on the different forms of science, I would like to suggest here that knowledge or science and its evaluation as 'good' or 'bad' depends on the way it is pursued and used as well as on the *sharʿī* rule on its pursuit and usage. The theoretical considerations advanced thus far will become clearer in the following section where a few bioethical issues are discussed in connection with Muslim scholars' juristic rulings on them.

---

[1] Hosam al-Din Shehadah *et al.*, *al-Istinsākh bayna al-ʿIlm wa al-Falsafa wa al-Dīn*, (Damascus: Markaz al-ʿIlm wa'l-Dirāsāt wa'l-Nashr, 1998), p. 129.

[2] Ibid., p.135ff.

[3] Ibid., p.140.

[4] Abdul Hadi Misbah, *al-Istinsākh bayna al-ʿIlm wa al-Dīn* (Cairo: al-Dār al-Miṣrīyah al-Lubnāniyyah, 1997), p. 9.

[5] Shehadah *et al.*, *al-Istinsākh*, p.128f

Critical Analysis of Juristic Views on Bioethical Issues

This section shall be devoted to looking into some specific medical and bioethical issues. Our task here is to crtically analyze and assess the juristic views and arguments advanced thereupon by contemporary Muslim scholars, particularly those leaning on *maqāṣid, unspecified benefits (maṣāliḥ mursalah)*, and legal maxims (*qawāʿid fiqhiyya*), and especially those deploying the maxim "*al-ḍarūrāt tubīḥ al-maḥẓūrāth*" (necessity renders the prohibited lawful) to support their opinions. The aim is to assess the extent, soundness and veracity of their dependence on the Sharīʿah reference framework. However, it should be pointed out that our examination of such juristic views is in no way comprehensive or exhaustive; it is rather partial and selective. Yet it is believed that the cases dealt with in this section represent the general trend prevailing among Muslim scholars.

1. Organ Transplantation

In the the biomedical field organ transplantation is one of the much-debated controversial topics by Muslim scholars together with its multitude of subissues. Without going into a detailed exposition of the issues involved in this topic, our focus will be on the most essential aspects thereof. As to the line of argumentation, it may be perceived that the view of permissibility of organ transplantation heavily relies on the principle of necessity (*ḍarūrah*). Basically, any (medical) intervention is an intervention into a person's *ḥurmah* or inviolability and needs a legal validation as well as moral sanctioning. Organ transplant involves the inviolable *ḥurmah* of two persons, the organ donor, be he dead or alive, and the recipient. Some scholars have ruled that organ transplantation, organ donation (during life or after death) and removing organs from a dead person are permissible arguing on the basis that necessity renders the prohibited lawful, and that the need for organ transplant is deemed a case of necessity if human life is endangered.

In 1988 the Jeddah-based Islamic Fiqh Academy, one of the OIC specialized bodies, made the resolution that organ transplantation from a living person is permissible as long as the organ is not a vital and essential one that will cause damage to the donor, such as the heart, or has a basic function, like the cornea. Transplants from a dead person are ruled as permissible, if it is essential to keep the beneficiary alive, or if it restores a basic function of the body, provided it has been authorized by the deceased person before his death or by his heirs after his death or with permission from concerned authorities if the deceased has not been identified or has no heirs. [1] The Academy's resolution draws on the objectives of the Sharīʿah stipulating that harmful effects which have appeared in some cases of organ transplantations have happened due to a disregard of the guidelines and objectives of the Sharīʿah.[2] The resolution bans the sale of human organs. [3] In another resolution, organs carrying hereditary traits are also not to be transplanted into another person's body.[4] The transplantion of organs from one part to another of the same body is ruled as permissible given that the benefits accrued outweigh the harmful effects.[5]

In contradistinction to what has been ruled by the Jeddah Islamic Fiqh Academy, there are more reluctant views in respect of the subject in question. Likewise, in 1989 the Islamic Fiqh Academy of India banned organ donation after death and declared a person's testament to this effect as invalid. [6] Al-Tantawi also permitted the use of body organs if a person has died in an accident, provided necessity requires the use of his

---

[1] IDB & IFA, *Resolutions and Recommendations*, Resolution No. 26, p. 54.
[2] Ibid., p. 51.
[3] Ibid.
[4] Ibid., Resolution No. 57, p. 114.
[5] Ibid., p. 53.
[6] http://www.iol.ie/~afifi/Articles/organ2.htm

organs to cure a patient.[1] However, we may stipulate that the view of the Jeddah Islamic Fiqh Academy is that of a majority of scholars today by virtue of the fact that its members and experts represent Muslim countries.

Some scholars, though, have argued that the definition of *ḍarūrah* does not apply in most of the cases of organ transplantation.[2] As defined in Islamic jurisprudence, a case of necessity must consist in a situation where a person has reached a stage of definite perishing if he does not consume what is prohibited to save his life. In other words, the situation does not allow for any alternative. If the person in question has not reached such a stage (of certain death), but is only experiencing hardship and pain, then *ḍarūrah* does not obtain, and what is prohibited (*ḥarām*) does not become permissible.[3] A scrutiny of cases of organ transplantation such as, for instance, kidney transplantation, reveals that many such cases are done as a precautionary method or as a way to improve life quality. Danger of death is not necessarily immediate or imminent. Kidney patients can be treated by dialysis and live longer with this treatment. They are certainly exposed to hardship, but can we qualify their situation as *ḍarūrah*? Also, necessity, from the established juristic definition, involves the person under duress. It cannot be expanded to the donor of an organ, or to establishing organ banks.[4] Transplantation of the cornea might, if successful, save a patient from blindness. The operation might considerably enhance his life quality, but it is not necessary to *save* his life.

We can clearly perceive that there is a paradigm shift involved in the interpretation of *ḍarūrah* and the reference framework resorted to. There is a particular reality in the

---

[1] http://www.islam_online.net/servlet

[2] See such criticism in, Mustafa al-Dhahabi of, *Naql al-Aʿḍāʾ bayna al-Ṭibb wa l-Dīn* (Cairo: Dār al-Ḥadīth, 1993).

[3] Ibid., p.70.

[4] Ibid., p.70f.

biomedical field: Ever since organ transplantation (of kidney, heart, lungs, etc.) has been established and proliferated as a model of medical treatment that relies heavily on technology and devices, alternative medical treatment of certain diseases affecting kidney, heart or lung have hardly been researched. The mere possibility of organ transplantation and the world-wide absorption of this medical model has deceived large parts of the public into believing that there is no other alternative. This model has thus gone unquestioned, but is it a *necessity*? Some scholars argue that there might be different forms of treatment; but as we do not know them, we still have to refer to what is available, even if it falls under a prohibited form of treatment, as it constitutes a necessity under the present circumstances.[1] This might apply in restricted cases of a real danger of imminent death. Yet this does not free us from the responsibility to search for other ways of treatment.

Possible negative effects as instances of *mafsadah* or *maḍarrah* affecting living organ donors are generally ignored in the juritistic discussions, although such dangers are widely known for medical experts and practitioners. Donors are thus exposed to the risks any operation carries, such as anesthesia side effects, and might even lose their lives.[2]

Relatedly, the specification of organ transplant as *ḍarūrah* has given way to a decision on another important issue: brain death. The discussion on brain death and whether it can be considered as death came into existence not only with the introduction of life support systems and more sophisticated apparatuses to measure brain currents, but also under the influence of the excessive practice of organ transplantation as a therapy, and hence a growing demand for "fresh" organs to be transplanted. So, the best chances of successful organ

---

[1] Arif Ali Arif, *Madā Shar'iyat al-Taṣarruf bi l-A'ḍā' al-Bashariyah: Dirāsah Muqāranah* (PhD thesis, University of Bahgdād, 1992), p. 27.

[2] Al-Dhahabi, *Naql al-A'ḍā'*, p. 74.

transplantation are the function of direct implantation from donor to receiver, and the time of declaration of death plays here a very crucial role.[1]

The OIC Islamic Fiqh Academy has ruled in its 10th meeting that brain death alone is no sufficient ground to declare death, and that other established signs, like the absence of heart beat, are essential to declare a person to be dead.[2] The majority of scholars seem to embrace this view. Contrary to this, al-Azhar Fatwā Council has decreed that brain death is a decisive indicator. If the brain-dead person has made a will or his family agrees, his organs might be removed for transplantation once he is declared brain dead.[3]

2. *Cloning and Genetic Engineering*

Being one of the newest topics in biological technology, cloning and genetic engineering have attracted a high degree of public attention, and a number of Muslim scholars have adavanced their (juristic) views on cloning in plants, animals and humans. The majority of them have ruled that the cloning of human beings is forbidden (*ḥarām*), as it involves a change of creation that manifests itself in several aspects that can be summarized as follows. As a theoretical possibility of *asexual reproduction*, the idea of cloning impinges on fundamental Islamic concepts about marriage and family and natural reproduction as the basis of human society. The conclusive argument against cloning is the changing of *fiṭrah*; that is, the alteration and distortion of the natural and innate constitution of human beings, the nature that surrounds them, and the order and system according to which

---

[1] For further detail, see the author's article, "The Dilemma of Islamic Bioethics in the 21st Century," *American Joutrnal of Islamic Social Sciences,* vol. 28, No. 1 (2011), pp. 45-75.

[2] Nada Muhammad Nuʿaym al-Daqr, *Mawt al-Dmāgh bayna l-Ṭibb wa l-Islām* (Beirut: Dār al-Fikr al-Muʿāṣir, 1999), p. 158.

[3] Ibid., p. 170f.

they live. Cloning human beings manipulates this order in many ways, as most of the contributions emphasize; thus, the make-up of humankind in sexes or pairs (*azwāj*) constituting the foundation of reproduction is undermined. Moreover, family bonds and social relations are absolutely uncertain and become questionable: Who are the parents of a clone? Shams al-Dīn sees the laws of inheritance vanishing and the institution of family so much endangered, as neither men nor women will be in need of a family to produce a child.[1]

The loss of the line of descent and the undermining of lineal indentity as a result of human cloning is usually referred to as a sufficient reason for prohibition and ban, as the relation between a cloned person and the clone is absolutely unclear: Is it the same person, or is it father or brother?[2] Nasr Farid Wasil, a former *muftī* of Egypt, underlines that cloning human beings would lead to the loss of kinship and filial ties (*ṣilat al-raḥim*), social and individual relations and the individual's rights and duties.[3] In this connection, Misbah points out that cloning does not cause only legal problems such as those relating to matters of inheritance, but most importantly it involves the danger of playing with human beings and violating their original dignity conferred on them by their Creator.[4] The erosion of the human natural social order as represented by *al-sunnah al-zawjiyah*, the creation in pairs or the matrimonial bond, is invoked by Wasil as a very important aspect of human existence: God has set the matrimonial bond as one of the norms of the Sharī'ah by means of which mankind's vicegerency (*khilāfah*) and trusteeship (*amānah*) on earth is to be realized. He goes as far as to say that

---

[1] Shams al-Dīn, in Shehadah *et al.*, *al-Istinsākh*, p. 121.

[2] Al-Qaradawi in an online-discussion with Saudi students (13/8/2000; *www.islam-online.net/fatwaapplication*); see also, al-Dhaouadi bin Bakhoush Qumidi, "al-Istinsākh fī al-Nuṣūṣ wa al-Qawā'id al-Shar'iyyah," *Majallat al-Iḥyā'* (University of Batna, Algeria), No.6 (10/2002), pp.385-392, at 389.

[3] Nasr Farid Wasil, in Shehadah *et al.*, *al-Istinsākh*, p. 125.

[4] Misbah, *al-Istinsākh bayna al-'Ilm wa al-Dīn*, p.42f.

experimenting on human beings by trying to create a new generation with outstanding qualities is an act of manifest disbelief (*kufr ṣarīḥ*).[1]

Al-Zuhayli gives as one of the reasons for rejecting cloning the fact that human beings' different characteristics belong to God's wisdom (*ḥikmah*) in His creation.[2] The principle of diversity (*tannawu'*) is inherent to the Divine order of creation, argues al-Qaradawi. Cloning contradicts this principle.[3] The *al-Ahrām* columnist Fahmi Huwaidi underlines that cloning is interference into the equilibrium of the existence as such, the results of which cannot be estimated yet.[4]

The scenario of breeding a human elite consisting of selected and predetermined characteristics as ordered on catalogue[5] is a recurring topic in juristic discussions on bioethical issues. What about making use of cloning in order to "improve" the characteristics of the next generation? Al-Zuhayli rejects the idea on the grounds that this would constitute sheer intervention in, and alteration of, God's creation (*taghyīr li-khalq Allāh*) and alteration of the different characteristics of human beings which are a manifestation of God's wisdom in the creation. Choosing and determining a baby's sex amounts to rebellion against the divine will.[6] In 1997 the OIC Islamic Fiqh Academy banned human cloning.[7]

Among the few voices not to subscribe to the prohibition of human cloning is Abdul Sabour Marzouq, vice president of the Supreme Council for Islamic Affairs in Egypt and professor

---

[1] Nasr Farid Wasil, in Shehadah *et al.*, *al-Istinsākh*, p. 124.
[2] Al-Zuhayli, in Fadlallah, in Fadlallah *et al.*, *al-Istinsākh*, p. 127.
[3] *Ibid.*, p. 125.
[4] Mohammad Sadiq Sabour, *al-Tansīl aw al-Istinsākh: Hal bi'l-Imkān Tansīl al-Bashar?* (Cairo: Dār al-Amīn, 1997), p. 66.
[5] Mohamed Bouzghiba, "al-Akhlāqiyāt al-Dīnīyah fī Zaman al-'Awlamah wa al-Ttiknūlūjiyā fī al-Gharb," *Majallat al-Iḥyā'*, No. 8 (2004), pp. 133-148, at 139.
[6] Al-Zuhayli, in Fadlallah, *et al., al-Istinsākh*, p. 127.
[7] IDB & IFA, *Resolutions and Recommendations*, Resolution No. 100/2/10, pp. 208-213.

of Internal Medicine at the University of ʻAin Shams. He bases his view on its possible benefits for mankind. For him, only politically motivated abuse of cloning to gain power over the world is a criminal act which deserves condemnation.[1] Marzouq would also like to see human society benefitting from the type of cloning he advocates, insisting that experiments should be made under clear legislation and constrictions.[2] He brings quite a different aspect into the discussion: Gaining back "treasures of humankind" by cloning historical personalities.[3]

The more diversified legal verdicts in related aspects of genetic and biotechnical engineering and cloning in animals and plants reveal a wider recourse to the objectives of the Sharīʿah. For example, al-Qaradawi explicitly refers to the concept of *al-maṣāliḥ al-mursalah* in respect of the question of genetic screening. In his opinion, any matter of legal relevance that is not expressly evidenced in the textual sources of the Sharīʿah can be judged in light of the benefit or harm (*maṣlaḥah/mafsadah*) resulting from it. If the benefit is overwhelming, then such matter constitutes what is legally required (*maṭlūb sharʿan*). On the contrary, if it is more harmful than beneficial, then it is unlawful and it is therefore forbidden from the point of view of the Sharīʿah (*mamnūʿ sharʿan*). Accordingly, al-Qaradawi advocates that genetic screening of marriage candidates be required by the state authorities. The decision on whether a man and woman ought to abstain from marriage in case of positive test of possible hereditary diseases should, however, be left to the candidates themselves. In this connection, al-Qaradwi emphasizes the protection of lineage (*nasl*) as one of the objectives of Islamic law. Accordingly, he declares the therapeutic application of cloning as permissible.[4]

---

[1] Marzouq, *al-Tansīl aw al-Istinsākh*, p. 65.
[2] Ibid., p. 92.
[3] Ibid., p. 89.
[4] *www.qaradawi.net/arabic/meetings/shreai&hayaa/prog-43.htm*

Al-Zuhayli's views on cloning and genetic technology run on a quite similar line of reasoning. If cloning and genetic engineering serve the wellbeing of mankind and the realization of human benefits (*maṣāliḥ*), they are permissible. If they endanger human life and cause harm rather than benefit, they are to be forbidden. For this he adduces the Sharīʿah rules according to which harm shall neither be inflicted nor reciprocated (*lā ḍarar wa-lā ḍirār*) and that averting harm precedes acquiring benefit (*dar' al-mafāsid muqaddam 'ala jalb al-maṣāliḥ*). Therefore, al-Zuhayli argues, the positive effects of genetic engineering like the possible elimination of hereditary or incurable diseases is welcome, whereas anything leading to morally, socially, legally, economically, psychologically or religiously negative consequences has to be avoided. Everything leading to evil consequences (*sharr*) is evil, whereas everything leading to good (*khayr*) is good.

Accordingly, whatever leads to benefit (*maṣlaḥah*) has to be welcomed, while anything leading to harm (*mafsadah*) has to be prevented. Should the divine equilibrium which has been instituted for the benefit and welfare of mankind be disturbed, the factor causing it is definitely bad and must, therefore, be avoided. Playing with God's creation by altering and changing its characteristics and violating the Sharīʿah objectives pertaining to the safeguarding of the self (*nafs*), intellect (*ʿaql*) and offspring (*nasl*), he expounds, is considered a crime and offence against mankind in the first place.[1] In the same vein runs the argument advanced by al-Qara Daghi who also invokes *maqāṣid al-sharīʿah* in his legal judgment on genetic treatment. As he argues, "the Islamic Sharīʿah is based on the realization of benefits and the prevention of harm; hence, wherever there is a real benefit, there lies the law of God. The complete Sharīʿah is just, and a mercy, and good, and anything in which there lies harm or hardship, or injustice or falsehood, or anything harmful, is not

[1] Al-Zuhayli, in Fadlallah, in Fadlallah *et al.*, *al-Istinsākh*, p. 127ff.

from this Sharīʿah."[1]

The kind of legal reasoning described above is also evident in the contribution by Bouzghiba, a professor at Tunisia's al-Zaitouna University. He tackles the issue of cloning and other related subjects mainly from an ethical point of view as opposed to the spirit of globalization which neglects moraliy and moral considerations. He also frequently refers to the doctrine of *maqāṣid al-sharīʿah* as the frame of reference for his argument. Bouzghiba supports the ISESCO's demand of establishing an Islamic organization for the ethics of the sciences whose task it should be to study and analyze new scientific developments from the point of view of the Sharīʿah objectives and to advise Islamic countries to adhere to them.[2]

It is frequently asked whether cloning can be regarded as a *therapy against infertility*. Muslim specialists in the fields of medicine, biology and the Islamic disciplines, especially *fiqh*, have been discussing the question of infertility and its lawful ways of treatment for a long time. Artificial insemination is generally regarded as lawful as long as the sperm and egg cell ensue from a lawfully married couple while both partners are still alive at the time of insemination.[3] The late Shaikh al-Azhar, Sayyid Tantawi, declared the bringing about of a human being without prior fusion of the egg and sperm as absolutely forbidden.[4] Like the introduction of a third party into the reproduction process, cloning has been considered as unlawful and not permissible as a medical therapy for infertile couples by the Islamic Fiqh Academy's 1997 resolution.[5] Marzouq

[1] Ali Muhiuddin al-Qura Daghi, *al-ʿIlāj al-Jīnī min Manẓūr al-Fiqh al-Islāmī, Majallat al-Iḥyā'*, No. 6 (2003), pp.51-74, at 63f &73.

[2] Mohammed Bouzghība, "al-Akhlāqiyāt al-Diniya fi Zaman al-ʿAwlamah wa al-Tiknūlūjiyā al-Gharbiya," *Majallat al-Iḥyā'*, No.8 (2004), pp. 133-148, at 144.

[3] As decided by the International Organisation of Muslim Scientists (IOMS) in its meeting in Kuwait, 1984 (*www.islamset.com/bioethics/index.html*).

[4] Misbah, *al-Istinsākh bayna l-ʿIlm wa al-Dīn*, p. 49.

[5] Fadlallah *et al.*, *al-Istinsākh:Jjadal al-ʿIlm wa al-Dīn wa al-Akhlāq*, Appendix, p. 3.

contradicts this view; he upholds cloning as an alternative for infertile couples to fulfil their desire to have children.[1] Wasil rejects cloning as an ultimate "therapy" for infertile couples arguing that such a situation of infertility, if confirmed, is a matter of fate and that one should not revolt against the will of God, as mentioned in the Qur'an (42: 50): "God's alone is the dominion over the haveans and the earth. He creates whatever He wills: He bestows the gift of female offspring on whomever He wills, and the gift of male offspring on whomever He wills; of He gives both male and female [to whomever He wills], and causes to be barren whomever He wills." The Islamic rule pertaining to medical treatment (*ḥukm at-tadāwī*), he says, does not apply here.[2]

Some scholars have seen human cloning as a treatment for barren couples by leaning on the idea that it concerns the crucial *maṣlaḥah* of safeguarding offspring (*nasl*). Majdah Zawawi, who critically presents this view, states that its application is "not as simple as it may seem."[3] She refers to the sub-categorization of *maṣāliḥ* into necessities (*ḍarūriyyāt*), needs (*ḥājiyyāt*), and embellishments (*taḥsīniyyāt*). She states that the desire to reproduce cannot be seen as a necessity (*ḍarūrah*), but rather a need (*ḥājah*). Therefore, it cannot act as a legal justification for cloning. Necessity (*ḍarūrah*) in this case is rather "to protect the whole society from being thrown into a state of chaos in trying to fulfil the needs of a few unfortunate couples."[4] "There is a probability", Zawawi further argues, "that cloning would disrupt the definition of *nasab* or lineage, causing confusion over family ties, which in turn would cause the problem of determining those who are in the prohibited degree of marriage; that in the

---

[1] Sabour, *al-Tansīl wa al-Istinsākh*, p. 89.
[2] Shehadah, *al-Istinsākh*, p. 125.
[3] Majdah Zawawi, *The Legal and Ethical Aspects of Human Cloning: A Comparative Study* (MA Thesis, Kulliyyah of Laws, International Islamic University Malaysia, 2000), p. 140.
[4] *Ibid.*

long run would cause the very destruction of the concept of family. In such a situation, reproductive cloning may not only be seen as a complimentary benefit (*maṣlaḥah ḥājiyah*) but could very well fall into the status of harm (*mafsadah*)."[1]

Furthermore, the unsettled position of human cloning itself contradicts one of the conditions of applying a *maṣlaḥah*, which is that it has to be genuine and is not only based on a plausible benefit. Also, it is not attested that the benefit serves the public at large as the second condition requires.[2] Referring to the question of conditions, Zawawi has brought up an important point which seems to have been neglected in most writings: the definition of *maṣlaḥah* in the biomedical field.

Stem cell research provides another example of the common reliance on *maṣlaḥah* by Muslim scholars. Stem cell research has widely been celebrated as an aspiration to find cures for a number of so far incurable diseases, like Alzheimer's, as stem cells can obviously be triggered to develop into cells of different specialization. The ultimate ethical problem is constituted by the source of stem cell material.[3] The most conveniently accessible source for stem cells is 'surplus embryos', i.e. those additionally fertilized cells not implanted in IVF procedures. It is not the only accessible source, though. Experiments have shown that stem cells taken from adult bone marrow possess a similar aptitude. More recent research has opened the possibility of using adult stem cells from nasal tissue or even breast milk, with more discoveries being made on a month-to-month basis. A number of *fatwās* do allow the usage

---

[1] *Ibid.*

[2] *Ibid.*, p. 141; see also Majdah Zawawi, *Human cloning: A comparative study of the legal and ethical aspects of reproductive human cloning* (Kuala Lumpur: Institute of Islamic Understanding Malaysia, IKIM, 2001).

[3] For a more eleaborate treatment of this topic see the present author's article, "Harvesting and Use of Human (Embryonic) Stem Cells: An Islamic Evaluation," *Journal of Bioethical Inquiry* (2017), pp. 97-108 (published online, 14 December 2016, *DOI 10.1007/s11673-016-9757-6*).

of 'surplus embryos' for stem cell research. The formal line of reasonong consists in arguing that those fertilized cells cannot be considered as human life before the decisive in-breathing of the soul (*rūḥ*) has taken place. Moreover, without artificial aid or implantation into a woman's womb, they would not survive. Most *fatwās* do not consider alternative sources for stem cells. They do not expound on the permissibility of "producing" surplus embryos for IVF either, but rather accept this as a given reality.

Shahid Athar, a Muslim medical doctor based in Indianapolis, USA expounds on the origin of this "cell material": Whereas he considers the interruption of a pregnancy for the purpose of research as not acceptable, "surplus material" stemming from IVF fertilizations are permitted.[1] Al-Qaradawi forbids the use of embryonic tissue as even the embryo does have a *ḥurmah*; that is, the integrity and inviolability of a human being.[2]

The idea of establishing a *human spare parts depot* by genetic engineering has met with vehement rejection. Al-Qaradawi advocates the permissibility of the cultivation of human organs by cloning once this becomes possible due to the inherent benefit (*manfaʿah*) and under the condition that no other person is harmed or has his/her dignity violated.[3] Marzouq points out that organ transplantation has already been positively sanctioned by international scientific and religious circles under the condition that it does not involve commerce, and explicitly welcomes the possibility of cloning human organs, though

[1] Dina Rashed, "Cloning is not playing God," *www.islamonline.net*, published on 9/2/2000. Dr. Shahid Athar is vice-president of the Islamic Medical Association (IMA), Chicago.

[2] Al-Qaradawi.online13/8/2000 (*www.Islam-online.net/fatwaapplication*).

[3] Al-Qaradawi online (*www.islam-online.net/fatwaapplication*); Abdul Sabour Marzouq expresses the same view (TV discussion published in *al-Ahram* 15/4/97); *cf.* Farid Wasil.

without specifying the ways and methods.[1]

Serour, a Cairo-based specialist in infertility treatment, would like to restrict the use of genetic engineering to therapeutic use only. He favors the somatic cell therapy aiming to correct defects in body cells as it promises medical treatment and cure. On the other hand, he asserts that enhancement genetic engineering (the implantation of a gene to improve certain characteristics) and eugenic genetic engineering (changing complex human characteristics) are not permissible, as they would clearly bring about a change in God's creation which might endanger the balance of the entire universe. As to germ line gene therapy, it should be restricted to therapeutic considerations.[2]

Differently from the unanimous prohibition of human cloning, most legal scholars do not ban cloning and/or the use of *genetic engineering in the realm of animals and plants.*[3] In this field, it is the increase of agro-economic production and "improvement of the kind", exactly the same argument forwarded against human cloning, which is praised as the benefit of genetic engineering. Al-Zuhayli clearly hails the benefits this kind of cloning holds for mankind, like increasing the productivity of plants, making use of animals for pharmacological aims etc. Reproducing animal or plant cell material in the laboratory and changing the qualities of genes or removing genetic defects are permissible as this produces benefits for human beings or averts harm from them, given that research abstains from playing with

---

[1] This statement was made during a TV program, the text was published in *al-Ahrām* of April 15, 1997. See Misbah, *al-Istinsākh bayna al-ʿIlm wa al-Dīn*, p. 51. It has to be mentioned here that Marzouq completely neglects legal Islamic ways opposed to at least some forms and conditions of organ transplantation.

[2] Serour Gamal I., "Islamic Perspectives on Genetic Technology and Information Use," in Jacquelyn Ann Kegley, ed., *Genetic Knowledge: Human Values & Responsibility* (Lexington, Ky: Paragon House, 1998), pp. 197-211.

[3] For a more detailed discussion on GMFs from an Islamic persopective see the author's article, "Islamic Legal Perspectives on Genetically Modified," Food," *American Journal of Islamic Social Sciences*, vol. 27, No. 1 (2010), pp. 1-30.

the creation and avoids things that are of no benefit to mankind.[1] Wasil expounds on the permissibility of anything leading to the benefit of mankind that does not involve experiments on the human being, like healing incurable diseases, supplying water, fighting poverty, etc. To attain such goals necessary steps leading to them are required by the Sharīʿah (*maṭlūb sharʿan*).[2]

In quite similar vein, Shaikh Mohamed al-Mokhtar al-Sallmi, former *muftī* of Tunisia, mentions that the legal verdict in these cases does not differ from the rule (*ḥukm*) concerning the production of other drugs for the benefit of humankind.[3] His juristic reasoning leads him to the conclusion that acquiring knowledge in this field of research might become a collective obligation (*farḍ kifāyah*) based on al-Shāṭibī's formulation that originally permissible (*mubāḥ*) or recommended (*mandūb*) matters may turn into an obligation (*farḍ*).[4]

Consolidating such views on cloning and genetic engineering, the Jeddah-based International Islamic Fiqh Academy made the following decision in 1997: "It is permitted by Sharīʿa to use cloning techniques and genetic engineering in the fields of microbiology, botanic and zoology, and thus within the limits prescribed by the Sharīʿa, in order to serve general interest and prevent inconvenience."[5]

Abdul Rahman al-Sanad is of the view that genetic modification of plants and animals is permissible if the intention behind it is to increase and enhance yield, based on the fact that God has made everything in the heavens and the earth subservient to mankind, as mentioned in the Qur'an (31: 20): "Are you not aware that God has made subservient to you all

---

[1] Al-Zuhayli, in Fadlallah *et al.*, *al-Istinsākh*, p. 127ff.

[2] Shehadah, *al-Istinsākh bayna al-ʿIlm wa al-Falsafah wa al-Dīn*, p.126f.

[3] Mohamed Mokhtar al-Sallami, *Majallat al-Hidāyah*, No.1/23, p. 23.

[4] *Ibid.*

[5] IDB & IFA, *Resolutions and Recommendations of the Council of the Islamic Fiqh Academy 1985-2000*, Resolution No. 100/2/10, p. 212.

that is in the heavens and all that is on earth, and has lavished upon you His blessings, both outward and inward?" Enhancing the quality of animals and plants by bringing about new kinds which are free of diseases is a realization of the benefit of mankind and is supported by *maqāṣid al-sharīʿah*. Al-Sanad stipulates that two conditions be satisfied for the implementation of genetic modification in plants and animals: 1. it should not lead to any harm (*maḍarrah*) by causing and spreading new diseases. The procedure needs to be safe of effects which lead to the dissemination of lethal toxins; 2. the procedure is not made use of to manipulate or change God's creation. The "enhancement" of human offspring by changing skin or eye colour and the likes is not part of this permission, he cautions.[1]

In light of the foregoing exposition, we are at a vantage point to make the following observations. Quite obviously, most of the scholars outweigh probable benefits over probable harms in their treatment of cloning and geneteic engineering in animals and plants. Issues like free and uncontrolled mutations and manipulations of plants, possible side effects on human health or the equilibrium of creation are hardly discussed as harms that should at least be heeded. Another striking characteristic in their debates is that there is hardly any consideration of the probability factor which is inherent to experimental sciences. What *might* accrue in terms of benefit is often treated as a real or existent benefit.

Negative side effects on consumers have either not been sufficiently investigated or the research has been carried out by the very companies that advocate its usage. Independent research hardly exists, as critics, mainly in NGOs platforms, frequently comment.[2] Some negative side effects, however, are

---

[1] Abdul Rahman bin Abdullah al-Sanad, *Masāʾil Fiqhiyyah Muʿāsirah*. (Beirut: Dār al-Warrāq, 2005), pp. 55-57.

[2] See Brian Tokar, ed., *Redesigning Life? The Worldwide Challenge to Genetic*

distinguishable, whereas others will probably only materialize after years of consumption. In addition, research on side effects will naturally focus on what is already known. We should not forget that, as genetically modified (GM) food is a new phenomenon, science may not know which side effects to search for in the first place, so that phenomena which might appear after decades may not be linked back to GM food at all. Prior to the arrival of GM food on the scene, human cultural history has recorded manifold changes in our diet. Humankind has had ample opportunity to gradually adapt to these changes. The quantitative changes in nutrition introduced by GM food, however, do not have any historical precedent, and the knowledge about possible side effects is with God alone.

Genetic engineering in plants (and animals) is advocated as one means to produce cheap medication available to all (especially in the developing countries), as this leads to the preservation of life (*nafs*) which is one of the essential objectives of the Sharīʿah. Wasil, as we saw earlier, focused on supplying water and fighting poverty in this regard. But what, evidently, has been left out of the discussion is to ask: Why is medication for a lot of diseases unaffordable to vast parts of the global population? The answer is quite simple indeed: Because their production is monopolized in the hands of a few multinational companies which prefer their increasing profits to global health, and because these companies eternalize their monopoly with a copyright on "their" products, thereby prohibiting their proliferation.

Considering these facts, would it not closer to reality and wisdom to present the Islamic alternative to this marketed copyright phenomenon prior to giving a legal rule based on an objective which, ironically enough, we will not see realized as long as this monopole is operated? The same might be said about global poverty, food and water supply. All these

---

Engineering (London & New York: Zed Books, 2001).

problematic issues are actually the product of an unjust global economic system. Any innovation in the field of genetic technology will ultimately be used to serve its vital interests and objectives of the free global market as long as the Islamic framework is not re-activated.

As the preceding analysis has shown, the real purposes and the rationale behind genetically modified organisms (GMOs) are not necessarily validated by the Sharīʿah. Moreover, scrutiny may show that there are texts establishing the *maṣlaḥah* involved as *mulghāt*, i.e. as an imaginary benefit to which the texts of Sharīʿah have already testified to the negative and which must therefore be discarded.

Conclusion

The theory of the objectives of the Sharīʿah has, in its foundations, been developed within an Islamic framework of reference. The same is true for legal maxims and *maṣāliḥ mursalah.* These principles have not, however, been undisputed, as we alluded to earlier. The crucial point in the usage of these legal concepts is the definition of *maṣlaḥah* and *mafsadah* themselves. Detecting a benefit or harm in a particular situation and linking them to the objectives of the Sharīʿah is based to a large extent on human judgment. This judgment ultimately depends on the surrounding circumstances and complexities of the socio-cultural realities. This may not have been as problematic in the time of al-Ghazālī or al-Shāṭibī as it is now, as their reality was dominated by the Islamic legal and value systems and imbibed by the Islamic worldview.

In today's world, and with the absence of Islam as a way of life, Muslims tend to judge as beneficial what is beneficial or merely advantageous or even merely judged so within a non-Islamic framework and based on non-Islamic criteria and values. As a matter of fact, we have seen that a lot of the discussions treat ostentatious, preliminary, or conjectural advantages as benefit (*maṣlaḥah*), and disadvantages of the same kind as harm (*maḍarrah*). It is an established fact that the Islamic *ummah* and its scholars today generally imitate or react to what other cultures have innovated rather than innovating on an original Islamic basis. Bearing this in mind we should make sure that what they understood as objectives of the Sharīʿah really remain *sharʿī* objectives and are not isolated from their texts or misinterpreted in a way that they legalise something that is not *sharʿī*.

Some Muslim scholars explicitly state that the subject matter, i.e. the bio-medical sciences themselves, needs to be Islamised in order to avoid the global catastrophe of an unguided usage.[1] It is indeed true that the guidance of Islam is bitterly needed to save mankind from destroying itself and the environment it lives in and prevent the worst scenarios of an abuse of genetic technology. The *dīn* of Islam does provide mankind with solutions to all existential problems. But this will only be achieved with the realization of the ultimate objective: the implementation of Islam as a way of life. Only with the realization of this first and foremost objective on a holistic scale can the preservation of the essential objectives be safeguarded and the emerging of harm be prevented.

As a matter of fact, what needs to be changed as a condition for any kind of Islamization to be successful is the framework under which these sciences are pursued. Otherwise, any attempt to Islamize with a reference to the objectives of Sharīʿah is doomed to fail, as it will operate in isolation from the original reference framework. The consideration of what we might refer to as authentic *maqāṣid sharʿiyyah*, i.e. what the Lawgiver has laid down as values and objectives, is not to be denied here. What I have tried to show is that there is a missing link needed to activate the theory properly. It is clear from the case studies this chapter has dicussed that most contemporary

---

[1] Arif Ali Arif, "Qaḍāyā fiqhyah fī l-jīnāt al-basharīyah min manẓūr islāmī," in, Umar SulaymAn al-Ashqar *et al.*, eds., *Dirāsāt Fiqhīyah fī Qaḍāyā Fiqhyah Muʿāṣirah* (Amman: Dār al-Nafā'is, 2001), vol. 2, pp. 735-803, at 736.

scholars embark on the generality of a *maqāṣidic* scheme, while leaving the definition of the respective harms and benefits to others. The case of GMOs for consumption has particularly shown that certain economic benefits may be mistaken as authentic *sharʿī* ones.

In summary we might state that the conclusions of this chapter are not confined to the biomedical field. We can, as a matter of fact, concede that the very same paradigm shift we expounded on in the beginning of this chapter has taken place in all aspects of life. The dichotomy of Islamic values and rules on one side and the implemented non-Islamic systems on the other is a phenomenon of our time. To counter this dichotomy by using *maqāṣid* al-*sharīʿah* within a non-Islamic context as a reference framework does in no way provide a solution to the problem. It rather confronts us with additional dangers: Authentic benefits or *maqāṣid* of the Sharīʿah are dependent on the texts and will be realized with a whole-scale implementation of Islam as a way of life. In the absence of this condition, the focus on *maqāṣid* may turn out to be a closing of ranks with utilitarianism, thus propagating particular interests in the garb of Islam. Likewise, *the ultimate objectives of the Sharīʿah can only be attained via a comprehensive total scale implementation of its system.* It is the implementation of the Sharīʿah rules that secures the realization of authentic legitimate benefits and prevention of harm. God Almighty has decreed (Q., 51: 56): "And [tell them that] I have not created the invisible beings (*jinn*) and men to any end other than that they may [know and] worship Me." And it is only then will the meaning of God's description of the Prophet's mission be truly realized: "And [thus, O Prophet,] We have sent thee as [an evidence of Our] grace towards all the worlds" (Q., 21: 107).

CHAPTER TEN

Maqāṣid al-Sharīʿah in the Prohibition of *Ribā* and their Implications for Modern Islamic Finance

Monzer Kahf

Introduction

Islamic finance was revived at the institutional level with the establishment of Islamic banks during the last quarter of the twentieth century. Along with the new institutions of Islamic banking, Islamic insurance companies and other Islamic finance companies came about new "financing" practices of a few classical contracts that, *inter alia*, include *murābaḥah* to the purchase orderer, *istiṣnāʿ* backed by a parallel *istiṣnāʿ* and financial lease. These and similar new practices of ancient contracts raised intensive discussions about the Sharīʿah validity of the addition of conditions to, and/or the combination of contracts for the sole purpose of transforming them into tools of financing. The dust of these discussions has not been settled yet and the raised red flags have not been lowered when, at the end of the century, a new stream of *fatāwā* came about on *tawarruq*, *ṣukūk* and paid-for guarantee (*kafālah bi-ajr*) that introduced new dimensions in the twenty-first-century Islamic finance hitherto considered as absolute taboos. These new dimensions include the provision of cash/personal financing to individuals and corporations and the hedging in future commodities and currencies. A closer look at these new *fatāwā* reveals that there is an exerted effort to deal with or mitigate the risks of Islamic financing and to make it match the interest-based finance.

This chapter aims at re-visiting, from the angle of modern finance, the objectives of the Sharīʿah with regard to the prohibition of *ribā* and examining the consistency of such *fatāwā* with these objectives and whether there are any Sharīʿah-intrinsic alternatives that satisfy the same finance purposes which such *fatāwā* were thought to achieve. The chapter consists of two sections. In the first section I discuss the objectives of the prohibition of *ribā*. I will further argue that there are certain "risks of Islamic financial contracts" that are an immediate outcome of the nature of the Islamic finance contracts. Carrying these risks by the finance provider is intended by the prohibition of *ribā*. I will therefore study the general characteristics of the financial contracts that are "named" in the classical Sharīʿah literature, the rationale of the prohibition of *ribā* and attempt to re-derive the objectives or "the *maqāṣid*" of this prohibition.

The second section discusses the implications of the *maqāṣid* of the prohibition of *ribā* and delineates the methodological principles of creating new financial products while preserving the objectives of the prohibition. It will also discuss the nature of Islamic financial intermediation, especially in its institutional form unknown in the classical *fiqh* literature. Finally, it will offer a few examples of *maqāṣid*-friendly modalities of reducing the risk of financing and will attempt to show that all the purposes used to justify some of the controversial *fatāwā* can be achieved by such modalities without taking the risk of *maqāṣid* violation or loosing some of the basic characteristics of which Islamic finance stand proud as compared to conventional interest-based finance.

The Objectives of the Prohibition of *Ribā*

Intrinsically and by its own nature, *ribā*-based financing is *purely personal* as it solely depends on the integrity (interpreted as ability to pay back) of the borrower and obtained collaterals. This also implies that *ribā*-based financing is *not target-oriented*; that is, it is detached from the objective for which financed means are going to be used. Detachment from the use of funds leads in turn to another problem that arises from the fact that personal financing can be put to any kind of usage *regardless of ethical principles and moral values*. In other words, *ribā*-based financing does not provide for a say about the moral criteria or ethical screening of the finance. It is also *assumptive* as it attributes a growth to debts while debts are a kind of asset that is not able to grow because of its abstract nature. The assumptive nature of *ribā*-based financing applies not only to assuming an increment, but also to assuming a rate of increment that is attributed to the non-able to grow asset.

Finally, *ribā*-based financing allows for the creation of multiple layers of pure financing on a small base of real market. This means that, because of its nature that permits attributing increment to a non-growing asset, it goes even farther from reality to allow pure debts exchanges and transactions so that the *size or amount of financing in any society exceeds by many folds the size of real market transactions.* Of course, one may argue that some of these problems can be tackled by additional means, regulations and laws, but this is incorrect as any regulations that violates the nature of a transaction are bound to die out because of the market pressure. Additionally, no regulations can cover all potential outcomes of the market forces once you found the market on unrealistic assumptions. This section consists of three headings: The Prohibition of *ribā*, Sharīʿah-friendly financing contracts and their characteristics, and finally deriving the objectives of the prohibition of *ribā.*

A. The Prohibition of Ribā (Usury/Interest)

Islam, like other monotheistic religions, condemns and prohibits *ribā* or usuary. The prohibition of ribā in Islam is given in the strongest and most clear-cut terms. The Qur'an (2: 275-278) decalres:

> Those who gorge themselves on usury behave but as he might behave whom Satan has confounded with his touch; for they say, 'Buying and selling is but a kind of usury'—the while God has made buying and selling lawful and usury unlawful... God deprives usurious gains (ribā) of all blessing, whereas He blesses charitable deeds with manifold increase. And God does not love... O you who have attained to faith! Remain conscious of God, and give up all outstanding gains from usury, if you are [truly] believers; or if you do it not, then know that you are at war with God and His Apostle."

No other sin is prohibited in the Qur'an with a threat of war from God and His Messenger!

The Traditions of the Prophet Muhammad contain several statements that condemn *ribā* and consider its practices as one of the gravest sins that invoke a curse or wrath from God. It is narrated by Jābir b. ʿAbd Allāh that "God's Messenger of (*pbuh*) cursed the taker and giver usury (*ribā*), the writer thereof, and its two witnesses, and then he said: 'they are all equally sinful'."[1]

Definitions of Ribā and Interest

Ribā is an Arabic word that means increment/increase. But the Qur'an did not mean any increment as it refers to an increment in a specific transaction, "the" *ribā* that was common and known among the Arabs and other nations at the time of revelation. This

---

[1] Abū al-Ḥussain Muslim b. al-Ḥajjāj al-Qushayrī al-Naysābūrī, *Ṣaḥīḥ Muslim* (Beirut: Dār al-Kutub al-ʿIlmiyyah, 1st edn, 1421/2001), "Kitāb al-Musāqāt", No. 1598, p. 620.

is why the reference in the Qur'an came to "the" *ribā*. This transaction was done in either of two ways: 1) deferment of an already existing and due debt to a new maturity provided the amount of debt is increased; and, 2) giving a loan that is due with an increment after a given period of time. The Qur'an (2: 279) itself implies this definition as it states: "But if you repent, then you shall be entitled to [the return of] your principal: you will do no wrong, and neither will you be wronged." This part of the verse has two important indications: 1) it defines *ribā* as any increment above the principal of a debt or loan; and 2) it describes such an increment as unjust. The exclusion of profit, being an increment in sale, is given by verse 2: 275, "… the while God has made buying and selling lawful and usury unlawful."

To be exact, *ribā* is defined, in regard to financial transactions,[1] as any contractual increment in a loan or debt due to the time element. This is exactly what we know today as interest. Both legally and financially, interest is defined as an increment paid by the debtor to the creditor for granting a loan or for extending the maturity of an existing debt. Obviously, the Sharīʿah does not recognize a counterpart for this increment. Consequently, once a debt is created (notice that a loan creates a debt), any increment above the principal of the debt is interest and it is *the* prohibited *ribā* according to the terminology of the Qur'an.

To understand why interest is prohibited we need to revisit the basic concept of debts. What is a debt? A debt is an interpersonal relation that is a liability on one party and an abstract asset to another. By its nature and in real life a debt is not liable to increase or decrease, it is not able to produce increments because it has no intrinsic utility other than being an ingredient of wealth. In other words, a debt cannot have different values at different times and places unless we create additions in the form

---

[1] We exclude from this definition *ribā al-buyūʿ* because of its irrelevance to financing as the time element is not necessarily an ingredient of it.

of assumptions; that is by creating a debt market and valuating or assessing debts in relation to time. Additionally, the amount of an increment in a debt is also assumptive; it depends on the conditions and externalities in the imaginary market that we create for debts.

Of course, this may sound astonishing to many of us who are accustomed to talking and hearing about debt markets and interest all through their lives! Are debts, in fact, able to increase or decrease or to produce increments? And how can this take place except in our imagination that we illusion to be true and real? Certainly, once a market is created for any thing, be it thin air, there will be a demand and supply for it on speculative grounds, exactly as people exchange indices, in a fantasy-created pure speculation-based index market, although indices are neither real assets nor goods or services! We must remember that the Sharīʿah recognizes real things and real growth whether by the nature of a real asset or by the effect of market forces on real assets, goods, or services.

Additionally, all real things/assets that may grow may also loose substance and/or value and the owners of such things/assets are exposed to losses exactly by virtue of the same argument that justifies their entitlement to increments. But a debt, among all assets, is not liable to decrease and does not expose its owner to such kinds of loss; brush aside the issue of default because every debt can be secured by all kinds of guarantees and collaterals and because the nature of default risk is different from the risk of increase and/or decrease that result from natural factors or from the interaction of market forces. A default risk is fault in the debt itself; it is of the kind of a faulty product or a product that does not maintain its normal characteristics; a defaulted debt is like delivering rotten apple in a sale contract that is very different from the price risk that affects the owner of the apple. This is why the default risk is compensated by a risk premium over and above the interest that is "the price of money".

It may be argued that a debt giver has made a sacrifice and that, acoordinfly, he/she deserves compensation without which he/she would have not made such a sacrifice. While the idea of a sacrifice is a legitimate one, the basic principles of private ownership prevent allowing any part of the increment of the debtor's property to be deserved by any other person, since any growth that may take place in the debtor's property can only be deserved by the owner of a property. In other words, since the property of the lender has been transformed to become an abstract asset that is not able to create increments by its own nature (a debt), it is inconsistent with the implications of the principle of private ownership for a lender to claim any part of the property of the debtor. [1] Furthermore, there are no measuring tools or criteria to estimate the contribution of a loan to increments especially since an asset is also exposed to decline by the same virtue it may develop increments. Consequently, a personal loan must remain personal and deserves thanks, gratitude and appreciation from the borrower and maybe reward from God too, but it is not a contributor to value creation.

B. *Alternative Financing Contracts and their Characteristics.*

Notwithstanding the several attempts to encode the Sharīʿah, the fact is that its bulk remains not coded in the form of articles of law but its rulings are found in the writings of Sharīʿah specialists through the centuries as Islam does not establish a religious hierarchy with a law-giving authority. We will study the Sharīʿah alternative financing contracts in an attempt to understand their essential characteristics and find out more about the Islamic financing principles and rationale of the prohibition of interest. It

[1] This is in contrast to giving the same sum on the basis venture capital by a sleeping partner. In this case the owner remains an owner of the asset that is in the hand of the active partner, even after the original capital is transformed into intermediate goods and/or final goods, and consequently she deserves increments that may take place her property.

has become known over the last four decades of theorization and practice that the Sharīʿah financing contracts are of three major kinds: sharing-based, sale based and lease-based.

On the other hand, from an historical point of view, Islamic financing products can be classified in two categories: 1) classical contracts that existed throughout centuries and are derived from the practice of the Prophet's community in Madīnah; and 2) hybrid contracts that are developed over the past half a century and are practiced in contemporary Islamic finance and banking.

Classical Financing Contracts

Classical writings on the Sharīʿah, some of which date back to twelve centuries ago, mention three essential sharing-based financing contracts, namely, equity sharing (*mushārakah*), equity sharing with a sleeping partner (*muḍārabah*) and crop-sharing (*muzāraʿah*). They also mention three sale-based financing contracts: deferred payment sale (*al bayʿ al-'ājil*), forward sale with cash advance (*salam*) and manufacturing financing sale (*istiṣnāʿ*). Lastly, classical writings also mention leasing (*ijārah*) as a form of financial contracting.

Although this chapter does not intend to go through the by-now well-known descriptions and conditions of each of these contracts, one stop is necessary at the deferred payment sale at a higher cost than the cash price because it provides a demarcation of interest *vis-á-vis* financing sale. The permissibility of deferred payment financing sale is mentioned in no less than the Qur'an itself, as stated in 2: 275: "they say, 'Buying and selling is but a kind of usury'."

Claiming that cash sale is just like interest lending is logically incorrect and exposes the claimant to be ridiculed and accused of foolishness, insanity or loss of rationale, because cash sale is very remote from interest lending and has no similarity to it. What is, obviously, similar to interest lending is deferred payment sale at a price that is higher than the cash price. Here the similarity is obvious.[1] Interestingly, the Qur'an did not ridicule this claim or accused it of irrationality; this is inspite of the fact that in many instances/occasions the Qur'an invokes rational reasoning and argumentation by such statements as: "Will they not understand?" "So you may understand," "Don't you understand?," "in order that you may rationalize;" all such phrases occur the same surah; and "have you no rationale?," "if you have reason," "don't you reason," "so that they may have mind to rationalize with!," and many similar verses throughout the entire Qur'an.

This implicitly means that some similarity is acknowledged; yet the Qur'an quickly directs the attention to the permissibility of the sale that is similar to interest lending and the prohibition of the latter; as if it says: while certain similarity is acknowledged there are differences that warrant the permissibility of deferred payment sale-based financing and the prohibition of interest/lending-based financing. This is why the overwhelming majority of scholars argue that the permitted sale in this verse, though general and applies to any kind of sale, refers specifically to deferred-payment [i.e., financing] sale. This is also supported by bringing in a verse (2: 282) about debts confirmation and documentation immediately after the verses that deal with the prohibition of interest and permissibility of deferred-payment sale financing (Q., 2: 275-281), since deferring the payment creates a debt that need to be documented.

The unavoidable immediate implication of verse 2: 275 is that debt-creating financing is permissible and recognized in the Sharīʿah, while the verse condemns interest-based lending and prohibits any increment on it. Thus, by rendering loan giving a

---

[1] Some may argue that even cash sale is similar to interest lending from the point of view that profit is an increment like interest. This kind of similarity seems very simplistic because of two reasons: 1) sale may involve a loss too but lending does not; and 2) profit is commodity/market-based while interest is time-based. And I may add that those who argue for such a similarity do not deny that the permissibility in the verse refers to both cash sale and deferred-payment sale.

non-profitable activity and shifting it from business arena to personal spheres, it approves a kind of sale that fulfills the same objectives including giving a reward for the time value of the sold commodity (rather than money lent). To put it fifferently, this verse establishes a very important rule that: *Debt-creating financing is an acceptable and rewarding business activity at the same time that it prohibits ribā (interest).* This plainly means that the creation of debts is not a thing that is discouraged or disliked in the Sharīʿah and avoidance of creating debts is not an objective of the prohibition of *ribā*.

The similarities between deferred-payment sale at a higher price than the cash price and interest lending are apparent and include: 1) the purchaser gets the asset/goods at the time of the contract and pays later; 2) the amount she may end up paying is about the same in both transactions; 3) the seller gets compensated for the time span between the contract and the maturity of the debt; and, 4) a debt is created. But the dissimilarities are not so clear and the verse did not elaborate on them.

Hybrid Islamic Financing Contracts and Financial Intermediation

The industry of financial intermediation is new to the Islamic Sharīʿah scholarship.[1] It has been developed in the Western countries over the past four centuries or so. Recognition of financial intermediation as an independent industry is vital to understanding the hybrid financial contracts, and those scholars and researchers who fail to recognize this industry still argue for preferences of sharing over other modes of financing instead of

[1] Although one has to recognize that classical Sharīʿah writings discussed the idea of "al-muḍārib yuḍārib" but the whole institutional setting and the idea of collecting savings from persons of excess savings and channeling them to persons of need for business and consumption activities was not known, especially that funds provision by intermediaries may take different methodologies that may not be *muḍārabah*-based.

taking such preference to be decided by players on the basis of market circumstances and forces.

When a merchant sells at a deferred price or lease an asset he/she is providing financing to the purchaser or the lessee. But if a corporation specializes in getting the savings of those who have them and channeling them to businesses that need them for investment, that is a specialized industry of financial intermediation. In other words, financial intermediation is a specialty of those who recruit deposits and provide funding while merchants and producers provide commercial credit from their own resources in dealing with the daily decisions of a production line or buying and selling of goods and services.

The role of Islamic financial engineering over the last four decades has been to develop contracts that fit this new industry. Its success and failure can be assessed on the basis of the extent to which new contracts maintain the main characteristics implied by the prohibition of *ribā* and preserve the objectives of this prohibition.

There are numerous Islamic financial products in the market and they are increasing by the day. New products are always developed through a process of combining existing contracts and arrangements. We have essentially *nine* main hybrid Islamic financing contracts practiced in Islamic banks today: *murābaḥah* to the purchase orderer, installment sale, *muḍārabah* investment deposit, current account deposit, three-party *istiṣnāʿ*, leasing to the purchase orderer, compound *salam*, *buy-back* and *tawarruq*. Although assessing how close/far each of these contracts to consistency with the objectives of the prohibition of interest is beyond the scope of this chapter, it must be said that some of the applications of new hybrids amounts to pure interest-based rescheduling of debts and are consequently in violation of the basic objectives of the prohibition of *ribā*.

General Characteristics of Financial Products in Sharīʿah

Islamic financial products are contracts that abide by the axioms and rulings of the Sharīʿah. The main principles that govern financial contracts in Islamic law are of two kinds: 1) general principles of contracting that include civil aptitude, consent and legal permissibility. These are common between all legal systems and societies, although there are variations in their minute details. For instance, while the Islamic law defines the civil aptitude for financial contracts as age 18 in addition to sanity, some states or countries carry the age limit to 21. 2) However, the second group of principles is important. It covers a specific Islamic view point and includes: moral commitment/ethical foundation, Sharīʿah permissibility, balance and realism or validity.

To be acceptable from a Sharīʿah point of view, a finance product must be *morally sound.* This is a general human standard preached and adopted by the Sharīʿah. It means that an Islamic financing institution can't use its resources to support drugs, alcohol, gambling, pornographic industry, environmentally harmful products, and/or any other production or distribution of any material or service that does not have a humanly acceptable ethical foundation. In this regard, Islamic financing is very similar to what is known as ethical investment. Yet, the following points will show that Islamic financing is, in fact, more demanding than ethical investment, as generally understood.

The principle of Sharīʿah permissibility refers to matters that Islamic law requires. These include pork and other swine products and other meat whose animals are not slaughtered in a manner that satisfies the Sharīʿah requirements. It also includes the prohibition of interest that will be discussed later.

The principle of *balance* requires that the obligations of each party be equivalent to the obligations of the other, so that there is no excessive load on either party. This principle rules out excessive overcharge and stands against the charge of interest too. As we will show later, interest is an obligation on one party against a presumed opportunity cost of the other. These obligations are obviously unbalanced!

Lastly, the principle of realism and validity means that all financing contracts must be *founded on real, in contrast to presumed or deemed*, transactions, exchanges or things and assets. This principle rules out any contract that is based on pure assumptions. Interest itself is one example, both in its very existence and in its rates, all are assumptive as we will discuss in more detail later. Another example is trading indices such as DJII or NASDAQ, because an index is a mere mental calculation that does not represent any real ownership. On the other hand, one can own and trade units in an indexed fund because the fund owns shares in companies that are represented in the index.

What is Wrong with Interest?

I argue that understanding the differences between interest-loan-based financing and debt-creating sale financing is extremely essential to comprehend the objectives of the prohibition of *ribā* (interest). This is because these differences elucidate the crucial point of the distinction between seemingly similar transactions.

The basic difference between interest financing and Islamic financing is that interest financing is done in a loan contract; hence it is based on a postulate that a debt may be assigned or may give entitlement to an increment while in reality a debt cannot produce any increment. This is at the same time very much linked to, or you may call it the other facet of, the property rights. Property rights entitle the owner of an asset to all and any increments that may happen in her/his asset and preclude any other person from any claim on increments that may happen in other persons' assets. In other words, a person whose asset does not produce any increment has no claim to an increment and consequently cannot and must not have any entitlement on increments that happen in other persons' assets.

This is the ideological foundation of the prohibition that is consistent with the characteristic of realism of the Sharīʿah, because in reality the lender's asset is a debt and a debt is abstract and, by its nature, canot create increments. The implications of accepting the idea that a debt has to have increment are:

1. It is a gross violation of the principles of private ownership that requires entitling an asset owner of all increments that may happen in her owned asset and that no entitlement may be assigned to any other person. Furthermore, because it is based on mere assumption, allowing any entitlement to increments to be assigned to any person other than the owner amounts to a gross disturbance in the property rights and gives room for other violations too.
2. You need another unrealistic assumption about the valuation of the increment (the rate of interest) that is to be assigned to an asset (a debt) that does not create increment.[1] This has been done by creating an artificial market for exchanging debts. This market is built in fact on pure speculation and purely speculative market forces, unlike markets of assets, goods and services; it is therefore very volatile by its nature.
3. Once you allow a debt to have an increment you will have to allow it to be rescheduled with increment and you will have to allow discounting with a reduction; both these two transactions do not create or add value in the economy; and,
4. You will have to allow other transactions on debts, pure, including exchanging them through inter-bank transactions and a whole set of pure financial or monetary transactions that do not essentially add value, but only transfer wealth from one person to another. The Sharīʿah takes a close look at these transactions and finds them done in isolation from real production and exchange; they do not affect inventories on the shelves of goods and services reaching consumers;

[1] This is in contrast with actual increase when you assign the increment to the owner of the asset that creates it.

they only enrich some individuals and impoverish others; they are like a zero-sum game; and finally

5. Withholding finance from activities other than those related to producing and/or exchanging goods and services helps channeling all finances in the economy to support activities that exclusively produce/exchange goods and services. This is not only economically wiser, but it is also socially more just. In other words, preventing finance that is provided solely on the credit worthiness of the user of funds regardless of the purpose of their use creates a better social justice environment than personal financing.

C. The Objectives of the Prohibition of Ribā

In light of the preceding exposition, we can proceed to establish the objectives of Sharīʿah concerning the prohibition of interest as follows:

1. Affirming the Sharīʿah characteristic of realism and maintaining its internal consistency in not allowing any transaction that is not a real-life activity. There are several forms of expressing the negative statement of this objective; one of these forms is preventing finance from activities that are not meant on their own or for what their nature defines or from activities that are used only as a vehicle to reach objectives other than what the nature of the contract implies. Another form is preventing return from being assigned to an asset that does not produce return. Yet another form is avoiding distributing any thing other than the real value added or value created in an asset.

2. Upholding the sanctity of property rights and respecting the consistency of entitlements with the rights of ownership.

3. Disallowing debts trade and exchange along with similarly unrealistic purely speculative transactions that are not based on real production or exchange such as creating unreal assets like index-units properties because these activities do not create value and only transfer wealth between individuals.

4. Redirecting or re-channeling the human and other resources used in purely speculative, non-value-adding activities, such as trading debts toward real production and exchange of goods and services.

5. Preventing debt discounting and rescheduling for increment, because these are non-productive activities as they only transfer wealth from one person to another. The alternative that the Sharīʿah provides for rescheduling is interestingly mentioned in the Qur'an within the same sequence of verses that deal with the prohibition of *ribā* (interest) that is: giving time to pay or even forsaking the principal of the debt itself. On the other hand, the Sharīʿah permits discounting for early payment provided it does not become a business practice (not in the contract and only between the two parties).

6. Preventing the use of business finances for what can be described as *ʿabath*, i.e., activities that have no disclosed purpose or whose purpose is not desired to be disclosed because of the embarrassment it may cause as such activities are either non-productive or involves certain degree of shame or do not belong to business although they may be honorable or legitimate.

7. Sending personal finance to where it belongs as a personal service based on direct contact and involvement between the finance provider and user. Thus, personal financing can be evaluated, judged and granted or not on the basis of the personal relations and bonds that exist between the user of funds and their provider. The answer to the question "who will give you a loan?" becomes, "your mother or a person who very well knows and loves you." This does not mean that a personal loan is not useful; it rather means that it must remain personal and not changed into a business activity that aims at making money. As such, giving a loan is rewardable by God as known in the Sharīʿah, because it becomes an act of benevolence.

8. Re-channeling all business financing toward the production and exchange of goods and services or toward value creation and closing doors in the face of all the uses of finance that

unnecessarily inflate the quantity/size of financing in a society relative to the real market of production and exchange.

Finally, it should be noted that the prohibition of *ribā* (interest) is never meant to be a prohibition or elimination of materially rewarding financing in general and of debt-creating financing in particular.

Implications of the Maqāṣid of the Prohibition of *Ribā*

There are two important results that arise from the objectives (*maqāṣid*) of the prohibition of *ribā*/interest: 1) A loan is a means of providing personal finance and it should remain "personal;" and, 2) any efforts that aim at creating new Islamic financial Hybrids should observe the *maqāṣid* in the process of developing new contracts. In this section, I will study these implications and proceed to look into the nature and characteristics of Islamic financial intermediation and give a few examples of Sharīʿah-friendly methodologies of risk mitigation.

i. Main Implications of the Prohibition of Interest Loans and Personal Finance

It is really enlightening that our traditional *fiqh* text-books assign loans and lending to the category of charities and benevolence, because when you talk about "personal" you need to have personal information, personal relation and personal touch, passion and care. These are the essence of benevolence and charity. This is why a loan is also due at any time because "there must be no charge on benevolence doers," as the Qur'an (9: 91) stipulates. In other words, it seems that the immediate implication of the prohibition of interest is to remove lending activities from the business arena and send them to the charitable arena that usually consists of both individuals who have close ties and bondages to each other and non-profit organizations that act also on the basis of creating personal data base and relations as a loan is given to a person who has temporary "needs" that call for "relief" with temporary liquidity. Loans and personal financing are not considered, in the Sharīʿah, as tools for mobilizing resources for investment, trade and business! Of course, this does not mean the prohibition of issuing loans to businesses; it simply means that lending to businesses is an exception not a rule and whenever it is done, it should *abide by the rules of benevolence and charity* not re-formulated as a profit generating activity.

1. Observing the Maqāṣid

I do not intend to go into the *uṣūlī* controversy over priorities between *maqāṣid* and direct or specific texts, but I want to argue that, from a financial-cum-economic point of view, the lack of full observance of the objectives of the prohibition of *ribā* may render a hybrid contract into a mere superficial cover-up of what is prohibited and makes Islamic financing completely ineffective and inefficient in performing its essential characteristics. For instance, while financing commodity trade is absolutely permissible and is consistent with the *maqāṣid*, the mere fulfillment of the conditions of owning/possessing is not a sufficient, although it is necessary, condition unless the objective (*maqṣad*) of helping/facilitating trade or exchange of goods and services is also observed. The criterion for this *maqṣad* is obviously the assurance that the financed commodity/service actually reaches a user.[1] To put it in other words, providing finances for contracts that are meant for what they are in contrast to contracts used for what they are not.

If this kind of *maqāṣid* observance is loosened, Islamic financing, as a unique financing methodology that is value-oriented and value-based, will loose its merits and substance because the moment you enter the arena of providing "personal

---

[1] Avoiding of vain (*ʿabath*) transactions can be achieved by defining the user of finance as either a business that uses it to help obtaining inputs (that may be assets, goods for sale or primary and intermediate goods for industry) for its business, or a final consumer.

finance" the financing methodology become incapable of fulfilling any moral and ethical standards and ceases to be real and value additive.

2. Nature and Characteristics of Islamic Financial Intermediation

Financial intermediation is an industry that recruits savings from persons who have them but do not know how or do not like to directly invest them and distribute financing to persons who need funding but do not have sufficient resources. It came into existence with the practice of bankers that notice that not all depositors (essentially for safety and convenience purposes) withdraw their savings at once, the point that allows bankers to provide some of these savings to users of funds without risking be unable to pay deposits on demand. Financial intermediation in the West uses the loan as a basic contract for deposits and for financing. This is done mainly for historical reasons: 1) it is a desired contract by depositors as it guarantees their deposits; so why not use it also for financing so that the banker would also be guaranteed? and 2) it was permissible for a Jew to take interest from the gentiles and most early bankers were Jewish.

The initiation and rise of Islamic banking in the last few decades of the twentieth century disturbed a four-century status quo! Islamic banks have been a blowing evidence that financing does not have to take the form of lending or a loan contract. With Islamic banking, financing is now redefined as *offering goods, services and means of investment for a delayed counterpart.* Accordingly, Islamic financial intermediation is also redefined as recruiting resources from those who have surpluses, either as sleeping partners with the intermediary institution (*arbāb al-māl,* sing. *rabb al-māl*) for depositors who want to use their savings for return generation or on loan basis from those who prefer guaranteeing their principles and giving financing to those who need them on the basis of *wakālah*, *ijārah* and/or venture capital (*muḍārabah* investment).

Funds in Islamic financial intermediaries come from three

sources that can be summed in two from the point of view of using them. 1. Shareholders' funds about which the management behavior is *wakālah*-based; 1. Demand deposit funds that are given to the bank, not to the management, as guaranteed loans in the *dhimmah* of the bank and the management acts on behalf of the bank on *wakālah* basis too since the funds become a property of the bank against "*inshighāl* of its *dhimmah*" that is represented as credit records in the bank accounts; and 3. Investment funds of *arbāb al-amwāl* through *muḍārabah* contracts with the bank, not simply its management. The management of an Islamic financial intermediary, as an institution, plays with the depositors' money on the basis of *wakālah* granted to the bank and assigned by its decision-making body to the management in regard to funds provided by investment depositors. The management also plays on the basis of *wakālah* granted by the decision-making body of the institution in regard to the institution's "own property." This "own property" term includes shareholders' equity plus demand deposits for which the institution's *dhimmah* is charged (*munshtaghilah*).

In other words, an Islamic financial intermediary institution is a *wakālah*-based entity. On the one hand, it is a *wakālah* from shareholders to management, like any other company, but with the exception that demand deposits are treated, from the point of view of investment decisions and profit/loss distribution on the same footing as if they were money shareholders. Furthermore, it is a *wakālah* from investment deposits' owners to the institution itself that is in turn reassigned to the institution's management.

This concept of *wakālah* implies extra precaution on two grounds: on the one hand, the *wakīl* in the Sharīʿah has a very limited power when it comes to *tabarruʿāt* (contributory) contracts. This requires specific permission from the property owner for giving *tabarruʿāt*. On the other hand, a *wakīl* is required to be extra cautious in selecting investments and uses of funds, something that might induce the *wakīl* to have a preference of more security over less of it and of less venturous uses of funds over risky alternatives. This may partially explain why Islamic bankers have been preferring *murābaḥah* and *ijārah* over *muḍārabah*, as a contractual vehicle, for their uses of funds.

A step further may be taken on a theoretical basis that is to dare saying that Islamic bankers must, on pure Sharīʿah grounds, have a preference for *murābaḥah* and *ijārah* over *muḍārabah* because of security and risk considerations.

We also question the wisdom of some traditional Islamic finance writings that have been calling on Islamic banks to use the *muḍārabah* contract on their asset side as if it is better, in the sight of the Sharīʿah, to take more risk. Some times this theoretical preference is mixed up with the maxim of *al-ghunmu bi al-ghrum*, as if taking risk is what justifies deserving a return and therefore the more risk an Islamic bank takes the better Islamic it is!

In fact, the Sharīʿah does not assign any moral value to risk taking; it does not have any reference to preferring more risk over less risk and it does not make risk the cause for earning a return.[1] The realism of the Sharīʿah is manifested in the axiom that one has an entitlement to a return either by expending human hours or by owning an asset that actually and factually produces a return;[2] this means that return in financing is only justified by owning an asset that is not only characterized by having a potentiality to create an increment but also that

---

[1] In fact, if risk taking justifies return the *kafālah*, which is a case of extreme risk taking, must be most rewarding in terms of return. But it is known, in the Sharīʿah as declared by the OIC Islamic Fiqh Academy's resolutions that a reward on *kafālah* is more prohibited than Ribā because it amounts to an increment on a promise to give a loan while Ribā is an increment on an actually given loan.

[2] What is added by some scholars that entitlement to a return can also be caused by "guarantee" refers to a special kind of a guarantee that is a guarantee of principal as in *sharikat al-wujūh* or of man hours as in the case of *taqabbul* in *sharikat al sanāʾiʿ*. Accordingly, this kind of guarantee boils down to labor or principal!

actually, in contrast to presumably or supposedly, has produced an increment. This is factuality as it exists on the ground!

Before we attempt to distinguish Islamic banking, as an alternative financial intermediary system, from direct financing, we need to revisit the idea of markup in *murābaḥah* and see how it is built up within the Islamic perspective of financial intermediation. Dates of payment and delivery have an effect on prices of goods and services. This is a known fact both in the Sharīʿah and conventional studies. Likewise, any commodity or service would have a spectrum of prices according to its date of payment and date of delivery. If we take, for the sake of simplicity, three of these prices, fix the date of delivery at a given point for the three of them and define them as: a) a price with payment before delivery; b) a price with payment at the time of delivery; and, c) a price with payment after the date of delivery, we will notice that, under the condition of "all other conditions or things are the same," price (a) is the lowest among then, them comes price (b) then the highest is price (c). This may be partially explained by the time value of commodities and means of payment but more important is the fact of the acquisition and use of a commodity. When you use a commodity without having to pay for it at the time of acquisition you are deriving utility from it and you would be willing to pay more for that. By the same token, when you pay for it but defer the acquisition, and use to a later date, you would like to pay less for the commodity. This is why we find our classical *fuqahā'* calling the *salam* sale as a sale of the *maḥāwīj* (the needy ones) or sale of *mustarkhiṣīn* (cheap price seekers). Once we establish that a commodity has such differences in prices because of the dates of payment and delivery, we can explain that a mark up in *murābaḥah* is neither derived from the interest concept nor it is based essentially on the time preference for money (although time preference of money is not inconsistent with it and we have no reason to argue against it).[1] The markup is essentially derived from the time structure of commodity prices.

Merchants usually provide commercial credit directly to their customers as is known and practiced, especially in trades between wholesalers and retailers; they use their own equity resources and very often depend on credit facilities from banks, especially by discounting commercial papers and promissory notes. On the other hand, Islamic banks undertake providing finance to individuals and businesses using the resources that consist mostly of depositors' funds. The kind of financing they provide is essentially based on financial intermediation. They do not need to open stores and show rooms to justify their earning of a markup as the latter is, financially and morally, justified by the fact that prices of commodities vary in regard to the dates of payment and delivery. Therefore, the price differential between the case of immediate payment and delivery (the buy price in *murābaḥah*) and the deferred-payment price (the marked-up sell price in *murābaḥah*) of a commodity is not a mimic of interest; it is rather a real market-base differential because people, in reality (and the Sharīʿah goes along with reality) do have such differences in prices because the dates of payment and delivery do in fact affect prices.[2]

---

[1] We argue that time value of money as a justification for interest is not a reality but an illusion because when we keep money on hand (or better, means of payment on hand) there will be no increase in it and no "time value of money" ever appears. Time value of money is only claimed to exist when we give money as a debt to another person or only when money is in another person's hand we claim an increment caused by "the time value of money." Furthermore, although human preference for cash on hand is a fact of life because such a preference gives us a higher degree of choice at each moment of time, this preference does not necessarily give us an "assured increment" as an alternative use may result in losses instead of increments. It is only when we create a market for interest loans (or rather increment in debts) that the alternative of keeping cash on hand becomes "assuredly positive." This we argued its unrealistic nature earlier in this chapter.

[2] This is obscured in today's practices of Islamic banking because of the

Finally, the distinctive feature of Islamic financial intermediation *vis-á-vis* direct commercial credit is the point that Islamic financial intermediaries must not act on their own initiatives in creating a financing process; they must only act on an initiative by a customer. This means that Islamic financial intermediary is not a direct investment industry; it is rather a support institution of businesses by providing financing to their investments and purchases. This also means that whenever Islamic banks undertake buying or owning assets on their own initiatives (of course outside buying goods and services for their own personal needs to practice their business), they are actually violating the basic definition of Islamic financial intermediation and turn into merchant direct commercial credit providers!

3. Examples of Sharīʿah-friendly Methods of Risk Mitigation

Khan and Ahmad have argued that Islamic banks not only face the type of risks that conventional banks face, but they are also confronted with new and unique risks as a result of their unique asset and liability structures. In their view, this new type of risks is an immediate outcome of their compliance with the Sharīʿah requirements. They added that even in regard to common or conventional risks, the risks that Islamic banks face differ in nature from those faced by conventional banks. The obvious implication of this argument is that Islamic banks need variant "risk identification processes" and different risk management approaches and techniques and require a different kind of supervision as well.[1] A Similar argument appeared a few years

---

structure of the market of financial intermediation. The financial intermediation industry is overwhelmingly dominated by interest-based lending to the extent that interest practices are a de facto price setter in this industry. The choice of Islamic banks is very limited to either go along the market or get out of business!

[1] Habib Ahmed & Tariqullah Khan, Risk Management in Islamic Banking," in M. Kabir Hassan & Mervyn K. Lewis (eds.), *Handbook of Islamic Banking* (Cheltenham, UK & Northampton, USA: Edward Edgar, 2007), pp. 144-158.

earlier in an IMF publication by Luca Errico and Mitra Farahbaksh.[1] Although they conceded that minimum capital requirement should take into consideration assets composition, i.e., the PLS investments versus non-PLS investments,[2] they argued that the minimum capital requirement needed to for risks' coverage should be higher in Islamic banks that in conventional banks because their PLS assets are not collaterized.

The main focus of these two writings on Islamic banks is addressed especially from the point of view of supervisory authorities and minimum capital requirement. While we agree with these writings on the things that Islamic finance entails, in fact, some kinds of risk that are different from the risks referred to, such as legal and litigation risks. These are purely procedural, being caused by the fact that courts are not yet fully familiar with Islamic finance.[3]

However, Islamic financial products pose a different kind of risk challenges that focus on the risks to investor and undertakers. Undertaker risk relates essentially to covering the issued product. The experience in the Middle East, South East Asia and Pakistan, in this regard, indicates that there is a strong appetite for Islamic financial products to the extent that each issue is always over-subscribed and purchasers and investors hold on to them to the extent that little room is left for a secondary market. This demand is derived essentially from

---

[1] Luca Errico and Mitra Farahbaksh, *Islamic Banking: Issues in Prudential Regulation and Supervision*, IMF Working Paper No. WP/98/30, 1998.

[2] *Ibid.*, p 17.

[3] I have argued elsewhere that the asset structure of Islamic banks is not substantially any different from conventional banks a fact that makes them in need to neither a different style of risk management nor more or stringier capital requirement. Additionally, since the larger portion of their deposits are *muḍārabah* -based investment deposits that basically shares risks with equities, the capital requirement may be less in Islamic banks than in conventional banks. See Monzer Kahf, "Basel II: Implications for Islamic Banking," paper presented at the 6th International Conference on Islamic Economics and Banking, Jakarta: Nov. 22-24, 2005.

religious enthusiasm rather than from economic calculation. Many researchers feel that with the enlargement of the Islamic financial market this enthusiasm may not continue, undertakers will then need to resort to economic rationale which appeals to all potential investors regardless of their religion and/or religiosity. Investors' risk is a matter of worry for beneficiaries of new Islamic financial products and Islamic bankers.

Promoters of Islamic public issues, such as *ṣukūk,* look for means of mitigating these risks in anticipation that religiously-motivated demand will sometime faint and a new motivation must be offered to investors. Here comes the role of new *fatāwā* that attempt to find out means to reduce risk of such issues and other new Islamic financial products. It is clearly noticeable that the pace of issuing *fatāwā* has been expedited, especially since the last few years of the past millennium and some of them seem to have been very controversial.

To understand the effects of some of the "new" *fatāwā* and assess their consistency with the specific *maqāṣid* of the prohibition of *ribā* we shall first review the extent and nature of risks involved in Islamic finance, then we shall suggest *maqāṣid*-friendly methodologies for risk mitigation that can be considered alternatives to the hazy "new" *fatāwā.*

ii. Risk Profile of Islamic Financial Contracts

Without having to reiterate the description and characteristics of the Islamic financial contracts, their risk profile can be described as being derived from the principle of realism. What goes on in real life is what is accepted in the Sharīʿah without any "additives" or assumptions. In other words, the nature of these contracts defines their risk profile. The fundamental financing elements in the Islamic financial contracts are:

1. There must asset basis to justify earning: Assets are either handed over to a manager (entrepreneur) or retained for leasing or obtained for resale.
2. The asset base of financing must be the kind that produces

increments either by its very nature (e.g., fruits or usufruct) or by the effect of real market forces (e.g., goods and services).[1]

3. The investor (property provider) earns by virtue of ownership of an asset that grows. This is apparent in sale and lease financing and implied in the agency content of sharing (continued ownership of money provider into bought assets).
4. Moral and Sharīʿah screening is essential for Sharīʿah compatible investment and financial contracts.

These characteristics have their own risk profile. The basic point (that Islamic financial products are essentially based on real market transactions, i.e., assets, goods and/or services) requires that we deal with the real risk of owning goods, services and productive assets. Hence, we have a combination of price risk and opportunity cost risk, the latter is usually expressed as interest rate risk as we live in a market that is over-ridden by interest![2] The credit risk or risk of default always exists

---

[1] How about money, can it be a principal in a sharing finance? One may quickly answer "no" because money does not grow. The classical Islamic literature on finance contracts recognizes this apparent fact but adds that money can be exchanged for other goods, assets and factors of production; it can, therefore, be used as a principal in sharing finance provided that the first step of using it (the step of buying goods, etc.) is founded on the basis of agency contract. In other words, by virtue of the agency contract, that is implicit in all sharing-based finances, the ownership of money provider is transferred to the asset an agent/partner buys and hence money becomes amenable to grow and can be used as a principal in a sharing finance contract. Debt is another real, though intangible, asset that cannot be used as a principal in sharing because it is not amenable to growth. It is not treated like money, in the Sharīʿah literature, because it is not readily available for purchasing good and factors of production as it takes time and effort to collect it. It requires an explicit and separate agency contract that may involve fees and/or other charges. But once it is collected, it becomes cash or other assets, then a sharing-based financial relationship may be contracted.

[2] As the Islamic finance accounts for only a small fraction of the interest-dominated conventional finance market, Islamic finance products and dealers are price takers, not price setters, in this globalized market if they want to be not thrown out! *Credit risk* or *risk of default* always exists whenever a contract creates a

whenever a contract creates a debt, and the moral hazard risk crops up in any inter-personal relationship.

What may be emphasized is that while price risk is uniquely important in Islamic financing, it is drastically reduced through the "binding promise" in *murābaḥah* and financial lease, while it remains an issue of consideration in other forms of finance (sharing and asset-based investment). As for moral hazard risk, it is apparently much greater in sharing finance than in lending-based finance, which means that if moving away from interest means adopting on *mushārakah* and *murābaḥah* the moral hazard risk will be multiplied many folds. On the other hand, on can hardly find any substantial difference in the nature and extent of opportunity cost risk and credit risk between Islamic finance and conventional finance.

iii. Examples of Maqāṣid-friendly Approaches for Risk Mitigation

In this subsection, I will discuss a few arrangements of risk mitigation that are intrinsic to the classical Sharīʿah literature and go on to imply that these arrangements provide a variety of potential applications that may reduce the need to using risk mitigation *fatāwā* that raise the Sharīʿah clouds that are dared sometimes by some products thrown in what is called "the Islamic capital market."

To minimize the investors' risk in new Islamic financial products, especially *ṣukūk* and corporate investments, a handful of arrangements can be used, namely, revenue sharing, service and usufruct-based finance, principal insurance, collaterals, third party guarantee, reverse *murābaḥah* and *murābaḥah* line-of-credit.

1. Revenue Sharing and Revenue Sharing Ṣukūk

The idea of revenue sharing is based on applying the *muzāraʿah* methodology to fund provision in *muḍārabah*. While *muḍārabah*

debt and the *moral hazard* risk crops up in any inter-personal relationship.

assigns a share of net profit to the fund provider (*rabb al-māl*), revenue sharing financing assigns a share of the gross revenue to the provider of assets that are used in the production process. Revenue sharing financing is thus a combination of *wakālah* to purchase or build fixed assets and a *muzāraʿah*-based partnership between assets' owner and assets' operator.

In a *ṣukūk*-type application, a trust (that represents the pool of investors) provides funds on *wakālah* basis to an SPV that constructs (through an *istisnāʿ* contract that may be concluded with the operator itself) the required airport, toll road or corporate factory and hands it over to the operator (the management) on revenue sharing. The construction is thus owned by the trust and investors receive a percentage of the total revenues of the airport. Revenue sharing may be applied to financing infrastructures as well as to corporate productive projects.

This arrangement allows investors to get a practically guaranteed positive (above zero) return because total revenues are always positive. Consequently, compared to *muḍārabah*, revenue sharing provides returns to investors even when the operator/management is losing. An element that reduces the worry about investors' return or to tp produce "new" *fatāwā* to guarantee returns that may be dubious from the Sharīʿah point of view such as issuing debt-based tradable *ṣukūk*.

On the other hand, revenue sharing arrangements do not provide protection against variations in the return of the investors; so it is still classified in the area of sharing finance like *muḍārabah* and *mushārakah*. Stability of projects and strength of their feasibility studies will be crucial for assuring smaller variations in return.

However, similar to *muḍārabah* and *mushārakah*, revenue sharing arrangements can be supplemented by either one of the following two structures or by both of them together: 1) a condition that imposes a cap on the net profit of the operator/management or on the return to investors whereby surpluses above the cap are either rendered to the other party or scaled at different percentages; and, 2) creating a fund, contributed to by deductions from investors' distributions and any concerned third party or by the surplus above the cap, for equalizing the investor's return over distribution periods as well as for principal guarantee.

2. Service and Usufruct-based Finance

In an economy of ever increasing inflation and rising cost of labor (improving level of living), service and usufruct-based financing and *ṣukūk* provide an excellent shelter against erosion of returns and/or principal. The reason is: payment of returns is in kind, i.e., in terms of either service units or units of usufructs. This is another Sharīʿah compatible hedge against inflation without resorting to dubious *fatāwā* vehicles that may involve a form or another of indirect interest.

3. Principal Insurance and Collaterals

The Sharīʿah rule on collateral taking is well known. It applies to debts. This means that any debt-creating finance or debt-representing *ṣukūk* may be supported by collaterals. Collaterals provide a tool to guarantee not only the debt of a principal, but also the debt of rentals as well as the in-kind debt of services and usufructs. Consequently, while services and usufruct financing hedge against inflation, they can also be supported by collaterals that guarantee, in fact, both principal and return. This is simply because financing of services and usufructs is based on the sale of *manāfiʿ* contract.

4. Third Party Guarantee: Deposit Guarantee

Third party guarantee can be offered by any entity/person that has interest in a financing contract without being a party to it. It may cover the principal as well as the return. For instance, a government, based on its own resources, may offer a third-party guarantee for a financier who provides funds, on *muḍārabah* or *mushārakah* basis, to certain strategic or infant industries so that a minimum return is guaranteed to investors in addition to guaranteeing their principals. The only requirement is that the guarantor must be financially and legally independent from the managing partner (*muḍārib*); this is because *muḍārabah* and *mushārakah* are *amānah*-hand contracts that can only be charged in case of neglect, abuse or violation of the contract conditions, but cannot be charged for commercial losses. Accordingly, we can always create an interested outsider-to-the-contract guarantor who can provide a third-party guarantee such as an SPV that is not owned by the managing partner.

The practice of third-party guarantee may also be applied to Islamic bank investment deposits when the government provides such a guarantee with no charge to the depository banks (being the *muḍārib*). This is done in the Sudan when the government created a deposit guarantee corporation nourished by contributions from *muḍārabah* depositors, the government and the central bank. Depository banks can also contribute to such a corporation for a special fund that covers operational risks.

However, the same principle is also invoked by deposit guarantee funds that are established by certain Islamic banks and nourished by deductions from the *arbāb al-māl*'s shares of profit before distribution. This practice started with the provisional act that established the Islamic Bank of Jordan; a few other Islamic banks do also practice it for the purpose of "smoothing out dividends distribution over the years." Similar funds can also be created for *ṣukūk* either for each issue alone or by creating an international *ṣukūk* guarantee corporation. Offered guarantee can be extended to cover the principal and a certain return as well.

5. Reverse Murābaḥah and Murābaḥah Line of Credit

The way of applying reversed *murābaḥah* is simple. Islamic finance providers for funding needs rely on their own resources and on deposits obtained either on loan basis or *muḍārabah* basis. More funds can be obtained on the basis of reversed *murābaḥah* in which the Islamic bank is the purchase orderer. Obviously, applying reverse *murābaḥah* to the purchases of the bank for its own use will limit financing through this methodology to a small amount. However, if we apply it to the purchases of the Islamic bank that are part of its own *murābaḥah* financing, it may extend to be a source of funding for a major part of its operation.

Reverse *murābaḥah* is a contract in which an Islamic bank is a finance user not a finance provider! Finance provider may be a central bank, another Islamic or a conventional bank or certain corporations/entities with large sums that need to be invested in an almost secured though modest return the same way *murābaḥah* gives the Islamic banks an almost secure and modest return.

The ground for Sharīʿah legitimacy of reverse *murābaḥah* is no different from that of *murābaḥah* itself. If, at the time of the second sale in *murābaḥah* the Islamic bank is permitted to make a markup gain that is known and predetermined for the period of the created debt, the Islamic bank can also be a purchaser is such a *murābaḥah*. The only condition that distinguishes such transactions from *tawarruq* is the realism or truthfulness property of the transaction. A reverse *murābaḥah* must maintain its truthfulness the same way truthfulness must be maintained in *murābaḥah* itself. It must be intended to transfer ownership of goods from the hand of a supplier to the hand of a user (that is the Islamic bank in reverse *murābaḥah*). Realistic conditions can be fulfilled if the transaction is genuine in the sense that it provides for the actual bank's purchases that it needs for its customer whereby the purchased goods and services actually change hands and end in the ownership of the bank and will then be genuinely sold to the Islamic bank's customers through *murābaḥah* or lease contracts. On the other hand, in *tawarruq* goods are purchased and sold only as a vehicle for financing as, unlike in reverse *murābaḥah*, they do not end up with a final user for actually using them for its own industry or consumption.

A simple way of creating genuine reverse *murābaḥah* is by adding a line of credit and a *wakālah* contract along with two accounts: one for a demand deposit and the other for a reverse *murābaḥah* deposit. In the case of certain *murābaḥah* financing where the Islamic bank wants to provide to its customers, it can transact a reverse *murābaḥah*, by virtue of the *wakālah*, for purchasing goods and services it provides to its clients and transfer funds from the current account of the finance provider to its reverse *murābaḥah* account, of course this will include the contacted markup.

Reverse *murābaḥah* arrangements can be used with the central bank, as a last resort fund provider to Islamic banks. It can also be used with large corporation deposits and as an alternative to inter-bank transactions-cum-financing. Some form of reverse *murābaḥah*, though without the name, has been used for decades by the Islamic Development Bank in financing national development financing institutions in Muslim countries by what it called "extending line of credit."

Finally, what needs to be noticed is that, like *murābaḥah*, reverse *murābaḥah* creates debts and cannot therefore be traded or discounted because of the prohibition of interest. In other words, no secondary market can be created for reverse *murābaḥah*; it is an arrangement that can be advanced prior to granting the *murābaḥah* to the bank customers.

6. Bundles/Packages of Financing: Applying the Majority Rule

The simple form of a bundle is common stocks. They represent a group of assets, tangible and intangible, including cash and receivables. Yet they can be traded at a market price that may be different from the face value if the majority of the assets they represent can have prices different than their face value. But if the majority of the group consists of assets subject to *ḥawālah* or *ṣarf*, then the rule that applies to the majority applies to the group. Consequently, the recognized ruling of the Sharīʿah is that common stocks may not be traded at a market price if the majority of the company's assets is in the form of receivables and cash.[1]

Creating bundles of goods, services, receivables and also cash and securitizing them is not restricted to common stocks; it can be done by Islamic banks and other financing and refinancing institutions. The IDB has been doing the same in transferring contracts to the Islamic Unit Investment Fund for two decades and it has been used as a means to discounting (securitizing) its investments at the IUIF.

Bundling lays the ground for a series of financial products that can respond to all personal financing needs and consequently has rendered baseless the argument for "a genuine need" for *tawarruq*. If there is a need for a certain form of "personal financing", it can be satisfied by means that do not allow themselves to be abused as what actually happens in the case of *tawarruq* that is often used to overcome the barriers placed by the prohibition of interest on rescheduling for increment and on abusing the financing for *ʿabath* or objectives that crisscross the moral screening of Islamic finance and can't be otherwise financed according to the Sharīʿah criteria.

7. Hedging Through Options (not trading options)

Lastly, hedging existing positions may be differentiated from trading options. While buying options for the purpose of price speculation may be argued as fictitious and profiteering without owning a real asset that may have an independent demand and supply for its own intrinsic utility/productivity, covering an existing position through buying or selling an option may be looked at as a means to reduce potential variations in prices and then tame price speculation. Accordingly, one-way hedging

[1] Although this is a theoretical case or at least very rare in real life as long as intangible assets are included because any difference between the book value and the market capitalization is attributable to these intangibles.

through options can be found useful and permissible, a matter that can also be used in Islamic financial innovation.

Conclusion

A word is needed for conclusion. This chapter is an attempt to determine and define the *maqāṣid* of the prohibition of *ribā* from the main texts of the Qur'an and in a contemporary context that takes into consideration a contemporary interpretation of the Islamic concept of returns/revenues generation. We noticed that although the condition of being asset based is a necessary condition for Islamic financing, it is not sufficient.

We need two more conditions to pass the criteria of Islamicity: the underlying asset must be of the kind that is liable to produce return, growth or increment and the transaction must be genuinely meant for what it is for or what defines it. Together, these three conditions channel financing contracts in the desired/designed direction meant by the prohibition of *ribā* and at the same time makes it, by the nature of described processes, subject to the moral/ethical screening that the Sharīʿah at large calls for and aims at.

We have within the limits of the *maqāṣid* of the prohibition of *ribā* a host of means that make risk management in innovative Islamic financial engineering a challenging arena that does not leave room to resort to dubious and counterproductive interest-mimicking approaches of financing that very often contradict the essence and basic objectives (*maqāṣid*) of the prohibition of interest as well as other regulations of Islamic financing.

CHAPTER ELEVEN

Dharā'iʿ and *Maqāṣid al-Sharīʿah*: A Study of Aspects of Islamic Insurance

Akhtarzaite Binti Abdulaziz

Introduction

Being a legal system based on God's final revelation to mankind, Islamic Law or the Sharīʿah encompasses all aspects of human needs and is suitable for application to all people under all circumstances till the Day of Judgment. In some important respects, the textual sources of the Sharīʿah (the Qur'an and Sunnah) provide only general rules and universal principles, thus allowing wide room for intellectual investigation and consideration of the needs and conditions of different locations and times in order to implement those rules and principles. Accordingly, *ijtihād* has been defined as the effort made by the jurists in the quest for knowledge of the Sharīʿah legal rulings through interpretation.

The classical jurists developed a specific methodology consisting of methods, rules and technical tools of interpretation and inference to deal with the textual sources of the Sharīʿah. Known as *uṣūl al-fiqh*, this methodology serves the purpose of systematic study and understanding of those sources as well as the proper derivation of legal rules (*aḥkām,* sing. *ḥukm*) enshrined therein. It also provides guidance on the proper application of such rules to their subject matter in the obtaining realities of life. One of those methods and tools is the theory of means or *dharāʾiʿ*. The jurists, however, disagreed on its reliability as a source of legal rulings.

This chapter attempts to examine the concept of *al-dharāʾiʿ* in its broad meaning, both at the preventive and proactive levels (*sadd* and *fatḥ al-dharāʾiʿ*). Though most of the jurists agreed that *al-dharāʾiʿ* included both meanings, their focus was mainly on *sadd al-dharāʾiʿ* or blocking those means which are lawful but lead to prohibited ends or unlawful results. However, the application of *al-dharāʾiʿ* at both levels plays a significant role as a practical mechanism for the realization of *maqāṣid al-sharīʿah,* due to the cause-effect relationship between means and objectives. Thus, the legality or the Sharīʿah value of an act could be determined based on its possible results in procuring benefits and/or preventing harms. While *maqāṣid,* especially those constituting the ultimate goals of the Sharīʿah known as *ḍarūriyyāt*, are eternal and unchangeable, a good deal of the means (*dharāʾiʿ* or *wasāʾil*) to attaining them are flexible and might differ from one situation to another, as they are based on the judgment of the possible results of actions to be evil or good in accordance with the prevailing circumstances. This is an important aspect of the flexibility and dynamism of Islamic law in addressing human individual and collective needs while pursuing the realization of the the higher objectives intended by the Lawgiver.

Islamic insurance has been considered as a new development in *fiqh al-muʿāmalāt.* The debate nowadays is, however, not on the question of legality of insurance as a concept and practice, but rather on how to provide an Islamic model of insurance that conforms to the criteria of the Sharīʿah and helps realize its objectives. Due to the unavailability of direct texts on this issue, some practical aspects of insurance depend largely upon the predominance of either beneficial or evil ends. This chapter will therefore look into some controversial issues prevailing in insurance practices and an attempt will be made to review the issues within the framework of realization of *maqāṣid al-sharīʿah* via the application of *dharā'iʿ* both at the preventive and proactive levels.

The Meaning and Types of *Dharīʿah*

The word *dharīʿah* (pl. *dharā'iʿ*) signifies the means or way of obtaining an end or attaining a goal. There are two positions in defining the technical meaning of *dharīʿah* as a source of derivation of legal rulings.

1. The Restrictive or narrow view on *dharīʿah:* This view is held by most classical jurists. They defined *dharīʿah* in a narrow sense to indicate those ways or means that are lawful but could lead to prohibited ends or unlawful results. For example, the great Mālikī jurist Muḥammad Ibn Rushd, grand father of Ibn Rushd the philosopher, defined *dharā'iʿ* as being "things which are apparently permissible but are used as a means to something prohibited."[1] According to Abū Isḥāq al-Shāṭibī, the rule of *dharā'iʿ* is "to use a benefit (*maṣlaḥah*) as an expedient to attain a harmful thing (*mafsadah*)."[2] Thus, in his view, the rule of *dharā'iʿ* means prohibiting a lawful act owing to the possibility of its leading to an unlawful result. It is important to mention here that not all lawful acts must be forbidden on the ground of the likelihood of harmfulness ensuing from them. In this connection, the jurists divided lawful acts into three categories:

A. Those that rarely lead to harmful results, like planting grapes that could rarely lead to wine making.

B. Those that usually lead to harmful results, like the sale of grapes to a winery and the sale of weapons to a known

---

[1] Abū al-Walīd Muḥammad Ibn Rushd, *al-Muqaddimāt al-Mumahhidāt* (Beirut: Dār Ṣādir, n. d.), vol. 2, p. 524.
[2] Abū Isḥāq Ibrāhīm ibn Mūsā al-Shāṭibī, *al-Muwāfaqāt fī Uṣūl al-Sharīʿah* (Beirut: Dār al-Maʿrifah, 1999), vol. 2, p. 556.

criminal.

C. Those in which there are equal probabilities of harm and benefit, such as marrying a woman with the intention to divorce her in order to enable her to remarry her former husband.

The first type does not fall within the purview of the rule of *dharāʾiʿ*, and an act that rarely leads to harmful results would not be prohibited. The jurists disagreed regarding the remaining two categories. According to the Mālikīs and Ḥanbalīs, they may be prohibited because they could lead to harmful results. In contrast, al-Shāfiʿī rejected this view, saying that what is permissible could not be prohibited on the ground of the likelihood that it might lead to a harmful result.

2. The second view, a boader and more liberal one, is to define *dharāʾiʿ* in a wider and broader sense, covering all means whether they lead to harmful or beneficial results. This means to prevent all means leading to harmful consequences (and is known as *sadd al-dharāʾiʿ*) or to open and encourage all possible means to beneficial ends (which is known as *fatḥ al-dharāʾiʿ*). Some classical jurists and the majority of contemporary scholars take this position. It should be noted here that the classical jurists agreed that beneficial acts must be encouraged, yet they did not lay sufficient emphasis on this aspect in their discussion on this issue. Rather, they mainly focused on *sadd al-dharāʾiʿ* or blocking the means. As the prevention of evil assumed more prominence in their discussions, the other part of the rule or doctrine of *dharāʾiʿ*, or the opening of the means to beneficence (*fatḥ al-dharāʾiʿ*), did not receive equal treatment from the jurists in their writings.

However, jurists like al-Qarāfī viewed *dharāʾiʿ* in its broad meaning mentioned earlier. Thus, he defined *dharāʾiʿ* "as being all means leading to specific ends." To this definition he added: "It should be noted that just as *dharāʾiʿ* must be blocked (when they lead to unlawful results), they also need to be opened, as they might be required (*wājib*), repugnant (*makrūh*), recommended (*mandūb*), or permissible (*mubāḥ*). Likewise, *dharīʿah* simply denotes the means; hence, just the means to what is prohibited must be prohibited, so too the means to what is obligatory must also be obligatory." [1] This broad and comprehensive definition of *dharā'iʿ* including the two aspects of both *sadd* and *fatḥ* has been upheld by most contemporary jurists, such as Muhammad Abu Zahrah, Wahbah al-Zuhayli, Abdullah al- Judayʿ, etc.[2]

Dharā'iʿ and *Maqāṣid*: The Cause-Effect Relationship

The idea or doctrine of *maqāṣid al-sharīʿah* has gradually captured the attention of an increasing number of contemporary Muslim scholars who consider it as a springboard for solving contemporary issues. This idea provides a guide and framework for the process of *ijtihād* in its endeavor to solve emerging issues creatively while complying with the will of the Lawgiver. Thus, *maqāṣid al-sharīʿah* as an independent discipline can be as a philosophy of law or a value system governing the Sharīʿah legal rules and reflecting the Islamic worldview in all its dimensions. Ibn Ashur defined *maqāṣid al-sharīʿah* as "the deeper meanings (*maʿānī*) and inner aspects of wisdom (*ḥikam*) considered by the Lawgiver (*Shāriʿ*) in all or most areas and circumstances of legislation (*aḥwāl al-tashrīʿ*).[3] He also explained the importance of the knowledge of *maqāṣid al-sharīʿah* for the *mujtahids* not only in understanding and interpreting the texts of the Sharīʿah but also to find solutions to the new problems facing Muslims on which

---

[1] Shihāb al-Dīn Aḥmad ibn Idrīs al-Qarāfī, *Sharḥ Tanqīḥ al-Fuṣūl* (Cairo: Maktabat al-Kulliyyāt al-Azhariyyah, 1993), p. 448.

[2] See for example, Muhammad Abū Zahrah, *Uṣūl al-fiqh*. Cairo: Dār al-Fikr al-Arabī, n. d.), p. 228; Wahbah al-Zuḥaylī, *Uṣūl al-Fiqh al-Islāmī* (Damascus: Dār al-Fikr, 1st edn, 1402/1986), Vol. 2, p. 879-895; Abdullah Yusuf al-Judayʿ, *Taysīr 'Ilm Uṣūl al-Fiqh* (Beirut: Mu'assasah al-Rayyān, 2000), pp. 203-208.

[3] Muhammad al-Tahir Ibn Ashur, *Treatise on Maqāṣid al-Sharīʿah*, trans. Mohamed El-Tahir El-Mesawi (London-Kuala Lumpur: The International Institute of Islamic Thought, al-Maqāṣid Research Centre and Islamic Book Trust, 2006), p. 67.

those texts are silent.[1]

Basically, the main objective of the Sharīʿah is to regulate human life and to protect the interests and benefits (*maṣlaḥah*) of people. *Maṣlaḥah* in the Islamic context and perspective means what is good and beneficial in the sight of the Sharīʿah. According to al-Ghazālī, the higher objectives of Islamic law consist of two types:

1. Religious or spiritual (*dīnī*) objective pertaining to the Hereafter: This purpose, which revolves around the preservation and promotion of religious faith (*ḥifẓ al-dīn*), is the utmost and ultimate purpose of the Sharīʿah. In its aggressive or positive aspect, the interest of religion is secured by facilitating ritual worship of God and establishing the pillars of Islam such as fasting, prayers, pilgrimage, and paying *zakāh*. In its defensive aspect, *jihād* is stated as a means to defending *dīn*, as it prevents the established pillars of Islam from being undermined or destroyed.
2. Worldly objectives (*dunyawī*) pertaining to mundane affairs of this world: This type includes all worldly interests and encompasses four major objectives. In accordance with their importance and order of priority, these objectives consist of the preservation and promotion of human life (*ḥifẓ nafs*), intellect (*ḥifẓ al-ʿaql*), progeny and offspring (*ḥifẓ al-nasl*), and property (*ḥifẓ al-māl*). According to al-Ghazālī, these five constitute the fundamental and ultimate principles of all kinds of of what it is good, *maṣlaḥah*.[2]

Upon close examination of the Sharīʿah rulings, one can safely conclude that they individually and collectively point out to the realization and protection of all these interests. As an example of the protection of human life, Islam has instituted a

---

[1] *Ibid.*, pp. 5-10.

[2] Abū Ḥāmid Muhammad ibn Muhammad al-Ghazālī, *al-Mustasfā min ʿIlm al-Uṣūl*, ed. Muhammad Sulayman al-Ashqar (Beirut: Muassassat al-Risālah, 1st edn, 1417/1997), vol. 1, p. 417.

severe punishment for murder by imposing the death penalty. As for the protection of progeny, it is realized through the institution of marriage and healthy family life. Islam encourages its followers to get married and have a family as a means to ensuring a balanced upbringing and a good life for the offspring, and to preventing human beings from committing such evil acts like adultery, fornication and cohabitation.

Human interests in all spheres of life can be classified into three levels according to their importance and impact on people's lives and existence, each one having its proper function in human life. These levels are strongly related to one another. The first and basic level of human interests consists of the *ḍarūriyyāt* or necessities.[1] All the five objectives comprising the preservation and promotion of the universals of *dīn, nafs, ʿaql, nasl* and *māl* belong to this fundamental level. They constitute indispensable interests on which the life of human beings essentially depends. If these are violated or undermined, the whole of human life would be subjected to corruption, disorder, injustice and, ultimately, destruction.

The second level of interests, which comes next to the *ḍarūriyyāt*, consists of the *ḥājiyyāt*.[2] These interests include what is needed to alleviate hardship and to bring ease and comfort in human life. Without them, people will suffer distress and difficulty in their observance of the Sharīʿah rules, though this is far less than the harm resulting from the disorder and corruption affecting the universals. This level includes all aspects of human affairs and applies to all spheres of legislation, whether in ritual worship, customary and daily life practices, contractual dealings or sanctioning and penalties. In other words, the the *ḥājiyyāt* serve to support and strengthen the necessities. Life can still exist without this level of interest but human beings will face difficulties and hardships in life. The

---

[1] al-Shāṭibī, *al-Muwāfaqāt*, vol. 2, p. 324.
[2] *Ibid.*, p. 326.

provision to break the fast during the month of Ramaḍān in the case of illness or a long difficult journey reflects this clearly.

The third level of interests is known as *taḥsīniyyāt* or complementarities. This level includes everything that promotes human well-being and makes people's life more comfortable.[1] The *taḥsīniyyāt* are not indispensably needed so that without them human life becomes deficient or the rules of the Sharīʿah inoperative. Their role is rather to improve and facilitate the quality of life and make the observance of the law easier and more comfortable. Ignoring this category is not detrimental to the *ḍarūriyyāt* or *ḥājiyyāt*, although it relates to the same areas of Islamic legislation. Al-Shāṭibī defined this level as adopting what conforms to the best of customs and, thus, avoiding those manners that are repulsive (unacceptable) to wise and refined people.

All these three levels are inter-related. The first level comprises the core and vital interests or ultimate objectives whose realization and preservation constitute the main purpose of the Sharīʿah. The other two levels are subordinate to the first, and serve the consolidation and advancement thereof.

As can be seen from the foregoing brief exposition, the theory of *maqāṣid* presents us with a comprehensive picture of the threefold order of the objectives of the Sharīʿah and a general philosophy governing its rules and provisions. It thus provides a systematic view of the human social order as envisioned by Islam, the scale of values determining the priorities and preferences of Islamic law and the criteria for policy-making in society.

Accordingly, the notion of *dharāʾiʿ* in its broad sense as explained above is closely related to the theory of *maqāṣid al-sharīʿah*, by virtue of the cause-effect relationship between means and objectives. Hence, the Lawgiver legalized certain acts or prohibited others on the basis of the benefit or harm they

---

[1] *Ibid.*, p. 327.

could lead to. Any act or type of conduct that is likely to result in something contrary to the objectives of the Sharī'ah must, therefore, be prevented, even though it might, in itself, be lawful in the first place. Similarly, any means that could possibly lead to beneficence must be legalized and encouraged in order to realize the *maqāṣid* or objectives of the Sharī'ah, no matter how inexplicitly mentioned in the texts.

Thus, allowing a clear measure of flexibility in Islamic Law, the rule or theory of *dharā'i'* also conforms to the spirit of the Sharī'ah and serves the purpose of realising its objectives. While the *maqāṣid* or objectives are eternal and unchangeable, the rule of *dharā'i'* is flexible and its implementation might take different forms from one situation to another, as it is based on the judgment of the possible results of actions leading to either evil or good. Likewise, *sadd al-dharā'i'* plays its role as a defensive or preventive tool in order to safeguard the *maqāṣid* by actively blocking whatever means that could hinder the realization of legal purposes. On the other hand, *fatḥ al-dharā'i'* is also important to proactively enhance the achievement of the lawful goals of the Sharī'ah by positively legislating all possible and lawful means in accordance with the prevailing circumstances.

In the the next section we will examine the application of the theory of *dharā'i'* in certain aspects of Islamic insurance. It is important, therefore, to give a general description of *maqāṣid al-sharī'ah* pertaining to wealth acquisition and property management. This is because the application of *dharā'i'* in this field will totally depend on the consideration of the higher objectives of the law in this regard. A set of goals and objectives must be clearly defined before it is possible to explore the means or ways to achieve those goals.

Maqāṣid al-Sharī'ah in Wealth Acquisition and Management

Wealth is part of God's bounties and blessings to His servants. Islam lays great emphasis on the importance of wealth management and protection to ensure that property is acquired and spent properly as allowed by the Sharīʿah. Among many others, the following Qur'anic verse provides proof of the positive attitude of Islam towards wealth: "And do not entrust to those who are weak of judement the possessions (*amwāl*) which God has made a means of support for you" (Q., 4: 5). This verse shows how Islam acknowledges material wealth as a vital factor in human life. While commenting on this verse, the great exegete Fakhr al-Dīn al-Rāzī stated that it means "your life and sustenance will not be established without such properties."[1]

As can be seen from the above, from their comprehensive analysis of the Sharīʿah legal rules based on thematic inference (*istiqrāʾ*), the jurists inferred and established five fundamental and vital needs of human life whose protection is given utmost priority by the Sharīʿah through its different rules and forms of legislation. As already pointed out, those needs revolve around religion, life, intellect, lineage and property. Thus, the protection of wealth or property is part of the ultimate goals of the Sharīʿah. Ibn Ashur explained in some detail the Sharīʿah objectives regarding wealth and property. He identified five criteria that the Sharīʿah observes in this respect.

These criteria constitute the goals of the Sharīʿah that have to be attained in wealth acquisition and management. They consist of *rawāj* (wide circulation of properties), *wuḍūḥ* (transparency), *ḥifẓ* (protection), *thabāt* (certainty) and *ʿadl* (justice). Since the third goal (protection) may not be considered to be something specific as it actually reproduces the general purpose governing the five fundamental universals (*al-kulliyyāt al- ḍarūriyyah*), only the other four goals, as explained by Ibn Ashur, will be discussed in the next section. However, it is important to add another aspect to the

[1] Fakhr al-Dīn al-Rāzī, *al-Tafsīr al-Kabīr* (Beirut: Dār al-Kutub al-ʿIlmiyyah, 1990), Vol. 5/9, p. 151.

protection and management of wealth and property, namely, the purpose of *takassub* and *istithmār* (acquisition and investment).[1]

1. Rawāj (Wide Circulation of Wealth)

This goal means that wealth and property should be circulated among the general public and actively transferred from one hand to another in the form of expenditures and investments.[2] For this, the Sharī'ah approves many forms of financial and economic transactions such as contracts of sale, lease, partnerships and many more in order to facilitate the proper circulation of wealth and smooth transfer of property ownership among the public. Thus, it is not allowed in the Sharī'ah to purposely keep wealth in all its forms idle. The Qur'an (9: 34-35) says: "But as for all who lay up treasures of gold and silver and do not spend them for the sake of God— give them the tiding of grieveous suffering [in the life to come]: on the Day when that [horded wealth] shall be healed in the fire of hell and their foreheads and their sides and their backs branded therewith." Following the mention of the parties eligible to be given shares of the spoils of war *(fay'* and *ghanīmah*), the Qur'an states in another verse (59: 7) that the reason for the distribution is to prevent monopoly of wealth by the rich and deprivation of the general public to benefit from it, thus it says: "so that it may not be [a benefit] going round and round among such of you as may may [already] be rich."

2. Wuḍūḥ (Transparency)

Wuḍūḥ or transparency means that all financial transactions must be conducted in such a manner that all parties are clear about all important facts of the transactions, thus, avoiding all causes of

---

[1] Ibn Ashur, *Treatise,* pp. 279-293.

[2] Yūsuf Ḥāmid al-'Ālim, *al-Maqāṣid al-'Āmmah li Al-Sharī'ah al-Islāmiyyah* (Herndon, Virginia: International Institute of Islamic Thought, 1412/1991), p. 497.

dispute, clash or damage to any party.[1] It is for this reason that the Qur'an (2: 282) recommends Muslims to keep all future transactions in record; it says: "O you who have attained to faith! Whenver you give or take credit for a stated term, set it down in writing. And let a scribe write it down equitably between you; and no scribe shall refuse to write as God has taught him: thus shall he write." The purpose of writing down a debt transaction is to make all information regarding the transaction clear and transparent in terms of subject matter, obligations and rights of all parties, so that this will serve as a reference in cases of dispute. This is particularly relevant to contemporary financial transactions that are always in the form of formal contracts duly signed by the parties concerned.

3. Thabāt (Certainty)

This purpose means that the rights of a party or parties to the ownership of property must be certain and there should be no doubt to those rights, unless there is certain public interest which could prevent individual privilege.[2] This implies three elements: i) the right of individuals to ownership, ii) freedom of disposal of property within the boundaries of the Sharīʿah requirements, and iii) guarantee of the privilege of ownership and prevention of encroachment on a person's rights without the owner's consent.[3]

The Qur'an has explicitly sanctioned the right of ownership in which respect it says (4: 29): "O you who have attained to faith! Do not devour one another's possession wrongfully—not even by way of trade based on mutual agreement—and do not destroy one another: for, behold, God is indeed a dispenser of grace unto you." This provides clear evidence that it is an objective of the Sharīʿah to guarantee the

---

[1] *Ibid.,* p. 525.

[2] Ismail al-Ḥasanī, *Naẓariyyat al-Maqāṣid ʿinda al-Imām Muḥammad al-Ṭāhir Ibn ʿĀshūr* (Herndon, Virginia: International Institute of Islamic Though, 1995), p. 117.

[3] Ibn Ashur, *Treatise,* pp. 291-292.

freedom of ownership and there is no way that the right can be transferred to others unless by contract of exchange or charity by the consent of the owner.

4. *'Adl (Justice)*

Justice is both a general principle of the Sharī'ah and one of its higher objectives. Thus, we read in the Qur'an (16: 90): "God commands justice and good deeds and liberality to the relatives and He forbids all shameful deeds, injustice and rebellion." Being one of the Sharī'ah goals in financial transactions and dealings, justice means to put wealth and property in its proper places, as commanded by the Creator. This includes the right to acquire wealth, to discharge all the duties related to wealth and to find the wisest way to spend or to invest it.[1]

5. Takassub and Istithmār (Earning and Investment)

Takassub means to exert oneself to earn what would help to satisfy one's needs, whether by physical labor or mutual consent with others,[2] whereas *istithmār* means the efforts made to increase the value of the properties through lawful means sanctioned by the Sharī'ah.[3] Thus, *takassub* means to acquire wealth and property, while *istithmār* means to add value to the existing wealth and property. These two aspects are strongly related to the purpose of wealth and property management. To achieve them, the Sharī'ah has approved numerous types of contracts and transactions. Likewise, the Qur'an recommends Muslims by saying (62: 10): "And when the prayer is ended, disperse freely on earth and seek to obtain [something] of God's bounty; but do remember God often, so that you might attain to a happy state!" This verse implies the obligation on all Muslims to earn a living. In a ḥadīth

---

[1] Al-'Ālim, *al-Maqāṣid al-'Ammah*, p. 527.
[2] Ibn Ashur, *Treatise,* p.276.
[3] Kotb Mustafa Sano, *al-Istithmār: Aḥkāmuhu wa Ḍawābiṭuhu fī al-Fiqh al-Islāmī* (Amman: Dār al-Nafaes, 2000), p. 20.

narrated by the companion Jābir b. Abdāllh, the Prophet (*pbuh*) pointed out people's duty to make efforts in order to enhance and increase the value of wealth and property; "Whoever possesses a piece of land must cultivate it or give it to one's brother another Muslim; if he refuses, he should simply let his land lie fallow."[1]

The five things explained above constitute the main objectives that should govern all financial transactions and economic dealings. It should be emphasised here that the application of the concept of *dharā'iʿ* in its broad meaning (both as *sadd al-dharā'iʿ* and *fatḥ al-dharā'iʿ*) aims at preventing all means which run against these five objectives and other established rules of the Sharīʿah, like *ribā* (usury or interest) and *gharar* (risk or uncertainty). Similarly, it aims at encouraging and opening all means that could enhance the realisation of these five objectives as far as they are lawful.

The next section deals with Islamic insurance or *takāful* and an attempt will be made to apply the concept of *dharā'iʿ* in its broad sense to some practical aspects of insurance.

Insurance in Islam: The *Takāful* Model

Insurance is one of the contemporary and recent developments in financial and economic activities. Therefore, the classical jurists did not discuss it. However, the philosophy behind the insurance industry is not totally absent from the basic Islamic teachings nor is it alien to the philosophy underlying them. Generally, insurance policy is a contract of mutual financing in which one party is expected to be protected materially against an unexpected loss or by the other party, in consideration of the payment of a particular amount of premium.[2]

---

[1] Abū 'Abd Allāh Muḥammad b. Ismāʿīl al-Bukhārī, *Ṣaḥīḥ al-Bukhārī* (Damscus/Beirut: Dār Ibn Kathīr, 1st edn, 1423/2002), "Kitāb al-Ḥarth wa al-Muzāraʿah', Nos. 2340-2341, p. 563.

[2] Mohd Masum Billah, *Islamic and ModernIinsurance: Principles and Practices* (Kuala

Insurance is, therefore, a contract of exchange between two parties whereby the insured buys protection from the insurer at a price (premium) against a prescribed risk. Contemporary Muslim jurists have examined the above model of insurance in a series of discussions held since 1976. Most of them are of the opinion that conventional insurance is not allowed in Islam mainly because of the elements of *ribā* and *gharar* it involves. Below are some conferences held to discuss this issue and the resolutions they reached.

i. The First Conference on Islamic Economy, Makkah, 1976: Conventional insurance as practiced today does not comply with the spirit of the Sharī'ah and does not fulfill the requirements which might render it permissible.

ii. 10th Conference of Prominent Muslim Scholars, Saudi Arabia, 1977: Confirmed by consensus of opinion that conventional insurance in all its types is not permissible, whether it is life insurance or general insurance (on property).

iii. The International Islamic Fiqh Academy, Jeddah ascertained in 1985 that conventional insurance is prohibited due to the uncertainties (*gharar*). Its committee suggested as an alternative an insurance system based on cooperation and *hibah* (*takāful*).[1]

Thus, the alternative for conventional insurance is a model of mutual insurance known as *takāful.*[2] Contrary to conventional insurance, a *takāful* or mutual insurance policy is not a contract

---

Lumpur: Ilmiah Publishers, 2003), p. 25.

[1] Nik Ramlah Mahmood, "Takaful: The Islamic System of Mutual Insurance—The Malaysian Experience," *Arab Law Quarterly,* vol. 6, No. 3 (1991), pp. 281-286; see also Masum Billah, *op. cit.*

[2] Malaysia *Takaful Act*, 1984, Section 2 defined *Takaful* as "A scheme based on brotherhood, solidarity and mutual assistance which provides for mutual financial aids and assistance to the participants in case of need, whereby the participants mutually agree to contribute for that purpose." (*Laws of Malaysia*, Act 312).

of exchange. Rather, it is a contract of mutual *hibah* or gratuity. In Islamic law, the elements of *ribā* and *gharar* are prohibited in exchange contracts (*ʿuqūd muʿāwaḍah*) and not operative in a contract of gratuity or *hibah*. In *takāful*, the policyholders are both the insurer and the insured, as they collectively and mutually guarantee each other against the stipulated risks. The relationship between the parties can be described as follows:

The relationship among the policyholders: All the policyholders are bound by the contract of partnership and hibah. They jointly own the funds in accordance with their contributions and undertake to mutually protect each other on the basis of hibah.

The *Takāful* Operator and the Policyholders: The relationship can be viewed from two sides. First, in its role as manager of the hibah funds and insurance claims, the company acts as an agent on behalf of the participants. Second, in its role as manager of the investment of the total funds accumulated, the *takāful* operator may play the role of *muḍrib* or entrepreneur in a *muḍārabah* contract or an agent with a fee. Thus, two models of *takāful* come into being: *muḍārabah*-based *takāful* as practiced by Syarikat Takaful Malaysia Berhad in Malaysia and *takāful* based on *wakālah* or agency as in *Takāful Taʿāwunī*, practiced by Bank al-Jazeerah in Saudi Arabia.

Syarikat Takaful Malaysia Berhad: A Muḍārabah Model

Syarikat Takaful Malaysia Berhad (STMB) is the first *takāful* operator in Malaysia to be incorporated on 20th November 1984. Being the operator, STMB accepts payment of *takāful* contributions (premiums) known as the *ra's al-māl* or the capital from the participants who are considered as *rabb al-māl* or the capital provider in a *muḍāarabah* contract. The ratio of profit-sharing among the parties shall be determined upfront in the contract.[1] STMB offers two types of *takāful* schemes: The first is family *takāful* or Islamic Life Insurance. The second is general *takāful* or the insurance on properties in relation to material loss or damage inflicted upon the property consequent upon a catastrophe or a disaster. [2] Under the Family *Takāful*, the installments of *takāful* contributions paid by the participants are divided and channeled by the company into two separate accounts:

1. The Participants' Account constituting most of the contributions.
2. The Participants' Special Account constituting the *tabarruʿ* proportion. It is from this account that the company shall pay the *takāful* benefits to the heirs of the participants who die before the maturity of the scheme[3]

Applying *Dharā'iʿ* to *Takāful*

This section attempts to apply the principle of *dharā'iʿ* to some selected practical aspects of *takaful* and to show its role in the realization of *maqāṣid al-sharīʿah* in some practical aspects of *takāful* as discussed above. The discussion will include both *sadd al-dharā'iʿ* and *fatḥ al-dharā'iʿ*.

i. Takāful as a Means to Preventing Ribā in Insurance Practices

The structure of *takāful* based on mutual help and solidarity eliminates the *ribā* element in insurance. As is clear from the above, *takāful* is actually a hybrid of contracts of partnership and *hibah*. The amount granted to a participant who encounters the

---

[1] BIMB Institute of Research and Training (BIMBIRT), *Takaful (Islamic Insurance), Concept and Operational System from Practitioners' Perspective* (Kuala Lumpur: BIMB Institute of Research and Training, 1996), p. 9.

[2] *Ibid.*., p. 69.

[3] Syed Waseem Ahmad, "Islamic Insurance in Malaysia," in Mohamed Ariff (ed.), *The Muslim Private Sector in Southeast Asia: Islam and the Economic Development of Southeast Asia* (Singapore: Institute of Southeast Asian Studies, 1991), p. 193.

risk insured is a donation agreed upon upfront by all participants collectively. Thus, it is not a consideration for the premium paid. Consequently, there is no requirement of hand-to-hand and equal value exchange as required fin the case of money for money exchange. Conventional insurance is *ribā*-based, as it is a contract of exchange of money in the future subject to the occurrence of the risks and at different value.

ii. Takāful as a Means to Prevent Gharar-Transactions in Insurance

Gharar or risk and uncertainty is prohibited in Islamic financial transactions. The existence of *gharar* may render a transaction invalid for lack of information. Al-Qarāfī stated that there are seven aspects of *gharar* that can possibly affect transactions. They pertain to the existence of the subject matter of a contract and its acquisition, to its genus and type, to its amount and to its identification.[1]

Gharar in the conventional insurance practice may occur in at least three of the seven categories listed by al-Qarāfī. First is *gharar* in existence, where the existence of the obligation of the insurance company to pay for the claim is not certain as it depends on the occurrence of the specified risk. Second is *gharar* in acquisition, where the policyholder is not certain at the time of the contract whether he/she will acquire the consideration for which he/she is paying the premium as the consideration again depends upon the occurrence of the insured risks. Third, *gharar* in amount is where both the insurance company and the policyholders are not certain about the amount of the premium that must be paid by the policyholders.

Takāful or mutual insurance can eliminate the element of *gharar* in insurance for two reasons: First, it is a gratuity contract (*ʿaqd tabarruʿ*) and not an exchange (sale) contract in the opinion

---

[1] Shihāb al-Dīn Aḥmad ibn Idrīs al-Qarāfī, *al-Furūq,* ed. Ali Gomaa Muhammad et al. (Cairo: Dār al-Salām, 2001), Vol. 3, p. 1051.

of the Mālikī jurists.[1] However, according to Shāfi'ī jurists, there is no difference between the two types of contract in the sense that both of them can be invalidated due to *gharar*. Second, even according to Shāfi'ī jurists, *gharar* can also exist in a *tabarru'* contract. In the case of *takāful*, the element of *gharar* can be eliminated. *Gharar* in existence, acquisition and amount are not present in *takāful*, as the participants are certain that they will acquire the *takāful* benefits in proportion to their contribution plus the surplus from *hibah* fund, if any.

Under the Family *Takāful* scheme, it is agreed by the parties that the *takāful* benefits shall be paid to the participants or their heirs in the following manner:

1. If the participant dies before the maturity of the plan, the heirs will be granted:

    A. The total amount of *takāful* instalments paid by the deceased from the date of his/her first instalment up to his/her death.

    B. His/her share of the profits from the investment of his paid contributions credited to his/her Participant's Account (PA) according to the *muḍārabah* ratio.

    C. The outstanding *takāful* amount which would have been paid by the deceased had he/she survived, calculated from his/her death up to the maturity date. This amount shall be recovered from the Participants' Special Account fund or the *Tabarru'* fund.[2]

2. If the participant survives the maturity date, he/she will be given:

    A. The total amount of *takāful* instalment paid by the participant during the tenure of his plan.

    B. The share of the profits from the investment credited

[1] *Ibid.,* Vol. 3, p .284.
[2] Ahmad, "Islamic Insurance in Malaysia," p. 194.

into his/her PA.

C. The net surplus allocated to the participant.

iii. Takāful as Means to the Realization of Sharīʿah Objectives Pertaining to Wealth and Property

As for *fatḥ al-dharāʾiʿ*, *takāful* or insurance based on cooperation and mutual help can undeniably provide an effective means towards the realization of *maqāṣid al-sharīʿah* in financial transactions and wealth and property management. With a well-defined structure and plan, all the five objectives of *rawāj* (wide circulation of property), *wuḍūḥ* (transparency), *thabāt* (certainty), *ʿadl* (justice) and *takassub* and *istithmār* (acquisition and investment) can be achieved.

As shown earlier, the threefold structure of the family *takāful* can be considered an effective means to realize the objectives of *rawāj* and *takassub/istithmār*, by saving regularly (via paying specified instalments), investing these savings with a view to earning profit in Sharīʿah-compliant economic and financial activities, and availing the cover of the payment of *takāful* benefits to the heirs and dependants in the case of death before the maturity.[1] In the event a participant wants to surrender the policy or discontinue the plan, he/she shall be entitled to the surrender benefit. This benefit consists of the proportion of his/her *takāful* installments paid and credited to his/her PA plus the profit from such installments. There is no forfeiture in the family *takāful* plan, as in conventional insurance. However, he shall not be entitled to be refunded from the PSA fund.

After the *ʿaqd* or contract has been made by the "proposer" (intended participant) and the *takāful* company, all the important clauses of the contract are recorded in the *takāful* certificate.[2] Before the issuance of the certificate, the *takāful* operator will

---

[1] *Ibid.*, p. 192.
[2] BIMBIRT, *Takaful*, p. 53.

issue a cover note, especially in the case of General *Takāful.* A cover note is a temporary document for the participant to be used as proof to make a fair claim against the risk if it occurs before the permanent *takāful* certificate is issued.[1] All the above arrangements and stipulations are means to realize the purpose of transparency, certainty and justice.

iv. Takāful and the Concept of Uberrimae Fidei

The concept of *uberrimae fidei* or agreement of utmost good faith in insurance means that the parties to the policy or *takāful* plan must disclose the truth of the facts or the matters affecting the policy.[2] Under the law, it is assumed that insurance contracts are entered into by all parties in good faith, meaning that they have disclosed all relevant facts and intend to carry out their obligations. Where lack of good faith can be proved, such as fraudulent application to obtain insurance, the contract may be nullified.[3]

Under section 28 of the 1984 *Takaful Act*, it is the participants' duty to disclose in the proposal form fully and faithfully all the facts which they know or ought to know, otherwise the *Takāful* Certificate issued may be void.[4] As indemnity provided in *takāful* contract is based on the mutual responsibility of all participants, it is inherently a duty of each of them to disclose all material facts affecting the contract in order to achieve the objectives of transparency and justice. Failure to disclose might render the possibility of benefiting from the *tabarru'* funds fraudulently at the expense of other participants.

---

[1] Masum Billah, *Islamic and Modern Insurance*, p. 249.

[2] *Ibid.*, p. 200.

[3] Harvey W. Rubin, *Dictionary of Insurance Terms* (New York: Barron Educational Series, 4th edn, 2000), p. 533.

[4] BIMBIRT, *Takaful*, p. 74.

v. Takāful Underwriting

Insurance underwriting is the process by which *takāful* operators consider and decide whether to accept participation of cover made by a "proposer" and the terms to be imposed. It is the process of examining, accepting or rejecting insurance risks and classifying those selected in order to charge the proper premium for each. Generally, the purpose of underwriting is to distribute the risk among a pool of insureds in a manner that is equitable for the insureds and profitable for the insurer.[1] The concept of underwriting is no less important in *takāful*, due to the solidarity and mutual assistance spirit inherent in *takāful* itself. Thus, the purpose of underwriting for Family *Takāful* is to maintain equity among the participants. In this case, each participant contributes to a common fund (*tabarruʿ* fund) from which *takāful* benefits will be paid to any participant suffering from the risks defined. Therefore, each participant should contribute according to the expected loss probabilities that he/she might transfer to the fund. The *takāful* company should estimate the expected loss exposure presented to it by the participant and charge a rate or percentage to be attributed to the *tabarruʿ* fund which is commensurate with that exposure.[2]

In the case of STMB in its family *takāful* scheme, the *tabarruʿ* proportion is worked out by the actuaries taking mortality by age into account using the method and techniques of determination as in the conventional insurance. The *tabarruʿ* proportion varies from two percent to nine percent of the installments to be credited into PSA.[3] Though it originates from conventional insurance practice to ensure the insurance company's adequacy to compensate for the loss occurred, the

---

[1] Rubin, *Dictionary*, p. 536.
[2] Ahmad, "Islamic Insurance in Malaysia," p. 193.
[3] *Ibid.*, p. 194.

process of underwriting can also be applied in the *takāful* industry. *Takāful*, being a mutual insurance and mutual help in protection against loss, requires a reliable step in determining the fund's adequacy and capability in providing protection against loss for all members. This in return is an effective means towards attaining the goals of transparency and justice, as the underwriting process provides transparency in determining the *tabarru'* portion and ensures that any participant will not take from the fund more than what he deserves at the expense of other participants.

vi. Takāful and Insurable Interest

Insurable interest means the financial interest a person has in the subject matter of the cover. For its validity, insurance requires that the insured shall be so related to the subject matter of the insurance that he/she will benefit from its survival or will suffer from loss or damage to it or may incur liability in respect of it.[1] The participant must stand in a relationship with the subject matter of the *takāful* whereby he benefits from its safety and well-being or freedom from liability and would be prejudiced by its damage or the existence of liability.[2] A policy without an insurable interest is like a gambling contract that is clearly prohibited in Islam, by which a participant hopes for a chance to gain instead of providing a mutual cooperation for security against a risk.[3]

However, under the 1984 *Takaful Act*, there was no expressed condition for insurable interest for a *takāful* plan. In the case of Family *Takāful*, whereby the insurable interest is the life itself, the question of requirement for insurable interest might not arise, as the participant in this case seeks to protect his/her and hi/hers family's interest. In *takāful*, the insured are

---

[1] BIMBIRT, *Takaful*, p.64.
[2] *Ibid.*
[3] Masum Billah, *Islamic and Modern Insurance*, p. 156.

themselves the insurers, and thus the element of gambling or the intentional self-inflicted harm will not obtain for lack of insurable interest.[1] Above all, the insurance benefit in a *takāful* policy shall be distributed on the basis of the Islamic law of inheritance, as it is considered as part of the participant's bequests.[2] The nominees in the policy are considered as mere trustees to administer the distribution of the *takāful* benefit after the participant's death.

The stipulation to administer the insurance benefit in accordance with the Islamic law of inheritance and will is no doubt on par with the goal of *thabāt* or certainty. It protects the deserving parties' rights to inheritance as prescribed by the Qur'an and Sunnah.

Conclusion

The concept of *dharā'iʿ* should be understood in a broad meaning. In the classical juristic literature dealing with the concept of *dharā'iʿ*, the jurists' emphasis was more on blocking the means to evil things than on opening the means to beneficence. Apart from that, opening the means to good can also operate through the general principle of *al-ibāḥah al-aṣliyyah* established in Islamic law, meaning that all material things and dealings are originally permissible. However, the application of *fatḥ al-dharā'iʿ* provides a more flexible and effective means to achieve the Sharīʿah goals by looking into the end result or consequences of an act or rule.

Insurance as a new development in the Islamic financial system and wealth management is an example of issues that require the application of the concept of *dharā'iʿ* in a broad sense with the ultimate view of achieving the five objectives of the Sharīʿah in wealth and property management as discussed

---

[1] Mahmood, "Takaful: The Islamic System of Mutual Insurance—The Malaysian Experience," p. 293.

[2] For a *fatwā* on this issue see *Malaysian Law Journal*, No. 1(1974).

above. The foregoing discussion has tried to show the relevance of the application of both *sadd al-dharā'i'* and *fatḥ al-dharā'i'* in some practical aspects of insurance based on the *takāful* model as practiced by STMB.

CHAPTER TWELVE

Re-embedding *Maqāṣid al-Sharīʿah* in the Essential Methodology of Islamic Economics

Mehmet Asutay & Isa Yilmaz

Introduction

The idea of Islamic economics burgeoned as a post-colonial counter-hegemonic attempt to address the observed developmentalist failures of Muslim societies in a period where old colonial legacies had overwhelmingly continued to shape socioeconomic institutions in the decolonized Muslim lands. Since the prevailing legacies are considered as impeding forces to the emancipation and empowerment of Muslim peoples and consolidation of their identity, obliterating their traces was seen as an essential concern in developing an authentic understanding of economy and society as part of identity search. Thus, Islamic economics emerged as a project to develop a new economic theory based on Islamic normative principles and substantive morality. This project aimed at coming to terms with the challenges Muslim individuals and societies have been facing with the mainstream materialistic conception of the economy in such a way as would rescue the meaning and function of human agency, land, labor and capital within the Islamic social formation based on participatory and sharing economy.

Consequently, considering the ideational mismatches

between Islamic and secular worldviews, Islamic economics would function to eliminate the dependence upon capitalist formation of economic life and help to construct a new social formation of Muslim societies in the light of Islamic ontology and epistemology. In achieving this, in the short-run, utmost importance is given to public policy oriented developmentalist agenda with the objective of eliminating underdevelopment, eradicating poverty and getting rid of weak politico-economic structures, while in the long-run an attempt is considered in developing Islamic social formation.

The theoretically defined aspirations of Islamic economics are invariably welcomed and encouraged as legitimate goals to be pursued and put into practice. Yet historical evidence has shown that the implementation and institutionalization process has departed from those aspirations and goals. That is, a drift has taken place whereby Islamic economic thinking has been reduced and limited to banking activities and financial transactions mostly divorced or, to just put it in a milder way, weakly connected to the realm of real economy, with an unsophisticated and theoretically shallow conception of Islamic finance. The general trend of Islamic economic studies has thus been moving towards a finance-and-banking centred view of Islamic economics in which financial operations constitute the pivot of economic activities.

The reasons behind the gap between aspirations and realities have been recurrently debated at various international conferences and forums that have resulted in a large volume of publications, thus boosting literature of Islamic economics and finance to quite an unprecedented level. The heatedly debated issues in academic studies have brought to the surface two opposing views on the right methodology to be followed in theory building of Islamic economics and finance. The first view grounds its basic argument on the idea of 'Islamization of knowledge' (IOK) devised by Ismāʿīl R. al-Fārūqī.

Although al-Fārūqī's IOK paradigm is highly sophisticated

both philosophically and methodologically, and hence deserves careful examination and assessment, in their *fiqhī* and modern constructs of Islamic finance, most Islamic finance experts have quite regularly made pragmatic references to IOK in an attempt to replicate conventional financial practices in disguise of 'Islamization' process, hence pre-fixing the word Islam and its derivatives to 'form' and loosing sight of 'substance'. Thus, IOK was simplified in the hands of Islamic finance practitioners as a method, and it has been instrumentalized in such a way as to espouse mainstream and conventional understanding of finance while eschewing philosophical contributions of al-Fārūqī and other proponents of IOK.[1] Following a clearly narrow legalistic approach to matters of the finance and banking industry in particular and the economy in general, this drift of focus and theoretical shallowness is in many cases presented as an exercise of Islamization or grounding (*ta'ṣīl*) has mostly ended up in clear mimicry of conventional finance through the

[1]The intellectual and academic movement known as Islamization of Knowledge (IOK) emerged towards the mid-1970s and gained momemntum over the subsequent decades in many Muslim countries; a number of institutions and bodies have been established to carry its mission out. Many eminent scholars and thinkers have made important contributions to its accumulating literature. They include people like Ismā'īl Rājī al-Fārūqī, Seyed Muhammad Naqib al-Attas, Malik Badri, Syyed Hossein Nasr, Seyed Ali Ashraf, AbdulHameed A. AbuSulayman, Taha Jabir al-Alwani, Mona Abdl Fadl, Mohamed Abul Gasim Haj Hamad, Ahmet Davotuglu, Eltigani Abdelgader and others. Regardless of the differences on details one may detect among the individuals involved in this movement, most of its members exhibit deep concern on epistemological and methodological issues in respect of how to go about doing Islamization of disciplines, especially in the social sciences and humanities, by recourse to the fundamental sources of Islam (the Qur'an and Prophetic traditions) and the high intellectual and scholarly tradion of Islamic civilzation. This concern is clearly steeped in a holistic view where ontology and the question values (or deontoly) occupy a prominent place. Almost without exception, the proponents of IOK shun narrow and merely legalistic approaches to Islamization of knowledge. For them, thinking on economic and other matters of human life has to be anchored in the Islamic worldview and its expressions of the relationship between God, the cosmos and man and the latter's position in the realm of creation as God's vicegerent on earth.—(Editor)

adoption of a hybrid of financial services. This explains much of the criticism leveled against IBF by committed Muslim intellectuals and scholars, such as its over-reliance on decontexualized juristic devices and legal tricks (*ḥiyal fiqhiyyah*) in justifying controversial issues and legitimatizing dubious products to conform to existing financial systems and practices, thus unwittingly taking the dominant coneventional economic models rooted in the secular worldview as a frame of reference.

The second view suggests the need to rely on the original scripts and reinterpret them in order to fathom out an ontologically authenticated and epistemologically substantiated Islamic paradigm of the economic system. The proponents of this view, who have harshly criticized the advocates of Islamizing existing financial systems and practices, stipulate a bottom-up redress of existing economic institutions by rejecting Western economic models as reference.

Interestingly enough, both the advocates of IOK in the profound and comprehensive sense and the proponents of Islamic banking and finance as just explained seem to converge on reviving the discourse of the juristic theory of *maqāṣid al-sharīʿah*[1] (the higher objectives and intents of Islamic law) in supporting their arguments. When closely examined, this convergence, however, is shown to be not more than superficial. The general juristic tendency among the latter group is rather pragmatic in its use of *maqāṣid al-sharīʿah*, as its main purpose revolves around using *maqāṣid* as simply a justificatory means to resolve actual and potential disputes pertaining to the Sharīʿah compliancy in the process of interaction between Islamic financial operations and conventional financial markets

[1] Literally, the term *maqāṣid*, singular *maqṣid*, connotes the meaning of objectives, ends, purposes, intents or goals. When attributed to the Sharīʿah in the of the compound form *maqāṣid al-Sharīʿah*, it refers to the wisdom and purposes underlying the Divine commands as being intended for the good and well-being of human beings as well as other creatures. As will be seen in this chapter, *maqāṣid al-Sharīʿah* have far-reaching implications in repsct of Islamic banking and finance.

and economic systems that are deeply rooted in the secular worldview, thus emptying this important theory of its true meaning and essence.[1] By doing this, it is believed, the process of integrating Islamic finance into the global financial system expedites, and Muslim societies would prosper and develop.

On the contrary, critiques of this approach reject such understanding of the meaning and role of *maqāṣid*, which is believed to blur the content of the term and pave the way for embracing toxic products and practices in the name of *maṣlaḥah*. Instead, they suggest using *maqāṣid al-sharīʿah* as a fundamental theoretical framework based on the taxonomy iniated by al-Ghazālī and agreed upon by most Muslim scholars after him, to identify and articulate the process and goals of developmentalism[2] with the objectives of the Sharīʿah. Grounded on such endeavor, various *maqāṣid* indices based on the Ghazālian five necessities[3] were developed to evaluate the

---

[1] Typical examples are evident in the legitimization of highly controversial Islamic financial instruments such as *tawarruq*, *bayʿal-ʿīnah* and specific *sukuk* applications.

[2] The authors recognize the value-loaded definition of 'developmentalism'. However, it also recognizes that Islamic aim is not only economic development but multi-faceted development within the parameters of *adalah, ihsan, rububiyah and tazkiyah* in the context of *tawhidi* paradigm (Mehmet Asutay, "Islamic Moral Economy as the Foundation of Islamic Finance," in Valentino Cattelan, ed., *Islamic Finance in Europe: Towards a Plural Financial System* (Cheltenham: Edward Elgar, 2013), pp. 55-68.) Hence, developmentalism is redefined within Islamic normativeness by essentialising human-centred development by re-defining individual as Islamic economics "aims at the study of human falah achieved by organising the resources of earth on the basis of cooperation and participation" (M. Akram Khan, "Islamic Economics: Nature and Need," *Journal of Research in Islamic Economics*, vol.1, No. 2 (1984), pp. 51-55., at 55). In this context, re-defined developmentalism is objected towards emancipation and empowerement in every aspect of life within the *iḥsāni* social formation.

[3] These consist in the preservation of faith, self, intellect, posterity, and wealth. Al-Ghazali was the first to enumerate them as making up the category of universal necessary (*ḍarūrī*) *maslahah* whose safeguarding is intended by the Divine Law (*sharʿ*) and which constitute the foundation of human society. See Abū Ḥāmid Muḥammad bin Muḥammad bin Muḥmmad al-Ghazālī, *al-Mustasfā min ʿIlm al-Uṣūl*, ed. Muhammad S. al-Ashqar (Beirut: Mu'assassat al-

performance of Islamic banks and economies in general. In doing so, *maqāṣid* is identified and interlinked with some popular concepts including corporate social responsibility (CSR), corporate governance (CG), environmental social and governance (ESG), sustainable development goals (SDGs), and human development (HDI). Furthermore, these concepts were appropriated and transferred into Islamic economics literature to show that *maqāṣid* already incorporates them all; thereby these initiatives represent only one aspect of the Sharīʿah objectives. In line with this, empirical studies on the nexus of *maqāṣid* and Islamic finance started to proliferate through following the popularization of abovementioned concepts under *maqāṣid* terminology.

As can be seen, theoreticians and practitioners on both sides tend to make use of *maqāṣid* merely as a 'floating signifier',[1] since the term is wittingly used for absorbing desired meanings into the concept of *maqāṣid.* Thus, at best, *maqāṣid al-sharīʿah* has been assigned the task of bestowing legitimacy in an instrumental manner for Sharīʿah-compliant products and practices in a formalistic way. Developmentalism, on the other hand, could not be reformulated with *maqāṣid al-sharīʿah* perspective in neither way, albeit the latter approach claims to reach it through developing some *maqāṣid* indices. Thus, what happened at the end is a pragmatic, instrumentalist and eclectic use of *maqāṣid* that eventually has led to the malaise of Islamic banking and finance (henceforth IBF) and diminished the close link between developmentalism and *maqāṣid al-sharīʿah* for the sake of yielding efficiency in the practices of IBF institutions. Due to such a failure, the current practice of Islamic finance has to be considered as the 'second best solution'[2] in relation to

---

Risālah, 1st edn, 1417/1997), vol. 1, p. 417.

[1] According to Oxford Reference Dictionary, the term means: "A signifier without a specific signified". Also known as an 'empty signifier', it is a signifier that absorbs rather than emits meaning.

[2] Mehmet Asutay, "Conceptualising and Locating the Social Failure of Islamic

developmentalist objectives.

This study argues that the prevailing conception of *maqāṣid al-sharīʿah* and its articulation in Islamic economics and finance is incapable of generating development due to market-oriented understanding of *maqāṣid* that is extensively applied in Islamic finance as a legitimization tool leading up to a new moral code of conduct for economic activities. Thus, a new and proactive *maqāṣid* understanding based on substantive morality should be developed and embedded in the theoretical underpinnings of Islamic economics to function as substantial methodology in deriving developmentalist oriented public policy beyond *maṣlaḥah*-based policy making.

A Review of Literature on *Maqāṣid* in Islamic Economics and Finance

It seems at first glance that *maqāṣid al-sharīʿah* has always been treated as an essential concept around which the theory of Islamic economics was constructed and Islamic financial services have been put into practice. While it is true that the founding fathers of Islamic economics, such as Muhammad Umer Chapra among others, put great emphasis on *maqāṣid* from the very beginning to provide a methodological base for theory construction; subsequent scholars, practitioners and policy-makers of Islamic finance have given recognition to its significance quite recently. A quick survey of the relevant literature affirms this observation, as the majority of *maqāṣid*-related articles and books were written in the last ten years, leaving a great gap between mid-1980s to 2000s.

Comparing the initial expressions by the founding fathers and the recent understanding of it, it is evident that *maqāṣid* has been wrested from the wider arena of Islamic economics to be

---

Finance: Aspirations of Islamic Moral Economy vs. the Realities of Islamic Finance," *Asian and African Studies*, Vol. 11, No. 2 (2012), pp. 93-113, at 109.

downsized to the sphere of Islamic finance. In this section, a survey of the *maqāṣid* related literature on Islamic economics and finance is presented in two subsections. The first subsection depicts quite extensively the emergence and essentialization of *maqāṣid al-sharīʿah* within Islamic economics in the works of the founding fathers, while the second focuses on the espousal of *maqāṣid* in the prevailing applications of Islamic finance. Thus, the divergence between theoretical and empirical studies is brought to the fore by showing how the theoretical articulation of *maqāṣid* is projected in practice.

1. Maqāṣid al-Sharīʿah and Islamic Economics: The Early Contributions

With the rise, expansion and institutionalization of modern sciences since the 17th century, Western philosophy experienced a radical shift from teleology to causality, which crystallized causal reasoning as the core of modern sciences in the face of teleology that basically explains a phenomenon in terms of its function and its 'purpose'. More precisely, modern Western philosophy, with its dominant positivist inclination, has been constructed exclusively in the form of a cause-and-effect dialectic within the framework of mechanistic explanations of natural and social phenomena, which entails causality and causal explanation as the central logical way of thinking. Therefore, teleological orientation in any theory or idea was regarded as metaphysical, nonsensical, and hence should be completely rejected.

In contradistinction to the positivist understanding, and in the context of Islamic philosophy and worldview, *maqāṣid al-sharīʿah* suggests a different understanding through its purposefulness and goal-seeking approach by embedding 'theologically' defined developmentalist ends in the relevant knowledge development and practice. In this respect, the founding fathers of Islamic economics attempted to detach themselves not only from the modern positivistic scientific methodology engulfed in the cause-effect nexus and mode of thinking, but also from the postmodern understanding, which proposes deconstruction of any sort of centrism (decentering) and universal truth constructions revolving around rationality assumptions.

Of the pioneering scholars of Islamic economics, Muhammad Umer Chapra's contributions in particular have played a significant role in guiding and inspiring following generations by emphasizing the concept of *falāḥ* or real well-being which constitutes the ultimate goal of the teachings of Islam.[1] Such well-being, Chapra maintains, cannot be attained merely by the satisfaction of just the material needs of the human personality, a matter that depends on the level of income and wealth.[2] Rather, there are other needs that have to be fulfilled, most of which "are spiritual and non-material in character and need not necessarily become satisfied as a result of increase in income."[3] Placing individual *falāḥ* at the centre of his theorization, Chapra adopts the essential taxonomy of *maqāṣid* initiated by al-Ghazali and upheld by subsequent Muslim scholars and jusrists, especially the five universal necessities which consist of the safeguarding of "faith (*dīn*), the human self (*nafs*), intellect (*'aql*), posterity (*nasl*) and wealth (*māl*)."[4] Within the framework of these core values, spiritual and non-material needs of the individual are given essential consideration in determining the goals of the Islamic economic system.

However, Chapra admits that these five things as delineated by al-Ghazali "are not the only *maqāṣid* aimed at ensuring human well-being;" there are many others stated in

---

[1] Muhammad Umer Chapra, *The Islamic Vision of Development in the Light of Maqāṣid al-Sharī'ah* (London: The International Institute of Islamic Thought, IIIT, 2008), p. 1.

[2] Ibid., p. 2.

[3] Ibid.

[4] Ibid., p. 4.

the Qur'an and the Sunnah or inferred from them by many scholars. For him, while these five can be seen as primary *maqāṣid* (*aṣliyyah*), the others may be considered as their corollaries (*tābiʿah*). The realization of the corollary *maqāṣid* is necessary as means to the realization of the primary ones. Furthermore, the primary *maqāṣid* are unchanging and constitute ends in themselves, whereas their corollaries are flexible "and may keep on expanding and changing with the passage of time."[1] In Chapra's categorization, the corollaries reflect the inherent dynamism of the Sharīʿah and they are such that they enable us "to ensure that all human rights are duly honored and that all the different human needs are adequately satisfied."[2] Both categories are consttituted in such a manner that human beings are seen as "the end as well as the means of development" process.[3]

Chapra's restructuring of *maqāṣid* into the realm of economy and economic developmentic realm, relies basically on strengthening the five universal necessities or essentials, namely the human self, faith, intellect, posterity and wealth, through fulfilling a set of corollary objectives. Likewise, he underlines the cruciality of policy goals geared towards attaining "security of life and property, removal of poverty, employment and self-employment, equitable distribution of income and wealth, education, good governance and development and expansion of wealth," all of which should result in the invigoratation of the human self (*nafs*) which "is one of the five primary objectives of the Sharīʿah."[4] Similarly, the enrichment of faith requires the establishment of certain 'rules of behavior (values)' and 'proper motivation' within Islamic worldview. Significantly, Chapra's reformulation of the

---

[1] Ibid., 4.
[2] Ibid., 5.
[3] Ibid., 6.
[4] Ibid.

theory of *maqāṣid* brings forward two very important features: one has to do with his espousal of the notion of 'enrichment' or 'invigoration' instead of the classical scholars' idea of 'preservation' or 'safeguarding' in delineating the five essentials; the other aims to incorporate societal aspects of *maqāṣid*, through corollaries, in relation to its economic dimension.

It can be deduced from the foregoing exposition that Chapra proposes a reformulation and extension of the notion of *maqāṣid* grounded in the Ghazalian basic structure of it, whereby special emphasis is put on the social dimension giving it a wider scope and more dynamic character expressed by such terms like 'enrichment' and 'invigoration'.

Siddiqi, another eminent figure of Islamic economics, approaches the objectives of Sharīʿah in a comprehensive manner in his quite recent book *Maqasid e Shariet: Ek Asri Mutala*[1], in which he mainly argues that contemporary Islamic scholars are mixing up the Sharīʿah objectives with the objectives of *fiqh,* as the intense academic debate evidences this fact in their writings. Thus, he suggests that those scholars confine the entire objectives of the Sharīʿah to *fiqhī* rulings and maxims. In addition to this, contemporary *maqāṣid* theorists appropriated the famous Ghazalian structure of *maqāṣid*, which, according to Siddiqi, must be enriched by incorporating the insights of Ibn Taymiyya and Ibn Qayyim al-Jawziyyah. The views of these two scholars constitute an important element in Siddiqi's *maqāṣid*-oriented thinking: Ibn Taymiyyah suggests considering securing benefits (*maṣāliḥ*) as one of the main goals of the Sharīʿah, to which Ibn al-Qayyim adds justice

---

[1] Muhammad Nejatullah Siddiqi, *Maqasid e Shariet: Ek Asri Mutala* (A Contemporary Study of the Objectives of Sharīʿah) (Islamabad: Institute of Islamic Research, 2009). The book is written in Urdu language and has not been rendered into English yet. Despite this limitation, it is possible to have an overview of the book thanks to its scholarly review by Abdul Azim Islahi published in *Journal of King Aabdulaziz University: Islamic Economics*, Vol. 23, No. 2 (2010AD/1431H), pp. 239-248.

as an essential objective. By invoking these two scholars and incorporating their views in his conception of *maqāṣid*, Siddiqi makes it clear that he rejects the idea of capturing the objectives into a finite list.[1]

Favoring Ibn al-Qayyim's ideas, Siddiqi expands *maqāṣid* through embedding such objectives of "cooperation at the world level, justice and equity, poverty alleviation, bridging gap between the poor and the rich, sustenance for all, peace and progress, moderation and balance, growth (*tazkiyah*), and justice (*qisṭ*)" into the five essentials.[2] Particularly, in evaluating the state of the art in IBF sector, Siddiqi considers the crux of the problem as being the general failure of examining the findings of Islamic banking and finance according to *maqāṣid al-sharīʿah* criteria.[3] In this manner, Islamic finance operations show that the *fuqahā'* mostly tackle the newly introduced financial products within a micro perspective, rather than putting their broader consequences into the agenda, and issuing their *fatwās* accordingly. However, as Siddiqi suggests, the principal objective of using *maqāṣid al-sharīʿah* as the methodology for the IBF sector must produce new public policies that reflect the substance of the theory of Islamic economics, and not just mere forms of hybrid products. The ideal *maqāṣid* methodology, Siddiqi further argues, must fulfil the specific objectives related to the IBF sector. Among them, utmost importance should be given to "encouraging businessmen and establishments for taking risks." Further,

---

[1] Ibid.; Muhammad Nejatullah Siddiqi, Keynote Address, *Round table on Islamic Economics: Current State of Knowledge and Development of the Discipline* (2004a) Held in Jeddah, Saudi Arabia on May 26-27, 2004, under joint auspices of the Islamic Research and Training Institute, Jeddah and the Arab Planning Institute, Kuwait. Accessed on 13th December 2006 at *http://www.siddiqi.com/mns/Keynote_May2004_Jeddah.htm.*

[2] Muhammad Nejatullah Siddiqi, *Maqasid e Shariet: Ek Asri Mutala* (A Contemporary Study of the Objectives of *Sharīʿah*), p. 239.

[3] Muhammad Nejatullah Siddiqi, *Riba, Bank Interest and the Rationale of its Prohibition* (Jeddah: Islamic Research and Training Institute, 2004b).

"justice, equity and benevolence should be necessary ingredients of finance so that not only one party would bear all the negative effects of the partnership and investment." Otherwise, any process of economic development based on financial operations that are oblivious to justice and benevolence would only lead to "bad consequences."[1]

Besides the contributions of Chapra and Siddiqi who attempted to develop a wider *maqāṣid* framework that aims to make *maqāṣid al-sharīʿah* essential to the methodology and substance of Islamic economics, there are other scholars who took it upon themselves to examine particular subjects in Islamic economics and finance through a general *maqāṣid* approach. Monzer Kahf, for instance, focuses on the Sharīʿiah goals intended by the prohibition of interest (*ribā*) and indicates their implications for IBF sector.[2] In light of an explication of the rationale behind the prohibition of *ribā* based on evidence from the Qur'an (i.e. 2:279) and the Prophet's sayings that strictly urge upon forbidding *ribā*, Kahf proceeds to discuss certain characteristics that should be observed in IBF products and have to do with their moral soundness, namely avoiding harmful products, Sharīʿah permissibility of the products, establishing obligational balance between each parties, founding all financing contracts on real exchanges and assets.[3] Then, he elucidates the primary objectives pertaining to the prohibition of *ribā* by determining eight objectives, some of which listed below:

- Preventing return from being assigned to an asset that does not produce return;

---

[1] Siddiqi, *Maqasid-e-Shariet*, p. 239.

[2] Monzer Kahf, "*Maqāṣid al-Sharīʿah* in the Prohibition of *Riba* and their Implications for Modern Islamic Finance", paper presented at IIUM International Conference on *Maqāṣid al-Sharīʿah*, Malaysia, August 8-10, 2006.

[3] Ibid., pp. 9-10. Editor's note: Kahf's paper referred to by the authors constitutes chapter 11 of the present book.

- Avoiding distribution of anything except the real value added or value created in an asset;
- Upholding the sanctity of property rights;
- Disallowing debts trade and exchange along with similarly unrealistic purely speculative transactions that are not based on real production;
- 'Preventing' debt discounting and rescheduling for increment.

In Kahf's delineation of the Sharīa'h objectives in the prohibition of *ribā* there is an undeniable protectionist approach that is clearly expressed by such terms as prevention, avoiding, disallowing and upholding have been chosen for the articulation of *maqāṣid al-sharīʿah*. This approach is indebted, not surprisingly, to the Ghazālian formulation and structuring *maqāṣid*, which is critically examined in this study in detail in a later section. Yet, Kahf's *maqāṣid* oriented interpretation of *ribā* constitutes a novel attempt to the critique of modern Islamic finance practices.

From another perspective, Ahmad critically addressed the role of Islamic finance in fulfilling al-Ghazālī's taxonomy of *maqāṣid.*[1] His *maqāṣid* oriented theorization focuses mainly on the 'protection of human life' and 'protection of Islamic religion'; the other three objectives are conceived to support these two cores and complement them. The former objective is built on two complementary *maqāṣid*; that is 'education' and 'justice' which ultimately pave the way for developing *ḥalāl* productive activities, educational and training programs in the financial capacity of markets.[2] The undertaking of these activities mainly requires the prohibition of *ribā* trade in debt and *gharar* so that *ḥalāl* ways of production would be

[1] Abdel-Rahman Yousri Ahmad, "Role of Finance in Achieving *Maqāṣid al-Sharīʿah*," *Islamic Economic Studies* 9/2 (2011), pp. 1-18.
[2] Ibid., pp. 6-7.

established. As for the second objective, it is essential to develop judicial and educational institutions in order to maintain and promote justice. Respect of private property rights, in the same vein, functions for protecting wealth, which plays a complementary role in achieving these objectives.

Ahmad determines, without much explanation, the chief goals of Islamic finance in its relation to realizing *maqāṣid* through incorporating them into al-Shāṭibī's three-level classification.[1] Amongst them, the first goal, namely low levels of development expressed as *ḍarūriyyāt* or essential needs, is addressed by the alleviation of poverty mainly through mobilizing resources and directing them towards sound projects. The second doal, medium stage of development in the form of *ḥājiyyāt* or complementary, can be achieved through facilitating, for example, better health systems and education and schooling system, and improving infrastructure. Lastly, the high stage of development or *taḥsīniyyāt* implying embellishments aims at satisfying luxurious necessities of individuals and society as long as it does not produce waste, consumerism and inequality; as having *taḥsīniyyāt* related consequences leads to improvement and the attainment in individual lives.

Under this structure, Ahmad gives some policy recommendations pertaining to the applications of Islamic finance:

- Giving up over-dependence on *murābaḥah* contract,
- Following and even developing the use of new types of contracts that have been first launched by countries such as the Sudan, the Gulf states and Malaysia,
- Putting the objective of financing the poor at the core,
- Finding some authentic benchmarks other than interest rates for determining the profit margin,

[1] Ibid.

- Expanding *sukūk* operations, but through avoiding some standards of it which have toxic nature.
- Discontinuing *tawarruq* contracts, which, in reality, does not differ much from interest-based loans.[1]

As surveyed above, the ong trajectory of theorizing on Islamic economics displays features of homogenous and dilatory development. Thus, the founding fathers and subsequent scholars have constructed their theories of Islamic economics within the boundaries of the Ghazālian *maqāṣid* framework and through non-substantiated attempts. In doing so, *maqāṣid al-sharīʿah* are essentialized within Islamic economics on the surface, yet embedding it as the substantial methodology is mostly missed, and the five-level essentials are favured with limited articulations. The next section demonstrates how contemporary proponents of Islamic finance are even narrowing the scope of *maqāṣid* to the preservation of wealth, which is rather evident in most empirical studies related to IBF.

2. Maqāṣid al-Sharīʿah and Islamic Finance: Eclecticism and Romanticism

Even though *maqāṣid al-sharīʿah* could not be profoundly embedded in the theoretical framework of Islamic economics in the efforts of the founding fathers, their contributions were of great importance since they established the theoretical base, dimensions and objectives of Islamic economics. It would, therefore, be expected that the successors would reap the benefits of these contributions both theoretically and practically by essentializing *maqāṣid* as a methodology. Yet the political economy atmosphere did not allow the emergence of Islamic economics both in theory and practice as an alternative economic system to flourish and play a central role in leading

[1] Ibid.

Islamic financing applications. Thus, the entire authenticity search in the end relegated to IBF, as the capital accumulation resulting from petro-dollars of the 1970s and 1980s urged and expedited the process of establishing Islamic financial industry as an 'integral' sector of the global financial system. In the initial stage, there was not much debate and intervention on the rise of Islamic finance in order to preserve the ongoing profitability. The *maqāṣid* related debate in the form of substantive morality, therefore, had to wait until 2000s when the social failure of Islamic banking started to be recognized.[1]

Highly influenced by these historical developments, the infant empirical literature on *maqāṣid* and Islamic finance nexus basically follows two main trends. The first type of literature stresses the need for a *maqāṣid*-based perspective to remove the social failure of Islamic finance. This literature highlights in a romanticized manner, highlights the debates of form *vs* substance, Sharīʿah-based versus Sharīʿah-compliant, debt finance vs equity finance, banks as profit-based oriented entities versus banks as socially oriented entities.[2] Although

---

[1] Mehmet Asutay, "Conceptualising and Locating the Social Failure of Islamic Finance: Aspirations of Islamic Moral Economy vs. the Realities of Islamic Finance," *Asian and African Studies* 11/2 (2012), pp. 93-113, at 109; also, "Conceptualisation of the Second Best Solution in Overcoming the Social Failure of Islamic Banking and Finance: Examining the Overpowering of *Homoislamicus* by *Homoeconomicus*," *IIUM Journal of Economics and Management*, vol. 15, No. 2 (2012), pp. 167-195.

[2] For an overview of these studies, see: Asyraf Wajdi Dusuki and Abdulazeem Abozaid, "A Critical Appraisal on the Challenges of Realizing *maqāṣid al-sharīʿah* in Islamic Banking and Finance," *IIUM Journal of Economics and Management*, Vol. 15, No. 2 (2007), pp. 143-165; Mustafa Omar Mohammad and Syahidawati Shahwan, "The Objective of Islamic Economic and Islamic Banking in Light of *Maqāṣid al-Sharīʿah*: A Critical Review," *Middle-East Journal of Scientific Research*, Vol. 13, No. 1 (2013), pp. 75-84; Noura El-Najar, "The Application of *Maqāṣid al-Sharīʿah* in Islamic Banking & Finance," *Conference Proceeding - 7th Quality Conference in the Middle East: Leading Transformation to Sustainable Excellence* (2014), pp. 2-10; Tawfique Al-Mubarak and Noor Mohammad Osmani, "Applications of *Maqāṣid* al-*Sharīʿah* and *Maslahah* in Islamic Banking Practices: An Analysis," paper presented at the International Seminar on Islamic Finance in India, Kochi,

delineating the aspects of failure is certainly important, the debate remained highly limited in the sense of suggesting authentic solutions with *maqāṣid* lens.

In addition to highlighting the failure in a discursive manner, another step of empirical character was made, which consists of efforts aimed at constructing a *maqāṣid* index and applying it to the economic performance of Muslim dominated countries. It would be therefore possible to diagnose to what extent economies perform in line with the objectives of the Sharīʿah. In terms of measuring economic, social and other performances together, *maqīʿid* index resembles multidimensional indices such as Human Development Index, Happiness Index, OECD Better Life Index, *etc.*

By using a *maqāṣid*-based index, it was aimed either to measure overall economic performance, or specifically Islamic banks' performance. The common characteristic of the index attempts is the adoption of the Ghazālian fivefold structure of *maqāṣid* framework, which is invariably and extensively utilized in the relevant academic studies. Looking at the country level *maqāṣid* performance studies, both primary and secondary data are selected in determining the variables for each dimension. Those selecting primary data mostly conduct questionnaires, in-depth interviews, surveys or using directly existing primary data such as World Values Survey and Gallup Analytics. As for the secondary data, World Bank, IMF, UNESCO and UNDP databases are opted for. The most appropriate approximation

---

India, 4-6/10/ 2010); Beebee Salma Sairally, "Integrating Environmental Social and Governance (ESG) Factors in Islamic Finance: Towards the Realization of *Maqāṣid al-Sharīʿah*," *ISRA International Journal of Islamic Finance*, vol. 7, No. 2 (2015), pp. 145-154; Younes Soualhi, "Application of Sharīʿah contracts in contemporary Islamic Finance: A *Maqāṣid* Perspective," *Intellectual Discourse*, vol. 23, Special Issue (2015), pp. 333-354; Luqman Zakariyya, "Harmonising Legality with Morality in Islamic Banking and Finance: A Quest for *Maqāṣid* al-*Sharīʿah* paradigm," *Intellectual Discourse* , vol. 23, Special Issue (2015), pp. 355-376.

of the five dimensions are sought in these databases, or surveys and questions are intended to meet each dimension. In this manner, Table 1 and Table 2 gives a selection of most commonly used proxies for the Ghazalian fivefold structure of necessities.[1]

Table 1. Variables for the Ghazalian Five-Level Dimensions (Secondary Data)	
ḥifẓ al-dīn	- Religious freedom - Crime rate - Corruption rate - Peace Index

[1] See, MB Hendrie Anto, "Introducing an Islamic Human Development Index (I-HDI) to Measure Development in OIC Countries," *Islamic Economic Studies*, vol. 19, No. 2 (2011), pp. 69-9; Daud Abdul-Fattah Batchelor, "A New Islamic Rating Index of Wellbeing for Muslim Countries," *Islam and Civilizational Renewal*, vol. 4, No. 2 (2013), pp. 188-214; Rafi Amiruddin, "*Maqāṣid al-Sharīʿah*: Are We Measuring the Immeasurable?," *Islamic Economic Studies,* vol. 22, No. 2 (2014), pp. 1-32; Mehdi Mili, "A Structural Model for Human Development, Does *Maqāṣid al-Sharīʿah* Matter?," *Islamic Economic Studies,* vol. 22, No. 2 (2014), pp. 47-64; Muhammad Mubashir Mukhtar, Hafiz Muhammad Safraz Nihal, Hafiz Abdul Rauf, Waleed Wasti, & Muhammad Shahid Qureshi, "Socio-Economic Philosophy of Conventional and Islamic Economics: Articulating *Hayat-e-Tayyaba* Index (HTI) on the Basis of *Maqāṣid* al-*Sharīʿah*," *Islamic Economic Studies,* vol. 22, No. 2 (2014), pp. 65-98; S. Salman Syed Ali & Hamid Hasan, "Towards a *Maqāṣid al-Sharīʿah* based Development Index," *IRTI Working Paper Series 1435-18* (2014), pp. 1-22; M. Fevzi Esen, "A Statistical Framework on Identification of *Maqāṣid al-Sharīʿah* Variables for Socio-Economic Development Index," *Journal of Business Studies Quarterly*, vol. 7, No.1 (2015), pp. 107-124; Rahmatina Kasri & Habib Ahmed, "Assessing Socio-Economic Development based on *Maqāṣid* al-*Sharīʿah* Principles: Normative Frameworks, Methods and Implementation in Indonesia," *Islamic Economic Studies*, vol. 23, No 1 (2015), pp. 73-100; Salman Ahmed Shaikh, "Developing an Index of Socio-Economic Development Consistent with *Maqāṣid* al-*Sharīʿah*," *Journal of King Abdul Aziz University - Islamic Economics*, vol. 30, No. 1 (2017), pp. 117-129.

Table 1. Variables for the Ghazalian Five-Level Dimensions (Secondary Data)	
ḥifẓ al- nafs	- Average life expectancy - Human rights index - Freedom Index
ḥifẓ al-ʿaql	- Education - Technology use - Number of researches - Articles published - School enrolment - Spending on education
ḥifẓ al-nasl	- Fertility rate - Life expectancy at birth - Health expenditure as percentage of GDP - Divorce rate - Child mortality rate
ḥifẓ al-māl	- GDP per capita - Household consumption - Gini ratio

The variables in the preceding table are chosen by many in an effort to best approximate the objectives of the Sharīʿah for different dimensions. The ultimate *maqāṣid* index, hence, would measure the overall economic performance of countries with respect to its conformity to the Sharīʿah. In order achieve this, some valuable indices were developed including Islamicity Index[1], *Hayat-a-Tayyaba Index,*[1] Islamic Human Development

[1] Hossein Askari & Hossein Mohammadkhan, *Islamicity Indices: The Seed for Change* (New York: Palgrave Macmillan, 2015); Hossein Askari & Scheherazade Rehman, "The Economic Development of OIC Countries: A Survey," in Zamir

Index,[2] *Maqāṣid al-Sharīʿah* based Development Index,[3] and Posterity Development Index[4].

Table 2. Variables for the Ghazalian Five-Level Dimensions (Primary Data)	
ḥifẓ al-dīn	- Attendance in religious services - Frequency in prayers/fasting - Charitable giving and Hajj attendance - Belief in God - Avoidance from Haram activities
ḥifẓ al- nafs	- Freedom of choice - War or terrorist attacks - Life satisfaction
ḥifẓ al-ʿaql	- High level of education - Avoidance from alcohol consumption and drug use - School attendance/achievements

Iqbal and Abbas Mirakhor, eds., *Islamic Finance and Economic Development* (Washington DC: World Bank, 2013), pp. 299-324.

[1] Mhammad M. Mukhtar *et. al.*, "Socio-Economic Philosophy of Conventional and Islamic Economics: Articulating *Hayat-e-Tayyaba* Index (HTI) on the Basis of *Maqasid* al-*Shari'ah*," *Islamic Economic Studies*, vol. 22, No. 2 (2014), pp. 65-98.

[2] M. B. H. Anto, "Introducing an Islamic Human Development Index (I-HDI) to Measure Development in OIC Countries," *Islamic Economic Studies*, Vol. 19, No. 2 (2011), pp. 69-96; Necati Aydin, "Islamic versus Conventional Human Development Index: Empirical Evidence from Ten Muslim Countries," *International Journal of Social Economics*, vol. 44, No. 1 (2016), pp. 1-45.

[3] Salman Syed Ali & Hamid Hasan, "Towards a *Maqasid al-Shariah* based Development Index," *IRTI Working Paper Series 1435-18* (2014), pp. 1-22; also: "Why a *Maqāṣid al-Sharīʿah* based Index for Socio-Economic Development?," *IRTI* (2017), pp. 1-22.

[4] Zahoor Khan, Jamaluddin Sulaiman & Zakaria Bahari, "Socioeconomic Human Well-Being and Posterity: A Newly Proposed Faith-Based Measurement Index," *Journal of Religion & Spirituality in Social Work: Social Thought*, vol. 34, No. 1 (2015), pp. 72-90.

ḥifẓ al-nasl	- Frequency of sickness - Access to health services - Homosexuality and prostitution - Abortion and divorce
ḥifẓ al-māl	- Employability - Income level / financial situation - Savings and consumption - Robbery and theft occurrences

Apart from country level performance, *maqāṣid* has also been employed for evaluating the performance of Islamic banks. In this regard, the wisdom and purpose behind financial activities are identified so that Islamic banks would observe them in their operations. However, constructing *maqāṣid* indicators alone is not enough; Islamic finance data must also be accessible and disclosed to evaluate Islamic banks' performances. One way of tackling this issue is to apply content analysis over the disclosed information in annual reports of Islamic banks. Mainly inspired by the distinguishing works of Islamicity Disclosure Index[1] and Ethical Identity Index,[2] content analysis-based *maqāṣid* studies determine some key concepts for each indicator, and through using the method of codifying text and content, the high frequency of concepts assumes much importance for related indicators. Table 3 depicts a selection of widely used indicators of *maqāṣid* in

[1] Shahul Hameed bin Mohamed Ibrahim, Ade Wirman, Bakhtiar Alrazi, Mohd Nazli bin Mohamed Nor & Sigit Pramono, *Alternative Disclosure & Performance Measures for Islamic Banks* (Kuala Lumpur: Department of Accounting, International Islamic University Malaysia, 2004).

[2] Roszaini Haniffa & Mohammad Hudaib, "Exploring the Ethical Identity of Islamic Banks via Communication in Annual Reports," *Journal of Business Ethics*, vol. 76, No. 1 (2007), pp. 97-116.

disclosure studies.[1]

Despite the degree of freedom of choice in determining the variables, one of the disadvantages of disclosure studies lies in too much reliance on the disclosed information in reports. Besides, this evaluation method in fact checks *maqāṣid* scores of Islamic reporting, not directly of Islamic banks' operations in the practical field. And lastly, it is very hard to reach a comprehensive performance measurement by using content analysis since the validity and reliability of data will always remain questionable. Despite all these shortcomings, Bedoui, and Bedoui and Mansour's contribution [2] is amongst the meritorious studies, which develops a conceptual measurement method for *maqāṣid* performances of Islamic financial institutions by extending and augmenting the concept of *maqāṣid* through introducing Abdel Majid al-Najjar's conceptualization of *maqāṣid.*[3] By adopting this structure, Asutay and Harningtyas[1]

---

[1] Siti Manisa Ngalim & Abdul Ghafar Ismail, "An Islamic Vision Development Based Indicators in Analysing the Islamic Banks Performance: Evidence from Malaysia, Indonesia and selected GCC Countries," *IRTI Working Paper Series 1436-02* (2014), pp. 1-33; Mehmet Asutay and Astrid Fionna Harningtyas, "Developing *Maqāṣid* al-*Sharīʿah* Index to Evaluate Social Performance of Islamic Banks: A Conceptual and Empirical," *International Journal of Islamic Economics and Finance Studies*, vol. 1, No. 1 (2015), pp. 5-64; Mohammad Abu Hurayra, "Achievement of *Maqāṣid al-Sharīʿah* in Islamic Banking: An Evaluation of Islami Bank Bangladesh Limited," *Global Journal of Computer Science and Technology: A Hardware Computation*, vol. 15, No. 1 (2015), pp. 9-15; Syhiza Arshad, Rahayati binti Ahmad, Wan Nazjmi Mohamed Fisol, Roshima Said, & Yusuf Haji-Othman, "*Maqāṣid al-Sharīʿah* in Corporate Social Responsibility of Sharīʿah Compliant Companies," *Research Journal of Finance and Accounting*, vol. 6, No. 6 (2015), pp. 239-247.

[2] Houssem Eddine Bedoui, "Ethical Competitive Advantage for Islamic Finance Institutions: How should They Measure Their Performance?" (Tenth Harvard University Forum on Islamic Finance: Islamic Finance and Development, 2012); Houssem Eddine Bedoui and Walid Mansour, "Performance and Maqāṣid al-*Sharīʿah*'s Pentagon-Shaped Ethical Measurement," *Science and Engineering Ethics*, vol. 21, No. 3 (2014), pp. 555-576.

[3] Most probably reference here is made to al-Najjar's seminal work entitled *Maqāṣd al-Sharīʿah bi-Abʿād Jadīdah,*first published from Beirut by Dar al-Gharb al-Islami in

conducted a content-based disclosure analysis and evaluated social performances of selected Islamic banks.

Table 3. Selected Variables Used in Disclosure Studies
- Prohibition of *riba*
- Opening *mudaraba* account
- Provide *maslaha* for all
- Microfinance activities
- Profit and loss sharing
- Employee education
- *Zakat* and Charitable activities
- Environmental responsibility
- Good governance
- Collaboration and sharing within bank staff

Another method of coping with the access-to-data problem is to conduct questionnaires and interviews and transform them into measurable variables through giving particular weights to each dimension.[2] In so doing, the interview method of data collection involves directing questions to scholars of Sharīʿah supervisory boards, staff, managers and directors of Islamic

2006.—Editor.

[1] Mehmet Asutay & Astrid Fionna Harningtyas, "Developing *Maqāṣid al-Sharīʿah* Index to Evaluate Social Performance of Islamic Banks: A Conceptual and Empirical," *International Journal of Islamic Economics and Finance Studies,* vol. 1, No. 1 (2015), pp. 5-64.

[2] Muslim Har Sani Mohamad, Muhammad Ahmar Ali, & Ros Aniza Mohd Sharif, "Determinants of *Maqāṣid al-Sharīʿah* based Performance Measurement Practices: The Case of Malaysian Islamic Banks," *International Journal of Economics, Management and Accounting,* vol. 24, No. 1 (2016), pp. 49-81; Salman Ahmed Shaikh, "Developing an Index of Socio-Economic Development Consistent with *Maqāṣid al-Sharīʿah,*" *Journal of King Abdulaziz University: Islamic Economics*, vol. 30, No. 1 (2017), pp. 117-129.

banks. The results are interpreted with some *maqāṣid* benchmarks, and scores are given accordingly. Similar to content analysis, this method is also less reliable, since internal staff or scholars sitting at bank boards are mostly likely not to enjoy giving negative responses regarding Islamic banks' levels of performance, which hence leads to response bias.

Lastly, the *maqāṣid* index is also constructed through determining objectives of Islamic banking with some ratio analysis.[1] Table 4 presents a set of widely used ratios that provide to assess *maqāṣid* performance of Islamic banks.

Table 4. Selected Ratios for Assessing *Maqāṣid* Performance
- Interest free income / Total income
- *Zakat* distribution / Net assets
- SME financing / Total investment
- Training and research expenditures / Total assets
- Employee retention ratio
- Education grant / Total income
- Profit / Total income
- Investment deposit / Total deposit

[1] See, Mustafa Omar Mohammed, Kazi Md. Tarique, and Rafikul Islam "Measuring the Performance of Islamic Banks using *Maqāṣid*-based Model," *Intellectual Discourse*, vol. 23, No. 1 (2015), pp. 401-424; Ismail Nizam & Mousa Larbani, "A *Maqāṣid* al-*Sharīʿah* based Composite Index to Measure Socio-economic Prosperity in OIC Countries," in Abdul Ghafar Ismail, Salman Syed Ali, & Latiba Bibi Musafar Hameed, eds., *Policy Discussion on Maqāṣid Sharīʿah for Socioeconomic Development* (Selangor, Malaysia: Penerbit Kuis, 2017), pp. 185-213); Salman Ahmed Shaikh, "Developing an Index of Socio-Economic Development Consistent with *Maqāṣid al-Sharīʿah*," *Journal of King Abdulaziz University - Islamic Economics*, vol. 30, No. 1 (2017), pp. 117-129; Aam S. Rusydiana and Salman Al Parisi, "The Measurement of Islamic Bank Performance: A Study Using *Maqāṣid* Index and Profitability," *Global Review of Islamic Economics and Business*, vol. 4, No. 1 (2016), pp. 1-14.

All these attempts at constructing *maqāṣid* indices are appreciated as they provide some inferences about economic performances. However, there are substantial problems inherent in developing such indices. First and foremost, it is debatable whether the Sharīʿah objectives in the economic sphere can be reflected with a limited number of dimensions. This question brings about another issue that concerns the validity of statistics as an adequate method to evaluate economic and social performance. As statistical methods require measurable forms of knowledge, the naturally immeasurable or unobservable factors are either declined or replaced with something different from the original. Taking the example of the preservation of *al-ʿaql* as one of the primary *maqāṣid*, most performance indices relegate it to 'education'. In order to measure and quantify education, the existing data are sought, and mostly 'education expenditure as percentage of GDP' or 'school enrolment' are chosen as they are readily accessible in the World Bank and other databases. As a result, a particular country (it can also be an economy or a bank) is evaluated for its contribution to the preservation of *al-ʿaql* with such proxies of education; and if it gets high score it is deemed and accepted as successful in conforming to the objectives of the Sharīʿah. Yet what happens in reality is nothing but the quantitatively increased education opportunities or funds reserved for it. In the case where a country's education system is underdeveloped, these proxies will contrarily imply biased results. More importantly, what al-Ghazālī intends with this dimension of *maqāṣid* should not be the proliferation of modern and positivist educational institutions as prevailing in Muslim countries.

This study does not claim that the *maqāṣid* index developers are all favoring such an approach; rather this is an inevitable route independent from subjective views once the need for measuring *maqāṣid* is taken for granted. If a particular dimension of *maqāṣid* is aimed to be measured, then there is no way other than to apply for the existing databases. Thus, even the best index that may be developed with appropriate components has to face the limitations imposed by mainstream databases. Considering also the data limitations of Muslim economies, *maqāṣid* indices eventually cannot go beyond a symbolic meaning. Similarly, this approach results in falling in the trap of judging advanced countries more Islamic, for the performance results give higher ranks to such countries.[1] Although it does not mean that advanced countries are performing less from the Islamic point of view, it is like comparing the superiority of apples over oranges. In other words, the value loaded dimensions of *maqāṣid* cannot be readily applied to different institutions emerged from different worldviews.

In summarizing the transformation of *maqāṣid* understanding and its application in Islamic finance throughout the decades, it can be said that the pioneering fathers' attempt at considering *maqāṣid al-sharīʿah* as the methodology of Islamic economics in defining its consequences did not pave the way for an authentic financial system based on Islamic values and norms.

Maqāṣid al-Sharīʿah: Towards an Essential 'Methodology'

In light of the foregoing critical survey of the contributions made by the founding fathers of Islamic economics and those who came after them, the remaing sections of this study will deal with the question as to how *maqāṣid al-sharīʿah* can function as an essential methodology for Islamic economics. In doing so, problems pertaining to the adoption of al-Ghazālī's *maqāṣid* framework and its use by Islamic finance scholars will be addressed. Then, an attempt will be made to bring to the fore the distinctive features as wel as the implications of a proactive

[1] See, for instance, Hossein Askari & H. Mohammadkhan, *Islamicity Indices: The Seed for Change* (New York: Palgrave Macmillan, 2015).

maqāṣid framework in relation to Islamic economics.

Methodological issues have always been the moot point, particularly in economic theorization, for they constitute the theory of knowledge or epistemological aspect of it. However, the scope of this chapter does not allow scrutinizing the mainstream methodology of economics in much detail, it is appropriate to touch upon its grounds to yield the necessary reflections on it.

Methodology in the economics science suggests that economic theory is part of the scientific knowledge and hence it must be verified by using empirical procedures in deriving objective facts and reason. Popper,[1] for example, proposes empirical methods for validating economic theorization through falsification process.[2] Together with much emphasis on empiricism, mainstream economic methodology also adopts the Darwinian principle of survival of the fittest in the market, *a priori* reasoning, utility maximization, and deriving economic theory 'from realities to doctrine'.[3] Additionally, the methodology of economics, following the Western Enlightenment philosophy, has mostly been developed around national interests and the political economy perspectives evidence that this methodology is subordinated to the legitimization and theorization of the real objectives of nation states.[4]

In responding to the 'poverty of economics', and with the

---

[1] Karl Popper, *The Logic of Scientific Discovery* (New York: Basic Books, 2nd edn, 1968).

[2] The term 'falsification' is used, in methodological sense, that since truth can never be known, scientific progress must be maintained by falsification of economic propositions.

[3] Waleed A. J. Addas, *Methodology of Economics: Secular vs Islamic* (Kuala Lumpur: International Islamic University of Malaysia Press, 2008).

[4] For example, Adam Smith's seminal work on 'the Wealth of Nations', far from being universally suggestible to every nation, aims to investigate the ways that leads advanced countries in the Western world to the achievement of prosperity.

emergence of post-modernism, the scope of economic analysis has gone beyond the traditional borders of 'pure scientific' approach by also considering institutions, political economy, values, cultures and religious behavior albeit as an exdogenous variable. The emergence of institutional economics, new political economy and public choice aims at expanding the horizon of economics by re-discovering the old wisdom of political economy suggesting the intersectionality of social sciences, which is also essential for Islamic economics, as it has always remained a moral and political economy in its broadest sense.

Despite all these developments in economic science, Muslim scholars have not systematically paid sufficient attention to methodological issues in theorizing Islamic economics; they oscillated between two opposite poles: the 'step-by-step approach' and the 'all-or-nothing approach'.[1] The first approach exploits the IOK paradigm in such a realist and pragmatist manner as would obliterate its essence, postulates and intentions. Likewise, it ends up in an evolutionary conception and construction of an Islamic theory of economics, thus neglecting the basic assumption—advocated mainly by Attas[2]—of practicing Muslim society in its pure economic theory making, beyond evolving economics into Islamic framework as part of the *tawḥīd*ic IOK paradigm developed by al-Fārūqī.[3] These two ramifications of methodological aspects pioneered in the literature, and *maqāṣid al-sharīʿah*, as mentioned above, are yet to burgeon to develop as a third alternative for the methodology of Islamic economics.

In light of the definition and function of methodology

---

[1] Zubair Hasan, "Islamization of Knowledge in Economics: Issues and Agenda," *IIUM Journal of Economics and Managment*, vol. 6, No. 2 (1998), pp. 1-40.

[2] Syed Muhammad Naqib al-Attas, *Islam and the Philosophy of Science* (Kuala Lumpur: International Institute of Islamic Thought and Civilization, ISTAC, 1989).

[3] Ismāʿīl Rājī al Fārūqī, *Al-Tawhid: Its Implication for Thought and Life* (Herndon, Virginia: The International Institute of Islamic Thought, 1412/1992).

mentioned above, this study, beyond the two oscillations, suggests recourse to *maqāṣid al-sharīʿah* as the fundamental methodology for the theorization of Islamic economics through which Islamic developmentalism is conceptualized and transformed into public policy making. When methodology is adjusted to the ambit of Islamic economics, *maqāṣid* functions to explain; (i) the way the primaty sources and origins of knowledge, the Qur'an and Sunnah, are articulated into the base of its economic theorization; (ii) the way the Islamic axiomatic approach is substantiated and instituted in such a way as to formulate and articulate the teachings enshrined in these sources into everyday socioeconomic life and realities; and lastly (iii) the way that the Islamicity of the institutional and non-institutional forms of these articulations are verified in both intentionalist and consequentialist ways. To further elaborate on these two approaches, owing to the intentionalist adoption, *maqāṣid* would provide theoretical, philosophical and also practical reference point to develop socioeconomic policies; the consequentialist approach, on the other hand, functions to filter out morally acceptable outcomes among others. Hence, it provides a methodological framework to measure the policy outcomes in relation to systematically formulated *maqāṣid* scheme, despite the fact that consequentialism has traditionally been ruled out as part of methodology in Islamic economics by the proponents of *fiqhī* approach.

Adhering to this view, together with the intentionalist and consequentialist approaches, *maqāṣid* would embed its distinctive epistemological spirit and methodological characterisctics into the economic system in such a way that the role of 'individual faculty, reason and rationality' in deriving knowledge, 'self-interest and utility maximization motives' in shaping economic behavior in line with *homoeconomicus*, market exchange and price mechanism in establishing justice and equity through allocating resources, and the harsh competition and craving for efficiency as the overall *modus operandi*, are all examined critically. Instead, the revealed knowledge as the source of epistemological knowledge, beneficence (*iḥsān*), altruism and cooperative behavior through expanded stakeholding understanding, substantive morality beyond instrumental reasoning, efficiency with equity, and ethico-economic relationship within Islamic order are located into the construction of authentic Islamic theory of *iqtiṣād* through the methodology of *maqāṣid al-sharīʿah*. At the end of this process, it is expected that *maqāṣid* embedded Islamic theory of *iqtiṣād* would generate a particular social formations that are distinct from capitalist social formations and capitalist modes of production. Hence, this process should lead to *iḥsānī* or 'good society' as opposed to capitalist commercial society.

Re-embedding *Maqāṣid al-Sharīʿah* into the Theory of Development

As has been shown in the survey of literature, the existing contributions in the theoretical construction of Islamic economics limitedly dealt with the notion of *maqāṣid al-sharīʿah* and its essential role in developing a fundamental methodology. Ironically, *maqāṣid* has later been accommodated into Islamic finance, which is one of the institutional constructs of Islamic economics, such that the Islamic financial transactions and the operations of Islamic financial institutions have implicitly been legitimized through *maqāṣid*. In addition, *maqāṣid* has also been used by the critics of Islamic finance to analyze and uncover its social failures. For example, Islamic financialization today, increasingly switching into the orbit of global financial gear, is being evaluated positively through various *maqāṣid* indices developed by contemporary econometricians.

The rationale for the exclusive interaction of *maqāṣid* with Islamic economics in such a way mainly stems from the retrieving and reintegrating well-formulated objectives in the Islamic intellectual history in today's environment, especially after recognizing the failure of the Islamic finance enterprise due to its mimicry of conventional finance. Thus, scholars believed that severe criticisms raised against Islamic finance could be obviated through a re-examination of the IBF applications by introducing *maqāṣid al-sharīʿah.* Accordingly, since al-Ghazālī's *maqāṣid* framework was ready to be adopted, Sharīʿah scholars at Islamic banks' boards used this particular frame to legitimize their products regardless of their divergence from the ideal position. This study, nevertheless, suggests that the Ghazālian approach to *maqāṣid* in producing an ideal methodology for Islamic economics is inadequate on the grounds of its inherent flaws in revealing developmentalism as discussed above.

Deficiencies in the Ghazālian framework with respect to its methodological functionality can be identified and explored under two main points. The first one, 'individual orientedness' or self-centredness (*fardiyyah*), is characterized by lacking explicit emphasis on societal aspects in relation to each objective. For instance, the objectives determined through the preservation of faith, soul, wealth, mind, offspring (and honor) all embraces individual preference, perspective and scope; hence the derivation of social consequences from these individually expressed five essentials is not plausible as the social dimension must be embedded in *maqāṣid al-sharīʿah per se* beyond instrumental or indirect ways. Indeed, the argument that the satisfaction of individual needs would, in return, lead to prosperity at the societal level is an arguable method in many aspects.

In theorizing the capitalist system, Adam Smith [1] had adopted a similar method, which can be termed as handicap of individuality, albeit the objectified consequences are in great contrast to Islamic premises, by claiming that the invisible

[1] Adam Smith, *An Inquiry into the Nature and Causes of the Wealth of Nations* (Indianapolis: Liberty Fund, 1994).

hand would establish social welfare and prosperity and lead to society's opulence so long as every single individual seeks the pursuit of his own gains in line with self-interest motives. In other words, Smith fancied a virtuous society in which prosperity and wealth can only be established at the societal level by setting some goals that confine its scope to the individual. This inductive method, however far from Smith's expectations, has not benefited society at large, as scattered historical evidence shows.

It is a methodological problem that the mere consideration of individual *falāḥ* does not necessarily bring out social justice, welfare, and developmentalism; thereby *iḥsān* (beneficence) as a societal objective should be conflated with *falāḥ* so that behavioral attitudes can be moulded by these two elements in order to reflect upon norms and values of society. In other words, societal objectives can be fulfilled through *falāḥ* surrounded with *iḥsānī* social capital. Here, it can be argued that the rationale for stressing individual centricity in developing the Ghazālian *maqāṣid* emanates from the fundamental exigency of developing and expanding the capacity and functioning of individual. Notwithstanding the greatness of the ultimate objective, the *tawḥīdī* understanding of Islam essentializes the concept of *iḥsān* in the process of fulfilling this fundamental objective so that each individual's capacity and functioning would harmonically contribute to the wellbeing of others. Consequently, such a process invalidates the individually acceptable but socially defective objectives and outcomes (or vice versa) through its *tawḥīdī* framework, which functions to set objectives in a harmonious and complementary way. Thus, eventually, human beings pursue *falāḥ* as part of their personal objectives, but they also increase *iḥsān* amongst their fellow citizens to establish socioeconomic justice and equity in this world and to reach eternal happiness in the hereafter, as the two-dimensional utility function of

Islam suggests.[1]

The second deficiency is 'the lack of proactivity' which becomes obvious with such words as 'safeguarding', 'preservation', 'prevention' and 'protection'; all referring to what al-Ghazālī uses as '*ḥifẓ*'. Thus, *ḥifẓ* evokes a closed system of objectives that is far from being dynamic in nature and hence unable to be adaptive to, and molder of, changing circumstances. As a counter argument to this statement, Chapra advocates:

> if we wish also to ensure the sustained development and well-being of a society, the word 'safeguarding' used by al-Ghazālī in the above quotation need not necessarily be taken to imply preservation of just the *status quo* with respect to the realization of the *maqāṣid.* We safeguard when we have reached the peak of achievement. However, this is not possible for human beings in this world. There is always room for improvement. The verdict of history is that unless there is a continuous progress in their realization through a movement in the positive direction, it may not be possible to safeguard them and to sustain the society's well-being in the long-run. Stagnation will ultimately set in and lead to decline.[2]

As can be seen, Chapra supposes 'safeguarding' to be realized when the 'peak of achievement' is ereached.[3] Yet since the peak is not reachable in this world, there should always be continuous search for, and pursuit of, betterment. Thus, Chapra aims with this statement to bring back the dynamic structure of

---

[1] Mehmet Asutay, "A Political Economy Approach to Islamic Economics: Systemic Understanding for an Alternative Economic System," *Kyoto Bulletin of Islamic Area Studies,* vol. 1, No. 2 (2007), pp. 3-18; also, "Conceptualising and Locating the Social Failure of Islamic Finance: Aspirations of Islamic Moral Economy vs. the Realities of Islamic Finance," *Asian and African Studies,* Vol. 11, No. 2 (2012), pp. 93-113, at 109.

[2] Chapra, *The Islamic Vision of Development*, p. 5.

[3] Ibid.

maqāṣid under *ḥifẓ*. This approach, albeit quite optimistic, widens the scope of the concept of safeguarding; that is why he prefers using 'invigoration'[1] in lieu of this concept.

As regards the 'prevention orientedness' as being a problematic approach, 'proactivity' transcends aforementioned prevention based (*ḥifẓ* approach and its variants in the contemporary era and sustains its authenticity and vividness in every time and place without any stagnation. The proactive *maqāṣid* approach, in this sense, echoes Mawlana Jalal al-Din al-Rumi's metaphor of a drawing compass[2] according to which one leg of the compass holds still and is rooted in a certain spot statically and the other leg arcs the entire surface without causing any translocation in the former part. By making use of this metaphor, proactive *maqāṣid* framework, in the same vein, takes nourishments from the entire historical intellectual pool by utilizing numerous philosophical contributions, *ijtihāds* and theories, and concurrently reforms and keeps alive itself without any disengagement from the ontological foundations of Islam. Nevertheless, if the former leg trends multiple shifts from the original spot towards others, then there will be plenty of circles drawn, which, in turn, reveal multiple intersection sets. In customizing to *maqāṣid al-sharīʿah*, consequently, the intersection sets hold a composite of various epistemological knowledge articulations derived from different ontologies. As a result, there will be a hybrid of *maqāṣid* understanding that is far from being authentic and distinct.

Rejecting the static and reductionist understanding of *maqāṣid* Ibn al-Qayyim explains the spirit of proactive *maqāṣid* through his identification of the Sharīʿah in the following momentous words:

---

[1] Ibid., p. 8.

[2] See, Ozkan Akman, "Compass Metaphor of Mevlana in Social Studies Education," in Wenxia Wu, Erol Kocoglu, and Ozkan Akman, eds., *New Approaches in Social Studies Education (I)* (Inonu University: ISRES Publishing, 2017), pp. 97-107.

> The Sharīʿah is based on wisdom and achieving people's welfare in this life and the afterlife. Sharīʿah is all about justice, mercy, wisdom, and good. Thus, any ruling that replaces justice with injustice, mercy with its opposite, common good with mischief, or wisdom with nonsense, is a ruling that does not belong to the Sharīʿah, even if it is claimed to be so according to some interpretation.[1]

In line with this elucidation, *maqāṣid* as the essential methodology of Islamic economics should be imbibed and molded by the moral principles and values discussed above in order to sustain its proactive nature and applicability down the ages. While the two main deficiencies, *fardiyyah* and the lack of proactivity, should be dealt with through the lens of proactive *maqāṣid* understanding, it should also be acknowledged that modern critiques to al-Ghazālī claiming lack of universal objectives in his *maqāṣid* framework such as justice and freedom,[2] socioeconomic reform, women rights, and abolishing slavery,[3] research and development,[4] mostly overlook the current inclusion of these elements into al-Ghazālian *maqāṣid* as absorbed and permeated through the theoretical foundations of his *maqāṣid* insights. Leaving aside the notion of justice which connotes the social dimension, other notions are, to a large extent, gathered into *maqāṣid* discourse by some reformist Muslim scholars with the aim of universalizing the problems of the Western world. This is a major fallacy in that by being adaptive and responsive to such specific problems as appeared in different formations of societies in the same time frame, it

---

[1] Jasser Auda, *Maqāṣid al-Sharīʿah as Philosophy of Islamic Law: A Systems Approach* (London: International Institute of Islamic Thought, 2007), p. xxi.

[2] Muhammad al-Ghazali, *al-Sunnah al-Nabawiyyah Bayna Ahl al-Fiqh wa Ahl al-Ḥadīh* (Cairo: Dār al-Shurūq, 11th edn, 1996).

[3] Yasir. S. Ibrahim, "Rashid Rida and *Maqāṣid al-Sharīʿah*," *Studia Islamica*, Vols. 102-103, No. 1 (2006), pp. 157-198.

[4] Muhammad Hashim Kamali, *Maqāṣid al-Sharīʿah Made Simple* (London: International Institute of Islamic Thought, 2008).

has been transmitted into Muslim intellectual world with the same content and form.

What is worse still is to judge previous Muslim scholars by anachronist reasoning, thus charging them of having neglected or omitted such imported issues in their theorization. To give an example, environmental concerns in public policy, when compared to embracing the term in the modern period, has not been emphasized in such a manner during the intellectual debates in the Muslim history, since both Muslim governors and philosophers dealt with the protection of environment under the broader theme of socioeconomic justice and equity. When environmental problems emerged in a particular society, then it used to be considered under the more general objective of establishing justice for future generations. Thus, coming back to the main debate, 'thinking outside the box' entails an approach that transcends the ambit of conjectural considerations of *maqāṣidic* thinking; thereby *maqāṣid* has to be cleared from politically or economically biased conjectural and expediential expositions. Yet this does not mean that such issues, which are free from bias, would not be located and evaluated within *maqāṣid* framework.

Besides the two main deficiencies in al-Ghazālī's *maqāṣid* scheme itself and the reformist Muslim scholars' misinterpretation of the overall Ghazālian *maqāṣid* framework, hedging *maqāṣid* around the essential levels of the traditional classification is another problematic that must be avoided. *Iḥsān* here, as this study essentialises, has a great impact on all three levels of necessities, needs and embellishmenst to realize *maqāṣid* in every sphere of life. Instead of hierarchically classifying *maqāṣid* as essentials (*ḍarūriyyāt*), exigencies or complementary (*ḥājiyyāt*), and embellishments (*taḥsīniyyāt*), it should be considered as a complete process at the end of which real and eternal happiness is achieved in both individual and societal level, as Islamic process relates to 'becoming process' permeates around ongoing development in every aspect including *iḥsān*-oriented development.

Likewise, *iḥsān* makes everything embellished, as the term connotes, and this everlasting embellishment process is nestled, instituted and expanded across the society and does not stop with any satisfaction or fulfilment of basic needs. In vitalizing embellishments Islamic economics should aim to develop structures to advance the degree of *iḥsān* in every step of individual interaction with his surroundings (with other individuals, environment, animals, machines, *etc*.). For instance, the introduction of coffee machines in every workplace all over the world is quite functional in terms of making life easier, especially for those who always rush for their jobs or businesses. However, beyond being functional and efficient, the *iḥsāni* approach also essentializes the existence of embellishment and aestheticism in every sphere through making things 'life-enhancing'. In this manner, the famous Japanese tea ceremony reflected the aesthetic and life-enhancing nature of Japanese culture, which coheres with the *iḥsān*-based perspective. Likewise, the articulation of *maqāṣid*-oriented thinking into institutional forms has to be expanded and scattered to the three levels in a holistic way without strict lines thereto, and transitivity of each level should be yielded easily within *iḥsān* approach so that the ultimate objective can be achieved in an interacted manner.

Distinctive Features of the Proactive *Maqāṣid* Framework

Based on the fundamental principle of proactivity, which entails an embedded and all-embracing character in identifying and implementing the Sharīʿah objectives, *maqāṣid al-sharīʿah* as a discourse embraces some distinctive features through which authenticity, vividness and dynamism of Islamic developmentalism are realized. Owing to the systems approach, these distinct features can be demonstrated as follows, together with comparing that of the stationary *maqāṣid* understanding:

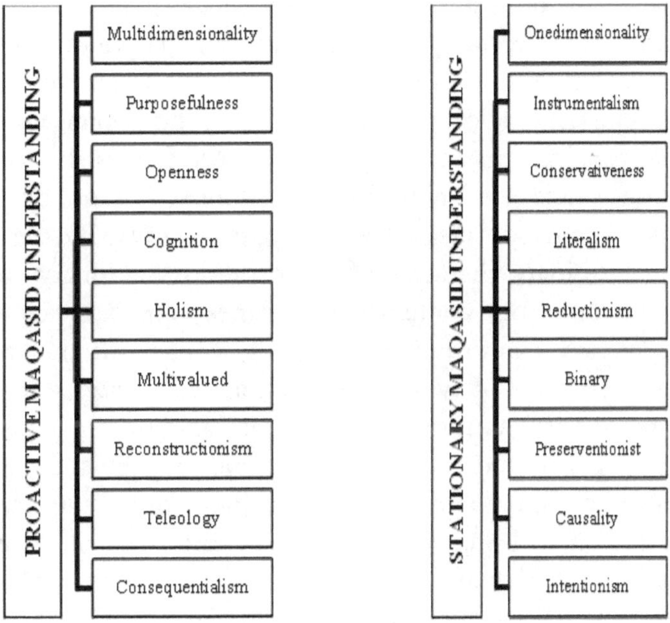

Each feature above demarcates and sheds light on the scope and substance of the proactive *maqāṣid* framework. In doing so, complementarity between each feature provides interdependency such that the scantiness of some features in the framework fades the strength of *maqāṣid.* Multidimensionality, in this sense, requires the existence of holistic, multivalued and *reconstructionist* characters to function smoothly, as opposed to the poorness of one-dimensional explanations. Therefore, in the *maqāṣid* realm, it entails conflating the level of necessities, the scope of the rulings and the level of universality simultaneously in its framework. In other words, the proactive *maqāṣid* approach should reflect the traditional classification characteraized by an *iḥsān* spirit and orientation as explained above and expand its scope to societal levels by eliminating the shortcomings posed by individuality, and also should capture the universal objectives through which particular and specific *maqāṣid* can be derived.

This perspective, explained with multidimensionality,

requires expanding the horizon of *maqāṣid*-inspired thinking by questing for different approaches and suggests pondering upon the possibility of more than one *maqāṣid* that are inherent in the related epistemological sources. However, the general tendency in internalizing *maqāṣid* into Islamic economics is towards adopting single evidence for the addressed issue by using *maṣlaḥah* in unsophisticated and pragmatic ways. By the same token, the binary character of the orthodox stationary *maqāṣid* understanding of contemporary times compels choosing between two contrasting alternatives, which are mostly the opposite far ends of two edges, such as *farḍ/ḥarām*, *ṣaḥīḥ/fāsid*, *salafi*/modernist, conservative/reformist and so on. However, the multivalued aspect urges to go beyond the zero-sum logic or black/white approach by introducing some intermediate categories that bring flexibility and transitivity in realizing *maqāṣid* identified goals. This problem, meanwhile, is not seen in the history of Islamic law, since scholars in those periods introduced intermediate categories and developed authentic views by adopting multivalued dimensions. In the case of IBF, *maqāṣid al-sharīʿah* should likewise consider financial operations by introducing multi filters amongst which the compliance to the *fiqhī* rulings constitutes only one aspect. Ideally, one would expect to achieve this goal more likely in today's post-modern world since the deconstructionist attitude of post-modernism would reveal multivalued characters in IBF. Nnevertheless, these approaches, when applied to Islamic law, still tend to be content with one-dimensional and reductionist explanations. As a result, moral objectives within IBF are mostly neglected or mentioned in an eclectic way at best.

It is an overwhelming fact that deconstructionist approaches to Islamic law applied by post-modernist Islamic scholars, contrary to the expectations, have deepened the divergence between *fiqh* and morality. More precisely, in search for *maqāṣid* of the rulings and past evidence, knowledge has been deconstructed in a right manner to crystallize the objectives, but deconstructed knowledge was decoupled from the original whole permanently and the reconstructive stage has never been reached, as it was before witnessed in the process of disciplinization of knowledge. However, the basic rationale for deconstructing knowledge would be to grasp the unseen at first sight in the whole picture with the aim of reconstructing it at the end lest it deviates from the original. Realizing *maqāṣid*, in the same vein, essentializes the complete process of deconstruction and reconstruction, as epitomized with the metaphor of drawing compass.

In order to make the entire process of deconstruction and reconstruction acting in concert, the holistic approach plays an important role here—remembering the complementarity nature of each feature emerged from *tawḥīd*—since it reminds us of the very basic idea that deconstructed and disentangled segments cannot display the whole picture on their own, but these segments rather give important expressions and understanding about it. Reductionist/partial or atomistic approaches to Islamic law, in this sense, neglect the holistic dimension of *maqāṣid al-sharīʿah*; hence it can never explain and link partial objectives within the main objectives due to relegating the entire process of deriving *maqāṣid* to the partial one.

Similarly, the idea of establishing an Islamic banking sector should be considered under the holistic objective defined by Islamic economics. In other words, the holistic approach explains IBF as an important component of Islamic economics that contributes to realize the ultimate objectives of *falāḥ* and *iḥsān*, whereas the reductionist approach treats IBF as a self-appointed and self-contained field that has its own objectives, which are subject to alter with the changing circumstances and are not necessarily connected with the ultimate objectives. One of the reflections of the latter approach implicitly suggests dealing with IBF as an isolated field, which does not necessarily aim to realize social objectives, but rather has its own financial objectives such as the everlasting passion to grow its assets and operations and exhibiting similar functions with conventional banking through being an important part of the global financial sector.

As one of the essential features of a proactive *maqāṣid* framework, purposefulness stands against the liberal notion of instrumentalism, as *maqāṣid al-sharīʿah* itself evokes a purposeful character beyond attaching an instrumental role to each dealing sepatrately. Therefore, every step in fulfilling a particular objective creates interdependent purposes, in a holistic way, complementing one another, without considering any of them as an instrumental part. In articulating purposefulness into Islamic economics, it is essential to accommodate 'substantive morality' at the core of its theorization, for the moral dimension must be embedded by its very nature of being a value-loaded system aiming to fulfil a particular objective. However, beyond purposefulness, the instrumentalist approach to morality breeds the notion of 'instrumental morality', which basically functions to deal with things as mere tools and instruments, thus eroding their essence. A good example of the instrumentalist approach to the moral dimension in Islamic economics can be given by the role of Sharīʿah experts in IBF field. Accordingly, moral issues are considered to be only an instrument in the hands of Sharīʿah experts who can decide on behalf of Islamic banking customers about the compliance of a contract to the principles of divine knowledge (*halalness*).

The purposefulness feature of *maqāṣid al-sharīʿah* brings about the issue of the tension between openness and conservativeness in approaching contemporary socioeconomic problems. As Muslim intellectuals face the challenges of establishing an authentic Muslim identity with its full characteristics in the post-modern world, two alternatives surface as a response to this situarion. One of them is adopting a conservative approach while confronted with modern scientific knowledge and its secular institutions. This approach is unable to construct the Islamic worldview in contemporary times, but rather it yearns for the same social formation of the Prophetic era to prevail again in the modern world. The openness approach, however, recognizes the existing conditions of Muslim world and aims to harmonize Islamic thought by proposing new ideas and establishing authentic institutions. In doing so, it adopts the aforementioned metaphor of the drawing compass. Forming an authentic *maqāṣid* framework, hence, necessitates the inclusion of openness character in order to get rid of anachronist expectations from the romanticized history and to allow for a dynamic and proactive thinking.

One of the aspects of the conservative approach is related to literalist or textualist interpretations of divine sources, which limits the boundaries of *maqāṣid* provisioning and undermines the burgeoning of *ijtihād* process therein. In contrast to literalism, the doctrine of *maqāṣid al-sharīʿah* revitalizes the cognitive aspects of Islamic law by suggesting a distinction between revealed knowledge and its cognitive parts that allow for re-functionalizing *ijtihād* in contemporary times.

A teleology-causality debate reflects another important aspect of the proactive *maqāṣid al-sharīʿah* framework. In this sense, as mentioned before, modern scientific thinking experienced a serious shift from teleology to causality through the essentialization of causal reasoning by introducing the cause-and-effect dialect which entails causality as the central logic of thinking. Thus, teleological adoption in any theory was regarded as metaphysical and hence completely rejected as irrelevant.

By acknowledging the distortions of causal positioning, *maqāṣid al-sharīʿah* suggests recourse to teleology by embedding 'theologically' defined developmentalist objectives. In this respect, modern scientific methodology that entails the causal way of thinking has to be replaced with teleology, which explains a phenomenon in terms of its 'purpose'.

Lastly, proactivity suggests that the intentionalist limits of presenting *maqāṣid* conceptions can be overcome by introducing consequentialism. To put it in more precise terms, intentionalist and consequentialist crosschecking simultaneously determines the framework of *maqāṣid* through establishing harmony between them. In the case of IBF, the observed mimicry and hybridization adopted by Islamic finance can be overcome, and authenticity can be achieved through this crosschecking system, since form-based interpretation and evaluation of the practices of Islamic finance cannot go beyond intentionalist limits and fails once consequentialist checking is applied.

Conclusion

Establishing authentic institutions to redesign prevailing social formations of a society is not a fledgling phenomenon peculiar to the post-modern era. Contrarily, every society somehow has faced the challenge of finding out the ways to embed shared norms, values and principles into its social, economic and political institutions. The idea of Islamic economics is such an attempt that has emerged in the post-modern atmosphere with an aim of establishing economic institutions that are subordinated to the whole objective of achieving a good life (*ḥayāt ṭayyibah*) from an Islamic perspective. Successful or not, the experience with and discussions under Islamic economics and finance ascertained that the initial concern with theory making should be on methodological issues, for knowledge can only be authenticated through a rigorous methodology.

In addressing the methodological dimension of Islamic economics, *maqāṣid al-sharīʿah* has almost been neglected in Islamic economics literature, although it has great potential to function as an essential methodology. Instead, it was made subservient to a justification mechanism engineered for the Islamic finance sector. Controversial and disputable issues within the sector have been resolved through a symbolic use of *maqāṣid* and *maṣlaḥah*, whereby Islamic finance would display a smooth parallel to mainstream financial progress. It is not surprising, in this regard, that *maqāṣid* perceptions of governments, the Sharīʿah scholars and some academics favoring self-regulated market economy are all homogenous. Therefore, an economic system which is conceived to reflect Islamic notions but in fact is not much different from capitalist framework can only reveal a *maqāṣid* understanding bounded with methodological individualism, and hence fails to go beyond the concern of utility maximization, essentialization of price mechanism, market exchange and efficient use of resources.

Beyond instrumental and eclectic approaches, theoretical grounds of Islamic economics should be re-examined in light of the proactive *maqāṣid al-sharīʿah* framework with its dimensions elaborated in the previous section. By so doing, the rationale behind the failure of realizing Islamic developmentalism in post-colonial Muslim nations can better be explained, since the proactive *maqāṣid* approach envisages a totally different philosophy, methodology and approach in respect of economic and scial development considerations when compared to existing applications of *maqāṣid* based on methodological individualism.

Finally, it must be reiterated, morality plays a central role in the entire process of knowledge authentication through *maqāṣid al-sharīʿah*, while the current use of *maqāṣid* in IBF demonstrates that it has been relegated to *fiqhī* injunctions and used as an instrument to legalise particular product and operation in a legalistically rational manner. This runs against the expectation that *maqāṣid al-sharīʿah* should constitute the essential base of methodology for Islamic moral economy, as deductive reasoning based on Islamic ontology and also historical practice suggests that we should constitute Islamic moral economy beyond the narrowly defined Islamic economics, as the latter refers to *fiqh* while the former is constituted through essential and proactive *maqāṣid.* Thus, substantive morality should be embedded through *maqāṣid* in the theoretical underpinnings of Islamic economics to generate Islamic moral economy to fit into *maqāṣid* expectations as a distinct system of economics,[1] so that the *maqāṣid* objective of 'whatever is done should be interest of human well-being' should be achieved.

This requires interpersonal and social relations not to be merely relegated to economic relations, but economics and finance should be embedded into norms and values of society through locating ethico-economic relationships across each system, so that morality would be articulated beyond impersonal market environment. Thus, *maqāṣid* or essentialization of human well-being in economic and financial activities takes place by motivating economic forces for economic and human development, which constitutes a base for the articulation of economic and financial choices to be linked to their 'consequences' beyond mere 'intentionalism'.

[1] Mehmet Asutay, "Islamic Moral Economy as the Foundation of Islamic Finance," in Valentino Cattelan, ed., *Islamic Finance in Europe: Towards a Plural Financial System* (Cheltenham: Edward Elgar, 2013), pp. 55-68.

Notes on the Contributors

Akhtarzaite Abdul Aziz is currently an assistant professor at the Department of Fiqh and Uṣūl al-Fiqh, Kulliyyah of Islamic Revealed Knowledge and Human Sciences, International Islamic University Malaysia (IIUM). She graduated from IIUM in LLB in 1995 and completed LLB (Shariah) in 1996. She also holds a Master's Degree (2000) and a PhD (2005) in Fiqh and usul al-fiqh from the same university. Her doctoral thesis written in Arabic on the the theory of *dharā'iʿ* and its application in modern financial transactions was published by Dār al Fikr, Damascus in 2008. Her research interest is modern issues in Islamic jurisprudence particularly in Islamic Banking, Islamic Capital Market and Takaful. She presented papers in several international conferences, the most recent as invited speaker in the First Salalah International Forum on Islamic Finance in Salalah, the Sultanate of Oman, August 2017. She has also contributed papers to international official bodies, such her paper on "Islamic Securities and its Modern Application and Trading" submitted and discussed in the Fiqh Academy Conference April 2009 held in Sharjah, UAE. She is currently Chairman of MBSB Shariah Advisory Committee, Chairman of Great Eastern Takaful Shariah Advisory Committee and a member of

Saadiq Standard Chartered Shariah Advisory Committee.

Anke Iman Bouzenita is an associate professor at the Department of Islamic Sciences, Sultan Qaboos University, Muscat, Oman. Born and educated in Germany, she holds a PhD from Ruhr-Universität Bochum in Islamic Studies, 2001. Dr. Bouzenita lectured and researched in Islamic Studies at the University of Bochum, Germany (1998-2001), the University of Batna, Algeria (2002-2004), the International Islamic University Malaysia, Kuala Lumpur (2004-2012) and Sultan Qaboos University, Oman (2013- date). She has published a number of books and many journal articles and has contributed papers to comferences and seminars in different countries. Her research interests include Islamic Bioethics, History of Islamic Law, Orientalism and International Relations. She can be reached at *bouzenita@squ.edu.om*.

Asyraf Wajdi Dusuki served IIUM as an Assistant Professor of the Kulliyyah of Economics and Management Sciences, the International Shariah Research Academy for Islamic Finance as Head of Research Affairs, and International Centre for Education in Islamic Finance as an Associate Professor. Throughout his academic service, he was known for his expertise in Islamic banking and finance. He was also the Chairman of the Shariʿah Advisory Committee and member of the Board of Director of Affin Islamic Bank Malaysia, member of the Shariʿah Advisory Committee of AIA Takaful Malaysia, Visiting Professor at the Malaysia University Kelantan and Shariah consultant and advisor to several financial institutions and advisory firms including London-based Mortgage Company Chain Mender Limited, Singapore-based IFIS Business Advisory Pte Ltd and AFTAAS Shariah Advisory Sdn. Bhd. He holds a Bachelor degree in Accounting from International Islamic University Malaysia, MSc. in Islamic Economics, Banking and Finance and Ph. D. in Islamic Banking and Finance from Loughborough University, United Kingdom. He has published in numerous international and local refereed academic journals and presented papers at both local and international conferences including London, Bahrain, Berlin, Dubai, Tehran, Jakarta, Singapore and Brunei. He also conducts training in Islamic banking and finance related areas to officers of Central Bank of Malaysia, banking practitioners, government officials and public. Malaysian politician. From July 2015 to May 2018 he was senator and Deputy Minister in the Prime Minister's Department of Malaysia in charge of Islamic affairs.

Bernard G. Weiss was professor of languages and literature at the University of Utah. He has an extensive publication record and is recognized as one of the foremost scholars in Islamic law, Islamic theology, Islamic philosophy, Islamic political thought, Arab history and Muslim discussions of linguistics and the origin of language. Weiss received his PhD from Princeton University in 1966 for his dissertation on "Language in Orthodox Muslim Thought: A Study of *waḍʿ al-lughah* and its Development". In addition to scores of articles and conference and seminar papers, Prof. Weiss has authored and co-authored a large number of books. They include *Studies in Islamic Law and Society; Religion and Law: Biblical-judaic and Islamic Perspectives; Studies in Islamic Legal Theory; A Survey of Arab History*; *The Spirit of Islamic Law; The Law Applied: Contextualizing the Islamic Sharīʿa; The Search for God's Law: Islamic Jurisprudence in the Writings of Sayf al-Dīn al-Āmidī.* Dr. Weiss died in February 2018.

Ibrahim Mohamed Zein is currently a Professor of Islamic Studies and Comparative Religion, College of Islamic Studies, Hamad Bin Khalifa University in Qatar. He was the former dean of the Faculty of Islamic Revealed Knowledge and Human Sciences and the International Institute of Islamic Thought and Civilization at the International Islamic University Malaysia (IIUM), Kuala Lumpur, in which he worked from 1993 to 2016. Prof. Zein obtained a B.A. (Hons) in Philosophy from the University of Khartoum in

1980, Master of Arts in Philosophy from the University of Khartoum in 1984, Master of Arts in Religion from Temple University in 1986 and a Doctorate of Philosophy in Religion from the same university in 1989. He published numerous articles, book chapters and book reviews. Through his academic administration of Islamic Studies programs, supervision of postgraduate research and teaching he has made a definite impact on the field. His first book was published in 1983 entitled *al-Sulṣah fī Fikr al-Muslimīn.* His research interests conver areas such comparative religion, legal philosophy, and ethics and values. He has to his credit a high score of journal articles and conference papers.

Isa Yilmaz is currently a PhD Scholar in Islamic Economics and Finance, at Durham Centre for Islamic Economics and Finance, Durham University Business School, UK. He has a BSc in Economics and Management from the Istanbul Bilgi University (Turkey) and BSc on the same subject from the University of London International Program (UK). He also completed his MSc in Islamic Finance, University of Durham. His PhD research explores novel issues in Islamic economics discourse, including constructing Islamic economic development, political economy of Islamic finance through conceptualising the financialization of Islamic finance sector, and *maqasid al-Shariah* and its application in Islamic economics as a methodology. Isa's research interests are on Islamic political economy and public choice, Islamic moral economy, Islamic banking and finance, *Maqasid al-Shari'ah* and social welfare, and political economy of developmentalism.

Louay M. Safi is a professor of political science and Islamic philosophy at Hamad bin Khalifa University (Qatar) and senior fellow at the Center for Muslim Christian Understanding, Georgetown University. He served as the editor of *American Journal of Islamic Social Sciences* (2001-2003), president of the Association of American Muslim Scientists

(2000-2003). He worked for many years at the Political Science Department, International Islamic University, Malaysia where he held a number of academic adminditrative positions. He is also the co-founder and first chair of the Syrian American Council (2005-2011), and co-founder and former board member of the Center for the Study of Islam and Democracy (1999-2007). He writes and lectures on issues relating to democracy, human rights, leadership, American Muslims, and Islam and the West. He is the author of nineteen books and numerous papers, including *al-Sharīʿah aw al-Mujatmaʿ* (2017), *The Qur'anic Narrative* (2009), and *Tensions and Transitions in the Muslim word* (2003).

Mehmet Asutay is a professor of Middle Eastern & Islamic Political Economy and Finance at the Durham University Business School; Director of the Durham Centre in Islamic Economics and Finance; Director for MSc in Islamic Finance & MSc in Islamic Finance and Management programmes, and Director of the Durham Islamic Finance Summer School. Asutay's teaching, research, publication, and supervision of research is all in Islamic moral economy, Islamic finance and banking, Islamic political economy, Islamic governance and management and the Middle Eastern political economies. His research articles interest have been published in various international academic journals and professional magazines. He has also published and edited a number of books on various aspects of Islamic moral economy and Islamic finance. Asutay's recent research includes the construction of Islamic moral economy and Islamic political economy, both of which are considered as incomplete projects since the early 1970s. Professor Asutay works on developing the discourse on 'social and developmentalist failure' of Islamic banking and finance in relation to the expressed ideals of Islamic moral economy by essentialising sharing, participatory and collaborative economy nature of Islamic finance. He is also researching the political economy of Islamic finance. Mehmet is also involved in empirical research in various aspects and dynamism of Islamic banking and finance.

Mohamed El-Tahir El-Mesawi is a professor at the Kulliyyah of Islamic Revealed Knowledge and Human Sciences, International Islamic University, Malaysia, IIUM in which has been working since 1994. He obtained a PhD from the Department of Usuluddin and Comparative Religion, IIUM (2004) for his dissertation on the topic of *maqāṣid al-sharīʿah* and the foundations of human society. He holds an MA in Islamic studies from the same university (1994) and a BA in economics from Oumdurman Islamic University, Sudan, 1988. Prior to that, he studied English language and literature at Ecole Normale Supérieure of Tunis, and philosophy and sociology at the University of Dhahr el Mahraz, Fez, Morocco. El-Mesawi has taught courses on *uṣūl al-fiqh*, *maqāṣid al-sharīʿah*, Islamization of knowledge, and contemporary Islamic political thought both at the undergraduate and postgraduate levels. He has presented papers in many conferences and seminars and published numerous articles, book chapters and book reviews and over ten books. His authored and translated books include, among others, *A Muslim Theory of Human Society; The Qur'anic Phenomenon; The Question of Ideas in the Muslim Word, A Treatise on Maqāṣid al-Sharīʿah.* El-Mesawi served as editor for the journals of *Islāmiyyat al-Marʿifah* and *at-Tajdid* and is member of the advisory boards for a number of journals. He also served as member of Sharīʿah committees for some Islamic financial institutions. His research interests include of Islamic legal theory, *maqāṣid al-sharīʿah*, values and social change, history of ideas, Islamic movements and reform, Islam, modernity and globalization.

Monzer Kahf is a professor of Islamic economics and finance at the College of Islamic Studies, Hamad bin Khalifah University, Doha, Qatar. He received his PhD in Economics from University of Utah in 1975. He has made significant contributions to Islamic economics and finance. His contributions include being a collaborating expert at the Islamic Fiqh Academy, IMF Consultant on Islamic Finance, and Resource person for IslamOnline.net and On Islam. Professor Kahf also served as the Head of Research in IRTI-IDB, Senior Research Economist, Director of Finance in the Islamic Society of North America, and a few other positions. He is the author of 35 books, more than 75 published articles and scores of conference papers and encyclopedia entries on *awqāf*, *zakāh*, Islamic finance and banking and other areas of Islamic economics.

Nurdianawati Irwani Abdullah is an associate professor in laws and Shari'ah at the Department of Finance, Kulliyyah of Economics and Management Sciences, IIUM. She is also member of the Shariʿah Advisory Board of AmMetlife Takaful Berhad and Shariʿah advisor to Khairul Anuar & Associates. Previously, she was the chairperson of the Shariʿah Advisory Board of Standard Chartered Saadiq Bank Malaysia, Research Fellow at the International Shariʿah Research Academy in Islamic Finance (ISRA) focussing in Takaful and Visiting Professor at the Malaysia University Kelantan. She has been serving the Association of Shari'ah Advisors in Islamic Finance Malaysia (ASAS) and IIUM Institute of Islamic banking and Finance as a Board member since its establishment. She is currently a member of the International Council of Islamic Finance Educators (ICIFE). Her areas of expertise cover Islamic law of banking, Shariʿah law, Fiqh Muʿamalat, Takaful, Corporate Governance, Islamic Capital Market, Business Law and Commercial Law. Dr. Irwani holds an LL.B (Shariʿah) and Master of Comparative Laws (MCL) from the International Islamic University Malaysia, and a Ph. D. in Islamic Banking and Finance from Loughborough University, United Kingdom. She has produced many journal articles and conference papers in the area of Islamic banking and finance, Takaful and Islamic commercial law. She also conducts training programs in areas related to legal and Shariʿah issues in Islamic financial products and Takaful. Apart from that, she is directly involved in the legal working committee for the Ministry of Domestic Trade, Cooperatives and Consumerism together with the Association of Islamic Banks of Malaysia (AIBIM) in respect to the legal reforms. Given her involvement and contribution to the Islamic finance education, research and consultancy, she was listed as among the World 50 influential women in Islamic Business and Finance 2017 by the Islamic Finance Review Special Report (ISFIRE).

Robert Dickson Crane started his professional career at Harvard Law School in 1956, where he received a Doctorate of Laws (J.D.) in comparative jurisprudence. This lifelong interest originated in the culture was passed on to him by his great-grandmother, who spoke Cherokee as her native language and helped to raise him as a custodian of the Cherokee Nation's indigenous religion borrowed in 1310 A.C. from the Mali Empire in Africa. At the age of 20 in 1949, in order to study the concept of justice and the practice of injustice, he joined the underground resistance movement in Eastern Europe and was perhaps the only person to have escaped twice from Stalin's Gulag Archipelago. In September, 1962, he was one of the four co-founders of the Center for Strategic and International Studies, Washington's most influential think-tank, as an expert on totalitarianism. In January, 1963, as a result of his publications there, Richard Nixon appointed him as his principal advisor on foreign policy and on Islam and interfaith cooperation. In January 1969, Nixon appointed him as Henry Kissinger's Deputy for Planning in the National Security Council, but this resulted in an existential clash of civilizations between Kissinger's paradigm of power as the ultimate foreign policy goal and Dr. Crane's indigenous paradigm of compassionate justice. Later in 1981, Dr. Crane was appointed by President

Reagan as the U.S. Ambassador to the United Arab Emirates. In 1982, Dr. Crane became a full-time Islamic activist as Director of Daʿwa at the Islamic Center in Washington, D.C., and Director of the Dialogue Commission in the Interfaith Conference of Metropolitan Washington. Since 1985, Dr. Crane has been associated in various capacities with the International Institute of Islamic Thought (IIIT) and has published books, monographs, and almost monthly articles as head of his own think-tanks, beginning in 1992 with The Center for Civilizational Renewal and its book, *Shaping the Future: Challenge and Response.* In the late 1990s he was Managing Editor of the *Middle East Affairs Journal* at the United Association for Studies and Research. From 2011 to 2015 he was a professor at Qatar Faculty of Islamic Studies and Director of its Center for the Study of Islamic Thought and Muslim Societies. He is currently the Editor-in-Chief of *Armonia* (www.armoniajournal.org), and Chairman of its sponsor, the Holistic Education Center for Civilizational Renewal.

Sherman Jackson is the King Faisal Chair of Islamic Thought and Culture, and professor of Religion and American Studies and Ethnicity at the University of Southern California (USC). He was formerly the Arthur F. Thurnau Professor of Near Eastern Studies and visiting professor of law and professor of Afro-American Studies at the University of Michigan (Ann Arbor). Dr. Jackson received his Ph.D. from the University of Pennsylvania and has taught at the University of Texas at Austin, Indiana University, Wayne State University and the University of Michigan. From 1987 to 1989, he served as Executive Director of the Center of Arabic Study Abroad in Cairo, Egypt. Dr. Jackson is a co-founder, Core Scholar, and member of the Board of Trustees of the American Learning Institute for Muslims (ALIM), an academic institution where scholars, professionals, activists, artists, writers, and community leaders come together to develop strategies for the future of

Islam in the modern world. Additionally, Dr. Jackson is a former member of the Fiqh Council of North America, former President of the Shariʿah Scholars Association of North America (SSANA) and a past trustee of the North American Islamic Trust (NAIT). He has contributed to several publications including the *Washington Post-Newsweek* blog, *On Faith*, and the *Huffington Post.* Professor Jackson is listed by the Religion Newswriters Foundation's ReligionLink as among the top ten experts on Islam in America and was named among the 500 most influential Muslims in the world by the Royal Islamic Strategic Studies Center in Amman, Jordan and the Prince Alwaleed Bin Talal Center for Muslim-Christian Understanding. His works include *Islamic Law and the State: The Constitutional Jurisprudence of Shihab al-Din al-Qarafi*, *On the Boundaries of Theological Tolerance in Islam: Abû Hâmid al-Ghazâlî's Faysal al-Tafriqa*, *Islam and the Blackamerican: Looking Toward the Third Resurrection*, *Islam and the Problem of Black Suffering*, *Sufism for Non-Sufis? Ibn Ata' Allah's Tâj al-'Arûs*, *Initiative to Stop the Violence: Sadat's Assassins* and the *Renunciation of Political Violence.*

Wael B. Hallaq is a renowned scholar of Islamic law, with numerous contributions to the field of Islamic legal studies and intellectual history. He is currently Avalon Foundation Professor in the Humanities at Columbia University, USA which he joined in 2009. His primary interests include the epistemic institutional ruptures created by the onset of modernity and the many socio-politico-historical forces that come with it, and the intellectual history and development of Orientalism. Hallaq is also concerned with the development of Islamic traditions of logic, legal theory, and substantive law along with the interdependent systems within these traditions. Hallaq's writings have explained the structural dynamics of legal change in pre-modern law and have recently been moving in the direction of asserting the centrality of moral theory to understanding Islamic law, past and present. He is the author of a dozen books, including *The Origins and Evolution of Islamic Law* (2005), *Sharīʿa: Theory, Practice, Transformations* (2009), *An Introduction to Islamic Law* (2009), *The Impossible State* (2013), and most recently *Restating Orientalism*, published in July 2018 by Columbia University Press. He's also edited or co-edited many books and has published numerous articles. His works have been translated into several languages including Arabic, Hebrew, Indonesian, Italian, Japanese, Persian, and Turkish. He joined McGill University as an assistant professor in Islamic law in 1985, after receiving his Ph.D. from the University of Washington in 1983. He became a full professor in 1994 and was named a James McGill Professor in Islamic law in 2005.

Select Bibliography

Abderrahmne, Taha, "Mashrūʿ Tajdīd ʿIlmī li-Mabḥath Maqāṣid al-Sharīʿah," *al-Muslim al-Muʿāṣir*, vol. 26, No. 103 (1422/2002).

Abdul Ghafar Ismail *et al.*, eds., *Maqāṣid al-Sharīʿah based index of Socio-Economic Development* (Gombak, Malaysia: IIUM Press, 2018).

AbuSulayman, AbdulHamid A., *Marital Discord: Recapturing the Full Islamic Spirit of Human Dignity Through the Higher Objectives of Islamic Law* (Herndon/London: The International Institute of Islamic Thought, 2nd edn, 1423AH/2003CE).

ʿĀlim, Yūsuf Ḥāmid al-, *al-Maqāṣid al-ʿĀmmah li Al-Sharīʿah al-Islāmiyyah* (Herndon, Virginia: International Institute of Islamic Thought, 1412/1991).

Alwan, Fahmi Muhammad, *al-Qiyam al-Ḍarūriyyah wa Maqāṣid al-Tashrīʿ al-Islāmī* (Cairo: al-Hay'ah al-Miṣriyyah al-ʿĀmmah li al-Kitāb, 1989).

Āmidī, ʿAlī ibn Muḥammad al-, *al-Iḥkām fī Uṣūl al-Aḥkām,* ed. Abdul Razzaq Afifi (Riyadh: Dār al-Ṣamīʿī, 1st edn, 1424/2003).

Ansari, Farid al-, *al-Muṣṭalaḥ al-Uṣūlī ʿinda al-Shāṭibī* (Cairo: Dār al-Assalām, 1st edn, 1431/2010).

Atiya, Gamal Eldin, *Towards Realization of the Higher Intents of Islamic Law, Maqāṣid al-Sharīʿah: A Functional Approach*, trans. Nancy

Roberts (Herndon, Virginia: The International Insttitute of Islamic Thought, 1428/2007).

Auda, Jasser, *Maqāṣid al-Sharīʿah as Philosophy of Islamic Law: A Systems Approach* (London: International Institute of Islamic Thought, 2007).

Bagby, Ihsan Abdul-Wajid, *Utility in Classical Islamic Law: The Concept of Maṣlaḥah* in *Uṣūl al-Fiqh*, unpublished Ph.D. thesis (the University of Michigan, 1986).

Bouhannach, Noura, *Maqāṣid al-Sharīʿah ʿinda al-Shāṭibī wa Ta'ṣīl al-Akhlāq fī al-Fikr al-ʿArabī al-Islāmī* (Algiers & Beirut: Manshūrāt Ḍifāf, 1st edn., 1433/2012).

Chahid, Elhassen, *al-Khiṭāb al-Maqāṣidī al-Muʿāṣir: Murājaʿah wa Taqwīm* (Beirut/Riyadh: Markaz Nama, 2013).

Chapra, Muhammad Umer, *The Islamic Vision of Development in the Light of Maqāṣid al-Sharīʿah* (Herndon/London: The International Institute of Islamic Thought, 1429/2008).

Ezzati, A., *Islam and Natural Law* (London: Islamic College for Advanced Studies Press, 1st edn, 2002).

Fasi, Allal al-, *Maqāṣid al-Sharīʿah al-Islāmiyyah wa Makārimuhā*, ed. Ismail l-Hassani (Cairo: Dār al-Salam, 1st edn, 1432/2011).

Ghazālī, Abū Ḥāmid Muḥammad ibn Muḥammad al-, *al-Mustaṣfā min ʿIlm al-Uṣūl,* ed. Muhammad Sulayman al-Ashqar (Beirut: Mu'assassat al-Risālah, 1st edn, 1417/1997).

Hallaq, Wael B., *A History of Islamic legal Theories* (Cambridge, UK: Cambridge University Press,

Hallaq, Wael B., *Sharīʿa: Theory, Practice, Transformations* (Cambridge: Cambridge University Press, 2009).

Hamid, Eltigani Abdelgadir, *The Qur'an and Politics* (London & Washington: The International Institute of Islamic Thought, 1416/1995).

Hassani, Ismail al-, *Naẓariyat al-Maqāṣid ʿinda al-Imām Muḥammad al-*

Ṭāhir Ibn ʿĀshūr (Washington: The International Institute of Islamic Thought, 1425/1995).

Ibn Ashur, Muhammad al-Tahir, *Maqāṣid al-Sharīʿah al-Islāmiyyah,* ed. Mohamed El-Tahir El-Mesawi, (Amman: Dār al-Nafaes, 4th rev. edn, 1440/2019).

Ibn Ashur, Muhammad al-Tahir, *Treatise on Maqāṣid al-Sharīʿah*, trans. Mohamed El-Tahir El-Mesawi (London & Washington: The International Institute of Islamic Thought 1427/2006).

Ibn ʿAbd al-Salām, ʿIzz al-Dīn ʿAbd al-ʿAzīz, *al-Qawāʿid al-Kubrā* known as *Qawāʿid al-Aḥkām fī Iṣlāḥ al-Anām*, ed. Nazih Hammad & Othman Jumʿah Dumayriyya (Damasucs: Dār al-Qalam, 1st edn, 1421/2000).

Juwaynī, Ḍiyā' al-Dīn Abū al-Maʿālī ʿAbd al-Malik b. ʿAbd Allāh b. Yūsuf al-, *al-Ghayyāthī: Ghiyyāth al-Umam fī Iltiyath al-Ẓulam,* ed. Abdul-Azim al-Deeb (Jeddah: Dār al-Mihāj, 3rd edn, 1432/2011).

Kamali, Muhammad Hashim, *Principles of Islamic Jurisprudence* (Petaling Jaya, Malaysia: Ilmiah Publishers, 2001).

Masud, Muhammad Khalid, *Shāṭibī's Philosophy of Islamic Law* (Kuala Lumpur: Islamic Book Trust, 2005).

Mesawi, Mohamed El-Tahir El-, "Human Nature and the Universality of Shariah: Fitrah and Maqasid al-Shariah in the Works of Shah Wali Allah and Ibn 'shur," *Al Shajarah*, vol. 14, No. 2 (2014).

Mili, Mahdi, "A Structural Model for Human Development, Does *Maqāṣid al-Sharīʿah* Matter!," *Islamic Economics Studies,* vol. 22, No. 2 (2014).

Najjar, Abdel Majid al-, *Maqāṣid al-Sharīʿah bi-Abʿād Jadīdah* (Beirut: Dar al-Gharb al-Isami, 2006).

Seyyed Hossein Nasr, *The Heart of Islam: Enduring Values for Humanity* (New York: HarlperCollins Publishers, 2002).

Nassery, Idris, Ahmed, Rumee & Tatari, Muna, eds., *The Objectives of*

Islamic Law: The Promises and Challenges of the Maqāṣid al-Sharīʿa (Lanham, Maryland: Lexington Books, 2018).

Nyazee, Imran Ahsan Khan, *Theories of Islamic Law: The Methodology of Ijtihād* (Kuala Lumpur: The Other Press, 2002).

Opwis, Felicitas, *Maṣlaḥah and the Purpose of the Law: Islamic Discourse on Legal Change from the 4th/10th to 8th/14th Century* (Leiden/Boston: Brill, 2010).

Qahtani, Musfir bin Ali al-, *Understanding Maqāṣid al-Sharīʿah: A Contemporary Perspective* (Herndon, Virginia: International Institute of Islamic Thought, 1436/2015).

Raquib, Amana, *Islamic Ethics of Technology: An Objectives' (Maqāṣid) Approach* (Kuala Lumpur: The Other Press, 2015).

Raysuni, Ahmad al-, *Imām al-Shāṭibī's Theory of the Higher Objectives and Intents of Islamic Law,* trans. from the Arabic by Nancy Roberts (London-Washington: The International Institute of Islamic Thought, 1427/2006).

Raysuni, Ahmad al-, *al-Kulliyyāt al-Asāsiyyah li al-Sharīʿah al-Islāmiyyah* (Cairo: Dar al-Kalimah, 2013).

Shāṭibī, Abū Isḥāq Ibrāhīm ibn Mūsā al-, *al-Muwāfaqāt fī Uṣūl al-Sharīʿah,* ed. Abd Allah Draz et al (Beirut: Dār al-Kutub al-ʿIlmiyyah, 1st edn., 1424/2004).

Shāṭibī, Abū Isḥāq Ibrāhīm ibn Mūsā al-, *The Reconciliation of the Fundamentals of Islamic Law: al-Muwāfaqāt fī Uṣūl al-Sharīʿa,* vols. 1 & 2, trans. Imran Ahsan Khan Nyazee (Reading: Garnet Publishing, 2011 & 2014).

Saghir, Abdelamjid al-, *al-Fikr al-Uṣūli wa Ishkāliyat al-Sulṭah al-ʿIlmiyyah fī al-Islām: Qirāʾah fī Nashaʾt Uṣūl al-Fiqh wa Maqāṣid al-Sharīʿah* (Beirut: Dar al-Muntakhab al-Arabi, 1st edn, 1415/1994).

Siddiqi, Muhammad Nejatullah, *Riba, Bank Interest and the Rationale of its Prohibition* (Jeddah: Islamic Research and Training Institute, 2004b).

Turabi, Hassan al-, *Qaḍāyā al-Tajdīd: Naḥwa Manhaj Uṣūlī* (Khartoum: Institute of Research and Social Studies, 1411/1990).

Ṭūfī, Najm al-Dīn al-, *Risālah fī Riʿāyat al-Maṣaḥah*, ed. Ahmad Abdulhamid al-Sayih (Cairo: al-Dār al-Miṣriyyah al-Lubnāniyyah, 1413/1993), pp. 25-48.

Ṭūfī, Najm al-Dīn al-, *Risālah fī Riʿāyat al-Maṣaḥah*, ed. Ahmad Abdulhamid al-Sayih (Cairo: al-Dār al-Miṣriyyah al-Lubnāniyyah, 1413/1993).

Weiss, Bernard G., ed., *Studies in Islamic Legal Theory* (Leiden/Boston/Köln: Brill, 2002).

Weiss, Bernard G., *The Search for God's Law: Islamic Jurisprudence in the Writings of Sayf al-Dīn al-Āmidī* (Salt Lake City: University of Utah Press & Herndon, Virginia: The International Institute of Islamic Thought, revised edition, 2010).

Weiss, Bernard G., *The Spirit of Islamic Law* (Athens, USA & London: The University of Georgia Press, 1998).

Index

A

ʿabath, 326, 328, 344
Abbasid, 206
  Dynasties, 211
Abdel Majid al-Najjar, xi, 395
Abdellah Jarbuʿ, 261, 262
Abdel-Malik al-Jaʿalī, 262
Abdel-Rahim, 265, 266
ʿAbdin Archives, 247
Abdul Rahman al-Sanad, 305, 306
Abdul Sabour Marzouq, 297, 303
Abdul Hamid Abu Sulayman, 173
Abdullah al-Judayʿ, 351
Abū Hurayrah, 229, 236
Abū Saʿīd al-Khudrī, 236
Abkār al-Afkār, 2
abrogation, 167, 173, 191
abstract
  judgments, 112
  universals, xix, 111
Abu Grun, 258, 260, 262, 263, 264, 268, 269
academy, xv, 96
ʿādah (course of things), 13, 72, 178
ʿādāt, 160
Adam
  Children of, 38
Adam Smith, 400, 404
ʿadl (justice), 249, 356, 366
Afghanistan, 173
  Sharīʿah law, 189
  State, 208
African, 115, 179, 244, 245, 258, 272, 286, 379, 389, 406
  Americans, 179
  continent, 286
Afro-Asian reformers, 148
Afrocentrism, 111
aggregate of proofs, 107
ahdāf, ix
ahl al-dhimmah, 135
  laws, 135
ahl al-kitāb (People of the Book), 258, 259
AIDS, 286
aḥkām (commands), 53, 170, 194, 258, 347
  aḥkām ahl al-dhimmah (the Rules of the Protected People), 258
  aḥkām kulliyah (universal rules), 194
aḥsan taqwīm (best of moulds), 166
aḥwāl al-tashrīʿ, 67, 351
Akhbaris, 162, 181
akhlāq (morality and ethics), 223
al bayʿ al-ʾājil (deferred payment sale), 318, 319
al-ahkām al-salṭāniyyah, 271
alcohol abuse, xx, 117
al-ḥaqq (the persistent), 130, 267, 268, 269
al-ḥaqq al-mukhtār (choice of the jurists), 130

al-ibāḥah al-aṣliyyah, 370
al-ḥikmah al-mutaʿāliyah, 184
al-ittibāʿ (following of the tradition), 270
al-kulliyyāt al- ḍarūriyyah (five fundamental universals), 356
ʿAlī b. Abī Ṭālib, 162
Allal al-Fasī, 66
all-purpose principle, 66, 67, 70, 88
al-maṣāliḥ al-mursalah, 129, 226, 298
al-Murshid al-Muʿīn ʿalā al-Ḍarūrī min ʿUlūm al-Dīn, 112
al-ʿadālah al-ijtimāʿiyyah (social justice), 265
al-ʿillah al-manṣūṣ ʿalayhā, 5
al-sunnah al-zawjiyah, 296
altruism, 230, 403
al-uṣūl al-khamsah, xii
al-Ṭuruq al-Ḥukmiyyah fī al-Siyāsah al-Sharʿiyyah, 105
al-Wāthiq Billāh, 202
amānah (trust), xxv, 40, 229, 239, 296, 339, 341, 428
  hand contracts, 341
  trusteeship, 239, 296
America, 30, 114, 115, 118, 164, 165, 166, 184, 425, 428
  Civil War, 158
  converts, 179
  Indians, 155
  Revolution, 165
American
  Classical, 171
Āmidī, Abū al-Ḥasan ʿAlī b. Abī ʿAlī Sayf al-Dīn al-, x, xvi, 1, 2, 3, 4, 6, 8, 9, 11, 12, 13, 14, 16, 18, 20, 29, 72, 126, 225, 287, 421, 431, 435
Amina Lawal, 189
ʿāmm (general), ix, xi, xiv, xix, xxiii, 7, 15, 20, 29, 35, 42, 47, 49, 53, 54, 55, 56, 58, 61, 63, 66, 67, 69, 71, 79, 80, 81, 85, 87, 91, 96, 104, 113, 114, 128, 131, 133, 136, 137, 140, 144, 145, 172, 178, 189, 191, 192, 194, 195, 199, 203, 219, 232, 234, 236, 243, 246, 260, 262, 263, 267, 268, 270, 273, 274, 275, 288, 289, 291, 305, 312, 319, 322, 327, 347, 354, 355, 356, 357, 359, 361, 363, 370, 374, 375, 376, 378, 384, 385, 409, 412
ʿAmr b. al-ʿAlā', 100
ʿAmr b. ʿUbayd, 100
analogical
  juristic reasoning, 195
  reasoning, 2, 4, 6, 18, 63, 191
analogous case, 3
analogy in legal argumentation, 4
ancillary objectives, 14
Andrew Haley, 185
Anṣār, 250
anti-analogists, 7
Anti-Christ, 180, 213
anti-religious tendencies, 207
applicability, 6, 53, 125, 167, 408
ʿaqd tabarruʿ (gratuity contract), 364
ʿaqīdah (faith), xxv, 18, 19, 20, 36, 39, 41, 43, 45, 57, 72, 73, 163, 164, 178, 212, 223, 224, 226, 227, 232, 234, 235, 268, 314, 352, 358, 367, 377, 381, 382, 404
ʿaqīdah, 178, 223, 268
ʿāqilah, 26
ʿaql (human mind), xix, xx, 4, 6, 7, 14, 50, 62, 97, 108, 112, 113, 114, 117, 119, 168, 184, 353, 398
Arab, ix, 48, 49, 56, 64, 99, 100, 101, 132, 159, 180, 199, 245, 253, 314, 361, 384, 421, 427
  Arabian Peninsula, 199
  Arabic language, xi, xxi, 38, 64, 104, 132
  Arabicate hermeneutic, 132, 133
  Arabicized non-Arabs, 100
  countries, 133
  world, ix
arbāb al-amwāl, 330
archetypes, 89

Arthur Anderson, 216
Asad, Muhammad, 38, 51
asfala sāfilīn (sink to the lowest of the low), 166
Ashʿarites, 84
 Ashʿarism, 112
Asia, 180, 206, 363
Aspen Institute, 185
asset, xxix, xxx, xxxi, 129, 313, 315, 316, 317, 320, 321, 323, 324, 325, 328, 331, 334, 335, 336, 337, 338, 339, 343, 344, 345, 385, 386, 397, 413
 based investment, 338
Asutay, xvi, xxv, xxxii, xxxiii, 373, 377, 378, 389, 395, 396, 406, 418, 423
atomistic approaches, 413
Austinian school of positivist law, 158
authoritative text, 5, 8
Awad al-Jeed, Ustaz, 258
awṣāf ʿāmmah (general characteristics), 68, 312
Aws, Banū al-, 199
Azhar University, al, ix, 119, 168, 271, 295, 300

B

Bagby, 63, 432
Baghdad, 2, 124, 161, 206, 226
baghy (treason), 260
Bahai religion, 182
balance, xvi, 17, 50, 131, 166, 230, 274, 275, 304, 322, 384, 385
bank, 238, 330, 331, 342, 343, 362, 384, 395, 396, 397, 398, 420, 425, 434
 activities, xxxii, 374
 bankers, 329
Bank al-Jazeerah in Saudi Arabia, 362
Barings, 216
Basel, 180, 335
Bedoui, 395
bāṭil (wrong), 193
belief, 19, 44, 46, 50, 58, 92, 97, 104, 111, 200, 201, 229, 268, 269, 272, 284
 system, 284
benefit, xxviii, xxix, 10, 64, 72, 84, 103, 125, 127, 130, 133, 225, 226, 237, 238, 241, 242, 275, 290, 298, 299, 302, 303, 304, 305, 306, 308, 349, 350, 354, 357, 366, 369, 370
bāʿith (elicit), 6
Bible, 95
bidʿah, 169
bioethical issues, xxviii, 281, 282, 290, 291, 297
biological
 survival, 76
 technology, 295
biomedical, 282, 309
 field, xxix, 291, 294, 302, 310
biotechnical engineering, 298
Blackamerican, xx, 96, 114, 116, 117, 428
 Muslims, xx
borrower, 313, 317
Bouzghiba, 297, 300
Brahma, 48
British, 146, 246, 247, 251, 252, 253, 278
 administration, 252
 colonial era, 251
 historiography, 246
Brotherhood, 40, 361
Buddhism, 155, 185
 Buddhist monastery, 185
 Buddhist monks, 155, 185
 Hinayana, 155, 185
 Tantrayana, 156, 185
Bukhārī, al, 50, 360
Bureau of Indian Affairs, 155
business, xxv, xxx, 21, 215, 216, 217, 219, 220, 221, 222, 223, 230, 233, 234, 235, 238, 240, 241, 320, 321,

326, 327, 328, 333, 334, 391, 394, 397, 410, 420, 422, 423, 425
finances, 326
financing, 326
Buti, al-, x, 234
buy-back, 321

C

Caliph, 202, 205, 206
Omar, 206
Camilla Adang, 104, 161
Cammack, 160
capital, xxxii, 131, 136, 152, 174, 175, 176, 177, 187, 210, 220, 317, 329, 335, 338, 362, 373, 389
accumulation, 389
intensive age, 174
ownership, 175, 176, 177, 187
punishment, 131, 136, 152
capitalism, 139, 151, 215, 269
capitalist
commercial society, 403
economy, 139
modes of production, 403
socio-economic thinking, xxxii
system, 404
worldview, 285
cardinal values, xvii, xxxiii, 18, 32, 44
Carolyn Fluehr-Lobban, 244, 247
Cassirer, 44
categories of objectives, 15
causality, xvi, 380, 415
cause-and-effect dialectic, 380
cause-effect nexus, 381
central bank, 341, 342, 343
certainty, xxxii, 44, 54, 59, 62, 103, 131, 356, 366, 367, 370
Shaping the Future, 184
Chapra, 224, 381, 382, 383, 385, 406, 432
Charles Long, 114
Cherokee Indian, 155
China, 139
Christian, 21, 49, 95, 96, 183, 205, 206, 208, 209, 212, 213, 225, 282, 422, 428
Christianity, 95, 189, 208, 210, 213, 269
Church, 282
church authority, 96
dhimmīs, 206
faith, 212
mystic, 183
circumstances, xxv, xxxiv, 24, 28, 30, 53, 56, 60, 63, 64, 67, 125, 167, 191, 216, 218, 233, 239, 263, 294, 308, 321, 347, 348, 351, 355, 406, 413
civic
institutions, 208
virtue, 207
civil
liberties, 208
society, xxiv, 203, 208
civilization, xviii, xxii, 37, 42, 57, 61, 115, 157, 164, 165, 169, 171, 178, 182, 183, 185, 186, 187, 217, 240, 283, 426
Civilizational clash, xxii, 157, 165, 186
classical
contracts, 311, 318
fuqahā', 332
Islam, xxii, 2, 8, 38, 42, 60, 167, 171, 172, 186, 337
Islamic, xxii, 8, 38, 42, 60, 167, 171, 172, 337
Islamic jurisprudence, 8, 60, 167
Islamic political theory, 42
Islamic scholarship, 38
Islamic thought, xxii, 171, 172
jurists, 20, 28, 29, 74, 75, 85, 96, 130, 195, 210, 347, 349, 350, 360
legal doctrines, 196
legal theorists, 54, 63
legal theory, 99, 104, 196

theory of law, 195
uṣūl al-fiqh, 101
cloning, xxviii, 295, 296, 297, 298, 299, 300, 301, 302, 303, 304, 305, 306
human beings, 296
human organs, 303
codification, xxv, xxvi, xxviii, 124, 146, 147, 243, 251, 259, 261, 273, 274, 275, 276, 278
codifying the *Sharīʿah* corpus, xxvii
of penal law, xxviii
collaterals, 313, 316, 338, 340
collective needs, 348
colonial
colonialist legal change, 136
era, xxvii, 252, 253
narrative, 122
Columbus, 164
commercial, xxx, 98, 129, 136, 240, 241, 321, 333, 334, 341, 426
commercialism, 247
commodities, 332, 333
prices, 333
common
law system, 252, 257, 274
sense, xix, 114
tendency, xviii, 98
communal
existence, 30, 145
legislation, 204
communism, 269
community, xxi, xxv, 12, 15, 20, 22, 23, 27, 30, 50, 51, 67, 73, 76, 80, 81, 82, 107, 131, 136, 137, 152, 156, 173, 175, 176, 178, 185, 187, 191, 192, 196, 197, 198, 199, 200, 208, 213, 215, 217, 219, 224, 230, 242, 318, 427
Compact, 198, 199, 200, 201, 217
of Madīnah, 199
Companions, 54, 102, 229
compassion, xxv, 214, 224, 231
compassionate justice, 156, 163, 171, 177, 179, 180, 184, 185, 186, 426
complementary, xxii, 57, 227, 232, 235, 386, 387, 405
compound salam, 321
concept, xvi, xvii, xix, xxii, xxviii, xxix, xxxi, xxxii, 8, 9, 11, 32, 35, 37, 39, 41, 42, 43, 45, 47, 51, 54, 61, 63, 66, 70, 84, 85, 86, 88, 89, 91, 92, 111, 114, 116, 121, 139, 158, 161, 162, 166, 167, 168, 169, 170, 171, 176, 178, 184, 192, 197, 200, 216, 218, 223, 224, 229, 230, 231, 236, 240, 241, 267, 268, 281, 286, 287, 295, 298, 302, 308, 315, 330, 332, 345, 348, 360, 367, 368, 370, 378, 379, 381, 394, 395, 405, 407, 426
conceptual framework, xvii
of CSR, 216, 229, 240, 241
of falāḥ, 381
of fiṭrah, 32, 35, 47, 70, 85, 88, 92
of justice, xxii, 51, 171, 426
of maṣlaḥah, 63, 66, 231, 236
condominium, 248, 252
Confucius, 48
consequentialism, 402, 415
consequentialist crosschecking, 416
consistency, 41, 62, 312, 321, 325, 336
contract
conditions, 341
of exchange, 359, 361, 362, 364
conventional
bank, 334, 335, 342, 414
finance, xxxii, 337, 338, 375, 404
financial markets, 376
financial practices, 375
insurance, 361, 364, 366, 368
Conventional
insurance, 361, 364
cooperative behavior, 403
Coptic, 213
core necessities, 14, 15

corporate
state, 160
corporate governance (CG), 218, 378
corporate social responsibility (CSR), xxv, xxvi, 215, 216, 217, 218, 219, 220, 221, 228, 229, 230, 231, 232, 234, 235, 237, 239, 240, 241, 378
commitment, 235
construct, 219
initiatives, 216, 220
literature, 217
corporation, xxvi, 215, 216, 217, 218, 219, 220, 221, 222, 229, 232, 236, 238, 239, 240, 241, 321, 341, 343
corpus juris, 141
corruption, xx, 29, 50, 57, 71, 73, 83, 109, 113, 117, 145, 166, 201, 207, 221, 225, 234, 353
in human nature, 50
Courts of Instantaneous Justice, 268
Covenant of Madīnah (*Ṣaḥīfat al-Madīnah*), 198
creation, 35, 38, 39, 51, 115, 160, 165, 174, 177, 202, 295, 296, 297, 299, 304, 305, 306, 313, 320, 375
of debts, 320
Creator, 19, 38, 39, 277, 290, 296, 359
Criminal Procedure Act (1983), 255, 256
criminal responsibility, 262, 270
criminology, 251, 259, 272, 275, 276
Crusaders, 206
Cuba, 139
cultivation of human organs, 303
cultural
authenticity, xxvii, 265, 266
heritage, 48, 266
identity, xxii, 165, 244
liberation, 266
cumulative meaning, 98
currencies, 312
current account deposit, 321

D

Dafaʿ Allah Al-Haj Yusuf, 257
Dakka, 182
Dalai Lama, 155, 185
dalīl, 104, 107
Daphna Ephrat, 161
ḍaraba, 173
Darfur, 246
ḍarūrah (extreme necessity), 12, 69, 293, 294
ḍarūrī, 12, 75, 76, 77, 78, 107, 377
category, 75, 76, 77
ḍarūriyyāt (essentials), xii, xxi, xxii, xxvi, 71, 72, 73, 76, 78, 80, 81, 85, 90, 91, 128, 130, 134, 160, 168, 227, 232, 234, 235, 236, 348, 353, 354, 382, 387, 409
Darwinian principle, 400
Dastagir, 182, 183, 184
Davies, 114, 217, 220, 221
Ḍawābiṭ al-Maṣlaḥah fī al-Sharīʿah al-Islāmiyyah, 234
dawn of Islam, 197
Day of Judgment, 20, 347
debate, xxiii, 2, 4, 189, 209, 210, 287, 348, 383, 389, 390, 409, 415
debt, xxix, xxx, 175, 177, 210, 239, 313, 315, 316, 317, 319, 320, 323, 324, 325, 326, 327, 333, 337, 338, 339, 340, 342, 343, 358, 386, 389
based tradable ṣukūk, 339
creating financing, 319, 327
creating sale financing, xxx, 323
finance, 389
debtor, 315, 317
declared, 71, 88, 136, 199, 279, 292, 295, 300, 331
deconstruction, 381, 413
deduction, 267
deductive
arguments, 123
syllogism, 106
default, 55, 316, 337
deferred

  payment sale financing, 319
  price, 321
dehumanization, 93
democracy, 30, 171, 187, 209, 423
democratization, xxiii, 189
dīn (faith), xxv, 18, 19, 20, 24, 36, 39, 40, 41, 43, 44, 45, 52, 57, 72, 73, 92, 163, 164, 178, 212, 224, 226, 227, 232, 234, 235, 259, 281, 287, 309, 314, 352, 353, 358, 367, 377, 381, 382, 404
dīn (religion), xvi, 1, 8, 18, 24, 42, 75, 77, 105, 108, 126, 127, 128, 184, 192, 210, 225, 237, 259, 287, 289, 290, 293, 296, 300, 304, 305, 351, 356, 364, 421, 433, 435
  al-fiṭrah, 40, 44, 92
dīnī (spirituo-religious), 43, 352
deposit
  guarantee, 341
  guarantee corporation, 341
deposit:, 321, 329, 330, 335, 341, 342, 343
depositors, 329, 330, 333
Depository banks, 341
dār al-maẓālim (the House of the rectification of injustices), 250
Deterrence, 277
Deuteronomy, 186
developmentalism, 377, 378, 404, 405, 422
developmentalist
  agenda, 374
  ends, 380
  objectives, 379, 415
dharā'iʿ, 348, 349, 350
  dharā'iʿ, definition of, 351
dhimmī (covenanters), 135, 205, 206, 330
dignity, 170, 173, 187, 191, 201, 296, 303
dimensions of *maqāṣid*, 399
discipline and punishment, 144
disciplinization of knowledge, 413
Divine, xvii, 3, 4, 5, 6, 13, 15, 17, 18, 30, 48, 57, 72, 114, 159, 165, 166, 179, 183, 184, 186, 193, 210, 211, 214, 222, 297, 299, 414, 415
  guidance, 47
  messages, 47
  Will, xxiii, 46, 167, 194, 195, 197
Diyar Bakr, 2
diyānah, 20
DJII, 323
doctrinal
  plurality, 202
  Sufism, 184
doctrine
  of necessity, 167
Dubos, 93
dunyawī (Worldly objectives), 352
Dutch colonialists, 160
dynamics of human society, 32
dynamism of Islamic law, 348

E

Eastern Orthodox Church, 165
economic, xxiv, xxv, xxix, xxxii, xxxiii, 69, 89, 117, 134, 136, 138, 139, 142, 147, 173, 182, 187, 199, 200, 203, 207, 218, 219, 220, 222, 223, 228, 236, 285, 287, 290, 304, 308, 310, 328, 336, 360, 373, 374, 375, 376, 377, 379, 382, 385, 388, 390, 392, 397, 398,뚜 400, 401, 402, 416, 417, 418, 422
  behavior, 222, 402
  economics, xxv, xxix, xxxiii, 158, 176, 218, 223, 373, 374, 379, 380, 388, 399, 400, 401, 402, 403, 404, 413, 414, 416, 417, 418, 422, 424, 425
  economics science, 400
  forces, 418
  man, 218
  objectives, 220
  performance, 390, 392, 398

system, 308, 376, 377, 388, 402, 417
theory, xxxii, 373, 400, 401
Edgar Bonham-Carter, 251
Egypt, 213, 252, 296, 297, 427
Ancient, 48
Egyptian historiography, 246
Egyptian rule, 246, 247
embellishment, 8, 16, 226, 227, 228, 232, 235, 236, 301, 387, 409, 410
categories, 232
emergency
rule, 256
Emergency Courts, 267
ends and means, 69
England, 161, 165
English
Common Law, 148, 251, 252
Common law system, 251
law, 248, 251, 278
Enlightenment, 34, 115, 400
philosophy, 400
Enron, 216
Environmental Social and Governance (ESG), 378
epistemological
argument, 61
significance, 75
theory of empiricism, xviii, 97
epistemology, xxxiv, 59, 178, 186, 266, 374
equal dignity, 212, 214
equality, xviii, 91, 175, 201, 207, 208
equilibrium
of creation, xxviii, 306
of the existence, 297
equitable balance, 51
equity, xxii, 160, 162, 166, 170, 173, 187, 212, 318, 330, 333, 368, 384, 389, 402
finance, 389
espistemic predicament, 123
essence of justice, 212
essential
methodology, xxxii, 399, 408, 416
needs, 234, 235, 387
essential values, 234, 287
essentialization, 380, 415, 417, 418
essentials
five, 383, 384, 404
five-level, 388
eternal wisdom, xxiii
ethical
guidance, xxvi, 221, 240
Identity Index, 394
investment, 322
principles, 222, 313
values, 40
ethico-economic relationships, 418
ethics and values, 91, 223, 422
European
Enlightenment, 38
grown import, 140
Renaissance, 170, 283
euthanasia, 65
evidence, 26, 43, 52, 62, 80, 83, 84, 124, 128, 174, 190, 211, 245, 310, 329, 358, 374, 385, 400, 405, 412
evil tendencies, 42
exchange of goods and services, 326, 328
exotericism, 100
explicit
individual, 104
texts, xix, 106
extended family, 26, 27

F

Fahmi Huwaidi, 297
faith, xxv, 18, 19, 20, 36, 39, 41, 43, 45, 57, 72, 73, 163, 164, 178, 212, 224, 226, 227, 232, 234, 235, 314, 352, 358, 367, 377, 381, 382, 404
based movements, 164
Fakhr al-Dīn al-Rāzī, xvi, 108, 225, 356
falāḥ, 405, 413
false

falsehood, 43, 299
universal, xix, 110, 111, 118
family, xiii, xxv, 2, 6, 24, 25, 26, 27, 28, 68, 69, 76, 89, 137, 168, 174, 211, 219, 224, 239, 295, 301, 353, 363, 366, 368, 369
and society, xxv, 224
law, 24, 137, 239
life, xiii, 24, 26, 353
takāful, 363, 365, 366, 368, 369
takāful scheme, 365
faqīh, 149, 151, 288
farḍ, 23, 82, 176, 282, 305, 412
farḍ kifāyah (collective duties), 23, 82, 176, 305
fatḥ al-dharā'i', 348, 350, 355, 360, 363, 366, 370, 371
fatwā (legal opinion), 16, 263, 295, 302, 311, 312, 336, 338, 339, 340, 370, 384
Fazlur Rahman, 61, 70, 133
fājir (non-righteous), 260
feminism, 111, 138
Fertile Crescent, 177
Festshrift, 178
Fethullah Gulen, 163
figurative interpretation, 98, 104
fiṭrah, xvii, 32, 35, 36, 37, 45, 47, 50, 52, 53, 61, 78, 83, 166, 179, 295
nafsiyyah, 166
fiṭrat Allāh, 166
filter mechanism, 232
finance, xxv, xxix, 238, 241, 311, 312, 313, 322, 325, 326, 328, 329, 333, 335, 337, 338, 339, 340, 342, 343, 374, 375, 380, 385, 389, 403, 404, 416, 418, 421, 422, 423, 425
financial
activities, 394, 418
and economic transactions, 357
interest, 369
intermediation, xxx, 320, 321, 332, 333, 334
lease, 311, 338
operations, 374, 385, 412
systems, 376
transactions, xxix, xxxii, 176, 315, 357, 359, 360, 366, 374, 419
Financial
intermediation, 329
financing
contracts, 313, 317, 318, 323, 345, 385
financing methodology, 328
fi'l (act), xxx, 7, 8, 19, 26, 38, 41, 46, 63, 64, 106, 126, 128, 129, 130, 131, 147, 165, 200, 205, 212, 221, 226, 271, 274, 297, 298, 301, 326, 327, 334, 341, 348, 349, 350, 355, 370
fiqh, 5, 16, 18, 29, 31, 59, 60, 106, 118, 132, 135, 148, 161, 190, 197, 225, 249, 252, 263, 282, 286, 300, 312, 327, 348, 351, 375, 383, 402, 412, 417, 419
approach, 402
literature, 16, 29, 312
rulings, 383, 412
fiqh al-mu'āmalāt, 348
First Conference on Islamic Economy, Makkah, 1976, 361
fitnah (dissension), 116, 260
fixed assets, 339
flexibility, 56, 149, 196, 223, 224, 233, 348, 355, 412
in Islamic Law, 355
Fluehr-Lobban, 247, 250, 253
formal contracts, 358
formalized ideologies, 116
Francis Fukuyama, 34, 35, 93
Frank Vogel, 157, 158
freedom
of faith, 202
of religion, 22, 169, 178, 186, 208, 213
of religion and faith, 209
French, 87, 115, 147, 286
Friedman, 230

Fuad al-Amin Abdel Rahman, 256
funds, 313, 320, 325, 326, 329, 330, 331, 333, 339, 340, 341, 342, 343, 362, 367, 398
fuqahā' (Muslim jurists), xvii, 3, 7, 11, 14, 17, 18, 23, 26, 54, 104, 118, 190, 193, 195, 197, 205, 225, 249, 263, 361
furūʿ al-fiqh, 161
furūʿal-fiqh (substantive law), 161, 254, 256, 428
future commodities, 312

G

general
  goal of the Sharīʿah, 67
  good, 219
  harm, 61
genetic
  engineering, xxviii, 295, 299, 303, 304, 305
  technology, 299, 308, 309
Genetically Modified (GM), 307, 308
Genetically Modified Organisms (GMOs), 308, 310
George Orwell, 117
German
  Civil Codes, 147
ghanīmah, 357
gharar (risk or uncertainty), 360, 361, 362, 364, 386
Ghazalian
  basic structure, 383
  fivefold structure of necessities, 391
  structure of *maqāṣid*, 383
Ghazālī, Abū Ḥāmid al-, xii, xvi, xix, xxxiii, 72, 105, 107, 108, 124, 128, 129, 130, 131, 168, 184, 191, 224, 225, 226, 227, 287, 288, 308, 352, 377, 398, 406, 408, 432
  maqāṣid, 408
  maqāṣid framework, 399, 404
  maqāṣid scheme, 409
  taxonomy, 227, 386
Ghazālian
  approach to *maqāṣid*, 404
  five fold, 390
  formulation, xxxiii, 386
  framework, 404
  maqāṣid emanates, 405
  maqāṣid framework, xxxiii, 388, 409
ghāṣib (unlawful appropriator), 127
global
  civilization, 48
  financial system, 377, 389
  nakbah, 181
  society, 213
globalization, 174, 216, 218, 300, 424
God, xvii, xxii, xxv, 1, 2, 8, 11, 13, 17, 18, 19, 24, 30, 35, 38, 39, 40, 45, 46, 47, 51, 53, 55, 57, 70, 73, 100, 102, 107, 113, 115, 116, 124, 126, 145, 149, 156, 161, 163, 165, 166, 167, 169, 170, 171, 176, 179, 182, 183, 184, 185, 193, 201, 210, 212, 225, 229, 230, 231, 232, 233, 234, 267, 269, 284, 288, 296, 297, 299, 301, 303, 304, 305, 307, 310, 314, 315, 317, 326, 347, 355, 357, 358, 359, 375, 393, 421, 435
  accountability to, 211, 233
  Almighty, 288, 310
  closeness to, 28
  exists, 19
  given disposition, xxii, 165
  given primordial nature, xvii
God-conscious believers, 201
Golam Dastagir, 182, 183, 184
Golden Rule, 212
Gordon, General, 246, 247
governance, 140, 141, 146, 209, 396, 423
  good:, 382
Government, 22, 30, 81, 142, 155, 157, 158, 166, 176, 177, 202, 213,

216, 218, 230, 245, 265, 285, 340, 341, 416, 421
Greek
contributions to medicine, 283
guaranteed loans, 330
Gulf, xxxi, 387
states, 387

H

ḥadd (punishment), 14, 46, 75, 77, 83, 89, 128, 136, 144, 145, 152, 227, 262, 267, 268, 270, 271, 272, 273, 274, 277, 285, 353
Ḥadīth, 162, 168, 236, 359
ahl al-ḥadīth, 4
ḥājah, 12
ḥajj, 78, 210, 211
ḥājī category, 78
ḥājiyyāt (exigencies or complementary), xii, xxvi, 71, 76, 77, 78, 79, 80, 81, 91, 129, 227, 228, 353, 354, 387, 409
ḥalāl, 60, 386
ḥanīf, 179
ḥaqā'iq (higher realities), 182
ḥaqq
al-dīn (protection of religion), 168, 172, 186, 191
al-hayāh, 167
al-ḥurriyhah, 173
al-karāmah, 170, 173, 187
al-mahd, 187
al-māl (or *amwāl*, protection of property), 168, 173, 175, 187
al-nafs (or *nufūs*, protection of the person), 168, 172, 186
al-nasl (or *ansāb*, protection of lineage or the family), 168, 172, 187
al-ʿilm (freedom for knowledge), 168, 170, 173, 178, 187
halalness (divine knowledge), 414
Hamurabi, 48
Hanbali, 2, 43, 164
Happiness Index, 390
haqīqah wa majāz, 103
ḥarām (forbidden), 3, 4, 5, 7, 15, 60, 124, 282, 295, 298, 299, 300, 349, 412
ḥarb, 23
hard sciences, 95
Ḥārith, Banū al-, 199
harmful result, 349, 350
Harningtyas, 395, 396
Hassan al-Banna, 163
Hayat-a-Tayyaba Index, 392
ḥawālah, 239, 343
ḥayāt ṭayyibah (good life), 416
Hazairin, 132, 159
healthy progress, 67
Heart of Islam, 181, 182, 433
hedging, 312, 344, 409
hegemonic claims of the modern West, 111
Henry Corbin, 180
Henry Regnery, 184
Heraclitus, 182
Hereafter, xxv, 223, 224, 228, 230, 285, 287, 352
Hermann Landolt, 179, 180
hermeneutical foundations of the law, xxi, 134
hermeneutics, 132, 151
heuristic methods, 101
hibah 239, 361, 362, 363, 365
takāful, 361
hierarchical classification, 71, 128
hierarchy, xxvii, 14, 27, 142, 172, 186, 274, 317
of objectives of the law, 14
of values, xxvii, 274
ḥifẓ (protection), xix, xx, xxxiii, 73, 74, 76, 77, 97, 108, 109, 110, 111, 112, 114, 117, 119, 168, 172, 175, 352, 356, 391, 392, 393, 394, 406, 407
ḥifẓ al-ansāb, 76, 77
ḥifẓ al-dīn, 73, 352, 391, 393

ḥifẓ al-nafs, 74, 172
ḥifẓ al-ʿaql (preservation of reason), xix, xx, 97, 107, 108, 109, 110, 111, 112, 113, 114, 117, 118, 119, 352, 392, 393
ḥifẓ al-nasl, 76, 77, 352, 392, 394
ḥifẓ al-ʿirḍ, 168
ḥikam (wisdom), xxviii, 5, 6, 10, 11, 16, 49, 52, 53, 58, 59, 60, 62, 67, 91, 108, 166, 178, 275, 288, 297, 307, 331, 351, 376, 394, 401, 408
ḥikmah (underlying rationale), 6, 10, 108, 178, 288, 297
higher objectives, 33, 69, 170, 348, 352, 355, 359, 376
higher paradigm of thought, 171
higher purpose, 7, 9, 10, 166, 167, 168, 288
  of the law, 7
higher transcendental aims, 145
highest principles or purposes, 186
highest priority, 172
highest transcendent good, 178
Hill, 215, 246, 247, 248
ḥirābah, 177
history, xii, xiv, xxii, xxviii, xxxiv, 20, 31, 47, 48, 52, 57, 62, 83, 96, 111, 122, 140, 150, 161, 170, 180, 181, 190, 192, 202, 244, 245, 246, 247, 248, 257, 260, 270, 287, 403, 406, 409, 412, 415, 421, 424, 428
  of mankind, 57
holistic
  approach, 43, 222, 413
  understanding of human nature, 70, 91
homicide, 14, 25, 26, 74, 127, 136, 248, 253
homoeconomicus, 402
Hujwīrī, Abū al-Ḥasan al- (Datta Ganjbaksh), 181
ḥudūd (punishment laws), 75, 77, 85, 189, 210, 262, 277
  ḥudūd law, 210
  ḥudūd penalties, 75, 77, 85
  ḥudūd punishments, 75, 189
ḥukm, 9, 163, 301, 347
human, xiv, xvii, xviii, xxii, xxiii, xxv, xxviii, xxxi, xxxii, xxxiv, 4, 5, 6, 7, 8, 11, 12, 13, 14, 15, 16, 17, 18, 19, 20, 24, 26, 27, 28, 29, 30, 32, 33, 34, 37, 38, 39, 40, 41, 42, 43, 44, 45, 46, 47, 48, 50, 51, 52, 53, 56, 57, 58, 61, 62, 63, 65, 67, 68, 70, 71, 72, 74, 76, 78, 79, 80, 82, 84, 85, 88, 89, 90, 91, 92, 93, 115, 116, 117, 119, 136, 145, 147, 156, 159, 164, 165, 166, 168, 170, 171, 172, 173, 174, 175, 176, 177, 178, 179, 182, 183, 184, 186, 187, 193, 194, 196, 197, 203, 204, 210, 211, 214, 215, 217, 221, 222, 224, 226, 227, 229, 230, 235, 241, 263, 267, 269, 275, 277, 282, 284, 285, 287, 288, 289, 290, 291, 292, 295, 296, 297, 299, 300, 301, 302, 303, 304, 306, 307, 308, 322, 326, 331, 333, 347, 348, 352, 353, 354, 356, 373, 375, 376, 377, 378, 381, 382, 405, 406, 418, 423, 424
  acts, 82
  agency, xxxii, 197, 373
  behavior, 42, 57, 193, 221
  being, xvii, xxii, xxv, 16, 17, 28, 30, 34, 38, 40, 43, 44, 46, 52, 53, 56, 68, 69, 71, 72, 82, 91, 92, 156, 165, 166, 171, 175, 177, 179, 194, 197, 211, 221, 222, 226, 229, 264, 269, 277, 287, 289, 290, 295, 296, 297, 300, 304, 353, 376, 382, 405, 406
  cloning, 296, 297, 301, 302, 304
  condition, xvii, xxxiv, 92, 116
  consciousness, 19, 58
  cultural history, 307
  culture, 57
  development (HDI), 378, 418

disposition, 263
existence, xxiii, xxv, 80, 194, 222, 282, 296
freedom, 19, 269
good, 32, 57, 58, 63, 79, 83, 90
heritage, 48
history, xxii, 34, 117, 145, 171
individual, 92, 147, 348
intelligence, 38
interests, xxxi, 210, 353
life, xviii, xxv, xxxiv, 12, 13, 26, 27, 28, 29, 30, 32, 33, 48, 51, 57, 58, 63, 65, 68, 70, 74, 76, 78, 79, 90, 183, 224, 227, 230, 282, 291, 299, 303, 352, 353, 354, 356, 375
life and existence, xviii, xxxiv, 70, 79
nature, 32, 33, 34, 35, 37, 40, 41, 44, 50, 51, 52, 53, 58, 61, 62, 70, 78, 83, 85, 88, 90, 91, 93, 159, 166
needs, 12, 32, 347, 382
offspring, 306
order, 166
personality, 41, 46, 381
procreation, 29, 76
psyche, 46
race, 45
rationality, 5
reason, xxiii, 84, 168, 194, 222, 263
resource management, 217
responsibilities, 164, 169
rights, xxii, 136, 169, 170, 171, 204, 214, 215, 217, 241, 382, 423
social existence, 78, 85, 88
social life, xiv, 17, 89
social order, 354
society, 12, 15, 33, 42, 72, 74, 78, 79, 90, 295, 298, 377, 424
socio-historical existence, 89, 91, 93
socio-political order, 33, 34
souls, 74, 173
species, 45, 47, 53, 67, 77, 173
thought and knowledge, 71
well-being, 11, 89, 90, 354, 381, 418
humanity, xi, 34, 35, 92, 93, 115, 182, 184, 187, 246, 289, 290, 375, 433
humankind, 153, 165, 170, 177, 284, 290, 296, 298, 305, 307
Humber, 221, 230
ḥurmah (inviolability), 291
ḥurriyat al-aqwāl (freedom of expression), 178
ḥurriyat al-iʿtiqād (freedom of religion), 22, 169, 178, 186, 208, 213
ḥurriyyah (freedom), xviii, 16, 17, 22, 30, 40, 49, 86, 90, 137, 165, 169, 170, 171, 173, 175, 178, 186, 187, 192, 199, 200, 201, 202, 204, 206, 207, 208, 213, 214, 269, 276, 358, 359, 369, 391, 395, 408
Hussain Hamid Hassan, 233
hybrid
Islamic financing contracts, 321
of financial services, xxxii, 376

I

ʿibād, 126, 127
ʿibādah (worship, 223
ʿibādāt (devotional matters), 60
IBF, xxxiii, 376, 378, 384, 385, 388, 389, 404, 412, 413, 414, 416, 417
sector, 384, 385
Ibn Ḥazm, 4, 102, 103, 161
Ibn Ashur, Muhammad al-Tahir, x, xii, xvii, xxii, 31, 32, 35, 36, 37, 38, 39, 41, 42, 43, 44, 46, 47, 48, 49, 50, 51, 52, 53, 54, 55, 56, 57, 58, 59, 60, 61, 62, 63, 64, 65, 66, 67, 68, 69, 71, 72, 73, 74, 75, 76, 77, 78, 79, 80, 81, 83, 84, 85, 86, 87, 88, 89, 90, 91, 92, 93, 105, 109, 111, 164, 165, 166, 167, 168, 169,

170, 171, 172, 173, 174, 175, 176, 177, 178, 351, 356, 357, 358, 359, 433
Ibn Barhān, 130
Ibn Khaldūn, 42, 87
Ibn ʿĀshir, 112
Ibn Qayyim al-Jawziyyah, xii, 43, 70, 105, 164, 192, 206, 288, 383, 384, 407
Ibn Rushd the philosopher, 349
Ibn Sīnā, Abū ʿAlī (Avicenna), 36
Ibn Taymiyya, xii, xix, 66, 70, 84, 105, 111, 114, 225, 383
Ibn Taymiyyah, xii, xix, 66, 84, 105, 111, 114, 225, 383
Ibrahim Ahmed Omer, 260, 266
ibtidāʿ (innovation), 270
IDB, 289, 292, 297, 305, 344, 425
idea of *maqāṣid*, xiv, xx, 31, 32, 58, 73, 88, 89, 91, 93
ideal social order, 23, 30
ideals of Islam, 275, 277, 423
identity of offspring, 76
identity politics, 157, 179
ifrāṭ (excessiveness), 50, 166
ihktilāf, 162
Ihsan Yilmaz, 163, 164
Iḥkām, al-, 1, 3, 4, 8, 9, 11, 12, 13, 72, 102, 103, 287, 431
iṣlāḥ ʿāmm (global reform), 178
iḥsān,
  iḥsān (beneficence), 405
  iḥsān (excellence), 148, 184, 214, 232, 403, 405, 410, 411, 413
  iḥsān approach, 410
  iḥsān spirit, 411
  iḥsān-based perspective, 410
  iḥsānī, 403, 405
  iḥsān-oriented development, 410
ʿIilm al-Maqāṣid, 71
ʿillah (ration essendi), 5, 6, 7, 8, 9, 29, 63, 108, 288
ʿilm al-ḥikmah, 178
ʿIlm al-Maqāṣid, 31, 79, 86, 87
ʿilm al-ʿadl al mutaʿālī, 184
ʿilm al-ʿadl, 180, 184
ʿIlm Maqāṣid al-Sharīʿah, xvii, 30, 31, 41, 58, 59
ijārah, 228, 239, 329, 331
ijmāʿ (consensus), 96, 102, 103, 104, 159, 162, 172, 178, 191, 196, 197, 225
ijmāʿ murakkab, 162
ijtihād, xiii, xiv, xvi, 56, 151, 159, 160, 162, 163, 168, 181, 191, 249, 250, 287, 288, 347, 351, 415
  ijtihād maqāṣidī, 288
  ijtihādic, 148, 151
  ijtihādic pluralism, 148, 151
  ijtihāds, 407
illusionary (*wahmiyyah*), 83
Illusionary maṣlaḥah, 84
images (*khayālāt*), 36
imagined community, 160
īmān, 184
Imām al-Shāfiʿī., 110
Imāmiyyah, 162
IMF, 335, 390, 425
impact, 29, 49, 52, 70, 84, 110, 206, 215, 217, 247, 265, 284, 286, 353, 409, 422
Imran Nyazee, 228
inborn disposition, 39
inborn inclination (*mayl jibillī*), 76
inbuilt mechanisms, 45
incongruity (*munāfarah*), 61
increments, xxix, xxx, 315, 316, 317, 323, 324, 333, 337
independent discipline, xvii, 31, 33, 87, 351
index, 179, 260, 300, 323, 325, 390, 392, 399, 431
indigenous interests, 136
indispensable (*ḍarūrī*), 75, 175
individual, xii, xviii, xxv, xxxiii, 14, 17, 20, 21, 24, 25, 26, 27, 28, 30, 33, 34, 46, 52, 54, 60, 63, 64, 73, 74, 77, 82, 83, 90, 98, 102, 103,

104, 105, 106, 133, 135, 147, 149, 163, 167, 174, 175, 177, 180, 183, 187, 190, 191, 193, 195, 196, 199, 203, 206, 208,뜌 210, 211, 223, 224, 228, 231, 238, 240, 285, 296, 358, 377, 381, 387, 402, 404, 405, 409, 410
individual *falāḥ*, 381, 405
individual lives, 387
individual morality, 190
individual privacy, 190
individual texts, xviii, 98, 104, 105, 106
individuality, 404, 411
Indonesia, xi, xxii, 132, 159, 391, 395
  Indonesian archipelago, 160
  Indonesian legal thinkers, 132
induction, xviii, xix, 53, 54, 76, 98, 105, 106, 108, 109, 111, 123, 170, 267
industry of financial intermediation, 320, 321
inebriants, xix, 124, 128
infāq, 174
inflation, 340
infrastructures, 339
inherent spiritual and mental disposition, 52
inheritance law, 14, 159
injunctions of the Sharīʿah, 50
injustice, 42, 163, 200, 201, 249, 299, 353, 359, 408, 426
innate constitution of human beings, 295
innate powers of reasoning, 8
installment sale, 321
instinctive cognition of God, 38
instinctive drives, 45, 82
instincts of mankind, 44
institutionalization of modern sciences, 380
instrumental morality, xxxiv, 414
instrumental reasoning, 403
instrumentalism, xxxiv, 414
insurable interest, 369
Insurance, 340, 347, 360, 361, 363, 365, 367, 368, 369, 370
  insurance in Islam, xxxi
  insured risks, 364
intellect, xxv, 36, 43, 67, 72, 191, 224, 226, 227, 232, 234, 286, 287, 299, 352, 356, 377, 381, 382
intellect (*ʿaql*), 36, 72, 224, 226, 299, 381
intellectual creativity, 37
intellectual *fiṭrah*, 36
intention (*niyyah*), 19
inter-bank transactions, 324, 343
interest, xii, xiv, xxx, xxxi, 2, 5, 46, 65, 70, 81, 85, 86, 88, 91, 108, 118, 145, 149, 175, 177, 207, 209, 215, 218, 225, 228, 230, 235, 236, 240, 245, 285, 288, 305, 312, 315, 316, 318, 319, 320, 321, 322, 323, 324, 326, 327, 329, 332, 333, 334, 337, 338, 340, 345, 352, 353, 369, 387, 388, 402, 418, 419, 423, 426
Interest, 314, 323, 327, 369, 384, 397, 434
  interest financing, xxx, 323
  interest-based finance, 312
  interest-based lending, 319, 334
inter-individual dealings (*muʿāmalāt*), 60
International Islamic Fiqh Academy, Jeddah, 361
International Islamic University Malaysia, xv, 86, 301, 394, 419, 420, 421, 425
inter-personal relationship, 338
interpretative communities, 161
interpretative modalities, xviii
interpretive presuppositions, 100
intoxicants, 5, 10, 107, 108, 113
intoxication, 5, 6, 7, 14, 108, 109, 125
intransigence (*tashdīd*), 52
intrinsic utility, xxix, 315, 344

investment, xxx, xxxii, 176, 215, 321, 322, 328, 329, 330, 334, 335, 337, 357, 362, 365, 366, 385, 397
investment industry, xxx, 334
investor, 335, 337, 340
inviolability of a human being, 303
inviolability of human rationality, 5
inviolability of the rational faculties, 7
invisibility of whiteness, 115
inward (*bāṭin*), 166
IOK, 374, 375, 376, 401
  IOK paradigm, 374, 401
Iraq, 173, 177
ʿirfān (gnosis), 184
ʿirḍ (honor), 77, 128, 135, 137, 158, 168, 180, 187, 404
irrelevant (*gharīb*), 125
Islam,
  abode of, 22, 23, 24
  advent of, 49
Islam and Muslims
  Essence and Practice, 156
Islamic and secular worldviews, 374
Islamic axiomatic approach, 402
Islamic bank, xiv, xxix, xxx, 235, 241, 311, 321, 329, 331, 332, 333, 334, 335, 336, 341, 342, 343, 344, 376, 378, 384, 389, 390, 394, 395, 397, 404, 413, 414, 420, 422, 423, 425
  Islamic bank investment, 341
  Islamic Bank of Jordan, 341
  Islamic bankers, 331, 336
  Islamic banking, xiv, xxix, 311, 329, 332, 333, 376, 384, 389, 397, 413, 414, 420, 422, 423, 425
  Islamic banking and finance, xiv, xxix, 376, 384, 420, 422, 423, 426
  Islamic banks' operations, 395
Islamic belief, 270, 284
Islamic capitalism, 139
Islamic character, 21, 151
Islamic civilization, 169, 282, 283
Islamic concept of justice, xxiv, 212
Islamic conception of human nature, 38
Islamic conception of law, 208
Islamic conception of religion, 39
Islamic consciousness, 163
Islamic constitution, 253, 254
Islamic corporations, 241
Islamic criminal law, 146
Islamic culture, 190, 282, 283, 284, 285, 286
Islamic culture and civilization, 190, 282
Islamic Development Bank, 289, 343
Islamic developmentalism, 402, 410, 417
Islamic economic studies, 374
Islamic economic system, 381
Islamic economic thinking, xxxii, 374
Islamic economic thought, xxix, xxxii
Islamic economics, xvi, xxxii, xxxiii, xxxiv, 174, 177, 373, 374, 377, 378, 379, 380, 381, 383, 384, 385, 388, 399, 401, 402, 403, 408, 410, 412, 413, 414, 416, 417, 422, 424
Islamic economics and finance, xvi, xxxiii, 374, 379, 380, 385, 416, 424
Islamic faith, 70, 80
Islamic feminism, 138
Islamic finance, xxxi, xxxii, xxxiii, 311, 312, 318, 335, 336, 337, 338, 341, 344, 374, 375, 377, 378, 379, 380, 384, 386, 387, 388, 389, 394, 399, 403, 404, 416, 422, 423, 425, 426
  Islamic finance and banking, 318, 423, 425
  Islamic finance companies, 311
  Islamic finance contracts, 312
  Islamic finance enterprise, 404
  Islamic finance experts, 375
  Islamic finance industry, xxxi
  Islamic finance operations, 384
  Islamic finance practices, 386

Islamic financial contracts, 312, 336
Islamic financial engineering, xxxi, 321, 345
Islamic financial Hybrids, 327
Islamic financial industry, 389
Islamic financial innovation, 345
Islamic financial intermediation, xxx, 312, 327, 329, 330, 334
Islamic financial market, 336
Islamic financial operations, 376
Islamic financial products, 321, 322, 335, 336, 337, 338, 426
Islamic financial services, 379
Islamic financial system, 370
Islamic financial transactions, 364, 403
Islamic financialization, 403
Islamic financing, xxx, xxxi, 312, 317, 318, 322, 323, 328, 338, 345, 389
Islamic Fiqh Academy, 289, 292, 300, 305, 425
Islamic goals, 266
Islamic Human Development Index, 391, 393
Islamic ideals, 196, 241, 257
Islamic insurance, xxxi, 311, 348, 355, 360, 368
Islamic insurance companies, 311
Islamic insurance or takāful, 360
Islamic jurisprudence (*fiqh*), x, xi, xvi, xxii, 1, 3, 8, 11, 24, 31, 58, 59, 60, 63, 70, 85, 160, 190, 191, 225, 233, 236, 237, 243, 282, 287, 293, 419
Islamic jurisprudence and legal theory, x
Islamic juristic, 31, 281
Islamic law, xvi, xxi, xxii, 16, 17, 27, 97, 100, 104, 112, 118, 123, 132, 136, 140, 141, 142, 143, 144, 145, 146, 148, 152, 156, 160, 181, 190, 192, 208, 209, 244, 252, 261, 263, 266, 270, 282, 287, 289, 290, 298, 322, 352, 354, 362, 370, 376, 412, 413, 415, 421, 425, 428
Islamic law of inheritance, 370
Islamic legal doctrine, 158
Islamic legal maxims, 237, 239
Islamic legal rules, 287
Islamic legal system, 70, 274, 282
Islamic legal theory, ix, xxiii, 88, 91, 112, 194, 225, 424
Islamic legal thought, 194, 225
Islamic legal tradition, xix, xxii, 99, 160
Islamic legislation, 55, 58, 67, 68, 69, 89, 261, 263, 264, 354
Islamic Life Insurance, 363
Islamic model, xxiv, 204, 207, 348
Islamic moral economy, 417, 422, 423
Islamic mysticism, 181
Islamic normative principles, xxxii, 373
Islamic penal commands, xxvi
Islamic penal law, 146, 251
Islamic penal precepts, xxvii
Islamic penal teachings, xxviii
Islamic penal values, 275
Islamic perspective, xxv, 216, 217, 230, 286, 332, 416
Islamic philosophy, 168, 380, 421, 422
Islamic philosophy of jurisprudence (*maqāṣid al-sharīʿah*), 168
Islamic political experience, 207
Islamic political system, 200
Islamic political thought, xxiv, 207, 208, 421, 424
Islamic polity, 198
Islamic punishments, 271
Islamic religion, 20, 23, 386
Islamic revelation, 200
Islamic scholars, xii, 225, 232, 237, 383
Islamic school, 163, 263
Islamic School of Law
  Evolution, Devolution, and Progress, 157, 158

Islamic sciences, 286
Islamic *Sharīʿah*, 157, 167, 172, 299, 320
Islamic *Sharīʿah* scholarship, 320
Islamic social formation, xxxii, 373, 374
Islamic social system, (*Uṣūl al-Niẓām al-Ijtimāʿī fī al-Islām*), 44
Islamic society, 282, 283, 284
Islamic state, 197, 198, 207, 259
Islamic teachings, 32, 50, 52, 56, 60, 61, 68, 88, 284, 360
Islamic theory of economics, 401
Islamic theory of *iqtiṣād*, 403
Islamic thought, xiv, 29, 37, 42, 159, 179, 184, 415
Islamic tradition, 214, 428
Islamic values, xxiv, xxix, 189, 193, 207, 209, 275, 286, 287, 310, 399
  Islamic values and ethos, xxiv, 207
  Islamic values and principles, 209
Islamic view of CSR, 222
Islamic view of human nature, 37, 40, 45
Islamic world, 32, 40, 45, 92, 286, 287, 289, 308, 351, 375, 382, 414
Islamic worldview, 40, 45, 287, 308, 351, 375, 382, 414
Islamicists, 245
Islamicity Disclosure Index, 394
Islamicity Index, 392
Islamist movements, 163
Islamization, 249, 257, 259, 264, 265, 266, 274, 275, 309, 374, 375, 401, 424
Islamization of human knowledge, 265, 266
Ismaʿīl Rājī al-Fārūqī, 182, 374, 375, 401
Ismāʿīlī philosopher, 181
istidlāl, 126, 129
  istidlāl bil-mursal, 129
istiṣlāḥ, (consideration of public good) 172, 190, 192, 193, 226
istiṣnāʿ, 311
istiḥsān (equity), 105, 172, 190, 192, 193
istiḥsān (juristic preference), 190, 192
istinbāṭ 169
istithmār (investment), 357, 359, 366
Ithnā-ʿasharī Imāmiyyah, 161, 162
IUIF, 344
ʿIzz al-Dīn b. ʿAbd al-Salām, xii, 214
ʿIzz al-Dīn ibn ʿAbd al-Salām, 59
ʿIzz ibn ʿAbd al-Salām, al-, 105, 191

J

Jafar Shaykh Idris, 266
Jalal al-Din al-Rumi's, 407
Jamāʿat al-Fikr al-lslāmī, 265
James Humber, 221
Jaʿfar al-Ṣādiq, 181
Jaʿfarī *madhhab*, 161
Japanese culture, 410
Jābir b. Abdāllh, 314, 360
Jeed, al-, 258, 260, 262, 263, 264
jāhiliyah, 174
Jesus, 48, 95
Jewish, 21, 162, 200, 329
Jews, 49, 200, 201, 212
  Jews of Banū ʿAwf, 200
jihād, 23, 128, 210, 248, 352
  jihād akbar, 41
Joseph Schacht, 159
Judaism, 269
judgment (*ḥukm*), 3
Judicial Revolution, xxvi, 245
Judiciary Act, 254, 255, 256
  Judiciary Act, 1983, 254, 255, 256
Judiciary Revolution, 254, 256, 259, 261, 264, 265, 269, 270, 274, 278, 279
jural system, 143
juridical procedures, 69, 89
jurisprudence, xxii, 2, 9, 31, 63, 112, 123, 156, 157, 158, 164, 165, 169,

180, 181, 185, 205, 213, 282, 289, 426
juristic consensus, 196
juristic empiricism, xviii, xix, 97, 99, 101, 103, 104, 106, 107, 109, 110, 119
juristic induction, xviii, 97, 98, 99, 106, 109, 110
Juristic induction, 99
juristic opinion (*ra'y*), 191, 192
juristic preference (*istiḥsān*), 191
juristic reasoning, 60, 69, 190, 193, 305
juristic speculation (*ijtihād*), 191
juristic tradition, 132
jurists (*fuqahā'*), xii, xvii, 7, 8, 18, 20, 22, 23, 29, 42, 54, 64, 70, 76, 77, 104, 127, 130, 143, 152, 162, 190, 191, 192, 193, 194, 195, 196, 204, 206, 210, 211, 225, 226, 233, 239, 347, 348, 349, 350, 356, 365, 370
just (*'adl*), 50
justice, xviii, xxii, xxiii, xxv, xxxii, 11, 30, 40, 51, 61, 86, 89, 91, 110, 129, 137, 142, 143, 145, 148, 152, 157, 158, 160, 165, 170, 171, 172, 175, 179, 186, 187, 194, 198, 199, 200, 201, 208, 214, 224, 227, 230, 240, 244, 245, 246, 247, 249, 250, 251, 252, 255, 256, 263, 267, 268, 278, 359, 367, 369, 383, 384, 386, 402, 408, 409
  administration of, 142, 243, 244, 247, 250, 257
  in Islam, 243
justification of punishment, 265, 268, 277
Juwaynī, Abū al-Ma'ālī al-, ix, xii, xvi, xvii, 31, 42, 71, 191, 192, 225, 433

K

Kahf, xxv, xxix, xxx, xxxi, 385, 386, 425
kalām (theology), 2, 13, 18, 70, 150, 182, 184, 421
  kalām scholars, 70
Ka'bah, 105
Karl Barth, 180
Karl Jaspers, 180
Karl Marx, 174
Kashf al-Maḥjūb, 181
kāfir, 180, 211
khalīfah (vicegerent), 39, 375
  Khalifah 'Abdullahi, 249, 250
  Khalifah 'Abullahi, 249
Khaliq Ahmad, 222
khalwah, 181
Khan, 222, 334, 377, 393, 434
Khartoum, 59, 61, 244, 250, 253, 256, 265, 271, 421, 435
  conquest of, 250
Khaybar, 204
khayr (good), 2, 5, 37, 41, 43, 44, 46, 51, 55, 57, 61, 62, 64, 65, 68, 71, 72, 79, 84, 95, 123, 127, 130, 144, 146, 151, 170, 178, 212, 220, 226, 229, 230, 234, 240, 241, 247, 253, 266, 269, 287, 289, 290, 299, 337, 348, 352, 353, 355, 359, 367, 370, 376, 382, 403, 408, 414, 416
khāṣṣah, 81
khāẓūq, 247
Khomeini, Ayatullah, 162
knowledge, xiii, xv, xviii, xxiv, 3, 5, 11, 18, 34, 37, 39, 40, 61, 62, 71, 72, 79, 87, 97, 104, 107, 115, 116, 118, 130, 150, 162, 165, 168, 171, 173, 182, 183, 207, 235, 267, 284, 287, 289, 290, 305, 307, 347, 351, 374, 375, 380, 398, 402, 407, 412, 415, 416, 417, 424
knowledge by presence (*'ilm ḥuḍūrī*), 62
kulliyyah (universal), xix, 80, 81, 110
kulliyyāt, 75, 83, 88, 168
  kulliyyāt ḍarūriyyah, 75
  kulliyyāt naṣṣiyyah, 83

kulliyyāt qaṭʿiyyah (definitive universals), 88
kurbaj, 247
Kurd, 177

L

labor, xxxii, 137, 174, 176, 187, 220, 331, 340, 359, 373
labor (*ʿamal*), 176
land, xxxii, 176, 189, 204, 360, 373
land (*arḍ*), 176
language of mystics, 183
later jurists (*al-mutaʾakhkhirūn*), 128
law
    grand purposes, 4, 5, 6
law (*fiqh*), 168
law and morality, 30
law of God, 299
lawful means, 355, 359
Lawgiver, 60, 67, 68, 133, 165, 170, 288, 309, 348, 351, 354
Lawgiver (*shāriʿ*), 67
Lawgivers, 140, 146
laws of marriage, 137
lease, 228, 318, 321, 337, 342, 357
    lease financing, 337
    leasing (*ijārah*), 228, 318
    leasing to the purchase orderer, 321
legal,
    legal actors, 255, 256, 276, 277, 278
    legal analogies, 29
    legal and political systems, 286
    legal autonomy, 205
    legal doctrine, 101, 196, 197
    legal ecology, 150
    legal education, 153, 252, 253
    legal epistemology, 106
    legal history, xxvi, 122, 123, 146, 244
    legal interpretation, 7, 98, 100
    legal jurisdictions, 190
    legal justice, 69
    legal maxims (*qawāʿid fiqhiyya*), 239, 289, 291, 308
    legal methodology, 1
    legal modernizers, xx, 133
    legal norms, 149
    legal orders, 15
    Legal positivism, 158
    legal reasoning, xxi, 59, 102, 134, 300
    legal responsibility (*taklīf*), 108
    legal rules, 130, 281, 282, 288, 347
    legal rulings, 192, 282, 348, 349
    legal scholars, 304
    legal sovereignty, 142
    legal system, xxvi, xxvii, 30, 32, 72, 145, 152, 157, 158, 169, 193, 204, 255, 274, 275, 322, 347
    legal theorist, xii, xx, 2, 71, 72, 88, 90, 159
    legal theory, *uṣūl al-fiqh*, 161
    legal tricks (*ḥiyal fiqhiyyah*), 376
    legal westernization, 138
legalistic approach, xvii, xxxii, 84, 85, 88, 375
legality of insurance, 348
legislation, 47, 48, 55, 59, 64, 67, 138, 203, 208, 254, 258, 260, 261, 262, 263, 264, 269, 274, 278, 298, 351, 353, 356
legislative strategy, 278, 279
legislator, 9, 10, 243, 261, 262, 271, 273, 274, 275, 276, 278
legitimate hermeneutic, 134
legitimization, 377, 379, 400
lending activities, 327
liability, xxix, 315, 334, 369
    liability structures, 334
liberation, 137, 265, 266
life (*nafs*), xiii, xvii, xxv, xxix, xxxiii, 5, 6, 11, 12, 15, 17, 18, 19, 20, 21, 24, 25, 26, 27, 28, 33, 37, 48, 65, 68, 71, 72, 75, 79, 89, 92, 93, 107, 116, 119, 127, 129, 130, 135, 136, 137,

152, 163, 167, 172, 174, 180, 182, 184, 187, 189, 191, 200, 203, 211, 223, 224, 226, 227, 229, 230, 232, 234, 235, 281, 282, 284, 285, 286, 287, 291, 293, 294, 308, 309, 310, 315, 325, 333, 336, 344, 348, 353, 354, 356, 357, 361, 369, 374, 377, 382, 392, 402, 408, 409, 410, 416
lineage, 37, 168, 287, 301, 356
lineal association, 76, 77
lineal indentity, 296
literal universals, 54
literalism, xviii, 95, 96, 97, 98, 99, 101, 102, 103, 104, 415
loan, xxx, 315, 317, 319, 323, 326, 327, 329, 331, 342
loan contract, xxx, 323, 329
Lord, 17, 19, 38, 39, 171, 180, 186, 249, 251
Lord and subject, 17
Lord Buddha, 180
Lord Cromer, 251
Lord Kitchener, 249, 251
loss, xxi, 33, 74, 152, 184, 199, 271, 284, 296, 316, 318, 319, 330, 360, 363, 368, 369, 396
Luca Errico, 335

M

M. Umer Chapra, 228
Madīnah Covenant, 198
Madīnah, *also known as* Yathrib, xxiv, 42, 49, 81, 197, 198, 199, 200, 201, 258, 318
Madīnan state, 201
madhhabs, 157, 159, 161, 162, 163, 164
madrasas, 161
maf'alah, 64
mafsadah (evil and harmful), xxxi, 64, 65, 72, 84, 288, 294, 298, 299, 302, 308, 349
mafsadah (harm), xxxi, 7, 10, 14, 52, 64, 65, 68, 72, 74, 77, 83, 84, 125, 127, 129, 130, 145, 187, 199, 224, 225, 226, 227, 231, 236, 237, 238, 239, 240, 241, 286, 288, 289, 294, 298, 299, 302, 304, 306, 308, 309, 349, 350, 353, 354, 370, 416
Mahayana Buddhism, 155, 185
Mahdi, al-, 61, 248, 249, 250, 251, 258, 260, 261, 265, 433
Mahdist state in the Sudan, 246, 248
Mahdiyyah, 248, 249, 251
Mahmoud 'Akkam, 290
maṣaḥah, 105
maḍarrah (harm), 294, 306, 309
maṣdar (the principal source of knowledge), 267
maṣāliḥ (benefits), xxi, 66, 67, 71, 73, 75, 78, 79, 82, 127, 134, 172, 175, 178, 224, 225, 226, 230, 232, 235, 240, 287, 288, 289, 291, 299, 301, 308, 369, 376, 381, 383, 405, 406
wellbeing of mankind, 299
maṣāliḥ mursalah, xxi, 134, 289, 291, 308
maṣlaḥah (benefit), x, xxv, xxvi, xxxi, 61, 63, 64, 65, 72, 75, 80, 81, 82, 83, 84, 126, 130, 132, 166, 172, 216, 217, 223, 225, 226, 227, 228, 233, 234, 235, 240, 288, 289, 298, 299, 301, 302, 308, 349, 352, 377, 379, 412, 416
  classification of, 81, 84
  conjectural, 84
  vertical categorization, 80
  maṣlaḥah ḥājiyah (complimentary benefit), 302
  Maṣlaḥah juz'iyyah, 81
  maṣlaḥah khāṣṣah, 65
  *maṣlaḥah mu'tabara*h, 172
  maṣlaḥah 'āmmah, 65, 81
  maṣlaḥah, doctrine of, xxv
  maṣlaḥah-based methodology, 228
  maṣlaḥah-based policy making, 379
  maṣlaḥah-mafsadah paradigm, 289
maintenance, 25, 29, 40, 200

Majdah Zawawi, 301, 302
major categories of objectives, 12
Makkah, 18, 43, 81, 179, 192, 288, 361
makrūh, 282
malaise of Islamic banking and finance, 378
Malaysia, 54, 189, 228, 283, 302, 361, 362, 363, 365, 368, 385, 387, 395, 397, 400, 420, 423, 424, 425, 431, 433
Malik, 33, 42, 192, 199, 225, 375, 433
managing partner (*muḍārib*), 341
mandūb, 282, 351
manāfiʿ contract, 340
maʿānī ʿurfiyyah ʿāmmah (universal conventional ideas), 61
manfaʿah (benefit), 225, 303
manṣūṣ (explicitly stated), 170
manifest disbelief (*kufr ṣarīḥ*), 297
mankind, 35, 42, 45, 47, 51, 53, 56, 57, 66, 72, 194, 224, 286, 290, 296, 298, 299, 304, 305, 309, 347
maʿnawiyyah (thematic), 53, 54, 76, 169, 356
manners
  good, 79
manufacturing financing sale (*istiṣnāʿ*), 318
Maqasid e Shariet
  Ek Asri Mutala, 383, 384
maqāṣid, ix, x, xi, xii, xiii, xiv, xvi, xvii, xviii, xix, xx, xxi, xxii, xxiii, xxv, xxvi, xxvii, xxviii, xxix, xxxi, xxxii, xxxiii, xxxiv, 2, 31, 32, 59, 61, 66, 68, 70, 71, 72, 84, 85, 87, 88, 91, 92, 96, 97, 104, 107, 109, 111, 119, 123, 124, 126, 129, 135, 137, 138, 139, 141, 146, 147, 150, 151, 152, 160, 164, 167, 168, 169, 170, 172, 173, 175, 178, 197, 214, 216, 217, 225, 228, 243, 273, 281, 287, 288, 291, 299, 306, 310, 312, 327, 328, 336, 345, 348, 349, 351, 355, 363, 366, 376, 377, 378, 379, 380, 381, 382, 383, 384, 385, 386, 387, 388, 389, 390, 392, 394, 395, 397, 398, 399, 401, 402, 403, 404, 406, 407, 408, 409, 410, 411, 412, 413, 414, 415, 416, 417, 418, 424
  complementary, 386
  essential taxonomy, 381
  essentializing, 388
  specific, 279, 336, 411
  study of, x, xi, xii, xiv, xvi, xviii, 59, 85, 86, 88
Maqāṣid al Sharīʿah
  Treatise on, 164
maqāṣid al-mukallaf (objectives of the human being), 273
maqāṣid al-sharīʿah (Objectives of the Sharīʿah), ix, xi, xii, xiii, xiv, xvi, xvii, xix, xx, xxii, xxv, xxvi, xxvii, xxviii, xxix, xxxi, xxxii, xxxiii, xxxiv, 2, 32, 59, 66, 84, 96, 97, 104, 107, 111, 119, 123, 164, 168, 214, 216, 217, 257, 273, 281, 299, 306, 310, 348, 349, 351, 355, 363, 366, 376, 377, 378, 379, 380, 384, 385, 386, 388, 389, 399, 401, 402, 403, 404, 407, 410, 412, 413, 414, 415, 416, 417, 424
Maqāṣid al-Sharīʿah al-Islāmiyyah wa Makārimuhā, 66
Maqāṣid al-Sharīʿah based Development Index, 391, 393
maqāṣid al-sharīʿah, doctrine of, xv, 240, 300, 351, 415
maqāṣid al-shārīʿ (objectives of the Lawgiver), 273
maqāṣid approach, 197, 214, 385
maqāṣid benchmarks, 397
maqāṣid discourse, 408
maqāṣid framework, 385, 390, 400, 408, 409, 415
maqāṣid ḍarūriyyah, 172
maqāṣid index, 390, 392, 397, 398
maqāṣid indicators, 394

maqāṣid indices, 377, 378, 398, 399, 403
maqāṣid khāṣṣah, 68
maqāṣid law, 151
maqāṣid methodology, 384
maqāṣid ʿāliyah, 172
maqāṣid ʿāmmah (general objectives), 67, 91, 273, 275
maqāṣid observance, 328
maqāṣid paradigm, 167, 178
maqāṣid philosophy, 147
maqāṣid qarībah, 172
maqāṣid realm, 411
maqāṣid scheme, 402
maqāṣid sharʿiyyah
 authentic, 309
maqāṣid studies, xii, xiv, 394
maqāṣid understanding, 399, 407, 410, 412, 417
maqāṣid universal, xxi, 135, 138, 139, 152
maqāṣid, doctrine of, xv, xxxi, 63, 240, 300, 351, 415
maqāṣid-based index, 390
maqāṣid-based perspective, 389
maqāṣid-friendly methodologies, 336
maqāṣidic, 243, 281, 310, 409
maqāṣidic framework, 281
maqāṣidic scheme, 310
maqāṣid-oriented thinking, 383, 410
maqāmah (a generic of Arabic prose), 261
maqṣad ʿāmm, 67
maqṣād, 175
maqṣūd al-Sharʿ, 72
maqṣūd, ḥaqq al-dīn, 169
maqṣid, 108, 109, 113, 170, 376
Marital Discord
 Recapturing the Full Islamic Spirit of Human Dignity, 173, 174, 431
Mark Cammack, 132, 159
market exchange, 402, 417
markets, 175, 316, 324, 386
markup, 332, 333, 342, 343
marriage, 11, 24, 25, 28, 29, 37, 68, 76, 78, 83, 125, 127, 129, 174, 295, 298, 301, 353
Marxism, 174
Marzouq, 298, 300, 303, 304
mashaqqah (hardship), xxv, 51, 56, 68, 78, 125, 224, 227, 293, 299, 353
material needs, 381
materialist paradigm, 92
materialistic philosophies, 89
matrimonial bond, 296
Maurice Strong, 155
Max Weber, 144
Maxim Litvinov, 171
May Revolution, 272
McGill University, x, 429
meanings (*maʿānī*), 67, 351
mechanistic explanations, 380
medicine, xxviii, 150, 282, 283, 286, 300
medieval Christian Europe, 213
medieval Muslim world, 21
Meister Eckhart, 183
Mejelle, 239
māl (wealth), xxv, xxix, xxxi, xxxii, 28, 69, 89, 139, 174, 176, 177, 187, 218, 224, 227, 230, 232, 315, 324, 325, 326, 329, 341, 352, 353, 355, 356, 357, 359, 362, 366, 370, 377, 381, 382, 387, 392, 394, 400, 404, 405
Mālik b. Anas, xii, 236
 Mālikī, 55, 59, 105, 119, 164, 191, 192, 250, 349, 365
 Mālikī jurist, 55, 164, 349, 365
 Mālikī schools of law, 191
 Mālikīs, 350
meta-cognitive truths, 116
Meta-law, 184, 185
metaphorical language, 103
metaphysical reality, 38
Meta-Religion

A Framework for Islamic Moral Theology, 182
mīthāq, xvii, 32, 37, 39, 45
methodological individualism, 417
methodology in Islamic economics, 402
methodology of economics, 400
methodology of Islamic economics, 399, 401
methodology of *maqāṣid al-sharīʿah*, 403
methods of verification, 87
Māturīdism, 112
Māwardī, Al-, 42, 142, 205
Michael Mumisa, 228, 232
Middle East, 99, 115, 118, 119, 121, 145, 159, 244, 335, 389, 423, 427
Midrash, 162
millah, 20
Milton Friedman, 218
mind, xii, xix, xx, 5, 6, 7, 8, 10, 13, 14, 62, 70, 83, 92, 110, 111, 113, 117, 125, 127, 128, 130, 139, 146, 150, 195, 209, 233, 261, 277, 289, 309, 319, 404
mind (*ʿaql*), 13, 19, 61, 127
minimalist approach, 4
minimum capital requirement, 335
Misbah, 290, 296, 300, 304
Mitra Farahbaksh, 335
Moderation, 50
Modern Age, 184
modern and post-modern worlds, 92
modern capitalism, 139
modern codification, 272
modern Islamic legal systems, 140
modern Islamic state, 259
modern legal history of Islam, 140
modern morality, 138
modern Muslim condition, 123
modern Muslim legal discourse, 104
modern Muslims, 96, 109, 111
modern nation-state, 135, 137, 142, 144, 152
modern secularism, 96
modern world, 29, 93, 97, 119, 122, 135, 415, 428
modernism, 184
modernist response, 182
modernity, xx, xxi, xxvi, 96, 115, 122, 123, 132, 133, 134, 135, 139, 152, 153, 243, 424, 428
modernization, xxii, 122, 160, 246, 252, 257, 275
modernization of the law, 252
Mohamed Allal al-Fasi, x
Mohamed al-Mokhtar al-Sallmi, 305
Mohamed S. R. al-Buti, 233
Mohamed Talbi, 39
Mohammad Anis Ubadah, x
Mohammad H. Kamali, 227
monetary transactions, 324
monotheistic religions, 5, 314
Monzer Kahf, 311, 335, 385, 424
moral, xxi, xxxiv, 16, 26, 30, 32, 34, 45, 89, 127, 134, 138, 151, 152, 153, 157, 160, 171, 176, 190, 193, 203, 204, 207, 208, 209, 210, 211, 212, 220, 221, 222, 223, 228, 229, 230, 231, 234, 283, 291, 300, 313, 322, 329, 331, 338, 344, 345, 379, 385, 401, 408,卄 412, 414, 417, 423, 428
moral agents (*khulafāʾ*), 203
moral and ethical standards, 220, 329
moral and political economy, 401
Moral and *Sharīʿah* screening, 337
moral community, xxi, 152, 153, 176
moral hazard risk, 338
Moral Law, 184
moral objectives, 412
moral order, xxi, 32, 152
moral order of human society, 32
moral responsibility, 230
moral screening, 344
moral theory, 221, 428
moral values, 45, 171, 283, 313
moral/ethical screening, 345

morality, xxiii, xxxiv, 58, 116, 138, 139, 148, 158, 167, 171, 178, 207, 208, 223, 412, 414, 417, 418
Morocco, xi, 424
Moses, 48
mubāḥ, 282
Mudathir Abdel-Rahim, 265
muftī, 143, 150, 151, 296, 305
Muhammad Prophet, x, 4, 19, 31, 36, 38, 39, 40, 41, 42, 43, 51, 54, 55, 56, 59, 61, 66, 72, 77, 86, 102, 105, 107, 109, 112, 116, 121, 133, 156, 162, 164, 165, 168, 192, 198, 223, 224, 228, 229, 236, 287, 289, 295, 351, 352, 364, 375, 377, 379, 381, 383, 384, 391, 396, 401, 408, 431, 432, 433, 434
Muhammad Abu Zahrah, 351
Muhammad Ali Chaudry, 156
Muhammad H. Kamali, 228
Muhammad Iqbal, 56
Muhammad Khalid Masud, x
Muhammad Mahdi Shams al-Din, 55, 289
Muhammad ʿAbdu, 41, 164
Muhammad Shahrur, 121, 133
Muhammad Umer Chapra, 379, 381
Muḥammad ibn al-Ḥasan al-Shaybānī, 204
Muḥammad ibn Idrīs al-Shāfiʿī, 190, 192
Muḥammad Ibn Rushd, 349
muḍārabah (equity sharing with a sleeping partner), 318, 320, 321, 329, 330, 331, 335, 338, 339, 340, 341, 342, 362, 365
  muḍārabah depositors, 341
  muḍārabah investment, 321, 329
  muḍārabah investment deposit, 321
  muḍārabah ratio, 365
  muḍārabah-based takāful, 362
muṭlaq (absolute), 54
mujtahid, 9, 150, 163, 351
Multidimensionality, 411
multi-religious societies, 190
muʿāmalāt, 69, 226
munāsabah (suitability), 9, 124, 125, 126, 130
munshtaghilah, 330
Muʿtazilah, 84, 100
Muʿtazilism, 112
Muʿtazilite, 100, 202
murābaḥah, 311, 321, 331, 332, 333, 338, 342, 343, 387
murābaḥah account, 343
murābaḥah contract, 387
murābaḥah financing, 342, 343
murtadd (apostate), 128
mushārakah (equity sharing), 318, 338, 339, 341
Muslim,
  classical, xvii, 20, 29, 60, 91, 225
  convert, 22
  society, historical, 208
Muslim Brotherhood, 260, 265, 266
Muslim community, 13, 20, 22, 23, 55, 107, 111, 130, 194, 195, 204
Muslim countries, ix, xxii, xxxi, 135, 137, 138, 140, 293, 343, 375, 398
Muslim cultural unity, 74
Muslim discourse, 121
Muslim economies, 399
Muslim family, 14, 24, 25, 26
Muslim government, 22, 23
Muslim identity, 19, 414
Muslim indigenous traditions, 122
Muslim inheritance law, 27
Muslim intellectual world, 409
Muslim intellectuals face, 414
Muslim judges, 205
Muslim jurisprudential thought, 4, 30
Muslim jurisprudents, xvii, 63, 178
Muslim jurist
  classical and modern, 86
Muslim juristic thought, 1, 8
Muslim jurists, xvii, 3, 7, 11, 14, 17, 18, 23, 26, 54, 104, 118, 190, 193, 195, 197, 205, 225, 249, 263, 361

classical, 29, 60, 225
Muslim lands, xxi, 373
Muslim law of homicide, 25
Muslim law of maintenance (*nafaqah*), 25
Muslim legal predicament, 133
Muslim legal theorists', 89
Muslim legal thinkers, xx, 132
Muslim Ṣūfīs, 183
Muslim peoples, 287, 373
Muslim political society, xxiv
Muslim scholars, xiii, xxiv, xxviii, xxxiii, 32, 38, 39, 84, 189, 191, 193, 202, 207, 213, 281, 283, 290, 291, 295, 302, 309, 351, 377, 381, 401, 408, 409
Muslim scientists, 283, 286
Muslim social structures, 146
Muslim societies, xviii, xxi, xxii, xxiii, xxiv, 73, 189, 193, 203, 207, 209, 213, 373, 374, 377, 401
Muslim theologians, 70
Muslim thinkers, 60
Muslim tradition, 112
Muslim *ummah*, 50, 51, 73, 81
Muslim unity, 80
Muslim world, ix, xi, xv, xxi, xxviii, 117, 118, 134, 136, 138, 139, 179, 206, 209, 281, 282, 415
Mustafa Zaid, 233
mutual assistance, xxxii, 361, 368
mutual *hibah*, 362
mutual insurance, 361, 364, 369
mutual knowing (*taʿāruf*), 48
Muwāfaqāt, 106, 107, 127, 193, 210, 222, 227, 287, 349, 353, 434
muzāraʿah (crop-sharing), 318, 338
muzāraʿah methodology, 338
mysterium tremendum, 114
mystical Shīʿa, 156
Mysticism, 179
mystics, 183

N

nazm, 186
nafʿ (benefit), 64
nafs (human self), 13, 24, 28, 41, 44, 45, 172, 224, 307, 352, 353, 381, 382, 392, 393
naṣṣ (univocal text), 103
Najāt, al- (Healing), 36
Najm al-Dīn al-Ṭūfī, x, 75, 105, 192
Najm al-Dīn ibn ʿAbd al-Qawīyy al-Ṭūfī, 168
Naʿim, al-, 248, 262
Napoleonic law system, 252
NASDAQ, 323
Nasr Farid Wasil, 296, 297
nationalism, 137, 159
nation-state, xx, xxi, 134, 135, 136, 137, 139, 140, 141, 142, 143, 144, 146, 149, 150, 151, 152, 160
nation-state's, 137, 143, 146, 149
nation-state's jural system, 143
native American religions, 185
natural (*jibillī*), 43
natural and hard sciences, xi
natural and revealed religion, 40, 45
natural disposition, 35, 166
natural disposition (*khilqah*), 166
natural inclination in human beings, 41
natural law, xxiii, 158, 187, 194
natural reason (*ṭabīʿah*), 103
natural reproduction, 295
natural sciences, xxviii, 282, 283
nature of existence (*wuqūʿ*), 72
necessary (*ḥājī*), 175
necessary objectives, 72
necessary universals, 75
necessities, 12, 13, 15, 25, 301, 353, 387, 409, 411
five, 13, 89, 377
five absolute, 107
necessities (*ḍarūriyyāt*), 301

necessity, 8, 12, 16, 42, 65, 75, 79, 118, 129, 146, 167, 203, 289, 291, 292, 293, 294, 301
need (*ḥājah*), xvii, xxii, xxvii, xxix, 3, 4, 8, 12, 15, 16, 21, 25, 29, 35, 41, 42, 43, 44, 47, 55, 70, 75, 78, 92, 122, 135, 138, 149, 155, 160, 175, 194, 204, 207, 209, 220, 221, 228, 235, 240, 269, 286, 288, 291, 296, 301, 315, 319, 320, 321, 324, 327, 329, 332, 333, 334, 335, 336, 338, 342, 344, 345, 350, 361, 376, 381, 389, 398, 406
negligence (*tafrīṭ*), 50, 166
Neo-Roman and Byzantine empires, 165
New World, 115
niẓām, 166
  niẓām al-ḥaqq, 166
  niẓām asāsī (constitutional law), 166
Nietzsche, 40
Nigerian *Sharīʿah* court, 189
nihilistic philosophical tendencies, 93
Nimeiri, 245, 254, 256, 259, 261, 265, 266, 268, 270, 272, 274
nomocratic civilization, 101
non-Islamic systems, xxix, 310
non-Muslim, xxiii, xxiv, 20, 21, 22, 23, 24, 80, 81, 118, 130, 178, 189, 198, 200, 201, 202, 204, 205, 206, 259, 260, 261, 264, 269
  non-Muslim communities, 22
  non-Muslim rights, 205
  non-Muslim subjects, 206
  non-Muslims, xxiii, xxiv, 22, 23, 118, 130, 189, 198, 200, 201, 204, 205, 259, 261, 264, 269
non-PLS investments, 335
non-productive activities, 326
non-profit organizations, 327
non-value-adding activities, 326
normalized domination, xx, 115, 116, 117
normative Islam, 164, 169
North-West Africa, xi
nuclear family, 27, 187
nuclear human family, 173
Nur al-Deen Madani, 260
nuwwāb (deputies), 250

O

objective of the law, 127
objectives,
  basic, xxxi, 321, 345
  five, xxv, 13, 289, 353, 360, 366, 370
  objectives (*maqāṣid*), 75, 327
  objectives of Islamic Law, 31
  objectives of the law, 96, 130
  objectives of the Legislator, 9
  objectives of the prohibition of *ribā*, xxx, 312, 313, 323, 328
  objectives of the *Sharīʿah*, 32, 78, 86, 106, 195, 273, 275, 276, 287, 292, 298, 308, 309, 312, 354, 355, 377, 383, 390, 392, 398
  objectives of this prohibition., 321
  objectivity, 110, 121, 196, 246
occasioning factor, 2, 9, 10
October Revolution of 1964, 254
OECD Better Life Index, 390
offspring, xvii, 28, 29, 38, 45, 72, 76, 127, 130, 135, 138, 299, 301, 352, 353, 404
offspring (*nasl*), 72, 127, 299
OIC Islamic Fiqh Academy, 295, 297, 331
Omer, 265, 266, 267
Oneness of its Creator, and to strengthen one's, 167
ontological basis, 30
ontological realities, 40
operational modalities, xiii
operationalization of *maqāṣid* in Islamic economics, xxxiii

optimistic interpretation of *fiṭrah*, 47, 61, 91
optimistic view of human nature, 85
order of priorities, xiii
order of the world (*niẓām al-ʿālam*), 65
organ, xxviii, 266, 291, 292, 293, 294, 303, 304
organ transplant, xxviii, 291, 292, 293, 294, 303, 304
organized religions, 206
Orientalism, 244, 420, 428
Orientalists, x, 156
original commands, 98
original covenant (*mīthāq*), 39
original disposition (*jibillah*), 83
original human nature (*fiṭrah*), 49
original religion, 39
Ottoman Empire, 141, 142, 143, 157, 158, 239
  Ottomans, 141, 142, 206
outward (*ẓāhir*), 166
overall goal of the *Sharīʿah*, 66, 67
own peculiar object (*mawḍūʿ*), 86
own peculiar problems (*masāʾil*), 86
owning (*tamalluk*), 176

P

paid-for guarantee (*kafālah bi-ajr*), 311
pairs (*azwāj*), 296
Pakistan, 133, 205, 335
paradigm, xxviii, 116, 169, 179, 184, 186, 230, 281, 287, 289, 293, 310, 376, 377, 390, 426
  paradigm shift, xxviii, 281, 287, 289, 293, 310
participants, xv, 361, 362, 363, 364, 365, 367, 368, 369
participatory and sharing economy, xxxii, 373
particular (*juzʾiyyah* or *khāṣah*), 80
particular rules (*aḥkām farʿiyyah*), 194
partnership, 339, 362, 363, 385
partnerships, 357
patriarchal structure, 28
patrilineal progeny, 29
peace covenant (*dhimmah*), 205
Penal Code, xxvii, 89, 251, 255, 257, 259, 260, 261, 262, 263, 264, 268, 270, 271, 274, 276, 278, 279
Penal Code, 1974, 257, 259, 260, 264
Penal Code, 1983, 255, 257, 259, 261, 262, 264, 268, 270, 271, 278, 279
penal commandments, xxvii
penal precepts, xxvii
penal system, 243, 255, 273, 275, 277, 278
penalties, 75, 82, 145, 353
Peri Bearman, 157, 158, 159, 161, 164
permissible (*mubāḥ*), 284, 305, 351
personal and public good, 65
personal finance, 326, 327, 329
  personal financing, xxix, 311, 313, 325, 326, 328, 344
personal freedom, xxiv, 17
Peters, 35, 157, 158
philosophical inquiry, 2
philosophical positivism, xxii, 158
philosophy, xxvi, xxvii, 2, 31, 150, 182, 184, 264, 266, 267, 268, 269, 272, 351, 354, 360, 380, 417, 422, 424
  philosophy of law, 31, 351
  philosophy of punishment, xxvii, 265, 268, 272
plenipotentiary minister (*wazīr tafwīḍ*), 205
PLS assets, 335
PLS investments, 335
pluralism, 141, 172
plurality of opinion, 148
policyholder, 362, 364
political economy, 388, 400, 401, 422, 423
political ideologies, 33, 92
political justice, 173
political oppression, 158

political rights, xxiii, xxiv, 189, 198, 201, 206
political structures, 207
political system, 33, 200, 203, 287
politics, 36, 176, 207, 224, 244, 259
polytheism, 179
Pope Paul VI, 186
Popper, 400
positive interpretation, 50
positive laws, 158
positivist international law, 173
positivist law, 161, 171
positivist secular framework, 259
positivist understanding, 380
positivistic scientific methodology, 381
possessions (*amwāl*), 356
post-colonial history, xxvi
post-colonial Muslim countries, 209
posteriori observation, 97
posterity, xxv, 224, 227, 232, 234, 377, 381, 382
posterity (*nasl*), 224, 381
Posterity Development Index, 393
post-human future, 35, 93
post-human future of mankind, 93
post-independence era, 248, 252, 253
post-independence Sudan, 246
post-modernism, 111, 182, 401, 412, 414
poverty alleviation, 384
poverty of economics, 400
pre-Islamic Arab tribes, 201
pre-modern, 143
  pre-modern Islamic law, 139
  pre-modern jurists, 97, 107, 114
  pre-modern legal sociology, 136
  pre-modern Sharīʿah, 121
preservation (*ḥifẓ*), xix, xx, xxxiii, 5, 14, 20, 23, 26, 28, 60, 65, 70, 74, 107, 109, 111, 117, 119, 128, 130, 136, 166, 173, 175, 226, 287, 307, 309, 352, 353, 354, 377, 383, 388, 398, 404, 406
  preservation of *al-ʿaql*, 398
  preservation of individual souls, 65
  preservation of life, 28, 136, 307
  preservation of Muslim community, 20
  preservation of private wealth, 175
  preservation of progeny, 14, 28
  preservation of reason (*ḥifẓ al-ʿaql*), 107, 109
  preservation of the essential objectives, 309
  preservation of the *fiṭrah*, 166
  Preservation of the religion, 24
  preservation of wealth, xxxiii, 388
preventing harm (*dafʿ al-ḍarar*), xxvi, 11, 236, 237, 239, 240,299, 310, 348
preventing the evil (*taḥṣīl al-maṣāliḥ wa ijtināb al-mafāsid*), 71
price mechanism, 402, 417
price of money, 316
primacy of scripture, 103
primary, 1, 16, 20, 26, 106, 124, 169, 170, 176, 190, 220, 232, 240, 328, 382, 385, 390, 398, 428
  primary *maqāṣid*, 382, 398
primordial covenant, 17, 19, 39, 40
primordial disposition, 53
primordial ontological covenant, 39
principle of balance, 322
principle of diversity (*tannawuʿ*), 297
principle of maṣlaḥah, 105, 217, 223, 241
principle of necessity (*ḍarūrah*), 291
principle of proactivity, 410
principle of punishment, 273
principle of realism, 323, 336
principles (*uṣūl*), 72
principles of the *Sharīʿah*, 192, 193, 233, 252, 254, 263
priori claims, xviii, 97

priorities, 118, 159, 167, 168, 235, 289, 328, 354
pristine human nature, 49
private ownership, 174, 317, 324
proactive *maqāṣid*, xxxiv, 379, 400, 407, 408, 411, 414, 415, 417
proactive *maqāṣid* framework, xxxiv, 400, 407, 411, 414
proactive strategy of the *Sharīʿah*, 75
proactive thinking, 415
probable or conjectural (*ẓanniyyah*), 83
process of codification, xxvii, 243, 267, 273, 274, 275, 276, 278
profit generating activity, 328
profit maximization, 218, 230
profitability, 177, 285, 389
progeny, 13, 28, 107, 173, 226, 352
progeny (*nasl*), 13, 28, 226
prohibited (*ḥarām*, 237, 293
prohibition of interest, xxxi, 317, 319, 321, 322, 325, 327, 343, 344, 345, 385
prohibition of *ribā*, xxx, xxxi, 312, 314, 320, 321, 326, 327, 336, 345, 385, 386
prohibition on fornication and adultery, 137
property, xvii, xxx, xxxii, 11, 13, 14, 18, 25, 72, 107, 125, 127, 128, 129, 130, 135, 139, 152, 168, 175, 178, 191, 204, 226, 234, 236, 286, 287, 317, 323, 324, 325, 330, 337, 342, 352, 355, 356, 357, 358, 359, 361, 363, 382, 386, 387
property (māl), 13, 72, 127, 226
property management, 355, 359
Property rights, 323
Prophet Muhammad, 20, 41, 45, 48, 49, 50, 52, 53, 54, 55, 64, 68, 83, 102, 103, 105, 162, 163, 173, 178, 191, 193, 197, 198, 204, 222, 229, 233, 236, 249, 283, 310, 314, 318, 360, 385
Abraham, 48
Prophet of God, 20
Prophetic era, 415
Prophetic message, 214
Prophetic Sunnah, 102
Prophetic teachings, 193
Prophetic traditions, 41, 55, 375
prophets, 20, 39, 47, 58
protecting offspring, 137
protection of faith and religion (*ḥifẓ al-dīn*), 73
protection of honor (*ḥifẓ al-ʿirḍ*), 77
protection of human life, 74, 352, 386
protection of human life (*ḥifẓ al-nafs*), 74
protection of lineage (*nasl*), 298
protection of progeny, 76, 353
Protestant—scholars, 95
PSA, 366, 368
psycho-religious, 45
public, ix, xiii, xx, xxxiii, 2, 21, 22, 25, 30, 62, 64, 68, 81, 82, 101, 105, 117, 121, 126, 127, 131, 137, 150, 172, 189, 191, 192, 198, 205, 206, 208, 209, 210, 211, 220, 224, 225, 226, 231, 233, 234, 235, 238, 242, 268, 271, 272, 273, 285, 294, 295, 302, 336, 357, 358, 374, 379, 384, 401, 402, 409, 421, 422
public good (*istiṣlāḥ*), 191, 192, 198, 225, 226, 234
public institutions, 206, 208
public interest, 68, 81, 82, 126, 127, 131, 211, 224, 225, 231, 238, 358
public interests (*maṣāliḥ ʿāmmah*), 68, 126, 211, 231
public morality, 137, 209
public policy, xxxiii, 172, 374, 379, 402, 409
punishment, 14, 46, 75, 77, 83, 89, 128, 136, 144, 145, 152, 227, 262,

267, 268, 270, 271, 272, 273, 274, 277, 285, 353
purchase orderer, 311, 321, 342
purpose, xiv, xxiii, xxv, xxviii, xxxiii, 7, 8, 11, 23, 39, 47, 48, 51, 59, 60, 63, 67, 69, 71, 75, 76, 79, 80, 82, 83, 84, 88, 89, 111, 163, 164, 165, 166, 167, 171, 174, 179, 185, 193, 194, 197, 224, 230, 237, 239, 251, 256, 263, 278, 303, 311, 325, 326, 341, 344, 347, 352, 354, 355, 356, 358, 359, 361, 367, 368, 376, 380, 394, 415
purpose of the *Sharīʿah*, xxiii, 82, 193, 354
purposes (*maqāṣid*), 191
pyramid of *maṣlaḥah*, xxvi

Q

qadhf, 77, 128
qadhf (slander), 77, 128
qadr, 170
qaṭʿ (certainty), 59
qaṭʿiyyah (definitive), 83, 88
Qajar period, 181
Qara Daghi, al-, 299
Qaradawi, al-, 296, 297, 298, 303
Qarawiyyīn, al-, x
Qarāfī, al-, 107, 108, 130, 350, 351, 364
qawāʿid (general principles), 68, 79, 191, 322
qawāʿid wa aḥkām, 68
qāḍī, 143, 149, 250
Qāḍī al-Islām,
Ahmed Ali, 250
Ahmed Jubara, 250
Qāḍī al-Quḍāt (Chief Justice), 250
Qārūn, 234
qiyās (analogy), xvi, 3, 4, 7, 18, 39, 79, 102, 103, 104, 105, 108, 163, 190, 191, 193, 226
qualities
good, 42
Quaraouiyine, al-, x
Quraysh, 198, 199

R

ra's al-māl (financial capital), 176
rabb al-māl, 329, 339, 362
rabb al-māl (fund provider), 329, 339, 343, 362
radical textualists, 7
Ramadan, x, 18
Rashid Rida, 132, 192, 408
ratio legis, 124, 125, 126, 128
rational judgment (*ḥukm ʿaqlī*), 112
rational necessity, 126
rational reasoning, 319
rationale, 2, 10, 130, 159, 255, 268, 308, 312, 317, 318, 336, 385, 403, 405, 413, 417
rationalist theologians, 112
rationality, xvii, 5, 10, 18, 381, 402
rationalized analogy, 5
rawāj (wide circulation of properties), 356, 366
Raysuni, Ahmad al-, 66, 102, 105, 108, 112, 114, 169, 192, 202, 222, 230, 232, 288, 289, 334, 363, 365, 368, 386, 387, 395, 434, 435
real assets, 316
real ideas or meanings (*maʿānī ḥaqīqiyyah*), 61
real market forces, 337
real market of production and exchange, 327
real production, 324, 325, 326, 386
realism, 322, 324, 325, 331, 342
realism of the *Sharīʿah*, 324, 331
realization of benefit, 11, 299
reason, xix, xx, xxiv, 6, 15, 44, 53, 54, 76, 77, 79, 95, 107, 108, 110, 111, 112, 113, 116, 117, 125, 159, 161, 163, 168, 178, 179, 182, 222, 240, 271, 296, 319, 333, 340, 357, 358, 400, 402

Reason and Inspiration in Islam, 178, 180
Theology, Philosophy, and Mysticism in Muslim Thought, Essays in Honour of Hermann Landolt, 179
reasoning by analogy (*qiyās*), 3
reciprocity, xxiv, 212
recommended (*mandūb*), 305, 351
reconstructing, 71, 413
rādiʿah (deterrent), 268
reductionist and secular theories of human nature, 34
reflection (*naẓar*), 13
reform (*iṣlāḥ*), 59, 60
regularity, 62
rūḥ (soul), 303
relevant (*mulā'im*), 125
religion, xvii, xxiii, xxiv, 13, 14, 18, 20, 21, 22, 23, 24, 33, 35, 38, 44, 49, 50, 53, 72, 73, 92, 96, 107, 114, 127, 130, 134, 135, 156, 157, 168, 169, 170, 171, 175, 179, 182, 185, 186, 200, 201, 207, 213, 234, 259, 260, 261, 285, 336, 352, 356, 422, 426
study of, 96
religion and human nature, 38
religion of nature (*dīn al fiṭrah*), 175
religious and secular ethics, xxiv, 212
religious belief, 33, 92
religious communities, 21, 107, 108, 205, 208, 213
religious community, 18, 212
religious education, 24
religious Fundamentalism, 95
religious law, 52, 105, 107, 202
religious laws (*sharāʿiʿ*), 52
religious morality, 138, 207
removing hardship (*rafʿ al-ḥaraj*), 236
Renaissance, 34
reproduction process, 300
reproductive cloning, 302
repugnant (*makrūh*), 350
rescheduling, 321, 326, 344, 386
responsible behavior, 220
restraining force (*wāziʿ*), 42
retribution (*qiṣāṣ*), 74
return, 23, 24, 25, 104, 192, 193, 207, 219, 237, 249, 315, 325, 329, 331, 339, 340, 341, 342, 345, 369, 385, 404
revealed law, 8, 166
revealed laws (*sharāi'iʿ*), 166
revealed religion, 50, 257
revelation, xxiii, 11, 19, 20, 47, 49, 56, 72, 80, 95, 101, 112, 124, 125, 130, 159, 161, 163, 166, 168, 179, 186, 192, 194, 202, 211, 214,222, 267, 269, 285, 314, 347
revelatory speech, 100
reverse *murābaḥah*, 338, 341. 342, 343
Revolution of May 1969, 254
ribā (usury or interest), xxix, xxxi, 118, 177, 311, 312, 313, 314, 315, 318, 320, 325, 327, 331, 360, 361, 362, 363, 385, 386
ribā-based financing, 313
right (*ḥaqq*), 16, 19, 81, 89, 93, 101, 160, 164, 166, 169, 170, 193, 198, 204, 210, 219, 230, 240, 296, 323, 324, 325, 358, 370, 386, 387, 392, 408
Rights of God (*Ḥuqūq Allāh*), 171, 210
rights of ownership, 325
Rights shared by God and his servants (Ḥ*uqūq Allāh wa-l-ʻIbād*), 210
Risālah, al- (The Epistle), 72, 75, 99, 105, 107, 168, 192, 224, 226, 287, 352, 378, 432, 435
risk, xxix, xxxi, 93, 312, 316, 327, 331, 334, 335, 336, 337, 338, 345, 360, 361, 364, 367, 368, 369
risk considerations, 331

risk mitigation, 327, 336, 338
risk profile, 336, 337
risks, 294, 312, 334, 335, 336, 341, 362, 364, 368, 384
Robert Davies, 217
Robert Gleave, 161
Roman Catholic, 165, 180
Roman Catholic Church, 165
Roman law, 177
Romano Guardini, 180
Rudolph Otto, 114
Rudolph Peters, 157, 158
rule (*ḥukm*), 305
rules (*aḥkām*), 80, 191

S

sadd al-dharā'iʿ, 348, 350, 355, 360, 363, 371
Sadiq al-Mahdi, al-, 258
Safavid period, 181
safeguarding offspring, 301
Saint John of the Cross, 180
ṣalāḥ (wellbeing and righteousness), 64, 67, 166
salam (forward sale with cash advance), 228, 318, 332
salam sale, 332
sale, 239, 292, 315, 316, 318, 319, 320, 328, 332, 337, 340, 342, 349, 357, 364
sale of *mustarkhiṣīn* (cheap price seekers), 332
sale of the *maḥāwīj* (the needy ones), 332
sales contracts (*buyūʿ*), 60
ṣāliḥāt, 170
samāḥah, 51, 52, 68, 178
Sanad, al-, 306
santri Islam, 160
ṣarf, 343
Satan, 108, 314
Saudi Arabia, 266, 361, 362, 384
savings, 176, 320, 321, 329, 366
Sayyid Qutb, 144
Sayyid Tantawi, 300
scheme of *maqāṣid*, 85
scheme of the *Sharīʿah*, 90
science, xxviii, 34, 70, 86, 87, 91, 93, 96, 101, 158, 177, 178, 180, 184, 221, 223, 271, 281, 282, 284, 286, 289, 290, 307, 401, 422
science (*ʿilm*), 86
science and progress, 34, 93
scientific knowledge, 287, 400, 414
scientific research, xxviii, 282, 286
scientific thinking, 415
scope, xxxiii, 43, 66, 69, 80, 84, 86, 138, 150, 199, 321, 383, 388, 400, 401, 404, 405, 407, 411
scope of *maṣlaḥah*, 66
Scottish Enlightenment, 165
scriptural interpretation, 96
scripture, 96, 101, 102, 104, 105
secular humanism, 92
secular institutions, 414
secular jurisprudence, 31
secular materialist thought, 92
secular mind, 93
secular paradigm, xxix
secular worldview, xviii, 376, 377
secularist paradigm, 35
secularization, 209, 287
Security, 22, 426
Sūfi, 270
self (*nafs*), 299, 382
self-centredness (*fardiyyah*), 404
self-destruction, 73
self-determination, 170, 173, 176, 187, 205
self-evident primary truths, 62
self-induced intoxicants, 113
self-knowledge, 185
self-regulated market economy, 417
semantic field, xxi, 133, 134
semantic possibilities, 99
sense of duty, 231
sense-observation, 97
sensibilia (*maḥsūsāt*), 36

Serour, 304
services, xxxi, 21, 22, 218, 316, 321, 324, 325, 329, 332, 334, 337, 340, 342, 343, 344, 393, 394
sexual behavior, 29
Seyyed Hossein Nasr, 93, 181, 182, 184, 433
Shahid Athar, 303
Shaṭibī, al-, 88
Shams al-Dīn, 77, 296
Shaping the Future
  Challenge and Response, 156, 427
Sharīʿah
  criteria of the, 348
  essential goals, xix
  essential objectives, 307
  five primary objectives of the, 382
  goals, xvii, 50, 68, 355, 356, 383
  higher objectives, 33, 69, 170
  historical, 121, 122, 197
  sovereignty of the, 262, 264
  specific objectives of the, 273, 276, 278
  spirit of the, 278, 355, 361
  ultimate goals, 348, 356
  ultimate objectives, xii, 310
  ultimate purpose, 89, 352
  universality and suitability, 56
Sharīʿah commands, xvi, xvii, 2, 37, 67, 85
Sharīʿah compliancy, 376
Sharīʿah framework, 233
Sharīʿah goals, xvi, 359, 370
Sharīʿah ideals, 274
Sharīʿah judgments, 80
Sharīʿah law, 3, 205, 206
Sharīʿah legal rules, 347, 351, 356
Sharīʿah objectives, 61, 67, 69, 70, 80, 216, 223, 227, 228, 235, 299, 300, 356, 378, 383, 398, 410
Sharīʿah of Moses, 48
Sharīʿah penal code, xxvii
Sharīʿah permissibility, 322, 385
Sharīʿah principles, xiii, 214, 239
Sharīʿah purposes, xxxii
Sharīʿah reform, 210
Sharīʿah requirements, 322, 334, 358
Sharīʿah rulings, 352
Sharīʿah scholars, xi, 404, 416
Sharīʿah sources, 80, 225
Sharīʿah supervisory boards, 396
Sharīʿah system, 69
Sharīʿah training, 235
Sharīʿah uppermost objectives, 224
Sharīʿah values, 274, 275, 276, 278
Sharīʿah-compliant economic and financial activities, 366
Sharīʿah-compliant products, 378
sharʿ (Divine Law), xxiii, 3, 4, 5, 15, 165, 168, 169 191, 193, 194, 226, 288, 290, 309, 310377
Sharʿī, 122, 141
sharr (evil consequences), 299
Shawkānī, al-, 126, 127, 128, 129, 130, 131, 135
Shaybānī, al-, 205
Shaykh Hasan Muddathir, 253
Shaykhi movement, 181
Shādhili *ṭarīqah*, 180
Shāfiʿī, xii, 2, 77, 99, 100, 191, 192, 226, 350, 365
  Shāfiʿī jurists, 192, 365
  Shāfiʿī, al-, xii, 2, 77, 99, 100, 191, 192, 226, 350, 365
  Shāfiʿīs, 2, 105, 164
  Shāfiʿite, 130
Shāṭibī
  Imām al-Shāṭibī's Theory of the Higher Objectives and Intents of Islamic Law, 66, 169, 434
  Shāṭibī, Ibrāhīm ibn Mūsā al-, x, xii, xiv, xvi, xvii, xix, 31, 54, 59, 66, 71, 86, 106, 107, 109, 123, 127, 164, 168, 170, 191, 193, 210, 214, 222, 224, 225, 227, 287, 288, 289, 305, 308, 349, 353, 354, 387, 431, 432, 433, 434

Shīʿa, 4, 157, 161, 162, 163, 177, 181, 184
  and Sunnī jurisprudence, 162
  doctrines, 160
  Shīʿism, 179, 180
  Shīʿite, 159, 161
shūrā (consultation), 200, 265
Shihāb al-Dīn al-Qarāfī, 55, 59, 225
Siddiqi, 383, 384, 385, 434
ṣilat al-raḥim (filial ties), 296
Sinnar, 246
siyāsah (government), 22, 81, 142, 148, 155, 157, 158, 176, 177, 202, 213, 216, 218, 230, 265, 285, 340, 341, 416, 421
  siyāsah sharʿiyyah, 148
social
  and moral fabric, xxi
  anthropologist, 245
  capital, 129, 405
  corporate responsibility, xxvi
  formations, 403, 416
  harm, 145, 152, 236, 238
  institutions, 33
  justice, xxiv, 30, 176, 325, 405
  life, 34, 207, 240
  order, 21, 29, 67, 73, 74, 76, 78, 79, 124, 130, 143, 144, 145, 147, 151, 269, 296
  organization, 42, 47, 48, 63, 142, 196, 253
  philosophies, 33, 92
  responsibility, xxv, 137, 218, 219, 221, 222, 230, 233, 235, 240, 241
  sciences, xi, 375, 401
  vision, xvii, 14, 17, 23
socialization, 62
society, xxiii, xxiv, 25, 26, 42, 43, 44, 49, 52, 60, 64, 65, 74, 77, 78, 80, 83, 89, 91, 93, 119, 129, 139, 140, 143, 144, 145, 151, 152, 158, 160, 173, 175, 189, 190, 193, 194, 196, 197, 198, 199, 200, 201, 203, 204, 206, 207, 208, 209, 212, 213, 214, 215, 216,뜌 217, 219, 220, 221, 227, 228, 229, 232, 233, 235, 237, 238, 240, 241, 267, 282, 283, 301, 313, 327, 354, 373, 387, 403, 405, 406, 409, 410, 416, 418
socioeconomic justice and equity, 405, 409
socio-historical existence, 71, 73, 90
sociological reasoning, 44
Socrates, 33
Solon, 48
Sophia Perennis, 178, 180
Sophists, 36
Sorbonne, 180
soul, xxxiv, 13, 14, 24, 43, 50, 131, 166, 183, 303, 404
South East Asia, xi, xxxi, 335
Sovereignty, 201
Soviet Union, 139
species, 37, 45, 76, 113
specific goals, 68
specific legislations, 64
speculation-based index market, 316
speculative market forces, 324
spiritual pursuit, 83
spirituality, 58, 178, 184
SPV, 339, 341
Stability of projects, 339
state, xxii, xxiv, xxvii, 10, 22, 23, 26, 28, 38, 42, 43, 44, 101, 115, 117, 122, 132, 134, 136, 137, 140, 141, 142, 143, 144, 145, 146, 147, 149, 150, 151, 152, 156, 159, 160, 161, 173, 174, 177, 190, 196, 197, 202, 203, 204, 206, 207, 208, 209, 210, 211, 249, 250, 251, 254, 256, 264, 279, 282, 287, 298, 301, 309, 310, 359, 384
  of emergency, 256
Stem cell research, 302
STMB, 362, 368, 371
subjective consciousness, 100
submission to God's command, 46

substantive morality, xxxii, xxxiv, 373, 379, 389, 403, 414, 417
Sudan, ix, xxvi, 244, 245, 246, 247, 248, 249, 250, 251, 252, 253, 254, 255, 257, 258, 260, 264, 266, 271, 275, 341, 387, 424
Anglo-Egyptian Sudan, 246, 251
Sudanese context, 265, 268
Sudanese experiment, xxvii, 243
Sudanese historians, 245
Sudanese laws, 251, 252, 254
Sudanese Penal Code, 243, 278
Sudanese people, 252, 269
Sudanese politics highly, 266
Sufism, 163, 180, 269, 428
Suhrawardī, 181
suitability, xvi, 9, 10, 18, 52, 53, 56, 61, 125, 126, 127, 128, 130
suitedness, xvi, 9
ṣukūk, 311, 336, 338, 339, 340, 341
sulṭān, 177
sulṭānī (governmental), 43, 204, 209
Sunnah, xiii, 3, 52, 53, 55, 56, 64, 106, 134, 191, 222, 225, 233, 249, 267, 283, 347, 370, 382, 402, 408
Sunnī, 99, 102, 157, 159, 162, 163, 164, 168, 169, 177, 224, 225, 243
Islam, 162, 243
world, 164, 168, 169
schools of law, 99
supplementary necessity, 12, 14
Supreme Reality or God, 183
surpluses, 329, 340
survival of the fittest, 400
sustainable development goals (SDGs), 378
ṣuwar kulliyyah (universal genres), 79
madhhab, 161
Suyūṭī, al-, 236, 237
Switzerland, 180
Syarikat Takaful Malaysia Berhad (STMB), 362, 368, 371
Syrian Christians, 206
systematic theology, 113
systematic theorization, 2
systematization, xxvii, 71, 86, 273, 274, 278
systematization of values, xxvii, 86, 273
systems approach, 410

T

ta'ṣīl (grounding), xvii, xviii, 18, 51, 61, 70, 85, 88, 92, 214, 375
tabarruʿ, 363, 364, 367, 368
tabarruʿāt (contributory), 330
tabula rasa, 34, 58
taghyīr li-khalq Allāh (God's creation), 297
Taha Jabir al-Alwani, Dr., 108, 169, 375
taṣawwuf, 181
taḥsīn, tawsiʿah (improvements), 129
taḥsīniyyāt (embellishments), xii, xxvi, 71, 79, 91, 172, 227, 228, 301, 354, 387, 409
takassub (acquisition), 176, 357, 359, 366
takassub (earning), 27, 176, 331, 333, 336, 357, 359, 366
takāful, xxxi, 360, 361, 362, 363, 364, 365, 366, 367, 368, 369, 371
certificate, 366
Certificate, 367
company, 366, 368
contract, 367
general:, 363
installment, 365, 366
insurance, xxxi
model of insurance, xxxii
operator, 362, 366, 368
plan, 366, 367, 369
schemes, 363
Takaful Act, 361, 367, 369
Taʿāwunī, 362
takfīr (charging one with disbelief), 211
takhfīf, 178

Talbi, 39, 40
talfīq, 163
talio, 26
Talmud, 162
taʿlīl (causality), xvi, 87, 124, 288
Tantawi, al-, 292
taqlīd, 163, 168
taqnīn al-sharīʿah (codification of the Sharīʿah), 274
taqwā (God-consciousness), 167, 170, 229, 230, 233
tasāmuḥ (tolerance), 86, 91, 141, 172, 221
ṭarīqahs, 179
tawarruq, 311, 321, 342, 344, 377, 388
tawḥīd, 58, 167, 184, 413
  tawḥīdī, 405
  tawḥīdī framework, 405
  Tawḥīdī paradigm, xxxiv
  tawḥīdic IOK paradigm, 401
taxonomy of maṣlaḥah, 84
tazkiyah (growth), xiv, 195, 313, 316, 317, 337, 345, 377, 384
teachings of Islam, xxxiv, 35, 203, 381
tābiʿah (corollaries), 382
teleology, 380, 415
  causality, 415
textualist-intentionalist, 8
thabāt (certainty), xxxii, 44, 54, 59, 62, 103, 131, 356, 366, 367, 370
theoretical shallowness, 375
theorization, xvii, xxvi, xxxiv, 30, 92, 318, 381, 386, 400, 402, 409, 414
theory
  of *dharāʾiʿ*, 355, 419
  of knowledge, 267, 400
  of knowledge in Islam, 267
  of *maqāṣid*, xvi, xx, xxii, xxiv, xxv, xxxii, 85, 92, 123, 124, 214, 354, 376, 383
  of *maqāṣid al-sharīʿah*, xvi, xx, xxii, xxv, xxxii, 92, 354, 376
  of punishment, 264, 267, 270
Thomas Jefferson, 171
three-party *istiṣnāʿ*, 321
Todd Lawson, 179
tolerance, 86, 91, 141, 172, 221
Torah, 68, 162
Toshihiko Izutsu, 181
trading indices, 323
tradition, xxiii, 49, 123, 133, 197, 245, 248, 251, 253, 257, 270
traditional
  African religions, 258
  Islamic finance, 331
  traditionalism, 184
Traditionalist
  Muslims, 156
  scholars, 210
transactions, xxx, 11, 69, 81, 175, 226, 228, 239, 240, 241, 313, 320, 323, 324, 325, 328, 337, 342, 357, 359, 364, 386
transcendent theosophy, 184
transitivity, 410, 412
transparency, xxxii, 175, 357, 367, 369
Transplants, 292
tribal division, 199, 200
Ṭūfī, al-, 226, 435
Tunisia, x, 164, 300, 305
Turabi, al-, 61, 251, 261, 263, 266, 435
Turkey, 163, 422
Turkiyyah, 246, 247, 249
Turks, 248, 249

U

U.N. Declaration of Human Rights, 171
uberrimae fidei, 367
uṣūl (fundamentals), ix, xii, xvi, xvii, 1, 18, 31, 52, 54, 58, 59, 60, 66, 72, 73, 84, 85, 95, 99, 101, 102, 151, 161, 176, 223, 289, 347, 424

uṣūl al-fiqh, ix, xii, xvi, xvii, 1, 18, 31, 58, 59, 85, 99, 101, 102, 161, 289, 347, 424
uṣūl al-fiqh studies, xii
uṣūl legacy, 60
uṣūl literature, 66
uṣūl scholars, 84
uṣūl theory, 54
uṣūlī tradition, 130
Uṣūl al Niẓẓm al-Ijtimāʿī fī al-Islīm, 178
Uṣūlīs (traditionists), 162
ultimate goal of suitability, 126
ultimate objective, xii, 23, 146, 309, 310, 354, 405, 410, 413
ultimate reality, xxiii, 156, 186
Umayyad, 211
ummah, 20, 73, 79, 80, 81, 198, 199, 200, 202, 203, 258, 309
ʿumūm (universality), xvii, xix, 15, 16, 48, 50, 52, 56, 61, 78, 88, 89, 91, 92, 110, 130, 131, 175, 196, 197, 411
ʿuqūd muʿāwaḍah (exchange contracts), 362
unanimous consensus of the jurists, 102
underdevelopment, 374
UNDP, 390
UNESCO, 390
unified in purpose, 57
United Nations, 155
United States, 30, 117, 136, 166
unity of vision, xxxiv
universal, xvii, xix, xxii, xxiii, xxxiii, 11, 12, 15, 16, 40, 48, 49, 53, 54, 56, 61, 63, 64, 67, 71, 72, 73, 75, 76, 78, 79, 80, 81, 83, 89, 90, 110, 111, 118, 123, 125, 130, 134, 135, 137, 138, 142, 146, 147, 156, 160, 167, 168, 169, 171, 174, 176, 178, 179, 187, 191, 194, 196, 201, 212, 213, 275, 281, 284, 347, 353, 356, 377, 381, 382, 408, 411
absolute universality, 196
benefit, 61
human rights, 135
ideal, 196
legislation, 54, 64
maṣaḥah, 80, 81
necessities, xxxiii, 12, 15, 73, 83, 381, 382
needs, 16
purposes, xxii, 160
society, 48
truth, 156, 179, 381
universalism, 110
universality of values, 89
universals
five, xxi, 90, 134
useful purposes, 68
usūliyyūn, 267
usufruct-based financing, 340
utilitarian/secularist approach, xxi, 134
utilitarianism, xxix, 63, 285, 310
utility, x, 64, 105, 110, 267, 332, 400, 402, 405, 417
maximization, 400, 402, 417
maximization motives, 402

V

validity, 7, 11, 44, 54, 106, 111, 112, 115, 126, 228, 233, 262, 269, 311, 322, 323, 369, 395, 398
value, xiii, xvii, xix, xxii, xxiii, xxvii, xxviii, xxix, xxxiv, 13, 17, 18, 23, 24, 28, 30, 32, 33, 41, 50, 53, 55, 57, 58, 63, 69, 79, 81, 90, 91, 92, 93, 96, 106, 107, 110, 111, 119, 124, 129, 134, 152, 171, 174, 194, 198, 201, 204, 208, 214, 221, 223, 225, 230, 234, 237, 273, 274, 275, 276, 277, 283, 284, 287, 290, 308, 309, 315, 316, 317, 320, 324, 325, 326, 328, 331, 332, 333, 343, 344, 348, 351, 354, 359, 364, 375, 377, 381, 382, 386, 399, 401, 405, 408, 414, 416, 418, 424

and norms Islam, xvii
creation, 317, 326
system of Islam, 79
systems, xxviii, 33, 287, 308
vertical order, 71
Vietnam, 139
virtue, xv, xxx, xxxiv, 6, 7, 10, 22, 25, 28, 40, 50, 51, 57, 64, 67, 68, 88, 143, 147, 170, 171, 178, 215, 272, 293, 316, 317, 337, 343, 354
vital interests, 18, 308, 354

W

W.E.B. Du Bois, 118
Wael Hallaq, 228
Wahbah al-Zuhayli, 289, 351
waḥdat al wujūd, 181
waḥy (revelation), xxiii, 11, 19, 20, 47, 72, 95, 112, 124, 125, 130, 159, 161, 163, 166, 168, 179, 186, 192, 194, 202, 211, 214, 267, 269, 285, 314, 347
wajaba al-wuqūf ʿindah, 103
wakālah, 329, 330, 339, 343, 362
based entity, 330
Warfare, 22, 23
wasā'il, 296, 301, 303, 305, 307
wazīr tanfīdh (executive minister), 205
weaknesses of human nature, 37
wealth
and property, xxxi, xxxii, 356, 357, 359, 366, 370
management, 356, 370
Weiss, Bernard G., x, xvi, 1, 8, 17, 32, 37, 73, 99, 100, 102, 126, 421, 435
wājib, 350
welfare, 28, 30, 32, 126, 225, 234, 241, 290, 299, 405, 408, 422
Weltanschauungen, 124, 146
West, xx, xxii, xxviii, 17, 95, 110, 118, 119, 158, 206, 217, 282, 290, 329, 423
Western
academy, 96
Anatolia, 2
business community, 240
conceptualization, 218
countries, xv, 140, 320
criminal codes, 146
cultural imperialism, 182
economic worldview, 218
empires, 180
Europe, 148
feminism, 138
Fundamentalism, 96
Fundamentalist, 104
humanistic theories, xxv, 222
jurisprudence, 158
law, xvi, 17, 157
model, xxviii, 122, 204
model of science, xxviii
model of the state, 204
philosophy, 380
positivist law, 156
scholarship, 101
Sudan, 249
thinkers, 35
thought, 34
westernization, 132, 246, 253, 257
westernized elite, 253
western-type law, 136
world, 400, 408
wāziʿ, 32, 41, 42, 43, 44, 45, 46
wāziʿ dīnī, 46
wāziʿ sulṭānī, 44
wāziʿ dīnī nafsānī (spiritual restraining factor), 45
Whig movement, 165
white man, 115
whose greatest, xxii, 165
wilāyat al-faqīh, 162
Wilfred Cantwell Smith, 181
Will of God, 179, 193, 301
William Brunyate, 251
William Chittick, 181
Winston, 117
wisdom
of human experience, 62

of the law, 6
and the law of God, 5
with self-interest motives, 405
women, xxiii, 22, 29, 125, 137, 144, 161, 189, 296, 408, 426
World, xi, xiii, xiv, xxii, xxv, 6, 13, 22, 23, 27, 28, 29, 33, 34, 37, 40, 42, 47, 48, 61, 66, 70, 73, 92, 112, 118, 126, 148, 150, 155, 156, 164, 166, 169, 170, 171, 173, 177, 179, 180, 182, 183, 185, 187, 190, 197, 206, 213, 217, 223, 224, 228, 230, 234, 240, 286, 287, 294, 298, 308, 352, 384, 405, 406, 410, 428
Bank, 390, 393, 398
Fiqh Council in Makkah, 169
religions, 155, 156, 171, 182, 187
War II, 180
WorldCom, 216
worldview, 30, 218, 223, 240, 285, 380, 399
worship of God, 28, 352
wuḍūḥ (transparency), xxxii, 175, 356, 357, 366, 367, 369

Y

yaʿqilūn, 113, 116
Yathrib, *also known as* Madīnah, 198
Yilmaz, xvi, xxv, xxxii, xxxiii, 373, 422
yusr (comfort), 78

Z

Ẓāhirī, 4, 102, 103, 161, 167
Ẓāhirism, 101, 102, 103, 104
Ẓāhirite legal theory, 102
Ẓāhirite, 102, 109
zakāh, 210, 228, 352, 425
duty of, 28
Zaki Mustafa, 244, 247, 254
zandaqah (charging one with heresy), 211
ẓann (conjectures), 191
Zawawi, 301, 302
Zaytuna Grand Mosque University, x, 164
Ziauddin Sardar, 223, 228, 283
zinā (adultery), 127
Zoroaster, 48
Zoroastrian, 21
Zuhayli, al-, 297, 299, 304, 305
ẓulm (injustice), 42, 163, 200, 201, 249, 299, 353, 359, 408, 426

www.ingramcontent.com/pod-product-compliance
Lightning Source LLC
Chambersburg PA
CBHW021757220426
43662CB00006B/83
* 9 7 8 9 6 7 0 5 2 6 5 5 3 *